Christian Missions and Conversion

Christian Missions and Conversion

A Historical, Sociological and Anthropological Study of the Depressed Castes of India, 1850-1950

Santha Kumari Varikoti-Jetty

CWI

Christian World Imprints

First Published in 2019 by

Christian World Imprints
Christian Publishing & Books from India
C-3, Shop No. 14, Ground Floor
Wazirpur Industrial Area, **Delhi-110052**
cwidelhi2017@gmail.com
www.ChristianWorldImprints.com
Phone: +91 11 41526079

ISBN: 978-93-5148-387-8 (HB)
ISBN: 978-93-5148-388-5 (PB)

Printed in India.

Dedicated

To

My beloved Father Lt. Sri. V.V. Prasada Rao (1946-2011)
&
My beloved Mother Lt. Smt. V. Nirmala (1951-1970)

Contents

Foreword

This book entitled, *Christian Missions and Conversion: A Historical, Sociological and Anthropological Study of the Depressed Castes of India, 1850-1950*, by Dr. Santha Kumari Varikoti-Jetty, documents the operation of six mission organizations which worked in six different locations in colonial coastal Andhra during the chosen period of study.

The narrative is clear, and is descriptive of the evangelization work of the missionaries, including their service in the fields of education, healthcare, social upliftment, humanitarian care, etc. The beginning, development and spread of the Christian religion among two Depressed Class (now termed as *Scheduled Castes* or popularly known as *Dalits*), communities—the Malas and Madigas--in Andhra make a substantial part of the narrative in the book.

The Depressed Classes as a category of caste communities were only nominally mentioned in the writings on Indian society, for they belonged to the subaltern people groups, and in many places were considered as slaves. They remained as deprived people for centuries in India. Though there have been attempts at their liberation by many social and religious reform leaders in India, they were noticed and their plight was brought to fore during the period of colonial modernity. It is a fact that the true story of these two Dalit communities was first narrated by the missionaries and thereafter the colonial government and later the society in general began to take note of them. This has been narrated in the book.

Missionary-mediated transformation of the consciousness of the Depressed Castes in Andhra in a colonial context forms another important aspect of this book. Missionary-mediated transformation and social consciousness of the Depressed Castes in Andhra in the colonial context forms an important aspect of this book. The foreign missionaries who came to work among the Malas and Madigas not only noted the peculiar customs, traditions, rituals and everything of their people, but were also shocked by the discrimination and oppression they suffered under the caste system. The plight of the Depressed Classes attracted global attention through voluminous writings of the missionaries, particularly Protestant ones. Their passionate enquiries into the nature of caste oppression were instrumental in changing the fortunes of the Depressed Classes. This book is a studied document of that sharp perception of the missionaries and their attempts at changing the situation of the Dalits.

The mediation of the missionaries was not just creating infrastructure for material empowerment of the Dalits, but also in instilling a stimulus for changing the self-image and self-perception of the Dalits themselves, by providing adequate socio-religious superstructure such as ideas, ideals and indoctrination. In missionary terms,it was 'salvation' of the convert, who otherwise would remain as a 'doomed' person that was offered to him/her. They seem to have facilitated the natives to have a critical understanding of the complexities of the consciousness of the Dalits. For the missionaries, liberation from the bondedness of the Malas and Madigas was intimately connected with the liberation teachings of the Gospels. Christianity was found as offering of an alternative worldview to the oppressed communities.

The author has skillfully woven this aspect into the narrative of the book. This is accomplished by giving a detailed description of the context, on the founding of the missions, preaching of the Gospel and demonstration of practical Christianity, besides narratives on the participation of the natives, and eventual devolution of responsibility and authority for constructing indigenous Christian communities. In fact, this is the cardinal argument of the book.

The author has skillfully tried to bring out the aspect of social transformation among the converts mediated by the mission agents, be it foreign missionaries or indigenous ones. The author has discussed in detail the pre-conversion contexts (social, religious, economic, political, and so on, of the Malas and Madigas and has woven the story beautifully, the apparent change (social, economic, educational, occupational, religious, etc) mediated among these convert communities.

The author has amassed a lot of sources from mission archives and libraries, and has created a narrative substantiated with historical sources, citing them almost at every sentence. Reliance on sources is her forte. I congratulate the author for presenting a source-rich narrative, but at the same time, weaving the mission perspective with a scholar's perspective.

Among the few books on Dalit Christians in Andhra Pradesh, this book stands out as a first-class document-based study on the conversion of Dalits in Andhra Pradesh and the post-conversion change among them. Of course, the epilogue in the concluding chapter, presents an anti-climax to the otherwise success story of socio-religious transformation mediated by the Christian missions, for in the post-1950 period, due to the Constitutional Order by the President of India, the Dalit Christians have not been granted constitutional protection in the form of reservations and hence deprived of their affirmative action status under the welfare- upliftment schemes of the Government of India.

The author has provided a handy tool for readers for a better understanding by giving quotations, references, and appendices. The book is very readable; its arguments are logical, data-based, contextualized and is based on careful and extensive research. Bringing new and unexplored source materials into focus, the book offers a kaleidoscopic perspective on how multiple American and European Protestant Christian Missions established new indigenous Christianity in collaboration with the native Indians.

I am sure the readers will find the book very enriching. Certainly, the book is a valuable addition to the existing body of scholarly books on Christianity in India. I congratulate Dr. Varikoti-Jetty for bringing out a well-researched book on the Christian Missions and conversion of the Malas and Madigas of Andhra.

Dr. Jose Kalapura, SJ
Executive Editor
Indian Church History Review

Preface and Acknowledgments

There has been a renewed interest in recent times among scholars to study social change among the subaltern/Dalit communities in India. Quite a few studies have focused on religious conversion and change among these communities. While most of the earlier studies have been done by missionary scholars, today, the whole theme has been taken beyond the missionary narrative. Scholars have critically looked at the process of conversion as a social movement among the subaltern/Dalit communities. This has happened particularly after the conversion movement led by Dr. B. R. Ambedkar among the Dalits. Ambedkar's conversion to Buddhism clearly demonstrated that Dalits converted *en masse* not because of any agency of missionaries, but due to attainment of a new social consciousness among them thanks to multiple socio-political, economic and religious factors during late nineteenth and early twentieth centuries in India. It may be noted that besides the agency of a modernized Indian context, the effective leadership of charismatic leaders have played a crucial roles in effecting conversion.

This book, entitled, *Christian Missions and Conversion: A Historical, Sociological and Anthropological Study of the Depressed Castes of India, 1850-1950*, substantiates these twin factors. As the title indicates, this research focuses on the conversion and the subsequent social change among two Depressed Class (Dalit) communities—Malas and Madigas—in Colonial Coastal Andhra during a period when not only Colonial Andhra, but the whole of India, was undergoing modernization due to a multiplicity of factors created by the Colonial administration, the main one of which was access to modern education. And the external agency or leadership in the case of these communities came from the missionaries. This book is the reconstruction of this story: the story of the historical movement of the Malas and the Madigas who embraced Christianity as a means of achieving social, economic, cultural and religious liberation from their earlier subaltern, depressed condition, thanks to the intervention of the faith-based missionary organizations and charismatic missionaries and native leaders.

One of my aims in this work is to bring the reader's attention to the imperfections that existed in the 19th century Indian society, namely social exclusion, deprivation of economic resources and the continuance of social oppression of the Depressed Castes within the Hindu social system. I have also attempted to narrate the story of Dalits' realization of their subalternity on one hand, and their determination to liberate themselves from the clutches of the oppressive structures within the Hindu society, on the other. The data show that conversion to Christianity had become a matter of conviction and a channel for achieving social mobility for the Depressed Castes.

This narrative on the conversion movement among the Malas and Madigas covers a period of one hundred years: from 1850-1950. The effervescent growth of the Mala and Madiga Christian communities began to be stifled after 1950 when the Government of India refused to recognize the Dalit Christians as Dalits and hence were deprived of all the benefits of affirmative action for Dalits in Indian society. Having grown up in Andhra, I always wondered why the Christian Dalits were deprived of affirmative action by the Government. Hence, the narrative on the conversion and post-conversion change among the Malas and Madigas ends in a brief comment in the form of an epilogue in the concluding chapter on the above predicament of the Dalit Christians in the post-1950 period.

There have been many studies on the Dalits in Andhra in general and the Malas and Madigas in particular from different perspectives. This study has adopted a historical perspective drawing substantial historical documents, both Government and Mission sources. The historical narrative here has been supplemented with sociological and anthropological data collected from the field. It is hoped that this research will contribute to the body of literature on Dalits in general, and Dalit Christians in India, in particular.

This book has emerged from my doctoral thesis, entitled, "Christian Missionaries and the Birth of New Social Consciousness among the Depressed Castes: A Case of the Malas and the Madigas in Colonial Coastal Andhra, 1850-1950." The writing of this book would not have been possible without the help of so many persons and institutions. I owe a debt of gratitude to all of them.

First, I express my deep gratitude and thankfulness to my Supervisor Prof. Amiya Prosad Sen, Department of History and Culture, Faculty of Humanities and Languages, Jamia Millia Islamia University for guiding this study. The thematic layout of the work and the comprehensive subject matter compilation are based upon his suggestions and directions. His supervision and encouragement enabled me to overcome many hurdles in this research. Despite being away from India as a distinguished Heinrich Zimmer Chair at the Heidelberg University, Prof. Sen constantly guided me and led the thesis study into a logical conclusion. I also thank for the support given by Prof. Rizwan Qaiser, who has agreed to be a co-supervisor at the end of my doctoral candidacy. My heartfelt thanks to Prof. Ravindran Gopinath, for his encouragement to start the doctoral studies in the first place. I also acknowledge and thank the other faculty and staff members of the Department of History and Culture, Jamia Millia Islamia University for facilitating this research during the doctoral research program.

My gratitude also go to the following institutions which provided their library and archival facilities and sources for my research: the National Archives of India (New Delhi), the Nehru Memorial Museum and Library (New Delhi), the Vidyajyoti College of Theology Library (Delhi), the Telangana State Archives (formerly the Andhra Pradesh State Archives) (Hyderabad), the State Central Library (Hyderabad), the City Central Library (Hyderabad), the Sundaraiah Vignana Kendram (Hyderabad), the Osmania University Library (Hyderabad), the Indira Gandhi Memorial Library of the University of Hyderabad, Sri Gowthami Regional Library (Rajahmundry), Sri Saraswata Niketan (Vetapalem), Sri Sarvothama Library (Vijayawada) and the State Regional Library (Guntur), Tribhuvan University Central Library and Kaiser Library, Kathmandu, Nepal.

I am also thankful to the management and staff of the United Christian Theological College (Bengaluru), the Andhra Christian Theological College (Hyderabad) and the Gurukul Theological Library (Chennai) for providing me with abundant source materials and other logistic support. I also express my sincere gratitude to a number of persons who went out of their way to assist me in my studies. I sincerely thank Mr. Mohd. Mahfooj Ahmad, Prof. Srinivas Bathula (JMI University), Prof. Yagati Chinna Rao (JNU), Prof. Peter Vethanayakamony (LSTC-Chicago), Prof. Usha Nair-Reichert (GA Tech, USA), Prof. David Raju Bezzam (ANU-Guntur), Dr. K.V.N Raju, Mr. Daniel Selvanayagam (World Vision East Asia), Mr. Velpula Chandrasekhar (Bharat Petroleum) and Mr. Challapalli Mani Kumar (National Secretary, YMCA). I also take this opportunity to thank the Rt. Revd. Graham Kings, former Bishop of Sherborne (Diocese of Salisbury), the Bishop of CSI Krishna-Godavari Diocese the Rt. Rev. T. George Cornelius and the President of Andhra Evangelical Lutheran Church Bishop K. Frederick Paradesi Babu for being excellent examples of leadership for the field of my study. I am also thanking for the advises given and scholarly conversations held with Emeritus Professor R.E. Frykenburg, Prof. Brian Stanley, Prof. Daniel Jeyaraj and Prof. Kirsteen Kim. It is my duty to specially uphold the spirit of scholarship and excellence instilled in me by my teachers at university level namely: Prof. Rekha Pande (HCU), Prof. Atluri Murali (HCU), Prof. Rattanlal Hangloo (VC-Allahabad University) and Prof. Sudhir Pillarisetty (AHA-USA) for their direction and encouragement at various stages of this study. I also thank the support given to me at research level by Prof. Chilkuri Vasantha Rao (Principal-UTC), Rev. Thathapudi Mathews Immanuel (BTESSC), Rev. Anuparthi John Prabhakar (Principal-ACTC) and Dr. James Elisha Taneti (UPSEM-Virginia).

In the publication of the thesis, I owe my sincere gratitude to the Vice-Chancellor, Jamia Millia Islamia for giving me permission to publish this research work. I also thank the Dean, the Registrar and the Controller of Examinations, Jamia Millia University, for facilitating the process of publication.

The doctoral thesis has undergone a revision to make it suitable for a monograph publication standards and I thank Rev Dr. Jose Kalapura, SJ, Director of Xavier Institute of Social Research, Patna for undertaking the editing work of this book. As a scholar on Christianity in India, and as the Executive Editor of the *Indian Church History Review*, he has used his expertise to make my thesis into a published book. I also thank his assistants for giving computer-based technical assistance.

I also thank Mr. Sudhanshu Kanda and Mrs. Anshul Kanda and the staff of the Christian World Imprints, New Delhi, for being very patient with this work and for publishing my book with wonderful professionalism and with highest competence.

I would not have completed my research and its publication without the support of my family members. Starting with my family elders, it is my first and foremost duty to express my utmost love towards my maternal grandparents Sri. Bezzam John Muniyya garu and Smt. Bezzam Anasuyamma garu for their dedicated and selfless efforts to raise me since my mother left for her heavenly abode. I owe my respectful honor to my paternal grandparents Sri. V. Francis garu and Smt. V. Saramma garu (CSI Krishna-Godavari Diocese) for being fascinating examples of Indian Christianity in the pre and post-independence period. I deeply commend my in-laws Sri. Jetty Samuel John garu and Smt. Jetty Suvarna Kamalamma garu for their dedicated efforts for the Andhra Evangelical Lutheran Church in Andhra Pradesh and for being the inspiring examples for this study. I also acknowledge the love and affection I received from my other family elders: Lts. Mrs. Mathe Sowbhagyamma, Bezzam Prasad, V. Charles Williams, V. Jaya Raju, V. Kshemabayamma, V. Susi Kantha Rao, Tadi Sayana Rao, Kapudasi Achyuta Kumar, Jetty Eliza Vara Prasad, and Jetty Jaya Raju.

On a very special note, I express my sincere and loving gratitude to my aunt Mrs. V. Rahel Bhavani who accompanied me in my research tours and for being my moral support. I also thank the generous help I received from my family members namely Bezzam Jawahar Babu, Bezzam Raghunath, V. Izak Lenin, Kapudasi Benarji and my sisters Mrs. Kapudasi Amrutha Vijaya and Mrs. V. Hymavathi. It is also my responsibility to recognize the love and care I have received from my near family members Mrs. T. Radhamma, Dr. Kapudasi

Subhashita Rao, Mr. Azariah Done, Mr. Kapudasi Sarat Babu, Mrs. P. Kasturi, Mr. Jetty Vijaya Kumar and Mr. Jetty Sudhir.

My family is my strength and my pride, and this opportunity gives me to express my appreciation and admiration for my husband Mr. Thimothy Jetty for his steadfast encouragement and affectionate support throughout this study and beyond. I affectionately bless my children Ms. Angela Swarnadeepika Jetty and Mas. Samuel Swarnateja Jetty for their constant patience and considerate understanding throughout the duration of my research study by fulfilling their academic duties diligently.

The two most important people of my life were my parents, my father Sri. V. V. Prasada Rao garu (1946-2011) and my mother Smt. V. Nirmala 'Kasulu' (1951-1970). Though my mother left for her heavenly abode at the very natal stage of my life, she made sure that I am in the best hands of my father who did a noble job of not only taking great care of me and also giving me the best educational foundation for life and making me a lifelong learner. My words of acknowledgement cannot match with the sacrifices he made to put me where I am in my life today and with an everlasting love and unceasing thoughts about these two noble souls, I sincerely dedicate this book to the eternal honour of my parents.

I take sole responsibility for this research study and for the assertions and affirmations contained in this book, and I declare that none of the above persons are responsible. Please direct your comments, questions and suggestions to my email address: santim2002@gmail.com.

Santha Kumari Varikoti-Jetty

September 7, 2019

List of Maps/Charts, Figures & Tables

Table List

Chapter 1

Introduction

The conversion and social change among the Depressed Castes[1] of Andhra Pradesh, especially the Malas and Madigas, since the second part of the 19th century is an interesting study to understand the processes and dynamics of upward social mobility in a traditional Indian society. Traditionally, the Malas were agricultural labourers and the Madigas, skilled leather workers.[2] For centuries they were marginalized from the mainstream society under the caste system. They were both included and excluded at the same time within the caste system: included to do all sorts of menial but essential occupations for the general society for which they were marginally remunerated, but excluded from the privileges of the four castes under the system. From a human rights perspective, they were bereft of any human rights. In a caste-based society, the depressed castes (today called the Scheduled Castes or Dalits), suffered centuries of inequalities and oppression.

Though there were many socio-religious reform movements which envisaged to bring about equality in society during the ancient and medieval periods, it was during the modern period, especially during the colonial period, reform became actualized in the life of the Depressed Castes. This was mainly because they were able to have access to and participate in the socio-economic and educational resources which were made available to them thanks to the mediation of certain external agencies, during the colonial period.

Among the several agents who facilitated this process, were the Christian missionaries whose philanthropic activities for growth of education and economic development resulted in the social upliftment of the Malas and the Madigas. In the case of Andhra Pradesh both Protestant and Catholic missionaries had well-networked systems of evangelization which essentially included humanitarian, liberative and empowerment programmes which were available to all members of the Indian society, but preferentially available to the poor classes and converts to Christianity.

Social change takes places due to a multiplicity of factors: it is often difficult to pin point a single factor. But a signal factor can trigger an avalanche of changes. Putting first things first, in the case of the Malas and Madigas in Andhra Pradesh, missionary presence, their evangelization and program for social upliftment came first. Then came conversion which was followed by upward social mobility, characterized by socio-religious and socio-economic changes, mediated through education. The basic imperfections in the 19th century Indian society, namely social exclusion and deprivation of economic resources, were said to be the reasons behind the depressed castes' choice of an alternative path for social upliftment.[3] In a context of oppressive social exclusion faced by the depressed castes, the evangelistic and philanthropic services of the Christian missionaries seem to have effected nearly one-fifth of India's depressed castes out of their depressed state.[4]

Though the services of the missionaries were available to all, it was the most marginalized sections of society which largely responded to their evangelization through conversion, accepting their religion. A large segment of the Malas and Madigas seem to have made 'conscious decisions' to break away from the fetters of the contemporary religiously-sanctioned caste system under Hinduism, and converted to Christianity. In their perception, Christianity as preached by the missionaries held out an alternative socio-religious system which believed in one God, as Father of all humans, and all humans as children, and hence brothers and sisters. There was no space for hierarchy of persons, all were considered equal and opportunities for human development were equally available to all. The decision to convert was personal, but there was group stimulus. Individuals, groups, and village communities responded *en masse*, making conversion a mass movement. Though missionary scholars have often variously described such a movement as 'mass movement' or 'group movement', 'birthing of a new group consciousness,' and so on, it was a conversion movement. And in this case, the movement was to Christianity.

Based on large amounts statistical and historical data, this study examines the mechanisms and dynamics of conversion and the post-conversion social, economic and educational changes among the Malas and Madigas, thanks to the mediation of the missionaries. Included in this study, is an attempt to understand the ethnographic, social, religious, cultural, economic and educational status of the Malas and Madigas in early mid-nineteenth century. The roles of the missionaries, their organizations, pastoral engagement, and so on have been studied using a large amount of mission sources. This is followed by an examination of the strategies and services of the missionaries. Also included in this study, is the response of the Malas and Madigas to missionary evangelism. Finally, in the epilogue, an attempt is made to understand the predicament of the Dalit converts in the post-Independence era.

1.1 The 19th Century Socio-Religious Reform Movements: An Overview

During the second part of the 19th century, a movement of social change occurred among the literate people due to their exposure to the colonial administrators, scholars and missionaries. This was characterized by attempt to reform from within given the self-understanding of the depth of social and religious degeneration in the Indian society. The establishment of schools and colleges by the colonial administrators and Christian missionaries contributed to a widespread zeal for social reform from within. There was awakened interest among the educated intelligentsia in the purification of their religion. There were also efforts by social reformers to establish Hindu religious life and worship more in accordance with the enlightened spirit of the age, which was a direct outgrowth of a spirit of rationality and reasoning.[5] The reform societies were oriented towards theistic reforms with a formalized abridgement of the supposed substratum of rationality contained within the Hindu tradition. The fundamental doctrine of the reformists was purification of the caste system and the removal of gross scandals and narrow exclusiveness in Hindu society thereby reorganizing the society based on equality and individual worth.

The 19th century social reform movements may be categorized into two: *Social Reformative Movements* that were conducted within the Hindu religious fold and led by the Hindu theistic societies and *Alternative Reformative Movements* that took place outside the Hindu socio-religious system which were led by the Christian missionaries.

Missionaries were instrumental in humanizing the efforts of the British government as manifested in the abolition of the practice of Sati and female infanticide. Great improvement were noted in the moral, religious and social life of the Indians thanks to the colonial legislations against certain inhuman practices such as human sacrifices, torture in religious rites, burning of widows, killing of female children, etc.

Foremost among the societies which ushered in reformative movement, was the Brahma Samaj (Society of God) founded by Raja Ram Mohan Roy which had a genuine desire to form a fair judgment of the merits of every creed and emphasized on pure monotheistic worship and the unity or oneness of God. The Samaj was open to the preaching of non-Hindu faiths and to accept what was good in them. The attempt of the Samaj was to restore the original purity of Hindu religion by discarding idol-worship as it was considered as non-belief in a living God. With an aim to reform the Hindu society, the Brahma Samaj strived for the removal of the social evil *Sati*, through legislation in 1829 which legislated that anyone who abetted the act of *Sati* was considered guilty of culpable homicide.[6] Another most important effort of the Samaj was getting the "Native Marriage Act", 1872 passed, which introduced the institution of civil marriage in Hindu society.[7] The Samaj also advocated against narrow exclusiveness of castes and fought for purification of the caste system.

The Arya Samaj, another reformative society, believed that the Vedas were the repository of knowledge and asserted its firm faith in the infallibility of the Vedas and their sufficiency for attaining salvation. It aspired to replace the then Hindu society with the Vedic society where one God was adored and only the Vedas were studied, accompanied by the sacrifice of homa with its elaborate ceremonies.[8] It had openly abandoned idolatry and publicly professed the principle of monotheism and called for annihilation of all caste distinctions. However, it advocated safeguarding of the hereditary professions or guilds and hence occupational mobility was stifled. The Arya Samaj strongly opposed social evils in society especially the practice of child marriage and achieved success in creating a public opinion in favour of fixing the minimum marriageable age at 16 for girls and 25 for boys. The Samaj laid down a remarkable educational network and special schools for the children of the depressed castes. The Arya Samaj had the distinction of re-admitting people from Islam and Christianity back into the fold of Hinduism.

An application of the ideals of the Arya Samaj was seen in the Sanskritisation movement, which was characterized by 'symbolic justification' wherein caste equality is appropriated by lower castes by caste up-gradation, through adopting the life styles, customs and rituals of the upper castes. A low caste person changes his/her customs, ritual, ideology and way of life in the direction of a high or the 'twice-born' caste in matters of language, cooking, clothing, jewelry and way of life.[9] According to Prof. M. N. Srinivas, an upward mobility has always been possible if a low caste was able, in a generation or two, to rise to a higher position in the hierarchy by adopting vegetarianism and teetotalism and by adopting the customs, rites, and beliefs of the Brahmins.[10] In other words, Sanskritisation enables a caste person to obtain a higher position in the hierarchy.[11] The process of Sanskritisation in Owen Lynch's words, involved emulation of three characters namely *identification*, *imitation* and *negation*.

One specific reference group could be cited as example: the Jatavs ('low' caste Chamars) of Agra who sought to raise their social position in the caste hierarchy to claim the status of Kshatriyas. The growth of education, political consciousness and change in economic structure had raised the position of the Jatavs in the caste hierarchy.[12] Another example of Sanskritisation can be seen in the *Chamars* of Uttar Pradesh, who were traditionally stigmatized leather workers, shoe makers and agricultural labourers. Bernard S. Cohn described the Chamars of Madhopur as traditional leather workers, shoe makers and agricultural labourers. The *Chamars* had been relegated to a polluted status due to their association with leather works of skinning, tanning and eating beef and were economically tied to the upper caste *Thakurs*,[13] through the system of *jajmani*. In the early part of the twentieth century, these Chamars set up tanning enterprises and became wealthy merchants with lucrative trading business.[14] They competed for higher rank through self-disciplined ways of life and achieved significant upward social mobility. Therefore, the low castes' effort to push themselves up within the Hindu system was possible provided, it was accompanied by upward economic mobility. Increased economic mobility led to increased social mobility and change in life style patterns.[15]

Similarly, the *Kammalans* of the Tamil region, the *Coorgs* of Mysore, the *Viswakarmas* and *Nayi Brahmins* of the coastal Andhra achieved upward mobility through Sanskritization.[16] However, the power of these movements and the levels of socio-economic change was limited due to the hegemonic hold of caste system in India.

In the opinion of M. N. Srinivas the 'pushing up' within the Hindu system through emulative practices did not attract the depressed castes in South India. It was in the form of self-consciousness that came with a deep dissatisfaction with the established order. The combination of both endogenous and exogenous factors contributed for the collective action for reform with precipitating mechanisms and structural changes in the society. Social mobility of the groups was symbolized and legitimated through a desire to move upwards on the social ladder and was rationalized in the form of group conversion movements.

There were alternative social reform movements which were characterized by protest ideologies which challenged the caste-bound systems. The social reform work of Mahatma Jotirao Phule consisted of disproval of caste privileges and liberation of women from their subordinate condition in patriarchal society. He consistently criticized the practice of untouchability and questioned the power and supremacy enjoyed by the upper castes.[17] He made considerable impact on the emerging intelligentsia of the Mahars of Maharashtra and provided inspiration for the building of an anti-untouchable movement in the middle of the 20th century.[18]

Another alternative reform movement through protest and pro-active action was initiated by Sri Narayana Guru (1854-1928) among the *Ezhavas* in Kerala. They were large endogamous groups known as *Thiyyas*, *Chovans* and *Thandans* and were considered to be lower in social position and hence, were consistently denied entry into Hindu temples and were denied other privileges. The Guru propagated the idea of "one caste, one religion and one God" through his organization (Sri Narayana Dharma Paripalanayogam-SNDP) to strengthen and spread spiritual reformation in the contemporary Kerala society. The temples which he established became centres of temple entry programs. The main goals of the organization were upliftment of the Ezhavas and reform of rituals in Hindu religion in matters of worship and customs. Advocating modern education and sanskritized practices, Sri Narayana Guru made efforts to transform the Ezhavas from an 'untouchable' group to be a liberated entity.[19] The movement of Sri Narayana Guru also checked, to a considerable extent, the movement towards conversion to Christianity, which had begun to occur among the Dalits in Kerala, due to the influence of the Christian missionaries in Kerala.[20]

The wave of socio-religious reform did not leave Coastal Andhra untouched. In the latter half of the nineteenth century, Coastal Andhra had seen social reform movements owing to the spread of English education and the growth of journalism. A class of social reformers imbibed with the spirit of social reform and liberal ideologies emerged. Foremost among the social reformers were Sri Kandukuri Veeresalingam (1848-1911) who was the father of renaissance movement in Andhra. He not only enlightened the people of Andhra by means of his literary, moral and social works, but also relieved the distress of a number of widows through widow-remarriages.[21] Also, Sri Gurajada Appa Rao (1862-1915) campaigned against the dowry system through his artistic play of *Kanyasulkam*.[22] Sri Raghupati Venkataratnam Naidu (1862 -1939) strived for eradication of untouchability and abolition of the devadasi system through his social purity movement.[23] Sri Chilakamarthi Lakshmi Narasimham (1867-1945) played an important role in the removal of untouchability effecting upliftment among the Harijans.[24] Sri Unnava Lakshminarayana (1877-1950) stood for the cause of the depressed castes by highlighting the problems faced by them through his work "*Mālapalli*".[25]

In the first part of the 20th century, Periyar E. V. Ranmaswamy Naiker initiated reforms in Tamil Nadu, wherein he rejected the Brahmanical priesthood and Sanskritic scriptural authority of the Brahmins which had largely driven the non-Brahmin populace to secondary citizens. His *Self-Respect Union* strived to restore dignity and pride in the Dravidian traditions and culture.[26]

Similarly, the conversion movement among the Depressed Castes under the influence of the Christian missionaries can be considered an alternative social reform movement. In the light of the proclaimed spiritual equality and the promise of a just society propagated by the Christian missionaries, a new wave of depressed caste adherents to Christianity emerged in Indian society. The depressed castes, in the words of Gordon, were influenced by the Gospel narrative of "the story of Jesus the son of God, became a poor man, performed miracles, died for sinners, arose from the dead and ascended to heaven."[27]

The socio-evangelistic mobilization of the Depressed Castes was achieved by the Christian missionaries by advocating them to disengage themselves from their old forms of life and worship practices. Missionaries had also been great pioneers of modern education, and had conducted schools both in vernacular and in English for all children irrespective of caste including the 'outcastes'.[28] Their proselytization combined with reform activities through education had created avenues for upward social mobility among the depressed castes' especially in South India.

Among the lower caste communities of South India, the *Nadars* (formerly a Dalit caste group called *Shanars*, known as *Nadars* since the 1920s) clearly present a powerful example of achieving social change through conversion in the 19th and 20th centuries.[29] Samuel Mateer and R. L. Hardgrave have described the substantial social change among the Nadars and the vital role played by the Anglican missionaries.

The Shanars of South Travancore were climbers of the Palmyra trees (toddy tapers), and were the first ones to embrace Christianity in large numbers. The Shanar social condition was as deplorable as that of the Malas and the Madigas of the 19th century coastal Andhra. But under the benign influence of Christianity, they had achieved material improvement and social change.[30] A new social consciousness emerged due to the efforts of the London Missionary Society which had not only provided the former with education and employment opportunities, but also pressed for legislative reforms to allow the Shanar women to wear the upper cloth after their conversion to Christianity, a privilege which was denied to the non-converts. As early as 1814, Colonel Munro had argued for the adoption of upper cloth to be worn by converted Christian women.[31] In 1859 the government of Travancore issued a proclamation regarding the adoption of wearing of the upper cloth by the lower castes.[32] The Shanars/Nadars also attained good educational progress and improved their position considerably in many spheres of remunerative and honourable labour.[33] R. L. Hardgrave observed that urbanization and new economic opportunities enabled the Shanars to abandon tree-climbing occupation and to become wholesale traders and merchants. Others, particularly the Christians, pursued education sufficiently to become teachers, advocates and lawyers. By the middle of the 20th century, the Shanars/Nadars experienced a large measure of material prosperity and were considered to be too advanced to be placed in the list of Scheduled castes in 1936. The uplift movement among the Shanars/Nadars of Tamil Nadu had been thoroughly organized within the caste solidarity and class based respect.[34]

The *Pulayas* (a Scheduled Caste community) of Kerala were agricultural laborers and were held in traditional bondage *(adirna)* or in client relationship with their high caste landlords, and could only claim a bare maintenance from the landlord.[35] The activities of the Christian missionaries had brought the Pulayas to large scale conversion into Christianity and an awareness of social identity sprang up among the Pulayas. Rev. George Matthan had observed that "strong fears existed among all classes of people that the enlightenment of slaves would be followed by their liberation and the consequent ruin of the interests of agriculture."[36] With a combination of the anti-slavery campaign and evangelistic efforts, the emancipation of the Pulayas was made possible. Through the government laws made in 1853 and 1855, the Rajah had proclaimed the elimination of slavery and provided for the Pulayas holding of property as freemen.[37] During the years 1915-16, the demand of covering breast cloth was adopted by the Pulaya women but the Nairs had expressed their bitter feelings and confronted the Pulayas.[38] Many Pulayas became converts to Christianity and experienced a rise on the social scale in regard to education and an ability to hold a social place for themselves.[39]

The Census of 1881 pertaining to Punjab described the *Chuhras* as the sweepers and scavengers in Punjab and some provinces of North India. They were one of the village menials proper, who had received a customary share of the produce in exchange of certain duties performed. The Chuhras lived in a condition of extreme poverty, insecurity and depended upon the higher castes for their livelihood.[40] C. B. Webster has described that the Chuhras, converted in large groups since the last part of the 19th century under the leadership of Rev. Samuel Martin and a native Christian convert named Ditt.[41] Conversion into Christianity led to social change among the Chuhra not only in matters of social esteem, but also in health, education and material advancement.[42]

1.2 Alternative Reform Movement among the Malas and the Madigas

Bishop Parker observed that the religion of the Malas and Madigas did not belong to orthodox Hinduism, but held on less firm practiced traditions. The Malas and the Madigas had readily received the Christian missionaries and their Gospels as a remedy to their social and religious problems. Besides, whatever was done for these people was considered as kindness or favour. Many of them had an urge towards '*moving on*',[43] to liberate themselves from their contemporary oppressed situation. On the Mission side, the missionaries readily received them into Christianity as a majority of the Malas and the Madigas was keen to embrace this new religion. Along with this, they were attracted by the social upliftment programmes of the missionaries especially education and vocational training, which they were convinced, were able to prop them up on a path of upward social mobility. On the other hand, the missionaries were challenged by the response of the upper castes who declined to convert saying "if these [meaning, Dalits] are received, we cannot enter your church."[44]

The main reason for the conversion of the Malas and the Madigas was to break away from their unclean occupations and free themselves from social discrimination at the hands of the 'caste people'.[45] Mahatma Gandhi, while holding his opinion that conversion is not a remedy for social problems, also expressed that "if a change of religion could be justified for worldly betterment I would advise it without hesitation. But religion is a matter of the heart."[46] It can be said that the Mala and the Madiga converts chose the path of conversion to ameliorate their depressed condition both socially and economically.[47] Our data on the number of Christians and the growth of Christianity from the year 1871 to 1951 show that converts belonged to different sub-castes among the Malas and Madigas.

1.2.1 Dalits' Interest in Christianity in Andhra

The London Missionary Society was the first missionary society to attract the attention of the Malas in the Ceded districts which was geographically placed adjacent to Coastal Andhra districts.[48] It was described that an Anglo-Indian civil servant, William Howell, who was stationed at Cuddapah during the early part of the nineteenth century, had the habit of visiting jails where he came across with a particular Atuku Nancharu, a Mala seller of thread.[49] Upon his release Nancharu met Mr. Howell and invited him to come to his village and preach the Gospel and thereafter Christianity began to find roots among the Malas since 1838.[50] Subsequently, the Malas in the adjoining Northern Circars and Nizam's provinces took interest in the work of the missionaries.

With regard to the Madigas, the first American Baptist missionaries Rev. Dr. Lyman Jewett and Rev. John E. Clough were initially perplexed to receive them, as their Gospel work among the *Súdras* was satisfactorily progressing. During the initial years, there were no Madigas in the Nellore church but the missionaries eventually agreed to admit the Madigas as they realized that they were bound to receive everyone who believed in Jesus Christ.[51] Besides, the Madigas also seem to have perceived missionary services as channels of social upliftment.[52] A very large movement among the Madigas was on its way after the first initiative taken by a certain Yerraguntla Periah, a Madiga who became the forerunner of the Madiga group mobility movement towards Christianity.

1.3 Scope of the Research

The study period for this study stretches from the year 1850 to 1950, during which time diverse social reform movements and political struggles took place in India. As noted above, the present study deals with an alternative reformative movement in coastal Andhra during the period, 1850-1950, initiated by Christian missionaries. The two Depressed Caste communities which converted to Christianity were the Malas and Madigas. This study deals with nearly one hundred years of their engagement with Christianity. They were socially known as 'Indian Christians'. It may be noted that in the post-independence era, the Mala and Madiga Christians in Andhra Pradesh tend to subscribe to twin nominal identities namely, '*Indian Christian'* which explicitly marks their religious identity as Christians, along with the official nomenclature given to the Depressed castes under the Constitution of India, namely, Scheduled Castes originally *'Adi-Andhra-Hindu'*. This liminal social status is due to the dilemma and contradiction created by the Presidential Order of 1950 wherein, Schedules Castes or Dalits exist only in Hindu, Buddhist or Sikh religion, whereas the converted Dalits to Christianity and Islam are denied Scheduled Caste status in a way to debar them from Government benefits of affirmative action (reservation in education and employment). Thus in the post-1950 era, the Dalit Christians in Andhra and elsewhere in India, live in a deprived state, due to constitutional disabilities. I shall discuss this aspect in the Epilogue. In the following chapters, I shall discuss the process of conversion and change among the Mala and Madiga Dalit Christians in coastal Andhra, initiated by the Christian missionaries.

1.4 Methodology

A *Historical-Descriptive* form of research is used for qualitative data analysis of historical resources for inductive results. Various primary and secondary sources have been used to narrate an ethnographic account of the Malas and the Madigas from sociological and anthropological perspectives. At the micro level, the study takes into account the case studies of pioneer individual converts and at the macro level it takes into consideration the collective action of specific groups of people (Malas and Madigas). To fit this work into a theoretical and conceptual framework, several missionary works and Church's official records pertaining to the work of Christian missionaries and the response of the people, were examined. A systematic and thematic approach has been adopted for illustrating the components and processes of social change by incorporating all the elements of the change among the Malas and Madigas.

By using the available primary and secondary sources, a narrative analysis of the historical factors was employed. The main strength of the study is drawn from the wealth of missionary sources.

The findings help us to understand the nature of change among the depressed castes in particular and the Indian society in general. By examining a variety of social issues pertaining to the people of India, the reliability of the study is assured for further researches on social issues for the progress of Indian historical research. The validity of the study is based upon the accurate interpretation of the sources and a genuine diffusion of ideas and observations. The content validity comes with historical verification and a qualitative account of the given constructs that represent all areas of social development. The work is also valid in the light of the accumulated evidence about the social consciousness-induced upward social mobility among the Malas and the Madigas. If any inadequacies are observed in this work, it is due to insufficient official and unofficial data pertaining specifically to the convert Christians of the Malas and the Madigas.

1.5 Sources of Research

The scope of the study covers an analysis of the life of the Malas and Madigas in all its varied forms and culture prior to their conversion and the post-conversion life, culture and changes. On examination of the plentiful sources, it is possible to trace the growth of a new social consciousness among the Malas and Madigas. As Government sources are limited and non-specific to the Malas and Madigas, I have had to rely upon the writings of the missionaries, missionary proceedings and documents. In spite of strenuous attempts to access Church's official registers such as Baptism Registers, which could have given the details of the different castes, it could not be done. Aside the wide variety of primary sources, I have made ample use of numerous secondary sources, including digital ones, to present this study as a logical narrative and interpretation of historical facts.

An identification of the past literature concerning the depressed castes' and the Christian missionaries in colonial Andhra help us to know the works of historical information pertaining to this area of research. The missionary works of various denominations give us valuable accounts of various aspects of development among the depressed castes.

The published official sources which are used in this research are the *Census Reports* from the year 1871 to 1951 and *District Gazetteers* (1907) pertaining to the districts of Ganjam, Vizagapatam, Godavari, Kistna and Nellore. Besides, the following official sources were examined in order to support and substantiate the secondary source materials. These are the *Report on Public Instruction in the Madras Presidency* and *Administrative Reports of the Harijan Welfare Department,* Charles E. Grover's *Results of Educational Census* (1871), Gordon Mackenzie's *A Manual of the Kistna·District in the Presidency of Madras* (1883), Henry Morris's account of *A Descriptive* and *Historical Account of the Godavari District in the Presidency of Madras* (1878), D. F. Carmichael's *A Manual Of the District of Vizagapatam in the Presidency of Madras (1869), The Imperial Gazetteer of India* (1909), *The Manual of the Administration of the Madras Presidency* (1885), *The Administrative Report of the Harijan Welfare Department, The Report on the Administration of the Police of the Madras Province,* Srinivasa Raghavaiyangar's *The Memorandum of the Progress of the Madras Presidency during the Last Forty Years of British Administration* (1893), *The Report on the Administration of the Madras Presidency* for various years and *The Report of the Commissioner for Schedule Castes* and *Scheduled Tribes.*

1.5.1 Mission Sources

Since the history and work of the Protestant Christian missionaries in coastal Andhra began with the London Missionary Society, the literature pertaining to their mission, personnel and activities become important. The two volumes, *The History of the London Missionary Society: 1795-1895,* (1899) by Richard Lovett gives a long chronology of events narrating the progress of the mission.

The Canadian Baptist Missionary activities have been described by John Craig in his work *Forty Years among the Telugus: A History of the Mission of the Baptists of Ontario* and *Quebec, Canada to the Telugus, South India 1867-1907* (1908) wherein facts about the beginning of the Canadian Baptist Mission and its evangelistic methods are narrated. In *The Enterprise; The Jubilee Story of the Canadian Baptist Mission in India, 1874-1924* (1925), by M. L. Orchard and Ms. K. S. McLaurin presents much information pertaining to the half-a-century of pioneering missionary work of the Canadian Baptist Mission and its influence on Indian society.

Much information about the beginning of the Godavari Delta Mission was found in various works of colonial personnel like Sir Arthur Cotton, Rev. Alexander Duff and Rev. C.T.E. Rhenius. For instance, the work of Ms. Elizabeth Reid Cotton, *General Sir Arthur Cotton, R.E.K.C.S.I., His Life and Work* (1900) may be used for information pertaining to the association between the East India Company's Chief Engineer Sir Arthur Cotton and Rev. Anthony Norris Groves, the principal force behind the founding of the Godavari Delta Mission. In the *Memoir of Anthony Norris Groves compiled chiefly from His Journals* and *Letters* (1869), Mrs. Harriet Groves gives an account of how the English Baptist missionaries strived among the coolies and the dam workers of the Dowlaishvaram area.

The beginning of the Church Missionary Society's (CMS) work in the Telugu areas is broadly narrated in Eugene Stock's four volume work, *The History of the Church Missionary Society: Its Environment, Its Men and Its Work* (1899). M. E. Gibbs, in his work, *The Anglican Church in India 1600-1970* (1972) shows the Anglican contribution for the evangelization of India and the rise of Indian Nationalism on Christian lines and the efforts of the Indian Christian clergy to become independent of the foreign missionary influence.

The history of the American Evangelical Lutheran Mission in the Telugu districts is depicted in George Drach and Calvin F Kuder's *Telugu Mission of the General Council of the Evangelical Lutheran Church in North America Containing a Biography of the Rev. Christian Frederick Heyer* (1914), in which the authors have discussed about the missionary work of Rev. Heyer and the growth of the Lutheran mission work in the Godavari and Kistna districts. L. B. Wolf has presented a historical sketch of the American Lutheran mission on the occasion of the Jubilee celebration of the mission in his *After Fifty Years: Or an Historical Sketch of the Guntur Mission of the Evangelical Lutheran Church of the General Synod in the United States of America* (1896). This book was written based on first sources and personal accounts about the advancement of Christianity among the people and their habits and customs.

The story of American Baptist Mission in the Telugu provinces is one of the success histories of missionary triumphs. Described from a missionary perspective, David Downie authored *The Lone Star: the History of the Telugu Mission of the American Baptist Missionaries Union* (1892). It is a compilation of the facts bearing on the Mission's work in leading the group mobility movements among the Madigas in the last part of the 19th century. A remarkable work of scholarly eminence was written by Mrs. Emma Rauschenbusch Clough for her husband Rev. John E. Clough titled *Social Christianity in the Orient: the Story of a Man, a Mission and a Movement* (1914), which is a detailed narration of events about the Madigas' group mobility movement towards Christianity in the Ongole and Nellore regions. This work about the Madigas could be viewed from the perspective of the reconstruction of modern Indian society on progressive lines.

1.5.2 Secondary Sources

The contemporary secondary sources that are relevant to the theme of Christian conversion and social change are varied in nature. Antony Copley's *Religions in Conflict: Ideology, Cultural Contact* and *Conversion in Late-Colonial India* (1997), Geoffrey A. Oddie's *Religious Conversion Movements in South Asia: Continuities* and *Change, 1800-1990* (1997), *Religion in South Asia: Religious Conversion* and *Revival Movements in South Asia in Medieval* and *Modern Times* (1977), and *Social Protest in India: British Protestant Missionaries* and S*ocial Reforms, 1850-1900* (1979), give us interpretative accounts of missionary efforts for the upliftment of the depressed castes in a complex social context.

Pertaining to the group mobility movements among the Malas, J. W Pickett has described the nature of the movements in his *Christian Mass Conversion Movements in India: A Study with Recommendations (1933)*, and in *Christ's Way to India's Heart* (1938), where he has tried to delineate the issue of material benefits from the spiritual quest of the converts. Dick Kooiman's *Conversion* and *Social Equality in India* (1989), Duncan B. Forrester's *Caste* and *Christianity: Attitudes* and *Polices on Caste of Anglo-Saxon Protestant Missions in India* (1980), Manickam Sundararaj's *The Social Setting of Christian Conversion in South India: The Impact of Wesleyan Methodist Missionaries on the Trichy-Tanjore Diocese with Special Reference to the Harijan Communities of the Mass Movement Area, 1820-1947* (1971) give accounts of Christian conversion and group mobility movements. C.

H. Swavely's *Hundred Years in the Andhra Country: A History of the India Mission of the United Lutheran Church in America* (1942) and *The Lutheran Enterprise in India 1706-1952* (1952) provide us with important information about the American Lutheran Mission in the Telugu provinces.

J. Mangamma's monographic account on Christian Missionaries and their contribution to education and medical care--*Andhra Desamulo Kraisthava Missionarila Seva* (1992)--is a brief but descriptive account of the Christian missionary activities in Andhra. A. T. Fishman's *Culture Change and the Underprivileged: A Study of* Madigas *in South India under Christian Guidance* (1941) and *For This Purpose: A Case Study of the Telugu Baptist Church in Its Relation with South India Mission of the American Baptist Foreign Mission Societies in India* (1958) deal in detail about the Madigas' conversion and subsequent upliftment from their depressed condition. Susan Billington Harper has narrated the efforts of Bishop Azariah to make the Indian Church free from the missionary influence since the year 1913, in her biographical account, *In the Shadow of the Mahatma; Bishop V.S Azariah and the Travails of Christianity in British India* (2000).

The above mentioned missionary accounts are only indicative of the list of sources which throw light on the social change among the depressed castes. Various official and contemporary source materials have been examined to understand the aspects of social change in the areas of religion, education, employment and social mobility of the subject communities in this study.

1.6 Chapterisation

This book deals with the conversion and social change among two Depressed Castes of Andhra Pradesh, the Malas and Madigas, from the second part of the 19th century till mid twentieth century. Various aspects of the process of conversion, namely the contextual factors, social factors, the dynamics and the level of upward social mobility achieved by these communities thanks to the missionary mediation, are covered in this study. As noted above in this introductory chapter, we have covered a general view of the 19th century socio-religious reform movements, besides making a note on the scope of the research, methodology, and sources of it.

Chapter 2 is an attempt to understand the 19th century social, economic, religious and political conditions of Colonial Coastal Andhra Pradesh, with special focus on the Malas and Madigas. It is envisaged that a historical, sociological, and ethnographic understanding of these two communities will enable the reader to understand, in some measure, the change in these communities, their achievements and upward social mobility after their encounter with Christianity. The chapter has three sections. Within these sections we have covered the socio-religious, educational and cultural condition, the social structures as part of the caste structures, the ethnography of the Malas and Madigas, their religious and cultural practices, the actual picture of their depressed condition have been re-constructed from numerous historical documents. Alongside, the various reform movements then in vogue in Andhra, the call for alternative path of reform made by the Christian missionaries have been noted. Faced with many hardships, the Malas and the Madigas chose to convert to Christianity when presented with the Gospel by the Christian missionaries, apparently with a hope of being liberated from their socio-religious fetters and of attaining better economic freedom.

Chapter 3 gives a detailed description of the work of the Christian missionaries in Coastal Andhra Pradesh. The early section of the chapter deals with the historical background of Christianity in Andhra, including the early Protestant missions in South India, the ecclesiastical policy of the British East India Company which then ruled the Coastal Andhra, the early Protestant Missionary Societies in Colonial Andhra, etc. The major sections of the chapter deal with the main six missionary societies, namely 1) the London Missionary Society, 2) the Canadian Baptist Mission, 3) the Godavari Delta Mission, 4) the Church Missionary Society, 5) the American Evangelical Lutheran Mission, and 6) the American Baptist Mission. The chapter also describes the missionary methods of these mission societies. The readers will note that the vast network of the Christian missionaries in colonial Andhra became a prominent feature of the social setting in Coastal Andhra where they undertook the role of 'agents of change' which brought forth a new social consciousness among the Malas and the Madigas.

Chapter 4 examines the process of conversion among the Malas and Madigas, particularly the spread, factors, and dynamics, besides a discussion on the role of the agencies in conversion. Further, an attempt has been made to uncover the motives of individual and group conversions and the purpose of the missionaries. What may be noted is that individual and group conversions seem to have occurred as a result of many contingent factors both spiritual and non-spiritual in nature. Also noted is the birth of a new consciousness among the Malas and Madigas. Conversion seems to have been their attempt to create a new identity for themselves and was the beginning of a great change in all aspects of life, particularly educational mobility, occupational mobility and social mobility. Though there were multiple agencies including the administration of the Colonial government, the work of the Christian missions was pre-eminent, in mediating the upward socio-religious and socio-cultural mobility among the Malas and Madigas.

Chapter 5 deals with another major engagement of the mission, namely providing education and modern health care to the people, both converts and non-converts. The first section explores the spread and depth of the educational enterprise of the Missions and examines the mediatory function of education in effecting social mobility among the Malas and the Madigas. The early part of the section has a review of the contemporary situation of education in Colonial Andhra, and the education policy of the Company Government. The missionary enterprise in education of the Malas and Madigas has been detailed out in separate parts. The second section explores the health care works of the missionaries. The chapter throws light on medical evangelism that is, preaching through medical care as an aspect of practical Christianity. Another aspect of this ministry was training the converts to become medical professionals as a means of employment and empowerment through adopting alternative occupations. Medical work among women through the Zenana Mission also has been dealt with in this section. That the medical mission became an important agency which not only improved the health condition of both converts and non-converts by alleviating their physical sufferings and pain, but also helped change the people's attitude to health care by discouraging obsolete and superstitious practices on one hand, and enhancing familiarity with the scientific understanding of diseases, besides instilling habits of hygienic living.

Chapter 6 is an interpretation of the missionary works among the Malas and Madigas keeping focus on both the mission agency and the target communities. Two broad areas of social change have been detailed out: socio-economic and socio-religious. Briefing describing the economic deprivation of the two communities in the given, entrenched caste system, the study analyses how the missionaries provided the people alternative packages of economic empowerment programs such as better agricultural techniques for better production, increase of irrigation facilities, establishing of agricultural settlements, imparting agricultural training, offering means of alternative professions, technical education, alternative employment avenues through teaching profession, preaching ministry, health profession, industrial financing, industrial production, etc. The chapter also makes a note of the higher level of socio-economic mobility which included their moving out from the former caste-bound traditional occupations by the Malas and Madigas. The second section deals with the socio-religious changes. In this area one is more certain about the powerful intervention of mission on one hand, and the conscientious decision of the converts to abandon their certain established rites, rituals, customs and traditions which they had been observing for centuries, in lieu of adopting new rites, rituals, customs and traditions which were part of their Christianization. In sum the chapter explains the construction of a Christian socio-religious identity by the converts in Andhra.

The concluding Chapter 7 gives an overview of the findings of the whole study besides an epilogue on the predicament of the converts in the post-Independence period, that is, from 1950s when socially the convert Malas and Madigas were accorded a different status under the Indian Constitution. They suffered a setback when they were excluded from the category of Scheduled Castes under the Presidential Order of 'Constitution (Scheduled Castes) Order, 1950'. While the non-Christian Hindu, Sikh or Buddhist members of the former Depressed Castes (Dalits) were categorised as Scheduled Castes and were given legal provisions and reservation in education and government jobs, the converted Depressed Castes were discriminated against on the basis that Christianity officially does not have caste. The chapter notes that the ground reality is otherwise. Not only that the convert Dalits continue to be treated as 'low castes' in the ambient general society, but also within the Christian community where they suffer deprivation due to their caste. Thus, Dalit Christians are 'twice deprived'. It implies that while the Constitution of India maintains clearly that India is a secular state and every person has a right to practice any religious faith, Dalit Christians are made to suffer discrimination because of their faith in a non-Hindu religion. The chapter concludes by saying that though class mobility and occupational mobility have taken place among the Dalit Christians in Andhra Pradesh after conversion, they continue to suffer caste discrimination and even untouchability, in the wider society and even in the Church.

Endnotes and References

1 A term used by the Colonial administration to designate those who were considered outside the four-fold varnas/castes. In the hierarchically ordered Indian society the 'caste people' were categorized again as upper castes and sudra castes (Backward/middle or lower castes). Traditionally, those outside the four-fold castes were called 'outcastes' or *panchamas* (fifth caste),' untouchables', etc. During the colonial period, these were categorised as 'Depressed Castes/Classes'. After Independence, the Depressed Castes/ Classes were officially called 'Scheduled Castes' and recently the generic term 'Dalits' is functionally adopted by the Scheduled Castes themselves. Throughout this study, I use the term 'caste people' (those within the four-castes) to distinguish them from the 'Depressed Castes'. For further explanation see Guenther Roth and Claus Wittich, *Max Weber: Economy and Society, An Outline of Interpretative Sociology* (Los Angeles: The University of California Press, 1978), 493; M. N. Srinivas, *Caste in its Twentieth Century Avatar* (New Delhi: Penguin Books India, 1990, Introduction.

2 Athelstane Baines, *Ethnography: Castes and Tribes* (Strassburg: Karl J. Trubner Publishers, 1912), 9.

3 T. K. Oommen, *Protest and Change: Studies in Social Movements* (London: Sage Publications, 1990), 30.

4 R. E. Frykenberg, "On the Study of Conversion Movements: A Review Article and a Theoretical Note" *The Indian Economic and Social History Review* 17 (1980): 128-129.

5 From an address by the Hon. John W. Foster, given at the Union Missionary Meeting of the Presbyterian Churches of New York City, at Carnegie Hall, November 15, 1895: James S. Dennis, *Christian Missions and Social Progress, A Sociological Study of Foreign Missions,* Vol. II (New York: Fleming H. Revell, 1899), 93.

6 Frank Lillingston, *The Brahmo Samaj and Arya Samaj in their bearing upon Christianity* (London: Macmillan Publishers, 1901), 50.

7 Ibid., 96.

8 Lajpat Rai, *The Arya Samaj: An Account of its Origin, Doctrines and Activities* (London: Longman Greens and Co, 1915), 38.

9 M. N. Srinivas, "A Note on Sanskritization and Westernization", *Far Eastern Quarterly* (1956): 482-484; Lucy Carroll, "Sanskritization, Westernization and Social Mobility: A Reappraisal of the Relevance of Anthropological Concepts to the Social Historian of Modern India", *Journal of Anthropological Research* 33 (4) (1977): 357.

10 M. N. Srinivas, *Religion and Society among the Coorgs of South India* (New Delhi: Asia Publishing House, 1952), 30.

11 M. N. Srinivas, *Caste in India: And Other Essays* (New Delhi: Asia Publishing House, 1962), 43.

12 Owen M. Lynch, *The Politics of Untouchability: Social Mobility and Social Change in a City of India* (Delhi: National Publishing House, 1974), 3.

13 Bernard S. Cohn, McKim Marriott & Alan R. Beals (ed), *The Changing Status of a Depressed Caste Village India; Studies in the Little Community Comparative Studies of Cultures and Civilizations* (Chicago: The University of Chicago Press, 1955), 61.

14 Mark Juergensmeyer, *Religion as Social Vision: The Movement against Untouchability in 20th Century Punjab* (Berkeley: University of California Press, 1982), 36-37.

15 M. N. Srinivas, "Caste in Modern India," *The Journal of Asian Studies* 16 (4), (1957): 531.

16 Ibid.

17 Oliver Mendelsohn and Marika Vicziany, *The Untouchables: Subordination, Poverty and the State in Modern India* (Cambridge: The Cambridge University Press, 1998), 93.

18 Masao Naito, *Marga: Ways of Liberation, Empowerment, and Social Change in Maharashtra* (New Delhi: Manohar Publishers, 2008), 96.

19 Oliver Mendelsohn and Marika Vicziany, op.cit., 97.

20 B. Kuppuswamy, *Social Change in India* (New Delhi: Vikas Publishing House, 1972), 225.

21 *Andhra Patrika*, Februray 11th 1899, in *Report on Native News Papers Examined by the Translators to the Government of Madras*, No 89 (1899), 45.

22 V. Ramakrishna, *Social Reform in Andhra, 1848-1919* (Delhi: Vikas Publishing House, 1983), 103.

23 Ibid., 124.

24 Ibid., 213.

25 Kasinadhuni Nageswara Rao, in Unnava Lakashmi Narayana, *Mālapalli* (1922), Preface.

26 J. Pandian, *Caste, Nationalism and Ethnicity* (Bombay: Popular Prakasan, 1987), 63.

27 John C. B. Webster, *Dalit Christians: A History* (Delhi: ISPCK Publishers, 1994), 71.

28 As early as 1859, government rules were made for the admission of low caste boys in Bengal and its lower provinces: *Government of India, Home-Education Proceedings*, no: 9-12 (February 5, 1858), 9.

29 R. L. Hardgrave, *Essays in the Political Sociology of South India* (New Delhi: Usha Publications, 1979), 164. "The label Nadar was originally a caste title of a particular caste named Shanar of Southern Tamil Nadu. With a general economic and educational transformation and advancement of the caste in the 19th century, the label Nadar became

the caste name. See J. Pandian, "Political Emblems of Caste Identity: An Interpretation of Tamil Caste Titles," *Anthropological Quarterly* 56 (October 4, 1983): 192.

"All Nadars are Shanars by caste, unless indeed they have abandoned caste, as many of them have by becoming Christians". Edgar Thurston, *Castes and Tribes of Southern India*, Vol. VI, P-S (Madras: The Government Press, 1909), 370.

30 Samuel Mateer, *The Gospel in South India: On the Religious Life, Experience, and Character of the Hindu Christians* (London: The Religious Tract Society, 1880), 225.

31 R. L. Hardgrave, op.cit.,154.

32 Samuel Mateer, *The Land of Charity: A Descriptive Account of Travancore and its People with Special Reference to Missionary Labour* (London: John Snow and Company, 1871), 62.

33 R. L. Hardgrave, op. cit., 149.

34 Ibid., 60.

35 George Oommen, "Dalit Conversion and Social Protest in Travancore, 1854-1890," *The Bangalore Theological Forum* XXVII (3 and 4), (1996): 69-84. Accessed from http://www.religion-online.org/showarticle.asp?title=1119, Sept 20, 2017.

36 *The Missionary Register of the Church Missionary Society* (London: W. Watts Publishers, 1852), 446.

37 Samuel Mateer, *The Land of Charity: op.cit.,*44.

38 K. Saradamony, *Emergence of a Slave Caste: Pulayas of Kerala* (New Delhi: People's Publishing House, 1980), 152.

39 Edgar Thurston, op. cit., 119.

40 John C. B. Webster, op. cit., 12.

41 Ibid., 47.

42 Ibid., 50.

43 Harlan P. Beach, *A Geography and Atlas of Protestant Missions: Their Environment, Forces, Distribution Methods, Problems, Results and Prospects at the Opening of the Twentieth Century,* Vol. I (New York: The Student Volunteer Movement For Foreign Missions, 1901), 372-373.

44 John E. Clough, *Social Christianity in the Orient: The Story of A Man, A Mission and A Movement* (New York: The MacMillan Company, 1914), 82.

45 'Caste people' meaning 'caste Hindus' indicates Hindus belonging to any of the four castes which can be upper or Sudra castes (middle or lower castes). Those outside the four-fold castes were traditionally called 'outcastes' or *panchamas* (fifth caste),' untouchables', etc., As noted above, during the colonial times, they were categorized as 'Depressed Castes' or 'Depressed Classes'.

46 Pervaram Jagannadham (ed), *Dr. Babasaheb Ambedkar Rachanalu-Prasangalu: Congress and Gandhi Antaranivariki Emi Chesaru*? (What Congress and Gandhi have done to the Untouchables?) (Hyderabad: The Government of Andhra Pradesh Publications, 2011), 40.

47 Kalaprapoorna Yendluri, *Telugunata Dalita Udyamamu* (Hyderabad: Samantara Publications, 2009), 27.

48 A prisoner from the Mala caste from Rudrawaram embraced Christianity. For a detailed account, see Richard Lovett, *The History of the London Missionary Society* (1795-1895), Vol. II (Oxford: Oxford University Press, 1899), 137-138.

49 Carol Graham, *Azariah of Dornakal* (London: S.C.M. Press Ltd, 1946), 66.

50 Ibid.

51 John E. Clough, op.cit., 84.

52 David Downie, *The Lone Star: The History of the Telugu Mission of the American Baptist Missionaries Union (1838-1927)* (Philadelphia: The American Baptist Publication, 1892), 40.

Chapter 2

Understanding the Malas and the Madigas: Social, Economic, Religious and Political Conditions in mid-19th Century

In this chapter the attempt is to have a comprehensive understanding of the Mala and the Madiga communities in mid-nineteenth century Andhra. Who were the Malas? Who were the Madigas? What are their ethnic identities? What were their socio-economic, political and religious conditions before their conversion? A historical, sociological, and ethnographic understanding of these two depressed caste communities will enable us to understand, in some measure, the change in their communities, their achievements and upward social mobility after their encounter with Christianity. Our enquiry is limited to the Malas and Madigas of coastal Andhra Pradesh during the period of our study. This chapter has three sections: 1) description of the locale of the study, the political and economic situation, II) the religious, educational, cultural and social situation, and III) ethnographic understanding of the Malas and Madigas.

I

2.1 The Locale of the Research

The geographic area chosen for this study is coastal Andhra Pradesh (see Map 2.1)[1] which was called the 'Northern Circars of the Madras Presidency' during the colonial period. The area comprised of 30,000 square miles along the 600-mile coast line, stretching from Chennai (formerly, Madras) in the south to the northern part of Ganjam district in the north-east direction. With the two deltas of rivers *Godavari* and *Krishna*, the region had large tracts of fertile agricultural land.[2] The people of this region are called *Telugus* because of the widely spoken vernacular language of Telugu. Politically, the region was generally at the receiving end. The natural wealth of the coastal region and its topographic advantages attracted invaders to win and occupy the region and hold sway over it for centuries. The ruling dynasties of Vakataka, the Vishnukundin, the Chalukya, the Rashtrakuta, the Kakatiya, the Bahamani, the Vijayanagar Raya and the subsequent rulers of the Deccan controlled the region in historical times.[3] In the 17th and the 18th centuries, the coastal Andhra strip was ruled by the Sultans of Golconda and the Nizams of the Asaf Jahi dynasty. With Colonel Ford's victory over the French Commander Bussey at Kondur in 1764, the Nizam had to hand over the Northern Circar districts, namely, Ganjam, Vizagapatam, Godavari and Kistna, to the British in 1766.[4] I have retained the colonial usage of the names of places. For instance, 'Vizagapatam'[5] for today's Vizagapatnam, 'Godavery' for today's Godavari,[6] 'Kistna,'[7] for today's Krishna district, etc.

2.1.1 The District of Ganjam

The district of Ganjam was part of north Madras Presidency and comprised of an area of 8,311 square kilometers including the Agency Tract with a population of 13, 88,976 in 1871.[8] When the English assumed charge of the district in 1766, they found that cultivation was under the *Zamindari* system with perpetual rights and Haveli lands were under small estates. The British introduced the Permanent Settlement in this district in 1804.[9] There were three taluqas (Berhampur, Chicacole, and Goomsur) and the *Zamindari*es were Aska, Ganjam, Itchapur, Jalantra, Narasannapet, Parlakimidi, Pratapagiri, Purushottampur, Sergada, Surada, Tekkali and Urlan. The Ganjam district comprised of 16 towns with 6879 inhabited villages.[10]

The district had hills covered with thick, dark jungles, and was one of the most beautiful districts in the Presidency.[11] Apart from agriculture, the chief non-agricultural activity in the district was weaving where ordinary cloths were woven in most of the villages.[12]

2.1.2 The District of Vizagapatam (Vizagapatnam)

The district of Vizagapatam in the north was the largest district of Madras Presidency and covered an area of 17,222 square miles with a population of 2,485,141 in 1871.[13] The number of villages was 12,032 and the number of towns, twelve.[14] The taluqas in Vizagapatnam were Anakapalle, Bimilipatnam, Bobbili, Chipurupalle, Gazapatinagar, Golgonda, Palkonda, Parvatipur, Salur, Srungavarapukota, Viravalli and Vizianagaram.[15] The soil of the district was of highly ferruginous red variety with sands and loams. The lack of advanced practices in agriculture in this district was attributed to the prevalence of the *Zamindari* system and the low level of intelligence of the average cultivator. Consequently, famines were frequent; prices of goods went up, causing much

Map 2.1: Telangana & Andhra Pradesh in 2018, showing Coastal Colonial Andhra

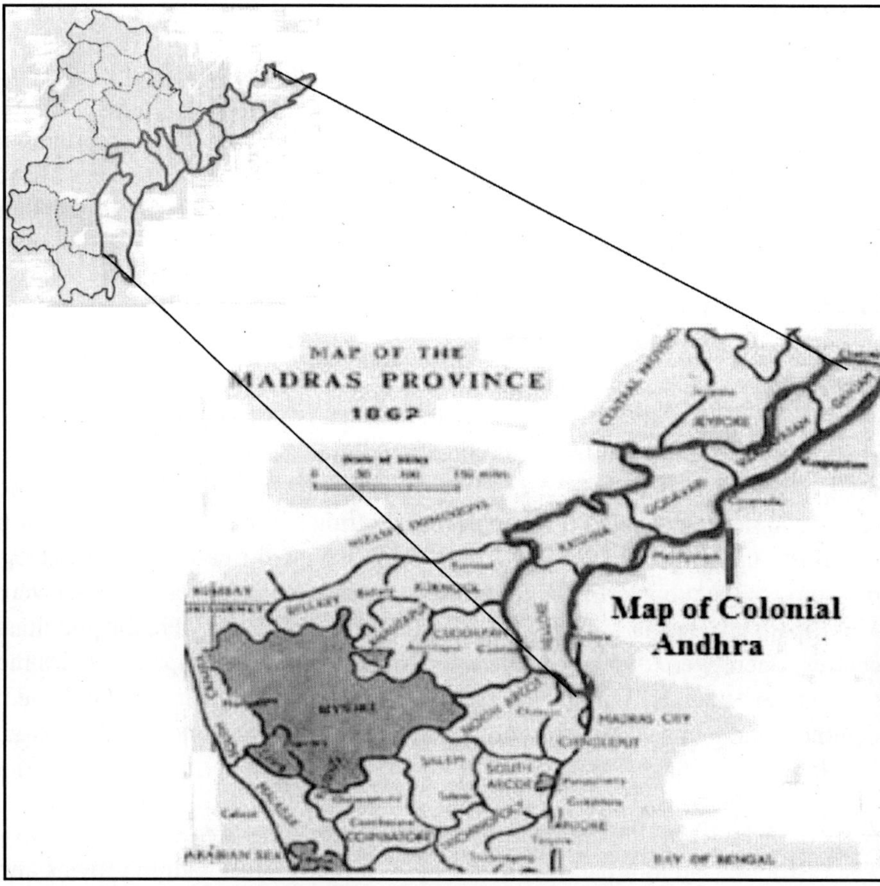

Source: https://www.researchgate.net/publication/225121263_Hegemony_Discipline_and_Control_in_the_Administration_of_Police_in_Colonial_India/figures?lo=1 (accessed on 17/08/2016).

economic distress to the inhabitants, forcing them to migrate elsewhere such as to Godavari delta area.[16]

2.1.3 The District of Godavari

The district of Godavari had an area of 7,972 square miles of which 3,897 square miles was government land and 4,075 square miles were under *Zamindari* and *Inam* tenures.[17] The district had a population of 1,5929,39 in the year 1871.[18] The district consisted of three different natural divisions namely, the Agency Tract in the north-west, the delta of the Godavari River and the upland taluqas midway between these two areas. The north-western Agency Tract along the

Eastern Ghats consisted of a series of broken and scattered hills rising from the lower uplands.[19] The upland and delta taluks differ widely in their agricultural conditions. The delta had the Lankas or islands with good fertile soil.[20] The taluqas were Amalapuram, Bhimavaram, Cocanada, Ellore, Narsapur, Peddapuram, Pithapuram, Rajahmundry, Ramachandrapuram, Tanuku, Tuni, Yernagudem and Bhadrachalam. The district of Godavari comprised 2, 678 villages of which 1,141 were in the Agency Tract.[21] Rice was the principal crop in the plains and ragi and cholam were staple diets.[22] In the year 1859, the districts of Rajahmundry, Masulipatnam and Guntur were merged into Godavari and Kistna (Krishna) districts.[23]

2.1.4 The District of Kistna (Krishna)

The district of Kistna had an area of 8,471 square miles with 13 taluqas and 1,818 villages and a population of 14, 523, 74 in 1871.[24] It was named after the perennial river Krishna which flows along much of its western side from the north-west to south-east and is its most striking natural feature. The extreme west of the district consisted of stony uplands dotted with rocky hills, the centre and north consisted of plain of black cotton soil and the eastern portion was made up of the wide alluvial delta. With irrigated rice-fields, the district had some of the most fertile land in Madras Presidency.[25] The chief towns were Masulipatnam, Bezwada and Guntur; and Chirala and Tenali were the populous centres. There were two *Zemindaries* of Nuzvid and Vissannapeta besides the government taluqas, namely Bapatla, Bezwada, Masulipatnam, Gudivada, Guntur, Nadigama, Narsaraopet, Nuzvid, Palnad, Repalle, Sattenapalle, Vinukonda and Vissannapeta.[26]

2.1.5 The District of Nellore

The district of Nellore had an area of 8,739 square miles with ten towns and 1,758 villages and a population of 13, 768, 11 in 1871.[27] The chief towns were Ongole and Nellore. The soil of Nellore was not naturally fertile, unlike the upper districts of coastal Andhra and a large portion of the land was either rocky wastes or covered with scrub jungle. Fine groves were occasionally found in villages. In some places bright green rice fields contrasts with dark clumps of trees forming a picturesque landscape.[28] The taluqas in Nellore were Atamakur, Gudur, Kandukur, Kanigiri, Kavali, Nellore, Ongole, Rapur, Udayagiri, Darsi (Z), Podili (Z), Poluru (Z) and Venkatagiri (Z).[29] The district of Nellore was renowned for a celebrated breed of cattle. The chief centres for breeding cattle were Ongole and Kandukur and Vinukonda in the north and Bapatla taluqa of the Kistna district.[30]

2.2 Nineteenth Century Colonial Andhra: Politico-Economic Situation

The late 19th century through the 20th century, was a period of changing political structures, society and economy, in coastal Andhra. The Northern Circars were always the prized possessions of its rulers owing to its fertile soil and the extent of sea coast. The Portuguese had first settled in Masulipatnam in 1606, the Dutch in 1608 and the English acquired it through a negotiated treaty with the Sultan of Golconda in 1611. The English activities on the Corommandel coast could be traced back to 1611 when numerous representations were made to the Mughal emperors. The English traders had succeeded in procuring a *Firman* from the Sultan in 1632 to trade from the port of Masulipatnam. In return, the Company agreed to import Persian horses and 'rarities' from Europe. It was considered as the *'Golden Firman'* and was the first written sanction from a ruler in India allowing a European Company the right to trade.[31] The French and the British negotiated and tried to avail themselves of the first opportunity to take possession of coastal Andhra.

Politically, the effectual determination of Aurangzeb brought the fall of Golconda at the end of September 1687 and the region of coastal Andhra came to be under the control of the Mughals.[32] In the year 1724, the Deccan Subedari was entrusted to the Viceroyalty of Mir Qamuruddin Nizam-ul-Mulk Asaf Jah. Until the acquisition of the Northern Circars by the English East India Company, politically it was a part of the Asaf Jahi Nizam rulers of the Hyderabad Subah. During the year 1756, the French under M. Bussy and the British under Col. Forde, took to hostilities to each other. The French forces were driven by the British forces from these districts by storming the fort of Masulipatnam and inflicting considerable loss. Upon the initiative of Mr. Palk, President of the Fort St. George, in October 1765, the Company directors obtained Sanads for all the five Sarkars in virtue of a *Firman* from the Emperor of Delhi. However, the efforts of the Nizam Ali Khan to take back the Northern Circars were only settled by an agreement by which the East India Company agreed to pay the Nizam an annual tribute of five lakh rupees each for the circars of Rajahmundry, Ellore, Mustaphanagar and two lakhs each, for the circars of Chicacole and Murtuzanagar. The circar of Guntoor came under the British Control in 1788, after the death of Basalat Jung, paying to the Nizam a sum of 916,665 rupees and 11 annas.[33]

2.2.1 Political Economy

The system of Permanent Zamindari had prevailed in Ganjam, Vizagapatam, Rajahmundry, Masulipatnam and Guntur, whereas village economic system had prevailed in Nellore.[34] Northern Andhra was controlled by the chieftains and *Zamindars,* an old politico-economic system under the Mohammedan Sultans of Golconda.[35] The Mughal administration had created the *Zamindari* system and appointed officials to run the revenue machinery.[36] The term '*Zamindar*' meant a "holder of the land," which technically referred to the control of the aggregate of the royal rights in the lands which were made over to the manager against a fixed payment of money.[37] They were hereditary landlords as well as ruling chiefs within their own estates. The Committee of Circuit which was appointed in 1775 reported that lands in the Northern Circars were principally held by the *Zamindars*. The *Zamindars* in the hilly areas were independent in the affairs of their territories, whereas the *Zamindars* in the plains were more under the control of the Government and had to pay a fixed amount of revenue to the Government and were allowed to appropriate the rents of their estates.[38] The vast peasantry had little in terms of land rights and the landless labourers toiled for their survival.[39]

The Northern Circars came into the possession of the Company in 1766 and the Company administration found that large portions of land called *zamindari* lands, were managed by the descendants of former landholders in Telingana and Orissa. They had maintained forts and armed forces for their defense and acted more like tributary chiefs than subjects.[40] The local chiefs who were also *zamindars* held the management of the revenues.[41] According to Baden-Powell, by the end of the eighteenth century, every ruler of a kingdom, whether Hindu or Muslim had established his claim to general ownership and the claim had stood for some generations at least in an extended meaning of the *zamindari* right of assignees.[42] The *zamindars* had maintained a large number of forces to defend their forts and were almost independent in the affairs under their control. A large part of every estate consisted of both cultivable and waste land and the *zamindar* was entitled to bring the waste land under cultivation. Hence the new cultivated land was virtually his own and he employed his own labourers known as tenants on the basis of contract.[43] The zamindars became powerful owing to their geographical position and a weak central supervision. The Muslim overlords granted titles to those *Zamindars* who had paid their tributes properly. These *zamindars* also maintained their own ships and conducted overseas business independently.[44] The *zamindars* held hereditary proprietary rights in their territories and enjoyed certain amount of political, economic and judicial power. Within the *zemindari* territories, there existed the 'village community system' from time immemorial which was a simple form of self-government that protected the cultivators of every village from the oppression of the *zamindars* and the Government.[45] They sub-let the lands to farmers on an annual basis and the revenue was collected from the *ryots* either in kind or cash.[46] The prominent chieftains and *zamindars* of this period were the Pusapati family of Vizianagaram, the Velamas of Bobbili, Vatsavayi family of Peddapuram and the Rajah of Pithapuram. Other principal *zamindaries* were in Nidadavolu,

Chintalapudi, Mylavaram, Bezwada, Munagala, Nuzvidu and Nadigama, Vinukonda, Repalle, Sattenapalle, Chilakaluripet and Devarakonda.[47]

2.2.2 Economic Condition

The 19th century economic life in Andhra was mostly under the control of the *zamindars* who acted as renters and farmers of their respective *zamindaries* and had the right of management of the revenue and of police. Besides the *zamindari* lands, there were certain lands called as Haveli lands which were farmed out by the Government to the agents or the highest rent bidders who employed oppressive means for collecting land revenues.[48]

During the colonial rule, the Circuit Committee made an enquiry of the economic condition, produce, number of inhabitants, manufacturing sector, fortified places, military strength of the *zamindars* and the expense of his household and troops and the means to cover these expenses in the Northern Circars.[49] In 1798, the East India Company, under Lord Cornwallis concluded a perpetual settlement with the *zamindars* based on the principle of 'permanent' fee and fixation of the assessment.[50] It was felt that a fixed permanent settlement gave the *zamindars* an irresistible inducement to promote cultivation of the land and welfare of the ryots.[51] According to the Settlement, the *zamindar* had to collect ½ of the total produce of the ryots and out of his collections the *zamindar* had to pay ⅔ as *peshcush* retaining ⅓ for his expenses.[52] During the first part of the 19th century the Company was in a stable position and appointed Collectors who depended on Dubashis for revenue collection.

2.2.3 Village Economy

Within the *zamindari* territories and in the Haveli territories, the 'Village Community system' had a 'self-sufficient economy.'[53] The economic organization with unalterable division of labour[54] in villages had continued from an earlier age and survived without much variation under various political hegemonies.[55]

The distinguishing features of the village system were:[56]

(1) The village was an isolated, economically independent unit.
(2) The division of labour was imperfect.
(3) The capital employed in each unit of industry was small.
(4) The direction of industry was in the hands of small craftsmen.

According to William Wiser, in the Indian village, each caste was expected to 'render a fixed type of service to each other caste', under the '*Jajmani* system'. There was an economic bond between the traditional *Jajaman* (overseer) and *Kamin* (labourer).[57] The village was constituted to be a single integrated system in which the basic economic, political, social, and religious dimensions of life were inseparable from one another.

Geographically, a village was a tract of land comprised of thousands of acres of arable and waste land and politically, it resembled a corporation or township.[58] The participants in the economic system had an absolute right to their hereditary professions and occupations. According to Monier Williams, the Indian village was not merely a collection of houses forming a village or town, but a division of territory, perhaps three or four square miles or more in extent, with its careful distribution of fixed occupations for the common good, with its intertwining and inter-dependence of individual, family, and communal interests. It had existed almost unaltered since the description of its organization in Manu's code, two or three centuries before the Christian era. It has survived all the religious, political, and physical convulsions from which India has suffered from times immemorial. Invader after invader has ravaged the country with fire and sword, internal wars have carried devastation into every corner of the land, tyrannical oppressors have desolated its homesteads, famine has decimated its peasantry, pestilence has depopulated entire districts, floods and earthquakes have changed the face of nature, folly, superstition, and delusion have made havoc of all religion and morality but the simple, self-contained Indian township has preserved its constitution intact, its customs, precedents, and peculiar institutions unchanged and unchangeable amid all other changes.[59]

The description of the village economy during the time of the Kakatiya rulers who had ruled the Andhra region between A.D 1000 to A.D 1323,[60] is worth noting. The country was devided into Sthalamu, Naadu, Vishayamu and Kampanamu. Village self-rule was in place with twelve Ayagars namely, the Karanamu, Peda kapu or Reddy, Talari, Purohithudu, Blacksmith, goldsmith, Carpenter, Potter, Washerman, Barber, Village Servant and leather-worker.[61] The Potail (Patel) or the Peda Kapu or Reddy acted as headman, the Curnum kept the accounts of cultivation, the Talari sought information of crimes and offences, the boundary-man, preserved the limits of the village, the Nirukattu was the superintendent of tanks and water courses. According to Romesh Dutt, the officers and servants constituted the hereditary 'establishment' of a village. The Brahmins had control over village worship, and were schoolmasters who initiated learning among children making them read and write on the sand. The other functionaries of the village were the Astrologer, the Smith and Carpenter, the potter, the washerman, the barber, the cow keeper, the doctor, the dancing-girl, the tenants-at-will and the share croppers.[62] According to Caldwell, the system was one of the simplest and most effective means of using the village's own resources and the services rendered were paid through renting of land or by a share of the grain. The whole system of decentralized and autonomous functional contracts ensured village solidarity and independence from outside political turmoil and economic disruption.[63] The relationship between two castes involved a *Jajmani* tie. Access to resources and control of village were based on hierarchical equation among castes.[64] Village administration tasks like accounts, revenue payments, cash and kind payments and certain customary prerequisites were in the hands of upper *Súdra* castes. The crucial pollution-removal tasks were entrusted generally to the Malas and the Madigas, apart from the lower *Súdra* castes such as washer men and barbers.[65]

2.2.4 The Company Administration

The East India Company's administration introduced a series of structural changes over land control and imposed new rules of governance for various classes associated with land-cultivation, which changed the existing agrarian relations. The system of 'permanent settlement' which was introduced in the Northern Circars between 1794 and 1802-08 failed owing to unequal revenue burden and insufficient knowledge about the revenue settlement procedure.[66] The other land revenue system was the *Ryotwari*, a non-landlord system where the landholders are the claimants of their own holding.[67] Under this system, the cultivating proprietor of the land was permitted to hold his land at a fixed assessment and the rent would not undergo any alteration.[68] The efforts of the British administrator Sir Thomas Munro in consolidating the revenue system in the Northern Circars may be noted. He appointed a body of trained revenue servants to become 'collectors' in the Northern Circars.[69] The new system of revenue was called as *Asara* and *Visabādi*. The main feature of Asara was ascertainment of the government land by actual measurement, while in Visabadi total assessment of land holding and revenue in each village occupied by the cultivators was imposed. Later, a joint revenue system of *Makta* was introduced in 1846 under which the annual demand on a village was settled once for all with no further interference by the government and the cultivators were jointly responsible for the whole demand.[70] This system was extended to all government lands in the Andhra districts and settlement rates were fixed separately for dry and wet lands.[71]

The Northern Circars was termed as '*the Granary of the Carnatic*' and agriculture formed the primary source of livelihood of the people. The area yielded rich harvest in grains and pulses like rice, bajra and juar.[72] Regarding the manufacturing sector, Barampuram for production of silk, Srikakulam for muslin, Ellore for carpet industry, Masulipatnam for dyeing industry and Nellore for Rumallu were renowned centres.[73]

The reason attributed for the disintegration of the village economy was the Colonial administration's efforts to enhance land revenue and centralize all economic powers.[74] A wave of natural calamities also resulted in famines and epidemics like cholera that plagued the Telugu population in the first part of the 19th century which made traditional industries fail to provide employment and resulted in migrations and population movements. The occurrence of famines desolated some parts of Andhra during the subsequent years of the 19th century and affected their occupational security. Due to over dependence on crops, people suffered when crops failed and during the years of drought. Another reason was that the money-lenders, who by their extortion methods, kept the tillers of the soil in a state of long indebtedness.[75] A cycle of famines struck the Madras Presidency in early 19th century particularly during the years 1805-07 with a reported high death rate.[76] During the famines of 1823 and 1833-34, the mortality rate was high in Northern Madras areas and the famine of 1854 put a considerable check on population survival. Mention may be made about the famines of 1865-66 and of 1876-78, the most terrible ones. Further, the Ganjam famine of 1888-89 put severe agricultural distress in the Northern parts of the Madras Presidency.[77]

Drought conditions also affected the textile industry in Andhra region between the years 1830-1835 causing quantitative setbacks on village employment.[78] Epidemics and mass hunger resulted either in massive deaths or group migration to neighbouring districts. Small land owners and tenants at will found that their cultivated lands could hardly yield any good crops and were faced with difficulties such as illnesses and deeper debts due to mortgaged lands which made them lose their lands to their creditors. Industries especially local handicraft industries suffered due to mechanization and rapid competition from England and cheap imports from Britain. Due to the decline in trade, ship building industry also suffered and resulted in loss of jobs. Many weavers migrated to Sri Lanka, Burma and Mauritius as indentured labourers. However, by the second half of the 19th century, the construction of the Krishna and Godavari anicuts somewhat bettered the agrarian conditions and accelerated commercialization of agriculture and contributed to the emergence of the middle classes.[79]

II

2.3 Socio-religious, Educational and Cultural Condition

Religion and religious beliefs from pre-ancient times had their own significance and controlled the daily life of a person in society. The 19th century religion in Andhra was essentially Hinduism with a medley of diverse traditions ranging from Vedic, Brahmanic and Animistic worship of village deities, besides Siva and Vishnu.[80] The majority of the people of Coastal Andhra in the early part of 19th century were Hindus, of either Vaishnava or Saiva tradition. Temples were the prominent centres of public worship and social activity in every town and village.[81] There prevailed various schools of thought such as *Advaita*, *Dvaita* and *Vishistadvaita*. According to Monier Williams, Indian way of life was sometimes conducted without any Vedic sanctions in such areas as the prohibition of widow-marriages, the general prevalence of child-marriages, the tyrannical sway of caste, the interdiction of foreign travel and the practice of idolatry."[82]

2.3.1 State of Education

Coastal Andhra had an excellent history of education that was placed within the reach of all privileged castes, but not the lower ones. The important educational centres were conducted in the Sangharama or Buddhist learning centres at Sri Parvata Nagrajuna Konda and Vengi.[83] The aim of education was to achieve self-realization through finding one's own relation to the world and realizing that all things have their beginning, life and end in God.[84] The individual is destined to take steps which their ancestors had taken to reach the highest pinnacle of human excellence. Accordingly, the pattern of learning of the individual was divided into three broad stages, namely opening of the mind, disciplining of the body and application of the principles into practice.[85] The control of education in Andhra was reserved for the privileged castes.[86] Teachers were poorly remunerated who were paid in kind or nominal fees. Pupils were taught fables and *Niti-sutras* from the *Panchatantra* and the rudiments of the arts of reading, writing and arithmetic together with moral precepts.[87] Scholastic education was held in Persian, Arabic or in Sanskrit. The *Madrasas* or *Maktabs* were attended by Mohammadans and by those who were attracted by the advantages of acquiring an acquaintance with the language of the law courts. Education among Muslims was conducted in Persian and teachers of Persian and Arabic languages were paid either by land grants or in cash.[88] The writings of Yogi Vemana, Dittakavi Narayanakavi, Kuchimanchi Timmakavi and Enugu Lakshmanakavi had earned the reputation of being the great literary works of Andhra in the 19th century.[89]

2.3.2 Cultural Life

The cultural life in Andhra was vibrant mainly under the aegis of the *zamindaries* namely the Bobbili, Vijayanagaram, Peddapuram and Pithapuram and Venkatagiri. Social and cultural life in Andhra came under severe scrutiny in the light of the rational spirit that critiqued the dark corners of traditional Hindu society during the 19th century. The Hindu society was riddled with social evils such as child marriages, enforced widowhood on women, prevalence of the Devadasi system and social discrimination. The position of women in Andhra society cannot be understood except in the light of the religious circumstances and under the sanction of superstitious premises.[90] Male population commanded women into submission quoting the sacred authority in which she had lacked any knowledge to his justification.[91] Women were regarded as an inferior order of beings and were denied education totally as it was quoted that "we have trouble enough with our women now and if we were to educate them, we would not be able to manage them at all."[92] However this condition was an exception for those women who were provided with education in their own homes. With regard to the position of widows, there was no hope for their future happiness as they had to practice the rules of virtue throughout the rest of their life.[93]

The institution of Nautch-girls or licensed courtesans continued to exist in the 19th century Andhra society where no entertainment, either religious or social was complete without their presence. At weddings and feasts, festivals and funerals their presence was necessary. In the name of honor, parents from the lower castes were persuaded by the *Brāhmins* to select beautiful little girls to be formally married to a deity in the temple. They were always richly dressed in silks and jewels, and their attractiveness made them a means of great gain to their priestly owners. They were trained to offer themselves up to the frequenters of the shrine where the monetary gains would go into the sacred treasury.[94]

Thus, the state of socio-religious affairs in Andhra during the nineteenth century was described to be in a state of want for reform and regeneration. The contribution of the Christian missionaries was a significant factor to bring change in the Indian society in general and the Coastal Andhra society in particular. The credit for initiating social reforms is owed to the earnest efforts of the Christian missionaries without whose support the colonial government would not ever have passed legislations of social reform.[95]

2.3.3 Social Structures: Evolution of Caste and Formation of Lower Castes

The institution of caste evolved to be an exclusive feature of Indian society and defines the core of Indian society.[96] A Hindu society and a Hindu person outside the fold of caste could not be imagined. It was also a unique and the chief socio-cultural institution with its hold on the entire society. The word "caste" was first used by the Portuguese travelers, and came from the word *casta*, meaning race or breed and was used to describe different sections of the Hindu community.[97] The Indian caste system was a complex and interrelated systems of *Jati* (clan) and family ties with Vedic sanctions and ran on the supporting columns of the caste structure – the social hierarchy, endogamous marriage arrangements, occupational inheritance and specialization[98] with tight restrictions on occupational mobility.[99] According to M. N. Srinivas, caste is a natural consequence of the territorial limits imposed by the political system where occupational specialization stress the interdependence, as each caste was dependent for its livelihood on the work done by the other castes. The tendency of economic ties to cut across caste barriers was also supported by political and religious ties.[100]

Social structure in India was built on stratified lines with hierarchically superposed classes, and was manifested in the existence of upper and lower layers on the social ladder. The members of the society were differentiated with a distribution of rights and privileges, duties and responsibilities, social values and customs that were set to be unequal in nature.[101] The institution of caste was rigorously hereditary and consisted of ritually sanctioned elements of purity and pollution[102] where hierarchy of purity was seen as a distinct social principle.[103] Louis Dumont's idea of "political and economic domains of social life were encompassed by the religious domain" is held true here.[104] The existence of social hierarchy and occupational ranking made the disposal of resources at a differentiated rate for different castes.[105] According to Max Weber, "Caste is an expression of hereditary status groups who maintain their identity by following certain socially imposed restrictions upon intermarriage and social intercourse with persons who do not belong to that status."[106] Sir E. A. Gait, the Census Commissioner of 1901, had observed that

The main characteristic of caste was the belief in a common origin and the possession of a traditional occupation with least possible deviation from the duties of caste. It was an endogamous group or collection of such groups bearing a common name, having the same traditional occupation, claiming descent from the same source.[107]

Sir H. Risley, colonial ethnographer and administrator defined caste as,

> A collection of families or groups of families bearing a common name which usually denotes or associated with specific occupation, claiming common descent from a mythical ancestor, human or divine, professing to follow the same professional callings and are regarded by those who are competent to give an opinion as forming a single homogeneous community.[108]

On the evolution of caste, Robert Shafer says that the *Nisādas* were *Súdras* in the sequence of order from the lowest to the highest: the *Nisāda* took the place of a *Súdra* because the *Súdra* was *Nisāda*, the only difference being that the former were partly aryanized. Citing from *Kausitaki Brahmana*, he says that one has to dwell successively with a *Nisada*, a *Vaisya*, a *Kshatriya* and a *Brahmin*.[109] The Sanskrit dictionary describes the *Dasyu*, as *an-ārya* or an enemy of *Indra* and *Agni*.[110] In William Hunter's view, another kind of non-Aryan stock, the Dravidians appear to have found their way into the Punjab by the northwestern passes and now inhabit the southern part of the three-sided tableland of India.[111] The invading Aryans found a flat nosed black Dasyus in the North West, evidently with proto-Australoid type of skulls, at Mohenjodaro[112] and the *Vedic Dasyu* was described as *'krsna-tvac'* or black-skinned, *'anās'* with flat-nosed *'mrdhra-vāc'* or of hostile speech,[113] and was called as the *Mlećcha-Jāti*.[114] Similar kinds of features were ascribed to the

Dravidian type of original inhabitants of India with dark complexion, dark eyes, broad nose depressed at the root which did not necessarily make the face appear flat.[115] William Hunter also opined that when the Aryans made their way eastwards through the Northern India, pushed down the black skinned races thereby reducing them to bondage.[116]

The *Purushasukta* of the *Rigveda* compared society with a giant organism with the *Brahmin*, *Kshatriya*, *Vaishya* and *Súdra* at its head, arms, belly and feet, respectively.[117] The four main categories namely, the *Brahmin* (scripture teacher), the *Kshatriya* (protector), the *Vaishya* (wealth manager) and the *Súdra* (labourer) proceeded from Brahma's mouth, arm, thigh and foot, respectively.[118] The Brahman was his mouth, of his arms was the Rajanya made, his thighs became the Vaisya, from his feet the Sudra was produced.[119]

The means of subsistence for the four classes as was devised by Manu was the following: the *Brahmin* by teaching of the Vedas and officiating at sacrificial ceremonies and receiving presents; the *Kshatriya* by military duties and bearing of arms; the *Vaisya* through trading of merchandize and looking after cattle and agriculture;[120] and the *Súdra,* by serving the twice born and engaging in menial works.[121] The classification thus structured the duties of the Brahmin as conducting priestly duties, Kshatriya of protecting the area under their control, the Vaishya, of undertaking commercial and agricultural activities and the Súdra of engaging in other service tasks of the society.[122]

The stratification of caste was also based on the colour scheme or *Varna* (colour) such that, the Brahmin was white (sita), the Kshatriya was red (lohita), the Vaisya was yellow (pitaka) and the Súdra was black (asita).[123] The *Manu Smiriti* also placed the category of mixed castes and the exterior castes at the lower bottom of the social structure.[124]

The hierarchy of the caste system could be illustrated with a pyramid diagram (Figure 2.1).[125] The Vedic sanction of the institution of caste and the graded ritual status of purity and impurity in a hierarchical manner were related to the socio-economic realms (Figure 2.2).[126]

Figure 2.1: Hierarchy of Castes

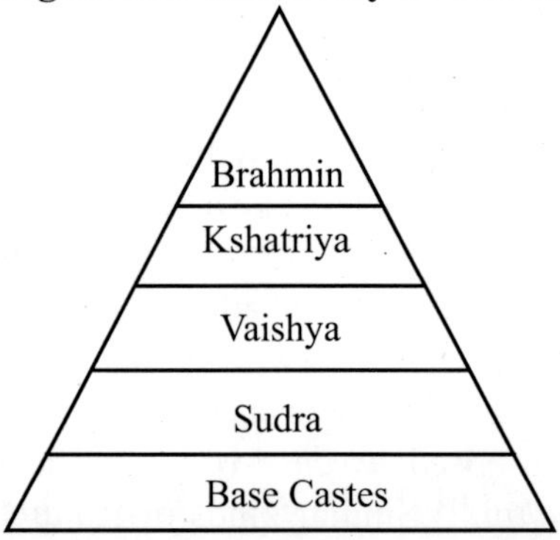

Figure 2.2: Hierarchy of Purity and Impurity

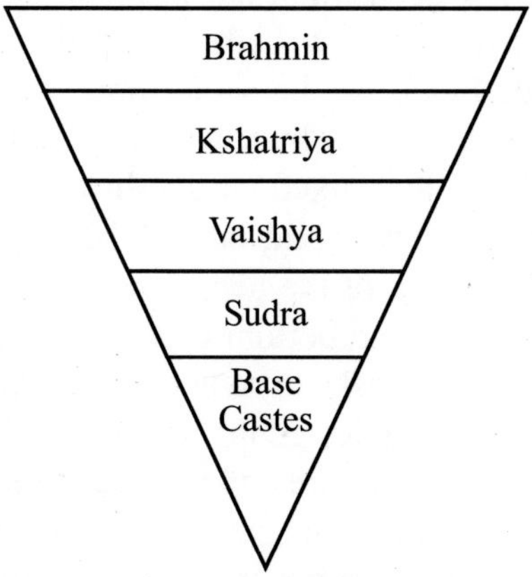

With the division of labour and specialization of professional skills, caste gradually evolved as a distinctive means of social identity.[127] Within the Hindu legal and ritual sanctions, each caste could pursue its own style of life, diet habits and customs.[128] In order to preserve the social and cultural identity of each caste, the rules of endogamy were enforced in which marriage was allowed only between equal caste groups.[129] However, mixed marriages were permitted during the time of Manu Smriti which noted an intermixture of groups out of *Viloma* (direct order) and *Anuloma* (indirect order) marriages, and hence the emergence of different sub-caste groups.[130] The intention for encouraging inverse order of social relations was to beget fifteen lower classes who would again beget still more base classes such as the *Ambashtaha* or *Vaidya*, *Nishāda*, *Ugra*, *Suta*, *Magadha*, *Vaideha*, *Ayogava*, *Cshattrĭ*, *Chandala*, *Sairindhra* (*Sairandhra*),[131] *Swapaca*, *Puccasa*, *Cārā-Vāra* and *Sopaca*.[132] The duties assigned to these mixed classes were curing of disorders, destroying filth, slaying of beasts, managing horses and chariots, travelling with merchandize, waiting on women, killing of animals, implementing royal warrants such as executions and carrying corpses, working with leather and punishing of criminals. The lower classes of the *Vratyas* (outcast *Brahmin*, *Kshatriya* and *Vaisya*) and *Súdra* were born within the confines of the *Varna* (color) scheme but were kept outside the pale of the Brahmanic structure.[133] Certain impure professions were enforced on the mixed classes and an element of impurity was ascribed to them. It was said in the Institutes of Hindu Law, the *Ayogava*, the *Cshāttri* and the *Chandāla* who were considered to be low, because of their origin from a *Súdra* father and from the inverse order of commercial (*Vaisya)*, military (*Kshatriya)*, and priestly classes of women (*Brahmin)* belonged to the three classes which were excluded from the performance of obsequies to their ancestors.[134]

From the above description, it may be observed that a person's degraded status was not due to his/her occupation but to the enforcement of the rigid rules by the early law makers who wished to keep themselves distant from the original inhabitants of India. At the same time, they could not prevent the women of the first three castes to mix with the *Súdra* through *Anuloma* marriages; hence the birth of the mixed castes. In the case of a twice born man marrying a *Súdra* woman, the child inherits his mother's caste and not of the father. Therefore, a section of the people who were placed outside the *Varna* scheme and were kept at the bottom of the society were assigned the functions of performing polluted tasks in society. As the conquerors inhabited larger portions of the land, they subjected the native population as rent-paying subjects, village labourers in agriculture and manufacturers of crafts and were to reside outside the village limits and perform obligatory services for the dominant people. Their traditional duties involved agricultural labour, village sanitation, scavenging, handling carcasses of dead animals, and working with leather, etc.[135] Louis Dumont had opined that the impure ritual status of the depressed castes was based on their social unhygienic practices. But it may be noted that their specialization in the prescribed tasks led to the attribution of permanent status of impurity on them.[136]

The social system in coastal Andhra was based on Hindu hierarchical system in which society was divided according to the four-fold division, and was governed by rules of endogamy and commensality. The 19th century Andhra society was divided into two broad social groups: the privileged, and the unprivileged. Broadly speaking, the *Brāhmin*, *Kshatriya* and *Vaisya* castes belonged to the first group and were called the 'twice-born'. The privileged *Brāhmin* was a hereditary teacher, an interpreter of the scriptures and *Shastras*, a hereditary priest and an astrologer. The section of the *Brāhmins* who confined themselves to the study of the Vedas and Shastras came to be known as the *Vaidiki* and the others were designated as *Niyogi* who held secular duties."[137] The second privileged group was the *Kshatriyas* in four gotras or sub groups namely *Vasishta*, *Kaundinya*, *Dhananjaya* and *Kashyapa*. The *Vaisya*, who were also called as *Komati* was shrewd in business matters and formed the third among the privileged castes. The *Súdra* castes were formed from various castes and were largely members of the unprivileged group who were debarred from the privileges of learning and reciting of the scriptures. However, the *Brāhmin* priests acted as instructors and family priests of some of the upper *Súdra* families. The Malas and the Madigas were considered outside the four castes and hence were placed at the bottom of the society with several social restrictions and were confined to specific 'task participation' in their respective village economic activities.[138]

The Mala and the Madiga castes of coastal Andhra were forced to undertake some of the indispensable tasks like agriculture labour, leather-work, guarding of villages, etc. The specific tasks performed by the Malas were farm labour, guarding of villages, burning of the dead, carrying messages and hereditary servile services for the *Súdras.*[139] The Madigas as ancient *Cārā-Vāra,* were leather workers who dealt with skins and hides.[140] Killing of the animals or taking charge of dead ox or buffalo, skinning and tanning dead animals, bearing burdens, making and beating drums at Hindu festivals, manufacturing of rude leather articles, especially sandals, trappings for bullocks and large leather well-buckets for irrigation purposes, were the professional duties of the Madigas.[141] W. H. Moreland argued that 'a servile labouring class was a normal element in the rural population up to the introduction of the British rule.'[142] These servile classes have existed from the time of the Aryan invasion (see details in Section III).

III

2.4 An Ethnographic Study of the Malas and the Madigas

Ethnography is the study of the principal characteristics of social and cultural life and examination of the human agencies that shed light on the relationship between social life and social structures.[143] The study of ethnography is to explore the scope and dimension of an explicitly ontological status of distinct social groups. The aim is not only to describe small-scale social events but also to study the methods and procedural rules of social life. This involves anthropological assumptions about the nature of the society in spheres of social, religious, material and cultural life with an embodiment of wholes and systems that go beyond the consciousness of individuals.[144] An examination of the fixed and unchanged status of peoples' lives in material and social life with bounded structures and customs help us to analyze the lives of the people. The Mala and the Madiga depressed castes in coastal Andhra were placed at the lower rungs of the social ladder for many centuries. They were heterogeneous groups with different *Jati* (*birth*) traditions and interaction styles. Despite having differentiated social standing and lack of homogeneity and having traditional animosity among the two, they were placed on the same category on the social ladder.

An ethnographic description of the non-Aryan origin of the Malas and the Madigas can be found in Gustav Oppert's work, *On the Original Inhabitants of Bharatavarşa or India* (1898). Sydney Nicholson has presented a brief history of the Malas in his scholarly article, "Social organization of the Malas: An Outcaste Indian People", in the *Journal of the Royal Anthropological Institute of Great Britain and Ireland* (1926), in which he states that the original Malas were the followers of Saivite faith and were divided into Right-hand and Left-hand sections. Edgar Thurston has described the traditions of the Malas and the

Madigas *in his Castes* and *Tribes of Southern India*, Vol. IV (1909). It provides information on the way of life and customs of the nineteenth century Malas and Madigas in Tamilnadu, Andhra and the Carnatic regions. The religious life and the worship of female deities by the Malas and the Madigas were discussed in Wilber Theodore Elmore's *Dravidian Gods in Modern Hinduism: A Study of the Local and Village Deities of Southern India* (1915) which also throws light on the customs and practices of the Malas and the Madigas.

The early 20th century I.C.S. ethnographers namely Edgar Thurston, Athelstane Baines, J. H. Hutton, W. W. Wilson and S. Nicholson attempted an impartial description of the life and traditions of these indigenous peoples. Athelstane Baines regarded the Malas as a Dravidian labouring caste whose chief occupation was labouring in the farm besides attending the *Súdra households and* the Madigas *as skilled leather workers.*[145] On the subject of social status of the Malas and the Madigas, Edgar Thurston noted that any job that required skill in a factory was conducted by the Malas and other trivial jobs were taken by the Madigas, therefore termed the Madigas as 'three-anna wage men.'[146]

Given the wave of conquest and migration of Aryans into mainland India,[147] the political atmosphere of the country experienced continuous disturbance and fighting within the Indian territories and there seems to be nothing abnormal in the claim that the Pariahs or the lower castes, were 'descendants of the original inhabitants' who were faced with rigid social practices and subversion of the Aryan and other kindred tribes.[148] The Malas and the Madigas belong to the Dravidian stock of the original inhabitants of India. According to Gustav Oppert, the word Mala has derived from mountain which was called as 'Mala' or 'Konda' in Dravidian languages.[149] R. C. Majumdar opined that throughout the greater part of India, the Proto-Australoid people had lived as lower castes with some pronounced or subdued physical features.[150] According to the law of Manu, the offspring of a *Súdra* man and a priestly class woman was directed to situate his dwelling near the mountains or in groves and should be engaged in servile works.[151] But these non-Aryan native inhabitants were never totally annihilated by the Aryan tribes but intermingled with the latter through intermarriages. When the victors intermarried freely, similar names were applied to the *Mār,* Mala and *Mahār,* who also claim relationship with the Rajputs of the Aryan Kshatriya origin and could be applied to all the tribes who bear the above names.[152] Some had settled down as cultivators, the chief trait attributed to the Malas, and were exposed to severe oppression and treated as *Pariahs*.[153]

2.4.1 The Malas

The Malas are spread throughout the undivided Andhra Pradesh.[154] The Malas were part of the larger Dravidian stock of race with names such as *Μαλλοί*

(Malloi) or *Malli*, *Mālaska*, *Mālasda*, *Mālas*ja, *Malla*, *Mallaka*, *Mallava*, *Mālas*, *Mālas*va, *Mālasvarti*, *Ballālas*, *Pālas*, *Pālis*, *Pallavas*, *Vellālar*, *Velamas* etc.[155] In Telugu they were known as *Mālavādu* or *Mālavāndlu* which originally signified to a mountaineer.[156] According to Monier William's Sanskrit dictionary, the word Mala indicates a particular tribe who were mountain dwellers.[157] According to Gustav Oppert, the term *Mallas* was preserved among the population all over India especially among the Malas, Mala-*Arayar*, Mala-*Arasar* and *Malacar*.[158] The two syllables r̲ and l̲ were used interchangeably and are equally apparent in the name of the *Maras* or Malas of Palamau, who derive their origin from Malva (Malava).[159]

The Malas' association with the *Brāhmin* comes where they claim to be the latter's elder brother, thereby setting a substantial proof of the origin of the low castes thanks to the relationship with *Brāhmin* women and low caste men.[160] The claim of the Malas regarding their Kshatriya origin[161] is validated by Manu Smriti's explanation of the *Ugra* tribe which was born from a *Cshatriya* father and a *Súdra* mother. The *Mallas* have been mentioned in the *Mahabharata*, *Harivansa* and the *Lalita Vistara*. The *Mallas* as a nation of Kusinagara and Mallithan of the Indus area came across with Alexander the Great.[162] The race name *Malasvā* as a powerful nation of *Μαλλοί* (*Malloi*) on the banks of the Indus River apparently indicates that they gave stiff resistance to Alexander. It was described that Alexander had nearly escaped from being cut into pieces by the *Malli*, who were club wielders and most warlike people in India.[163] We may notice that the Malas of the present day are club wielders and wrestlers (*Mallayodhas*). But Alexander's master strategy rooted out the *Malloi* and extinguished their military power before any help came from the neighboring lords.[164] Gustav Oppert regarded the *Pariah* or the *Palla* or the *Malla* as part of the ancient Dravidian population.[165] A wheel of misfortune turned on the *Malla*, though the name itself was once thought to bring prosperity and enjoyment of wealth and power. Eventually they were defeated and degraded and reduced to a low position in society, as can be gleaned from the term *Mālavādu* used for the Telugu *Pariah*.[166] The representative names of the *Malla*, *Malli*, *Palla* and *Palli* are part of the surnames of the Malas such as *Pallikonda*, *Pallapati*, *Mallavarapu*, *Nagamalla* and *Malli*. Therefore, there is absolutely no resemblance between 'Maila' (dirt) as described in C. P. Brown's Telugu dictionary[167] and the caste name Mala as per the classical and credible historical information mentioned above.

2.4.2 The Mala Endogamy

A vast number of castes in general belong to the Right hand or Left hand factions throughout South India. The castes that belonged to the Right hand division were the *Súdras* and the *Pariahs* (Malas) who held a closer relationship with the village land.[168] The masters of the Malas were the *Súdras* where the former had worked for the latter in agricultural fields and in households.[169] Historically, they were more identified with the rural territory and were directly dependent on the produce of the soil as intensive agricultural production was their major economic concern.[170]

The Malas were a homogeneous group with various sub groups with different *Jati* (birth) traditions and customs. Sydney Nicholson has described the Malas as originally belonging to the '*Kudipaita*' or Right hand caste where their women wore the cloth over their right hand shoulder.[171] They possessed broad facial and nasal features and well-built bodies with dark brown skin.[172] They were the labouring caste of Andhra whose main occupation was agriculture labour and weaving.[173] They were obliged to hire themselves out to the *Súdra* castes in cultivating the soil in return for a minimum wage.[174] For the reason of being weavers, they were also called as *Netapanivandlu* (weaving workers) who had the job of producing coarse white cotton fabric usually worn by men.[175] The Mala weavers had the practice of working for the *Súdra for generations.* The latter supplied the cotton which was spun by the Mala women of the village for remuneration.[176]

Among the Malas too, there were Right hand and Left-hand sections. The Right-hand section was called the *Reddi- Bhūmulavāndlu* and the Left-hand sub sections were called the *Murikināti* and *Pōkanāti.*[177] It was said that the *Reddi-Bhumulavandlu* came to Andhra along with the Reddy population presumably their masters, and hence the name. The Right-hand division followed the Saivite faith prior to their conversion into Christianity.[178] The numerous sub-divisions among the Malas might have contributed to exogamous practices among them. The prominent surnames of the *Reddi Bhūmi* are *Bandi, Bejjam, Dhidla, Gera, Kaila* and *Silam*. Among the *Pōkanāti*, the prominent surnames are *Allam, Dara, Gone, Maggam, Pasala* and *Thummala*. The *Sarindla* section bear the surnames of *Challa, Chinthala, Duddu, Kaki, Ballem* and *Boori*. The *Dāindla* Malas bear the surnames of *Dasari, Doddi, Gonji, Kommala, Marri* and *Thumma*.

2.4.3 Culture and Life Style of the Malas

In matters of civil authority, the *Peda* Mala or the village elder along with a council of elders sorted out all the disputes arising among the Malas.[179] Elaborate marriage ceremonies were held with *Chinna Tambulam,* an initial arrangement for a future wedding, and *Pedda Tambulam,* the engagement ceremony. The wedding ceremony took place in the presence of six Malas and a priest. The bridegroom would tie the *Thālibottu* (golden disc) which was considered to be the *Brahma* knot.[180] When a child was born in the family, a feast was arranged by the parents of the child's mother and the child was named on the same day.[181] Death was regarded as pollution like in any other caste and different kinds of ceremonies were followed on the occasion of the death of Mala person of both Vaishnavite and Saivite sects.

It was said that the Malas would not accept food prepared or touched by the *Kamsala, Medara,* Madigas, *Beri Chetti, Boya* and the *Bhatrazu.*[182] Howeve, an instance of better cooperation between the Malas with other castes of a village was noted where a Mala medicine-man prescribed medication for a *Brāhmin* tahsildar (revenue officer). In some districts, the Malas also acted as hereditary custodians of the idol of *Gauri* (a deity of the *Kapu* and *Balija* castes) and her jewels and the *Súdra* castes need to gain permission from the Malas whenever they wanted to worship the deity.[183] Usually, the *Brāhmin* of the village fixed auspicious dates and time for the marriages of the Malas.[184] The Malas carry the dead of the *Brāhmin* and burn at the ghat.[185]

In Kistna district, the Malas had their own dancing-girls called *Mala Bogam,* own barbers known as *Bainedis* and own priests called the Mala *Dasari.*[186] The *Dāsari* officiated at the burial ritual where the dead body was covered with leaves at the time of burial.[187] The blood relations accompanied the actual burial. The rituals for the dead widow were done by her brothers (*Puttintivāru*). A typical custom of sending the widow's cloths to a washer man (*Tsakali*) which she was wearing during the time of her widowhood existed even to the present day.[188]

The Malas' houses were placed quite apart from the village proper and were made out of thatched roof and mud walls.[189] They rendered allied services like temple services (garland making) and held *Jatara* or festival services.[190] For the allied services rendered to the village peasant communities, they could claim a share of the harvest.[191] During the village ritual of offering sacrifices, certain groups among them did the jobs of musicians and storytellers.[192] The Malas also discharged the functions of gravediggers where they held proprietary rights to burial and cremation grounds.[193] One of the functions of the Mala messengers was to carry messages for the *Súdras* especially during the occurrence of death in the latter's household.[194]

Since the second half of the 19th century, there was a great movement of the Malas towards Christianity and the Christian converts were enumerated as Christians. Though the entry of the Malas was irregular, they were found in considerable numbers in every district of coastal Andhra. The districts that contained the highest number of Mālas were the Kistna, Godavari, Nellore and Guntur. We shall discuss the Mala engagement with Christian missions in the coming chapters.

2.4.4 The Madigas

The Madigas are found throughout undivided Andhra Pradesh.[195] According to the Sanskrit dictionary, the *Carma-Kāra* (Charmakara) was a shoe maker and a worker in leather whose origin was either from a *Candāla* woman and a man from the fisherman caste.[196] The Madigas were also denoted by the name *Kārāvara*, as a man of mixed and low caste, born from a *Nishada* father and *Vaidehi* mother who had worked with leather and hides.[197] According to Gustav Oppert, the Madigas claim to be the descendants of *Adijambavu*[198] and the word Mạdiga was a corrupted form of *Mātanga*[199] which signifies a wild mountaineer.[200]

Vincent Smith opined that the *"Siboi"* or a rude folk clad in the skins of wild beasts and armed with clubs, had submitted themselves to Alexander the Great during his invasion of the lower Indus River and were allowed to retain their freedom.[201] According to N. G. Chetty, the Madigas belonged to the 'left hand caste' or the *Edamapaitavaru*.[202] The Left hand faction comprised of the *Vaisyas* or trading classes and the *Panchalas* or the five artisan castes who drew their functional support from the Madigas or Chucklers.[203] The Madigas earned their living by performing manufacturing jobs by employing their hereditary skills.[204] The Madigas were termed as the 'great leather working caste of Andhra and traded with dead cattle and skinning of dead animals.[205]

2.4.5 The Madiga Endogamy

The Madiga social division was based on *Kula* (clan) and called themselves as *Pedda Intivaru*. The Madigas lived in thatched hamlets at a considerable distance from the dwellings of the caste people in villages.[206] The main reason for their poverty was poor compensation for their labour which ranged from sharecropping to slavery. They were often paid in kind and obtained fodder for their buffaloes. Their diet was poor, clothes were few and unclean and houses were small and fragile and the people appeared unhealthy and helpless in debt.[207] The Madigas' dwellings were squalid to the extreme and the odour of their hamlets was said to be repulsive. It was further stated that in the Northern districts, the Madigas were attached to one or more families of ryots and supplied them with sandals, belts for bulls and all the accessories of agriculture and for which they had to find the requisite leather themselves, with the exception that for larger articles their masters provided the leather.[208] The despised position of the Madigas was mainly attributed to their handling of leather and hides and the jobs of removing, skinning and tanning. They took charge of the ox or buffalo as soon as it was dead and ate the carcass, an act which made their touch polluting.[209] The endogamous sub-divisions among the Madigas were called as Gampa Dhompti (basket offering), Ginna Dhompti (cup offering), Bhumi (earth offering), Chatla (winnowing), Sibbi (brass vessel offering), and Chadarapa (square space offering).[210]

2.4.6 Culture and Life Style of the Madigas

The hereditary office of the *Pedda* Madiga (chief) was assisted by two elected officers called *Dharmakartha* and *Kulambantrothu*. The *Kula-*

Panchayat resolved disputes and solved disagreements among members of the community.[211] The marriage ceremonies of the Madigas were said to be elaborate and were conducted with much noise due to the quantity of liquor consumed. The *Pedda* Madiga conducted the ceremonial duties of *Pradhanam* (Betrothal) by using the *Bonthu* (unbleached cotton thread) round the bride's neck, the *Bashingam* (a string soaked in turmeric and tied around bride and bridegroom's foreheads) and the *Thalibottu* (a disc of gold and a marriage badge). The practice of disposing of the dead either by burial or cremation was prevalent. An interesting custom was that the grave was dug by a *MalaVetti* followed by *Chinnadhinam* (small ceremony) which was conducted on the third day and the *Peddadhinam* (major ceremony) was performed at the close of the third week after a person's death, usually on a Wednesday or Sunday.[212]

As traditional leather workers, the Madigas also did the job of drummers, played musical instruments, especially during marriages, birth ceremonies and funeral processions. A section of the Madigas was called *Sindhuvallu* who acted scenes from the *Mahabharatha* and *Ramayana* or the stories of the village deities. The Madiga *Chindu* or sword-dance was performed in honor of the village goddess during the time of threshing of corn, building of a new house or the opening of a newly-dug well. The ritual was generally accompanied by a song containing indecent comments against the Malas.[213] A curious illustration of this Mala and Madiga antagonism was described by J. Chartres Molony, Superintendent of Census Operations for Madras in 1911, who had cited from H. R. Bardswell, I.C.S., who said that the dance performed by the Madigas was the main objection and infuriated the Malas. The music for the dance was played on a particular instrument of tom-tom called '*tappeta*', a large round instrument with the skin hide only on one side. This instrument was also used for the playing of *Koluva* music. The *Chindu* dance consisted of waving of a cloth and brandishing of a stick, to represent a sword.[214] Abbe Dubois described that the right and left hand factions of Malas and Madigas nurtured traditional animosities and were sources of perpetual riots and disturbances in public peace.[215]

2.5 Religious and Cultural Practices Prior to Conversion

It is important to make a note of the religious and cultural practices of the Malas and the Madigas prior to their conversion to Christianity. In the 19th century, the Malas and the Madigas were considered to be followers of Hinduism but their variety of Hinduism was different from those of the higher classes. They were actually worshippers of animistic deities and village idols. According to Augusta Highland, in India, there were more idols than there were people.[216] The great number of Indian Christian converts came from the depressed castes who were outside the proper Hindu fold or who had never been thoroughly Hinduized.[217] The religious practices of the Malas and the Madigas occupied an important place in village festivals. The mode of worship comprised of primitive forms of idol worship, serpent worship, worship of Mother Nature and demon worship.[218]

2.5.1 Animistic Worship

The Primitive man who had evolved from the depths of animal existence found himself face to face with mighty and mysterious natural forces. He had personified and idolized the natural forces whose powers had impressed upon him and hence tried to propitiate them.[219] The original inhabitants of India followed animistic and nature worship for all practical purposes.[220] There were the ghosts of their forefathers, river spirits, forest-spirits, well-demons, mountain-demons, and a mighty host of unseen beings all of which should be kept in good humor.[221] The religion of the masses was concerned about keeping peace with a host of natural spirits. The belief in spirits and unseen objects of inconsistent abstraction was symbolized in a concrete endowment of natural objects, artifacts and animal figures which were regarded as invisible beings that follow their own laws and influence the destiny of people.[222] The worship of *Gramadevatas* was in principle identical to the Mother Goddess worship which was a primitive form of worship.[223]

2.5.2 The Seven Sisters

Traditionally the Malas and the Madigas *were worshippers of animistic deities along with a pantheon of Saivite* and *Vaishnavite* deities. Animal sacrifice to these deities was a common feature.[224] The worship of Mother Goddess is evident in terracotta figurines. The principle of the female energy or *Sakti*[225] was represented by the local goddesses called *Gramadevatas* or the seven sisters namely, *Poleramma, Ankamma, Muthyalamma, Dilli Polasi, Bangaramma, Mathamma* and *Renuka.* Besides, there were *Peddamma, Pochamma, Ellamma, Gangamma, Mutyalamma, Ravelamma* and *Mahalakshmamma,*[226] who were worshipped along with their younger brother called *Potu Razu.*[227] *Potu Razu* was personified in a ritual by a Madiga by killing the sacrificial goat by strangling it with his teeth and tearing open its throat.[228] The sacrifice of animals, particularly of goats was the most characteristic feature of the worship of *Sakti* (the great power of nature) and the most significant survival rite as per the known sources of the Indus Valley religion.[229] Some of the Malas and the Madigas were also members of some medieval sects such as of Ramanuja.[230]

The prevalence of polytheistic faiths and of the universal worship of tutelary deities among the non-Aryan races does not seem to be an imported factor,[231] but developed in the later centuries through amalgamation of non-Aryan deities with those of the Aryan ones, as for instance, *Candi, Kātyāyanī* and the glorification of the *Dēvi.*[232] The aim of the ordinary peasant's religion was to gain deliverance from evil forces inflicted by demons, and also to escape calamities which they believed occurred due to demoniac presence, planetary and atmospheric influences.[233]

Though the Malas did not perform the actual sacrifice, they participated in the singing of praises (Mala *Āsādhi*) of the goddess, while a buffalo was carried for offering and a procession taken out through the village to ward off demons.[234] The shrines of these deities were rarely imposing structures. Prayers, flattery, offerings and sacrifices were there to propitiate the deity to offset the irritable, uncertain and spiteful nature of the deity whose wayward temperament might be offended by neglect.[235]

Apart from this, the Madigas were also worshippers a number of other Hindu deities such as *Ellamma*, *Katamma*, *Muneeswara* of *Saivite* and *Vaishnavite* pantheons. Each *Kula* (group of sub-castes) maintained their own deities of folk goddesses namely, *Kalamma*, *Chandamma*, *Yallamma* and *Gangamma*. Among the Madigas, some men underwent initiation ceremonies and were called *Asādi*, who in the company of the *Mātangi* (dedicated temple woman) recited the story of *Ellamma* in her praise.[236] The worship of Parvathi in the form of the great *Shakti* was also prevalent.[237] The invariable traits of village goddesses were as follows: *Ellamma,* the *Sakti* in *Existence;*[238] *Mutyalamma,* presiding over small-pox and cholera;[239] *Peddamma* or *Sunkulamma* and *Chinnamma,* prevent crops failure or cattle death in large numbers;[240] and *Mālaskshmi* and *Poleramma,* who ward off devils and evil spirits.[241]

2.5.3 The Institution of Mātangi

Mention may be made about the institution of *Mātangi*, who was a '*vestal virgin*' or an unmarried Madiga woman, initiated as a special representative of the goddesses. If in a village there happened to be only one *Mātangi,* "she knows no moral restrictions."[242] The Madiga *Mātangi* may be differentiated from the '*Rajamatangi*' of the *Dasha-Mahavidyas*. The former was a human and her primary duty was to abuse and spit upon the assembled people irrespective of their caste status,[243] while the latter was an embodied form of *Devi* (Shakti in existence) in Hinduism. In his *Dravidian Gods in Modern Hinduism,* Elmore described that:

During the festival the *Mātangi* becomes possessed by the goddess and runs among the people, touching them with her stick, spurting toddy from her mouth over them, and backing up against them, all the time uttering strange wild cries... as she rushes about spitting on those who under ordinary circumstances would almost choose death rather than to suffer such pollution from a Madiga, she breaks into wild, exulting songs, telling of the humiliation to which she is subjecting the proud caste people. She also abuses them all thoroughly, and… they appear to expect it and not to be satisfied without a full measure of her invective.[244]

2.5.4 The Institution of Basavi

The Malas also had an institutionalized system of dancing girls called the *Basavi,* who were consecrated for divine services and could never be widowed. In Nicholson's observation, the institution of *Basavi* was an age old practice where it was a custom to dedicate girls to temple service. The girl would go through a ceremony with a knife, which was placed in front of the deity. If a man wishes to gain a proprietary right over her, he may obtain it by paying an amount of money and the consent of village elders.[245] The Malas also took part in the *Velpu* festival of the *Kois* of greater Godavari regions of Bastar, Bhadrachalam and Dummagudem.[246]

2.5.5 Animal Sacrifices

When villages faced epidemics like cholera, small-pox, cattle plagues and other misfortunes, the villagers hurried to propitiate the rage of the goddesses by animal sacrifices which were often described to be revolting in nature.[247] The sacrificial buffalo was brought forward and a Madiga person killed it by cutting its throat or head. The chief of the Madigas sacrificed the buffalo and sprinkled its blood over a basket of boiled rice, with the buffalo's head kept on top of it and a lighted lamp on top of the buffalo's head and placed on the head of another Madiga who makes his way around the village boundaries for the purpose of warding off the demons.[248] Interestingly, the intestines were put over the neck of a Mala and its liver was placed in his mouth, while another Mala takes the basket of rice soaked in blood and mixed with the entrails of the buffalo. The man with the liver in the mouth was to be in a state of frantic excitement as he was supposed to be possessed by the goddess.[249]

Bishop Henry Whitehead observed the sacrificial procedure at Masulipatnam performed by the Malas and the Madigas where the images are smeared with turmeric and dots of *kumkuma* and a male buffalo, called *Devara-Potu* is brought before the image and its head cut off by the head Madiga of the town. A procession took place which was called as *'bali-haranam'* where the dead buffalo's blood was collected in a vessel and sprinkled over some boiled rice and the head, along with the right fore-leg in the mouth, was placed before the shrine on a flat wicker basket. With a lighted lamp on the top of the buffalo's head, another Madiga carried it on his head round the village to draw a kind of cordon on every side of the village to prevent the entrance of evil spirits. Anyone in the village who refused to participate in the festival was debarred from the procession and left to the mercy of the devils.[250]

In the Kistna district *inams* or rent-free lands were held from the Government by some families of the Madigas for performing the sacrifices. But, in the town of Masulipatnam, a Madiga was specially licensed by the local administration for the purpose. Besides the buffalo, large numbers of sheep, goats and fowls were sacrificed, each householder giving at least one animal. The head Madiga would actually perform the sacrifice and distribute the flesh among the members of his family.[251]

In prosperous villages near Gudivada in the Krishna delta region, the ritual was somewhat simpler where the sacrificial animal was simply killed by a Madiga who cuts off its head with a large chopper in front of the image of the principal deity *Pallalamma* and the blood was allowed to flow on the ground. The head was claimed by the pujari and the offerer took away the carcass for a feast in his house. The practice of pouring water over the sheep's back was done to test whether the animal shivered. If the animal shivered, it was a sign that the deity had accepted it. If it did not shiver, it was taken as a sign that the deity did not accept the animal and it was taken away to be replaced by another animal.[252]

In the Coconada region, offerings were made to *Nukalamma* every day, regardless of her temper. One custom noted in this region was that after the sacrificial animal was slaughtered, it was put before the shrine and water was poured on it to see whether the mouth was opened and it was taken as a sign that the sacrifice was accepted. At Ellore, during the annual festival of *Mahalakshmamma*, rich people sent as many as twenty or thirty animals and a bulk of animals were sacrificed in one day with blood flowing into the fields.[253] A woman of the Mala caste after her conversion to Christianity described her previous religious life as:

> A visit to our village some twenty years ago would have shown you men, women and children living together in wretchedness and misery, all ignorant and debased, worshipping the little gods that are daubed over with yellow and red, kept under daubed earthen pots in a miserable mud-walled *'gudi'* or temple. Of the dreaded goddess, cholera should come, wild orgies were engaged in and the men, all drunk with toddy would wildly sacrifice hens, chickens and goats in order to appease the goddess and sent her away.[254]

Suffice it here to say that the religion of the Malas and Madigas was replete with worship of a pantheon of gods and goddesses, a plethora of rituals, and rites. Their beliefs, rituals and customs remained practically unchanged and unchallenged for many centuries until the coming of the Christian missionaries. Due to the Christianization efforts of the missionaries their pre-conversion idol worship and animistic practices began to disappear as the converts accepted Christian ways of worship, beliefs and rituals.[255] I shall describe the Christianization of the Mala and Madiga converts in the coming chapters.

2.6 Depressed Condition of Malas and Madigas

A caste was considered dominant when it enjoyed a high ritual status in the caste hierarchy and also could wield economic and political power on the subordinate castes.[256] Whether it was ritually sanctioned or historically evolved over the centuries, the 19th century socio-economic condition of the Malas and the Madigas presented a degenerated state of affairs that needed serious reform and social action.

2.6.1 Social Discrimination

The relation of the Malas and the Madigas with other castes was based on a sort of *jajmani* (patron-client) system, wherein super-ordinate and subordinate interaction existed as patrons and suppliers of services, respectively.[257] Though the Malas and the Madigas were economically integrated with village productive occupations, they were socially rejected as their abode must be out of town; their clothes must be the mantles of the dead; no man should hold any intercourse with them.[258] In Abbe Dubois' words,

> The idea that he was born to be in subjection to the other castes is so ingrained in his mind that it never occurs to the *Pariah* to think that his fate is anything but irrevocable. Nothing will ever persuade him that men are all made of the same clay or that he has the right to insist on better treatment than that which is meted out to him.[259]

The Malas and the Madigas were socially excluded, though included through a local variety of jajmani system. According to Frykenberg, many societies of the world through the making of the historical past have had slaves, but no other society designated 1/5 of its population to be innately subhuman and hence relegated to a permanent state of hereditary thralldom.[260] "Social exclusion should be viewed as a process that restricts the access of certain social groups to valued resources and entitlements, relegating them to the status of social outsiders."[261]

Untouchability, as 'cumulative domination,' shaped into a threefold discrimination of low ritual status, oppressive economic condition and devoid any political power.[262] Although, the extent of the discrimination varied from region to region, in many places, they were not allowed to access the streets and houses of the upper castes. J. R. Kamble described thus the extent of restrictions on the depressed castes in an example from the delta area of the Andhra district: that a depressed caste person had to wait for hours before being ferried across over a river as a *Brāhmin* and a *Pariah* would never be taken together and the *Brāhmin* would always get a priority over others.[263]

Traditionally, the Malas and the Madigas were placed under the cumulative domination of the *Súdra* castes and were attributed to permanent impurity as a result of which their means of livelihood was also relegated to varied levels of impurity.[264] They were denied to hold any property and therefore had to depend on their masters. Due to doing polluted tasks, restrictions were placed such as prohibition of drawing water from the common wells and entering into the temples. They were denied ministrations of the *Brahmins* with a few exceptions.[265] Their dwelling places were set aside from the rest of the village and houses were ill-lighted and unventilated and appeared as water-tight furnaces in hot weather and stifling black holes in the cold.[266] Their routine tasks demanded hard labour and hence the consuming of all types of alcoholic beverages and tobacco.[267] In Rev. Henry Whitehead's observation, during the time of festivals held in honour of the village deities, there was wild excitement and a large amount of drunkenness and immorality.[268]

2.6.2 Economic Hardships

Caste system in India based on hierarchical division of labour and reciprocal interdependence not only decided social ranking but also controlled material life. The village agricultural production was geared to the needs of the villagers on a non-market oriented subsistence pattern.[269] Occupations were hereditarily passed on to succeeding generations. Thus for generations the Malas did agricultural labour and weaving, [270] and the Madigas did curing and tanning of hides to manufacture leather articles.[271]

The Malas and the Madigas were indispensable workforces in the village economy without whose assistance the functioning of a village economy would come to a standstill.[272] The Malas were the petty cultivators of the village lands, called '*Paulaloo*' (un-saleable), under an arrangement made for them so as not to desert their master, or if they did, they would lose the cultivable lands.[273] They were also the hereditary serfs and domestic servants in the service of the landlords and the authority of the masters was not legally enforced.[274]

Despite the Slavery Abolition Act of 1843, the Malas remained in a subjugated condition in order to repay their creditors and lived in a state of abject bondage.[275] The low income generating tasks coincided with ignorance and poverty. Owing to the debts borrowed from money lenders, they were oppressed and were left with no choice to improve their economic condition.[276] Their food was simple as they lived mainly on Conjee (ganjee or boiled rice water), relished with onions and green chillies, which they could procure from the farm without buying. They generally consumed ragi or cumbu which they procured as part of their wages. The females of households picked up the droppings of cattle and dry twigs and used these as firewood.[277] Limited access to resources and differential distribution of income along with intemperate habits and accumulated debts increased their poverty. Burdensome social customs such as dowry and extensive wedding feasts further worsened the already economic depressed condition of the Malas and the Madigas.

2.6.3 Educational Backwardness

Traditionally, the Malas and the Madigas were denied the right to education and acquiring of knowledge. They were not allowed to attend the *pathshalas* or the *pyal* schools but had to follow their hereditary occupations of their forefathers. They were economically exploited, socially oppressed and devoid of acquiring knowledge. Throughout history, their society was controlled and hegemonised wholly according to the interests of the top privileged groups, under the caste system.[278] Until the second half of the 19th century, education was not within the reach of the depressed castes who had to content themselves with the acquisition of skills that enabled them to carry out their hereditary professions.

2.6.4 Social and Cultural Restrictions

The Malas and the Madigas were socially and culturally restricted in the village. Some of the restrictions were:[279]

- That the Adi Dravidas [Malas and Madigas] should not wear ornaments of gold and silver;
- That the males should not be allowed to wear their clothes below their knees or above their hips;
- That their males should not wear coats or shirts or baniyans;
- No Adi Dravidas shall be allowed to have his hair cropped;
- That the Adi Dravidas should not use vessels other than earthenware ones in their homes;
- Their women shall not be allowed to cover the upper portion of their bodies by clothes (*ravikas* or *thavanies*);
- Their women shall not be allowed to use flowers or saffron paste; and
- The man shall not use umbrellas for protection against sun and rain nor should they wear sandals.

Strict linguistic restrictions were also imposed while addressing their caste masters. There were restrictions on free movement during the day and night on grounds of pollution. They were expected to adopt a servile and obsequious attitude when addressing the caste people.[280]

2.7 Conclusion

During the second part of the 19th century, social reformation in the Indian society occurred through the efforts of Christian missionaries and western educated Indian intelligentsia. With the introduction of a set of fundamental truths based on faith and reason and with a spirit of scientific rationalism, the impetus for discarding the traditional faiths in place of new ones started to emerge. The reform and emancipation ideologies were based on elements of justice and righteousness of humanity which were aimed at reestablishing the social order by eliminating the obsolete, immoral and unjust practices of the Hindu society. The emancipation agenda was set to uproot morally unjustified practices such as that of idolatry, burning of the widows, prohibition of widow-marriages, child marriages, the interdiction of foreign travel, and so on. Through various reform channels and personal persuasion techniques, they initiated goal orientated activities, provided direction, energy and persistence, to the depressed communities

In the given context, a call for deliverance of the oppressed was made by the Christian missionaries who took a leading role sometimes supported by a few enlightened individuals. In condemning the gross evils, an uncompromising attitude was displayed by the Christian missionaries who stressed the principles of the Fatherhood of God and the brotherhood of humans. Faced with many social hardships, the Malas and the Madigas, chose to convert to Christianity when presented with the Gospel by the Christian missionaries, apparently with a hope of being liberated from their socio-religious fetters and of attaining better economic freedom.

Endnotes and References

1 The State of Andhra Pradesh, formed in 1950s was recently bifurcated into two states, Telengana and Andhra Pradesh. The coastal area pertaining to this study falls in Andhra Pradesh as shown in Map 2.1

2 Y. Sudershan Rao, *Andhra between the Empires* (Hanmakonda: Sulekha Publishers, 1991), 1.

3 Khadavalli Lakshmi Ranjanamand Balendu Sekharam, *Andhras through the Ages* (Hyderabad: Sri Saraswati Book Depot, 1973), 88.

4 Ibid., 11.

5 D. F. Carmichael, *A Manual of the District of Vizagapatam in the Presidency of Madras* (Madras: The Lawrence Asylum Press, 1869), 1.

6 Henry Morris, *A Descriptive and Historical Account of the Godavery District in the Presidency of Madras* (London: Trubner and Co Publishers, 1878), 1.

7 The 'Kistna' district was formed in December 1859 under the order of Governor Sir Charles Trevelyan: Gordon Mackenzie, *A Manual of the Kistna District in the Presidency of Madras* (Madras: Lawrence Asylum Press, 1883), 1; Also *The Imperial Gazetteer of India*, Vol. 15, Karachi to Kottayam (Oxford: Clarendon Press, 1908), 319.

8 Lewis McIver, *Census of India*, 1881, Madras Presidency, Operations and Results, Vol. II (Madras: The Government Press, 1882), 444 b.

9 *The Imperial Gazetteer of India,* Vol. 12 (Oxford: Clarendon Press, 1909), 155.

10 *Ibid.,* 147.

11 W. Francis, *The Gazetteer of South India,* Vol. 1 (New Delhi: Mittal Publications, 1988), 194.

12 *The Imperial Gazetteer of India,* Vol. 12, op. cit., 151.

13 *The Imperial Gazetteer of India*, Vol. 24 (Oxford: Clarendon Press, 1909), 322.

14 Lewis McIver, op.cit., 444 b.

15 *The Imperial Gazetteer of India*, Vol. 12, op. cit., 328.

16 *Ibid.,* 333.

17 *The Imperial Gazetteer of India,* Vol. 12, op. cit., 288.

18 Lewis McIver, op.cit., 444 b.

19 W. Francis, *The Gazetteer of South India,* Vol. 1, op. cit., 268.

20 *The Imperial Gazetteer of India,* Vol. 12, op. cit., 288.

21 *Ibid.,* 286.2

22 *Ibid.*

23 Gordon Mackenzie, op.cit., 1. Also in *The Imperial Gazetteer of India*, Vol. 15, op. cit., 319.

24 *The Imperial Gazetteer of India*, Vol. 15, op. cit., 319.
Also in Lewis McIver, op.cit., 444 b.

25 W. Francis, *The Gazetteer of South India,* Vol. 1, op. cit., 299.

26 *The Imperial Gazetteer of India*, Vol. 15, op. cit., 323.

27 *The Imperial Gazetteer of India,* Vol. 12, op. cit., 11. Also in Lewis McIver, op. cit., 444 b.

28 W. Francis, *The Gazetteer of South India,* Vol. 1, op. cit., 340.

29 Ibid., 12. 'Z' denotes *Zemindar.* W. Francis, *Gazetteer of South Indi.*

30 W. Francis, *The Gazetteer of South India,* Vol. 1, op. cit., 15.

31 Henry Morris, op. cit., 180. Also in William Wilson Hunter, *The Indian Empire: Its People, History and Products* (London: Trubner and Ludgate Hill Publishers, 1886), 368.

32 Henry George Briggs, *The Nizam: His History and Relations with the British Government*, Vol. I (Delhi: Manas Publications, 1861), 19.

33 Ibid., 73.

34 John William Kaye, *Administration of the East India Company: A History of Indian Progress* (London: Richard Bentley Publishers, 1853), 224.

35 J. Talboys Wheeler, *India under British rule from the Foundation of the East India Company* (London: Macmillan, 1886), 132.

36 Romesh Dutt, *The Economic History Of India Under Early British Rul*e, Sixth Edition, Kegan Paul (London: Trench and Trubner Publishers, 1901), 110.

37 Baden B. H. Powell, "The Origin of Zamindari Estates in Bengal," *The Quarterly Journal of Economics* 1 (1896): 42.

38 Ibid., 117.

39 D. N. Dhanagare, *Peasant Movements in India 1920-1950* (Delhi: The Oxford University Press, 1983), 29.

40 R. Ricards, *India or Facts Submitted to Illustrate the Character and Condition of the Native Inhabitants*, Vol. 1 (London: Smith Elder and Company Publishers, 1829), 426.

41 Baden B. H. Powell, *The Land Systems of British India: Being a Manual of the Land Tenures and of the systems of Land Revenue Administration prevalent in the Several Provinces*, Vol. I (London: Clarendon Press, 1892), 291.

42 Ibid., 510.

43 Baden B. H. Powell, "The Origin of Zamindari Estates in Bengal," *The Quarterly Journal of Economics*, No. 1 (1896): 43.

44 Y. Sudershan Rao, *Andhra between the Empire*s, op. cit., 156.

45 Romesh Dutt, op. cit., 118.

46 R. Ricards, op. cit.,406.

47 Gordon Mackenzie, op. cit., 8.

48 Ibid., 117.

49 Henry Morris, op. cit., 154.

50 J. Talboys Wheeler, op. cit., 132.

51 John Clark Marshman, *History of India from the earliest period to the close of the East India Company's Government* (Calcutta: The School Book Society, 1873), 226.

52 Baden B. H. Powell, "The Origin of Zamindari Estates in Bengal," *The Quarterly Journal of Economics,* No. 1 (1896): 49.

53 Ibid., 118.

54 Irfan Habib, *The Agrarian System of Mughal India* (New Delhi Asia Publishing House, 1963), 122.

55 R. Ricards, op. cit., 46.
A detailed description of the Ryotwari village see, Baden B. H. Powell, "The Origin of Zamindari Estates in Bengal," *The Quarterly Journal of Economics*, No. 1, 1896: 154-157.

56 Theodore Morison, *The Economic Transition of India* (London: John Murray Publishers, 1911), 153.

57 William Wiser, *The Hindu Jajmani System: A Socio-Economic System Interrelating Members of a Hindu Village Community in Services* (Lucknow: Lucknow Publishing House, 1958), 116.

58 Romesh Dutt, op. cit., 118.

59 Monier Williams, *Brahmanism and Hinduism or Religious Thought and Life in India: As Based on the Veda and other Sacred Books of The Hindus* (London: John Murray Publishers, 1891), 455.

60 Khadavalli Lakshmi Ranjanam, *Kakatiya Yugamu* (Hyderabad: Andhra Pradesh Sahitya Academy Publishers, 1975), 1.

61 Ibid., 70.

62 Romesh Dutt, op. cit., 118-119.

63 Bruce J. Caldwell, *Jajmani System: An Investigation* (New Delhi: Hindustan Publishing Corporation, 1991), 9.

64 Ibid., 21.

65 Richard L. Brubaker, "Barbers, Washer men and other Priests: Servants of the South Indian Village and its Goddess," *History of Religions* 19(2), (1979): 135.

66 *Manual of the Administration of the Madras Presidency: An Illustration of the Records of Government and the Yearly Administration Reports* (Madras: The Government Press, 1885), 80.

67 Baden B. H. Powell, "The Origin of Zamindari Estates in Bengal," *The Quarterly Journal of Economics*, No. 1 (1896): 144.

68 Romesh Dutt, op. cit., 139-140.

69 J. H. Beaglehole, "Sir Thomas Munro," *The Indo British Review* 1-2, (1968-69): 24.

70 W. Francis, *The Gazetteer of South India,* Vol. 1, op. cit., 283.

71 Ibid., 314.

72 Charles Francis Greville, *British India Analyzed: The Provincial and Revenue Establishments*, Vol. III (London: R. Faulder and Co Publishers, 1795), 659.

73 P. Raghunadha Rao, *History of Modern Andhra Pradesh* (Delhi: Sterling Publishers, 1988), 74.

74 Ibid., 120.

75 Ibid., preface.

76 William Digby, *Prosperous British India: A Revelation from Official Records* (London: T. Fisher Unwin Publishers, 1901), 127.

77 P. Raghunadha Rao, op. cit., 129.

78 Konrad Specker, "Madras Handlooms in the Nineteenth Century," *The Indian Economic and Social History Review* XXVI (2), (April-June 1989): 138.

79 Y. Vaikuntham, *Education and Social Change in South India,* Andhra: 1880-1920 (Madras: New Era Publications, 1982), 3.

80 Henry Whitehead, *The Religious Life of India: The Village Gods of South India* (Calcutta: The Association Press, 1921), 14.

81 Wilber Theodore Elmore, *Dravidian Gods in Modern Hinduism: A Study of the Local and Village Deities of Southern India* (New York: Self- Published, New York, 1915), 17.

82 Monier Williams, *Brahmanism and Hinduism or Religious Thought and Life in India: As Based on the Veda and other Sacred Books of The Hindus*, op. cit.,18.

83 Y. V. Krishna Rao, *Andhra Pradesh Darshini*, (Hyderabad: Vishalandra Publishing House, 1976), 1119.

84 Nogendranath Mazumder, *A History of Education in Ancient India* (Calcutta: Macmillan Co Ltd Publishers, 1916), 51.

85 Ibid., 57.

86 Kapil Fathima Kutty, *Education and Social Change in India* (New Delhi: Radiant Publishers, 1990), 9.

87 Nogendranath Mazumder, op. cit., 67.

88 Charles E. Grover, *Results of Educational Census, Madras-1871* (Madras: The Governemnt Printing Press, 1872), 60.

89 Khadavalli Lakshmi Ranjanam, *Andhrula Charitra Samskriti* (Madras: Bala Sarawathi Book Depot, 1951), 386.

90 Ross C. Houghton, *Women of the Orient: An Account of the Religious, Intellectual, and Social Condition of Women* (New York: Cranston and Stowe Publishers, New York, 1877), 31.

91 Ibid., 32.

92 Ibid., 82.

93 Ibid., 379.

94 Ibid., 334.

95 James S. Dennis, *Christian Missions and Social Progress, A Sociological Study of Foreign Missions,* Vol. II (New York: Fleming H. Revell, 1899), 61.

96 Nicholas B. Dirks, "Castes of Mind," *Representations*: *Imperial Fantasies and Postcolonial Histories*, Special Issue (37), (1992): 56.

97 Monier Williams, A *Sanskrit-English Dictionary* (Oxford: Clarendon Press, 1872), 452. Also L. S. S. O'Malley, *Indian Caste Customs* (London: Curzon Press, 1974), 1.

98 D. F. Pocock, *Essays on the Caste System by Célestin Bouglé* (Cambridge: Cambridge University Press, 1971), 82.

99 Noel P. Gist, "Caste Differentials in South India," *The American Sociological Review* 19 (2), (1954): 129.

100 Srinivas, M. N., *Caste in Modern India: And Other Essays* (New Delhi: Asia Publishing House, 1962), 16.

101 Pitirim A. Sorokin, *Social and Cultural Dynamics: A Study of Change in Major Systems of Art, Truth, Ethics, Law and Social Relationships* (New Jersey: Transaction Publishers, 1962), 570.

102 Andre Beteille, *Castes: Old and New: Essays in Social Structure and Social Stratification* (New Delhi: Asia Publishing House, 1969), 35.

103 Louis Dumont, *Homo Hierarchicus: The Caste System and Its Implications* (Chicago: University of Chicago Press, 1970), 78.

104 Nicholas B. Dirks, op. cit., 57.

105 Morton Klass, *Caste: The Emergence of South Asian Social System* (Delhi: Manohar Publishers, 1980), 163.

106 Reinhard Bendix, *Max Weber: An Intellectual Portrait* (Berkeley: University of California Press, 1977), 144.

107 Cited in Nripendra Kumar Dutt, *Origin and Growth of Caste in India*, Vol. I (Calcutta: Firma K.L Mukhopadhyay, 1968), 1-2.

108 Shridhar V. Ketkar, *The History of Caste in India: Evidence of the Laws of Manu on the Social Conditions in India During the Third Century A. D, Interpreted and Examined*, Vol. I (New York: Taylor and Carpenter Publishers, 1909), 14.

109 Robert Shafer, *Ethnography of Ancient India* (Wiesbaden: Harrassowitz Publishers, 1954), 8.

110 Monier Williams, A *Sanskrit-English Dictionary*, op. cit, 406.

111 William Wilson Hunter, *A Brief History of the Indian Peoples* (Oxford: Clarendon Press, 1893), 49.

112 Bimal Kanthi Majumdar, *The Military System in Ancient India* (Calcutta: The World Press Limited, 1955), foot note 71, 28.

113 Robert Shafer, op. cit., 9-10.

114 "A generic term applied for a person speaking any language but Sanskrit and not conforming to the usual Hindu institutions and also used in terms of a man of an outcast race". See Monier Williams, A *Sanskrit-English Dictionary*, op. cit., 800.

115 J. D. Anderson, *The Peoples of India* (Cambridge: Cambridge University Press, 1913), 24.

116 William Wilson Hunter, *The Indian Empire: Its People, History and Products*, op. cit., 55.

117 A. R Gupta, *Caste Hierarchy and Social Change: A Study of Myth and Reality* (New Delhi: Jyotsna Prakasan, 1984), 34.

118 William Jones, *Institutes of Hindu Law or the Ordinances of Menu: According to the Gloss of Culluca: Comprising (the Indian System of Duties, Religious and Civil* (London: Printed by Order of the Government, 1796), 5.

119 *The Rig Veda*, Book 10, Translated by Ralph T.H. Griffith.

120 William Jones, op. cit., 299.

121 Ibid., 300-302.

122 A. R Gupta, op. cit., 38.

123 Robert Shafer, op. cit., 7.

124 John Henry Hutton, *Caste in India: Its Nature, Function and Origins* (Cambridge: The University Press, 1946), 122.

125 Based on Louis Dumont, op. cit., xii.

126 John Henry Hutton, op. cit., 125.

127 J. D. Anderson, op. cit., 24.

William Wilson Hunter, *The Indian Empire: Its People, History and Products*, op. cit., 14.

128 Andre Beteille, op. cit., 90.

129 Ibid., 31.

130 William Jones, op. cit., 290-293.

131 The surnames of given by Thurston about the *Sarindla* sub-division of the Mala may indicate that they might be the Sairindhra family of class. *Challa* (Butter-Milk), *Chinthala* (Tamarind), *Duddu* (money), *Kaki* (Crow), *Ballem* (Spear) and *Boori* (Cake), *Uyyala* (See-Saw), *Karna* (Ear), *Gali* (Wind/Fanning), etc., indicate names related to domestic jobs. In Telugu, *indra* means 'house', *sari* means 'to make it right', and therefore the task of the *Sairindhra* was house-keeping, Edgar Thurston, *Castes and Tribes of Southern India*, Vol. IV, K-M (Madras: The Government Press, 1909), 348.

132 William Jones, op.cit., 293.

133 R. C. Majumdar, et al, *An Advanced History of India*, Fourth edition (New Delhi: Macmillian Publishers, 1967), 44.

134 William Jones, op. cit., 291.

135 Edgar Thurston, op. cit., 292.

136 Louis Dumont, op. cit., 47.

137 Khadavalli Lakshmi Ranjanam and Balendu Sekharam, *Andhras through the Age,* (Madras: Sri Sarawaṭhi Press, 1973), 28.

138 J. A. Abbe Dubois, *Description of the Character, Manners and Customs of the People of India and of their Institutions, Religious and Civil* (London: Longman and Hurst Publishers, 1816), 24.

139 William Jones, op. cit., 295.

140 Ibid., 293.

141 Edgar Thurston, op. cit., 308-309.

142 Dharma Kumar, *Land and Caste in South India: Agricultural Labour in the Madras Presidency* (London: Cambridge University Press, 1965), 188.

143 John D. Brewer, *Ethnography* (Philadelphia: The Open University Press, 2000), 51.

144 Ibid., 30.

145 Athelstane Baines, *Ethnography: Castes and Tribes* (Strassburg: Karl J. Trubner Publishers, 1912), 9.

146 Edgar Thurston, op. cit., 294.

147 Ibid., 74.

148 Gustav Oppert, *On the Original Inhabitants of Bharatavarşa or India* (Westminster: Archibald Constable and Co, 1898), 51.

149 For example: The *Himalaya,* the *Tirumala* and the *Nallamala* hills.

150 R. C. Majumdar (ed), *History and Culture of the Indian People: The Vedic Age* (Mumbai: Bharatiya Vidya Bhavan, 1996), 147.

151 William Jones, op. cit., 295.

152 Gustav Oppert, op. cit., 48.

153 Ibid.

154 K. E. Rajprakukh, *Dalit Christians of Andhra: Under the Impact of Missionaries* (New Delhi: Serials Publications, 2008), 96-97.

155 Gustav Oppert, op. cit., 18.

156 Ibid., 21 and 56.

157 Monier Williams, A *Sanskrit-English Dictionary*, op. cit., 774.

158 Gustav Oppert, op. cit., 21.

159 Ibid., 37.

160 William Jones, op. cit., 293. Also in Gustav Oppert, op. cit., 51.

161 Athelstane Baines, op. cit., 74.

162 Alexander Buenes, *Travels Into Bokhara: Being the Account of a Journey From India to Cabool, Tartary and Persia*, Vol. III (London: John Murray Publishers, 1834), 114.

163 Plutarch, *Alexander* (New York: Philips and Hunt Publishers, 1883), 12.

164 Vincent A Smith, *The Early History of India: From 600 BC to the Muhammadan Conquest* (Oxford: Clarendon Press, 1904), 97.

165 Gustav Oppert, op. cit., 31.

166 Ibid., 21.

167 Charles Philip Brown, *A Telugu-English Dictionary*, 2nd Edition (Madras: The Society for Promoting Christian Knowledge, 1903), 0985.

168 J. A. Abbe Dubois, *Hindu Manners, Customs and Ceremonies,* Third Edition (Oxford: Clarendon Press, 1906), 25.

169 Gustav Oppert, op. cit., 65.

170 Brenda E. F. Beck, "The Right-Left Division of South Indian Society", in Rodney Needham (ed) *Right and Left: Essays on Dual Symbolic Classification* (Chicago: The University of Chicago Press, 1973), 780.

171 The right blocs of castes were dominated by a body of rural landlords. Allied with them were several groups who were economically dependent on land, in particular, castes who could claim a share of the harvest of a particular area in return for ritual services rendered to local peasant communities. See Sydney Nicholson, "Social organization of the Mālas: An Outcaste Indian People," *The Journal of the Royal Anthropological Institute of Great Britain and Ireland* 56 (1926): 92. Also in Brenda E. F. Beck, op. cit., 780.

172 N. K. Singh, *Global Encyclopedia of the South Indian Dalit's Ethnography* (New Delhi: Global Vision Publishing House, 2006), 491.

173 Athelstane Baines, op. cit., 9.

174 J. A. Abbe Dubois, *Hindu Manners, Customs and Ceremonies,* Third Edition, op. cit., 49.

175 Edgar Thurston, op. cit., 344.

176 Hibbert G. Ware, *Christian Missions in the Telugu Country* (Westminster: The Society for the propagation of the Gospel, 1912), 82.

177 Sydney Nicholson, op. cit., 92.

178 Ibid., 91.

179 Ibid., 96.

180 Edgar Thurston, op. cit., 362.

181 Ibid., 370.

182 Ibid., 344.

183 Ibid.

184 Ibid., 355.

185 Ibid., 349.

186 W. Francis, *Census of India*, 1901, Vol. XV-A, Part II, Imperial Tables, Madras (Calcutta: The Government Press, 1902), 166.

187 Edgar Thurston, op. cit., 377.

188 "She was stripped of all the jewels she wore as a married woman. Afterwards she is taken inside by some widows, and, after bathing, dons a cloth which has been brought for her by her brothers. Her own cloth is left outside, and must be sent from there to the washer man", Edgar Thurston, op. cit., 378.

189 Ibid., 348.

190 Ibid., 349.

191 Brenda E. F. Beck, op. cit., 780.

192 Edgar Thurston, op. cit., 305.

193 Ibid., 349.

194 Ibid., 350.

195 K. E. Rajprakukh, op. cit., 96.

196 Monier Williams, *Brahmanism and Hinduism or Religious Thought and Life in India: As Based on the Veda and other Sacred Books of The Hindus*, op. cit., 318. Also in William Jones, op. cit., 290-293.

197 Monier Williams, *Brahmanism and Hinduism or Religious Thought and Life in India: As Based on the Veda and other Sacred Books of The Hindus*, op. cit., 221.

198 Gustav Oppert, op. cit., 465.

199 Ibid., 66.

200 Monier Williams, *Brahmanism and Hinduism or Religious Thought and Life in India: As Based on the Veda and other Sacred Books of The Hindus* (London: John Murray Publishers, 1891), 768. Also in Gustav Oppert, op. cit., 17.

201 *The Early History of India: From 600 BC to the Muhammadan Conquest* (Oxford: Clarendon Press, 1904), 97.

202 Edgar Thurston, op. cit., 295. The 'left' bloc was led by the artisans. This latter division included a number of communities who lived mainly by marketing their skills and paid for their individual job. They were the 'specialists' who learned and practiced some particular inherited occupation rather than the 'generalists' whose fortunes were linked directly to agricultural production. See Brenda E. F. Beck, "The Right-Left Division of South Indian Society", in Rodney Needham (ed) *Right and Left: Essays on Dual Symbolic Classification* (Chicago: The University of Chicago Press, 1973), 780.

203 J. A. Abbe Dubois, *Hindu Manners, Customs and Ceremonies,* Third Edition, op. cit., 25.

204 Brenda E. F. Beck, op. cit., 780.

205 Athelstane Baines, op. cit., 9.

206 Edgar Thurston, op. cit., 294.

207 John C. B. Webster, *Dalit Christians: A History* (Delhi: ISPCK Publishers, 1994), 71.

208 Edgar Thurston, op. cit., 309.

209 Ibid., 308.

210 Ibid., 318.

211 Ibid., 319.

212 Ibid., 322-323.

213 Ibid., 315.

214 Chartres J Molony, *Census of India*, 1911, Vol. XII, Part I, Report (Madras: The Government Press, 1912), 162.

215 J. A. Abbe Dubois, *Hindu Manners, Customs and Ceremonies,* Third Edition, op.cit., 25.

216 Augusta Highland, *India* (Rock Island, IL: Lutheran Augustana Synod Centennial Committee, ND), 9.

217 *The India Mission of the Free Church of Scotland* (Edinburgh: The Edinburgh Press, 1891), 10.

218 John E. Clough, *Social Christianity in the Orient: The Story of A Man, A Mission and A Movement* (New York: The MacMillan Company, 1914), 93. Also in Monier Williams, *Brahmanism and Hinduism or Religious Thought and Life in India: As Based on the Veda and other Sacred Books of The Hindus*, op. cit., Preface.

219 John E. Clough, op. cit., 209.

220 Hibbert G. Ware, op. cit., 86.

221 William Wilson Hunter, *A Brief History of the Indian Peoples*, op. cit., 46.

222 Guenther Roth and Claus Wittich, *Max Weber: Economy and Society: An Outline of Interpretive Sociology* (Los Angeles: The University of California Press, 1978), 401.

223 Gustav Oppert, op. cit., 473.

224 Nandu Ram, *Encyclopedia of Scheduled Castes in India (*New Delhi: Gyan Publishing House, 2007), 472.

225 Monier Williams, *Brahmanism and Hinduism or Religious Thought and Life in India: As Based on the Veda and other Sacred Books of The Hindus*, op. cit., 185.

226 Henry Whitehead, op. cit., 70.

227 Wilber Theodore Elmore, op. cit., 19.

228 Gustav Oppert, op. cit., 461.

229 Kashinath Narayan Dikshit, *Pre-Historic Civilization of the Indus Valley* (Madras: The University of Madras, 1967), 5.

230 John E. Clough, op. cit., 93.

231 Ibid., 436.

232 Ibid., 436.

233 Monier Williams, *Brahmanism and Hinduism or Religious Thought and Life in India: As Based on the Veda and other Sacred Books of The Hindus*, op. cit., 210.

234 Edgar Thurston, op. cit., 329.

235 Monier Williams, *Brahmanism and Hinduism or Religious Thought and Life in India: As Based on the Veda and other Sacred Books of The Hindus*, op. cit., 222.

236 Edgar Thurston, op. cit., 61.

237 John E. Clough, op. cit., 148.

238 Edgar Thurston, op. cit., 306.

239 Ibid., 58.

240 Ibid., 337.

241 Ibid., 296.

242 Wilber Theodore Elmore, op. cit., 30.

243 Ibid., 295.

244 Ibid., 31.

For a detailed account of the Institution of *Mātangi*, also see Emma Rauschenbusch Clough, While Sewing Sandals or Tales of a Telugu Pariah Tribe (London: The Selwood Printing Works, 1899), 62-76.

245 Edgar Thurston, op. cit., 384.

246 The Vēlpu is a large three-cornered red cloth, with a number of figures of various ancestors roughly cut out of different colored cloth, white, green, blue, or yellow, and stitched to the main cloth. Whenever any important male member of the family dies, a new figure is added to commemorate his services. It is usually kept in the custody of the leading man of the family, and taken round by him to all members of that family once a year, when each member is bound to give an offering to the Vēlpu. Edgar Thurston, op. cit., 62.

247 Hibbert-Ware had described the ritual in the following words: "A male buffalo is brought which has been provided by the Súdras and selected for the chief sacrifice. The buffalo is decorated with garlands of margosa leaves, which are hung round its neck, and with turmeric (a yellow stain). It is then taken in procession by the Malas and the Madigas round the village from house to house. An Mala person lead the buffalo, and an Madiga beat tom-toms and dance and sing. As the animal makes its progress, it is worshipped by the people. At an appointed hour the buffalo is brought in front of the newly erected shrine of the goddesses. There it is killed by an Madiga who cuts off the victim's head and one of its legs. The head is placed before the goddess, the leg is fixed in its mouth, and a lamp burning the fat of the buffalo is then placed on the head. The light on the buffalo's head is put out, and the head itself carried off by the Madiga who slew the animal as his perquisite" in Hibbert G Ware, op. cit., 88-89.

248 Wilber Theodore Elmore, op. cit., 22.

249 Henry Whitehead, op. cit., 52.

250 Ibid., 62-63.

251 Edgar Thurston, op. cit., 314.

252 Ibid., 54-55.

253 Ibid., 64-66.

254 John Craig, J. R. Stillwell, I. C. Archibald and A. E. Baskerville, *Telugu Trophies: The Jubilee Story of Some of the Principal Telugu Converts in the Canadian Baptist Foreign Mission in India from 1874 to 1924* (Toronto: The Canadian Baptist Publication Society, NY), 56-57.

255 Jacob Chamberlain, *In the Tiger Jungle and other Stories of Missionary Work among the Telugus of India* (New York: Fleming H Revell, 1896), 173.

256 M. N. Srinivas, *On Living in a Revolution and Other Essays* (New Delhi: The Oxford University Press, 1992), 308.

257 Harold A. Gould, *The Hindu Caste System* (Delhi: Chanakya Publications, 1987), 138-139.

258 William Jones, op. cit., 295.

259 J. A. Abbe Dubois, *Hindu Manners, Customs and Ceremonies,* Third Edition, op. cit., 50.

260 R. E. Frykenberg, "On the Study of Conversion Movements: A Review Article and a Theoretical Note," *The Indian Economic and Social History Review* 17, (1980): 128-29.

261 A. K. Lal (ed) *Social Exclusion* (New Delhi: Concept Publishers, 2003), 151.

262 T. K. Oommen, "Sources of Deprivation and Styles of Protest: The Case of the Dalits in India," *The Contributions to Indian Sociology* 18, (1984): 46.

263 J. R. Kamble, *Rise and Awakening of Depressed Classes in India* (Delhi: The National Printing Press, 1979), 12.

264 T. K. Oomen, *State and Society in India: Studies in Nation Building* (New Delhi: Sage Publications, 1990), 25.

265 E. A. Gait, The Census Commissioner of India, "Notes on Census Returns of Hindus," (Simla: 1910), cited in Wilber Theodore Elmore, op. cit., 11.

266 Srinivasa S. Raghavaiyangar, *Memorandum of the Progress of the Madras Presidency during the Last Forty Years of British Administration* (Madras: The Government Press, 1892), 97.

267 Guenther Roth and Claus Wittich, op. cit., 402.

268 Henry Whitehead, op. cit., 153.

269 D. N. Dhanagare, op. cit., 28.

270 Hibbert G. Ware, op. cit., 81-82. Also in John Henry Hutton, op. cit., 287.

271 Edgar Thurston, op. cit., 309.

272 Andre Beteille, op. cit., 92.

273 Dharma Kumar, "Caste and Landlessness in South India," *The Comparative Studies in Society and History* 4 (3), (1962): 339.

274 Ibid., 349.

275 G. A. Oddie, *Social Protest in India: British Protestant Missionaries and Social Reforms 1850-1900* (New Delhi: Manohar Publishers, 1979), 113.

276 Edgar Thurston, op. cit., 350.

277 Srinivasa S. Raghavaiyangar, op. cit., 96-97.

278 V. P. S. Raghuvanshi, *Indian Society in the Eighteenth Century* (Delhi: The Associated Publishing House, 1969), 11.

279 J. R. Kamble, op. cit., 9.

280 Robert Deliege, *The Untouchables of India* (Trans) Nora Scott (Oxford: Berg Publishers, 1999), 90.

Chapter 3

Christian Missions in Coastal Andhra: Organization, Evangelization and Conversion

3.1 Introduction

Christian Missions, missionaries and their works had a significant role in the making of modern India and as such are part of modern Indian history. Christianity in India is as old as Christianity itself, for it was preached in Kerala by St. Thomas, an Apostle of Christ himself, in the second half of the first century. Ever since, the Christian community has been a part of Indian society though was limited to Kerala and adjoining regions, for over fifteen centuries. Modern Christian evangelization work by missionaries began only in the 16th century, after the arrival of the Portuguese in Goa. For the next two hundred years Catholic missionaries such as the Franciscans, Dominicans, Jesuits, Augustinians and the like, began to evangelise various communities in India as in other parts of Asia. Since early 18th century, Protestant Christian missionaries made their presence, first in Tamil Nadu, and later in other parts of India. Their work in Andhra picked up momentum from mid-eighteenth century. This study being related to the evangelization and conversion of the Malas and Madigas of coastal Andhra, in this chapter, we shall focus on some of the main Protestant missionaries who had worked in this region, during the period, 1850-1950. The missionaries were of different national identities: English, Scottish, Canadian, American, Australian, New Zealander, Danish, German and Swedish.

Christian Missions were institutions for preaching of the Gospel, through example, word and action. Christian missionaries through their dedicated lives preached through lived example, through scriptures, works of mercy, and liberative and empowering action such as education, health care, and the like.

They were indispensable in Gospel propagation and church building.[1] They were essentially community builders rather than church builders. Studies have shown that the impact of their work was felt in the lives of the people, especially of the marginalized sections in terms of socio-religious, economic, cultural, educational and occupational changes among them. In the perception of the people, they had genuine empathy for the poor and the underprivileged. This enabled the latter to respond positively to their preaching by accepting baptism as individuals, in kin groups, families and as communities. Consequently, there seems to have emerged a new social consciousness among the converts. Our attempt in this chapter is to explore the founding and growth of mission organizations, method of evangelization and mission works among the people of coastal Andhra, particularly among the Malas and Madigas. In this narrative process, attempt has been made to include the profile and prominence of certain pioneer missionaries.

3.2 Christianity in Andhra

The first Christian presence in Andhra begins in early 16th century with the arrival of the Portuguese ambassador from Goa, Louis de Salvador to Vijayanagar to negotiate an alliance between the Vijayanagar Empire and the Portuguese and to obtain permission to preach the Gospel in Andhra. It was through him that the first contact of the Telugus with (Catholic) Christianity was established.[2] The Jesuit missionaries having arrived in Goa in 1542 sent a delegate to the court of the Vijaynagar Emperor then stationed at Venkatagiri in 1599. They extended their work in the interior in two places: Bijapur and Bisnagar. Christian doctrine, namely, the catechism, was translated into Telugu in 1600. As the Jesuits could not continue in Bijapur, the Goan Bishop Matteo de Castro tried to organize Christianity in Andhra area which was within his Vicariate of Bijapur.[3]

Subsequently, other missionary societies such as the Carmelites, the Theatines and the Augustinians worked among the Telugus. However, there was a gradual decline in the mission work among the Telugus in the areas around Hyderabad, Warangal, Vijayawada, Guntur, and Visakapatnam. There was some sporadic mission work for the next one hundred years and more in these dioceses, while there was a 'mass movement' towards conversion among the Telugus in the same period in the present day Kumool, Nellore and Bellary dioceses.[4]

During the second missionary efforts of the Jesuits under their Carnatic Mission (1700-1773), Christianity spread again in a big way among the Telugus.[5] The Mission was wounded up due to the Suppression of the Jesuits in 1773. But by that time the Mission had nearly 40,000 converts belonging mainly to upper castes such as the Kammas and the Reddys of the Royalasema region. Subsequently this Jesuit Mission was handed over in 1788 to the Foreign

Missionaries of Paris (MEP) headquartered at Pondicherry. The history of the Telugu Christians under the MEPs was identified with the life and work of Clement Bonnard, known as the Father and Apostle of the Telugus.[6]

Evangelization in Andhra was subsequently undertaken by the Mill Hill Missionaries (MHM), who began a new chapter in conversion work in mid 1870s, in south Andhra region. Two decades earlier, mid 1850s, another Catholic society (Missionaries of St. Francis de Sales) had begun evangelization work in the Vishakapatnam region. Though Catholic Christianity continued to spread in most regions of Andhra, Catholics form only 26% of the total Christian Population in Andhra.[7]

It may be noted that the Protestant missionaries began to evangelize in Andhra only by mid 1850s, although Protestant presence had begun in coastal Andhra with the arrival of the East India Companies of the English and the Dutch in the second decade of the 17th century.[8] Once coastal Andhra came under English colonial administration following the defeat of the Golkonda Sultan, Protestant mission societies began to have more access to Colonial Coastal Andhra.

The main narrative of this chapter being the missionary work of the Protestant Missions in Colonial Coastal Andhra, I shall elaborate on their work in the coming sections after this brief note below on the overall picture of the Christian Churches in Andhra today.

Today, the major Churches/Denominations in Andhra Pradesh are the Roman Catholic Church (RCC), London Missionary Society (LMS), Church Missionary Society (CMS), Society for the Propagation of the Gospel (SPG), American Baptist Mission (ABM), Canadian Baptist Mission (CBM), Mennonite Brethren Church (MBC), Godavari Delta Mission (GDM), Brethren Assemblies (BA), Wesleyan Mission (WM), Methodist Church in Southern Asia (MCSA), Free Methodist Church (FMC), American Lutheran Mission (ALM), South Andhra Lutheran Church (SALC), and Salvation Army (SA). There are also followers of smaller sects or movements such as Bro. Bakht Singh's Movement, Pentecostal and Charismatic Movements, Indian Missionary Society, Bible Mission, India Mission, Bro. G.R. Lorne's Assemblies, Leymen's Evangelical Fellowship, etc.[9]

Today, Christians constitute only 1.6% of the total population of Andhra Pradesh. The Dalits, mostly Malas and Madigas, constitute nearly 98% of the total Andhra Pradesh Christian population, the remaining being from castes like Kamma, Reddy, Kapu, etc. Of all the Christian Churches in Andhra, the Catholics, Baptists, Church of South India and the Lutherans have made significant progress.[10]

3.3 Early Protestant Missionaries in South India

The foundation of the Indian evangelical work was laid under the auspices of King Frederick IV of Denmark and by two Protestant missionaries Bartholomew Ziegenbalg and Henry Plutscho of the Danish Mission who had sailed to Tranquebar on 9th July 1706.[11] During the initial years of the mission work at Tranquebar, it was hard for these two missionaries to impress upon the minds of the natives due to the corrupted lives of the Christians lived there and the idolatrous worship of the natives.[12] Rev. Ziegenbalg and Rev. Plutscho had learned the Portuguese and Malabarick languages to preach the Gospel and to translate the Scriptures. They were much helped by the Society for the Propagation of Christian Knowledge (SPCK) of England with the supply of a printing press, six hundred weights of Roman and Italic type, one hundred reams of paper and a printer man.[13] The work of Ziegenbalg from 1706 to 1719 could be assessed in terms of his accomplishments such as 355 converts and numerous catechumens, a native church, a complete New Testament in Tamil, a dictionary, a mission seminary and schools. He was termed by Dr. Alexander Duff, as "a great missionary, considering that he was the first, inferior to none, scarcely second to any that followed him."[14]

It was not until the year 1728, that the SPCK formally began its Indian mission under Rev. Benjamin Schultze.[15] Schulze had a pioneering experience in the printing of the Tamil Bible and was responsible for the Tamil Scriptures through the press at the Francke's Orphan House.[16] The beginning of the German Lutheran missionaries from Halle began with the arrival in India of Rev. Christian Frederick Schwartz (1726-1798) of the Tanjore Mission. He had a pioneering work to his credit for forty-eight years at Tanjore, having not gone back to Europe once during his time.[17] He was appointed as the superintendent for the Christian schools and churches south of the river Cauvery.[18] He was credited for the conversion of the *Pariahs* and the *Súdras*. It was said that his garden was filled from morning till late in the evening with natives of every rank who came to him to have their differences settled...and the number of those who came to him to be instructed in Christianity was great. Every day individuals attended and requested him to establish a Christian congregation in their part of the country.[19] The monument which was erected in his honor in 1807 reads as:

He, during a period of fifty years went about doing good, manifesting in respect to himself, the most entire abstraction from temporal views, but embracing every opportunity of promoting both the temporal and eternal welfare of others.[20]

There was a growing enthusiasm for missionary work in England from the beginning of the 19th century. The denominational missionary societies in England namely, the Baptist Missionary Society founded in 1792, the London

Missionary Society founded in 1795, the Scottish Missionary Society founded in 1796 and the Church Missionary Society founded in 1799 were destined to be '*Societies for Missions to Africa and the East'*. These missionary societies possessed an eagerness to enlighten the public mind in England on the question of introduction of Christianity not only in India and but also in the colonial possessions of the Crown.[21] In 1792, Rev. William Carey, 'the founder of modem missions' published a work called "An enquiry into the obligation of Christians to use means for the conversion of the heathens, in which the religious state of the different nations of the world, the success of former undertakings, and the practicability of further undertakings are considered," and it marked a new beginning of the work of the Protestant Christian missions in India.[22]

3.4 Ecclesiastical Policy of the British East India Company

The East India Company followed a hostile policy in granting permission to the missionaries and held a firm opposition to any European missionary setting foot on British Indian soil without a license.[23] Therefore, it was not possible for any missionary to gain a license.[24] The chaplains who were appointed by the East India Company were made to confine themselves to their work as Church of England's clergyman and were made to discharge their duties such as conducting church worship services for the European residents and soldiers in the barracks, in the hospitals and in their own private houses.[25] The Company, having a strict policy of non-interference in the religious and social affairs of the natives of India, was apprehensive that the missionaries might seek some sphere of influence in the Company's territories which might jeopardize its trade interests.[26] Further, the missionaries were also warned against obtaining an asylum in a foreign settlement with an intention to gain access to the Company's territories.[27] Therefore, the *Serampore Triumvirate*, Dr. William Carey, Dr. Joshua Marshman and Mr. William Ward resolved to settle in Serampore, a Danish settlement fifteen miles from Calcutta.[28]

However, a Company official, Charles Grant was the force behind the inspiration of the missionary enterprise in India.[29] He had published an elaborate pamphlet titled *"Observations on the State of Society among the Asiatic Subjects of Great Britain"* in 1790 and in 1793 William Wilberforce, who under the influence of Grant, took up the 'first battle for toleration'[30] and moved a resolution in the Parliament to facilitate missionary work in India. The resolution was read as:

> It is the peculiar and bounden duty of the legislature to promote, by all just and prudent means, the interests and happiness of the inhabitants of the British dominion in India and that for these ends, such measures ought to be adopted as may gradually tend to their

> advancement in useful knowledge and to their religious and moral improvement.[31]

However, Wilberforce failed to pass the resolution as the East India Company had held a strict policy against any such resolution.[32] Prior to the passing of the Charter Act of 1813, William Wilberforce, Charles Grant and Babington sought a grant of measures from the Prime Minister Lord Liverpool on the subject of the evangelization of India and the Premier had consented to grant a seminary at each of the Presidencies and provision of consecrating bishops for India, by the Board of Control rather than by the Company's Court of Directors.[33]

The Charter Act of 1813 was passed on 16th June 1813, through the efforts of Wilberforce and Charles Grant, in which the 12th and 13th Resolutions received the Royal Assent.[34] The Act gave direction to the Company to allow the activities of the missionaries as long as they had conformed to the regulations.[35] An Ecclesiastical Establishment would direct the Company to afford facilities to persons desirous of promoting moral and religious improvement of the natives of India and an obligatory clause was inserted upon the Company to set apart a sum of not less than one lakh rupees each year for the revival and improvement of English language, literature and sciences among the inhabitants of the British territories of India.[36] During the formative years of the British Protestant Evangelism in India, the famous 'Five Chaplains' (David Brown, Claudius Buchanan, Henry Martyn, Daniel Corrie and Thomas Thomason) did much evangelical work.[37]

The progress of Christianity in India between 1850 and 1950 was remarkable owing to the combined efforts of the early missionaries, the translation and dissemination of the scriptures, the spread of education and an enthusiastic body of native workers from the ranks of converted Christians. The large-scale increase in the number of Christians in South India can be viewed as an expression of the discontent of the depressed castes.[38] It may be noted that, when the missionaries started to work among the Malas and Madigas, they had a comprehensive package of evangelization: preaching, educating, empowering, and helping the poor depressed castes. At the same time, they maintained cordial relations with caste Hindus and local zamindars.

It may be noted that the evangelical efforts of the Christian missionaries in the beginning were aimed at converting the higher castes as the missionaries believed that Gospel teachings would flow downwards from the higher castes onto the lower ones. Experience showed, however, that except for a few converts from among them,[39] the vast majority came from the depressed castes. Naturally, most mission organizations began to concentrate on evangelizing the latter castes.

Mission organizations in India became widespread and strong due to the financial, spiritual and managerial support from their home countries. There was growing enthusiasm for evangelical work in India among the British Congregationalists.[40] The proselytizing responsibilities of the missionaries started with the initiative of the London Missionary Society in Northern Andhra.

3.5 Protestant Missionary Societies in Colonial Andhra

For the present study, only six missionary societies are considered, namely 1) the London Missionary Society (Vizagapatam), 2) the Canadian Baptist Mission (Cocanada), 3) the Godavari Delta Mission (Dowlaishvaram and Narsapur), 4) the Church Missionary Society (Masulipatnam and North Kistna), 5) the American Evangelical Lutheran Mission (Guntur and South Kistna) and 6) the American Baptist Mission (Nellore and Ongole). As noted above, each mission society had different territory as its operating area. The choice of mission territories was made based on mutual consensus.

3.5.1 The London Missionary Society (LMS)

The London Missionary Society was the first mission to lay the foundation of a mission centre in coastal Andhra in early 19th century. Though the present study starts from the year 1850, it is necessary to know about the contribution made by the missionaries of the LMS in early years, as they were the first missionaries to introduce Protestant Christianity in colonial Andhra.

i) Revs. George Cran and Augustus Des Granges

The LMS was established in the year 1795 with a subsidy of the Directors of the East India Company until 1840.[41] The evangelistic work of the LMS among the Telugu people was conducted at four centers: Vizagapatam, Bellary, Cuddapah and Nandyal. However, this study considers only the Vizagapatam station. In the year 1804, two missionaries were sent out with the permission of the Honorable Governor in Council. Rev. George Cran and Augustus Des Granges got a cordial reception by the Europeans and natives at Vizagapatam.[42] The missionaries gave utmost attention to the study of Telugu language and met constantly with the natives to achieve progress in the spoken language.[43] When they were able to speak fluent Telugu, they started visiting the surrounding villages and preached the Gospel to all castes.[44] A free school was started with the help of the European residents who not only helped in erecting the school building but also took charge of its monthly maintenance by paying fees for students who could not afford.[45] Revs. Cran and Des Granges initiated the task of translation of the Holy Bible into Telugu and were actively helped by a Mahratta convert *Brāhmin*, Subbrayer. Subbrayer had taken the name of Anandarayer upon his conversion. He had to face rejection from his caste-mates and had suffered persecution.[46] The method of preaching the Gospel was visiting populous villages thrice in a week and reading the portions of the scriptures in Telugu and conducting conversation on the read scriptures.[47]

After the death of Cran in 1809 and of Des Granges in 1810, the directors of the LMS sent Revs. John Gordon and William Lee, who carried on the missionary work jointly until the end of 1812, when Rev. Lee was sent to Ganjam to open a new mission. Rev. Edward Pritchett arrived at Vizagapatam in 1812 and achieved considerable progress in learning Telugu and engaged himself in the translation of the Scriptures. After the distribution of the first edition of the Gospel, more copies were needed especially in the south of Vizagapatam.[48] Rev. Lee's missionary efforts were hindered by a malignant fever in 1815 and due to the invasion of the Pindarees.[49] Rev. Edward Pritchett and James Dawson were joined by Rev. Gordon in 1815. Rev. Gordon had committed himself for the completion of the translation of the New Testament and also utilized the translation services of Mr. Anandarayer.[50] The New Testament in Telugu was printed in Madras in 1818 under the supervision of Rev. Pritchett.[51]

The mission's activities were taken over by Rev. James William Gordon and Rev. E. Porter in 1835. Mrs. Porter was instrumental in carrying forward the girl's school that was established by Mrs. Drew in 1932.[52] Rev. Gordon (1834-1875) had acquired good knowledge of Telugu and committed himself diligently to the translation of the Old Testament into Telugu.[53] In 1836, the first Protestant chapel among the Telugus with a capacity for 300 people was built. The number of Sunday-school pupils was one hundred and fifty. A printing press was established in Vizagapatam to print and circulate scripture translations, books and literary tracts in coastal Andhra.[54] A revised version of the New Testament and portions of the Old Testament and twenty thousand tracts were printed. Besides, school books, other works such as the *Pilgrim's Progress* and *Peep of Day* were printed and circulated.[55]

In the early part of the 19th century, evangelical work was a hard task due to poor response of the people, as becoming Christian, they feared, would entail losing their caste ties even though they appreciated the doctrines of Christianity.[56] In 1847, a wave of opposition and violence from the caste Hindus was experienced following the conversion of a certain Pulipaka Jagannadham. Even military forces were called to suppress the disturbance.[57] Pulipaka Jagannadham became a teacher in the Vizagapatam school and was ordained as a preacher in the Chicacole mission where he became a renowned Telugu Christian lyricist. In 1840, Rev. John Hay joined the mission and contributed much to educational work. Known as the 'best Telugu scholar among the missionaries', he gave a great deal of attention to the revision of the Old and New Testaments in Telugu. About him it is said, 'among the apostles of India there has risen none greater than John Hay.'[58]

ii) Spread of the LMS Missionary Work

In the year 1850, the LMS had 144 Christian converts.[59] In 1855, Rev. John S. Wardlaw of the Bellary Mission joined the Vizagapatam mission to work in close cooperation with Rev. Hay for the preparation of an accurate translation of the Scripture into Telugu.[60] Caste distinctions were largely discouraged by the missionaries while admitting students in their schools. It was quoted that "*Brāhmin* and the *Pariah* have been seen in close fellowship, aiding each other in the preparation of their tasks."[61] Between 1858 and 1860, considerable progress was made by the mission in Mala villages, where the Malas evinced interest in converting to Christianity.[62] The Vizagapatam mission station was entwined with Chicacole mission to become the greater Northern Telugu mission. By 1881, four missionaries were in charge of these missions under the supervision respectively, of Rev. M. Thomas, Rev. H. J. Goffin and Rev. John Hay.[63] In 1883, at Vizagapatam there were about 223 native converts connected to the LMS stations of Vizianagaram and Chittivalasa.[64] The congregations in the villages grew larger due to awakened interest and enthusiasm for the new faith.[65]

Towards the end of the 19th century, a greater number of Christian converts within the LMS mission areas was drawn from the lower castes. The adjoining Ceded Districts became centres of group conversion movements which began to spread to colonial Andhra. In the district of Cuddapah, mass conversions were reported among the Malas. The movement also spread among the low-caste *Súdra* in 1890 and it was reported to have exceeded the outcastes' conversions.[66] Notable missionaries of the LMS were Rev. William Dawson (1838, Chicacole), Rev. L. Valett (1857), Rev. John Hay (1863-returned) Mr. E. Midwinter (1876), Mr. H. J. Goffin (1876), Mr. Morris Thomas (1878), G.H Macfarlane (1882) and Rev. John Knox (1888).

The mission station of Vizagapatam maintained by the LMS's missionaries lasted till the end of the 19th century, though the mission personnel suffered some setbacks such as ill health, transfers, resignations and other contingent factors. In the year 1911, the LMS sold its undertakings (the Union Chapel, high school, Telugu church, Hope Hall Girls' School, mission bungalows, etc.) for a sum of Rs. 40000.[67] However, the progress and continuity of the mission work went unhindered due to the quality of work of its native workers until the merger of the LMS in the Church of South India union in 1947. In conclusion, the London Missionary Society, in collaboration with other missionary societies, laid a strong foundation of a flourishing Christian community in colonial Andhra.

3.5.2 The Canadian Baptist Mission (CBM)

i) The Baptist Missionary Beginnings in Andhra

Initially the work of the Baptist Mission in Andhra was a combined effort of the English Baptist Missionary Society, the American Baptist Missionary Society and the Canadian Baptist Missionary Society of Quebec and Ontario. The English General Baptist Missionary Society was founded in 1792 with a motto: "Enlarge the place of thy tent, and let them stretch forth the curtains of thine habitations…and thy seed shall inherit the Gentiles and make the desolate cities to be inhabited". The Foreign Bible Society was formed in 1804 and three missionaries, Mr. William Carey, Mr. Joshua Marshman and Mr. William Ward were sent to the Danish settlement of Serampore. These missionaries submitted a proposal to the Home Committee for the translation and publication of the Holy Bible into Indian languages such as that of Bengali, Hindustani, Oriya, Telugu, Karnata, Marathi and Tamil.[68] In the year 1807, the New Testament was translated by William Carey into Telugu,[69] which he had learnt from a Telugu pundit.[70] Rev. Amos Sutton from the English Baptist Mission was stationed at Balasore in 1826. Rev. Brown pitched his tent in Berhampur town, in Ganjam District and preached both the Telugu and Oriya inhabitants since 1836.[71] The American Baptist Mission also established its presence in Bimlipatnam and Bobbili.[72]

The first Canadian Baptist Foreign Missionary enterprise was founded in 1814 which was called the "Nova Scotia Baptist Association" at Chester[73] with the motto "where currents of living water are to flow, the channels need to be hewn by careful labour on well directed lines," a motto which missionaries applied to their mission in the region of great Godavari River that flew through the southern section of colonial Andhra bringing the secret of life and fertility to millions of people and thousands of acres.[74] The Ontario and Quebec Baptists carried their missionary work with renewed interest, greater liberality and in close cooperation with other foreign missionary enterprises. In 1832, the Nova Scotia Baptist Association began to promote Foreign Missions in Burma and India.[75] The earliest contribution in the Telugu region by the Canadian Baptist Mission was made by Mr. William Craig, who had worked some time with Rev. Samuel. S Day of the American Baptist mission till 1858.[76]

ii) Association with American Baptist Mission

In 1867, during the Baptist Convention of Ontario and Quebec at Ingersoll, Rev. A. V. Timpany and Mrs. Jane Bates Timpany were endorsed and appointed to work among the Telugus. In 1869 they were joined by Rev. John McLaurin and Mrs. Mary Bates McLaurin who were largely supported by the Canadian Auxiliary but under the auspices of the American Baptist Missionary Society.[77] Rev. A. V. Timpany had the distinction of being the founder principal of the

Ramapatnam Theological Seminary in 1872 to train native evangelists and pastors.[78]

During the time of Rev. Clough's furlough, Rev. John McLaurin took charge of the Ongole mission station, which was the largest and most fruitful field, in the *"Lone Star Mission"* with a Church membership numbering 1,658, comprised mainly of Madigas.[79] Before leaving Canada, Rev. McLaurin was advised to establish a mission independently as it was opined that Canadian Baptists will never do their best until they have a mission of their own possession.[80] An opportunity came from Taleru Marayya alias Thomas Gabriel, who gave up his position as a telegraph operator and began preaching in the town of Cocanada which had about 20,000 inhabitants. It is said that Thomas Gabriel had been associated with other mission societies such as the English Plymouth Brethren of the Godavari Delta Mission and the Lutherans at Rajahmundry, but he wanted to be in association with the Baptists. He opened up a tannery to support the Kollair Mission in 1870 but struggled for financial support and wanted an affiliation with a foreign missionary society. Once on his way to Madras to request help from the English Baptists, he stopped at Ramapatnam, met Rev. McLaurin and shared about his mission, his troubles and his quest.[81] In 1873, upon the appeal of Thomas Gabriel, the Cocanada Mission station was taken over by the Canadian Baptists of Ontario and Quebec. Rev. McLaurin tendered his resignation to the American Foreign Mission Board and went to Cocanada to start the CBM's missionary enterprise in 1874[82] and was termed as the 'Father of the Cocanada Mission.'[83] In 1881, the CBM had 1,530 baptized members with 21 congregations and three missionaries at Chicacole, Bimlipatam, and Bobbili.[84]

The Madigas in the Godavari delta associated themselves with the CBM in Cocanada due to their traditional association with the American Baptist Mission in Nellore and Ongole. Before any Baptist presence was known in the Godavari delta region, trade relations existed between Godavari delta area and South Andhra region and the converted Madigas from the Ongole region shared their experiences about the new religion, to their brethren elsewhere. Until the establishment of the CBM in 1874, the Madigas did not have a choice but to join the nearest Anglican mission of the Church Missionary Society and American Evangelical Lutheran Mission at Rajahmundry.[85]

iii) Foundation of the CBM in Cocanada

The CBM started its evangelical activities in Cocanada in 1874 and Cocanada was the only CBM mission between the southern half of the territory between Bengal Presidency (of the English Baptists) and Nellore in Madras Presidency (of the American Baptists).[86] In 1879, the McLaurins were joined by the Timpanys and a chapel was built in 1882 with a terraced roof, a veranda hall round and a tower over the front entrance.[87]

Work among the children proved to be the most effective method of getting access to the homes of the people, which subsequently opened the door for women missionaries. The 'English Free school' (est. 1833) (later called as the Timpany Memorial school) and the Cocanada Girls' Boarding School (1876) were the two schools supported by the CBM in Cocanada which had rendered remarkable educational service to all around, especially to the converted Christians, helping them build their Christian character and personality.[88] Miss Mary Jane Firth was sent by the Toronto Women's Society to work among women and children of Cocanada. Miss Firth opened the Zenana work in Cocanada.[89] She also visited many homes, assisted by Miss Charlotte Gibson and Mrs. De Beaux, along with two other Bible-women.[90] With its four mission compounds, comprised of thirty acres of land and five bungalows, the Cocanada station won the distinction of being the principal mission station of the CBM. In 1925, the CBM had one hundred missionaries, eighty churches with 17,000 members and a total staff of over one thousand Telugu workers.[91] The educational and economic contribution of the CBM is dealt extensively in Chapter 5.

iv) The Pioneer Missionaries

With Cocanada as their headquarters, the mission had Rev. McLaurin at Cocanada and Samalkota, Rev. G. F. Currie at Tuni, Rev. J. E Chute and Mr. Craig in Akidu. Some other notable missionaries were C. B. Mwere, Rev. and Mrs W. F. Armstrong, Mrs. Boggs, Rev. and Mrs. George Churchill, Rev. and Mrs. Rufus Sanford, Rev. J. R. Stillwell, Rev. E. G. Smith, Rev. M. L. and Rev. I. C. Archibald, Rev. and Mrs. Orchard, Rev. John Hardy and Rev. A. D. Matheson. The chief Canadian Baptist stations were in the towns of Vizagapatam, Bimlipatnam, Tekkali, Gunnanapudi (1875), Tuni (1879), Akidu (Akividu) (1880), Samalkota (1882), Vuyyuru (1882), Bodagunta, Yelamanchili (1890), Bobbili, Avanigadda, Ramachandrapuram and Pithapuram.

v) The Vizagapatam Station

When the Canadian Baptist missionaries ventured to start a mission at Vizagapatam (a town of 50,000 inhabitants), they found that the town had few Christians, although it was formerly an important mission station of the London Missionary Society. The Vizagapatam station had 320 villages with a congregation of Christians of 'out-caste' origin.[92] The pioneers of CBM in Vizagapatam were, Rev. Boggs, Rev. Churchill, Rev. Sanford and Rev. Armstrong. Churches were organized in the adjoining four stations of Bimlipatnam, Vizianagaram, Bobbili and Parlakimedi. Rev. George Churchill befriended the Bobbili Raja who gifted the missionary a plot of land for building churches. So he established churches at Bimlipatnam and Bobbili in 1875 and 1876, respectively. In 1879, Miss Carrie Hammond took over the Bimlipatnam station from Mrs. Sanford where she became in-charge of the Bible classes and the Verandah Telugu services.[93] In 1892, Mrs. and Rev. L. D. Morse succeeded Dr. Sanford at Bimlipatnam. With the help of native workers he converted not only the outcastes but also some caste Hindus namely Somalingam, Veeracharyulu and Sooriyanarayana.[94]

vi) The Chicacole Station

The principal work of the missionaries was to manage station affairs, directing native workers, supervising boarding and day schools and touring of the mission field. The members of the 'Serving Seven', W. F. Armstrong and Mrs. Norris Armstrong were in charge of the Chicacole station since 1877. Miss Hammond, Rev. and Mrs. J. R. Hutchinson were the successors of the Armstrongs in 1880 and 1881, respectively. The evangelistic work in Chicacole was mostly among the Mala and Madiga communities. Rev. I. C. Archibald secured a plot of land near a Mala hamlet, built a church and a school, where children were given daily instruction in the Bible. An eager crowd of people gathered frequently in the school shed to receive Gospel instruction.[95] Rev. I. C. Archibald was also credited to have worked hard with an aggregate of 101 Christian native workers until his retirement in 1923 when the mission was taken over by Dr. and Mrs. Eaton. The Malas and the Madigas of Chicacole became anxious to hear more of the Gospel and wished that their children be taught in a mission school and expressed willingness to arrange a house and payment for the teacher.[96]

vii) The Tekkali Station

Mission work in Tekkali station became very active when this station was formed into a separate mission station in 1898 under the supervision of Mr. Higgins. Under his guidance native preachers and teacher-evangelists were employed at various mission centres and hence church membership steadily grew from just thirty one in 1898 to ninety-four in 1903. In order to preach among the Malas and Madigas, a body of native workers who were willing to live in the midst of the people, was employed by the mission. These native workers and preachers were expected to take interest in the daily lives of the people, visit them in sickness and win them for Christ. For a designated place for dwelling for the native preachers, the mission secured land in those hamlets which they served and erected comfortable houses for them.[97]

viii) The Vizianagaram Station

Vizianagaram (*City of Victory*) had been a mission station of the LMS since 1852 and continued till 1889, when the society (LMS) decided to sell its properties to the Maritime Baptist Mission. In 1875, the Baptists built a church there and placed it under Rev. Das Anthravady with occasional assistance from

Dr. Sanford. Rev. W. V. Higgins and Mrs. Higgins and Rev. M. B. Shaw and Mrs. Shaw achieved good progress in mission work.[98] Efforts were made for the evangelization not only of the Malas and the Madigas but also caste Hindus.[99] The services of Miss Flora Clarke were valuable owing to her industriousness and progressive views. In order to create employment for the converts, Miss Clarke founded a knitting factory, purchased knitting machines, and gainfully employed them. Consequently, this station became a self-supporting and self-propagating native church.[100]

ix) The Akidu Station

Close to the Kolair lake was Akidu, where some of the relatives of Thomas Gabriel had lived and were influenced to become Christians owing to caste allegiances. The Malas of Akidu became Christians upon the conversion of the village elder's family, the Karre brothers, namely Karre Samuel (village headman), Karre Peter and Karre Andrew. Karre Peter became the first ordained minister and Karre Andrew became a deacon.[101] In 1875, a church was established in Gannanapudi and it became an important church due to strong native leadership and mature Christianity.[102] In 1880, Akidu became an independent mission station and was handed over to Rev. Craig by Rev. John McLaurin.[103] Tremendous progress was recorded at the Akidu station where hundreds of strong and self-reliant Christians lived in eighteen to twenty different villages. By end 1884, church membership at Akidu was reported to be at 1,118.[104] In 1884, Rev. Timpany took charge of Akidu and Rev. Craig, in 1888. Rev. Dr. Jesse Chute and Dr. Pearl Chute took charge in 1895 and rendered pioneering service as preachers and medical missionaries and established a school and a hospital in 1897. Miss Fanny Stovel was the first woman to have toured among the villagers along with a native Bible woman Pantagani Annamma.[105] Together they built a strong Christian community fulfilling the evangelistic policy of the mission.[106] Incidentally, the open confession of a caste Hindu in 1887 encouraged many more Malas in Akidu to become Christians.[107]

x) The Pithapuram Station

Pithapuram was a stronghold of orthodox Hindus and put strong, organized opposition to the caste-ignoring Christian missionaries. Though small in area, Pithapuram became a centre of medical mission of the CBM, also because there was no other hospital around forty miles and medical help was needed constantly for the sick. The people were helped by a contingent of trained medical assistants. Pithapuram was served by Rev. Armstrong, Dr. E. G. Smith and Dr. Chute. They also started a school as well as a nursing school there. The Bethesda Hospital of Pithapuram had not only trained compounders and medical assistants but also preached the Gospel in remote areas. The services of Miss M. Helena Blackadar, assisted by Dr. Smith since 1915 have been well remembered for her dedication in medical work.[108] The adjacent Tuni field was placed under Rev. and Mrs. Currie in 1876 and a church was organized in Tuni in 1879 where many Madiga families converted in to Christianity.[109]

xi) The Samalkota Station

Since the beginning of the Cocanada mission, its sub-station at Samalkota occupied an important place for its theological college, the second such institution in coastal Andhra after the one at Ramapatnam. In 1882, Rev. John McLaurin started a church and a theological seminary and became its first Principal. The Rajah of Samalkota donated some land which was used for missionary and educational activities of the mission. Cocanada being a large mission territory, Revs. Timpany and McLaurin had to travel frequently to its sub-stations which were eventually divided into five or six different mission districts under the charge of resident missionaries. The theological seminary continued to operate in Samalkota for training the Telugu pastors in a competent manner until 1912 when it was shifted to Cocanada under the leadership of Rev. H. E. Stillwell.[110] Dr. Smith opened a dispensary at Samalkota and was assisted by native Christian assistants. Gradually it enjoyed the confidence of the Hindus who also visited the dispensary.[111]

xii) The Vuyyuru Station

Amongst all the CBM mission fields, Vuyyuru station was the farthest from Cocanada station. In fact it was more adjacent to the Church Missionary Society's mission stations of Masulipatnam and Bezwada. Vuyyuru was part of Akidu mission. Under the supervision of Rev. Craig (until 1891) and later under Rev. J. G. Brown, Vuyyuru was developed as a separate field station, which became an important station for medical services in the lower Godavari region.[112] The stations at Avanigadda and Bodagunta were within the ambit of Vuyyuru station. Increasing conversions in Vuyyuru were not tolerated by the ambient communities: the missionaries and converts had to face persecution in the form of threats, boycotts and blows.[113] A well-organized boarding school was supervised by the missionaries' wives, namely Mrs. Harry Stillwell, Mrs. Cross, Mrs. Bensen and Mrs. Gordon.[114] Economic self-sufficiency was achieved in Vuyyuru field owing to the efforts of Dr. Wolverton, Mr. Cross, and Rev. Gordon who contributed substantially for the economic development of the Malas and the Madigas through organized co-operative unions (see discussion in Chapter 6)

xiii) The Fields of Avanigadda and Bodagunta

The missionaries at Avanigadda were native converts, two illiterate Christian women of Bodagunta, who had begun to believe in the Gospel much before the CBM established its mission in Cocanada. They were mobile vendors of onions who carried their goods in baskets on their heads. They voluntarily took to preaching and sang hymns in villages until requests came for missionary visits. The converted men of Avanigadda furthered Gospel preaching after their baptism and strived to influence their relatives in villages where no missionary had ever visited before. This native initiative in Gospel preaching was encouraging as one heart set the other on fire.[115] By end 1900, there were 1,080 members and in end 1907, there were nearly 1,736 members.[116] Sectarian differences and caste prejudices were overcome when the Madigas worked with the Malas in a spirit of humility and service, to the credit of Pastor Todeti Abraham.[117] In 1914, a church and a school were established in Avanigadda with the support from Toronto Sabbath School. Bodagunta's Mala hamlet experienced perceptible change after the conversion of most members, under the influence of the missionaries, native Christian teachers and Bible women.[118]

3.5.3 The Godavari Delta Mission

The Godavari Delta Mission ***(GDM)*** was an independent mission created as an alternative to the mighty Church of England. It originated through the efforts of Mr. Anthony Norris Groves, Mr. William Bowden and Mr. George Beer who were greatly influenced by the principle of 'precedence of the scriptures' over 'Ecclesiastical Authority and Church'. The members of this Church formed a fellowship of believers, who gave prominence to the scriptures.[119] Rev. Anthony Norris Groves was said to be the first of the Plymouth Brethren, a Christian sect,[120] and was also the originator of the faith-based missions in India called Brethren Missions. It is said that he was the forerunner of native Pentecostal preachers, Rev. M. Devadas and Rev. Bhakta Singh.

i) Rev. A. N. Groves and Sir Arthur Cotton

Mr. Groves was born on February 1, 1795 in Plymouth, England and after his good education, became a doctor and practiced dentistry at Devonshire. He is said to have been influenced by two spiritual pastors whose teachings impacted him to become a missionary in the East.[121] While reading the New Testament, which he did regularly, Groves became convinced that he was destined to become a missionary. He published a booklet entitled *Christian Devotedness* in 1825 which encouraged his fellow believers to give away their savings and assist in proclaiming the Gospel throughout the world.[122] In 1833, Rev. Groves was visited by Captain Arthur Cotton, a military engineer, who had been working in India.[123] The latter invited Groves to come to India to explore the possibilities of evangelical ministry.

ii) Foundation of Godavari Delta Mission (GDM)

With great enthusiasm and zeal for missions among the Indian people, Rev. Groves accomplished the founding of the GDM. It can be compared to the works of the American Lutheran Mission near Guntur and Rajahmundry. In fact, he had reportedly written a letter to the Synod of the American Lutheran Churches in 1834 seeking support to help the labours of the German CMS evangelist Rev. C. T. E. Rhenius of Tinnevelly.[124] The American Lutheran Mission came to help the missions in Andhra. Hence Groves is credited to have facilitated the founding of the mighty missionary enterprise of the American Evangelical Lutheran Mission in coastal Andhra.

Besides, Groves also tried to establish a Plymouth Brethren Mission in coastal Andhra. In 1835, he managed to get a fresh team of missionaries namely, Mr. Parnell, Mr. William Bowden and Mr. George Beer along with their wives, to work in India. He was also the force behind the arrival of the *Barnstaple Party* or the families of William Bowden, George Beer and Mr. Parnell in Masulipatnam in 1836. They learned Telugu for about eight months and ministered to the European population by giving Bible lessons twice a week in the home of Mr. and Mrs. Hughes. Further, the 'un-ordained Baptist missionary work' in Godavari region was started through the efforts of Mr. Groves who tried to negotiate between the much prosperous Church of England's Church Missionary Society (CMS) and the English Baptists by putting away formal differences.[125]

The Mission suffered much due to natural tragedies. It was a time of terrible financial suffering owing to the great famine of 1833 due to failure of rains for three successive years from 1836 to 1838. In 1839, a devastating cyclone with its mighty tidal waves swept the coast from Narsapur to Visakhapatnam and wiped out many villages.[126]

iii) Mr. William Bowden and Mr. George Beer of Godavari Delta Region

Rev. Groves tried to negotiate with other mission societies to find financial support. The CMS missionaries stationed at Masulipatnam refused to provide financial help apparently for his "unconventional views". Rev Groves also approached the Collector of Kistna, Mr. Henry Stokes Esq to support his evangelical activities. But not much help came. Rev. Groves, was a believer of '*three-self schemes*', namely self-governing, self-supporting and self-propagating. To realize his dream he launched various schemes like cultivation of silk and other self-supporting educational enterprises at Chittoor and Madras.[127]

The GDM at Narsapur, established in 1837, eventually became its headquarters in the Godavari delta region.[128] A second mission station was established at Palakol and Thomas Gabriel (mentioned earlier), worked with the Bowdens and made the Kolair Lake region as one of the fields of their missionary activities.[129] Rev. Bowden taught the Gospel to the coolies in the fields and the missionary women gathered village women to teach the scriptures. The village women were said to have listened to the Gospel quite attentively.[130] Despite its struggled existence in matters of finance, the GDM succeeded in spreading the Gospel through preaching and education in the Godavari delta villages.[131] The GDM tried to maintain collaboration with the CMS and the German Lutheran missions in Rajahmundry.[132]

In 1847, the building of the diversion dam across the Godavari River by Captain Arthur Cotton and his corps of engineers was being undertaken at Dowlaishwaram. Captain Cotton, upon hearing that some missionaries were working nearby at Narsapur and Palakol invited them to preach the Gospel among the 10,000-odd workers labouring at the anicut.[133] The CMS' Rev. Henry Fox and Mr. Bowden frequently visited the labourers for preaching the Gospel.[134] For two years they got the opportunity to preach the Gospel to thousands of people who were working at the dam site and were said to have reaped good 'harvest of souls.'[135] The Bowden and Beer families suffered bitter financial hardship for seven years but were sustained with support from Mr. Groves.[136]

In 1865, the missionaries were told that the huge pilgrim crowds at festival of Antharvedy, a pilgrim site at the merging of Godavari River with the Bay of Bengal, were eager audience to hear the Gospel. The pilgrims, who had pitched their tents at the site, listened to the preaching of Rev. Bowden and Rev. Heelis with much attention.[137] Many converted after the preaching. Though the converts faced scorn and ridicule from the caste Hindus, they spoke about the fullness of their hearts regarding their redemption.[138]

Though the GDM had a humble beginning and confronted many constraints, it initiated a movement towards Indian management of mission. In August 1860 the journal *Church Missionary Intelligencer* reported that "it is indeed a new era in Indian Missions that of lay converts going forth, without purse or scrip, to preach the Gospel of Christ to their fellow-countrymen and that with a zeal and life we had hardly thought them capable of."[139] The educational activities of the GDM and the growth of education among the Malas and Madigas are discussed in the Chapter 5.

The fruitful and extensive work done by the GDM grew in various branches and attracted many Indian native missionaries from Kerala and Tamil Nadu regions. The India Pentecost Mission was established in Andhra in 1932 in Eluru by P. M. Samuel and Rev. P. T. Chacko. Native pastors P. M. Samuel, P. L Param Jyothi, C. Anandam, C. Raja Ratnam, K. R David, J. C. Sudarsanam and A. S. Paul strengthened the Brethren mission's work at Bezwada, Eluru, Tadepalligudem, Visakhapatnam, Amalapuram,

Antharvedipalem and Rajahmundry.[140] In 1938, the Bible Mission was established by Rev. Mangamuri Devadas (1875-1960). The mission at present is engaging the coastal Andhra regions of Kistna and Guntur Districts through faith-based healing ministries. With its headquarters at Peda Kakani in Guntur District, it is a fast-growing denomination in Andhra Pradesh with branches all over Andhra and other parts of India.[141]

3.5.4 The Church Missionary Society

i) Anglican Christianity in Masulipatnam Since the 17th Century

The Church Missionary Society (CMS) was the only missionary society that was associated with the British Colonial Government. Therefore its policies and practices were associated with, controlled and patronized by the British Government. The CMS' missionary activities were centred at Masulipatnam which was the chief station of the Anglican Church in coastal Andhra. Therefore, it is necessary to know about the beginning and emergence of Masulipatnam as the chief station of Church of England's evangelical propagation. It was the principal trading town of the Northern Circars from the 17th century and is credited to have had the first English factory on the Coromandel Coast. At the end of 1762, the towns on the coast came under the control of the East India Company, which set up military centres in these towns. Nellore, Ongole, and Masulipatnam each had one company of European infantry, and a company of artillery was founded at Rajamundry.[142] Masulipatnam with a fortification, was the headquarters of the Northern Division of the Army.[143]

The earliest connection of missionaries with Masulipatnam was in 1610, when the missionaries called '*Chaplains for Southwards*' travelled to Masulipatnam in the ship *Globe*. The early chaplains who stationed at *Metchlepatam* (Masulipatnam) were James Rynd, Thomas Friday and Patrick Copeland. After them, a number of chaplains were associated with the factories at Masulipatnam and ministered amongst the soldiers.

Till early 19th century the presence of the Anglican missionaries was not felt much except in church services for the company's military personnel. Although, the *Society for Promoting Christian Knowledge* was founded in 1698, and the *Society for the Propagation of the Gospel in Foreign Parts* in 1701, Great Britain did not enter into the field of missionary evangelism until the beginning of the 19th century. The CMS was formed through the efforts of the 'Electic Society' in connection with the 'Evangelical agenda of the Church of England'. It was formed through the joint efforts of Rev. William Goode, Charles Grant, Josiah Pratt, John Venn and Charles Semeon, on Friday, April 12, 1799.[144]

The chapel at Masulipatnam was built by General Pater. In 1810 Rev. Edward Vaughan was commissioned by the Archbishop of Canterbury to consecrate the church and the burial ground at Masulipatnam.[145] In 1793, a church was built at Ellore, as it was one of the frontier stations of the East India Company where the 4th battalion of the Company's Europeans resided[146] and was placed under the military Chaplaincy of Sir Charles Oakeley and Rev. R. H. Kerrin in 1795.[147] According to the *Ecclesiastical Proceedings of the Home Department*, the Chaplain‘s duties at the military station comprised of conducting Sunday worship services and admission of holy communion twice in a month and conducting occasional services like baptisms and burials. They were also directed to show an interest in the progress of schools by visiting and catechizing among the employees' children.[148]

ii) The Visionaries Bishop Daniel Corrie and Rev. John Tucker

Between 1812 and 1824, the work of the CMS was mainly in the Black town area of Madras where Telugu people resided where they opened a few vernacular schools.[149] The Charter Act of 1833 provided for the establishment of two new bishoprics, viz Madras and Bombay and in 1835 Bishop Corrie was consecrated as the first Bishop of Madras. He was the visionary of the CMS' evangelical programme in the Telugu country.[150] He was the animating and unifying personality and 'soul' of all CMS operations.[151] Rev. John Tucker was credited to be the organizer of the CMS' Telugu mission. But the supply of missionaries from the home country was very much inadequate and it was only in 1841 that the Telugu mission was formally founded by two CMS missionaries. The Collector of the Kistna district, Mr. John Goldingham contributed for the founding of the mission in 1836. He was concerned about the well being of the Telugu people whom he loved for their "great manliness of character and strong natural affections."[152]

iii) 'The University Men': Robert Turlington Noble and Henry Watson Fox

The leading members of the South India CMS Committee at Madras organized a fund of £2000[153] which was donated by two university graduates, Robert Turlington Noble of Sidney Sussex, University of Cambridge and Henry Watson Fox of Wadham, Oxford, respectively.[154] They were directed to work in two different fields: Rev. Noble was to open a school similar to that of Alexander Duff's in Calcutta, and Rev. Fox to initiate and lead village preaching services. In 1843, an English school was opened by Rev. Noble with the help of a Eurasian missionary Rev. J. E. Sharkey, who was proficient in spoken Telugu.[155] For many years, the missionaries spent time in preaching to the servants of the missionaries and other European officers. In 1844, two servants of the Noble household were admitted into baptism.[156]

Rev. Noble was convinced that it might not be possible to reach the Hindus of good social standing by preaching in the bazaars and therefore

Christian schools would act as agencies of conversion.[157] The Noble school was meant for caste Hindus, a plan devised by Rev. Noble to influence the *Brāhmin* and other caste students to convert to Christianity. There was no provision for admitting pupils from the Mala and the Madiga castes due to the fear of losing the caste students.[158] However, the strategy of Rev. Noble did not yield much result during the first ten years, as only a few caste Hindus were converted and admitted into the Church. The Church Missionary Society in Masulipatnam did not record any considerable results for a decade owing to the conservative policies of Rev. Noble. The rate of conversions was very slow as it was reported that the students of the Noble school reacted to Rev. T. K Nicholson that, "you may preach Christianity in Masulipatnam forever, but you will never get a convert from us."[159] There were only two caste Hindu converts: Manchala Ratnam, a *Brāhmin* and Ainala Bhushanam, a *Vellama,* in the year 1852. Since 1855, there was a gradual increase in the number of baptisms, by Rev. Noble, of converts from various castes/sections of people, namely, Mulayya and Ganugapati Krishnayya (*Brahmins*), P. Davidu (a *Súdra*) and Jani Ali (a *Mohammadan*).[160]

All through these years, Rev. Noble persistently refused admission of the Malas' children in his school for fear of opposition from the *Brāhmins.* He even convinced CMS Committee at Madras on sticking to the upper castes. The particular four lower castes that were excluded from his school were the *mat-maker*, the *pariah*, the *shoe-maker* and the *sweeper*.[161] The CMS Committee's directives for admitting all children irrespective of caste background and the affiliation of the Noble school with the Madras University were opposed by Rev. Noble. But the CMS Committee directed that in its Ellore School, there should not be any conditions on the basis of caste. On this issue, Rev. Noble went as far as tending resignation to his post that was averted with much difficulty out of reverence to him.[162] But the controversy came to an end when the Committee allowed Rev. Noble to follow his policy, but was immediately discontinued after his death.[163]

However, Rev. Noble had started a vocational school for the depressed castes in his compound and the curriculum was based on vocational and artisanal works. An interesting sight took place during the time of Rev. Noble's funeral when his body was taken to the burial ground by six Christians from the *English*, *Brāhmin*, *Vellama*, *Súdra*, Mala and *Mohammedan* that marked a sign of respect for Rev. Noble's devoted work in Masulipatnam.[164]

Later, the policy of CMS changed. In the subsequent years the Malas in the Kistna district formed the vast body of the Telugu Anglican Church, thanks to opening up the schools for them.

iv) Preaching Services of *Itinerant* Rev. Fox

Rev. Fox's missionary career lasted for about seven years and was much interrupted by his ill health and family conditions. Rev. Fox worked as a village preacher in towns such as Chintalapudi, Kurukulapadu, Challapalli, Nidumolu, Pamarru, Gollapalli, Bezwada, Mangalagiri, Eluru, Guntur, Kondapalli, Valluru and Gannavaram, where he had reported about the progress of the evangelistic work among the Malas. Apparently, the Madigas asked Rev. Fox, "If we become Christians what will happen to our dead cattle"?[165] Rev. Fox employed a lady from the Malas to be caretaker for his son Henry much to the annoyance of the *Brāhmins*.[166] The little boy, Henry Elliot Fox became the Honorary Secretary of the Church Missionary Society in later years.[167] Rev. Fox showed dedication towards his work. He laid the foundation for the village itinerant mission in coastal Andhra. He died a few days after his thirty-second birthday, in 1848.[168]

v) Village Preaching Services of Rev. Sharkey

Rev. Edmund Sharkey was an Anglo-Indian, born in 1821 at Masulipatnam where his father was a government servant. He was educated in Madras at Bishop Corrie's school and spent two years with Rev. Noble for the study of Telugu and was regarded by Rev. Noble as an amiable and studious catechist.[169] Edmund Sharkey became the chief assistant of Rev. Noble until his ordination in 1847 and married Miss Ann Amelia Nailor (1813-1878), the daughter of a well-to-do merchant in Madras.[170] He undertook to continue the mission of Rev. Henry Fox and mainly occupied himself with village preaching and contributed largely to the growing Telugu congregation. He started a vocational school in Masulipatnam and Mrs. Sharkey played a leading role in opening a girl's boarding school which became a model school for many schools in the region and was called as the Sharkey Memorial School.[171]

Rev. Sharkey was also a gifted writer; he was the editor of a Christian magazine called *Hitavadi*.[172] With his good command in Telugu, Rev. Sharkey preached the Gospel among the Malas of Kodur, Vuyyuru, Gudivada, Pattametta (Patamata, Bezawada), Poranki, Kankipadu, Tirukotur, Bantumilli, Munipadu and Chintalapudi, besides in the Godavari region of Bhimadolu, Rajahmundry and the Nizam's dominion of Khammamettu. He was asked by the Malas of Pattametta whether they could wear the Sharai (shortpant) if they were to convert to Christianity.[173] This may be taken as an evidence to show the aspiration of the Malas to change the way they appeared to the outer world (as mentioned earlier, the depressed castes were not allowed to wear clothes below their knees or above their hips). It was further said that the Mala's mode of living (in in Telugu, *Malala Jeevana Vidhanamu*) attracted the missionaries to take an interest on the Malas.[174]

vi) Rev. F. W. N. Alexander and the CMS Ellore Station

Ellore was one of the East India Company's frontier stations which had quartered the Company's European force. The CMS missionaries conducted Gospel preaching in the villages around Ellore and an English school was started under Rev. Noble's guidance. At the end of the year 1857, Rev. F. W. N. Alexander (Australia) and his wife came to Ellore in fulfillment of Rev. Noble's wishes to establish a permanent mission there.[175] Rev. Alexander worked with great zeal for 54 years[176] using thorough evangelistic and diligent methods at the Ellore mission station.[177] In 1864, the church in Ellore was built, followed by another church in Polasanapalli. The activities of the CMS spread to the surrounding villages of Naidugudem, Pedapadu, Siriwada, Nuzvid, Kanumolu, Bhimadolu and Chintalapudi.[178] The fruitful missionary work of the CMS mission was witnessed even overseas where a catechist from Tinnevelly discovered twenty-one Telugu immigrants in Mauritius prepared for baptism by Rev. F.W.N. Alexander.[179]

vii) Rev. Thomas Young Darling and the Bezwada Station

During Rev. Fox's time in Masulipatnam, the town of Bezwada (presently called Vijayawada) was not accommodative of missionary preaching, due to the Brahmin domination there. Hence, missionaries considered this town as the last one to settle down. However, it became a centre of itinerating preaching by 1858, when even an Anglo-Vernacular school was founded there.[180] Earlier, in 1857, Rev. C. Tanner and Mrs. Tanner came to the Bezwada station and later Rev. Thomas Young Darling was deputed there where he preached at the *melas* (fairs) and street gatherings. Active missionary work began among the Malas in 1860.[181]

In 1847, the Kondapalli villagers were covered by Gospel teachings. Since 1851 the Malas also started converting to the Christian faith. The acceleration of the conversion movement happened because of the conversion of Pagolu Venkayya, a leader of a band of violent men in 1859.[182] In various villages in the Kistna district, the Malas became the chief supporters of the CMS missionaries.[183] In course of time, the activities of CMS were extended to the districts of Guntur, North Kistna and East Godavari.

Rev. Thomas Young Darling was a notable missionary and an enthusiastic clergyman who, besides conducting the Anglo-Vernacular school, preferred to preach at street gatherings and to visit the surrounding villages. In his diary, he had noted about the Madigas that, “only evangelization and conversion would alleviate them from their degraded position.”[184] Though Rev. Darling once resented the Malas for their rigid, strange beliefs, he worked zealously among them in villages such as Gudur, Kappaladoddi, Vinnakota, Balapuram, Shemakanapalli, Devapudi, Bogalingala, Kaikaluru, Avanigadda,

Pavuradapalli, Koduru, Raghavapuram, Kondapalli, Kancikacharla, Penuganchiprolu, Mailavaram, Rayavaram, Gannavaram, Kalavapamula, Gudlavalleru and Pedana. Since 1858, Rev. Darling played a leading role in the mass conversion movement among the Malas of Bezwada, Raghavapuram and Indupalli.[185]

viii) The Raghavapuram Village and Pagolu Venkayya

Raghavapuram village can be said to be the birth place of group conversion movement among the Malas in Kistna District. It was situated on the banks of River Kistna, about twenty-eight miles from Bezwada. One of the first converts of the CMS mission there was Pagolu Venkayya, baptized by Rev. Darling in 1859. A detailed description of Venkayya's conversion is discussed in Chapter 4. Pagolu Venkayya's influential testimony brought fellow Malas and their families into the Christian faith.[186] In 1862, there were eighty converts in a cluster of nine villages under the charge of a native schoolmaster, who used to conduct a school for boys and another one for girls, on week days and led two worship services on Sundays.[187]

A committee of six people was appointed there to collect and administer church funds and donations received either in grain or money.[188] For the first time in the history of Andhra Church, Europeans, *Brāhmins*, *Súdras* and Malas met together to conduct the affairs of the church.[189] A community meal was organized by the church in 1859, on the eve of Christmas celebration, in which people from all castes participated and served each other. It was an experience of equality and practice of equal treatment to all castes. Indeed, it was a step towards achieving social equality. The direction for self-government and self-supporting of the churches was made in September 1876. The First Telugu Native Church Council was held in 1876 in Raghavapuram under the leadership of Rev. Darling in which Christians from different castes namely, *Brāhmins* and *Súdras* sat with the Mala delegates.[190] In 1876, Rev. James Stone was appointed to Raghavapuram and for several years he rendered his valuable services not only in Raghavapuram but also in adjoining Khammamet and Dornakal, which were in Nizam's territory.[191]

There were 260 native Christians by end 1861, that is, twenty years after the foundation of the CMS Mission. The number kept increasing: in 1871, it was 1,700 and in 1878, it was 4,000. The rapid increase was sign of a general mass movement towards Christianity among the Malas. The movement began to spread to the surrounding districts. The fast pace of Malas' Christian conversion was chiefly due to kinship and caste affinities, as was the cause of all mass conversion movements.

ix) The Great Cyclone of 1864

The Telugu mission suffered heavy loss due to a terrible cyclone in 1864, which brought sorrow and mourning to the CMS mission. It was one of the worst cyclones that South India had seen. The wide flat delta between Kistna and Godavari rivers was ravaged by heavy floods and drowned some 30000 people.[192] Though the missionaries, Rev. Noble and Rev. Sharp and their families, narrowly escaped, many people associated with the mission perished among whom were thirty-three girls of Mrs. Sharkey's Boarding School.[193] In the next year Rev. Noble, who was shocked by the disastrous cyclone, passed away: after long twenty three years of service at Masulipatnam.[194]

x) Rev. and Mrs. Harrison at Bezwada

Rev. John Harrison was a distinguished CMS missionary credited with 42 years of service at Bezwada.[195] Taking charge of the mission in 1867, he engaged himself with educational and social relief activities. Besides working with the Mala converts, he was credited for the establishment of a school for caste girls in 1870, with the active cooperation from the Rajah of Nuzvid. In 1872, Rev. Harrison converted some *Brāhmins* namely Kalpata Srinivasam, Malladi Venkataratnam, Buddha Seshayya, Midde Lakshmayya and Kanaparthi Sivaiah. Rev. Harrison strived to spread the Gospel not only in Bezwada but also in the surrounding villages of Kuntamukkala and Kolavennu. Mrs. Emma Henrietta, wife of Rev. Harrison was an equally zealous woman and helped her husband in the challenging missionary work of the Bezwada field.[196]

xi) Other Notable CMS Missionaries

Rev. John Cain became in-charge of the remote station of Dummagudem on the banks of Godavari River.[197] Mr. John Thornton and Rev. J. E. Padfield[198] successively held the Vernacular Training Institution or the Vernacular Theological Institution at Masulipatnam that supplied catechists and school-teachers to the Telugu districts.[199] Mrs. Padfield had conducted the Sharkey's Girls' Boarding School in an efficient manner.[200]

Other notable missionaries at the Telugu mission were Revs. W. Ellington, W. Clayton, W. G. Baker, H. W. Bales, Albert Henry Arden, Mr. Martin Browne (the Ellore schoolmaster), W. G. Peel and E. Noel Hodges. Some missionaries had served longer, such as Mr. Goodman for 22 years, Arthur W. Poole and C. W. A. Clarke for 21 years each, H. W. Eales for 35 years. They had all occupied themselves with preaching and teaching responsibilities of the mission.[201]

The CMS Telugu mission and its native evangelists continued to expand their service of preaching the Gospel beyond the British territories, into the Nizam's dominions. The adjoining district of Khammamett became an additional centre in 1887 under the supervision of Rev. J. B. Panes, who had baptized hundreds of rural (Mala) population.[202] Also, some Mala Christians from Khammamett migrated and settled down in Bezwada town in Kistna District and became members of the CMS mission there.[203]

xii) Growth of Native Clergy and Laymen

A prominent aspect of the CMS Telugu mission was the effective growth of native clergy. In 1864, Bishop Rev. Gell ordained the first two native clergymen, Manchala Ratnam, and Ainala Bhushanam, both caste converts of Rev. Noble, who had rendered faithful service for the mission.[204] Revs. Atsanta Subbarayudu, Ganugapati Krishnayya, and I. Venkata Rama Razu, all of whom were caste converts, worked in schools as teachers and superintending pastors.[205] The rank and file of the CMS Telugu church was mainly composed of the Malas. They converted as individuals or along with their families or in groups in hundreds, year by year, initiated by the missionaries and the native clergymen.[206] For example, in the most Anglican district of the Kistna, if there were 36,194 Christians in 1881[207] there were 177,607 Christians in the same district according to the census reports.[208] The conversions took place in spite of occasional persecutions and general apathy of the caste Hindus.[209]

A class of agricultural cultivators, the Mala community was strong in caste spirit and carried the same spirit into the church, after its conversion. To quote Rev. Azariah, "Caste structures provided natural and effective instruments for publicizing the gospel and vehicles for encouraging group conversions along caste lines, which were much less socially disruptive than individual accessions."[210]

The CMS Telugu Church also witnessed development of native leadership even among the Mala converts. In 1884, the Mala converts, Marumudi David and Kandavilli Peter[211] and Domatatti Stephen were ordained as pastors, whose lives, in missionaries' opinion were examples for all.[212] Rev. Dhanwada Anantam had worked earnestly in the evangelical, educational and literary fields (maintained the monthly magazines of *Sakshi, Hitavadi*, and *Satyaduta*)[213] in Bezwada and Masulipatnam. In recognition of his services he was '*canonized*' and appointed by Bishop Henry Whitehead as Canon of the Madras Cathedral.[214]

xiii) Firm Roots of Anglican Christianity in Coastal Andhra

Between 1882 and 1895, the Telugu Church grew tremendously: from 6000 adherents to 11,000. Both baptized and 'communicant' members increased year by year.[215] It was reported by Rev. Henry Elliot Fox, a member of the Winter Mission of 1887-1888, and son of Rev. Henry Watson Fox (one of the first two CMS missionaries at Masulipatnam), that in the year 1888, there were 8,000 Christian adherents in Masulipatnam.[216] We may note that the infant H. E. Fox was looked after by a Mala woman during his father's missionary service in

Masulipatnam around the year 1847. Rev. H. E. Fox became the Honorary Secretary of the CMS Mission in London in 1895.[217] At Masulipatnam, there were three schools and a vernacular theological institution for the training of native Christian preachers. The CMS's Khammamett station was placed successively under the charge of Mr. Panes, Mr. Peachey, Mr. Tanner and Mr. Woodhouse.[218]

The Census Reports of 1891 mention the success of the missionaries in the districts of Kistna and Guntur districts. There were 7,670 Christians in the Kistna district in 1871 (with Guntur);[219] the number increased to 10,802 (without Guntur): Guntur alone stood at 79,479 in 1891.[220] Without differentiating between Mala Christians and Madiga Christians, the Census reports have based on the Malas' traditional allegiance to the Anglican Christianity, as it was the CMS mission that had mainly worked and mediated change among the Malas. In 1901, together with Guntur, the Christians of the Kistna district had formed a higher proportion of the population than in any other district north of the Madras city.[221] Be that as it may, according to the Imperial Gazetteer of India, the Baptists in Nellore and Ongole counted at 88,967 and the Lutheran adherents of the Kistna and Godavari districts stood at 20,000 at the close of the 19th century.[222]

During the first decade of the 20th century, there was an increase in the number of native clergy and teachers who also contributed much to the evangelistic work and the pastoral care of the converts. There were a total some 28,000 adult baptisms besides 7,000 catechumens. In 1910, a modest group conversion movement started among the Malas at Khammamett. The Bishop of Winchester along with Bishop Henry Whitehead baptized 35 of the 127 aspirants.[223] Subsequently, group conversions became a prominent feature among the Mala and Madiga castes at Ellore, Bezwada and Raghavapuram districts. Besides, a similar movement of conversion occurred among the lower *Súdra* castes. In 1907 during Bishop Whitehead's visit, 102 *Súdras* received baptism.[224]

The World Missionary Conference held at Edinburgh in 1910, gave greater impetus to evangelization. Missionaries were advised to undertake unprecedented, rapid expansion of their evangelical activities with thoroughness.[225] The Conference also set up a Continuation Committee, a sort of representative body of all the missionary societies of the world, with a view to promoting closer co-operation and unity among the mission bodies in foreign missions.[226] The president of the Conference, Rev. John R. Mott toured the Indian missions where he noted organizational need to sustain and promote unity and co-operation among missionaries and indigenous leaders.[227] But this initiative did not continue for long as there was a growing demand among the Indian Christian clergy for independence and self-direction in the affairs of the church and a demand to separate the Church from the mission.

xiv) The Diocese of Dornakal and Bishop V. S. Azariah

The United Diocese of Madras comprised of a vast episcopal territory with varied evangelical needs. According to a resolution passed by the Episcopal Synod in 1910, the Dornakal mission area was widened to include all the mission stations of both the CMS and the SPG (Society for the Propagation of the Gospel) in the Telugu areas which included Kistna District's Masulipatnam and Bezwada, and Godavari District's Dummagudem, Ellore and Khammamett.[228]

On December 29th 1912, a native pastor Vedanayagam Samuel Azariah was consecrated Bishop in St. Paul's Cathedral, Calcutta and was made in-charge of the new CMS mission station of Dornakal.[229] The significance of this event was that Bishop Azariah was the first Indian native to be consecrated as a bishop in the Anglican Church.[230] Rev. Azariah was the chief inspiration behind in furthering mass conversion movements. He is credited to have brought nearly 200,000 Malas, Madigas and *Súdra*s into the fold of the church. By this time the number of foreign missionaries and foreign staffs had gradually dwindled and the number of Indian clergy grew steadily. Rev. Azariah, assisted by Rev. Cranswick, had some 100 lay teachers working in 75 villages with 3,384 baptized Christians and 1,451 catechumens. There was an increase in the number of baptisms to 4,271 and catechumens to 2,372 during the year 1914.[231]

xv) Self - Directed and Self-Governing Churches

The rise of Indian nationalism in civil society was gaining momentum in the early decades of the 20th century. It had its reverberations in the Indian Church. The desire for self-governing and self-directed churches began in the year 1910 and largely affected missionary work in the Telugu districts. A parallel movement, characterized by strong denominational allegiance and a demand for Home Rule in the Anglican Churches for a progressive strengthening of the indigenous priesthood on one hand, and decreased strength, authority and power of the American and British missionary societies, on the other, was taking place.[232] Rising nationalism among the Indian Christians was aimed at glorifying everything Indian, and opposing everything foreign including the presence of Christian missionaries. Despite the initial understanding and mutual trust between the Indian National Congress and the Christian missionaries, at later stages, they looked upon each other with growing disfavour.[233] The Nationalist movement also gave the Indian Christians a desire for self-direction to control the affairs of the church independently. As the Canadian Baptist missionary Dr. J. R. Stillwell observed:

As soon as there are converts they were organized into churches. The Telugu churches were organized with their own pastors and deacons who had the local authority with regard to the leading and developing of the churches.

During the times of conventions, missionaries are allowed to speak but not given the right to vote. They were only lending moral support for the churches to become independent, evangelistic and self-supporting.[234]

xvi) Devolution of the Indian Church

In the context of the nationalistic political situation in India, the institutional presence of foreign missions was challenged. It was felt that the work of the Church in India should be entrusted to the newly emerging Indian leadership and all resources and missionary co-operation should be provided for native organizations. Further, the National Missionary Council, set up in 1914 and its Committee on 'Indian Church' called for the need to organize all missionary activities as 'church-centered' rather than 'mission-centered.'[235] The Evangelistic Forward Movement which began in 1915 worked for uniting all the Christian workers of all denominations, which eventually paved the way for the formation of the Church of South India in 1947. In preparation for this, the National and Provincial Missionary Councils, formed in 1914, set up separate departments to conduct surveys about the Councils' evangelistic opportunities, church finances, literature distribution and medical work.[236]

The self-management movement gained momentum after 1916; thousands of workers cooperated in conducting rural campaigns, spreading of Christian literature, organizing conferences of ministers and workers and for disseminating Christian instruction.[237] Demand by Indian church leaders for 'devolution' or 'Home Rule' or the transfer of leadership and control, became louder within the Provincial councils.[238] A prominent voice was of Bishop Azariah, the Chairman of Indian Church Department of the National Council, who reminded the missions of the need of 'Indianisation of the Church' in matters of Church hierarchy, administration and control of the Church's affairs,[239] and the need to transfer control and handing over of the responsibility of the churches to Indian Christian hands.[240]

In 1922, Provincial Councils were established and were directed to work towards removing of certain social disabilities and to raise the economic levels of the people.[241] Further possibilities aimed at were securing trained leaders and strengthening of communities by appointing committees to deal with high schools, Christian homes, youth work and economic life of the Church for a sustainable development.[242] In 1923 the National Missionary Council was renamed as National Christian Council, and declared a policy on the 'Unification of Indian Churches.'[243]

Corresponding to the two sections of nationalists in civil society (the liberals and the moderates) since the early part of the 20th century, the movement for indianisation of the churches gained momentum. Devolution of the authority and responsibility of the foreign missionaries and vesting the responsibility in the hands of the Indian Christian clergy, were expected to take place in a gradual manner. The International Missionary Council of 1928, held in Jerusalem, urged missionary agencies to establish cordial relations with the younger native Churches, based on mutual cooperation rather than longing to play a leadership role.[244] By 1931, Bishop Azariah was successful in getting the Telugu areas under the control of 25 Deanery Chairmen, each responsible for the affairs of as many as 10,000 Christians.[245] In the Annual Evangelistic Campaign in 1937, more than 11,000 Christians took part. Indianisation of the CMS's Indian missions also gave great spurt in evangelization work. It is recorded that 1027 villages were visited where some 3000 aspirants decided to become Christians.[246] In 1939, the Christian adherents of the CMS Mission in the Kistna district alone stood above 124,000.[247]

xvii) The Unification of the Episcopal and Non-Episcopal Churches in 1947

The activities of the CMS were expanded all over Andhra including the Telangana areas and in 1947 this Society was renamed as *Church of South India* (CSI) with the Dioceses of Medak, Dornakal, in Krishna, Godavari and the Rayalaseema. A Bishop was appointed for each diocese to head the affairs of the churches and schools.[248] In 1939, negotiations had started for the union of the churches at the Sixteenth Session of the National Christian Council's meeting at Madras.[249] Rev. Azariah also played a leading role in church unity negotiations, when deliberations were held for the amalgamation of the Church Missionary Society with other missionary societies namely, the London Missionary Society, the Society for Propagation of Gospel (SPG), the Society for Propagation of Christian Knowledge (SPCK) and the Anglican Methodist Church.[250] The most significant union occurred on 27th September 1947 when the Episcopal and non-Episcopal denominations of Anglicans, Methodists, Presbyterians and Congregationalists formed into one body of the CSI and paved the way for Anglican Ecclesiastical unity of the Indian Churches.[251]

Thus, the CMS played a significant role in altering the social setting in colonial Andhra with its devoted and faithful missionaries and established a vast Christian church that has been playing a leading role in the life and experiences of the people in Andhra Pradesh. The educational and philanthropic activities of the CMS are discussed in Chapter 5.

3.5.5 The American Evangelical Lutheran Mission

The Lutheran Foreign Missionary enterprise had its beginnings since the beginning of Lutheranism. According to the Herzog's Encyclopedia, Martin Luther always reminded his hearers of the distress of the 'heathens' and the Turks and urged them to pray on their behalf and to send a missionary for them.[252] The first Lutheran missionaries to ever land in India were Bartholomew

Ziegenbalg and Henry Pluetschau on July 9, 1706.[253] But it was not until the middle of the 19th century that the active Lutheran missionary work started in colonial Andhra, by the American Evangelical Lutheran Missionary Society.

The History of the American Lutheran missionaries in India is unique in the history of Indian Christianity as it was the only body which enlisted close cooperation and active participation of other European missionary bodies, such as the North German Missionary Society of Hamburg, the Leipzig Society of Dresden, the Lutheran Augustana Synod and the Augustana Women's Missionary Society. The Hagerstown meeting of 1837 urged the enthusiastic Germans living in America, suggesting the establishment of the German Foreign Missionary Society. At the Baltimore meeting of the General Synod in 1841, the Telugu field was chosen under the society's new name, *The Foreign Missionary Society of the Evangelical Lutheran Church in the United States.*

i) Rev. John Christian Frederick Heyer of the Pennsylvania Ministerium

Upon the request of the missionary CTE Rhenius of the CMS Tinnevelly Mission,[254] the Foreign Missionary Society decided to send Rev. John Christian Frederick Heyer to India in 1841. Rev. Heyer served in the American Lutheran mission fields of Guntur and Rajahmundry between the years 1841-1871.[255]

The American Lutheran Missionary Society in Andhra was partly founded due to the interest of Mr. Henry Stokes, Esq., Magistrate-Collector of Guntur District, who expressed the desire to secure a resident missionary for Guntur. As a member of the Church of England he had appealed to the CMS for a missionary at Guntur. The Society advised Mr. Henry Stokes to persuade Rev. Heyer of the Pennsylvania Ministerium to be stationed at Guntur and Mr. Stokes formally placed him at the Anglo-vernacular school in 1842. Rev. Heyer was an ideal missionary who can be considered as the founder of the Guntur Mission of the American Evangelical Lutheran Mission on July 31 1842.[256] For a year, he conducted worship services for the English officials and European residents who were engaged in the East India Company's civil, military and commercial pursuits.[257]

Rev. Heyer's missionary service in India stretched for three terms over a period of 30 years from 1841 to 1871. According to Rev. L. B. Wolf, "Rev. Heyer had a world vision and his soul was restless unless it was in touch with the whole world. He saw what few in his day were able to see, that the Church stands for one supreme work, which must be performed in the whole world and for all men."[258] Educational activities occupied Rev. Heyer's evangelistic activities for which he started schools in the Collector's compound and one each at Prathipadu, Kothapeta and Nallapadu.[259] It was considered that schools were suitable for the planting of the Gospel seed.[260] By the end of 1842, a children's Sunday school was also started.[261] Rev. Heyer was an excellent disciplinarian and a good instructor, having possessed with an ability to organize schools. [262] He made substantial progress in establishing and supervising schools and enrolled 150 pupils and employed seven teachers.[263]

The Telugu field of the American Lutheran Mission was divided into two mission fields namely Rajahmundry (on the north part of the Godavari River) and Guntur (on the South of the Kistna River). Each mission field was divided into several taluks and the serving missionaries lived in the mission centres of these talukas.[264]

3.5.5 A. The Guntur Mission field

In 1844, Rev. Walter Gunn was sent to assist Rev. Heyer in the Palnadu area. Rev. Gunn started to learn Telugu and taught English to the Hindu boys besides conducting regular Bible study classes attended by the English residents. Mrs. Gunn began to teach English and needle-work to a small class of Hindu girls.[265] Rev. Walter Gunn laboured vigorously despite his feeble health.[266] At the end of the year 1844, five Lutheran missionaries were stationed at Guntur namely, Rev. Heyer, Rev. Gunn, Rev. Valett of the North German Missionary Society and two missionaries of the Leipzig Society, namely Revs. Ochs and Schwartz.

i) The Extended Field of Palnadu

In 1850, Rev. Heyer undertook a mission to establish a Christian colony near Gurjala on nine acres of land, donated by Mr. Stokes, the Collector. Rev. Heyer's preaching strategy comprised of visiting villages and distribution of Bibles and tracts. During the year 1850, Rev. Heyer baptized nearly 126 adults and children.[267] He undertook missionary tours in Gurajala, Veldurti, Dachepalli, Polepalli and Tumurucotta. A number of other missionaries from the neighbouring mission stations visited him, among whom mention may be made about Rev. J. E. Sharkey and Rev. T. Y. Darling of the CMS mission. The American Bible Society and the Madras Auxiliary Society had supplied Bibles and scripture tracts for free distribution.[268]

Rev. Heyer and Rev. Valett undertook preaching tours through the Palnadu taluk, where Malapati John from Polepalli had converted[269] and was baptized in 1847, under the auspices of Rev. Gunn.[270] In 1849, Rev. Gunn baptized twenty two persons belonging to the Mala caste of Polepalli who had received Christian instruction from Malapati John. Rev. C. W. Grönning of the North German Society worked in Guntur, Ellore and Rajahmundry, and possessed a missionary career that marked the beginning of large number of conversions in the Palnadu District.[271] In 1849, Rev. Grönning was stationed at Ellore where, besides preaching the Gospel, he organized two Telugu schools, for about twenty pupils each.[272]

ii) The Extension of the Guntur Field

Rev. William E. Snyder started his missionary service in 1852 and was active in maintaining the mission schools, especially the English school and conducting tour of villages until his death due to cholera in 1859.[273] The native Christians who collaborated for evangelical work were Mala converts Cornelius, James, Jerripotu William, Tota Joseph and Nelaprolu Paulus, all of whom proved to be efficient workers.[274] Rev. and Mrs. Snyder took Tota Joseph into their home and treated him like their own child.[275]

Rev. Dr. Erias Unangst took the charge of the Guntur mission field in 1859 and worked for over a decade in cooperation with Rev. Grönning. Between the years 1862 to 1863, he undertook several preaching tours in the Palnadu region and administered the Lord's Supper to one hundred communicants in six congregations.[276] He was also a member of the Committee for Revision of the Telugu Translation of the Bible.[277] Also, Rev. Dr. Lemon L. Uhl, served the mission for fifty years since 1873, with remarkable success both in evangelistic work as supervisor of the schools in Guntur.[278]

After the extensive evangelical service for three terms from 1841 to 1871 at Guntur and Rajahmundry mission stations, Rev. Heyer left India at the close of 1871 and passed away at the age of 81 on 7th of November 1873.[279] After twenty-five years of work of the American Lutheran Missions in the Telugu field, there were four mission stations of Guntur, Rajahmundry, Samalkota and the Palnadu. The number of baptized persons at the close of 1867 was 1,140 and the number of Christians stood at 680 and that of regular communicants was about 350 people. In twenty-two schools, there were about 300 pupils.[280]

iii) Famine Relief Measures

During the terrible famine of 1876-77, Rev. Rowe successfully managed the funds of the *"Mansion House Relief"*, as in-charge of the missions in Repalli and Bapatla taluks, where he combined Gospel work and famine relief work.[281] He also won commendation for his plans and efforts, from Mr. William Digby, the superintendent of the fund in Madras.[282] The famine gave the missionaries large access to the "inquirers" where many sought baptism between 1876 and 1880. With the exception of a few who were motivated by selfish motives, the majority of the converts renounced their old faiths and were baptized as direct or indirect result of the famine relief work, and remained faithful to build a substantial native church.[283] Miss Kate Boggs was the first unmarried lady missionary to work in the Guntur mission from 1880 to 1883. She worked with great zeal and persistent interest.[284]

In 1885, Rev. L. B. Wolf assumed the charge of the Guntur Mission High School and the Boys' Boarding School from Rev. L. L. Uhl. Rev. N. E. Yeiser took the charge of the mission work in Vinakonda, Narasaraopet and Kanigiri in 1892.[285] The Narasaraopet field became a prominent Lutheran mission station with a permanent mission bungalow called the 'Nichols Memorial.'[286]

iv) Rev. Dr. J. H. Harpster and the 'Famine Kitchen' of 1900

Rev. Dr. John Henry Harpster served the General Synod Mission at Guntur and later in the General Council's Rajahmundry Mission for two terms from 1872 to 1876 and from 1893 to 1902.[287] He took charge of the Guntur Mission District and contributed for the growth of the church. There was an increase in the number of baptisms from 1,906 to 3,593.[288] Rev. Harpster's first term was marked by the advancement of the mass-movement among the depressed castes into Christianity in the Telugu districts.[289] Rev. Harpster played a key role in advancing church membership from 3,861 in 1893, to 8,194 in 1901.[290] Rev. Harpster is specially remembered for his hard and energetic work during the great famine of 1900 when he conducted a 'famine kitchen' from which over two thousand people were fed daily. When the distressed condition came to end, he organized the remaining funds in laying the foundation of an orphanage by purchasing a site of 40 acres and assumed the care of about one hundred orphan boys and girls.[291] He showed great love for his native converts and devoted most of his time to work among them. Through mass conversion movements, he had hoped to find leaders who were worthy to lead people in their struggle against caste tyranny and traditional socio-economic and socio-religious bondages. He took delight in working for the Malas and the Madigas, even though their social habits were resented by him.[292]

v) The Zenana Mission

In the year 1880, an organization of the Zenana Conference was founded under the leadership of Ms. Fannie M Dryden. She managed both Zenana schools and conventional schools at Bapatla, Perala, Cherala, Amaravati, Mangalagiri, Ponnur and Chebrole. Another lady missionary Ms. Susan R. Kistler supervised the schools at Narasarowpet, Chilakalurpet, Rompicherla, Vinukonda and Dachepalli.[293] Besides, Ms. Amy L Sadtler managed the girls' boarding schools as well as Zenana work at Guntur. Mr. and Mrs. Aberly, along with Miss Amy L Sadtler did remarkable mission service in 1890 in Bapatla and Repalli stations that brought order and deepened the faith of the converts.[294] The Lutheran missionaries undertook a number of social activities in fields of education, health care, zenana work and vocational training for men and women (see discussion in Chapter 5).

vi) Medical Mission

Rev. Heyer was a medical missionary and he used his medical knowledge and skills to treat patients.[295] Rev. Unangst was another medical missionary who, being aware of the Indian hot climate, adapted his ways of treatment and even practiced healing art for the treatment of common diseases. The contribution of yet another medical missionary, Dr. Anna Sarah Kugler is worthy of mention for her valuable and dedicated medical services in the Guntur Lutheran mission field.

3.5.5 B. The Rajahmundry Mission Field

As mentioned earlier, the American Evangelical Lutheran Mission worked in close association with the North German Missionary Society in Rajahmundry since 1845.[296] Louis P. Menno Valett of the North German Society was invited by Rev. Heyer in 1843 and the former established a mission station at Rajahmundry.[297] In 1846, Rev. Valett was joined by two additional missionaries, Charles W. Grönning and Ferdinand August Heise.[298] On 1st January 1851, the Executive Committee of the American Evangelical Foreign Missionary Society agreed to take charge of the Rajahmundry mission station and hence the resident missionaries came under the control of the General Synod of the Foreign Missionary Society.[299] The two missionaries, Revs. Valett and Heise, remained in the Rajahmundry mission station till the year 1862.[300] During the years from 1863 to 1865, Rev. Grönning baptized nearly forty adults and admitted them into Holy Communion.[301]

i) Rev. William I. Cutter and Mrs. Cutter

After the takeover of the mission station by the General Synod in 1851, Rev. William I. Cutter and Mrs. Cutter were placed at Rajahmundry in 1852, and became in-charges of the Anglo-vernacular school. Mrs. Cutter founded the first girls' school with financial aid from her friends abroad.[302] In 1854, at the second meeting of the Synod at Rajahmundry, three native Christians namely, Chinsa Ramurdu of Rajahmundry, William Barnabas of Passavant and Tota Joseph of Guntur, were recommended for training as catechists and pastors.[303] After 1858, Rev. Adam Long conducted the mission station of Rajahmundry, and even opened a new station at Samalcota.[304] After about eight years of busy work, Rev. Adam Long fell a victim to smallpox on 5th March 1866 and thence Rajahmundry was left without any Lutheran missionary.[305]

In 1866, when Rev. Unangst visited Rajahmundry, he observed that unless a Lutheran missionary occupies the Rajahmundry mission station, the Lutherans might lose the station permanently to those mission societies which do not share the same ideological platform.[306] Therefore, Rev. Unangst decided to transfer the Rajahmundry-Samalkot mission stations to the CMS at Ellore which shared the similar ideology, under Rev. Alexander. However, it was averted with the timely interference of Rev. Heyer and Rev. Grönning and hence Rajahmundry station remained with the General Council of the Evangelical Lutheran Church in North America.[307] Educational work in Rajahmundry showed better results than that of Guntur even though the progress of conversions could not compete with that of the Guntur mission field.[308]

A comparatively slow progress of the Lutheran Telugu mission during the first decade of its work was due to the confinement of evangelistic work only to the towns of Guntur and Rajahmundry. These missionaries relied more upon education work as a medium of evangelization and seldom took to the tour of villages in the districts. Besides, lack of native helpers who could have prepared the way for missionary or followed up missionary preaching, became a big drawback in the progress of conversions.[309] Though the new converts were faithful to the mission's cause, yet they were uneducated and untrained.[310] It was expected that the educated children of the converts would become native helpers with some competence after some years of schooling. But many years had passed before these schools produced some such competent graduates.[311] Regarding the competence of the missionaries, the Council of the India Mission had decided that once a missionary was assigned to a mission, he/she should undergo two-year language training in Telugu and study of Hinduism.

At the end of 1871, the number of congregations at Guntur was 32 and the members of the Church stood at 2,150, of whom 638 were communicants from 52 villages. At Rajahmundry, the Lutheran mission had 320 converts and 93 communicants in 1871.[312] Rev. Schmidt was in-charge of the Rajahmundry station from where he rendered various services as preacher, teacher and administrator of mission's properties.[313]

ii) Extension of the Rajahmundry Field

Rev. Schmidt took charge of Dowlaishwaram, Velpur, Jagganathpuram, Mallipudi and Agartipalem and appointed Mr. Nelaprolu Paulus, a native Christian as the catechist in 1876.[314] The mission work of the Rajahmundry mission station spread far and wide in villages, such as Metta, Peddapuram, Gowripatnam, Muramunda, Jegurupadu, Peravaram and Lolla, where both Christian families and new inquirers became eager to know the Gospel.[315] During the period of natural disasters, such as the famine of 1876 and 1877 when cholera epidemic made it worse for the people, missionaries advanced monetary help to both converts and Hindus. In Rev. Schmidt's own words, 'it was a great help to the poor people.'[316]

Rev. Iver K. Poulsen, in association with Rev. Schmidt since 1871, took charge of the educational work at Rajahmundry.[317] However he was more interested in the Samalkot station, where he had prepared a number of inquirers for baptism.[318] He undertook supervision of the mission work and extended his area of operation to wider Godavari region comprised of the towns of Muramunda, Jegurupad, Dulla, Peravaram, Lolla, Amalapur, Samalkot, Rajanagaram, Gokavaram, Jaggampet and Korukonda. He conducted regular village visits during the time of village festivals.[319] While touring the villages, the missionaries lived in tents which were pitched just outside the village or in the open field under a large tamarind or margosa tree.[320] Generally the touring missionary was accompanied by one or two catechists who took the responsibility of gathering the people and assisted the missionary in Bible reading and singing.[321]

Rev. Augustus B. Carlson, a Swede, became the General Council's foreign missionary in the Rajahmundry field from the year 1879 to 1882. Rev. Carlson was an educational missionary who later became in-charge of the CMS' educational work at two of its boarding schools at Masulipatnam.[322] Mrs. Carlson was succeeded by Mrs. Schmidt as teacher in the sewing class and the Sunday school which was conducted daily on the verandah of Carlson's bungalow. The missionary along with his wife used a mission-boat, the *Dove of Peace,* for conducting preaching tours in water-surrounded Godavari delta villages.[323]

In 1880 came Rev. and Mrs. Horace G. B. Artman who undertook school work and achieved rapid development by enforcing strict discipline and high level of efficiency. Eleven native Christian teachers were employed to manage many village schools.[324] Mrs. Artman is particularly remembered for her initiative in starting Zenana work among the caste women. She had made an observation that caste women were more interested in learning English and were attracted to fancy work rather than plain sewing and learning Telugu.[325]

In 1881, the adherents at the American Evangelical Lutheran Mission increased to 7,988, with 2,404 communicants, 120 congregations, 95 preachers and teachers, 59 schools and 1,965 scholars.[326] A review of Lutheran mission statistics has noted that with over 300 percent increase in baptized membership, the native Christian community doubled itself every decade. The missionaries had hoped that if the same rate of increase were to continue, the whole of the depressed castes' population would be gathered into the Church within thirty years.[327]

iii) Native Teachers

Rev. Poulsen employed a number of native teachers namely, Joseph and Lakshmiah as catechists, Amelia, the wife of Lakshmiah as teacher at Peddapur, David as teacher at Rajagopalem and Francis at Katlamur, in various stations under his supervision.[328] Church services were conducted in Telugu every Sunday at the missionary's bungalow where teachers and Christians came from villages and Holy Communion was administered to them.[329] Christians were found in large numbers in the three districts of Godavari, Kistna and Nellore. These belonged to Lutheran, Baptist and Anglican denominations and were part of the two million and half Christian population of the Madras presidency.[330] The contribution of the native Gospel workers was considerable. They had been educated in the mission schools and had had nearly twenty five years of Christian exposure and experience thanks to the preaching of the missionaries. There were about 450 native workers in Guntur mission who looked after the spiritual needs of the multitudes.[331] Teaching of the Bible was given a prominent place and the Catechism was included in every service in the schools. All un-ordained workers who wished to be confirmed in the mission's work were expected to be free from all objectionable caste prejudices and possess the requisite intellectual and moral qualities.[332] They had worked in organized groups in Gospel preaching and establishing congregations. In this work, they were largely helped by ordained pastors, catechists, evangelists, teachers, Bible women and other native Indian workers.[333]

iv) Industrial and Vocational Work

Rev. Frederick James McCready, a Eurasian, was appointed as the missionary in-charge of the Samalkota and Tallapudi stations in 1885. He worked hard for his converts from the Mala and Madiga castes.[334] He was successful in creating employment opportunities through manufacturing tiles, building of churches and mission bungalows. However, his request for the industrial work of tile making as a regular branch of mission work was not accepted by the Foreign Mission Board. Mrs. Catharine Taylor McCready taught vocational courses of crochet, knitting and lace making for the Christian women in Tallapudi.[335]

v) 'The Children's Missionary': Rev. Adam Rowe

The American Lutheran Mission also laid the foundation for the Children's Foreign Missionary Society to give more support to the Sunday school work. The Society supported Rev. Adam Rowe, known as 'Children's Missionary', for his innovative and creative involvement among children,[336] since 1874. It also enhanced evangelistic work among the natives, organized village congregations better, started and strengthened Sunday schools among them, and increased the number and efficiency of the native workers.[337]

vi) Notable Lutheran Missionaries

Some of the other prominent Evangelical Lutheran missionaries who worked with dedication at Guntur and Rajahmundry mission stations were: Ms. Christina Erickson (1915-1930), Rev. E. Edman (1890-1903), Ms. Hilma Levine (1915), Rev. H. E. Isaacson (1893-1914), Ms. Charlotte Swenson (1895-1908), Edwin A. Olson (1915-1921, Hedwig Wahlberg (1900-1908), Ms. Verna A. Lofgren (1923), Rev. O. O. Eckhardt (1906-1916), Rev. Oscar L. Larson (1906-1923), Ms. Ruth Hildegarde Swanson (1924), Dr. Betty A. Nilsson (1908), Ms. Ada E. Kron (1929-1933), Rev. T. A. Holmer (1912-1933), Rev. R. L. Cunningham (1936), Ms. Agnes Christenson (1915) and Ms. Margaret Hawkinson (1939-1944).

The Evangelical Lutheran mission work in Guntur station was under the guidance of the General Synod and was divided into seven subdivisions at Palnad, Satenapalli, Narasaraopet, Vinakonda, Guntur, Bapatla and Repalli.[338] The work of the Lutheran missionaries in the Telugu field grew rapidly in the beginning of the 20th century due to increase in the number of missionaries, their increased interest in the Telugu field as well as the availability of trained native workers.[339] In 1918, the 'American United Lutheran Church' was formed from the three foreign missionary units of a) the General Synod, b) the General Council and c) the Southern United Synod and continued the activities of the mission in India. The mission stations of Guntur and Rajahmundry which were separated in 1869 were re-united in 1918.[340]

3.5.5 C. Development of the Andhra Evangelical Lutheran Church

The India mission of the American Lutheran Church was the largest Lutheran Mission in the world and the most productive and prosperous all over India. As the Indian Lutheran Mission developed and matured, it became a self-managing Church. Eventually the Andhra Evangelical Lutheran Church (AELC) emerged from it in 1927. Some of the missionaries and clergymen who led the church as Presidents successively were, Dr. S. C. Burger, Dr. R. M. Dunkelberger, Dr. J. R. Fink, Dr. E. Neudoerffer, Dr. J. Roy Strock, Dr. L. W. Slifer, Dr. J. R. Fink, Dr. E. Prakasam, Dr. H. H. Moyer and Rev. A. N. Gopal. Dr. E. Prakasam was the first Indian President of the Lutheran Church, elected in 1944.[341] The membership of the AELC was drawn mostly from the Mala and Madiga castes whose number stood at about two hundred thousand in the second decade of the 20th century. Since 1920, some *Súdras* also started coming into the fold of the Church.[342]

The Augustana Synod helped in the building up of the Charlotte Swenson Memorial Bible and Training school at Rajahmundry for helping the deserted Christian women and caste women converts who had to face terrible sufferings upon their conversion.[343] The Society also provided funds for the building and equipment of the Augustana Hospital at Bhimavaram in 1934. The development of the missionary institutions opened opportunities for employment for Mala and Madiga men and women.[344]

Although, the American Lutheran enterprise thrived for a long time, by the first quarter of the 20th century difficulties grew owing to the lack of supply of funds, harsh climatic conditions, low salaries and the high cost of living. As calls for *Indianisation* and self-support of the Church was gaining momentum, the foreign missionaries started to lay stress on choosing native men and women for future leadership of the church. They realized that the time has ripened for their exit and the Indian Church has developed to be independent and could walk on its own feet.[345] In the words of Prof. Sunil Bhanu, former President of the Andhra Evangelical Lutheran Church of Andhra Pradesh, the committed and dedicated efforts of men with good educational backgrounds, together with increased zeal for evangelistic work as well as national fervor, the Lutheran Church in Andhra was founded firmly for a bright future.[346]

In 1942, Centennial Celebrations were organized to commemorate the commencement of the India Mission. By then, the Indian pastors and delegates had outnumbered foreign missionaries.[347] At a convention held at Guntur on 18th and 19th September 1944, the India operations of the American Lutheran Mission were officially transferred to the Andhra Evangelical Lutheran Church.

In conclusion, the American Evangelical Lutheran Mission contributed much to bring about change in the lives of men and women who were associated with it. The Mission had substantially contributed to the betterment of life of the Malas and the Madigas in a special way, by undertaking educational service and eliminating intense poverty through schemes such as industrial and vocational training. The Lutheran missionaries brought a vision of hope, opened avenues of development, and constructed a Christian fellowship for the depressed caste converts. A substantial number of converts advanced in social mobility so as to become professionals such as doctors, nurses, teachers and service personnel in pre and post- independent Andhra.

3.5.6 The American Baptist Mission, a 'Miracle' Mission

The American Baptist Mission among the Telugus was termed as "the miracles of modern missions", but had a humble beginning at the Eighth Triennial Meeting of the General Missionary Convention held in the city of Richmond, Virginia, in 1835. The Convention was addressed by the English Baptist Missionary, Rev. Amos Sutton of the Orissa Mission who gave a clarion call for immediate attention to the evangelical needs of the Telugu people to the South of Orissa. The Convention recognized an imperative need for the enlargement of the Baptist Church.[348] Filled with missionary enthusiasm and zeal, the American Baptists passed a Resolution for the immediate establishment of a mission among the Telugu people, sufficiently supported with a gratified treasury surplus and liberal contributions of the members. A number of missionaries under the leadership of Rev. Howard Malcom were entrusted to visit the mission fields in Asia. While Rev. Elisha L. Abbott led a team of missionaries to the Karen Mission in Burma, Rev. Samuel S. Day chose to come to the Telugu people of India.[349]

i) The Lone Star Mission of the American Baptist Missionary Union in Nellore

Rev. Samuel S. Day and Mrs. Rowena Clarke Day landed in Vizagapatam and came into contact with Rev. Purushottam Choudhary, an senior Telugu Christian convert. However, they were directed to proceed to Madras. As things turned out, a Tamil man from Nellore, invited Rev. Day to Nellore, where he decided to pitch his tent along with Rev. Stephen Van Husen in the year 1840.[350] Rev. Day toured the interior Telugu districts, some forty towns and villages, where he saw the inviting fields of missionary labour. There was not even one missionary nor any native Christian, in these towns and villages.[351] Putting his heart and soul, Dr. Day conducted his evangelical services in Nellore for the next twenty-six years. The result was tremendous: there was all-round development of the people, particularly the converts so much so that the station was termed as the '*Lone Star of the Telugu Mission.*'[352]

The first Telugu convert named Venkappah was baptized by Rev. Day in the Pennar River on September 27, 1840. Three other converts were baptized in August 1843.[353] However, it took many years for the people there to recognize the faithful labours of the missionaries.[354] There was much opposition and often assaults on the missionaries. In one instance, Rev. Day while on his preaching tour, was beaten severely and paraded through the narrow streets, by a group of people instigated and led by the Brahmins. Rev. Day narrowly escaped from being trampled to death.[355] In 1844, the mission in Nellore being comprised of only four missionaries and only four converts, it was decided to abandon it.[356] The lack of progress in the number of converts made the American Baptist Missionary Union (ABMU) to even abandon the Telugu mission.[357]

In 1848, the question of discontinuing the Telugu mission was discussed at the anniversary of the Union.[358] In 1849, Mr. and Mrs. Day returned to Nellore accompanied by a new missionary, Dr. Lyman Jewett and his wife.[359] Due to their intense efforts, there were 250 children in the schools established by Dr. and Mrs. Day and a Sabbath-school, with 200 students.[360] In 1850, there were a few converts namely, Luchama (Ruth), wife of Venkappah who had converted after ten years of long opposition to her husband's conversion, and Julia from the boarding school of Mrs. Day. These women aided Mrs. Jewett in her efforts to teach the Gospel at the festival gatherings of Nellore.[361] The early Baptist missionary preaching strategy was to visit Hindu festivals (where there was easily a gathering of 30,000 or 40,000 people) and distribute Bible tracts and scripture portions, which only produced mixed results.[362]

A resolution to continue the mission despite the discouraging results was adopted at the annual meeting of the Missionary Union held in Albany, New York in 1853, by naming the Nellore mission as '*Lone Star*', suggested by Samuel F. Smith, the author of the American national Anthem.[363] In 1853, Dr. and Mrs. Jewett together with Christian Nursu, a native preacher, Julia and Ruth, both Bible women, visited Ongole, a town with a population of six thousand.[364] The new year of 1854 began with a celebrated prayer meeting on top of a hill overlooking the village of Ongole (Prayer Meeting Hill), with an inner longing for a missionary to be sent to Ongole.[365] Rev. Day's determined resolution to live and die among the Telugus prevented the American Baptists from withdrawing from the mission.[366] In 1854, owing to ill health, Dr. Jewett left India and the mission work was passed into the hands of Mr. and Mrs. Douglass.[367] During the Sepoy Mutiny of 1857, the church membership was only twelve, and the missionaries had to leave Nellore as the British Captain expressed inability to give protection for the missionaries in case of an attack.[368]

At the same time, the persistently low number of converts attracted much opposition from the ABMU which, at its annual meeting in Providence, in 1862, seriously deliberated a third time on abandoning the Telugu mission. But the matter was finally resolved at the insistence of Dr. Lyman Jewett, not only to continue the mission, but also to strengthen and reinforce it. The end result was the beginning of great missionary success in the history of Indian Christianity: the coming of Rev. John Everett Clough, the 'future missionary for Ongole' and Mrs. Harriet Clough, who reached Nellore on April 22nd 1865.[369] During his short stay at Nellore, Rev. Clough baptized four converts and was hoping for a great multitude to come out of their heathenism.[370] Rev. Clough compiled a booklet called, "*Messages for all*" which was a collection of Bible verses.[371] He also distributed thousands of Gospel tracts, aided by the American Bible Society and the Madras Auxiliary Society.[372] Distribution of Bible tracts was a method followed by the Baptist missionaries similar to the methods of Lutheran and CMS missionaries. Since the year 1865, there was a gradual growth of the American Baptist Mission (ABM) with the establishment of the Ongole mission station.

ii) Admission of the Madigas into the Church

In 1866, Dr. Jewett, along with Rev. Clough and Canakiah, visited Ongole where they heard about a certain Yerraguntla Periah, a Madiga leather-dresser who was eager to meet the missionaries to get baptized.[373] At his initiative he was baptized. It was he who mediated the conversion of hundreds of his caste-mates, the Madigas. Periah shared his experience as:

> Four years ago, I went north to Ellore, where I heard for the first time the Gospel from Rev. Alexander of the CMS. After that I went to Palacole and heard from Mr. Bowden, and saw the native Christians. After my return, the Lord enlightened my mind, and I began labouring for the conversion of my family. After eighteen months, my wife was converted, and several others were awakened.[374]

The religion of the Madigas was already discussed in the previous chapter. It was characterized by fear of the unseen forces of the non-Aryan cults. Yerraguntla Periah had maintained contact with the Ramanuja sect which was filled with Vaishnavite beliefs and had also practiced Rajayoga. It was said that he was in a much-elevated position both religiously and socially when compared to an ordinary Madiga.[375] The admission of the Madigas into the Church was a perplexed issue for the missionaries, as all the early converts of the Baptist mission consisted of only the *Súdra* castes. Eventually, they decided to receive the Madigas into their Church, which positively set in motion a group movement of conversion of the Madigas in the ensuing years. The missionaries did not realize that the conversion of Yerraguntla Periah would usher in a whole multitude of the Madigas into the fold of Christianity.[376]

iii) The Foundation of the Ongole Church

In the month of September, 1866, Rev. Clough and his family were placed at Ongole.[377] Rev. Clough was assisted by his sister, Miss Vina Ruth Clough who was filled up with deep missionary spirit and desire for the salvation of souls.[378] After a visit to Ongole, the native preachers Canakiah, Rungiah and Rungashia undertook a preaching tour to the Northwest part of Nellore that included Talakondapadu where they met Periah with burning zeal for the souls of his fellow-men.[379] Rev Clough assisted by the native preachers, was determined to turn his attention to the conversion of the Madigas. Though he had started an Anglo-vernacular school in 1866, he closed it and devoted all his energies to train a group of native helpers to preach the Gospel, which step was to bring in high results.[380]

iv) The First Ingathering at Talakondapadu

In 1866, Rev. Clough launched his Madiga mission programme at Talakondapadu. He put up a tent in a tamarind grove and began to preach. Many people started to arrive to meet him. Nearly thirty to forty people brought with them supply of provisions and cloths for several days and were seeking baptism after his instruction. It was not a time of famine or any such natural calamity but they professed and wanted to be baptized. After a five-day consultation, twenty-eight converts were baptized.[381]

But the first converts had to face trials and persecution. The faith of the new converts was tested when they returned to their villages. They were forbidden to pass through the streets, and were denied water from the wells. They were presented before the magistrate on charges of cattle poisoning.[382] In Markapur town, the converts were whipped, fined three rupees each and were ordered to be jailed. They were to do forcible work in the vicinity of the Vishnu temple.[383] All through these ordeals, the missionaries stood by the Christians, defended them and negotiated with the *Tahsildar* to let the converts practice their new faith. The Tahsildar relented and ordered that the three rupees fine be paid back to them besides rice for seven days.[384]

The firm stand taken by the Christians influenced others to join them.[385] Rev. Clough and his preachers stood by the Madiga Christians.[386] Consequently, the preaching of the Gospel was welcomed in other villages. The preachers visited nearly eight hundred villages where over seventy thousand pages of tracts and scripture portions were distributed. Rev. Clough now occupied himself with receiving the inquirers, superintending the building of a chapel and visiting villages. Villages with converted Christians were directed to send one or two men to Ongole immediately after harvest for instruction, so that they would return and teach the rest of the villagers.[387] Conversions increased in several villages. At the end of 1867, the Church in Ongole had seventy-five members and had a new chapel built for them, besides a school. The credit of starting a school in Ongole is owed to Mrs. Clough, who along with the wives of the native preachers, took to frequent tours to preach to village women.[388] In 1869, Rev. Clough constructed a baptistery in the garden of the Ongole mission compound and baptized forty-two converts.[389] During his preaching tours of the pariah villages, Rev. Clough not only preached the good news of salvation in the Bible, but also enlightened the pariahs about their general vices such as superstitions, prejudices, ignorance, drunkenness, lust, deceit, cunningness, etc. which, he convinced them, were the cause of their low state. His mission became a success, as the Madigas responded positively and sought baptism. He is said to have baptized three hundred and twenty-four by the end of that year.[390]

v) The Mission Station of Ramapatnam

With an extensive work in sight and the necessity for trained preachers to teach the multitudes and the requests of people for teachers paved way for the opening up of new stations. Also, with the increased number of converts (23) in Nellore and (68) in Ongole pressed the need for more missionaries to cater to further requests from more than 800 villages.[391] Due to the indispensable need for trained preachers, a mission station and a theological school for training of pastors and evangelists of the American Baptist Telugu mission were established at Ramapatnam by Rev. R. R. Williams in 1869.[392] Rev. A. V. Timpany and Mrs. Jane Bates Timpany joined the mission at Nellore, and were placed at Ramapatnam in February, 1870. Rev. Edwin Bullard and Rev. John McLaurin along with his wife Mrs. Mary Bates McLaurin also arrived in 1870 and proceeded to Ramapatnam. The new out-station, Alloor, where the baptized converts were numbered at thirty-eight, was placed under the care of a native preacher.[393] In 1869, the government decided to transfer the headquarters of the English magistrate from Ramapatnam to Ongole and the large compound of nearly one hundred acres with two buildings were placed in the hands of the Baptist missionaries, where Rev. Timpany established a school besides a theological school.[394]

The church was organized in Ramapatnam in March, 1870 which consisted of thirty-five members to which nearly seventy baptized converts were added by the year end.[395] From 1870 to 1872, Rev. Clough worked in cooperation with Rev. McLaurin. The church membership in Ongole was

1,658.[396] Rev. John McLaurin undertook missionary work at Ongole with great discretion and he baptized over seven hundred converts in a single year.[397] The training of the native pastors and preachers that was begun by Dr. Jewett took its best shape in the founding of a theological seminary by Rev. A.V. Timpany in April, 1872, in Ramapatnam, with eighteen students. The seminary accommodation was later upgraded to for nearly hundred students.[398] The Brownson Theological Seminary, founded at Ramapatnam in 1872, had the capacity to accommodate some 200 students.[399]

In 1873, Rev. David Downie and his wife joined the Telugu mission during the time when Rev. McLaurin was directed to establish a new station for the Canadian Baptists at Cocanada.[400] At the end of that year, the members at the Baptist mission stations were: 336 at Nellore, 2,761 in Ongole, 675 in Ramapatnam and 60 at Alloor.[401] In 1874, a printing-press was set up to cater to the print needs of the mission.[402] In January 1874, Rev. Clough returned to Ongole accompanied by Rev. and Mrs. W. W. Campbell and with Miss Peabody.[403] In the years 1875-76, Miss M. A. Wood and Rev. D. H. Drake and his wife, Rev. A. Loughridge and his wife and Rev. A. A. Newhall were added to the working force of the American Baptist Mission.[404] Miss Mary M. Day, daughter of the founder of the American Baptist mission, Rev. Samuel S. Day, also joined the mission to help reap the harvests of the seed sown by her parents.[405] These new missionaries occupied themselves with visiting towns and villages where they had examined and baptized hundreds of eager candidates and supported them in times of persecution and strengthened their adherence to the new faith.[406] The persecutors of the Madiga Christians met with a punishment of three months in prison and Rs.30/- as fine.[407] Rev. and Mrs. Timpany left Ramapatnam in 1876, to be placed at the newly established mission station of Cocanada of the CBM about which we have already discussed in the previous pages. Since the starting of the American Baptist Mission in 1841, until the onset of the terrible famine in 1876, that had lasted for two years (1876-1878), the number of baptized members in the Telugu Baptist mission was 4,394.[408]

vi) The Great Famine of 1876-1877 and the Second Ingathering

During the year 1876, Rev. Clough baptized 656 converts,[409] however, the course of action was hindered by an onset of the dark days of famine in the Telugu districts. With complete failure of the harvest, it was reported that people ate only once in three days. The situation got further worsened as the caste traders refused to sell food for the Christians.[410] Evangelistic work was suspended in some departments and the efforts were directed towards saving the lives of people by undertaking and superintending of the public works that provided temporary employment for the starving multitudes. Rev. Clough felt that he should not accept members into the church who came with pecuniary motives. Therefore, all appeals for baptism were denied during the fifteen months of famine, despite the genuine requests by true believers.[411] A well anticipated caution was issued for the genuine converts to be separate from those who seek baptism for mercenary motives.[412] Rev. Clough used the opportunity of taking part in the Colonial government's public works of gigantic nature and found a way to give employment for the starving people. The construction of the Buckingham Canal came handy, as it passed through the regions in Nellore and Ongole, where the Christians lived.[413] Rev. Clough took keen interest in the work on the Buckingham Canal as it would generate remunerative employment for the starving multitude. Rev. Clough offered his services to work in conjunction with the government officials whereby he agreed to provide bullock carts to transport eight thousand tons of rice from Burma to Cumbum.[414]

In addition, during an epidemic cholera in Ongole, Rev. Clough distributed ten thousand cholera pills among the natives.[415] With a determined conviction and cooperation from the native Christian converts, Rev. Clough decided to take active part in the canal work to seek benefit for the Christians.[416]

Pitching his tent at Razupalem, a few miles south of Kothapatnam from February 5, 1877 for a period of four months, he began to supervise the massive canal work.[417] The Buckingham canal stretched from the north of Madras to Bezwada.[418] The digging of the twelve feet deep canal began on February 24, 1877 with eight hundred coolies, both men and women, taking part.[419] An unexpected large company of coolies approached the camp seeking labour. The whole area looked like a Christian coolie camp.[420] Upon instructions from the Engineer in-charge for a larger work force, the numbers of coolie workforce was increased to three thousand. About half of those coolies were Christians, and the other non-Christian half presented an opportunity for preaching of the Gospel.[421] The workers at digging sites were entirely Madigas. Without discrimination based on caste all were given equal treatment based on Christian ideals, whether in catering of food, or distributing relief materials, or giving employment.[422] By August, 1877, nearly one hundred miles of canal digging work was completed which brought appreciation from the Chief engineer of that section, as is evident from his comments: "this portion of the canal is uniform and is the best on the whole line."[423]

An organization for distribution of money for famine relief was set up from the 'Mansion House Fund' of which enterprise Sir William Digby, Esq., was the leading spirit.[424] The severity of the famine forced the mission functionaries to temporarily abandon regular mission work; village schools were closed; preaching schedules were suspended and admission of baptisms did not take place since March, 1877. Rev. Clough firmly decided that, "so long as the famine lasted, no one would be received."[425] When the rains followed at the end of 1877, Rev. Clough was again faced with the demands by a multitude of seekers for baptism. Despite his repeated dissuasion, the multitudes from many villages persisted, requesting thus: "Baptize us! We all are going to die of hunger! Baptize us first!"[426] At this Rev. Clough relented and agreed to administer baptism. This group conversion event took place in a tamarind grove in Vellumpilly village on the banks of the Gundlakamma River. On a single day, 3rd July 1878, some 2,222 people converted receiving baptism (see discussion in Chapter 4).

vii) Accelerated Pace of Accessions

In June 1879, the Decennial Missionary Conference for South India and Ceylon was held in Bangalore where much deliberation was contemplated about the recent accessions to the Christian missions located in famine areas.[427] Dr. David Downie of the American Baptist Mission presented the informed facts relating to the American Baptist Mission in Telugu areas defending the missionary strategy of Rev. Clough. While pushing away the idea of inquisitorial investigation into the recent accessions in the American Baptist Mission, the Conference felt that the spiritual condition of the converts should be given utmost care and the missionaries ought to share the responsibility.[428] The remarkable work of evangelism in the Ongole field is evident from the number of conversions. In 1880, the number of baptisms was 2,757; during the first half of 1881, it was 1,669 and reached a total of 16,846.[429] With 600 villages under the influence of the American Baptist Mission, the strength of the mission in 1882 was ten American missionaries, forty six ordained native preachers, two hundred and forty nine un-ordained native preachers, two hundred theological students, 20,757 Church members and 53,000 estimated Christian adherents.[430] It may be noted that there were stimulus for conversion among the depressed castes elsewhere too: the leather workers in Northern India flocked into the fold of the Church after the example of the Madigas.[431]

viii) Extended Field of the American Baptist Mission

The American Baptist mission stations were extended to other places such as Allur, Atmakur, Udayagiri, Kavali, Kanigiri, Bapatla, Donakonda, Podili, Narsaraopet, Vinukonda, Sattenapalli, Gurajala, Cumbum, Markapur, Nandyala and Gadwal.[432] Rev. Clough arranged for a system of organizing churches on village lines wherein the village council or *Panchayat,* consisted of five men led the affairs of the village congregations. They were to meet Rev. Clough in quarterly conferences to discuss the progress and strengthening of the village churches.[433] Gradually changes in their social and cultural life began to take place. The converts decided to discard some of their un-Christian ancient customs and traditions and to adopt the new communal life on the basis of Christian teachings.[434]

The extent of the work was too large to be managed from one station and so a division of the mission field became necessary. The station of Cumbum was placed under Rev. W. B. Boggs, Vinukonda under Rev. G. N. Thomssen, Narsaraopet under Rev. R. Maplesden and Bapatla under Rev. E. Bullard.[435] In October, 1892, the Telugu mission received thirteen missionaries who had contributed for further expansion of the fields at Kandukur, Kanigiri, Podili and Markapur. Dr. and Mrs. Boggs successfully worked for the interests of the mission in the absence of Rev. Clough, assisted by staffs and helpers who were also filled with matching enthusiastic spirit.[436] Rev. D. K. Rayl and Mrs. Lily Johnson Rayl located themselves at Ongole and took active part in the maintenance of the English worship services.[437] Dr. Downie in Nellore was succeeded by Rev. J. F. Burditt in April, 1882 till October 1884. In December 1891, Prof. Lewis E. Martin took charge as the principal of the high school in Ongole.[438] Miss Emma Rauschenbusch, an appointee of the Woman's Society of the West, took charge of the boys' school and the responsibility for the Bible woman's work in 1893.[439]

In the predominantly CMS region of Bezwada, there had been a Baptist community of converts since 1904. This was because people migrated to Bezwada for livelihood from South Andhra areas of Ravipadu, Allur, Atmakur, Udayagiri, Kavali, Kanigiri, Bapatla, Donakonda, Podili, Narsaraopet, Vinukonda, Sattenapalli, Gurajala, Cumbum, Markapur, Nandyala and Gadwal.[440] In that year, Rev. S. Curtz established a church in the midst of "Ravipati Huts" and named it as Baptistpalem and made Rev. Jonnalagadda Nathaniel as pastor in-charge. In 1906, Rev. Velpula George and his wife did remarkable service in the same field.[441]

ix) The First Telugu Baptist Convention at Ramapatnam, 1897

In 1891, Dr. Ashmore, along with Rev. Henry C. Mabie, the Home Secretary of the Missionary Union visited the Telugu mission from where they had received a request from the Christians for two more missionaries for Nellore.[442] He also visited the students of the Ramapatnam Seminary and gave instructions, counsel and encouragement.[443] The need for a Telugu General Convention was planned in 1894. However, the actual event could take place only in 1897, at Ramapatnam. It was a huge gathering of enthusiastic native converts who had by then become partners in the mission for carrying the Gospel to their benighted fellow countrymen and women. At the end of 1905, the numerical strength of the mission stood at 96 missionaries, 1,477 Indian workers and 54,807 members in congregations.[444]

Since the year 1905, five regional associations were set up covering the whole area of the mission so that missionaries and converts could share and mutually exchange plans.[445] The leadership in church organizations was displayed by the new more mobile, educated young men.[446] The quality of leadership and organization at the Ongole station was such that, in the year 1908, the All-India Christian Endeavour Convention in which large number of delegates attended, was successfully held at Ongole under the supervision of Rev. James M. Baker.

Prominent among the delegates were Dr. W. Carey, the great grandson of Rev. Dr. William Carey who spoke at the Prayer Meeting Hill,[447] Rev. J. Heinrichs, Rev. John Newcomb, J. A. H. Curtis, C. R. Marsh, Rev. Alfred C. Fuller, Rev. James M Baker, F. Kurtz, Rev. F. P. Manley, Rev. Henry Huizinga, Rev. W.T Elmore, Rev. C. H. Brock, Rev. Arthur G Boggs, Ms. Gertrude Boggs, Rev. Thorlief Wathne, Ms. Helen Bailey, Dr. J.W. Stenger and Mrs. Alice Stenger (daughter of Dr. David Downie), Ms. Sigrid Johnson, Ms. Bertha Wathane, Ms. Amelia Dessa, Ms. Eva Gruen and Ms. Sarah Kelly, all of whom rendered valuable service in the villages, maintaining schools, medical work and promoting Christian life.

x) Strong Missionary Leadership

The vast mission field of the American Baptist mission had seen three leading missionaries for eighty years. The first was Rev. J. E. Clough, the '*Father of the Ongole Mass Movement*' who served actively from 1867 to 1895 in the Ongole field and adjoining towns and villages. The second was Rev James M. Baker, '*the touring missionary*,'[448] who as an itinerant missionary and an outstanding educationist built up the institutions of the Telugu Baptist church, till his retirement in 1931. The third one was Rev. Thorlief Wathane, who nurtured the Ongole church with efficient pastoral care from 1929 to 1953. He baptized 1,205 believers in 1932, the largest number since the time of the ingathering of 1878.[449] At the end of the year 1935, there were 110,000 Christians, 337 churches and 1,244 village schools conducted by the American Baptist Mission.[450] In 1939, the Ongole parish alone had consisted of 196 churches, with a membership of 71,953, having 246 schools and 8,910 pupils.[451] Despite war emergencies,[452] political agitations and reduced missionary personnel, the work of the American Baptist mission continued its service in education and medical care.

The American Baptist mission in Ongole had revolutionized missionary policies. It saw masses flocking to it in 'tumultuous tides'. It was suggested that its evangelistic methods should be emulated by all the missionaries in India.[453] The profile of and the level of social mobility achieved by the Christian converts in Ongole is evident in the following comment of Mrs. Clough: "Our Christians thus far have come, almost without exception, from the Malas and Madigas, the outcasts of the Telugu people. Comparatively few have to suffer persecution, when they turn to Christianity. On the contrary, they rise in social standing."[454] We shall discuss more on this theme in the coming chapters.

xi) Competent Native Preachers

The mission had facilitated the emergence of a body of competent native leaders from among the converts. The excellent group of trained native preachers and workers strived to spread the Gospel among their fellow caste men. Mention may be made chiefly of Yerraguntla Periah of Talakondapadu, Thota Joseph, Nelaprolu Paulus, Medikonduru Nathaniel and Bethala John, Baddepudy Abraham, Thaluri Daniel, Munangi Anumiah, Bezwada Paul, Kola Peddaiah, Tupili Rungaiah and Tupili Lutchmiah, Thomas Gabriel, Jonathan Burder, Pastor Karre Peter and Karre Samuel of Vuyyuru, S. Venkataswamy, M. Peter, K. Philemon, P. Joseph and M. Jagannaikulu, Das Antharvedy, Thomas Gabriel of Masulipatnam, Pidatala Periah, Bezwada Paul of Atmakur, Baddepudy Abraham, Thaluri Daniel, Rev. N. Kanakiah of Nellore, Munangi Anumiah, Kola Peddiah, Rev. Perivalli Abraham and others.

3.5.7 Self-management and Indianisation of the Church

We have discussed the unification attempts among the Episcopal and Non-Episcopal Churches and the final formation of the Church of South India in 1947. Similar attempts took place among the American Lutheran Churches too.

By the year 1930, several local conventions had been organized under the aegis of the Telugu Baptist Convention. The delegates passed a resolution to 'plan and work together.'[455] Between the years 1931-1950, several joint efforts were made which brought together different churches. Networking did take place among the 442 churches comprised of 140,172 members. In 1947, the Joint Evangelistic Committee organized a 'Crusade for Christ' program of the American Baptist Convention churches and distributed teaching materials to conduct Bible study classes.[456]

Parallel to the nationalist struggle for autonomy in the Indian political arena, there was growing enthusiasm for Indianisation and struggle for autonomy in the Church. While there was a clamour among the native missionaries for self-governance in the church, there was also a perception among the foreign missionaries that the Indian Christians had reached maturity and had the ability to handle their own affairs. At the same time the considered opinion of some members from both the sections was that native leaders were to be accorded a place of authority alongside the foreign missionaries as equals.[457] Functionally, both sections worked in collaboration with each other as each needed the other. For instance, in the new stations of Donakonda, Markapur and Kanigiri, local churches were organized in cooperation with the Regional associations which comprised mainly of native workers. However, the expenses related to the pastors and teachers, study courses, conduct of quarterly meetings, building churches, schools, orphanages, etc., the native missionary received help, especially financial help, from the foreign missionaries.

The missionaries understood the political undercurrents among the nationalists as well as among the Indian Christians and saw that their role in relation to the Indian Church was to step aside and leave the initiative, leadership and the direction of Christian work in the hands of the Indian Christians.[458]

3.6 An Overview of the Missionary Methods

The missionary work in Andhra was informed by evangelistic vision of a new society based on Christian values, which was shared by all the above-mentioned missionary societies, though there might have been variations in their approach, perception of the ground realities and methods. Overall, all of them engaged in preaching, teaching of the Bible, and making Christian communities. The package of mission work consisted of not only building churches and chapels for worship, but also opening educational institutions, hostels, training institutes, medical centres, and doing humanitarian works such as relief work, food for work, etc. The end result was spiritual and material upliftment of the people, particularly the most marginalized sections of society, namely the Malas and the Madigas. What we have noticed is a gradual transfer of leadership from foreign personnel to native Christian leaders.[459] In this section, I shall elucidate the main method of mission work in coastal Andhra, during the period of our study.

i) Street Preaching

In the beginning, teaching of the Gospel was constrained due to lack of familiarity of the local language, among the foreign missionaries. Nevertheless, they trained themselves in the local language so that they could effectively communicate the Gospel message. The means of disseminating the essence of the Gospel was many folded that ranged from bazaar preaching to gatherings in chapels, halls and school buildings. Preaching to the crowds in bazaars and streets often attracted and gathered enthusiastic audiences as it had happened in the case of Rev. Sharkey of Masulipatnam and Rev. T.Y. Darling of Bezwada. During *melas* (religious festivals) where thousands gathered, the missionary usually found a chance to preach to the people with the help of his native assistants. During village visits, it was customary to put a tent on the outskirts of the village for a day or two or locate themselves in a village for a particular period to cover many villages. While preaching after dark in the open air, the lantern was used where a sheet is hung between two trees thus making a stereopticon of the missionary and permitted him to make himself heard and people remained silent for hours listening to the connected story.[460]

ii) Dissemination of the Bible Message

The missionaries of the LMS chose the method of visiting populous villages thrice a week by rotation. After reading a portion of the scriptures, conversation was conducted in Telugu. The missionaries also found that in several villages, few persons besides the *Brāhmins* were able to read or willing to learn though they were given copies of the New Testament and Gospel tracts.[461] As a first step, a catechist was sent to a village to prepare the people and also to gather information about them and understand the level of their interest in the Gospel. In some cases the missionaries were invited by the village elders.[462] Then the missionary would go to the village to preach the Gospel.

After a few years, the missionaries found that street preaching was not a viable option and started to rely on educational work. Invariably, most students in mission schools would have learnt about the Bible, or received instruction on Christian faith, tenets and teachings.[463] The missionaries' pastoral work among the Malas and the Madigas consisted of instruction for baptism and confirmation, conducting worship and administering Holy Communion to the baptized converts. Besides, they also undertook the task of preparing and printing vernacular Christian literature, production of hymn books in local language.[464]

Centralised work from a mission station became increasingly difficult as the mission territory expanded and the number of converts increased. So they divided the mission field into districts for better organization. In each the district, they deputed a preacher and an assistant.

iii) The Role of Bible Men and Women

The missionaries sought active cooperation from the native pastors, evangelists, Bible women, musicians and drummers from the Mala and Madiga castes. The Bible women played an important role in organizing societies such as the *Women's Help Meet Society* at the meeting of the Kolair Association in 1898. As very few women could read, the work of the Bible women was to fill the minds of women with scripture passages and sang beautiful hymns.[465] Many western hymns were translated into Telugu and Telugu Christian hymns were written by native converts under standard linguistic expressions which were used in chapels and boarding schools.[466] Mission documents have noted the case of the Bodagunta women onion peddlers who went on preaching the Gospel by singing hymns and telling the story of Christ.[467]

3.7 Conclusion

In the beginning, the missionaries had earnestly wanted to convert caste Hindus for two reasons: to bring the prosperous caste people into the Christian faith and to elicit their support in mission work. At the same time, they were convinced that they would work among the poor, who were generally of 'low' castes. Indeed, they experienced that few among the caste Hindus converted, whereas a large majority of the poor castes, particularly the Malas and the Madigas welcomed the message of redemption and liberation.[468] They also realized that caste, more than religious faith and traditions, hindered the higher castes to convert. Caste being a perennial socio-religious structure with its tenacious hold over the everyday life of the people, continues to define the social and ritual status of a person even today. History has shown that caste distinction and discrimination continues to remain even when they changed religion.

The experience of the missionaries in Andhra was not different. Though the missionaries did not accept caste-based status ascriptions, the converts, hailing from different castes as they were, continued to maintain caste distinctions in the church. Often, the pattern of conversion was also guided by caste considerations. It was observed that: "When Christianity first enters a place, should those who first embrace it be of the Mala caste, others still lower will join, but should the first converts be the Madigas, the Malas keep themselves aloof from that church.[469] So also do the higher castes. Thus, the experience of the missionaries in Andhra concurs with that of other places in India and elsewhere: conversion always took place on kin, family, clan or community or caste lines. If one member of a particular caste community converts, others in the same caste would easily follow into that church. But if there are converts from among other castes which are traditionally higher or lower, they would be wary of converting into that church, perhaps they may choose a different church.

Overall, the progress of Christianity was remarkable in colonial Andhra region. For example, in the Guntur district, there were 153,510 Christians in 1921 that increased to 237,772 in 1931.[470] The increase of Christianity in the "East Coast North", i.e. the five districts of the present study, was a continuous gain where the people who followed the Christian faith had increased at a rate above the population growth with relative disparities (see Chapter 4).[471] Guntur had the distinction of being the '*Most Christian District*', replacing Tinnevelly (in Tamil Nadu) from its predominant position.[472] The American Evangelical Lutheran Mission reported a leap in number of baptisms to over 300 percent between the year 1870 and 1880 and 168 percent of the mission's share of the Christian population.[473] The Lutheran mission drew its members mainly from the Mala caste and it was believed that whole of the Mala population would come into the fold of the Church within thirty years.[474] The missionaries believed that though the progress of Christianity had always been fruitful among the Depressed Castes, it was also embraced by the other Hindu castes since 1920s in the Kistna district.[475]

Thus, the movement towards Christianity from the Depressed Castes could be marked as an evangelical success both in the history of the Christian missions as well as in the history of Indian Christianity.[476] In the year 1950, after 135 years of missionary work, ten million Christians were present in the country and Christians had formed four percent of the population of the Andhra state.

In conclusion, we can say that the vast network of the Christian missionaries in colonial Andhra became a prominent feature of the social setting in coastal Andhra where they undertook the role of *'agents of change'*. The socially reconstructive role played by the missionaries in the growth of social consciousness among the Malas and the Madigas and their subsequent social upliftment is dealt in the ensuing chapters.

Endnotes and References

1 Edward Lawrence, *Modern Missions in the East: Their Methods, Successes and Limitations* (New York: Harper Brothers Publishers, 1895), 35.

2 Y. Antony Raj, 2001, *Social Impact of Conversion: A Comparative Sociological Study on the Christians of Scheduled Caste Origin and Scheduled Caste Hindus* (Delhi: ISPCK, 2001), 38.

3 Hanugundla Solomon, *Structures of the Church in Andhra Pradesh: An Historico-Juridical Study* (Secunderabad: Karuna Sri Printers, 1997), 33.

4 Antony Raj, op. cit., 39, quoting Ibid., 44.

5 The term *Carnatic Mission* indicates the French Jesuit Mission territory from north of Pondichery covering the Royalaseema region of south and south west Andhra Pradesh. The Mission was founded in 1700 and ended with the suppression of the Society of Jesus in 1773. By then, the Mission had some 40,000 converts from different castes, particularly Kamma and Reddy castes. For details see, Fr. S. Joe Sebastian, S. J., *The Jesuit Carnatic Mission: A Foundation of Andhra Church,* (Secunderabad, Andhra Jesuit Province Society, 2004), 3-11.

6 Antony Raj, op. cit., 39; K. E., Rajprakukh, *Dalit Christians of Andhra: Under the Impact of Missionaries* (New Delhi: Serials Publications, 2008), 32.

7 M. E. Prabhakar, "Caste-class and Status in Andhra Churches and Implications for Mission Today: Some Reflections," *Religion and Society* XXVIII (3): 17.

8 Stephen Neill, *A History of Christianity in India: 1707-1858 (*Cambridge: Cambridge University Press, 1984), 274; Also Penny Frank, *The Church in Madras: The History of the Ecclesiastical and Missionary Action of the East India Company in the Presidency of Madras from 1805 to 1835* (London: John Murray Publishers, 1912), 69.

9 Manasseh Pasupuleti, *A Historical Overview of Christianity in the Telugu States and its Impact on Telugu Language, Literature & Culture* (Hyderabad: Andhra Christian Theological College, 2015; for a history see, Rev. R. C. Paul, *History of the Telugu Christians* (Madras: Good Pastor Press, 1929); A Father, *History of the Telugu Christians* (Trichinopoly: St. Joseph's Industrial School Press, 1910).

10 K. E. Rajprakukh, op. cit., 30.

11 John Rutherford, *Missionary Pioneers in India* (Edinburgh: Andrew Elliot Press, 1896), 5.

12 In Ziegenbalg's own words. John Rutherford, Ibid.

13 John Rutherford, op. cit., 15.

14 Ibid., 32.

15 Eugene Stock, *The Romance of Missions: Beginnings in India* (London: The Society for Promoting Christian Knowledge, 1917), 6.

16 Fleming Stevenson, *The Dawn of the Modern Mission* (Edinburgh: A.C. Armstrong, 1888), 153.

17 John Rutherford, op. cit., 34.

18 Fleming Stevenson, op. cit., 38.

19 Ibid., 52.

20 James Hough, *The History of Christianity in India: From the Commencement of the Christian Era, 1706-1816*, Vol. I (London: Seeley Burnside, 1845), 644.

21 Ibid., 165.

22 John Rutherford, op. cit., 99.

23 Ibid., 107.

24 Ibid., 103.

25 A. Thomson, *Great Missionaries: A Series of Biographies* (London: T. Nelson and Sons Publishers, 1870), 251.

26 M. A. Sherring, *The History of Protestant Missions in India from their Commencement in 1706 to 1881 (*London: The Religious Tract Society, 1884), 32.

27 John Rutherford, op. cit., 108.

28 Ibid., 107.

29 Anthony Copley, *Religion in Conflict: Ideology, Cultural contact and Conversion in Late Colonial India* (Oxford: Oxford University Press, 1997), 37.

30 Eugene Stock, *The History of the Church Missionary Society: Its Environment, Its Men and Its Work*, (hereinafter, *The History of the Church Missionary Society),* Vol. I (London: The C.M.S Publications, 1899), 55.

31 Henry Morris, *Charles Grant: Director of the East India Company and Member of Parliament* (Madras: M. E. Publishing House, n. d), 29.

32 Penny Frank, op. cit., 22.

33 James Hough, op. cit., Vol. I, 192.

34 Ibid., 193.

35 Penny Frank, op. cit., 22.

36 Henry Morris, *A Descriptive and Historical Account of the Godavery District in the Presidency of Madras*, 38. Also George Smith, *The 'Conversion of India from Pantaenus to the Present Time, A.D. 193-1893 (*New York: Young Peoples Missionary Movement, 1903), 108.

37 Eugene Stock, *The History of the Church Missionary Society, Vol. I, op. cit.,* 55.

38 *The Imperial Gazetteer of India*: *The Indian Empire, Descriptive,* Vol. I (Oxford: Clarendon Press, 1909), 445.

39 Paul D. Wiebe, *Christians in Andhra Pradesh: The Mennonites of Mahbubnagar* (Bangalore: The Christian Literature Society, 1988), 14.

40 M. A. Laird, *Missionaries and Education in Bengal 1793-1837* (Oxford: Clarendon Press, 1972), 36.

41 Penny Frank, op. cit., 600.

42 James Hough, *The History of Christianity in India:* op. cit., Vol. I, 36.

43 Ibid., 257.

44 Ibid., 258.

45 Ibid., 258.

46 Ibid., 36 and 263.

47 James Hough, op. cit., Vol. II (London: Nisbet Publishers, 1845), 267.

48 Ibid., 270.

49 Ibid., 272.

50 Richard Lovett, *The History of the London Missionary Society 1795-1895*, Vol. II (Oxford: Oxford University Press, 1899), 38.

51 Ibid., 55.

52 Ibid., 56.

53 James Hough, op. cit., Vol. II, 504; Also, George Cousins (ed.), *The Chronicle of the London Missionaries Society for the year 1890* (London: The Directors of London Missionaries Society, 1891), 60.

54 James Hough, op. cit., Vol. I, 504.

55 David Downie, *The Lone Star: The History of the Telugu Mission of the American Baptist Missionaries Union (1838-1927)* (Philadelphia: The American Baptist Publication, 1892), 26.

56 Richard Lovett, op. cit., 39.

57 J. Mangamma, *Andhra Desamulo Kraisthava Missioanrila Seva* (Hyderabad: Telugu Academy Publishers, 1992), 26.

58 Richard Lovett, op. cit., 334.

59 M. A. Sherring, op. cit., 422.

60 Ibid., 131.

61 Ibid.

62 Richard Lovett, op. cit., 138.

63 Ibid., 133.

64 *Manual of the Administration of the Madras Presidency*, Vol. I (Madras: The Government Press, 1885), 140.

65 Richard Lovett, op. cit., 141.

66 Norman Goodall, *A History of London Missionary Society* (Oxford: Oxford University Press, 1954), 18.

67 Mary S. McLaurin, *25 Years on: 1924-1949* (Toronto: The Canadian Baptist Foreign Mission Board, 1950), 46.

68 John Rutherford, op. cit., 114.

69 Ibid., 126.

70 Ibid., 120.

71 Amos Sutton, *Orissa and its Evangelization: Interspersed with Suggestions Respecting the More Efficient Conducting of Indian Missions* (Boston: William Heath Publishers, 1850), 301.

72 *Manual of the Administration of the Madras Presidency*, Vol. I, op. cit., 140.

73 M. L. Orchard, *Canadian Baptists at Work in India* (Toronto: Missionary Education Department of the Foreign Mission Board, 1922), 31.

74 M. L. Orchard and K. S. McLaurin, *The Enterprise: The Jubilee Story of the Canadian Baptist Mission in India: 1874-1924* (Toronto: The Canadian Baptist Foreign Mission Board, 1925), 11.

75 Ibid., 16.

76 Ibid., 135.

77 Ibid., 32.

78 Ibid., 32.

79 Ibid., 167.

80 Ibid., 176.

81 Ibid.

82 Ibid., 177.

83 *Report of the Canadian Baptist Telugu Missions,* January 12-16, 1900 (Madras: M.E. Publishing House, 1900), 18.

84 M. A. Sherring, op. cit., 418.

85 John Craig, *Forty Years among the Telugus: A History of the Mission of the Baptists of Ontario and Quebec, Canada to the Telugus, South India 1867-1907* (hereafter, *Forty Years among the Telugus*) (Toronto: The Canadian Baptist Foreign Mission Board, 1908), 76.

86 Ibid., 34.

87 M. L. Orchard and K. S. McLaurin, op. cit., 205.

88 Ibid., 222. Also see John Craig, op. cit., 173.

89 The word *Zenana* is of Persian origin—*Zan* means a woman and usually means the apartment or group of apartments where the women of the household live. Irene H. Barnes, *Behind the Purdah: The Story of C.E.Z.M.S Work in India* (New York: Thomas Y. Crowell Company, 1897), 41.

90 Irene H. Barnes, Ibid., 219.

91 M. L. Orchard and K. S. McLaurin, op. cit., 330.

92 Ibid., 115.

93 Ibid., 59.

94 Ibid., 113.

95 *Report of the Canadian Baptist Telugu Missions,* January 12-16, 1900, op. cit., 63.

96 Ibid., 65.

97 Ibid., 73-74.

98 M. L. Orchard and K. S. McLaurin, op. cit., 71.

99 *Report of the Canadian Baptist Telugu Missions,* January 12-16, 1900, op. cit., 80.

100 M. L. Orchard and K. S. McLaurin, op. cit., 24.

101 Ibid., 175.

102 Ibid., 256.

103 Ibid., 206.

104 Ibid.

105 John Craig, J. R. Stillwell, I. C. Archibald and A. E. Baskerville, *Telugu Trophies: The Jubilee Story of Some of the Principal Telugu Converts in the Canadian Baptist Foreign Mission in India from 1874 to 1924* (Toronto: The Canadian Baptist Publication Society, NY), 139.

106 M. L. Orchard and K. S. McLaurin, op. cit., 220.

107 John Craig, *Forty Years among the Telugus,* op. cit., 74.

108 Ibid., 71.

109 *Report of the Canadian Baptist Telugu Missions,* January 12-16, 1900, op. cit., 40.

110 M. L. Orchard and K. S. McLaurin, op. cit., 97.

111 Ibid., 137.

112 Pathuri Joseph, *Bharatiya Baptist Prarambha Charitra Parishodhana* (Ohio: Transworld Ministries, 2005), 85.

113 M. L. Orchard and K. S. McLaurin, op. cit., 265.

114 Ibid., 232.

115 Ibid., 263.

116 John Craig, *Forty Years among the Telugus,* op. cit., 128.

117 John Craig, J. R. Stillwell, I. C. Archibald and A. E. Baskerville, op. cit., 160.

118 John Craig, *Forty Years among the Telugus,* op. cit., 115.

119 Olive Rogers, *The Origins of the Godavery Delta Mission and Its Distinctive Tenets* (Secunderabad: Andhra Christian Theological College, 1980), 5. Also Tracy G. Gipson, "Anthony Norris Groves and the Godavery Delta Mission," *The Indian Church History Review (*1984), 60.

120 George Smith, *Life of Alexander Duff,* Vol. I (New York: A. C. Armstrong and Sons Publications, 1879), 266.

121 Tracy G .Gipson, op. cit., 58.

122 Robert Bernard Dann, "The Legacy of Anthony Norris Groves," *The International Bulletin of Missionary Research* 29 (4), (2005): 199.

123 Lady Hope Elizabeth Reid Cotton, *General Sir Arthur Cotton R .E .K.C.S.I: His Life and Work* (London: Hodder Stoughton, 1900), 578.

124 Harriet Groves, *Memoir of Anthony Norris Groves: Compiled Chiefly from His Journals and Letters*, Third Edition (Bristol: James Nisbet and Co, 1869), 551-552.

125 Ibid., 426.

126 Olive Rogers, op. cit., 150.

127 Harriet Groves, op. cit., 644.

128 Kenneth Scott Latourette, *History of the Expansion of Christianity*, Vol. VI (New York: Harper and Brothers Publishers, 1938), 66.

129 John Craig, J. R. Stillwell, I. C. Archibald and A. E. Baskerville, op. cit., 8.

130 Harriet Groves, op. cit., 644.

131 M. A. Sherring, op. cit., 417.

132 M. Moses, *Andhra Pradesh Kraisthava Sangha Charitra* (Tenali: Kraisthava Satya Grandhasala, 2004), 128.

133 Martin L. Dolbeer, *A History of Lutheranism in Andhra Desa: The Telugu Territory of India* (New York: Board of Foreign Missions, 1959), 39.

134 Sir Arthur Cotton, *The Madras Famine with Appendix Containing a Letter from Ms. Florence Nightingale and Other Papers* (London: Marshall Simpkin and Co Stationers, ND), 153.

135 Harriet Groves, op. cit., 648.

136 M. Moses, op. cit., 128.

137 Harriet Groves, op. cit., 645.

138 Ibid., 646.

139 *Church Missionary Intelligencer: A Monthly Journal of Missionary Information* (London: James Nisbet and Co Publishers, 1860), 4.

140 M. Moses, op. cit., 108.

141 Ibid., 28.

142 Penny Frank, op. cit., 350.

143 Ibid., 689.

144 Eugene Stock, *The History of the Church Missionary Society,* Vol. I, op. cit., 64.

145 Penny Frank, op. cit., 689.

146 In later years between 1794-95, the 4th battalion moved from Ellore to Masulipatnam: see Penny Frank, op. cit., 415.

147 Penny Frank, Ibid., 682.

148 *Home and Ecclesiastical Proceedings,* No 13-18 (Calcutta: April 1, 1871).

149 Eugene Stock, *The History of the Church Missionary Society,* Vol. I, op. cit., 201.

150 Ibid., 299.

151 John William Kaye, *Christianity in India: An Historical Narrative* (London: Smith Elder and Co, 1859), 521.

152 Frederik Gledstone, *Andhra Christian Church Founders :John Goldingham, Collector of Kistna* (Madras: Diocesan Press, 1940), 2.

153 The members were: Mr. James Hough, the former Tinnevelly Chaplain, Mr. Joseph Fenn, the former Travancore missionary and Mr. J M Strachan, the former Madras Treasurer. See Eugene Stock, *The History of the Church Missionary Society,* Vol. I, op. cit., 327.

154 Eugene Stock, Ibid., 376.

155 Ibid., 327-328.

156 Frederik Gledstone, *Andhra Christian Church Founders*: *Robert Turlington Noble* (Madras: Diocesan Press, 1941), 6.

157 Eugene Stock, *The Romance of Missions: Beginnings in India,* op. cit., 102.

158 Ibid., 43.

159 M. E. Gibbs, *The Anglican Church in India* (Delhi: ISPCK Publishers, 1972), 153.

160 Eugene Stock, *The History of the Church Missionary Society,* Vol. II (London: The C.M.S Publications, 1899), 179.

161 Frederik Gledstone, *Andhra Christian Church Founders*: *Robert Turlington Noble,* op. cit., 10.

162 Eugene Stock, *The History of the Church Missionary Society,* Vol. II, op. cit., 531.

163 Frederik Gledstone, *Andhra Christian Church Founders*: *Robert Turlington Noble,* op. cit., 10.

164 *The Church Missionary Atlas: Containing an Account of the various Countries in which the Church Missionary Society Labours and of its Missionary Operations* (London: Seeley Jackson and Halliday Publishers, 1879), 103.

165 Frederik Gledstone, *Andhra Christian Church Founders*: *Henry Watson Fox (*Madras: Diocesan Press, 1941), 9.

166 Ibid., 4.

167 Eugene Stock, *The History of the Church Missionary Society,* Vol. IV (London: The C.M.S Publications, 1899), 24.

168 Ibid., 12. Also B. E. Devaraj, *Bharatadesa Kraisthava Sangha Charitra,* Andhra Christian Theological Literature Council (Tenali: A.S.R. Power Press, 1969), 139.

169 M. E. Gibbs, op. cit., 152.

170 Frederik Gledstone, *Andhra Christian Church Founders*: *Sharkey Jeevitha Charitra* (Madras: Diocesan Press, 1941), 2.

171 Gerald H. Anderson, *Biographical Dictionary of Christian Missions* (Grand Rapids, Michigan: W. B. Eerdmans Publishing Company, 1999), 614.

172 M. Moses, op. cit., 36.

173 Frederik Gledstone, *Andhra Christian Church Founders*: *Sharkey Jeevitha Charitra*, op. cit., 7.

174 Ibid., 7.

175 John Noble, *A Memoir of the Rev. Robert Andhra Pradesh Kraisthava Sangha Charitra Turlington Noble: Missionaries to the Telugu People in South India* (London: Seeley Jackson and Halliday Publishers, 1867), 260.

176 Eugene Stock, The History of the Church Missionary Society, Vol. IV, op. cit., 241.

177 John E. Clough, *Social Christianity in the Orient: The Story of A Man, A Mission and A Movement* (New York: The MacMillan Company, 1914), 95.

178 M. Moses, op. cit., 36.

179 Eugene Stock, The History of the Church Missionary Society, Vol. II, op. cit., 469.

180 Gujjarlamudi Krupachary, Telugu Sahityaniki Kristavula Seva (Guntur: Navodaya Publishers, 1988), 43.

181 Eugene Stock, The History of the Church Missionary Society, Vol. II, op. cit., 178.

182 Frederik Gledstone, Andhra Christian Church Founders: Robert Turlington Noble, op. cit., 9.

183 M. Moses, op. cit., 35.

184 Frederik Gledstone, Andhra Christian Church Founders: Robert Turlington Noble, op. cit., 5.

185 Gerald, H. Anderson, op. cit., 169. Also in Gijjarlamudi Krupachary, op. cit., 43.

186 B. E. Devaraj, op. cit., 143-144.

187 Eugene Stock, *The History of the Church Missionary Society,* Vol. II, op. cit., 420.

188 Ibid., 420.

189 *The Church Missionary Atlas*, *op. cit., 104.*

190 Eugene Stock, *The History of the Church Missionary Society,* Vol. III, op. cit., 165-167.

191 Eugene Stock, *The History of the Church Missionary Society,* Vol. IV, op. cit., 241.

192 *The Imperial Gazetteer of India*, Vol. 16 (Oxford: Clarendon Press, 1909), 246.

193 Eugene Stock, *The History of the Church Missionary Society,* Vol. II, op. cit., 545-546.

194 Ibid., 545-546.

195 Eugene Stock, *The History of the Church Missionary Society,* Vol. IV, op. cit., 241.

196 *The Church of South India, Krishna Godavari Diocese* (2010), 41.

197 Eugene Stock, *The History of the Church Missionary Society,* Vol. III, op. cit., 165.

198 Ibid., Vol. IV, 241.

199 Ibid., Vol. III, 166.

200 Ibid.

201 Ibid.

202 Ibid., 478.

203 Personal Testimony of Smt. V. Saramma (1903-1998) from Khammamett.

204 Eugene Stock, *The History of the Church Missionary Society,* Vol. II, op. cit., 522.

205 Eugene Stock, *History of the Church Missionary Society,* Vol. III, op. cit., 165-167.

206 Ibid., 166.

207 Gordon Mackenzie, *A Manual of the Kistna District in the Presidency of Madras*, op. cit., 291.

208 S. Venkateswaran, *Census of India*, 1951, Vol. III, Madras and Coorg, Part II B, Tables (Madras: The Government Press,1953), 145.

209 Eugene Stock, *History of the Church Missionary Society,* Vol. III, op. cit., 761.

210 Susan Billington Harper, "The Dornakal Church on the Cultural Frontier" in Christians, *Cultural Interactions and India's Religious Traditions,* (eds.) Judith M. Brown and Robert Eric Frykenberg (Grand Rapids, Michigan: William B. Eerdmans, 2002), 193.

211 Eugene Stock, *The History of the Church Missionary Society,* Vol. IV, op. cit., 241.

212 Ibid., Vol. III, 459.

213 G. Daivasirvadam, "Dhanyajeevi Canon Dhanwada Anantam," in *The Church of South India* (Machilipatnam: The Krishna Godavari Diocese, 2010), 50-51.

214 Eugene Stock, *The History of the Church Missionary Society,* Vol. III, op. cit., 242.

215 Ibid., 47.

216 Ibid., 680.

217 Ibid.

218 Cecil John Grimes, *Towards an Indian Church: The Growth of the Church of India in Constitution and Life* (London: SPCK, 1946), 262.

219 W. R Cornish, *Census of the Madras Presidency*, 51-1871: Containing the Census arranged in Standard form prescribed by the Government of India, Vol. I, Appendix Tables (Madras: The Government Gazette Press, 1874), 102.

220 H. A. Stuart, *Census of India,* 1891, The Report, Vol. XIII (Madras: The Government Press, 1893), 69.

221 *The Imperial Gazetteer of India,* Vol. 12 (Oxford: Clarendon Press, 1909), 324.

222 *Ibid.,* 76.

223 Eugene Stock, *The History of the Church Missionary Society,* Vol. IV, op. cit., 242.

224 Martin L. Dolbeer, op. cit., 50.

225 World Missionary Conference, *Report of Commission 1: Carrying the Gospel to all the Non-Christian World* (Edinburgh: Oliphant Anderson and Ferrier Publishers, 1910), 160.

226 Harlan P. Beach, *The Findings of the Continuation Committee Conferences held in Asia, 1912-1913* (New York: Student Volunteer Movement for Foreign Missions, 1913), 306-7.

227 Ibid., 7.

228 M. E. Gibbs, op. cit., 342.

229 Cecil John Grimes, op. cit., 262.

230 Eyre Chatterton, *A History of the Church of England in India Since the Early Days of the East India Company* (London: Project Canterbury, SPCK, 1924), NP.

231 Eugene Stock, *The History of the Church Missionary Society,* Vol. IV, op. cit., 244.

232 Brian Stanley (ed), *Missions, Nationalism and the End of the Empire* (Grand Rapids, Michigan: William B. Erdman Publishers, 2003), 21.

233 Susan Alexander, *The Attitudes of British Protestant Missionaries Towards Nationalism in India: With Special Reference to Madras Presidency, 1919-1927* (New Delhi: Konark Publishers, 1994), 9.

234 M. L. Orchard and K. S. McLaurin, op. cit., 345-347.

235 *Proceedings of the Tenth Meeting of the National Christian Council of India, Burma and Ceylon* (Mysore: Wesley Press, 1946), 51.

236 Kaj Baago, *A History of the National Christian Council of India 1914-1964* (Mysore: Wesley Press, 1965), 20.

237 Ibid., 21.

238 Ibid., 28.

239 Ibid., 4.

240 Harlan P Beach, op. cit., 105.

241 Cecil John Grimes, op. cit., 143.

242 *Proceedings of the Tenth Meeting of the National Christian Council of India, Burma and Ceylon,* op. cit, 9-10.

243 Ibid., 44.

244 Susan Billington Harper, *In the Shadow of the Mahatma: Bishop V.S. Azariah and the Travails of Christianity in British in India* (hereinafter, *In the Shadow of the Mahatma:)* (Surrey: Curzon Press, 2000), 213.

245 Ibid., 215.

246 *The Report of the Church Missionary Society*, 1937-38, op. cit., 35.

247 *Annual Report of the Committee of the Church Missionary Society for Africa and the East, 1947-48* (London: The C.M. S Publications, 1948), 41.

248 Gujjarlamudi Krupachary, op. cit., 44.

249 *Proceedings of the National Christian Council Review*, Vol. XVIII, 1940 (Mysore: Wesley Press, 1941), 75.

250 Susan Billington Harper, *In the Shadow of the Mahatma:* op. cit., 359.

251 J. I. Packer, *The Church of South India and Reunion in England, Conference of Evangelical Churchmen* (Oxford: Church Book Room Press, 1968), 249.

252 L. B. Wolf, "Lutheran Missions and Missionaries before Carey: From 1555 to 1800" in *Missionary Heroes of the Lutheran Church, (ed.)* L. B. Wolf (Philadelphia: The Lutheran Publication Society, 1911), 3.

253 W. G. Polack, *Into All the World: The Story of Lutheran Foreign Missions* (St. Louis, Missouri: Concordia Seminary, 1930), 64.

254 Ibid., 109.

255 During the early decades of the nineteenth century the activities of the Lutheran Church in North America were confined to two bodies, namely, the Ministerium of Pennsylvania and the General Synod: Ibid., 111; Also see George Drach and Calvin F. Kuder, *Telugu Mission of the General Council of the Evangelical Lutheran Church in North America Containing a Biography of the Rev. Christian Frederick Heyer* (Philadelphia: General Council Publication House, 1914), 12.

256 L. B. Wolf, *After Fifty Years: or an Historical Sketch of the Guntur Mission of the Evangelical Lutheran Church of the General Synod in the United States of America* (hereafter, *After Fifty Years*) (Philadelphia: The Lutheran Publication Society, 1896), 87.

257 George Drach and Calvin F Kuder, op. cit., 52.

258 L. B. Wolf, "Christian Frederick Heyer" in *Missionary Heroes of the Lutheran Church*, (ed), L. B. Wolf, op. cit., 114.

259 J. Mangamma, op. cit., 36.

260 George Drach and Calvin F Kuder, op. cit., 123.

261 Ibid., 54.

262 L. B. Wolf, "Christian Frederick Heyer", op. cit., 105.

263 George Drach and Calvin F Kuder, op. cit., 53.

264 Augusta Highland, *India* (Rock Island, IL: Lutheran Augustana Synod Centennial Committee, ND), 15.

265 Ibid., 63.

266 George Drach and Calvin F. Kuder, op. cit., 77.

267 Ibid., 82.

268 Ibid., 65.

269 L. B. Wolf, *After Fifty Years,* op. cit., 254.

270 George Drach and Calvin F. Kuder, op. cit., 79.

271 Ibid., 83, 86 and 113.

272 Ibid., 86.

273 L. B. Wolf, *After Fifty Years,* op. cit., 115.

274 George Drach and Calvin F. Kuder, op. cit., 145.

275 Ibid., 145.

276 Ibid., 123.

277 L. B. Wolf, *After Fifty Years,* op. cit., 122.

278 W. G. Polack, op. cit., 114.

279 L. B. Wolf, *After Fifty Years,* op. cit., 102.

280 George Drach and Calvin F Kuder, op. cit., 127.

281 L. B. Wolf (ed), *Missionary Heroes of the Lutheran Church (*Philadelphia: The Lutheran Publication Society, 1911), 187.

282 Ibid., 135.

283 Ibid., 188.

284 L. B. Wolf, *After Fifty Years,* op. cit., 156.

285 Ibid., 153.

286 Ibid.

287 L. B. Wolf (ed), *Missionary Heroes of the Lutheran Church*, op. cit., 79.

288 L. B. Wolf, *After Fifty Years,* op. cit., 128.

289 L. B. Wolf (ed), *Missionary Heroes of the Lutheran Church*, op. cit., 154.

290 Ibid., 157.

291 Ibid., 158.

292 Ibid., 166.

293 L. B. Wolf, *After Fifty Years,* op. cit., 218.

294 Ibid., 131.

295 George Drach and Calvin F. Kuder, op. cit., 80.

296 The first station was at Ellore. George Drach and Calvin F Kuder, op. cit., 83 and 86.

297 Ibid., 86.

298 Ibid.

299 Ibid., 90- 91.

300 L. B. Wolf, *After Fifty Years,* op. cit., 83 and 86.

301 George Drach and Calvin F. Kuder, op. cit., 124.

302 L. B. Wolf, *After Fifty Years,* op. cit., 117.

303 George Drach and Calvin F. Kuder, op. cit., 101.

304 L. B. Wolf, *After Fifty Years,* op. cit., 76.

305 Ibid.

306 George Drach and Calvin F. Kuder, op. cit., 126.

307 Ibid., 130.

308 Ibid., 120.

309 Ibid., 105.

310 Ibid., 106.

311 Ibid., 105.

312 M. A. Sherring, op. cit., 414.

313 W. G. Polack, op. cit., 115.

314 George Drach and Calvin F. Kuder, op. cit., 178.

315 Ibid., 141.

316 Ibid.

317 Ibid., 162.

318 Ibid., 152.

319 Ibid., 170.

320 Julia M. Harpster, *Among the Telugoos: Illustrating Mission Work in India* (Philadelphia: Lutheran Publication Society, 1902), 16.

321 Ibid., 20.

322 George Drach and Calvin F. Kuder, op. cit., 197.

323 Ibid., 201.

324 Ibid., 200.

325 Ibid., 205.

326 M. A. Sherring, op. cit., 415.

327 L. B. Wolf, *After Fifty Years,* op. cit., 276.

328 George Drach and Calvin F. Kuder, op. cit., 162.

329 Ibid., 208.

330 H. H. Risley, *Census of India*, 1901, Vol. I, Part I, Report (Calcutta: The Government Press, 1903), 387.

331 Julia M Harpster, op. cit., 22.

332 L. B. Wolf, *After Fifty Years,* op. cit., 303.

333 Augusta Highland, op. cit., 28.

334 Ibid., 227.

335 Ibid., 284.

336 L. B. Wolf (ed), *Missionary Heroes of the Lutheran Church*, op. cit., 182. Also, L. B. Wolf, *After Fifty Years,* op. cit., 137.

337 L. B. Wolf (ed), *Missionary Heroes of the Lutheran Church*, op. cit., 186.

338 L. B. Wolf, *After Fifty Years,* op. cit., 46.

339 Augusta Highland, op. cit., 14.

340 M. Moses, op. cit., 55.

341 C. H. Swavely (ed), *The Lutheran Enterprise in India* (Madras: Federation of Evangelical Lutheran Churches in India, 1952), 229.

342 Augusta Highland, op. cit., 14.

343 C. H. Swavely (ed), op. cit., 20.

344 Ibid., 15.

345 Augusta Highland, op. cit., 20.

346 Interview held on 14/07/2012 with Prof. Sunil Bhanu, President of The Andhra Evangelical Lutheran Church, Guntur.

347 Augusta Highland, op. cit., 30.

348 Edmund F. Merriam, *A History of American Baptist Missions* (Philadelphia: American Baptist Publication Society, 1900), 132.

349 Ibid., 44.

350 S. F. Smith, *Missionary Sketches: A Concise History of the Work of the American Baptist Missionary Union* (Boston: W. G. Corthell Publishers, 1883), 193.

351 Ibid., 192.

352 Ibid., 42-44.

353 *The Missionary Jubilee: An Account of the Fiftieth Anniversary of the American Baptist Missionary Union with Commemorative Papers and Discourses* (hereafter, *The Missionary Jubilee)* (New York: Sheldon and Company, 1871), 189.

354 Edmund F Merriam, op. cit.,131.

355 Ada C. Chaplin, *Our Gold Mine: The Story of American Baptist Missions in India* (Boston: W. G. Corthell Publisher, 1889), 342.

356 Ibid., 342.

357 Edmund F. Merriam, op. cit., 134.

358 *The Missionary Jubilee, op. cit.,* 189.

359 Ada C. Chaplin, op. cit., 343.

360 *The Missionary Jubilee, op. cit., 189.*

361 Ada C. Chaplin, op. cit., 344.

362 *The Missionary Jubilee, op. cit.,* 190.

363 Edmund F. Merriam, op. cit., 134.

364 Ibid., 135.

365 S. F. Smith, op. cit., 199.

366 E. B. Bromley, *They were Men Sent from God* (Bangalore: The Scripture Literature Press, 1937), 65.

367 John Craig, op. cit., 16.

368 Ada C. Chaplin, op. cit., 345.

369 John Craig, op. cit., 16.

370 S. F. Smith, op. cit., 202.

371 John E. Clough, *Social Christianity in the Orient: The Story of A Man, A Mission and A Movement* (New York: The MacMillan Company, 1914), 78.

372 George Drach and Calvin F. Kuder, op. cit., 65.

373 Ada C. Chaplin, op. cit., 351.

374 David Downie, op. cit., 62.

375 John E. Clough, op. cit., 93.

376 Ibid., 84.

377 Ibid., 78.

378 Ibid., 217.

379 Ibid., 63.
380 Ibid., 84.
381 Ada C. Chaplin, op. cit., 356.
382 Ibid., 356.
383 Ibid., 358.
384 Ibid., 360.
385 David Downie, op. cit., 87.
386 Herbert Waldo Hines, *Clough: The Kingdom Builder in South India* (Philadelphia: The Freedom Press, 1929), 86.
387 Ada C. Chaplin, op. cit., 356.
388 David Downie, op. cit., 84.
389 Ibid., 86.
390 S. F. Smith, op. cit., 206.
391 Ibid., 205.
392 Edmund F. Merriam, op. cit., 146.
393 S. F. Smith, op. cit., 205.
394 John E. Clough, op. cit., 226.
395 S. F. Smith, op. cit., 206.
396 David Downie, op. cit., 88.
397 S. F. Smith, op. cit., 207.
398 Ibid., 208.
399 M. A. Sherring, op. cit., 407.
400 S. F. Smith, op. cit., 208.
401 Ibid., 209.
402 Ibid., 210.
403 Ibid., 208.
404 Ibid., 210. Also David Downie, *The Lone Star, op. cit.,* 138.
405 S. F. Smith, op. cit., 211.
406 Ibid., 208.
407 *The Jewett Vision*, (Ongole: Jewett Memorial Baptist Church, May 2012), 22.
408 S. F. Smith, op. cit., 138.
409 Ibid., 212.
410 Ibid., 209.
411 David Downie, op. cit., 111.
412 S. F. Smith, op. cit., 212.
413 John E. Clough, op. cit., 239.
414 Ibid., 240.
415 Ibid.
416 Ibid., 241.
417 Ibid., 242.
418 Emma Rauschenbusch Clough, *While Sewing Sandals or Tales of a Telugu Pariah Tribe* (London: The Selwood Printing Works, 1899), 274.
419 John E. Clough, op. cit., 243.
420 Ibid., 245.

421 Ibid., 246.
422 Ibid., 249.
423 Ibid., 256.
424 Ibid.
425 Ibid., 263.
426 Ibid., 268.
427 Ibid., 305.
428 Ibid., 306.
429 S. F. Smith, op. cit., 218.
430 M. A. Sherring, op. cit., 410.
431 John E. Clough, op. cit., 308.
432 M. Moses, op. cit., 33.
433 Herbert Waldo Hines, op. cit., 167.
434 Emma Rauschenbusch Clough, op. cit., 307.
435 Ibid., 348.
436 David Downie, op.cit., 116.
437 Ibid., 221.
438 Ibid., 132.
439 Ibid., 128.
440 *Bezwada Baptist Sangha Golden Jubilee Souvenir* (1906-1956).
441 M. Moses, op. cit., 34.
442 Ibid., 75.
443 Ibid., 76.
444 A. T. Fishman, *For This Purpose: A Case Study of the Telugu Baptist Church in Its Relation with South India Mission of the American Baptist Foreign Mission Societies in India* (Madras: Diocesan Press, 1958), 77.
445 Ibid., 42.
446 *A Report from Rev. C. R. March of Markapur:* see A. T. Fishman, Ibid.
447 James Millard Baker, *Contending the Grade in India* (Ashville: The Biltmore Press, 1947), 124.
448 Ibid., 251.
449 Ibid., 287.
450 C. H. Smiley, "God at Work in the Telugu Area," *The National Christian Council Review* XIII, (January to December), (Mysore: Wesley Press, 1935), 188.
451 James Millard Baker, op. cit., 288.
452 The RAF established a Coastal watch center at the Southside of Ongole. James Millard Baker, op. cit., 292.
453 Edmund F. Merriam, op. cit., 150.
454 James S. Dennis, *Christian Missions and Social Progress: A Sociological Study of Foreign Missions*, Vol. III (New York: Fleming H. Revell, 1896), 262.
455 John E. Clough, op. cit., 53.
456 Ibid., 59.
457 A. T. Fishman, op. cit., 78.

458 A. Mathew, *Christian Missions, Education and Nationalism: From Dominance to Compromise 1870-1930* (New Delhi: Anamika Prakasan, 1988), 189.

459 George Drach and Calvin F. Kuder, op. cit., 267.

460 James M. Thoburn, *The Christian Conquest of India (New York: Young People's Missionary Movement,* 1906), 170.

461 James Hough, *The History of Christianity in India,* Vol. II, op. cit., 267.

462 Jacob Chamberlin, *In the Tiger Jungle and other Stories of Missionary Work among the Telugus of India* (New York: Fleming H. Revell, 1896), 135.

463 George Drach and Calvin F Kuder, op. cit., 105.

464 Eugene Stock, *A Short Handbook of Missions* (London: Longmans Green and Company, 1904), 16.

465 John Craig, op. cit., 234.

466 A. T. Fishman, op. cit., 79.

467 John Craig, op. cit., 235.

468 George Drach and Calvin F. Kuder, op. cit., 159.

469 Ibid., 230.

470 John Craig, op. cit., 235.

471 Ibid., 235.

472 Ibid., 324.

473 L. B. Wolf, *After Fifty Years, op. cit.,* 276.

474 Ibid., 276.

475 Ibid., 278.

476 John E. Clough, op. cit., Introduction.

Chapter 4

Conversions among the Malas and Madigas: Spread, Factors, Agency and Dynamics

4.1 Introduction

We have discussed the socio-economic and socio-cultural life and the religion of the Malas and the Madigas in Coastal Andhra in Chapter 2 and the work of the Christian missions and spread of Christianity in the area from mid 19th century to mid 20th century, in Chapter 3. In this chapter, we shall focus on the evangelical work of the missionaries and the factors that led to the conversions, besides discussing the role of agencies in conversion. Scholars have discussed mass conversions among the marginalized sections of people in late 19th to early 20th century. Most conversions were from Hindu religion to Islam, Buddhism, Christianity, and Sikhism.[1]

It is often commented that the conversions among the deprived classes were not out of conviction, but of convenience, meaning to secure socio-economic mobility which was made possible due to the work of the Christian missionaries who not only preached a new religion, but offered channels for human development. The latter means, it is alleged that were fraudulent means for eliciting conversion. It would imply that those who converted were not capable of making decisions about their personal religious life. Perhaps what the converts were looking for was an escape from their deprived condition, through any channel that offered freedom from not only economic and social bondage but also religious bondage. Using scores of historical sources, I shall attempt to uncover the motives of conversion and genuineness of purpose of the missionaries to verify such interpretations. Besides discussing the individual and collective nature of the conversion, I shall analyze the dynamics of conversion in the last part of the chapter.

4.2 Missionary Evangelization among the Malas

4.2.1 The London Missionary Society (LMS)

The LMS was the foremost of the missionary societies to conduct Gospel work among the Malas. In the Ceded district of Cuddapah, there was a Mala seller of thread, Atuku Nancharu, who had heard the Gospel from an Anglo-Indian civil servant, William Howell.[2] When the Gospel was propagated among the Malas in his village, the villagers accepted it. This is the first account of conversion of the Malas to Christianity of the Anglican tradition. This was the beginning of the work of the LMS among the Malas in the Ceded districts.[3]

4.2.2 Evangelization by the Church Missionary Society (CMS)

The CMS began the work of evangelization in 1847 in Kistna District. In 1851, the Mala village headman of Kondapalli village accepted the Gospel and was the first to convert.[4] He shared the Gospel with not only among his fellow caste men in his village, but also in the neighbouring hamlets where it was reported that more than 100 men were placed under Christian instruction.[5] A year before (1850), the Malas living in the Pattametta area of Bezwada sought to be baptized by Rev. Edmund Sharkey, the preacher. The evangelical efforts of Rev. Sharkey and companions such as Rev. Henry Fox, Rev. Thomas Young Darling, and Rev. F. N Alexander continued at various places such as Bezwada, Masulipatnam, Ellore, Raghavapuram, and in Khammamet District.[6] There was an increased interest and enthusiasm among the Malas in these places. Earlier, Rev. Noble had preached the Gospel among the upper castes. According to Rev. T. K Nicholson, they told him that "you may preach Christianity in Masulipatnam forever, but you will never get a convert from us."[7] Since he did not receive any enthusiastic response from them, he and others turned their attention to the lower castes. Besides, some Malas, were associated with CMS missionaries in Masulipatnam, as domestic helpers or care givers for the missionaries' children, because of which, they were familiarized with Christianity.

i) The Native Preacher Pagolu Venkayya of Raghavapuram

Under the leadership of a native convert preacher Pagolu Venkayya in Raghavapuram, groups of Malas sought baptism in Christianity. His example is illustrative of conversion out of conviction.[8] He was the leader of a band, who, being displeased with his own way of life, wanted to know the real path of salvation. He had heard from his fellow caste men that in the Palnadu region a new faith was spreading. He was interested in this new faith. It so happened in 1859, during the Siva Rathri festival in Bezwada, some 40,000 people had gathered to have holy bath in the River Kistna. With dilemma and confusion in the mind, Venkayya stood beside the river, without bathing. At that time, a

Brāhmin asked him why he was not bathing in the river, to which Venkayya replied that the water was so foul that the river cannot wash the body, let alone cleanse the soul.[9] Then the Brāhmin pointed out to him a bungalow on the top of the hill adjacent to the river where a Christian missionary was stationed. At this Venkayya along with his companions, went to visit the missionary, had a conversation with him and told him about his spiritual quest for true meaning in life. At the end of this interaction, Venkayya reportedly said, "This is my God and this is my Savior. I have long been seeking for Him, now I have found Him."[10] Convinced of the Christian way of life, he sought baptism. At the age of about forty-seven, Venkayya took a decision to renounce his practice of idol worship and began to pursue a new journey in religion. The baptisms of Venkayya, his wife, his five children and sixteen other men took place at Raghavapuram on March 9, 1859.[11] The CMS missionary, Rev. Thomas Young Darling who baptized him had been in despair for eight years because nobody had sought conversion earlier in spite of his Gospel work.[12] The case of Venkayya was noted by A. D. Nock:

> …the reorientation of the soul of an individual, his deliberate turning from indifference or from an earlier form of piety to another, a conscious decision that the old means was wrong and the new way is right. Such conversion is in its essence a turning away from a sense of present wrongness at least as much as a turning towards a positive ideal.[13]

This event of conversion marked the beginning of the group conversion movement in Kistna District particularly in Bezwada, Raghavapuram, Polasanapalle, Nuzvid, Ellore, Khammamet, and the adjacent Godavari region. Subsequently, due to the zealous work of the missionaries and with native collaboration, thousands of Malas converted to Christianity in these areas.

The Christmas celebration in Raghavapuram in 1859 was said to be an unforgettable event for the newly converted Christians. The worship service was led by Rev. Darling. Two caste convert pastors from Masulipatnam, Rev. Ainala Bhushanam and Rev. Manchala Ratnam, along with some non-Christian Malas of the village attended it. A great spiritual fervor was felt in Raghavapuram and the missionaries convinced the converts that they were no more called as Malas (which had a pejorative identity) but as members of the Church with a fraternal bond.[14] In 1862, there were eighty converts in a cluster of nine villages. These converts were placed under the charge of native school masters.[15] Rev. Hibbert Ware reported that in the beginning of the 20th century, Masulipatnam became the chief station for the CMS activities. Subsequently, there were mass conversions in the adjacent areas eventually counting nearly six thousand Christians with five hundred catechumens.[16]

ii) The CMS Bezwada Mission Station

The Bezwada station, founded in 1858, had also witnessed mass conversions. By the year 1912 there were nearly four thousand Christians and two thousand catechumens.[17] This necessitated re-organization of the station: Bezwada and Raghavapuram were made into two separate stations in 1870.[18] Rev. J. E. Harrison was stationed in Bezwada in 1867. He rendered remarkable work in his fields of evangelization and in the training of the native Gospel workers who preached among the masses. In 1872, Rev. J. E. Padfield noted,

We have much cause for joy and rejoicing at the workings of the Spirit amongst the poorer portion of the rural population. The seed cast abroad in faith for twelve years was now rapidly springing up. From village after village the cry comes for a teacher of the word of life. No sooner is a fresh post occupied than urgent entreaties come from another still further on. In my last tour, I brought away no less than fifty-two idols, given up by new inquirers.[19]

The statistics on the mass conversions in Kistna District, noted in the *Manual of the Kistna District,* was reported at the Bangalore Missionary Conference of 1879: Christians in Masulipatnam, 1,414; in Bezwada, 516; in Raghavapuram, 756 which made a total of 2,686 Christians.[20]

Besides Pagolu Venkayya, the other converts such as Budda Seshayya and Kama Muthayya became native preachers and travelled wide in other areas to preach among the Malas.[21] Many Mala converts from Raghavapuram were trained to be village school teachers or voluntary preachers who went on long tours to preach.[22] Even church worship services were led by the Mala converts about whom a CMS missionary in Bezwada observed:

> It [the church] looked fairly full with the 139 people that were counted in it. The men and boys sat in front, the women and girls behind. In the centre, looking like the patriarch of his tribe, with a grave and somewhat heavy-looking countenance, sat Venkayya, the first convert. Nearer us on either side were three or four young Christian schoolmasters. The people present had come from various Christian villages, one of which is twenty miles distant. The service commenced with a hymn sung to a native tune and portions of the prayers were read in Telugu.[23]

iii) The Evangelistic Work of Rev. Alexander in Ellore

Considerable mission work was done at the Ellore mission station under the guidance of Rev. Canon. F. N. Alexander from 1857 to 1911. The church in Ellore with its territory reaching as far as the Nuzvid Zamindari, had nearly six thousand baptized converts.[24] From 1860s and 1870s, a large number of Madigas also were contacted by the missionary Rev. Alexander. With his undaunted work for 50 years at the Ellore mission station, he tried to keep both the Mala and the Madiga converts united under one church congregation. The CMS mission carried on with the evangelistic work in a fruitful way under successive missionary leaders such as Rev. Panes, Rev. Padfield, Rev. Peachey, Rev. Tanner, Rev. Eales, Rev. Harrison, Rev. Woodhouse, Rev. Cranswick, Rev. Anthony B. Elliott and Rev. Cain and Mrs. Cain.

iv) Expansion to Nizam's Territories

The group conversion movement in Colonial Andhra gradually made its way into the adjoining Nizam's State of Hyderabad, further into the towns of Khammamet and Dornakal. Since 1900s large scale group conversions occurred in Khammamet and Dornakal under the missionaries of the Indian Missionary Society of Tinnevelly (IMST), which was stationed at these places. Between the years 1906 and 1909, the Malas were taught by the missionaries of the IMST and Bishop Henry Whitehead baptized 1600 Malas at Dummagudem.[25] During the year 1908, Rev. Samuel Pakhyanadham and Solomon Pakhyanadham worked earnestly among the Mala, Madiga, Vaddara and Erukala castes and converted people in large numbers. In the year 1913, Rev. Vedanayagam Samuel Azariah was appointed as the Bishop of Dornakal and was made in-charge of all the CMS work in and around Khammamet and Dornakal.[26]

As per the Church statistics, during the year 1910, there were five Telugu pastors with 100 lay teachers working in 75 villages and the baptized Christians were 3,384 with 1,451 catechumens. A year later the baptized membership grew to 4,271; catechumens 2,372 with seven pastors and 115 lay teachers.[27] Later on there were 9,200 adult baptisms and the total number increased from 11,700 to 28,000, besides 7,000 catechumens in the Dornakal region.[28] Recognizing the need for of the time, the Bishop of Madras had requested other missionary societies to help out by urgently supplying teachers and preachers to the Telugu speaking areas.

v) Rev. V. S. Azariah and the Group Conversion Movement

The group conversion movement in Andhra saw a fast pace during the leadership of the first Indian Bishop of Dornakal, V. S. Azariah. Under his guidance, the movement brought the membership of the Telugu Anglican community from 56,681 in 1912 to 225,080 in 1941. The Christian population in the area grew at a faster rate with an average of 12,855 per month.[29] In Carol Graham's words, "he entered into a great heritage of opportunity at a time when India was ripe for a deep stirring of the Spirit and, to some extent, reaped where other men had sown."[30] In 1918, a Mass Movement Commission of the Protestant Churches was appointed whose members visited various missionary denominations working in various parts of India.[31] The mass movement progress in the CMS areas was largely attributed to the utilization of services of the newly trained Indian clergy and teachers.

Initially group conversion occurred mostly among the Malas and the Madigas but a few, about 102, *Súdra* caste people were admitted and baptized by Bishop Whitehead in 1907.[32] In the beginning of the 20th century, the movement became so intense that more requests for Gospel preachers came from several un-reached villages. The period witnessed a sort of tidal wave of conversion. Bishop of Winchester and the Bishop of Madras (Rt. Rev. Henry Whitehead) were so astonished to see those seeking conversion came walking 30 to 40 miles to be present at a baptismal service at Khammamet in February 1910.[33] In 1918, there were 43,500 Christian adherents whose number increased to 122,500 in 1928, in Kistna District.[34] At the time unification of Anglican, Presbyterian and Methodist Churches in 1945, the Anglican membership in Andhra stood at 50,000.[35]

4.2.3 The Ministry of the Godavari Delta Mission (GDM)

Much before the well-known story of the Mala convert Pagolu Venkayya, there was a certain Chinnaiah of the Dasari caste, who was converted by GDM missionaries. He had studied in a school established by Rev. E. S. Bowden of the GDM. He convinced his villagers of Velpur about the noble message of the Gospel and was instrumental in eliciting their interest towards the new faith and requested Rev. Bowden to confer baptisms.[36] When Rev. Bowden turned down the request of Chinnaiah, he and the villagers proceeded to Rajahmundry to meet Rev. C. F. Heyer of the Pennsylvania Ministerium and were baptized. This was a significant beginning of the conversions of the Malas in the Godavari Delta Region.[37]

The GDM was established with the active leadership of Rev. Anthony Norris Groves, in 1836. Thereafter, the Mission conducted significant evangelistic works through preaching, educational activities and distributing tracts among the Malas and Madigas. During the construction of the anicut across the Godavari River at Dowlaishvaram in 1847-48, thousands of coolies were employed by the chief engineer, Sir Arthur Cotton, who had invited Rev. Beer and Rev. Bowden to preach the Gospel.[38] In 1861, a church was built in Palakol upon the initiative of Rev. Bowden. Marlapudi Emberu from village Siddelagudem was the first native convert. The native Christian brethren played an important role in establishing churches and village congregations in the surrounding villages.[39] By 1880, six native preachers had been fully engaged in preaching the Gospel. Three hundred converts founded a local Christian fellowship, covering some thirty villages, spread in a large area.[40]

4.2.4 The Canadian Baptist Mission (CBM) among the Malas

Mr. Thomas Gabriel (pre-convert name Taleru Marayya), a Mala employee of the Telegraph Department of the government, was a native pastor, who had been influenced by two Churches, the Plymouth Brethren of Narsapur and the American Lutheran Mission at Rajahmundry. He had laboured single-handedly for seven years in Coconada.[41] In July 1873, Mr. Gabriel reported the baptism of thirty-one converts at Gunnanapudi and eight at Chinnamilli.[42] When the Canadian Baptist Mission (CBM) started its activities in Cocanada, it was found that Mr. Gabriel had already been working in the Kolair region and was persuaded to proceed to Vuyyuru and preach in the surrounding areas. The conversion and baptism of the Malas in the upper Kistna basin, chiefly owed to the efforts of Mr. Thomas Gabriel. In 1874, there were nearly one hundred and thirty-three baptized persons. Their number increased to two hundred and nineteen in a few years.[43]

The work of the CBM chiefly spread to Moturu, Gunnanapudi, Akidu, Vuyyuru and Avanigadda of the Kolair Mission station. Frequent group baptisms in these places were reported in Gunnanapudi thanks to the native leadership of Rev. Karre Peter. It may be noted that the conversions there did not occur in a deprived condition of the people, nor under famine conditions. These areas were well-irrigated and in the arable lands of this coastal area the Mala cultivators did not have to suffer much. Yet, there was a great increase in church membership from this caste. This remarkable increase of conversions has been attributed to the zeal and enthusiasm of the native preachers and the Malas themselves who became convinced that Christianity offered an alternative path to social up-gradation and social equality.[44]

4.2.5 The American Evangelical Lutheran Mission (AELM) among the Malas

The two main agencies of the AELM, the General Synod at Guntur and the Pennsylvania Ministerium at Rajahmundry, were responsible for a steady stream of conversions through their evangelical and educational programs. Similar to the CMS, the work of the AELM too had attracted the Mala caste in the Kistna-Godavari and Guntur regions.[45] They had converts from among the *Súdras* as well. Much before the conversion of Pagolu Venkayya, the AELM's evangelistic and educational work under the leadership of Rev. C. F. Heyer had made a huge impression on the Malas in the Palnadu region.

In 1894, there were nearly two thousand Mala Christians in Bhimavaram, who were active in church building and consecration of churches under the AELM. Karre Peter from Gunnanapudi, Barnala David from Narsapatnam, Tuluri Cornelius from Tuni, Karre Krupanandam from Gollapalli and

Addepally Mariamma from Muramanda were the notable native preachers and faithful evangelists among the Malas.[46]

The missionaries of the Lutheran mission were quite successful in their evangelistic work which began in 1844. Rev. Heyer baptized three persons, a man, a woman and a child (Isaac, Ruth and Prakasam),[47] in 1845. Later he baptized eighteen adults and six children.[48] Small scale group conversions took place among the Malas in Polepalli village. In 1850, Rev. Heyer baptized 126 adults and children.[49] Rajahmundry and Samalkot were the chief Lutheran mission stations in the Godavari Delta region. Gurajala, Polepalli, Veldurti and Macherla became the chief centres in the Palnadu region. With the growing network of schools, enrollment of students increased to 1,036. The work of the AELM was remarkable in raising the social standards of the Malas. Around 1859, when other missionary societies were struggling to get even a single convert, the number of baptisms in the AELM recorded forty four, besides sixteen confirmations and one hundred and nine communicants.[50] In 1867, the number of Christians under the Lutheran mission's influence stood at six hundred and eighty with three hundred and fifty communicants.[51] In end 1893, the number of Christians stood at 3,757 with 1,224 baptized members and 1,441 communicants.[52] Under the able guidance of Rev. J. H. Harpster, the membership of the Church grew to 8,194 in 1901. In 1905, Dr. Harpster reported to the Board of the General Council, that there were 11,938 baptised members in the Church and about the extent of his work in Godavari District.[53]

The evangelical work in the Guntur region was more fruitful owing to the earnest efforts of some notable native pastors namely, Thota Joseph, Nelaprolu Paulus, Medikonduru Nathaniel and Bethala John who had worked as village teachers cum evangelists.[54] These native preachers were not motivated by any material advantages, but were very devoted and faithful in the mission of the Church to win over souls.[55]

In 1909, the baptized members of the General Council were 16,316 and of the General Synod, 38,236. In 1919, the number of Christians in both Rajahmundry and Guntur fields was placed at 91,700.[56] The notable AELM missionaries who were responsible for group conversions among the Malas were Rev. Dr. C. F. Heyer, Dr. Lemon L. Uhl, Rev. Charles William Groenning, Rev. Erias Unangst, Rev. Hans Christian Schmidt and Rev. Christian Friedrich, Rev. Johan Becker, Rev. Horace, Rev. G. B. Artman, Rev. Iver K. Poulsen, Rev. Frederick, Rev. James McCready and Dr. John Henry Harpster

4.2.6 Mission Work by American Baptists and Other Denominations

The work of the American Baptist Mission in Ongole started with the conversion of a prominent Mala, a village priest, named Tupili Lutchmiah. Before his conversion, he used to go round with idols in some thirty villages in Ongole to conduct idol worship. Initially he grew angry over the missionaries for preaching the Gospel. Later, he decided to meet Rev. Clough and inquired how he could be saved. Convinced of salvation in Christianity, he received baptizm on December 24, 1865. He became the first fruit from among the Malas of the American missionary's labour in evangelization.[57]

Other denominations also did notable work among the Malas in Guntur and Kistna districts which had several group conversion events. The Salvation Army and the Brethren Church led many people among the Malas to conversion. In Masulipatnam, nearly 400 people embraced Christianity within a short span of 3 days at a function led by Rev. Bandela Raja Ratnam in 1944. Mass conversions took place in the South Andhra town of Kanigiri led by the Brethren Church.[58] Thus, individual and group conversions among the Malas were mediated not only by the missionaries of different Churches, but also by native leaders, whose leadership and example became so persuasive as to attract hundreds of Malas into Christianity in Colonial Andhra.[59]

4.3 Missionary Evangelization among the Madigas

4.3.1 The Work of the American Baptist Mission (ABM)

The Madigas' interest in Christianity came as a surprise for the missionaries of the ABM as they were pre-occupied with the conversion of the Súdra castes in Nellore since the year 1840.[60] The first Telugu convert of the ABM was Venkappah, baptized in the Pennar River in September 1841.[61] For unknown social reasons, the Súdras in this South Coastal Andhra region wanted to embrace the new faith. It was said that the quest for conversion among the Sudras emerged due to the attempts of a frustrated Súdra old man who approached the missionaries in the Ongole field.[62] Among the few converts from the Súdra castes in Nellore were Kanakiah, the first native convert and Julia, a female convert.[63] These two converts got married in 1856 and Kanakiah was ordained a preacher in December 1861.[64]

The Madiga converts of the Kistna-Godavari basin shared their experiences with the traders of their fellow caste men from Ongole who came to buy cattle hides and skins at a cheaper price due to a poisonous insect disease.[65] These trade travelers became the principal leaders of the Ongole group conversion movement among the Madigas. In the absence of a Baptist mission station, the converted Madigas at Vuyyuru, Gudivada and the surrounding villages joined the CMS at Ellore or Masulipatnam.[66] In mid nineteenth century, caste affinities played a big role while associating with the Churches: if the Malas joined in a particular Church, the Madigas joined in a different Church.

i) The Talakondapadu Ingathering

Group conversions at Talakondapadu started initially around the year 1867. Thirty to forty people were admitted into baptism on a single day. In response to the preaching of the missionaries, people in big numbers gathered in 1867 at the Baptist Church in Ongole.[67] Hailing from different villages, they came with food provisions for several days, asking to be baptized.[68] By 1869, the number of converts grew to more than six hundred owing to the evangelistic work of two missionaries: Rev. Clough and Rev. McLaurin.[69] This led to the establishment of a separate mission centre at Ramapatnam by Rev. R. R. Williams, in 1869.[70] Subsequently, Rev. A. V. Timpany started a theological seminary in Ramapatnam in 1872 for the training of teachers and preachers.[71]

Group conversion movement among the Madigas began to gain momentum under the strenuous efforts of Rev. Clough, Yerraguntla Periah, Bangarapu Thatiah and Bezwada Paul. The number of Christians grew from 1,103 in 1870 to 1,745 in 1872. In 1876, two years before the ingathering of Vellumpally, the number increased to 3,000 in about 160 villages.[72] The first converts worked towards building a strong church and facilitated the conversion of the fellow Madigas. The majority of the believers were young men and women between twenty and thirty years of age.[73]

Natural calamities also were factors of conversion. A devastating flood had destroyed many hamlets in Nellore in October 1874, when Christian and non-Christian people approached the missionaries for shelter. The men were accommodated in the chapel and women and children were cared for in the missionary's bungalow.[74]

As the congregation was growing by hundreds, Rev. Clough and his associate missionaries were not eager for any miracles to happen during the onset of the great famine of 1876-78. The missionaries there had made it clear that no one would be given baptism during the time of natural calamities, as it would be construed as bait for getting conversions. It was an evidence to demonstrate that conversions *en masse* were not the results of the famine relief activities. In Rev. Clough's view material benefits should be separated from the spiritual needs.[75] But Rev. Clough realized that "their [people's] minds were not fixed on rupees, they wanted salvation for their souls."[76] The reluctance of Rev. Clough to receive people into the Church attracted much criticism from the Roman Catholic Mission in that region. The latter had conveyed to Rev. Clough that in principle, they had no restrictions in receiving the multitudes.[77] As a matter of fact, there was a dividing line between the converts who were converted before the occurrence of famines and those who converted after the famine relief experience. The former spoke about their conversion with certain pride than the latter who came to be known as 'famine converts.'[78]

ii) The Great Famine of 1876-1878 and the Buckingham Canal Work

The great famine or "Dhaata Karuvu" of 1876-1878 devastated the entire Nellore and Ongole regions. A great number of people had perished in Guntur, Kistna and Nellore districts.[79] Rev. Clough had realized that a famine and an impending epidemic of cholera were imminent in South Andhra. He had planned to take part in the government relief work projects and had managed to get a contract to dig a three-and-a-half-mile section of the Buckingham canal being constructed by the government.[80] The canal work came as a relief in the distressed condition of the people as it created opportunities for paid employment to thousands of people, who would otherwise have died of starvation. According to A. T. Fishman, thousands of able bodied men and women were saved from the ravages of starvation by the remunerative employment at the canal work.[81] Rev. Clough's camp was located at Razupallem near Kothapatnam. When the canal work began on February 24, 1877, thousands of coolies, almost half of them Christians, were employed in the work.[82] The teachings and illustrations about the Gospel miracles attracted many Madigas in the camp and they believed in the message of redemption.[83] Rev. Clough emphasized on three essential instructions namely 'do not work on Sunday, do not eat carrion and do not worship idols.'[84] A famine fund named the Mansion House Fund was raised by the Governor of Madras for which requests were sent abroad for immediate economic aid with the caption "Thousands of Christians starving, please solicit subscriptions". The fund was meant for the Baptist societies in Assam and Burma as well.[85]

iii) The Second Ingathering at Vellumpilly

By end 1870s Rev. Clough had realized that time had ripened to admit thousands of converts into the fold of the Church and so he looked for local leaders from the Madiga community. A meeting was called in the town of Vellumpilly near Ongole owing to the fear of cholera that may accompany the large number people flocking to see Rev. Clough in Ongole. The Madigas pleaded with Rev. Clough saying, "we do not want help. By the blisters on our hands we can prove to you that we have worked and will continue to work. If the next crops fail, we shall die. We want to die as Christians. Baptize us, therefore!"[86] On 16th June 1878, he baptized one hundred and two people of whom seventy-four were male heads of families from Ongole.[87]

The native preachers brought large contingents of people from different provinces namely Darsi, Podili, Kanigiri, Markapur and Cumbum. The notable preachers who led this movement were Yerraguntla Periah, his wife Nagamma, Obulu, Baddepudi Abraham, Thaluri Daniel, Munangi Anumiah, Bezwada Paul, Kola Peddaiah, Tupili Rungaiah, Tupili Lutchmiah, Oogriah and Sreeram Solomon.[88] Filled with a Pentecostal spirit, a large number of people gathered in the Vellumpilly tamarind grove, close to the Gundlakamma River, under the leadership of four preachers. Group baptism of six hundred and fourteen people took place that day, 2nd July 1878. The total number of Madiga baptisms was 2222.[89] Between 2nd and 4th July 1878, some 3536 baptisms took place.[90] At the end of 1878, the number of baptized Madiga converts stood at 9606. The Ongole Church membership stood at 12804 in four hundred villages.[91] At Ramapatnam, over 600 converts were baptized, similar to the ingathering event at the Ongole mission in 1878.[92]

Conversion to Christianity was expected to bring concurrent changes in the religious life, worship and customs of the people. The missionaries wished to see in their Madiga converts a complete stop of drinking the intoxicating *Sarai* and of eating the carrion. Observing rest on Sundays and abandoning of worship of idols were also expected.[93] To ensure church life in the community of converts, select village elders holding traditional authority in villages were appointed as deacons.[94] A spirit of clan and of family prevailed among the converts.

iv) Increased Pace of Accessions

The Madiga group conversion movement took a big turn with the ingathering in Vellumpilly. Hundreds of seekers had been expressing their desire to be baptized and to live as Christians.[95] In the beginning of 1880, the church membership in Ongole was at 14872.[96] The vastness of the Ongole field necessitated division of the territory. Twenty six churches such as that of Cumbum, Vinukonda, Narsaraopet and Bapatla, were created.[97] The ABM in Kistna District had five thousand two hundred and forty five baptized communicants and an estimated fifteen thousand followers.[98] The theological seminary at Ramapatnam had an enrolment of 200 students that demonstrated the need for trained preachers to provide for the growing number of congregations in the Telugu provinces.[99] In 1880, twenty four native preachers were ordained at Ongole by Rev. Clough, Rev. David Downie and Rev. R. R. Williams.[100] The effect of the great ingathering continued well into the first decade of the twentieth century. During the year 1905, when it was time for Rev. Clough to leave India, the ABM Telugu Church had one hundred missionaries, sixty thousand members and nearly two hundred thousand adherents.[101]

Bezwada also became a prominent place for the Baptist Church due to a wave of migration by the Madiga Christians from the Palnadu region. They had settled in an area that came to be known as Ravipati Huts which was subsequently named as Baptistpalem. From 1904, Rev. Kurtz had been doing remarkable missionary service in Bezwada and in 1906, Rev. Velpula and Mrs. Velpula George came from Bapatla to serve in the Bezwada church. In the years 1931 and 1935, the Iasraelpet and the Fraserpet Baptist churches were established to serve the growing number of adherents.[102]

4.3.2 The Church Missionary Society (CMS), Yerraguntla Periah and the Madigas

As mentioned earlier, the Madigas were leather workers by occupation and held some trade links with their fellow caste men. While passing through the town of Ellore, Yerraguntla Periah, a skin trader came across with the CMS missionary Rev. F. W. N. Alexander[103] and Rev. E. S. Bowden, who resided there.[104] When he returned to his village of Talakondapadu in the Kanigiri taluq, he started to persuade his family members to convert into the new faith.[105] He was baptized in 1866, along with his wife Nagamma, by the American Baptist missionary Rev. Clough. Since then, Nagamma and Periah, who was a practitioner of Raja Yoga became Christian preachers and carried on the Gospel mission in many villages as far as 80 miles and became the chief inspiration for the Madigas.[106] He worked diligently with dedicated conviction for the evangelization of the Madiga community for 31 years.[107] There was also another Madiga convert named Bangarapu Thatiah, a guru of Raja Yoga, who took much interest in the spread of the new faith.[108] In 1867, the first ingathering took place at Talakondapadu under the leadership of Periah.[109] During 1869, Rev. Clough baptized forty-two converts and a number of others joined the ranks of the church there.[110]

4.3.3 The Canadian Baptist Mission (CBM) and the Madiga Conversion

The Canadian Baptist Mission established itself and thrived where the London Missionary Society had relinquished its activities in places such as Vizagapatam, Tekkali, Tuni, Parlakimidi, Pithapuram, Bobbili, Bhimunipatnam, Yalamanchili, Rayagada, Vijayanagaram, Srikakulam, Samarlakota and Sompeta.[111] On the northern side of the Kistna delta, the town of Vuyyuru became the centre of the CBM's activities under the leadership of Rev. Timpany and Rev. Craig. The Vuyyuru Church was organized in November 1885 when eighty-two people from the surrounding villages were baptized. The membership of the church grew steadily with more conversions and baptisms. In 1887, the Gospel activities of the Vuyyuru and Akidu mission fields were brought in close association.[112]

In the end of the nineteenth century the CBM held eighty churches in Cocanada, Kollair, Akidu and Gunnanapudi. With an aggregate membership of about seventeen thousand Christians, these church congregations had maintained a vast circle of village communities who were guided by teacher-evangelists. Due to rapid expansion of the Gospel work, the mission was divided into two parts, namely Godavari Association with ten Telugu churches and seven hundred and fifteen members, and the Kolair Association with thirteen churches and one thousand eight hundred and seventy four members.[113]

The poor and illiterate Christian women of Bodagunta initiated the task of voluntary Gospel preaching while selling onions in surrounding villages. Thereafter, the villagers requested for a missionary to be sent to them for furthering their Christian understanding.[114] The newly converted and baptized men of Avanigadda did evangelization work amongst their relatives and brought more results than what a missionary could do.[115] The missionaries' role in this peoples' spiritual enterprise was to give guidance and moral support.[116] Some notable native preachers in this region were Jonathan Burder, Pastor Karre Peter, Karre Samuel, S. Venkataswamy, M. Peter, K. Philemon, P. Joseph and M. Jagannaikulu, whose earnest efforts contributed to the increase in the number of baptisms in this region.

The Madigas' interest in the Baptist denominations was due to group conversions in the Ongole field. One reason why the Madigas preferred CBM was because the other Churches like CMS and AELM were dominated with the presence of Malas. Natural caste opposition between the two led the former to choose a different denomination.[117]

In 1906, a nation-wide revival movement was launched among the Churches for quickening evangelization and deepening of the spiritual life of those who were already Christians. It strengthened the mission churches and boarding schools where groups of Christians made sustained efforts at increasing the number of baptisms, and deepening of spirituality. The campaign doubled the number of Christians.[118]

Table 4.1: Population of Hindus, Muhammadans and Christians, 1851-52/1856-57

Districts	Total Population 1851-52	Hindus	Mohammadans	Christians	% of Christian Population
		1851-52	1856-57	1856-57	
Ganjam	926930	921832	4536	549	0.05
Vizagapatam	1254272	1238590	16489	1213	0.09
Rajahmundry	1012036	991210	20998	430	0.04
Masulipatam	520866	497796	27331	742	0.14
Guntoor	570083	534725	33629	3521	0.61
Nellore	935690	894034	42916	868	0.09
Total	5219877	5078187	145899	7323	1.02%

Source: W. R. Cornish, *Census of the Madras Presidency*, 1871, Census Results, Supplementary Tables, Vol. II, (Madras: The Government Gazette Press, 1874), 9 and 12.

The devolution of the Indian Mission Churches had begun in 1910 which was characterized by a gradual change of leadership of the Churches to Indian preachers and clergymen. Thus, the conversions and baptisms that took place in the following decades were largely attributed to the work of native Christian leaders. During 1920s and 1930s undoubtedly the missions and churches showed a larger increase in membership though it was not uniform in all the Churches. For example, the Canadian Baptist Mission has advanced 62 percent conversion during the decade, the United Lutheran Church, 59 percent, the Church Missionary Society in the Dornakal Diocese, 58 percent, the Wesleyan Methodist Church, 100 per cent and the American Baptist Telugu Mission had registered 40 percent conversions.[119] It was estimated that nearly 20% of the Depressed Castes in West Godavari, 32% in the Kistna and 57% in the Guntur district had become Christians.[120] Table 4.1 shows the number of Christians in Coastal Andhra districts in the beginning of the missionary period, indicating their small percentage in the total population.

4.4 Factors that Led to Conversions

It is a surprising factor that Christianity became an answer to various social, economic, religious and spiritual problems in the second part of the 19th century. Whether it was from the prosperous river deltas or from the drought stricken arid region, the Malas and the Madigas had one intention: to embrace Christianity. Therefore, it is important to examine the factors responsible for the individual and the group conversions in the late nineteenth and early twentieth centuries in Colonial Andhra. Scholars have studied and analyzed the factors that led to mass conversions in elsewhere in India[121] and Andhra.[122] They have identified diverse factors ranging from spiritual zeal to material gain, quest for social liberation to desire for attaining economic upward mobility, yearning for freedom from caste-based occupational bondage to seeking freedom to acquire alternative occupations for socio-economic development, quest for human dignity amidst degrading 'out-casted' existence in Hindu society, and so on. From our data, it is evident that a majority of the Malas and the Madigas chose alternative occupations seeking liberation from caste bondages as other means of social change was closed for them.[123] Often multiple factors were present in a single conversion. We shall discuss these in this section.

4.4.1 Passion for Christianity

Some scholars tended to have given undue weightage to the quest for social and economic upward mobility of the Depressed Castes, undermining their quest for spirituality. In the several case studies we have on record, the primary factor of spiritual thirst among the Malas and the Madigas was not given due importance.[124] A visible passion for Christian faith was exhibited by some Malas and Madigas as has been illustrated for instance, through narratives on the personal life Pagolu Venkayya (Yerraguntla Periah), the leader of a band of violent men. The search for higher principles of life to satisfy their spiritual needs was indeed a remarkable feature in some of the individual conversions among the Depressed Castes.[125] Describing the spiritual zeal of the Malas and Madigas, Hibbert Ware noted:

The common characteristics of this class, which are found in some of them in a high degree, are that they pass through a period, sometimes before they have had their first encounter with a Christian preacher or book, of seeking after God, that, often through remarkable circumstances, they come within the hearing of the Gospel; that they quickly, and sometimes immediately, find in it the satisfaction of their highest desires and finally, that they become leaders to their own race.[126]

The Malas' eagerness to find out the new truths could best be described in the case of Pagolu Venkayya, the first among the Raghavapuram converts, who was said to have been in great sorrow when he lost his child despite making sacrifices to the village goddess. He realized that the idols were made by village carpenters and were impotent things. Thereafter he refused to believe in them. Venkayya readily agreed to renounce idol worship and was at the same time, interested to know about the missionary who had been preaching in the surrounding areas.[127] The message that appealed to him most was that, "the world was made by one God and that He loved all men irrespective of any man made distinctions."[128]

The Madiga skin traders of the Ongole region held trade relations with the fellow Madigas in the Kistna and Godavari river basin. The Christian converts among them found occasions to share the Gospel with the non-Christian caste-mates, some of whom evinced interest in the new faith influenced by the change of behaviour of the Christians. They were ready to forego their Hindu worship practices and bad habits.

Some group conversions were induced by the inspiration and leadership of certain convert leaders. For instance, Yerraguntla Periah (1826-1897), a member of the Ramanuja sect but also followed the teachings of the Saivaite reformer, Yogi Pothuluri Veerabramham (1610-1693), was a powerful witness to Christian way of life and was able to effect change of faith in many Madigas. He was one of the virtuous personalities who was revered by the Telugu people for his views on caste prejudices and his proclaimed faith-based conviction that all men are equal.[129] His personal convictions convinced others, his example inspired others, and his leadership led others to Christianity. In Rev. Clough's words, the converts' minds were not fixed on rupees but wanted salvation for their souls. The people pleaded with Rev. Clough in the following words:

> We are very poor, our huts are fallen down, and we have not much to eat but leafs. But we do not ask you for money. We will not ask you for the smallest copper coin, even though we starve to death, we believe in Jesus, we want to be baptized.[130]

It is surprising that such choices of faith were made at a time when Colonial Andhra had not faced a dearth of social reform activities. A possible reason may be that they were strongly attracted by and were touched in the heart, by Christ's message of acceptance, forgiveness, love and compassion of the poor and the despised, rather than an intellectual understanding of Christian principles and doctrines. It may be noted that baptism was not administered to them, until they demonstrated their acceptance and perseverance in the Christian faith.[131]

4.4.2 Humanitarian Relief Works During Natural Calamities

In the second half of the 19th century, natural calamities such as famines and diseases like cholera and plague devastated the whole of Andhra region from time to time. During the famines of 1870, 1877 and 1890, Christian missionaries collaborated with the government in reaching relief to the affected people. They also engaged in rehabilitation works by undertaking many large scale public works in collaboration with the government. The American Baptist Mission in Ongole took the burden of the 1877-78 famine when people were too weak to reach the canal to take up any paid work and so the mission distributed relief materials directly to the affected.[132] Public works such as the construction of the Buckingham Canal on behalf of the government, by the American missionary Rev. Clough near Razupalem, a few miles south of Kothapatnam in 1877, to ease the drought condition, was appreciated by all.[133]

The severe famine of 1877-78 had affected the entire population especially the Depressed Castes due to their dependence on their caste masters for their livelihood. However, owing to the relief efforts of the missionaries in the form of great public charity, undertaken under the 'the Mansion House Fund', helped mitigate their sufferings to a large extent.[134] The immediate economic assistance enabled the Madigas to escape starvation and death in the short run. But the solid economic assistance by the mission enabled them to better their lives in the long run.[135] The pattern of group conversions among the Madigas suggest that conversions to Christianity occurred only at the end of the epidemic period or famine period, contrary to the common notion that struggle for survival in times of famine and drought made them to become Christians.[136]

4.4.3 Colonial Agrarian Policy, Dislocation of the Village Economy

The economic organization in India had continued without much variation through many centuries though political organization had changed from time to time.[137] Economic relations were largely governed by the Jajmani system in which different occupational castes and agricultural castes in a village mutually depended on mutual exchange of services and goods. According to William Wiser, each caste in a village was assigned a fixed type of service that was based on Jajman and Kamin (owner-tenant) relations.[138] Under the Jajmani system, agricultural activities and other allied works were allocated according to caste ranking and the landowning castes were obliged to distribute grain to the service castes, which fulfilled the caste-based services for the whole village.

But during the latter half of the nineteenth century, the British administration expanded its commercial interests and the traditional village economic system was replaced with a structural economy (primary, secondary and tertiary). Increased demand for manufactured goods resulted in the commercialization of agriculture that made the traditional industries suffer and created economic displacement of traditional occupations.[139] According to Dharma Kumar, a class of landless agricultural labourers was wholly created during the British period due to the impoverishment of the peasant proprietor and the village craftsman.[140]

As for the Malas, weaving was one of their traditional occupations apart from their being agricultural peasants. But during the middle of the 19th century when Indian raw material was exported to Britain, many occupations including weaving became less remunerative and hence they sought new avenues.[141] Any hope of social improvement without economic freedom was not achievable and unthinkable. The deteriorated economic situation and break up of economic ties made the Depressed Castes seek alternative means of secure living. The initiative and leadership came from deeply discontented individuals and groups in the form of conversion to Christianity.[142] In Duncan Forrester's opinion, conversion among the Depressed Castes was the result of the "cumulative effect of the western impact on India" and the dislocation of village life due to new social and legal systems.[143] According to some scholars, the breakdown of the *Jajmani* system along with famine and distress, the desire for social upliftment, social and economic security and freedom from oppression were the contributing factors of the conversion of the Malas and the Madigas to Christianity.[144]

By the end of the 19th century, the British government began to convert ranked economic rights into absolute economic rights by monetizing the rural economy.[145] According to Duncan Forrester, economic conditions in villages were affected in the second half of the 19th century when the traditional productive relationships were disturbed either by natural calamities or through commercialization of agriculture. The introduction of railways and communication facilities opened up new opportunities for the Depressed Castes. Conversion to Christianity offered a new social identity for the converts.[146] The growth of both vernacular and English education contributed to greater mobility. New avenues of empowerment were made available to the Depressed Castes in general, and the Malas and the Madigas in particular, by the missionaries. The marginalized communities were able to achieve much progress in life through education and remunerative employment. In short, Christian missionary undertakings in India was not just for evangelization of the people, meaning preaching of the Gospel, but to show practical Christianity by empowering the poor and the rejected in society through material means.[147]

4.4.4 Escaping Persecution from Caste Hindus

Converts to Christianity had to suffer mild and violent persecution at the hands of the caste Hindus. First, conversion implied dislocation of the inherited, traditional occupation-patronage relationship (jajmani) in villages. Some of the so-called 'degraded' occupations such as cleaning hide and leather work, scavenging and so on were imposed on the Depressed Castes by the upper castes, under the caste-based jajmani system. And because of these 'polluting' occupations, the former were perennially considered out-castes. The converts refused to be degraded by discarding the so-called 'polluting' occupations, which tilted the jajmani system in the village. This was unacceptable to the upper castes who began to harass and persecute the converts for challenging the system. Although Christianity accorded dignity to all occupations, in the given circumstances, missionaries did discourage the so-called 'polluting' occupations and eating impure foods.

Christianity's arrival seems to have disrupted the existing caste-based occupational structure and notions of purity and pollution. This was the main cause of harassment, intimidation and persecution of the converts by the caste Hindus. Sometimes, the converts had to face strong reactions of the *Súdra* castes who were afraid that conversion would deprive them of the traditional employee service of the Malas and Madigas. The new converts had often refused to perform their traditional roles if it came into conflict with their new faith.[148] Often Christians had to face indiscriminate vengeance by the upper castes whose aim was to disturb the lives of the converts. Rev. Timpany of the CBM had noted that more than one hundred false cases were brought against the Christians in one church within a span of ten years.[149] There were numerous attempts to discourage enquirers from accepting the new faith by physical threatening. In Raghavapuram, there were instances of the converts' cattle driven off or seized, while the converts were forced to give up their rent-free lands, victimized with verbal abuse, imprisonment, beating and other forms of physical violence.[150] Sometimes, the missionaries helped converts by offering legal advice.[151]

When the missionaries delayed the admission of baptism, it produced some drop out candidates as they had faced harassment and persecution by their caste employers. But many believers persisted and joined the ranks of the Christian church, in spite of persecution.[152]

There was also an account of some *Súdra* farmers, the *Kammas,* who had persecuted the Malas by putting all their cattle in the pound without cause and not allowing the opening of schools for the benefit of the converts' children.[153] Converts often showed their disapproval to carry out traditional duties at village festivals such as the beating of drums or dancing before the idols. The convert Malas and the Madigas refused to pay the taxes charged of them to cover the cost of Hindu festivals and for the upkeep of the temples. This challenged the Sudras and upper castes. During animal sacrifice rituals, a question of *who* was raised, when the Madiga converts refused to sacrifice animals or beat the drums and remove animal carcasses.

Various forms of persecution took place such as beating, burning down of houses, poisoning of the wells, impounding of the cattle, making false charges, boycotting, etc.[154] In some cases the converts lost their remunerative jobs and were denied their traditional rights to gather fire-wood in wastelands and to dig fresh water tanks during drought.[155] A missionary had observed that, "no individual has any expectation of receiving the smallest extra income for his change of faith, but, on the contrary, stands a good chance of losing it."[156] The giving up of work on Sundays, particularly during the busy harvest period, was strongly opposed by the *Súdra* landlords.[157] The refusal of the converted Malas and the Madigas to work on Sundays met with harsh lessons from the *Súdra* employers who denied the former their share of the grain.[158]

Persecution was borne by the converts in a truly Christian spirit and indeed deepened the faith of those who endured it.[159] The landlords and moneylenders raised a hue and cry saying that conversion was used as an opportunity by the Malas and the Madigas to escape their traditional duties on one hand, and put the blame on the missionaries for encouraging unrest among the converts, on the other.[160] Sometimes the caste Hindus held that conversions 'angered' the deities and resulted in the occurring of natural calamities and outbreak of diseases like cholera and violent types of fever.

Nevertheless in all cases of persecution, as in the case of LMS missionary Mr. Johnston, the Sudras' anger was due to their jealousy: they could not tolerate the fact that the children of the Malas and the Madigas began to get educated and employed in blue or white collar jobs than their children could not achieve.[161]

4.4.5 Liberation from Caste-based Structural Oppression

The system of caste in India became a structural determinant owing to its ritualized sanctions that placed individuals' occupations in fixed physical spaces thereby reducing them into typical role takers to perform their routine jobs. However due to exposure to new and rational values, the rigid lines of social division started to change in the latter half of the 19th century. The social hardships that were endured by the Depressed Castes were mitigated due to availability of alternative choice of occupations after their Christian conversion.[162] The active intervention on the part of the Christian missionaries worked as an effective means for the social upliftment of the Malas and Madigas. We have discussed in Chapter 2, the depressed condition of the Malas and the Madigas in mid 19th century.

4.4.6 Quest for Social Upliftment and Alternative Socio-religious Identity

During the nineteenth century, the social environment in Andhra was filled with deep discontent among the Depressed Castes. They aspired to elevate their social position by ameliorating their degenerated condition.[163] In Rev. Clough's observation, people who were eager to improve their social position, approached him to be admitted into baptism rather than seeking to obtain material benefits.[164] According to Duncan Forrester, their yearning for human dignity, self-respect, and social equality on one hand, and the new context of missionary-supported institutions, on the other were powerful incentives for their conversion to Christianity.[165] Forrester says that conversion to Christianity was used by the Malas and the Madigas as an instrument to advance on the social scale.[166] An individual seeks to break the power of oppressive social structures to "escape from the origin state."[167] The Canadian Baptist Missionary Rev. Malcolm Orchard had described that the outcaste aspired schooling for his children, sympathy and brotherhood for himself and attainment of his long lost rights in the community.[168]

Among the most significant outcomes of the mass conversions in Colonial Andhra was the desire of the people to get education for their children rather than tending the cattle of the landlord.[169] The main reason for the missionaries' success in gaining the hearts of the converts was their emphasis on the values of individualism and equality of all human beings that were often accompanied by attempts at socially uplifting them through programs related to education, health care and economic development. In order to educate and instruct the new converts, the missionaries gave priority to training of teachers and pastors to work in village congregations. The mission, in all the areas under its supervision provided a catechist and a schoolmaster each.[170] Village teachers were responsible for elementary education and literacy classes for adults. They offered simple remedies for common diseases, undertook temperance campaigns, and built and maintained village chapels and schools.[171] The expectations of the missionary, on the other hand, is reflected in the words of Eugene Stock, "when a whole body of low caste or out-caste people desired to become Christians for mixed motives, who after instruction in missionary schools for their children, will distinctly rise in character."[172] In Rev. Clough's words, the converts had begged for teachers to be sent to their villages.[173] The boys and girls who had received education in mission schools had formed the base of the intelligent members of the Christian community.[174]

4.4.7 Evangelistic Zeal of the Missionaries

The chief biblical call for evangelization namely, 'Go ye therefore and teach all nations' was followed by the Christian missionaries.[175] They were endowed with firm faith in God, had deep devotion to duty, and had the courage to travel to new and strange lands. They worked with people whose language, mode of life and customs were unknown to them.[176]

The 19th century Christian missionaries were engaged in a variety of evangelistic activities such as that of preaching in villages during large gatherings of people.[177] They distributed scripture portions and tracts which were written in Telugu.[178] Considerable amount of time was devoted to individual inquirers.[179] The missionary and the mission bungalow were always accessible to the people.[180] They established warm relations with the converts who were treated as their own people.[181] The missionary became a source of inspiration, instruction, advice and love.[182] The wife of a missionary was a resourceful and uncomplaining woman who supplemented the work of her husband.[183]

The missionary occupied an important place in the lives of the people. Both Christians and Hindu caste people alike felt that they had someone with them far above the ordinary.[184] During times of natural calamities the missionaries became a ray of hope not only for the Depressed Castes but also for the caste people who trusted the missionaries with their valuables.[185] During their missionary work they had had to suffer often personal losses, diseases and face unsuitable weather conditions.[186] Their children were left in their home countries under the care of their relatives while they rendered their services in India.

The remark of an uneducated woman is worth noting: "a no-man's land has separated us very effectively from the caste part of the village, and no caste man or woman ever stepped into our doorway. But the missionary came, and the mission school was opened, and so much of what was dark, has become light."[187] In the words of Rev. John R. Mott, a pioneer who initiated group conversion,

> The work of the missionaries presented a most powerful witness of the Christian faith for raising the standard of the depressed castes in moral, spiritual and social spheres of life. The Depressed Castes' conversion to Christianity brought them out from a state of degradation and servitude under Hinduism for the last two thousand years. The movement impacted the whole people of India, especially the educated classes.[188]

4.4.8 Influence on Súdra Conversions

The Depressed Castes' interest in Christianity was like a fire that kindled other fires in the villages in Colonial Andhra. It kindled after the coming of the Christian missionaries. The impact of group conversions was felt in a significant way not only on the Malas and the Madigas, but also among other caste people, many of whom also sought conversion. Rev. Pickett observed that "about ninety percent of all higher caste converts interviewed attributed their conversion wholly, or in part, to the influence upon them of changes they had observed in converts from the depressed castes."[189] The report given by the Andhra Christian Council showed the remarkable social progress among the Malas and the Madigas in the Dornakal and Kistna dioceses and the willingness of the caste Hindus to hear the Gospel.[190]

The rapid growth of Christianity among the Malas and the Madigas attracted the lower non-*Brāhmin* castes who were also partakers of the social suffering though on a much lesser scale compared to that of the Malas and the Madigas. Mention may be made about the Kammas, Reddis, Telagas *and the* Gollas *besides the* Odderas *and the* Erukulas, *who sought conversion.*[191] Seemingly after witnessing the improvement in the lives of the Malas and Madigas, they were attracted towards Christian teachings and converted in large numbers.[192] The Lutheran missionary writer M. L. Dolbeer had observed that a friendly village with a faithful Christian congregation was selected to preach among the *Súdras.* The *Súdras* had expressed their eagerness for Christian preaching in the following words: "we thought Christianity was only for the Malas and Madigas, but now we see it is for everyone and now you come to preach to us instead of going always to the outcaste palem."[193] The United Lutheran Church Mission had worked among the *Súdras* in Guntur, East Godavari, West Godavari and Nellore districts. During the year 1930, there was an estimated three thousand and three hundred converted Christians from the *Súdras.*[194] Table 4.2 below shows the increase of conversions to Christianity after fifty years of missionary work.

Table 4.2: The Number of Christians in Coastal Andhra Districts in 1901

Districts	Total Population	Christians	% of Christians
Ganjam	16,891,42	2,426	0.12
Ganjam Agency	321,114	923	0.58
Vizagapatam	20,82,662	4.191	0.16
Vizagapatam Agency	850,988	3,155	1.13
Godavari	21,41,917	16,153	0.19
Godavari Agency	159,842	729	1.00
Kistna-Guntur	21,54,803	202,827	9.41
Nellore	14,96,987	36.249	8.24
Total	1,331,944	196,02	13.72%

Source: W. Francis, *Census of India,* 1901, Vol.15A, Part II, Imperial Tables, (Madras: The Government Press, 1902) 6.

As Rev. Pickett noted, in early twentieth century the converts from the *Kamma* caste said that, "none of our people would have become Christians if they had not first seen what happened to Malas."[195] The Christian influence on the caste Hindus is substantiated through a literary work by Raja M Bhujanga

Rao Bahadur, who described himself as "an old soldier, now a local Rajah, not a Christian, who translated the Gospels of St. Matthew, St. Luke and St. John into 'rhythmical Telugu.'" He published it with a preface apparently by a Christian.[196] Large scale conversion of caste Hindus did not occur unlike among the Depressed Castes because of the fear of losing their caste privileges.

4. 5 Conversions in Coastal Andhra: Processes and Mechanisms

4.5.1 Individual and Group Conversions

Individual conversions occurred when persons became convinced of the proposed new religion was the right one for attaining salvation. The initial conversions in Colonial Andhra occurred following the preaching of Christianity by the missionaries. The initiative was first taken by the missionaries who arrived in the midst of the people, preached their religion, holding out a new path of religious life for the people. Unlike in other regions, there was hardly any native initiative in Colonial Andhra of inviting the missionaries from elsewhere to come and preach Christianity. Secondly, slow and gradual conversions took place in the region, at the initiatives of certain individual pioneers. Neither Mission records, nor any government reports mention any use of coercive methods to force Christianity among the people. We have discussed the initiatives of some pioneers, who in turn, became preachers themselves. Eventually this gave rise to group conversions which became a feature in many areas. In this section we shall discuss how and why individual or group conversions occurred in Coastal Andhra.

4.5.2 Peoples' Initiative

Long before any social reform activities took place in Colonial Andhra, the Malas of Bezwada and Guntur asked the missionaries about the chances of getting uplifted if they were to convert. They had seen the level of social upliftment which missionaries elsewhere had mediated among the Depressed Castes. The people understood that education provided opportunities to achieve occupational mobility which could replace occupational bondage under the jajmani and caste system in traditional society. They also seem to have understood how missionary institutions such as churches, mission compounds, hospitals, schools and Sunday schools offered alternative channels of development to the converts. Visible evidence of social change was observed in the life and character of the converts who gave up some of their harmful habits on one hand, and attained higher economic status, on the other.[197] Every individual was considered as an integral part of the local church and therefore the person's consent and co-operation was enlisted.[198]

Individual conversion was liable to immediate excommunication often from one's own family or clan and definitively from one's own caste, and from the larger village community. This implied subsequent lose of the means of livelihood, and ostracisation. Therefore group conversion was preferred because it gave a sort of security and group strength to the converts. One can see a sort of tribal spirit in group conversions.[199] All these factors seem to have played together in augmenting group conversions, which eventually became a movement when many group conversion instances occurred.

In group conversion, the sluggish nature of individuality was won over by corporate action while changing allegiance towards a new religion.[200] The ties of kinship were also preserved through endogamous marriage relationships.[201] In Andrew Wingate's opinion, "a vital relationship exists between the family, friends, ethnic group, religious community and neighbourhood, which create a sense of identity."[202]

The missionaries also convinced village elders and headmen who were called *Kula Peddalu* (elders of clan) of the Mala and Madiga communities that they could become a body of capable leaders if they became preachers.[203] After a suitable period of instruction, they were baptized. Subsequently, they began to lead their fellow caste men to conversion.[204] The missionaries had exercised caution while receiving the crowds and every possible effort was taken to instruct the people much in advance before administering baptism to them.[205] The spread of the Gospel was rapidly facilitated on occasions like weddings, funerals, business deals, etc. Sometimes conversion was a prerequisite condition for marriage between a Christian and a Hindus of the same *jati.*[206] Group conversions in Colonial Andhra were also rural in character. Villagers came from far off villages to the towns of Bezwada, Ellore, Rajahmundry and Ongole to meet the missionaries seeking instruction and baptism. Table 4.3 shows the high increase of the Christian population in Colonial Andhra as the 1941 Census.

Table 4.3: Distribution of adherents of three major faiths in Colonial Andhra, 1941.

Districts		Population	Hindus	Mohammadans	Christians	% of Christians
Ganjam		38,45,944	35,072,24	29,122	20,503	0.53
Vizagapatnam	Agency	221,437	79,675	407	632	0.28
	Plains	36,24,507	34,275,49	28,715	19,871	0.54
Godavari East		21,61,863	18,974,15	32,801	39,117	2.53
Godavari East	Agency	271,569	1,640,75	3,410	6,878	2.53
	Plains	18,90,294	18,233,40	29,391	32,239	1.70
Godavari West		13,80,088	6,359,39	29,728	83,271	6.0
Kistna		14,44,294	12,32,212	76,722	134,434	9.30
Guntur		22,77,283	17,97,256	183,318	293,768	12.89
Nellore		16,17,026	14,16,178	120,004	80,246	4.96
Total		**18,734,305**	**45,25,321**	**533,618**	**710,959**	**41.26**

Source: N. W. M. Yeats, *Census of India*, 1941, Vol. 1, Part 1 (Madras: The Government Press, 1942), 331.

4.5.3 Caste/Clan, Kin and Family Affinities in Conversion

While individual conversions continued throughout the hundred-year period of our study, there occurred quite a few group conversions, particularly among the Malas and Madigas in coastal Andhra. Group conversions indicate collective social action and group solidarity. Such conversions invariably took place due to clan/caste or family/kin or race affinities. In fact most group conversions to Christianity or any other religion were characterized by such affinities. In some countries race was the stimulating force behind group conversion. In India, by and large, conversions occurred due to clan or caste or kin or family affinities, meaning, if one family converted it became a stimulus for other families of the same clan, if not the same caste. The history group conversions elsewhere in India has shown that caste cohesiveness was the stimulating force behind the conversion of a substantial number of members of a particular caste.

In the case of the Malas and Madigas, kin/family and clan/caste affinities were evident as our data on conversions show. This is substantiated in the processes of group conversions. If one caste converted to a particular Church, another caste which considered itself either below or above that caste, would invariably convert to another Church, not the same Church. Here the Church's identity and teaching were subsumed because caste affinity was stronger. Thus caste linkages were a major factor of conversion.[207] People tended to move within their caste boundaries *en masse* towards conversion.[208] The motive was primarily to protect themselves from the persecution of the upper caste employers and to continue their congregational life based on caste allegiances.

The issue of Congregational allegiance was overlooked by the missionaries while encouraging group conversion. They had followed a policy of neutrality and non-interference with regard to the entry of caste within the church, thereby risked schisms in the churches.[209] In the CMS mission fields, the large presence of the Malas was enough for the Madigas to stay away from that Church. Pagolu Venkayya, a Mala, was rebuked by some of his own people for eating with the Madiga Christians.[210] Large accessions to a particular missionary denomination had been almost exclusively from the same caste, either Malas or Madigas. For example, the Malas were dominantly present in the CMS and AELM, whereas the Madigas were prominent in the Baptist congregations.[211] It was a given fact that if one missionary denomination attracts the Malas, the other would keep aloof from attending that particular mission's activities. Growth of separatism was also due to the fact that when a mission starts its working with one caste group, that community starts to think that all the resources of that mission ought to be spent for the betterment of that caste community only.[212]

Some historians viewed group conversion movements as essentially 'caste movements' where caste was carried and promoted in the Church even after conversion.[213] But there were a few cases of overcoming of mutual caste hostility such as among the Malas and the Madigas who were once baptized together in the CMS missions roughly in equal numbers during the last part of the nineteenth century.[214] The Madigas' accession to Christianity can be traced to the Gospel preaching of Pagolu Venkayya.[215] On the contrary, in the ABM mission of Ongole, where the Madigas' presence was in large numbers, church worship was conducted side by side with the Mala' worshippers.[216] As Bishop Pickett observed, the Christian Malas had shown a sense of responsibility for the conversion of the other castes especially of the Madigas.[217] When all the converts started worshiping together caste hostility subsumed and a new Christian brotherhood began to sprout. They also began to accept the presence of higher caste Sudra members of the church and considered the church as a communion or corporate body of believers in the same church of Christ.[218]

Church functionaries also strove to construct a cohesive, united community of Christians out of disparate caste converts, through Christianization of the converts. After witnessing change among the Malas and the Madigas, it was noticed by the missionaries that these castes had desired for development and above all attempted to escape from their degraded status in society.[219] The missionaries became the forbearers of change in terms of introducing a new faith and in creating an aspiration for better life. They exhibited a sincerity of purpose with ingenious methods and enthusiasm.[220] By combining the proselytizing and philanthropic services the missionaries had laid a foundation for an assimilative incorporation of the Depressed Castes into a church community.[221]

4.5.4 Motives of Conversion

In the light of the group conversions missionaries have been criticized for encouraging swelling number of converts rather than checking the purity of their motivations. Further, the whole work of social upliftment of the marginalized by the missionaries has been condemned as 'allurement' to enhance conversions to Christianity. The main criticism is based on the influx of converts with mixed motives and the missionaries' methods of dealing with the crowds. The late nineteenth century membership of the Christian church was not an attempt by the missionaries to produce statistics for their home societies.[222] The genuine character of the missionary work should be measured in terms of the upward social mobility mediated by them.[223] The fact is that in the absence of an alternative reformative system that could bring them out of their depressed position, the Malas and the Madigas took the help of the Christian missionaries to achieve progressive social upliftment. M. N. Srinivas opined that the depressed castes had limited chances of pushing themselves up in the social system[224] and hence chose to follow an alternative path for social mobility.[225]

4.5.5 Reaction/Response of an Alarmed Ambient Society

The late nineteenth century conversion of the Depressed Castes into Christianity was viewed by some scholars as attempts to undermine the religious supremacy of Hinduism and a challenge to the foundation of Indian social structure. When the British government proposed to provide for separate electorates for the Depressed Castes in 1932, it became an issue of concern for the Indian National Congress because of an apparent fear of losing grip of the upper castes over the Depressed Castes.[226] Politically, Christian conversion became an explosive issue since 1930 as India witnessed a surge in voluntary defection from Hinduism.

In 1935, Mahatma Gandhi, who advocated removal of untouchability and upliftment of the Depressed Castes, strongly criticized mass conversions. Though he desired the upper castes to treat the 'untouchables' as humans, he never wanted equity and occupational mobility for them. He was a believer in the caste-based Hindu social structure which did not allow occupational mobility to certain castes and out-castes. So, he termed conversion into Christianity as an irrelevant and unpatriotic response to the problems of the untouchables. He did not accept the reality of conversion as 'a change of heart from sin to God brought about by Christ alone' and declared that this phenomenon might be applicable to only individual conversion, not to mass conversion.[227] He would have liked the missionaries to be mere reform workers without touching the religious beliefs of the Indians. During the socially turbulent period of 1930-35, the Indian national leaders were quite alarmed by the emerging confidence of the Indian Christian leaders who asked for equality of citizenship to members of all religions. But the former were not comfortable to accommodate the Christians as equal partners in the struggle for Independence.[228] In response to this criticism, a conference on group conversions was held by the National Christian Council in December 1936, at Nagpur. It discussed the unrest among the Depressed Castes, their motives, methods and results of mass conversion,[229] and justified mass conversion movement as a genuine struggle for freedom from socio-religious bondage.

4. 6 Role of Agents: Mediating Social Change

4.6.1 Role of Christian Missionaries

The comprehensive objective of the missionaries was to evangelize the nations by preaching the Gospel and reaching it to every individual. Among the manifold motives that drove the Christian missionaries to far off countries was their passion for the spread of Christianity. According to Horner, the missionary is a necessary person, involved in essential functions in the life of the church, because it is through him that the church fulfills its obligation to reach out in the mission. The aim and method of the Christian mission is always evangelism or evangelization.[230]

The Christian missionaries in Andhra acquired knowledge about the social and economic condition of the people in general, and of the poor, depressed caste Malas and Madigas in particular. They also acquired a fairly good knowledge about the culture and religion of the people. This knowledge helped them to understand the people and also in devising various schemes for the upliftment of the poor. In Chapters 5 and 6 we shall explore in detail about the uplitment programmes and humanitarian action of the missionaries in areas of education, health care, economic life, occupation, etc. Their contribution in these areas seems to have been more than their agenda of mere evangelization.[231]

Here there is a need to understand what evangelization meant to them. Evangelization according to them was not just oral preaching of the tenets of Christianity to an audience. It was practical Christianity that they preached. Preaching was much less in words than in deeds and action. Christianity as a 'social religion' created institutions for the betterment of society on the basis of egalitarian values. Reaching to the periphery, the poor, the marginalized peoples who needed more urgent help than others, the missionaries showed what practical Christianity was. Besides, the life witness, dedication, kindness and compassion for all, becoming a refuge for the homeless and so on, they became endearing persons for and among the people.

The reason behind their winning the trust of the Malas and the Madigas was their understanding of the people and their problems. In working with the Malas and Madigas, the missionaries had aimed at the improvement of their living conditions, along with teaching the Bible and telling about Jesus Christ.

The Christian missionaries also tried to fulfill their social obligations with humanitarian works. They understood that it was their duty to feed the hungry, give drink to the thirsty, visit the sick and so on, as the Bible teaches. There was no other way to serve humanity.[232] The missionaries used humanitarian works as part of evangelical works.[233] Within the primary aim of preaching the Gospel, the missionaries translated into action practical Christianity through their services. Thus, in the perception of the people, they came to be identified with the type of service they engaged in: evangelistic missionaries, educational missionaries, medical missionaries, itinerant missionaries, industrial missionaries, zenana missionaries, and so on.[234]

Mission records are replete with narratives on the remarkable personal qualities of some of the missionaries. Their character was marked by self-denial, selfless devotion to duty, unquestioning fidelity for the establishment of the mission, and deep love for their flock (people).[235] The modest and unwearied missionary was often accompanied by his amiable wife who both proved themselves to be the right people with a sense of mission.[236] During natural calamities like famines and diseases, the charitable conduct of the missionaries was appreciated not only by the depressed communities but also by the caste people.[237] Revs. Cran and Des Granges (LMS), Rev. Henry Watson Fox (CMS), Rev. William E. Snyder (AELC) and A. V. Timpany (CBM) were among those who had lost their lives while in missionary service in Colonial Andhra. Credit must also go to the hundreds of native missionaries and assistants who shared the burden of the missionaries and who made commendable contribution to bettering the lives of the people of Coastal Andhra.[238]

In organizing mission work, the missionary societies appear to have been very careful and sensitive to each other. As early as in 1850, missionaries in different parts of India felt the need to meet regularly in conferences to discuss the common interests of their work, so that one society may not intercept others' works and also to avoid 'sheep stealing' (weaning away converts from one church by another).[239] Cooperation and comity were established between missionary societies to avoid the risk of different missionary societies encroaching into each other's physical boundaries.[240]

4.6.2 The Question of Material Inducements, Judicious Approach in Relief Work

The missionaries' offer of help during times of need was a matter of suspicion and some scholars in the past as well as in the present tend to call the humanitarian service of the missionary as 'allurement' to elicit conversion. Our records show otherwise. During times of bitter famine and emergencies of catastrophic nature, missionary aid was distributed not only for the converts or prospective converts, but to all others including the caste people.[241] Missionaries were judicious in using the public funds for the benefit of all people, whereas they were free to use privately donated funds for the benefit of the converts.[242]

No assurance of any kind was given to the beneficiaries of relief service, that they could obtain any gains by conversion. The poor were not told at any time that the acceptance of Christ would bring them release from their burden of serfdom or from their debts.[243] Nevertheless, becoming Christian generally enabled the Depressed Castes to make social and economic improvement with education and vocational training from the mission.[244] Often the converts were termed as 'Rice Christians', a claim which was disproved by Rev. Clough who followed a dictum, 'first profess the faith, then baptism'. He never baptized anybody without ensuring that he or she professed Christianity for spiritual and religious reasons, rather than for any material ones. Many a time, seekers were kept in waiting for months for admission into baptism and into the Church.[245] Elsewhere we have noted the earnest request for baptism and admittance into the church, of some very poor Malas and Madigas who declared that they would not need any monetary or material assistance, come what might, even death.

4.6.3 Influence of the Christian Press and Literature

The importance of the Christian press and literature as missionary instruments was perceived by all missionary societies which worked in Colonial Andhra. These instruments were used to strengthen the faith of the Christians and to evangelize the non-Christians.

When the modern printing press was a technological luxury in those times, missiaonries ensured that they set up presses as they understood its effectiveness. Included in the Christian literature were "all books, tracts, and magazines published in India in English or in vernacular languages, with the purpose of expounding the teachings of Christianity, in illustrations of biography and history and applying it to home life and social life."[246]

The earliest literary works in Telugu language on the Christian faith were the *Tobhya Charitra* or *Sarvesvara Mahatya* of Pingali Erranarya or Pingali Ellanaryudu (1602) and *Vedanta Rasayana* and *Anuruddha Charitra* of Mangalagiri Anandakavi (1750).[247] The German Lutheran missionary Benzamin Schultze had translated the New Testament into Telugu in 1727, though it never appeared in print but the manuscript was found at Halle.[248] Rev. Schultze also had prepared a Telugu-English Dictionary in 1728, for use of the missionaries.[249]

The Foreign Bible Society was formed in 1804 and three missionaries, Mr. William Carey, Mr. Joshua Marshman and Mr. William Ward were sent to the Danish Settlement at Serampore, on the banks of Hooghly River, West Bengal. The three missionaries had submitted a proposal to the Home Committee for the translation and publication of the Holy Bible into Indian languages such as Bengali, Hindustani, Oriya, Telugu, Kannada, Marathi and Tamil.[250] In 1807, the *New Testament* was translated by Rev. William Carey into Telugu.[251] A translation of the St. Luke's Gospel by the LMS's Rev. Des Granges was printed in 1810. The Telugu version of the *New Testament* that was prepared by the Serampore missionaries was printed in 1818.

In later years, the Bellary Tract Society, the Madras Tract and Book Society, the Vizagapatam Tract Society, the American Baptist Mission at Nellore and the Narsapur Mission succeeded in printing Gospel tracts in Telugu.[252] The Madras Auxiliary Society in particular played active role in the preparation and distribution of a number of Gospel tracts at free of cost to the Telugu missions.[253] In the year 1849, Mr. Newill, Esq., the Assistant Collector of Guntur played active role in the preparation of a number of Gospel tracts, a Telugu hymn book and an almanac and got these printed and published from his personal resources.[254] The London Missionary Society was the forerunner of all literary and translation activities in the Telugu provinces. For more than thirty years, the *New Testament* published by Rev. Gordon and Rev. Pritchett in 1818 was in circulation. Although, the *Old Testament* was translated simultaneously, it was not printed until Revs. Johnson and Gordon prepared the final proofs in 1850.[255]

The primary objective of translation of the Bible in native languages was to bring the knowledge of the Gospel to the natives. In 1865, under the leadership of the Foreign Bible Society and Rev. John Hay of the London Missionary Society, a committee for a comprehensive translation of the Holy Bible into Telugu, was undertaken in collaboration with all concerned missionary societies, namely the American Baptist Mission, the Hermannsburg Lutheran Mission of Naidupet, the General Synod of the Lutheran Mission of Guntur, the General Council of the Lutheran Mission of Rajahmundry, the Church Missionary Society of Masulipatnam, the Plymouth Brethren, the Godavari Delta Mission and the London Missionary Society of Vizagapatam and Bellary.[256] Access to the Holy Bible in Telugu indeed helped the people to understand Biblical teachings and the life of Christ.

Literary pursuits rose out of an eagerness to reach out to a large number of people who could read and write. The contribution of the missions towards the development of Indian literature was referred to by the first Prime Minister of India, Jawaharlal Nehru: "the desire of the Christian missionaries to translate Bible into every possible language thus resulted in the development of many Indian languages. Many of them as scholars, historians, sociologists or lexicographers earned a high place in oriental literature and had written books with lasting utility.[257] In the words of Dr. Jacob Chamberlain, the Holy Bible in its suitability for all the races and all the languages of mankind met the spiritual wants of the Hindus, from the intellectual *Brāhmins* to the most illiterate Pariahs. It became an imperative need for the missionary to make the scripture portions and Gospel tracts available to the people in their missionary fields of operation.[258]

The literary tracts were widely used by the missionaries and native preachers to disseminate not only the Gospel teachings but also practical living and social development. Table 4.4 below shows some of the works that were translated from English and other languages into Telugu, during the second half of the 19th century.[259] The press and literature also had a major role in disseminating new ideas of reform among people.

Table 4.4: List of Christian Literary Works

Sl. No.	Name of the Tract	Author	Original Language	Year
1	The Indian Pilgrim	Rev. W. Howell	English	1830
2	A View of the Christian Religion	Rev. S. S. Day	Burmese	1839
3	Good Tidings	Rev. J. Reid	Marathi	1841
4	The Parallels which Christ Spoke	Rev. J. E. Sharkey	English	1848
5	The Jewel Mine of Salvation	Purushottam Chaudhary	Oriya	1849
6	Truth for All	Rev. J. Hay	English	1849
7	Believe and Live	Rev. J. Hay	English	1850
8	The Peep of Day	Rev. J. W. Gordon	English	1854
9	Come to Jesus	Rev. J. W. Gordon	English	1855
10	The Ayah and Lady	Rev. E. Porter	English	1855
11	The True Religion Demonstrated	Rev. William Dawson	English	1856
12	God's Gift of Grace	Rev. T. Heelis	English	1859
13	A Dialogue on Salvation	Rev. R. D. Johnston	English	1861
14	History of the Everlasting Gospel	H. Newill Esq.	English	1861
15	Mothers in South India	Mrs. T. Clarke	English	1861
16	On Caste	Purushottam Chaudhary	English	1861
17	On Idolatry	Purushottam Chaudhary	English	1861
18	The True Way of Salvation	Rev. W. Dawson	English	1861
19	Messages for All	Rev. J. E. Clough	English	1868
20	Pilgrim's Progress	Rev. J. Hay	English	1868

Source: own compilation from various Mission sources.

The Tract and Christian Literature Society undertook the tasks of production, publication and distribution of Christian literature. The Christian magazines in circulation were the *Hitavadi* from Masulipatnam with 1000 copies in circulation, the *Messenger of Truth* by Rev. Dhanwada Anantam of the Church Missionary Society with 5760 copies in circulation, *Ravi* from Cocanada and *The Telugu Baptist* by Rev. H. C. Stillwell of Samalkota, with equal number of copies in circulation.[260] In 1901, the number of Telugu speaking people was estimated at 20.70 millions.[261]

The Madras Conference Report recognized the emerging need for Christian literature for which efforts were directed in the preparation and circulation of suitable books, tracts, and leaflets. For this purpose, missionaries with literary aptitude were assigned for the preparation of literary work in the linguistic area of their work. The literature was intended to reflect the needs of the native people and to enlighten their minds. Hence, the authors were free to add, alter, and adapt the contents to suit the native readers. But in the case of Bible translation, the translator was to strictly follow the canonical norms regarding Bible translation.[262] While preparing Christian literature, the writers were expected to recognize the important elements in the native religion, literature, customs and practices by keeping in mind the target readers. Clear printing of the text with suitable pictorial illustrations was required.[263]

The circulation of the Christian literature was entrusted to the colporteurs, school teachers, Zenana visitors, Bible women and hospital workers. They were to keep sufficient stock of books, leaflets and tracts to be sold or freely distributed.[264] The formation of the All India Federation of Christian Tract and Book Societies in 1916 succeeded in unifying the activities of different publishing societies in matters of methods of work and activities through adequate intercommunication between them.[265]

In the initial years of Gospel preaching, Christian literature was not widely used among the Malas and the Madigas as the missionaries scarcely found any one able to read among these castes. Nevertheless, owing to the rapid increase of education and aspiration for upward mobility, literary works became more in demand.

The new Christian literature helped expose the deplorable condition of the Depressed Castes and proposed to them the message of redemption and freedom from social bondages.[266] The growth of a new social consciousness among the Malas and the Madigas could also be attributed to the availability of Christian literature. The literature also contained helpful items such as prayers, hymns, songs, for worship services. In this context, the Andhra Christian Hymnal was a prominent one. It was first published by the Christian Literary Society in 1893. The native Christian converts had composed and contributed many hymns on various themes such as praise to God, Christian life and hope, Marriage, Baptism, Faith and love, Salvation, Redemption, etc., to this book. Notable among the writers were Daniel Jonnakuti, Daniel Thupili, Mallela David, Kadiyam Gabriel (1876-1937), Nelaturi Luther (1892) Gollapalli Nathaniel (1839-1914), Chikkala Paulus (1865-1912), Kuchipudi Rajaratnam (1888-1946), Bontha Samuel (1911), Mamuduri Simon (1869-1946), Sarella Samuel Subbayya (1888-1944), Chadalavada Thomas (1856-1906), Abraham Kesanapalli, Daniel Eddu (1900), and Chadalavada Zecharia (1876-1951). In hymns such as *Yehova Naa Mora Laalinchenu* (The Lord God heard my distressed voice), *Dikku Leni Vaadano Prabhu* (I am a destitute), *Deva*

Samsthuthi Cheyave Manasaa—Chaavu Gothi Nundi Ninnu (Praise the Lord for redeeming from the death trap), *Yesunannu Preminchinaavu* (Jesus, you loved me), and other hymns were concrete poetic expressions of the distress of the people who sought to be redeemed through conversion.

The National Christian Council's Theological Committee called the attention of the theological colleges to the need of translation of standard theological books and modern apologetic literature into Indian languages.[267] A conference of Christian authors and artists was held at Bezwada in 1946 which approved the establishment of the *Telugu Christian Weekly Newspaper.*[268] Thus, the dissemination of Christian values, ideals, tenets and the message of salvation in the Bible were effectively carried out by the missionary bodies to cover a wide range of people, both converts and the general public.

4.6.4 Role of Native Leaders

Along with the foreign missionaries there was a large body of native preachers and leaders whose combined work augumented group conversions in Colonial Andhra. Mention has been made elsewhere in this book about some of the prominent foreign as well as native missionary leaders. A few of the latter ones were Rev. N. Kanakiah of Nellore, Pagolu Venkayya of Raghavapuram, Das Antharvedy, Thomas Gabriel of Gunnanapudi, Yerraguntla Periah of Talakondapadu, Pidatala Periah, Bezwada Paul of Atmakur, Baddepudy Abraham, Thaluri Daniel, Karre Peter of Vuyyuru, Munangi Anumiah, Kola Peddiah and Rev. Perivalli Abraham. The native preachers were first converts themselves who became the principal force behind the group conversion movement. They became pillars of the local church and strove to keep the mission fields thriving.[269] They were not perfect literates to interpret the Holy Bible, but through their simple preaching and other ministerial acts, they gained thousands of converts.[270] They never grew tired of preaching and they preached in a language that was plain and easy to understand even by the most ignorant.[271] To the astonishment of the missionaries, the native preachers, who were idol worshippers only a few years ago, exhibited remarkable knowledge of the Christian doctrines with adequate theological training at the Ramapatnam Seminary.[272]

The pioneers of group conversions had maintained strong faith and led the movement in a steadfast way. For example, throughout his life Venkayya had remained an ardent Christian preacher and converted nearly ten thousand people from villages such as Kallur, Lankapalli and Kishtaram, besides Raghavapuram from among the Malas and Madigas.[273] The mass movement which Venkayya had initiated in Kistna and Godavari areas increased church membership from 260 in 1861 to 11,356 in 1894.[274] Though he was an illiterate man, he proclaimed the Gospel with utmost conviction and zeal. He died in 1891 at the age of 82.[275] His fascinating leadership in effecting group conversion was remarkable as the Malas simply decided to get converted in droves. In the words of Rev. Hibbert-Ware, Venkayya was "the type of a well-recognized class of men who in all parts of India where the Gospel has newly come and is being accepted have been the immediate human instruments to lead their fellow-countrymen to Christ."[276]

Similar was the case with Yerraguntla Periah, the pioneer of group conversions among the Madigas. He had shown sincerity in faith, simplicity in thought and nobility in service and was regarded as the patriarch of the Madiga conversion to Christianity. Narrating his Christian persuasion, Periah says, "What the teachers of Yoga told me was good. But nothing satisfied my soul till I heard of Gospel of salvation."[277] The burning zeal of Yerraguntla Periah was noticed by native preachers Rev. Canakiah and Rungiah who were astonished to find him far ahead of themselves in his desire to preach the Gospel.[278] In the words of Rev. Clough,

> Yerraguntla Periah was a personality, a man with a spiritual history. He had taken more distinct steps in his religious experience than falls to the lot of most white men to take. His request to me was practically that I should let this Christian movement go in the channels formed by Indian movement's own means of enhancing spiritual significance.[279]

4.7 Understanding the Dynamics of Group Conversions

We have explored the course of the conversions of the Malas and the Madigas, both individual and group ones, in the preceding pages. Individual conversions of a few over a period of time cannot be considered as a mass movement. But as we have seen in the preceding pages and also in other chapters, individual conversions led to regular occurrence of group conversions due to kin/family, clan/caste affinities, which became a pulling factor. Just as group social reform movements were taking place in the Hindu society during late nineteenth and early twentieth centuries, group conversion movements to Christianity also were taking place in several parts of India from mid 19th century to roughly about 1930s.[280] These movements were triggered by the coming of the Christian missionaries.

We have seen that in coastal Andhra, it was the Protestant missionaries who initiated this process. Conversions of a good number of individual Malas and Madigas, seem to have initiated groups of Mala and Madiga families to convert. The whole process began in the 1840-45 period which was the time when six major Protestant missionary societies began to work in Colonial Andhra.

It may be noted that group conversions were influenced and triggered by some individual conversions among both the communities. It was a particular convert, Dasari Chinnaiah, who studied in the school of Rev. E. S. Bowden of the Godavari Delta mission, who convinced the villagers of Velpur (Tanukutaluq) about the goodness of the new religion, Christianity.[281] In the Kistna and Godavari deltas, the Malas, who converted were primarily occupied with agriculture, were industrious and were relatively independent of the caste people because of which that they could make free decisions to convert without fear of any reprimands from the caste overlords.[282] In G. A. Oddie's observation, the Malas and the Madigas living in the Kistna and Godavari delta were free from the recurrent famines as compared to the South Andhra region and therefore economic independence might have contributed for their orientation and initiative to convert to Christianity without any fear of reprisal.[283] So also, since 1857, quite a few Madigas were influenced by the missionary, Rev. F. W. N. Alexander at Ellore. The village of Polepalli was where some of the early Madigas converted under the influence of Rev. C. F. Heyer in 1844.[284] The influence of the pioneer Venkayya and Yerraguntla Periah on a large number of members of the their respective Mala and Madiga communities was noted above.

Significant momentum of the movements was noted after 1853 in the Telugu districts due the missionaries' methods of reaching the people with their educational work and social upliftment programs.[285] Quite contrary to the expectations of the missionaries, who believed in the 'downward percolation theory' that is, the Gospel would first reach the English educated intelligentsia, which would, in turn, influence the wider Indian population, it was the Depressed Caste people who began to show much interest in Christianity. The profound pessimism expressed by Abbé Dubois in early 19th century did not apply to the Depressed Caste converts from the Telugu districts.[286] Contrary to his belief and prediction that, 'Christianity would percolate downwards slowly until at last the untouchables would also be gathered in' was not the case in coastal Andhra.[287] The massive majority of the converts, nearly 95%, came not from the Sudra or upper castes, but from the Depressed Castes (Malas and Madigas).[288] This impetus for upward social mobility seems to have derived its strength from the mobility achievers elsewhere in the Madras Presidency. Mission's success stories were commonly circulated by the missionaries in newer areas where nascent converts lived. The stories of the Depressed Castes movement in Tinnevelly and Travancore regions had given great fillip to the new converts on Coastal Andhra.[289] This took the missionaries by surprise.[290]

The principal towns and the catchments that came under the influence of group conversion movements were almost all the chief towns and adjoining villages of colonial Andhra namely, Vizagapatam, Vizianagram, Bobbili, Cocanada, Samalkot, Rajahmundry, Tuni, Dowlaishvaram, Akidu, Ellore, Bezwada, Raghavapuram, Masulipatnam, Vuyyuru, Guntur, Narasaraopet, Rentachintala, Cumbum, Vinukonda, Bapatla, Ongole, Kanigiri and Nellore.

The movement grew in physical spread across the Madras Presidency and the adjoining Nizam's territories of Dornakal, Hanmakonda, Nalgonda, Khammamet, Warangal and Karimnagar. Table 4.5 below shows the growth in the number of Christians during the 100-year period of the Christian Missions in Coastal Andhra.

Table 4.5: Growth in the Number of Christians during 1851 to 1951

	1851	1861	1871	1881	1891	1901	1911	1921	1931	1941	1951
Ganjam/ Srikakulam	549	556	1043	1,537	2,292	2,426	2,367	1,969	2,691	--	9,102
Ganjam Agency				14	521	923	1,896	1,395	5,893	--	108
Vizagapatam				3,408	3,914	4,191	4,983	8,656	11,882	19,871	10,095
Vizagapatam Agency	1,213	739	2,185	8	130	3,155	9,753	13,772	22,242	632	212
Godavari Agency	742	1316	1,483	8	442	729	1,616	2,436	4,365	6,878	7419
Godavari East				3,856	2,871	4,768	8,240	14,237	25,212	32,239	42,091
Godavari West					5,766	11,385	18,968	37,189	62,661	83,271	96,885
Kistna	3,521	5,387	7,670	36,194	10,802	17,801	49,863	53,898	101,289	134,434	177,607
Guntur	868		--	--	79,479	167,225	123,707	153,510	237,772	293,768	356,039
Nellore	549	1,617	3,012	20,794	34,875	36,249	44,298	52,498	65,593	80,246	104,750
Total	7,742	9,615	15,393	64,819	141,092	248,852	265,691	339,560	539,600	651,339	804,308
% Increase/ Decrease	---	24.19	37.53	76.25	54.05	43.30	6.33	21.75	37.07	17.15	19.01

- Sources: W. R. Cornish, *Census of the Madras Presidency, 1851-1871: Containing the Census arranged in Standard form prescribed by the Government of India,* Vol. I, Appendix Tables (Madras: The Government Gazette Press, 1874), 9 & 12;
- Lewis McIver, *Census of India*, 1881, Madras Presidency, Operations and Results, Vol. II, (Madras: The Government Press, 1882), Op cit, 10.
- Gordon Mackenzie, *A Manual of the Kistna District in the Presidency of Madras*, (Madras: Lawrence Asylum Press, 1883), 291.
- H. A. Stuart, *Census of India*, 1891, The Report, Vol. XIII (Madras: The Government Press, 1893), Op cit, 69.
- W. Francis, *Census of India*, 1901, Vol. XVA, Part II, Imperial Tables, (Madras: The Government Press, 1902), Op cit, 26.
- Chartres J Molony, *Census of India*, 1911, Imperial and Provincial Tables, Part II, Table VI, Vol. XII (Madras: The Government Press, 1912), 272.
- G. T. Boag, *Census of India*, Imperial and Provincial Tables, Part II, Vol. XIII (Madras: The Government Press,1922), 63.
- N. W. M. Yeats, *Census of India*, 1931, Vol. I, Report, Part I, Appendix I, (Madras: The Government Press, 1932), Op cit, 62.

- D. H. Elwin, *The Census of India*, 1941, Vol. II, Part I, Provincial Tables (Simla: The Government Press, 1942), 60-63.
- S. Venkateswaran, *The Census of India*, 1951, Vol. III, Madras and Coorg, Part II B, Tables (Madras: The Government Press,1953), 145.

4.7.1 Birth of a New Consciousness

The missionaries believed that evangelization was man's work and conversion as the act of God. The primary purpose of the missions/missionaries was to proclaim the Gospel message and to bring out the converts out of 'heathenism' for the formation of the 'Ecclesia' (Church community).[291] Conversion is an event or process that brings change in the life of a person and in his beliefs, attitudes and behaviour.[292] It insists on a real change, a decisive turn of a regenerative nature.[293]

The process began with the arrival of the missionaries who set up mission houses, went about preaching the Gospel, promising spiritual salvation to the souls, and liberation from bondage and poverty in the material life. A teacher-evangelist was assigned to teach in the village household to strengthen the process of conversion.[294] The propagation of the Gospel invariably involved setting up educational institutions, providing health care facilities, skill and technical training, as well as succor during times of suffering due to natural calamities.[295] W. S. Hunt has described group conversion movement as:

> Repeated occurring acts in churches, schools, in mud and palm leaf sheds, under trees in the open air, in rivers and tanks, a repeating scene of families or group of families getting baptized collectively by the missionaries of Anglican, Wesleyan, Congregational, Presbyterian, Baptist, Lutheran, European and American.[296]

It is important to understand the dynamics of group conversions which became a movement in coastal Andhra. The response of the people to missionary preaching begins when a person decides to become an inquirer and then decides to convert. Group conversions (*Gumpula Sanchalanamu,* in Telugu) occurred due to the choice of groups of families and villagers to convert *en masse* to Christianity. The process was set in when people comprising of individuals, families and village entities worked in their own network of *Jat* or family ties.[297] In group conversion, the convert chooses to move along with his family and relatives belonging to the same *jati* (caste or sub-caste) into the fold of another religion and strive to preserve the basis of their social environment.[298]

Group conversions in Andhra did not experience any surging mobs of people 'gate crashing' their way into Christianity. The number of conversions was substantial but not huge. This was because there was no stimulus for triggering massive movements. However, the number of conversions in groups or families among the two castes (Malas and Madigas) over a period of some

50 years had had the characteristics of a mass conversion movement. All the factors inherent in the spread of group conversions and its processes indicate that a new socio-religious consciousness had begun to take root among them. It was the articulation of their quest for a new way of life, a new social status with a distinct religious identity as Christians.[299]

An examination of the course of the group conversion movements can provide us with insights into the relation between conversion, social relations and inter-caste dynamics. In the late nineteenth century, the numbers involved in group conversion movements were unusually large as converts came in caste groups rather than as family groups or groups of individuals.[300] It was evident that the Malas and the Madigas had chosen an alternative route of social change under the leadership of prominent persons or community leaders.[301] There might also have been a desire not to be left out, when many members of the community were moving ahead. There might have been an eagerness to be identified with the new religion, which was accepted by a substantial numbers among them.[302] We have discussed the work and strategies of the missionary societies in Chapter 3. It may be understood that the beneficiaries of the missionary aid might have felt more empowered having received better education, training, health care, etc (see Chapters 5 and 6).

That alone would not have effected a change of perception in their lives which would eventually enable them to take a different religious and cultural orientation by accepting an alien religion. Undoubtedly this was something force, some ideals that seem to have gripped them to make such a momentous decision to change one's religion.

In the mind of the missionaries, whatever they did by way of giving education, skill training, health care, and so on was to translate the essential message of the Gospel in real life. The message of the Gospel was called 'good news'. The 'good news' articulated in their preaching has been recorded in many Mission records. I can only reconstruct the essence of what they preached. 'The 'good news' was that 'God created all humans and all are sons or daughters of the one God, who is like Father of all. Being children of the one Father, all are born equal with equal dignity. Therefore man-made distinctions and inequalities are sinful structures. The glory of God is the full development of man. Therefore the vocation of humans is to enhance the quality of life on earth. The aim of human life is to have communion with God, which was 'salvation'. God wills that all human beings be saved. We have come to announce this good news of salvation.'

In the context of the Malas and the Madigas, the key message was that God created all men equal and there existed no divisions between men such as that of caste barriers. The Biblical maxim of "God has chosen the poor and the despised rather than the rich and mighty, as the first fruits of His saving grace" was a welcoming message for the converts from the Mala and Madiga castes.[303] The ideal of equality of all human beings inclusive of the 'outcastes' might have been experienced by them in the lived life of the missionaries. The Christian missionaries had established a relation between scriptural writings and hope of an egalitarian society in the here and now which seem to have made an appeal to their listeners.[304] Thus, this message of salvation seems to have touched the Malas and Madigas who otherwise were considered 'outcastes' in the contemporary Hindu society. For centuries, they had lived a subaltern life, having internalized their society-imposed lowliness and rejection or fate.

Thus, beyond the material advancement achieved through the mediation of the missionaries, was the enlightening of their minds, gaining of abilities, gaining more confidence in themselves and above all, the touching experience of the heart—the acceptance of the Malas and Madigas as persons with dignity by the endearing, welcoming and accepting attitude of the missionaries—all these together seem to have created a new consciousness among those who came across with the missionaries. This seems to be the reason why groups of families and villagers decided to forego their centuries-old socio-cultural structures and the religions of their ancestors—Hinduism—and accept an alien religion, Christianity. A proper perception of the teachings or doctrinal Christianity might not have been there, but the experience of Christianity as the lived religion of the missionaries seems to have been deep. This was the birthing of a new consciousness among the Malas and the Madigas.

This new social consciousness seems to have goaded the Malas and the Madigas to make conscious efforts, individually and collectively, to liberate themselves from the given depressed condition, to a better level of life.[305] Social consciousness is a purposive effort in Durkheim's words "of the individual mind as the 'collective consciousness is incarnated in the individual."[306] "Collective action for common ends is the essence of society, and in taking counsel together for the good of the tribe each one learns also to take counsel with himself for his own good."[307] Social consciousness is a byproduct of 'self-consciousness with reference to the one self.[308] New consciousness occurs from the mobility of a few individuals' exposure to new ideas and impacting those ideas upon their own people.[309]

The dynamics of social change can be seen at the macro level: change in the social structures and at the micro level, change in the life of the individual.[310] The influence of individual effort impacts collective effort; as also collective effort can influence individual efforts, making it a two-way movement. Social mobility is followed by 'social action' where the actions of individuals were meaningfully related to the behaviour of other persons in *'wholes'* towards a specific action to achieve some objective values.[311] According to Durkheim, social mobility is a system of rules emanating from a group which are imposed upon its members of the clan or tribe.[312] Christian missionaries and their activities seem to have induced the Malas and the Madigas to convert to Christianity. This displayed the dynamism of both individual consciousness and collective consciousness. Mobility takes place when people experiencing some instinct or seeking achievement of some purpose, make collective decisions at the initiative and leadership by leaders and pioneers. Mankind has always expressed its inner self and externalized its needs, desires and possibilities in a collective manner.[313] The collective conscious decision making was not an imagined entity but a real process of social engineering beginning with individual conscious decision makings.[314]

Group conversion movements of the Malas and the Madigas into Christianity were apparently attempts to achieve a new collective identity as Christians, rejecting the existing identity as 'outcastes' and distancing themselves from their past faiths. At the same it was also their attempt towards upward mobility for a qualitative change in life.

The 19th century group conversion movements contained an element of voluntary acceptance of Christianity and shifting the roots of their old identity to a new one.[315] Around the years 1920 and 1930, the group conversion movements that occurred among the Malas and the Madigas into Christianity were to be viewed as an attempt to improve their lives where baptism became the dividing line between the old and new way of life.[316] The divine sanction of religion had found its expression into man's ideological beliefs, customary rituals and practices and profoundly influenced the individual's economic and social way of life. The conversion of the Malas and the Madigas in groups was neither a pre-planned event nor hoped by the missionaries.[317]

The growth of social consciousness and the aspiration for social change among the Christian converts of the Malas and the Madigas during the second half of the 19th century was a byproduct of their interaction with the Christian missionaries. Social change is a process where an idea or ideas is/are perceived as an illuminating influence for social mobilization.[318] Alvin Boskoff opined that "social change is an intelligible process in which we can discover significant alteration in the structure and functioning of the social systems."[319] In Romila Thapar's opinion, Christian missionaries were moved by the condition of the depressed castes who were oppressed by the *Brāhmins* and other upper castes from the period of Aryan invasions.[320] Social and economic bondages started to lose grip on the depressed castes due to colonial government's policies and an awakened consciousness that took a definite shape with the help of the missionaries. A degree of social mobility occurred among these castes as a consequence of their conversion, education and occupational mobility. During the second half of the 19th century, Christian missionaries acted as agents of change and presented the depressed castes with alternative strategies for social change.

The late nineteenth century group conversion movement was characterized by elements of spiritual restlessness, quest for new faiths and striving for betterment of life.[321] Given their experience of inclusion-exclusion within Hinduism, it was not hard for them to convert, though it entailed several challenges and even sufferings.[322] The resolve to join the ranks of the new faith rose from a conviction about the essential truths of the Gospel.[323] Certain other material motives for attaining social, educational upward mobility also played a role in their decisions.[324] Overall, the deprived condition of the people and their quest for a better life on one hand, and the purposive, goal-oriented, external action of the missionaries on the other, seem to have brought about the change in the Malas and Madigas. The 'push and pull factors' may be referred here: the push factors constituted the existential oppressive social, economic and religious structures of the Malas and the Madigas; the pull factors comprised of the new consciousness, new understanding of another religion and aspirations for a better life and future.[325]

Historically the birth of the new social consciousness among the Mala and the Madiga Christian converts can be explained in terms of a combination of some historically contingent factors. "Consciousness of oppression may well be as old as the system of untouchability itself, but the conditions for its development into militancy were put in place only during the period of direct British rule after the uprising of 1857."[326] In the case of Colonial Andhra the new consciousness did not erupt into incipient or sporadic revolts, nor was it articulated as protest conversions. Quite differently, the conversions in Andhra were mobility-oriented and voluntary.

4.8 Conclusion

Thus group conversion movements in Andhra seem to have occurred as a result of many contingent factors of both spiritual and non-spiritual nature. The lead for the group mobility movements came from the leading men of the clan.[327] The dire poverty, wretched homes, unremitting toil and physical sufferings were also behind the Malas' and Madigas' conversion into Christianity.[328] The fact that many converts remained steadfast under severe pressure was a sign that they were not actuated by want of immediate gains and temporal benefits.[329]

Theoretically, conversion lifted the converted individual and his family out of depressed condition and created a place for them in the contemporary society filled with an egalitarian ideology.[330] The Christian missionaries had influenced the Malas and the Madigas towards a positive affirmation of a new social identity. The converts had made a conscious effort to make changes in their behavioural patterns and life styles to enhance their social status.[331]

In conclusion, the group conversion movements among the Malas and the Madigas was an attempt to create a new identity for themselves and was the beginning of a great change in all aspects of life that was characterized by educational mobility, occupational mobility and social mobility. The most important outcome of the group conversion movements was the accomplishment of spiritual gain, thanks to the evangelistic activities. The series of movements created avenues for the Malas and the Madigas to move out of their traditional spaces into alternative and new spaces in society.[332] Thousands of Malas and Madigas who had passed through the missionary schools had experienced change in their lives through education and improved economic conditions. It was a collective decision of a number of individuals that enabled them to become Christians, while maintaining full ties with their non-Christian relatives, thereby enabling the latter to follow the faith after suitable instruction.[333] The aim has always been transformation of the collective towards upward status or position with the help of an external agency, which, in Colonial Andhra was the Christian mission. But the Christian mission was not the sole agency: there were other contemporary external agencies or forces such as the Colonial Government and its program of inclusive education of the Depressed Castes, public works programmes, modernization of economy, political empowerment, and a number of others. However, in the case of the Malas and Madigas of Coastal Andhra, the most significant external agency which mediated their upward socio-religious and socio-cultural mobility, was the missionary society.[334]

Endnotes and References

1 For a dossier on conversions in India during the peak period of 1930s led by Ambedkar, see Anon, *The Depressed Classes: A Chronological Documentation,* Part I-XI, 1931-1937 (Kurseong: St Mary's College (presently Vidyajyoti College of Theology, Delhi), 1937): 1-587+ xx.

2 Carol Graham, *Azariah of Dornakal* (London: S.C.M. Press Ltd, 1946), 66.

3 For a detailed account see Richard Lovett, *The History of the London Missionary Society, 1795-1895*, Vol. II (Oxford: Oxford University Press, 1899), 137-138.

4 M. Moses, *Andhra Pradesh Kraisthava Sangha Charitra* (Tenali: Kraisthava Satya Grandhasala, 2004), 35.

5 Richard Lovett, *The History of the London Missionary Society, 1795-1895*, Vol. II (Oxford: Oxford University Press, 1899), 138.

6 G. A. Oddie, "Christian Conversion among Non-Brāhmins in Andhra Pradesh with special Reference to Anglican Missions and the Dornakal Diocese, c. 1900-1936" in *Religious Conversion and Revival Movements in South Asia in Mediaeval and Modern Times*, ed. G. A. Oddie (New Delhi: Manohar Publishers, 1977), 73.

7 M. E. Gibbs, *The Anglican Church in India* (Delhi: ISPCK Publishers, 1972), 153.

8 Frederick Gledstone, *Andhra Christian Church Founders: The Life Story of Thomas Young Darling* (Madras: Diocesan Press, 1941), 9.

9 Hibbert G. Ware, *Christian Missions in the Telugu Country* (Westminster: The Society for the propagation of the Gospel, 1912), 189.

10 *The Church Missionary Gleaner* (London: Seeley Jackson and Halliday Publishers, 1881), 190.

11 Frederick Gledstone, Andhra Christian Church Founders*: The Life Story of Thomas Young Darling*, op. cit., 9.

12 *The Church Missionary Gleaner* (London: Seeley Jackson and Halliday Publishers, 1881), 89.

13 A. D. Nock, *Conversion: The Old and the New in Religion from Alexander the Great to Augustine of Hippo* (Oxford: Clarendon Press, Oxford, 1933), 8.

14 Frederick Gledstone, *Andhra Christian Church Founders: The Life Story of Thomas Young Darling*, op. cit., 10.

15 Eugene Stock, *The History of the Church Missionary Society: Its Environment, Its Men and Its Work* (hereafter, *The History of the Church Missionary Society*), Vol. II (London: The C.M.S Publications, 1899), 420.

16 Hibbert G. Ware, op. cit., 186.

17 Ibid., 191.

18 Ibid.

19 Eugene Stock, *The History of the Church Missionary Society,* Vol. II, op. cit., 527.

20 Gordon Mackenzie, *A Manual of the Kistna District in the Presidency of Madras* (Madras: Lawrence Asylum Press, 1883), 289.

21 G. A. Oddie, "Christian Conversion in the Telugu Country, 1860-1900: A Case Study of One Protestant Movement in the Godavery Kistna Delta," *The Indian Economic and Social History Review* XII, (1975): 75.

22 Ibid., 75.

23 *The Church Missionary Gleaner*, Vol. XIX (London: The CMS Publications, 1869), 35.

24 Hibbert G. Ware, op. cit., 191.

25 Eugene Stock, *History of the Church Missionary Society,* Vol. IV, op. cit., 242.

26 M. Moses, op. cit., 65.

27 Eugene Stock, *The History of the Church Missionary Society,* Vol. IV, op. cit., 244.

28 Ibid., 242.

29 M. Moses, op. cit., 184.

30 Carol Graham, op. cit., 61.

31 P. Y. Luke and John B. Carman, *Village Christians and Hindu Culture: Study of Rural Church in Andhra Pradesh, South India* (New Delhi: ISPCK Publishers, 1969), 18.

32 V. S. Azariah and Henry Whitehead, *Christ in the Indian Villages* (London: Student Christian Movement Press, 1930), 27.

33 Eugene Stock, *The History of the Church Missionary Society,* Vol. IV, op. cit., 242.

34 V. S. Azariah and Henry Whitehead, *Christ in the Indian Villages*, op. cit., 27.

35 M. Moses, op. cit., 30.

36 E. Hrangkhuma, *Christianity in India: Search for Liberation and Identity* (New Delhi: ISPCK Publishers, 1998), 87.

37 Ibid.

38 M. Moses, op. cit., 130.

39 Ibid., 132.

40 M. A. Sherring, *The History of Protestant Missions in India from their Commencement in 1706 to 1881* (London: The Religious Tract Society, 1884), 417.

41 Ibid., 418.

42 John Craig et al, *Telugu Trophies: The Jubilee Story of Some of the Principal Telugu Converts in the Canadian Baptist Foreign Mission in India from 1874 to 1924* (hereafter, *Telugu Trophies)* (Toronto: The Canadian Baptist Publication Society, ND), 10.

43 Ibid., 11.

44 M. L. Orchard and K. S. McLaurin, *The Enterprise: The Jubilee Story of the Canadian Baptist Mission in India: 1874-1924* (hereafter, *The Enterprise*) (Toronto: The Canadian Baptist Foreign Mission Board, 1925), 279.

45 George Drach and Calvin F. Kuder, *Telugu Mission of the General Council of the Evangelical Lutheran Church in North America Containing a Biography of the Rev. Christian Frederick Heyer* (Philadelphia: General Council Publication House, 1914), 301.

46 M. L. Orchard and K. S. McLaurin, *The Enterprise*, op. cit., 266.

47 George Drach and Calvin F. Kuder, op. cit., 58.

48 Ibid., 66.

49 Ibid., 82.

50 Ibid., 115.

51 Ibid., 127.

52 Ibid., 291.

53 Ibid., 355.

54 M. L. Orchard, *Canadian Baptists at Work in India* (Toronto: Missionary Education Department of the Foreign Mission Board, 1922), 52.

55 Gustav Warneck, *Outline of a History of Missions from the Reformation to the Present Time: Contribution to Modern Church History* (New York: Fleming H. Revell, 1901), 281.

56 M. Moses, op. cit., 55.

57 John E. Clough, *Social Christianity in the Orient: The Story of A Man, A Mission and A Movement* (New York: The MacMillan Company, 1914), 76.

58 E. Hrangkhuma, op. cit., 86

59 P. Y. Luke and John B. Carman, op. cit., 18.

60 John E. Clough, op. cit., 83.

61 David Downie, *The Lone Star: The History of the Telugu Mission of the American Baptist Missionaries Union (1838-1927)* (Philadelphia: The American Baptist Publication, 1892), 36.

62 John Craig, *Forty Years among the Telugus: A History of the Mission of the Baptists of Ontario and Quebec, Canada to the Telugus, South India 1867-1907* (hereafter, *Forty Years among the Telugus*) (Toronto: The Canadian Baptist Foreign Mission Board, 1908), 14.

63 Julia was a caste convert. David Downie, op. cit., 50.

64 John Craig, *Forty Years among the Telugus,* op. cit., 16.

65 John E. Clough, op. cit., 95.

66 John Craig, *Forty Years among the Telugus,* op. cit., 75.

67 Ibid., 19.

68 John E. Clough, op. cit., 102.

69 Ibid., 214.

70 Edmund F. Merriam, *A History of American Baptist Missions* (Philadelphia: The American Baptist Publication Society, 1900), 146.

71 M. L. Orchard and K. S. McLaurin, *The Enterprise*, op. cit., 135.

72 *American Baptist Missionary Union: Fifty Seventh Annual Report: With the Proceedings of the Annual Meeting held in Chicago*, May 23 (Boston: Missionary Rooms, 1871), 60-61.

73 John E. Clough, op. cit., 103.

74 David Downie, op. cit., 68.

75 Ibid., 267.

76 Ibid., 263.

77 Ibid., 273.

78 John E. Clough, op. cit., 225.

79 Tathapudi David, *Telugu Baptist Mission History*, NP, ND, 9.

80 John E. Clough, op. cit., 239.

81 A. T. Fishman, *Culture Change and the Underprivileged: A Study of the Madigas in South India under Christian Guidance* (Madras: The Christian Literature Society for India, 1941), 5.

82 John E. Clough, op. cit., 246.

83 Ibid., 249.

84 A. T. Fishman, op. cit., 5.

85 John E. Clough, op. cit., 255.

86 Ibid., 279.

87 Ibid., 275.

88 Herbert Waldo Hines., Clough: *The Kingdom Builder in South India* (Philadelphia: The Freedom Press, 1929), 85.

89 M. Moses, op. cit., 32.

90 John E. Clough, op. cit., 286.

91 Ibid., 289.

92 David Downie, op. cit., 115.

93 John E. Clough, op. cit., 283.

94 Ibid., 282.

95 Ibid., 279.

96 Ibid., 335.

97 John Craig, *Forty Years among the Telugus,* op. cit., 29.

98 Gordon Mackenzie, op. cit., 290.

99 Ibid., 347.

100 John Craig, *Forty Years among the Telugus,* op. cit., 28.

101 Ibid., 394.

102 M. Moses, op. cit., 34.

103 John E. Clough, op. cit.

104 Ibid., 95.

105 Ibid., 216.

106 Hibbert G. Ware, op. cit., 202.

107 M. Moses, op. cit., 233.

108 Rev. Alexander of Ellore had assured Periah and Thatiah about a new missionary (a white teacher) who would be coming to Ongole. John E. Clough, op. cit., 92, Also in Hibbert G Ware, op. cit., 202.

109 David Downie, op. cit., 64.

110 Ibid.

111 Ibid., 28.

112 John Craig, *Forty Years among the Telugus,* op. cit., 86.

113 Ibid., 258.

114 Ibid., 263.

115 Ibid.

116 Ibid., 279.

117 Ibid., 258.

118 M. L. Orchard and K. S. McLaurin, *The Enterprise*, op. cit., 263.

119 Azariah, V. S., "Evangelization and its Challenge" in the Andhra Christian Council Meeting, *The National Christian Council Review* (Mysore: Wesley Press, 1933), 10.

120 G. A. Oddie, "India: Missionaries, Conversion and Change," in *The Church Mission Society and World Christianity 1799-1999*, eds. Ward, Kevin and Brian Stanley (Grand Rapids, Michigan: W. B. Eerdmans Publishing Company, 2000), 228.

121 K. C. Alexander, "The Neo-Christians of Kerala," in *The Untouchables in Contemporary India*, ed. J. Michael Mahar (Arizona: The University of Arizona Press, 1972; Robert Clark, *The Missions of the Punjab and Sindh* (London: SPCK, 1904); Walter Fernandes, *Caste and Conversion Movements in India* (New Delhi: Indian Social Institute, 1981); J. W. Gladstone, *Protestant Christianity and People's Movements in Kerala: A Study of Christian Mass Movements in Relation to Neo-Hindu Socio-Religious Movements in Kerala, 1850-1936* (Trivandrum: The Seminary Publications, 1984); Dick Kooiman, *Conversion and Social Equality in India: The London Missionary Society in South Travancore in the 19th Century* (New Delhi: Manohar Publications, 1989); S. Manickam, *The Social Setting of Christian Conversion in South India,* Franz Steiner (Verlog: Wiesbaden, 1977; G. A. Oddie, (ed) *Religion in South Asia: Religious Conversion and Revival Movements in South Asia in Medieval and Modern Times* (New Delhi: Manohar, 1991); J. W. Pickett, et, al, *Christian Missions in Mid India: A Study of Study of Nine Areas With Special Reference to Mass Movement*, (Jabbulpore: The Mission Press, 1938).

122 Y. Antony Raj, *Social Impact of Conversion: A Comparative Sociological Study on the Christians of Scheduled Caste Origin and Scheduled Caste Hindus* (Delhi: ISPCK, 2001); K. E. Rajprakukh, *Dalit Christians of Andhra: Under the Impact of Missionaries* (New Delhi: Serials Publications, 2008).

123 Duncan B. Forrester, "The Depressed Classes and Conversion to Christianity, 1860-1960," in *Religion in South Asia,* ed. G. A. Oddie (Delhi: Manohar Publishers, 1977), 45; Also in M. N. Srinivas, "Caste in Modern India," *The Journal of Asian Studies* 16 (4), (1957): 531.

124 L. Stanislaus, *The Liberative Mission of the Dalit Christians* (Delhi: ISPCK Publishers, 1999), 143.

125 Samuel Jaya Kumar, *Dalit Consciousness and Christian Conversion: The Work of SPG Missionaries, Historical Resources for a Contemporary Debate, Mission Theology in an Asian Context* (Delhi: ISPCK Publishers, 1999), 238.

126 Hibbert G. Ware, op. cit., 187.

127 Ibid., 188.

128 V. S. Azariah and Henry Whitehead, *Christ in the Indian Villages*, op. cit., 25.

129 Emma Rauschenbusch Clough, *While Sewing Sandals or Tales of a Telugu Pariah Tribe* (London: The Selwood Printing Works, 1899), 119.

130 John E. Clough, op. cit., 264.

131 Emma Rauschenbusch Clough, op. cit., 5.

132 A. T. Fishman, op. cit., 6.

133 John E. Clough, op. cit., 242.

134 Ibid., 253.

135 Duncan B. Forrester, op. cit., "The Depressed Classes and Conversion to Christianity, 1860-1960," in *Religion in South Asia*, ed. G.A. Oddie, op. cit., 43.

136 J. W. Gladstone, op. cit., 97-8.

137 R. Ricards, *India or Facts Submitted to Illustrate the Character and Condition of the Native Inhabitants*, Vol. 1 (London: Smith Elder and Company Publishers, 1829), 46.

138 William Wiser, *The Hindu Jajmani System: A Socio-Economic System Interrelating Members of a Hindu Village Community in Services* (Lucknow: Lucknow Publishing House, 1958), 116.

139 Jurgen Habermas, *Religion and Rationality Essays on Reason, God, and Modernity* (London: Polity Press, 2002), 61.

140 Dharma Kumar, *Land and Caste in South India: Agricultural Labour in the Madras Presidency* (London: Cambridge University Press, 1965), 47.

141 Duncan B. Forrester, "The Depressed Classes and Conversion to Christianity, 1860-1960," in *Religion in South Asia*, ed. G. A. Oddie, op. cit., 43.

142 Ibid., 43.

143 Duncan B. Forrester, *Caste and Christianity: Attitudes and Policies on Caste of Anglo-Saxon Protestant Missions in India* (Richmond, Surrey: Curzon Press, 1980), 74.

144 Duncan B. Forrester, "The Depressed Classes and Conversion to Christianity, 1860-1960," in *Religion in South Asia,* ed. G. A. Oddie, op. cit., 43.

145 Romesh Dutt, *The Economic History Of India Under Early British Rul*e, Sixth Edition, Kegan Paul (London: Trench and Trubner Publishers, 1901), 170.

146 Duncan B. Forrester, *Caste and Christianity: Attitudes and Policies on Caste of Anglo-Saxon Protestant Missions in India*, op. cit., 77.

147 K. K. Kuruvilla, "The Christian Approach to the Unprivileged," *The National Christian Council Review* XV (Mysore: Wesley Press, 1937): 547.

148 Duncan B. Forrester, "The Depressed Classes and Conversion to Christianity, 1860-1960," in *Religion in South Asia*, ed. G. A. Oddie, op. cit., 46.

149 M. L. Orchard and K. S. McLaurin, *The Enterprise*, op. cit., 264.

150 Eugene Stock, *The History of the Church Missionary Society,* Vol. II, op. cit., 91.

151 John Craig et al, *Telugu Trophies,* op. cit., 130. Also, John E. Clough, op. cit., 324.

152 G. A. Oddie, "Christian Conversion in the Telugu Country, 1860-1900: A Case Study of One Protestant Movement in the Godavery Kistna Delta," *The Indian Economic and Social History Review* XII, op. cit.: 77.

153 John Craig et al, *Telugu Trophies,* op. cit., 130-131.

154 Hibbert G. Ware, op. cit., 60.

155 G. A. Oddie, "Christian Conversion in the Telugu Country, 1860-1900: A Case Study of One Protestant Movement in the Godavery Kistna Delta," op. cit.: 74.

156 Hibbert G. Ware, op. cit., 213.

157 John E. Clough, op. cit., 161-162.

158 Ibid., 162.

159 Ibid., 39.

160 Walter Fernandes, op. cit., 24.

161 Richard Lovett, op. cit., 147.

162 John E. Clough, op. cit., 126.

163 John R. Mott, *The Decisive Hour of Christian Missions* (New York: Student Volunteer Movement for Foreign Missions, 1910), 87.

164 John E. Clough, op. cit., 279.

165 Duncan B. Forrester, "The Depressed Classes and Conversion to Christianity, 1860-1960", in *Religion in South Asia*, ed. G. A. Oddie, op. cit., 42-43.

166 Duncan B. Forrester, "Indian Christian Attitudes to Caste in the Twentieth Century," *The Indian Council of Historical Review* IX (1), (1975): 7.

167 Jurgen Habermas, op. cit., 64.

168 M. L. Orchard, *Canadian Baptists at Work in India*, op. cit., 119.

169 G. A. Oddie, "Christian Conversion in the Telugu Country, 1860-1900: A Case Study of One Protestant Movement in the Godavery Kistna Delta," op. cit., 73.

170 Eugene Stock, *The History of the Church Missionary Society,* Vol. IV, op. cit., 171.

171 Susan Billington Harper, *In the Shadow of the Mahatma: Bishop V. S. Azariah and the Travails of Christianity in British in India* (Surrey: Curzon Press, 2000), 191.

172 Ibid.

173 John E. Clough, op. cit., 302.

174 Ibid., 381.

175 Anthony Copley, *Religion in Conflict: Ideology, Cultural Contact and Conversion in Late Colonial India* (New York: The Oxford University Press, 1997), 6.

176 George Drach and Calvin F. Kuder, op. cit., 49.

177 M. A. Sherring, op. cit., 284.

178 C. B. Webster, *Dalit Christians: A History* (Delhi: ISPCK, 1994), 36.

179 John E. Clough, op. cit., 339.

180 Ibid., 96.

181 M. L. Orchard, *Canadian Baptists at Work in India,* op. cit., 80.

182 M. L. Orchard and K. S. McLaurin, *The Enterprise,* op. cit., 274.

183 Ibid., 263.

184 Ibid., 309.

185 John E. Clough, op. cit., 255.

186 Frederik Gledstone, *Andhra Christian Church Founders*: *Henry Watson Fox* (Madras: Diocesan Press, 1941), 9.

187 This was an observation of the local Mala and Madiga converts in Ramachandrapuram. John Craig et al, *Telugu Trophies,* op. cit., 57.

188 John R. Mott, op. cit., 91.

189 John E. Clough, op. cit., 60.

190 *Proceedings of the Seventh Meeting of the National Christian Council* (Madras: Diocesan Press, 1937), NP.

191 Susan Billington Harper, "The Dornakal Church on the Cultural Frontier," in Christians, *Cultural Interactions and India's Religious Traditions,* eds. Judith M. Brown and Robert Eric Frykenberg (Grand Rapids, Michigan: William B. Eerdmans, 2002), 186.

192 G. A. Oddie, "Christian Conversion among Non-Brāhmins in Andhra Pradesh with special Reference to Anglican Missions and the Dornakal Diocese, c. 1900-1936," in *Religious Conversion and Revival Movements in South Asia in Mediaeval and Modern Times*, ed. G. A Oddie, op. cit., 91.

193 Martin L. Dolbeer, "The Caste Mass Movement in the Telugu Area," *The National Christian Council Review* (Mysore: Wesley Press, 1933), 420.

194 Ibid.

195 J. W. Pickett, *Christian Mass Movements in India* (Lucknow: Lucknow Publishing House, 1933), 52-53.

196 Eugene Stock, *The History of the Church Missionary Society,* Vol. II, op. cit. 243.

197 D. F. Pocock, *Essays on the Caste System by Celestin Bougle* (Cambridge: The Cambridge University Press, 1971), 82.

198 F. Whittaker, "Evangelism: Opportunities and Difficulties in Relation to Mass Movements," *The National Christian Council Review* XVII (Mysore: Wesley Press, 1939), 125.

199 John E. Clough, op. cit., 280.

200 W. S. Hunt, *India's Outcastes: A New Era* (London: The CMS Publications, 1924), 5.

201 Sundara Raj Manickam, *The Social Setting of Christian Conversion in South India : the Impact of the Wesleyan Methodist Missionaries on the Trichy-Tanjore Diocese with special reference to the Harijan Communities of the Mass Movement Area 1820-1947* (Wiesbaden: Franz Steiner Verlag, 1977), 100.

202 Andrew Wingate, *The Church and Conversion* (Delhi: ISPCK Publishers, 1997), 259.

203 John E. Clough, op. cit., 214.

204 P. Y. Luke and John B. Carman, op. cit., 216.

205 K. K. Kuruvilla, op. cit., 549.

206 C. B. Webster, op. cit., 58-59.

207 L. Stanislaus, op. cit., 143.

208 M. A. Sherring, op. cit., 409.

209 Duncan B. Forrester, "The Depressed Classes and Conversion to Christianity, 1860-1960," in *Religion in South Asia,* ed. G. A. Oddie, op. cit., 39.

210 Quoted in G. A. Oddie, "Christian Conversion in the Telugu Country, 1860-1900: A Case Study of One Protestant Movement in the Godavery Kistna Delta," *The Indian Economic and Social History Review* XII, op. cit.: 70.

211 David Downie, op. cit., 130.

212 V. S. Azariah, Bishop of Dornakal, "Evangelization and its Challenge," in Proceedings of the Sixth Meeting of The National Christian Council (1933).

213 Sundara Raj Manickam, *Studies in Missionary History: Reflections on a Culture-Contact* (Madras: The Christian Literature Society, 1988), 55-56.

214 *Church Missionary Society Annual Report, 1886-87*, 157 in G.A. Oddie, "Christian Conversion in the Telugu Country, 1860-1900: A Case Study of One Protestant Movement in the Godavery Kistna Delta," *The Indian Economic and Social History Review* XII, (1975): 69.

215 *The Church Missionary Intelligencer*, Vol. XVII, (London: Seeley Jackson Halliday Publishers, 1892), 906.

216 G. A. Oddie, "Christian Conversion in the Telugu Country, 1860-1900: A Case Study of One Protestant Movement in the Godavery Kistna Delta," *The Indian Economic and Social History Review* XII, op. cit.: 78.

217 J. W. Pickett, *Christian Mass Movements in India*, op. cit., 130-131.

218 Ibid.

219 G. A. Oddie, "India: Missionaries, Conversion, and Change" in ed. Kevin Ward and Brian Stanley, The Church Missionary Society and World Christianity 1799-1999, op. cit., 251.

220 Gustav Warneck, op. cit., 37.

221 Ibid., 404.

222 Alice B. Van Doren, "Christian Mass Movements in India: A Review in Laymen's Foreign Missionary Inquiry Reports", Vol. I, *The National Christian Council Review*, (Mysore: Wesley Press, 1933), 139.

223 J. Mangamma, *Andhra Desamulo Kraisthava Missioanrila Seva* (Hyderabad: Telugu Academy Publishers, 1992), Introduction.

224 M. N. Srinivas, op. cit., 531.

225 Sebastian C. H. Kim, *In Search of Identity: Debates on the Religious Conversion in India* (New Delhi: Oxford University Press, 2003), 32.

226 Ibid., 24.

227 Ibid., 31.

228 Ibid., 34.

229 Ibid., 32.

230 Norman A. Horner, *Protestant Cross Currents in Mission: The Ecumenical-Conservative Encounter* (New York: Abingdon Press, 1968), 122.

231 James S. Dennis, *Christian Missions and Social Progress: A Sociological Study of Foreign Missions*, Vol. III (New York: Fleming H. Revell, 1906), 23.

232 Graham Taylor, *Religion in Social Action* (New York: Mead and Co Publishers, 1913), 88.

233 David W. Bebbington, *Evangelism in Modern Britain: A History from the 1730s to the 1980s* (London: Unwin Hyman Publishers, 1989), 2-3.

234 Edward A. Lawrence, *Modern Missions in the East: Their Methods, Successes and Limitations* (New York: Harper Brothers Publishers, 1895), 43.

235 George Drach and Calvin F Kuder, op. cit., 50.

236 Ibid., 110-11.

237 Ibid., 179.

238 M. L. Orchard and K. S. McLaurin, *The Enterprise*, op. cit., 335.

239 Bengt Sundkler, *Church of South India: The Movement towards Union, 1900-1947* (London: The Lutterworth Press, 1954), 23.

240 R. E. Frykenberg, *Christianity in India: From Beginnings to the Present* (Oxford: Oxford University Press, 2008), 262.

241 Rev. Clough's Dairy: They had given to more than six hundred people of all castes an aggregate of nearly four thousand rupees: John E. Glough, op. cit., 259.

242 Ibid., 259-260.

243 Sundara Raj Manickam, op. cit., 110.

244 Chad M. Bauman, Christian *Identity and Dalit Religion in Hindu India* (Grand Rapids, Michigan: W. B. Eerdmans Publishing Company, 2008), 83.

245 John E. Clough, op. cit., 273.

246 A. C. Clayton, *Christian Literature in India and Ceylon: An Account of the Christian Literature Published in the Vernacular Languages and in English by Protestant Missions* (Madras: The Christian Literature Society, 1920), 14.

247 P. Chenchayya and Raja M. Bhujanga Rao Bahadur, *A History of Telugu Literature* (Calcutta: The Association Press, n. d.), 105.

* Vedanta Rasayana was a Kavya in four cantos dedicated to Nidimamilla Dasayamatya, a member of an influential family that had adopted the Christian faith.

248 Schultze was present in Halle to see the New Testament printing through the press at the Francke's Orphan House. Fleming Stevenson: See *The Dawn of the Modern Mission*, (Edinburgh: A. C. Armstrong, 1888), 153. Also Gerald, H Anderson., *Biographical Dictionary of Christian Missions* (Grand Rapids, Michigan: W. B. Eerdmans Publishing Company, 1999), 604.

249 Douglas H. Shantz, *An Introduction to German Pietism: Protestant Renewal at the Dawn of Modern Europe* (Baltimore: The John Hopkins University Press, 2013).

250 Rutherford, John, *Missionary Pioneers in India* (Edinburgh: Andrew Elliot Press, 1896), 114.

251 Ibid., 120.

252 John Murdoch, *Catalogue of the Christian Vernacular Literature in India: With Hints on the Management of Indian Tract Societies* (Madras: Caleb Foster Publishers, 1870), 238.

253 George Drach and Calvin F. Kuder, op. cit., 78.

254 Ibid., 78.

255 L. B. Wolf, *After Fifty Years*, op. cit., 40-41.

256 In 1865 a Committee of delegates was formed by the Madras Auxiliary Bible Society to co-operate with Rev. John Hay in the translation of the Bible. Among its members were A. H. Arden, Jacob Chamberlain, J. Clay, Pulipaka Jaganatham, Lyman Jewitt, E. Lewis and Manchala Ratnam. See L. D. Barnett, *A Catalogue of the Telugu Books in the Library of the British Museum* (London: Longmans and Co Publishers, 1912), 33.

257 Raj Bahadur Sharma, *History of Christian Missions: North India Perspective* (New Delhi: Mittal Publications, 2005), 178.

258 Jacob Chamberlain, *The Kingdom in India: Its Progress and Its Promise* (London: Fleming H. Revell, 1908), 41.

259 John Murdoch, op. cit., 239-242.

260 *Report on the Vernacular Papers as examined by the Translators to the Government of Madras,* No 27, (1909), 467.

261 Harlan P. Beach, *India and Christian Opportunity* (New York: Student Volunteer Movement, New York, 1908), 84.

262 Ibid., 84.

263 Ibid.

264 Ibid.

265 A. C. Clayton, op. cit., 92.

266 A. Satyanarayana, *Dalits and Upper Castes: Essays in Social History* (New Delhi: Kanishka Publishers, 2005), 136.

267 *Proceedings of the Tenth Meeting of the National Christian Council of India, Burma and Ceylon* (Mysore: Wesley Press, 1946), 21.

268 *Ibid.,* 57-58.

269 John. E, Clough, op. cit., 360.

270 George Drach and Calvin F. Kuder, op. cit., 325.

271 Ibid.

272 John Craig, *Forty Years among the Telugus,* op. cit., 29.

273 B. E. Devaraj, *Bharata Desa Kraisthava Sangha Charitra*, Andhra Christian Theological Literature Council (Tenali: A.S.R. Power Press, 1969), 144; Also see Hibbert G. Ware, op. cit., 90.

274 G. A. Oddie, "Christian Conversion in the Telugu Country, 1860-1900: A Case Study of One Protestant Movement in the Godavery Kistna Delta," op. cit., 67-69; Also, B. E. Devaraj, op. cit., 144.

275 W. S. Hunt, op. cit., 9-10.

276 Hibbert G. Ware, op. cit., 187.

277 John E. Clough, op. cit., 95.

278 Yerraguntla Periah used to stir the preachers up long before daybreak to go to villages at a distance. The weather was at its hottest, and Periah would carry a big pot of buttermilk on his head for the preachers: David Downie, op. cit., 63.

279 John E. Clough, op. cit., 100.

280 Anon, op. cit., 1-587+ xx.

281 E. Hrangkhuma, op. cit., 87.

282 John Craig et al, *Telugu Trophies,* op. cit., 144.

283 G. A. Oddie, "Christian Conversion in the Telugu Country", 1860-1900: A Case Study of One Protestant Movement in the Godavari Krishna Delta," *The Indian Economic and Social History Review* XII, op. cit., 70.

284 George Drach and Calvin F. Kuder, op. cit., 79.

285 Ibid., 105.

286 J. A. Dubois, *Letters on the State of Christianity in India: In which the Conversion of the Hindoos is considered as Impracticable: To which is added a Vindication of the Hindoos, Male and Female* (London: Longman and Company Publishers, 1823), 2.

287 Duncan B. Forrester, "The Depressed Classes and Conversion to Christianity, 1860-1960," in *Religion in South Asia,* ed. G. A. Oddie, op. cit., 36.

288 Regunta Yesuratnam, *Bharatavanilo Kraisthava Sangham* (Hyderabad: Telugu Kraisthava Vedanta Sahiti Samiti, 1998), 60.

289 John R. Mott, op. cit., 87.

290 Eugene Stock, *The History of the Church Missionary Society,* Vol. II, op. cit., 178.

291 Eugene Stock, *A Short Handbook of Missions* (London: Longmans Green and Company, 1904), 7.

292 Ibid., 129.

293 Andrew Wingate, op. cit., 237.

294 M. L. Orchard, *Canadian Baptists at Work in India,* op. cit., 53.

295 Gordon Mackenzie, op. cit., 289.

296 W. S. Hunt, op. cit., 4.

297 J. W. Pickett, *Christian Mass Movements in India*, op. cit., 25.

298 G. A. Oddie, "Christian Conversion in the Telugu Country, 1860-1900: A Case Study of One Protestant Movement in the Godavery Kistna Delta," *The Indian Economic and Social History Review* XII, op. cit., 61.

299 R. E. Frykenberg, "On the Study of Conversion Movements: A Review Article and a Theoretical Note," *The Indian Economic and Social History Review* XVII, (1980): 133.

300 Duncan B. Forrester, "The Depressed Classes and Conversion to Christianity, 1860-1960," in *Religion in South Asia*, ed. G. A. Oddie, op. cit., 35.

301 J. J. Ellis, "Christward Movements in South India," in *The Social Setting of Christian Conversion in South India : the Impact of the Wesleyan Methodist Missionaries on the Trichy-Tanjore Diocese with special reference to the Harijan Communities of the Mass Movement Area 1820-1947,* ed. Sundara Raj Manickam (Wiesbaden: Franz Steiner Verlag, 1977), 100.

302 Andrew Wingate, op. cit., 82.

303 George Drach and Calvin F. Kuder, op. cit., 159.

304 W. S. Hunt, op. cit., 86.

305 Warner Fite, "The Social Implications of Consciousness," *The Journal of Philosophy, Psychology and Scientific Methods* 10 (14), (1913): 367.

306 Charles Elmer Gehlke, *Emile Durkheim's Contributions to Sociological Theory* (New York: Columbia University, 1915), 181.

307 The New Encyclopedia Britannica, Vol. 20 (Chicago: Encyclopedia Britannica Incorporation, 1997), 84.

308 Charles H. Cooley, "Social Consciousness," *The American Journal of Sociology* 12 (5), (1907): 676.

309 Barbara R. Joshi, *Democracy in Search of Equality: Untouchable Politics and Indian Social Change* (Delhi: Hindustan Publishing Corporation, 1982), 34.

310 Jay A. Weinstein, *Social and Cultural Change: Social Science for a Dynamic World* (Lanham, Maryland: Rowman Littlefield Publishers, 2005), 9.

311 Guenther Roth and Claus Wittich., *Max Weber: Economy and Society: An Outline of Interpretive Sociology* (Los Angeles: The University of California Press, 1978), 1375.

312 Charles Elmer Gehlke, op. cit., 181.

313 Thomas H. Groome, *Christian Religious Education* (San Francisco: Harper and Row Publishers, 1980), 110.

314 Maurice Halbwachs, "Individual Consciousness and Collective Mind," *The American Journal of Sociology* 44 (6), (1939): 815.

315 Philip E. Hammond, *Religion and Personal Autonomy* (Columbia: University of South Carolina Press, 1992), 5.

316 Susan Billington Harper, *In the Shadow of the Mahatma: Bishop V. S. Azariah and the Travails of Christianity in British in India,* op. cit., 191.

317 F. Whittaker, op. cit., 125.

318 R. S. Mann, *Social Change and Social Research: An Indian Perspective* (New Delhi: Concept Publishing Company, 1988), 18.

319 Alvin Boskoff, "Social Change: Major Problems in the Emergence of theoretical and Research Foci," in *The Modern Sociological Theory in Continuity and Change*, ed. Howard Becker and Alvin Boskoff (New York: Holt, Rinehart &Winston, 1957), 263.

320 Romila Thapar, "The Theory of Aryan Race and India: History and Politics," *The Social Scientist* 24 (1/3), (1996): 11.

321 Lewis R. Rambo, *Understanding Religious Conversion* (New Haven: Yale University Press, 1993), 168.

322 *The Church Missionary Intelligencer of Missionary Information: A Monthly Journal of Missionary Information*, Vol. VIII (London: The CMS Publications, 1872), 45.

323 C. B. Webster, op. cit., 33.

324 Chad M. Bauman, op. cit., 74.

325 Anthony Copley, op. cit., 54.

326 Oliver Mendelsohn and Marika Vicziany, *The Untouchables: Subordination, Poverty and the State in Modern India* (Cambridge: The Cambridge University Press, 1998), 77.

327 Gustav Warneck, op. cit., 404.

328 Robert Hall Glover, *The Progress of World-Wide Missions* (New York: Harper and Brothers Publishers, 1924), 23.

329 J. P. Jones, *The Yearbook of Missions in India, Burma and Ceylon* (Madras: Christian Literature Society of India, 1912), 255.

330 J. W. Pickett, *Christian Mass Movements in India*, op. cit., 78.

331 Duncan B. Forrester, "The Depressed Classes and Conversion to Christianity, 1860-1960," in *Religion in South Asia*, ed. G. A. Oddie, op. cit., 45.

332 Alice B. Van Doren, op. cit., 139.

333 This was an observation made specifically on the Malas and Madigas: see Donald McGavran, *Understanding Church Growth* (Grand Rapids, Michigan: W. B. Eerdmans Publishing Co, 1970), 298.

334 *The New Encyclopedia Britannica*, Vol. X, 15th Edition (Chicago: Encyclopedia Britannica Incorporation, 1997), 921.

Chapter 5

Christian Education and Health Care Services in Coastal Andhra

5.1 Introduction

The Christian missionary enterprise in coastal Andhra from mid 19th century had several enabling tools for social empowerment in their package of evangelization of the people. Conversion aimed at not just change of religion, but change in life many aspects—social, economic, educational, cultural and so on. Along with teaching of religion, teaching the three R's was a key aspect of missionary work. In fact, a major engagement of the mission was providing education to the people. Though the education service of the missionary was available to all, it was preferentially available to the convert Malas and Madigas in the mission area. So also, health care of the sick was considered a humanitarian service by the missionary. Medical missions have added much to the credible work of the missionaries through which a lot of physical suffering was alleviated with the introduction of western medical practices.[1] Christian medical work came as a relief as it was embodied with care and love towards human beings by dispelling superstitious practices and prejudices held for many centuries.[2]

In my study of the impact of conversion and social change among the Malas and Madigas of coastal Andhra, I found that a major part of the mission resources were spent on education and health care. This chapter is an exploration of the educational and health care services of the missionaries in coastal Andhra. The two sections of the chapter are 1) education and 2) medical care. In the first section I explore the spread and depth of the educational engagement of the missionaries and examine the mediatory function of education in achieving social mobility among the Malas and the Madigas. In the second section, I explore the health care works of the missionaries. The Protestant Christian medical missionary work in Andhra had three-pronged aims: a) to provide health care to the converts, b) to practice practical evangelism among the converts and non-converts, and c) to train the converts in medical service which was envisaged to provide employment. The aspect of providing employment will be dealt with in detail in Chapter 6 on the economic development among the Malas and Madigas.

I

5.2 Education and Evangelization

"The true cure of darkness is the introduction of light,"[3] so said a historian of English Education in India. A cursory reading of the social history and social change in India in the 19th and 20th centuries shows that this dictum was translated into reality by many social reformers and missionaries. Education was a great factor that brought social transformation in India,[4] particularly in the lives of the Depressed Castes. From the second half of the 19th century, dissemination of education was viewed as a determining 'change agent' which produced knowledge and awakened individual consciousness to achieve a new social identity and self-image.[5]

Education is an "act or process of acquiring knowledge, skill, competence or desirable qualities of behavior especially by a formal course of study, instruction or training."[6] In M. S. Gore's opinion, "education is a flame or light of knowledge and a major agency of social change and its nature is to ensure continuity of change and educational institutions serve as socializing agents for different sub-cultures."[7] It was said that an individual's mind that was lacking in ideas, feelings and habits can be filled with a constructive education.[8]

Scholars have studied about the co-relation between education and upward social mobility, particularly of the marginalized communities. Several studies have substantiated that the power of knowledge acquired through education has not only enlightened the ignorant, but also empowered them in all aspects of life.[9]

As for the missionaries, education was not used not only as a tool of empowerment of the marginalized, but also as a medium for communicating the message of the Gospel. The message of the Gospel, they seem to have understood, was communicating the love of God to all by enlightening the ignorant, empowering the weak, freeing the bonded, helping the helpless and so on. In other words, education was not an appendix to evangelization, but an essential aspect of it.

Evangelization was articulated in the educational enterprise of the missionaries where it had formed to be a part of the total work of the 'Church building' program in India. 'Educational Evangelism' was aimed at the laying of a solid foundation for the spread of Christianity in India.[10] Rev. Benjamin Rice, a pioneer of the London Missionary Society's early educational enterprise, looked upon education as an important means of diffusing the Gospel in India, especially good English education based on Christian principles."[11]

The missionaries chose the strategy of education as an "indirect means of proselytization" to bring the Gospel to the listeners, as it was understood that through schools and colleges they might reach many people. The British historian Kenneth Ingham said that, among all the activities the missionaries undertook, the most important activity to consider was the establishment of the missionary schools and disseminating knowledge through a systematic network of educational institutions.[12] The benefits of the missionary educational services were reaped only by those people who had perceived that those services were significantly relevant for them. The school was the chosen field of the missionary where his/her influence was felt.[13]

Modern India witnessed the pioneering educational services of missionaries such as Rev. Alexander Duff (1830-1863), Rev. John Wilson (1829-1875), Rev. John Anderson (1837-1855), Rev. Stephen Hislop (1844-1863) and Rev. Robert Turlington Noble (1841-1865) and others.

In Andhra, as we shall see below, all the missionary societies had engaged in education work, during the period, 1850-1950. My attempt in this chapter is to show the extent of the educational work carried out by the selected six missionary organizations in coastal Andhra during the period of this study. Further, I shall critically study the impact of education in the lives of the subject communities under this study—Malas and Madigas. Whether and how education together with other support systems of the mission, effected upward social mobility in these communities, will also be dealt with in this and the subsequent chapters.

Though missionary educational institutions were established for all the sections of the Indian population, the general apathetic attitude and suspicion about the missionaries among the caste Hindus came as hurdles to their taking advantage of missionary education. The latter, on the other hand, turned their attention towards the Depressed Castes. Thus, it turned out to be that mission's educational facilities were preferentially available to the latter castes.

It may well be noted that the progress of education among the Malas and the Madigas occurred within the broader framework of the Colonial government's educational policies and support or no support to the missionaries. Therefore to have a comprehensive view of the missionary's role in education, it is necessary to look into the historical Acts and legislations with regard to education under the Colonial dispensation. I have considered the following steps or legislations for closer study: the Charter Acts of the East India Company, Dispatches of the Government of India, Education Commission

Reports and Constitutional Provisions in a chronological order. The official reports pertaining to the education of the Depressed Castes are the Census Reports, Reports of the Public Instruction for Madras Presidency and Harijan Welfare Reports of Madras Government. The limited government sources aside, attempt has been made to peruse the large amount of primary mission sources such as policy statements, reports, proposals, etc., to reconstruct the story of the educational empowerment of the Malas and Madigas in coastal Andhra.

5.3 Education Under the British East India Company, 1800-1850

The British East India Company's primary interest was trade and it would not venture into any social field which might jeopardize its trade prospects. Even after the East India Company became a Company Government in 1765, invested with the responsibility of civil and political governance, it refused to take any responsibility for education of its Indian subjects. Also it stayed away from interfering with the religious affairs of the Indian subjects due to the sheer fear that it would negatively affect their trade. Hence, when the missionaries requested permission to preach their religion and engage in education in British ruled areas, the Company's categorical response was 'no'.

The Court of Directors' hostile attitude towards both the Christian missions and the spread of education came in for discussion in the British Parliament when Mr. Wilberforce pleaded the House to grant permission to spread the truths of Christianity to the native peoples of India for their voluntary acceptance.[14] The missionaries, on the other side, considered education as an important tool for propagation of the Gospel teachings.[15] Moderate, but daring attempts were made by some missionary societies to impart education. The London Missionary Society's missionaries were pioneers in education in coastal Andhra: they had started their educational work in Vizagapatam right from the beginning of the 19th century, even before the Charter Act of 1813 which permitted missionary education.[16] In 1805, they opened a school for the native children and a charity school for Eurasian children in Vizagapatam.[17] In 1815, three missionaries were supervising 14 schools where English, Geography, History, Mathematics, music and drawing were taught. Two missionaries were stationed at Vizagapatam and Anakapalle along with a few staffs of European origin, long before the Colonial Government initiated its efforts towards the spread of education.[18]

The growth of a liberal spirit in England was evident in the passing of landmark legislations such as the Factory Legislation and Suppression of Slavery, which apparently contributed to a change of perception and attitude of the East India Company in favour of assuming greater responsibility for civil governance in India. The passing of the famous Charter Act of 1813 was the consequence of this change. It may be noted that missionaries were party to or asked to collaborate with the government in the drafting of certain clauses in the Act. The Clause 43 of the Charter Act of 1813 largely owes to the missionaries and may be regarded as the foundation stone of English education in India. It reads as:

It shall be lawful for the Governor General in Council to direct any surplus funds which may remain realized of the rents, revenues, and profits arising from the said territorial acquisitions. A sum not less than one lakh rupees in each year shall be set apart and applied to the revival and improvement of literature and the encouragement of the learned natives of India and for the introduction and promotion of knowledge of the sciences among the inhabitants of the British territories in India.[19]

In 1822, Sir Thomas Munro, the Governor of Madras, asked the Board of Revenue to conduct an enquiry into the actual state of indigenous education in Madras Presidency. Subsequently it was found out that the standard of education of the natives was very low, mainly due to economic backwardness of the people. It was also found that education was a closely guarded prerogative of the privileged upper castes in traditional Indian society. Munro stated that in certain districts, reading and writing were almost entirely confined to the Brahmins and the merchant classes.[20] Therefore a system was proposed for the improvement of mass education in the indigenous schools.[21]

In a Minute dated March 10th, 1826, Sir Thomas Munro suggested the establishment of two principal schools in each Collectorate, one for the Hindus and the other, for the Muhammadans, besides an inferior (elementary) school in each Tahsil.[22] The medium of teaching adopted was vernacular languages for Hindu students, while Mohammadan students were taught in Hindustani, Persian and Arabic. A provision was also made for the basic teaching of the English language, European Literature and Science.[23]

The efforts of a visionary like Sir Thomas Munro were remarkable in their consequences for the spread of education among the masses, which otherwise would have been limited to the privileged classes only. Lord Elphinstone also proposed for the formation of high schools at major towns with a view to raising them eventually to college levels and be connected to Madras University. Therefore, four schools (one each at Trichinopoly, Masulipatnam, Bellary and Calicut) were established for the benefit of the Tamil, Telugu, Kanarese and Malayalam speaking people respectively.[24]

The education policies of the Government of India were shaped by its political and administrative decisions. The Charter Act of 1833 announced that no native of India would be disabled from holding any place, office or employment, because of his religion, place of birth, descent or color.[25] This measure pushed for the promotion of English education because it entitled Indians to enter into government service. In a resolution passed by Lord William Bentinck on 7th March 1835, it was envisaged that "the great object of the British government was the promotion of European literature and science among the natives of India, and that the funds appropriated to education would be best employed on English education alone."[26] The Macaulay's Minute of 1835 aimed at westernization of higher education by raising the standard of instruction among the Indians that would eventually produce quality of thought among the learners.[27] English was introduced as the medium of instruction in place of local languages in all government schools and the funds were devoted for the same.

5.4 Education Under the British Colonial Government, 1850-1950

A new era in the history of Indian education began with Wood's Despatch of 1854, known as the "Magna Carta of English Education" in India.[28] It was the first comprehensive and conscious effort of the British government to take up the responsibility of education of the natives on official lines. A separate Education Department was created under the Director of Public Instruction.[29] A well planned system of education was introduced in every Presidency whose principal features were:

(1) The constitution of departments in the several provinces or presidencies for the administration of education.
(2) The establishment of Universities at the Presidency towns.
(3) The creation of training schools for teachers for all classes of schools.
(4) The maintenance of the existing government colleges and high schools, and the increase of their number when necessary.
(5) The establishment of new middle schools.
(6) Increased attention to vernacular indigenous schools for elementary education.
(7) The introduction of a system of government grants-in-aid.
(8) The provision of Vernacular school books and
(9) The annual examination for government rewards.[30]

The Despatch acknowledged that the education of a great percentage of the people was totally neglected due to their utter incapability to obtain any education worthy of the name and that the Government should provide for the education in such a disadvantaged situation.[31] Therefore the Despatch suggested that the Government should spend more resources on popular education and grant scholarships for capable wards. A system of Grants-in-Aid came into existence and came to the reach of the missionaries and educational enthusiasts.[32]

Caste distinctions in theory were eradicated as per the Despatch: "no boy be refused admission to a government school or college merely on the grounds of caste...in every institution which is wholly maintained at the cost of public funds, whether provincial, municipal or local."[33] Provision for the establishment of special schools for children of low castes was encouraged in places where there were a sufficient number of children to form such separate schools.[34] In a specific order that was passed in 1857, the departmental schools were made open to all castes and communities including outcastes.[35] In 1858, it was directed by the Government that schools and colleges should be open to every caste, class and creed.[36] Therefore, the Despatch of 1854 was a great achievement for the Depressed Castes as well as the missionaries, who hailed it a moral and religious victory. In their efforts to give a lead as well as to collaborate with the Government, they worked hand in hand with the latter and benefitted from grants-in-aid system.[37] However, the missionaries faced some difficulties as some of the government schools were conducted in the immediate vicinity of the mission schools, which affected their prospective clientele.[38]

In the Report of the Indian Education Commission of 1881 (the Hunter Commission) it was declared that "every branch of education should justify the fostering care of the State, and the State should direct its efforts for the elementary education of the masses, its extension and improvement."[39] In other words, the Commission opined that primary education should be devoted for the instruction of the masses and its provision, extension and improvement should be part of the educational system and strenuous efforts of the State should be directed in a larger measure than before. The Commission recommended that through the system of grants-in-aid, progressive devolution of the primary, secondary and the collegiate education could be passed on to the private enterprise.[40] Therefore, the policy of the government in broadening the base of education for the benefit of the masses of population had contributed for the growth of education among the Malas and the Madigas also.

Taking the lead from missionary initiatives and progress of education among the Indian Depressed Castes, Indian nationalists and educational enthusiasts recognized the importance of quantitative advance of education among the Indian people. The 1904 Resolution of the Government called for an expansion of primary education and called the State to improve elementary education by continuous encouragement of privately managed schools by government inspection, recognition, control and aid of government funds.[41] In 1906, the Calcutta Session of the Indian National Congress adopted a Resolution urging people to take up education that would suit to the requirements of the country on technical and scientific lines.[42] A Department of Education was created in 1910, to deal with the subjects of education, hospitals, public health, municipalities and local boards and ecclesiastical matters.[43] The Indian Educational Policy of 1913 laid down in principle that liberal provision should be made for giving free elementary instruction to children whose parents could not afford to pay school fees. Local governments were ordered to extend the application of the principle of free elementary education amongst the more backward sections of the population. The Government had also aimed at the qualitative improvement of the pupils' habits through instruction, health awareness, recreation and discipline. Much attention was given to the modification of moral habits to reform their social life and betterment of the environment by practicing hygienic habits and cleanliness.[44] These measures were attuned to the missionaries' advocacy to remove social ills such as the four demons of dirt, drink, debt and disease.[45] The Gokhale Bill of Education of 1911 also had emphasized on free and compulsory primary education as it was felt that the well-being of millions of children depended on the humanizing influence of education.[46] Gopal Krishna Gokhale was the champion of free and compulsory primary education.[47] It was emphasized that education would increase efficiency of the individual, a higher level of intelligence and strengthening of the moral backbone of the country. On a more secular front, the Depressed Classes Mission Society of India was organized in 1917 through which the educated people from the Depressed Castes demanded compulsory and free education for their castes.[48]

The Montage-Chelmsford Reforms of 1919 introduced the policy of placing the responsibility of education on the hands of a separate Education Ministry with steps taken towards increasing elementary education among the backward sections of the society.[49] Under the Report of the Public Instruction for the Madras Presidency 1918-1919, the educational schemes for the Depressed Castes got further encouragement as the Government insisted that schools be situated in accessible places in order to enable regular attendance of the Depressed Caste students. Through the successive orders issued in 1919, 1920 and 1922, emphasis was laid on the necessity of admitting the Depressed Caste children in schools under public management.[50] The District Boards were ordered to admit Depressed Caste pupils without any discrimination and the Assistant Labour Commissioner warned of losing subsidies and grants had they failed to comply with the government policy in admitting children of the Depressed Castes.[51] In 1921, a Labour Department was created and separate labour schools were established for the promotion of education among the Depressed Castes. Only Mala and Madiga students were enrolled here and teachers were also appointed from the same caste backgrounds.[52] The primary aim of the Labour Department was promotion of elementary education among the Depressed Castes by admitting them into government-run schools and providing financial assistance through scholarships, fee concessions, etc.[53] The Director of Public Instruction had also asked the local boards and municipalities to work towards removal of caste prejudices by admitting students from all backgrounds.

The Hartog Committee Report of 1929 had envisioned the growth of education for a bright future for India. A large increase in the enrolment of the pupils from the Depressed Castes in the primary schools testified that the traditional indifference towards the education of these castes was breaking down.[54] The Abbot-Wood Report of 1936-37 advised the expansion and integration of vocational and technical education as part of the general education where subjects were taught in non-vocational schools as well, as in the vocational schools.[55] The Wardha Scheme of Education which was designed by Mahatma Gandhi in 1937 stressed the need for correlating school education with the activities of practical nature. The seven years of basic education was to include teaching of basic crafts along with the curriculum subjects. It was aimed at enabling the pupils to pursue an occupation in basic crafts such as spinning, weaving, carpentry, agriculture, fruit and vegetable gardening, leather work or any other craft that suited to local and geographical conditions.[56] It was realized that academic education was mainly designed to achieve higher forms of instruction leading to government services such as engineers, mechanics, electricians, revenue officers and railway personnel without giving importance to the technical aspect of instruction as part of the basic general education.[57] According to the Harijan Welfare Department Report of 1948-49, Industrial training was given in carpentry, cabinet making, spinning and weaving, engraving, drawing, fitting, blacksmithery, knitting, electric wiring, metal work, paper making, shorthand, typewriting, book keeping, etc.[58]

The Lindsay Commission on Christian education (1929) suggested that Christian colleges should contribute to the upliftment of village communities through social work and thus strengthen the Church in India.[59] The Report by the Central Advisory Board of Education or the Sargent Scheme of 1944 recommended that missionary schools managed by the Christian denominations would continue to exist under the new system of educational reconstruction.[60] Therefore, the education of the Indian population including that of the depressed castes (Malas and Madigas) was held within the administrative framework of the Colonial Government.

5.5 State of Education in Coastal Andhra

The pre-British education system in coastal Andhra was that of *Patshala* and *Gurukul* maintained by teachers who generally belonged to the *Brahmin* caste. The education method traditionally followed was rote learning wherein various branches of knowledge were memorized, and therefore students were unable to think on scientific and critical lines. It was characterised by an absence of independent thinking and spirit of enquiry among the learners. The teachers recited religious and mythological stories or rhymed arithmetical rules to pupils and employed manuscripts. The average duration of study was eleven or twelve years. There were no girls' schools; however, the privileged families sometimes instructed their daughters in writing and accounting with a view to empowering them in the event of an early widowhood.[61] The Telugu *Brahmins* were liberally provided with jobs as scribes and priests by the *zamindar*s, and enjoyed *inams* (gifts) and land grants.[62] There was also another system of education that existed in the 18th century which was called *Pyal* school, a school held on platforms raised two or three feet above the level of the adjacent road.[63] These schools taught subjects related to astronomy and Vedic literature.[64] The *Pyal* system of education attracted the attention of Rev. Dr. Andrew Bell, the eminent founder of the Madras Education System.

Until the second half of the 19th century, education was not within the reach of the Depressed Castes. They could not pursue learning either in *Pathshalas* or in *Pyal* schools but had to be content themselves with acquisition of skills through apprenticeship that is, learning from elder professionals, so that they could carry on the traditional or hereditary occupations. Education among the Muslims was conducted in Persian language and teachers of Persian and Arabic languages were paid either through land grants or in cash.[65]

The state of education among the Malas and the Madigas is evident in the note made by Rev. Wolf of the American Evangelical Lutheran Mission: "for centuries our converts largely were slaves, mere things in the hands of a superior race, with no intellectual training, no cultivated tastes for learning or books, and no chance to improve themselves."[66] But the desire of the Malas and the Madigas to acquire education was expressed in the following words, "we do not want our children to be as we are, give us a school."[67] In group conversions, where a group of villagers proposed to convert to Christianity *en masse,* the first request that came invariably to the missionaries was to open a school and to send a teacher.[68] Self-help among depressed caste children was observed by a missionary: the poor converts' children gathered under a tree to make letters and figures on sand as they could not afford a slate or a copy book.[69] Therefore, the missionaries' empathy naturally was oriented to the education of the Depressed Castes (Malas and Madigas) who wished to elevate their social condition from a depressed position.

But not all missionaries did undertake education of the Malas and Madigas. Some initially refused them admission to the mission schools. For instance, Rev. Noble of the CMS mission at Masulipatnam had persistently refused admission of the depressed castes' children in his school for fear of opposition from the *Brahmins.* The CMS Committee's directive to admit children irrespective of their caste background was opposed by Rev. Noble who even went as far as to offer his resignation in protest, in 1859.[70] In some cases, where no caste restrictions were entertained, *Brāhmin* students had refused to sit on the same bench with the depressed caste Christian and non-Christian students. In such situations, the missionaries were determined to dispense education for all students irrespective of their caste backgrounds because the success of the mission schools did not depend on the *Brahmins* or their objections.[71] For instance, under the headship of Rev. John Anderson at the St Andrew's School in Madras, three *Pariah* boys wearing caste-marks entered the school but their deception was soon detected. A number of boys from caste families were withdrawn, but Anderson stuck to his point and would not refuse admission to any boy who was competent to enter the school. The result was the *Pariah* boys stayed on in the school.[72]

The government too had faced numerous difficulties from caste Hindus on every attempt to make the advancement of the depressed castes.[73] That aside, there were caste distinctions within the Malas and Madigas themselves. In 1879, the parents of the Mala children did not allow the Madiga boys to sit with their children in the Ellore school. The Mala parents insisted that Mala converts should not fraternize with people whom they regarded as 'unclean' and 'lower' on the social scale, much to the frustration of the missionary, Rev. Alexander.[74]

The bold efforts of the government took a definite shape when the subject of education of the Depressed Castes gained official attention of the Lieutenant Governor of Bengal. He made an enquiry as to find out whether there existed any rule or practice that had prohibited admission of the children from 'low' castes into the government schools in the lower provinces and in what proportion the boys of low castes were in general found to frequent these schools.[75] On a more provincial note, the Madras Government's commitment towards the education of the Depressed Castes was expressed by its call for perfect equality in educational matters, and the admission of all sects and castes to its benefits.[76]

5.6 Christian Missionary Educational Enterprise in Coastal Andhra

Educational ministry always appealed the missionaries as it enabled the converts to read the Bible and to become preachers and teachers. The Christian converts also always looked for a school for their children and the missionaries promptly made efforts to help the new Christian communities.[77] In order to understand the extent of the missionary educational enterprise, a detailed account of the educational institutions founded and managed by the six missionary societies, namely, the London Missionary Society (LMS), the Godavari Delta Mission (GDM), the Canadian Baptist Mission (CBM), the Church Missionary Society (CMS), the American Evangelical Lutheran Mission (AELM) and the American Baptist Mission (ABM), in coastal Andhra are examined.

The Christian missionaries began to impart education to the natives with the initiative of a government official, Collector John Goldingham Esq. of Masulipatnam. It was with his support that Rev. Robert Turlington Noble of the CMS established a school in Masulipatnam.[78] What came to be known as 'The Noble school', was started with two teachers (Rev. Noble and Rev.

Sharkey) and two students, in 1843.[79] Mention may also be made about the establishment of a school in Guntur where the Magistrate-Collector, Mr. Henry Stokes, Esq, had offered Rev. Heyer of the American Lutheran Pennsylvania Ministerium to use part of the Collector's building for a school.[80] During the initial years of the AELM Mission (1848-1850), Rev. Heyer established schools in Palnadu, Gurajala, Polepalli, Veldhurthi, and Macharla where he was able to enroll a good number of Mala students.[81] Since 1854, some 400 Christian Mala children attended the village schools of the CMS mission at Masulipatnam, Ellore and its surrounding taluqas.[82]

Fostering elementary and vernacular schools was one of the promoted policies of the Court of Directors.[83] A general opinion that was held by the missionaries was that education taught in the vernacular tongue would become the best means of opening up of the evangelistic work in rural settings.[84] English education was also encouraged by the missionaries with the rationale that 'only through the medium of some other language than their own, that any education, in the proper sense of the term could be given to the people.[85] Despite the higher expenditure incurred by the Madras Government exclusively on English education, the cultivation of the vernacular languages did not suffer as it was realized that a greater number of people could only be educated through the medium of vernacular dialects.[86] Elementary education was in the vernacular medium without any distinction.[87] The importance that Rev. Alexander Duff gave for vernacular instruction helped promote it and led to the establishment of more vernacular primary schools.[88] The prominence of vernacular education in coastal Andhra is evident from the fact that, Mr. G. N. Taylor (the Sub-Collector and the architect of the Rate schools of the Godavari region), brought to the notice of Sir Walter Elliot, the Commissioner of the Northern Circars, that he had received applications for the establishment of primary vernacular village schools from the inhabitants of twenty-four villages in 1854.[89]

The learning schedule in schools began with basic instruction in the Christian doctrines followed by classes on the basics of language. When adequate numbers of Christians were formed in a village, a primary vernacular school was started to provide basic education that was subsidized by the government. Basic instruction in English also began at the primary level, besides teaching arithmetic, geography, outlines of history, mensuration of land, and calculation of areas, all taught in the vernacular.[90] In order to appeal to caste Hindus, Anglo-Vernacular schools were started where secular subjects were taught, besides daily Bible lessons, by the Christian teachers. Both Christian and non-Christian children were admitted and made to pursue the study of the Bible. It was reported that such schools and students produced productive results.[91] Generally, the missionary's office functioned as the central office for the mission's educational work. In some districts the missionary was the manager of as many as forty schools.[92]

With a desire to impart education on the Gospel as well as in secular subjects, to the converts and their children, the missionaries introduced the boarding school system, which was understood as a more progressive institution beyond village schools for rural Christian children.[93] The boarding school worked as a place where better learning took place with more discipline and a regulated dormitory life. It is said that another motive behind the establishment of boarding schools was to free the parents from the responsibility of monitoring their wards' study, so that more parents could be deployed in evangelistic activities of preaching and teaching.[94] Julia Harpster reported that, "only the daughters of Christian parents are admitted to the school as boarders."[95] Due to the poverty and financial hardships of the people especially the Malas and Madigas, only a small amount of the cost of supporting the students was paid by the parents and the larger burden had rested on the mission. The missionaries came forward to pay for the expenses of providing accommodation, food, clothes, books, and tuition fees for the students.

Missionary boarding schools were a great help for the parents to get their girls educated in boarding schools, secure government scholarship for normal training that could guarantee a livelihood for them. A boarding school also provided a different environment from that of a village setting in matters of social behavior and social cooperation. It gave ample opportunities for self-expression and self-discipline. The missionary's quarters were also situated within the vicinity of the boarding schools where there were facilities for teachers' training and vocational training.[96] After completing middle level education, pupils were sent for teacher training to teach in village schools. Thus through the medium of boarding schools, the education of the Christian children of the Mala and Madiga castes was promoted.[97]

The extensive growth of village primary school could largely be credited to the Christian missionaries and the native teachers.[98] Facility for education at various levels was made. A high school level education could lead either to university education or to vocational and practical training which benefited the Christian children of the Malas and Madigas. The following provisions and concessions from the government also helped the general growth of education of the Christian and non-Christian Malas and Madigas.[99]

(1) Special training schools for the Depressed Castes under the public management with an additional stipend of Rs 2 per month for each pupil;

(2) Establishment of special schools by local boards and municipalities for the Depressed Castes in all villages, where they were in large numbers;
(3) Allotment of government waste lands to schools for the Depressed Castes;
(4) Payment of stipends at 50% above standard rates to the Depressed Caste pupils attending government schools and in grant-in-aid schools; and
(5) Night schools for the labouring classes.

It was also decided to appoint Inspectors of Schools by the missionaries who were especially interested in the welfare of the Depressed Castes than appointing other caste officers.[100] Thus, more care was given to the education of the Depressed Castes, thanks to the efforts of the Christian missionaries and through the system of grant-in-aid.[101]

According to the Report of the Public Instruction of 1905-06, the education of the Depressed Castes increased in strength and size in public institutions. But it may be difficult to know the percentage by caste as the Depressed Caste Christians frequently returned as Christians without caste appellations.[102] The Census Commissioner of 1911 observed that "although converts to Christianity are recruited mainly from the aboriginal tribes and the lowest Hindu castes who are almost wholly illiterate, they have in proportion to their numbers three times as many literate persons as the Hindus and more than four times as many as the Muhammadans.[103] This observation was substantiated by the supporting information from A. G. Fraser, the chairman of the Village education commission of 1920 that Christians compare well with other religious communities in India. Taken as a community they were surpassed only by the Parsees (71.1%), Jains (27.5%) and Buddhists (22.9%) with 20.6%, followed by Hindus (5.5%) and Mohammadans (3.8%).[104] The educational progress of the Christians mediated by the missionaries can be appreciated, given the earlier level of illiteracy of the Christian Malas and Madigas (see **Table 5.1**).

Everything did not go smoothly with the missionaries. Sometimes they faced indifferent attitude from their 'Home churches' which would send meagre funds to conduct the missionary work. Protests were aired by the field missionaries against this policy and took the matter to their home countries through an established group called the 'General Council of Education in India' in 1878.[105] In the opinion of Naik and Nurullah, whose work traces the development of modern education in India.

The early missionaries found that their work began, rather than ended, 'with conversion', and that their main task was not so much the conversion of the people to Christianity as the improvement of the social, cultural and economic condition of the converted people, an object which could only be secured by conducting schools.[106]

Table 5.1 Growth of Education among the Malas and the Madigas, 1871

Districts	Hindus			Muhammadans			Christians		
	Population	No. of persons able to read and write	Proportion	Population	No. of persons able to read and write	Proportion	Population	No. of persons able to read and write	Proportion
Ganjam	13,82,561	34,448	2.5	4,826	528	10.0	679	207	30.5
Vizagapatam	18,20,944	40,644	2.2	21,030	1,027	4.9	882	214	24.0
Godavari	15,55,981	45,223	2.9	35,173	1,551	4.4	585	44	7.5
Kistna	13,65,709	55,951	4.1	78,941	1,801	2.3	7,380	277	3.8
Nellore	13,08,014	53,398	4.1	65,670	1,801	2.7	2,653	158	7.1
Total	74,33,209	229,664	15.8	205,640	6708	3.26	12179	900	72.9

Source: W. R. Cornish, *Census of the Madras Presidency*, 1871, Supplementary Tables, Vol. II, (Madras: The Government Gazette Press, 1874), 252.

The ignorance, helplessness, and poverty among the Depressed Castes called the attention of the missionaries, who in turn, called the attention of the colonial government to initiate socially ameliorative measures.

It can be explicitly stated that missionary educational institutions particularly served the convert and non-convert Malas and Madigas with an evangelistic motive. Credit also must go to the determination of the Malas and Madigas to get educated in order to move upward on the social scale. The first generation converted Christians largely entered public service employment as teachers, railway staff and military personnel.[107] By the year 1898, despite the occurrence of natural calamities like famines and cyclones, the education among the converts had increased nearly by 5% among boys and 8% among girls in the Madras Presidency.[108] Scholarships, fee concessions, grants-in-aid, supply of clothes and books by the missionaries as well as by the local bodies contributed for the spread of education among the Malas and Madigas.

5.7 Education among the Convert Malas and Madigas

5.7.1 Education of the Males

The missionaries of the London Missionary Society (LMS) were pioneers and forerunners of missionary educational activities in colonial Andhra. As mentioned in the earlier part of this chapter, the LMS missionaries had opened a native school as early as in 1805. In 1835, Rev. J. W. Gordon was responsible for the supervision of schools in Vizagapatam. Mrs. Gordon and Mrs. E. Porter started a girls' boarding school with one hundred native girls.[109] In 1836, a Sunday school was attached to the first Protestant chapel with one hundred and fifty children. The introduction of the printing press owed to the earnest efforts of the LMS missionaries which contributed to the development and dissemination of Christian and secular literature.[110] In 1840, Rev. John Hay undertook the translation of several useful and popular works from English to Telugu. He was also instrumental in establishing a printing press where the Holy Bible and several works such as the *Truth for All* (1849), *Peep of the Day* (1854), *True Religion Demonstrated* (1856) and *Pilgrim's Progress* (1868) were printed.[111] At the English school at Vizagapatam, Rev. Pulipaka Jagannatham, an LMS Telugu convert had contributed to the expansion of the school.[112]

In 1845, the Director of Public Instruction proposed that all the small vernacular schools in Vizagapatam to be merged into one Native Anglo-Vernacular High School and it became the only school of its kind in the whole of Madras Presidency.[113] But the spread of Christianity among the Malas and the Madigas did not occur until 1850 and so the effect of the LMS educational initiatives did not reach both these castes except in the Ceded district of Cuddapah. Upon their baptism, the Mala converts placed themselves under Christian instruction and showed intense desire for Christian teachers to be sent to their villages.[114] Thus it can be said that the missionary and educational services of the LMS prepared the ground for the other missionary societies in coastal Andhra.

The educational work of the Godavari Delta Mission (GDM) was mainly confined to the Godavari River delta and the Anicut areas. These areas were covered by the missionaries of the CBM from its centre at Cocanada and the missionaries the AELM operated from Rajahmundry. Sir Arthur Cotton as the principal architect of the Anicut near Dowlaishvaram on the Godavari River, encouraged both evangelistic and educational work. Revs. George Beer and William Bowden taught the Gospel to the coolies who were employed in the Anicut works and the missionary women gathered the village women from the villages and taught them.[115] At this time the "Rate School System" of Mr. G. N. Taylor was in place but it did not prove to be useful for the Malas and the Madigas who could not afford to pay the 'special rate' owing to their economic hardships.[116] This necessitated special intervention of the missionaries to make provision for the education of the children of these two castes.

The GDM contributed much to the education of the Malas and the Madigas by conducting schools in the Godavari delta region, where it was said that Rev. Bowden hardly could get school masters to work among these two castes.[117] Mr. Beer's Boys' School at Narsapur and Rev. Bowden's Normal

School also provided education for the converts. The GDM drew its converts mainly from the Madiga caste[118] and so native preachers and leaders were few. Rev. Bowden wished that much of the opportunity would become fruitful if a greater number of native preachers were prepared at their educational institutions.[119] The initial educational work of the GDM became a trajectory for launching the mighty educational work of the Canadian Baptist Mission (CBM) and the American Evangelical Lutheran Mission (AELM) in the last quarter of the 19th century.

During its Jubilee year (1874-1924), the CBM had maintained 400 village schools with daily average attendance of more than ten thousand pupils, ten boarding schools with nearly 1,000 boarders, two high schools with about 1,500 boys, one industrial school, one normal school, one Bible women's school and one theological seminary.[120] The mission's schools were conducted in the towns of Cocanada, Samalkot, Srilakulam, Vizagapatnam, Sompeta, Yalamanchili, Akidu, Tuni, Tekkali, Vuyyuru and Avanigadda. In 1874, Rev. McLaurin started the CBM's educational work, by establishing a school with thirteen boys and a few girls from the Christian families.[121] The school was conducted in a rented house which was successively headed by Rev. and Mrs. Timpany, Jonathan Burder, Mrs. Craig, Mrs. Davis and Miss Baskerville.[122] In 1876, Rev. and Mrs. Sanford started a school in the church building at Bhimunipatnam with an attached boarding home, for imparting elementary education to the converts and the downtrodden children.[123] The students were supplied with free books, food, shelter and clothing and this institution had produced many outstanding and useful Mala and Madiga citizens.[124] By the year 1880, the CBM had maintained 38 schools with 435 students.[125] The tiled school-house was built in 1880 thanks to the donation of land by the Rajah of Pithapuram.[126] In 1884, another school was opened at Gunnanapudi for the convert Mala Christians.[127] The CBM's school at Akidu was started in 1888 where 100 boys and 60 girls who came from the surrounding twelve villages, stayed as boarders.[128] The Bimlipatnam Central Boarding School had 295 boys where regular and vocational training were imparted both for Christian and Hindu pupils.[129] At the Samalkota Boys' Boarding School, academic and non-academic performance of the students delighted the missionaries. The boys had excelled in academics as well as class room activities, gardening, scouting and sports.[130]

The Church Missionary Society's missionaries were said to be 'school masters first and preachers secondly'. Rev. Noble, the "great educational missionary"[131] established a school at Masulipatnam.[132] In 1843, the Native English School was established by Rev. Noble in Masulipatnam with the help of the Eurasian missionary Rev. J. E. Sharkey.[133] The school grew into a high school in 1855 and in 1864, it was upgraded into a college which had catered to the higher educational needs of the students in the Northern Circars, until the establishment of the Andhra Christian College in Guntur in 1873.[134]

The syllabus at the Noble School was designed to include lessons from the New Testament, the Bhagavad Gita and the Koran and the students were invited to weigh and compare the non-Christian scriptures with the New Testament. During its initial years, the school did not make provision for admission of the Depressed Caste children as Rev. Noble had apprehensions of opposition by caste Hindus. But the CMS Committee at Madras did not accept his decision and insisted that 'low' castes should not be discriminated. But the strong caste opposition controlled Rev. Noble till his death. On the other hand, the principal John Barton of St. John's College, Agra did not consider caste as a criterion for barring the lower castes.[135] Later, upon the initiative of a Mala convert, Kurimella Joseph, Malas and Madigas were admitted into the school.[136] Students from the mission's village schools were sent to high school where they were trained to be clergymen, assistant-surgeons and school masters.[137] Sir Charles Trevelyan, the Governor of Madras described the school as the "South Indian Cambridge."[138] The Bishop of Madras looked for adequate supply of well-trained teachers for the schools throughout the CMS mission fields.[139] In 1849, a school for children of the lower castes was opened in Masulipatnam under Rev. R.T. Noble, for which teachers were drawn from the Noble school.[140]

The development of education in the CMS station at Ellore started in 1854 soon after Rev. George English opened a mission station there. He observed that the inhabitants there were longing for education and so he founded a school in the old hospital and guard-room of the fort.[141] Rev. F. W. N. Alexander who was appointed as the station in-charge in 1857, started twenty village schools in Telugu medium, for some 400 Mala children. As the Malas sought baptism, he founded an elementary school exclusively for the converts.[142] There was also a boarding-school for the Christian girls in the mission compound where about forty pupils received instruction up to the fourth standard. In 1862, Rev. Alexander's wife also started a boarding school at Ellore with nearly 90 pupils, again meant for the children of the Christian converts who were admitted free of charge owing to their financial backwardness.[143]

In 1880, the CMS maintained 84 vernacular village schools, with some 1170 students.[144] For the year 1881, M. A. Sherring has given the cumulative number of pupils for the coastal Andhra districts of Ganjam, Vizagapatam, Kistna and Godavari at 6,573 (male and female) in 256 mission schools having 180 Christian teachers.[145]

In the CMS Bezwada station, an Anglo-Vernacular school was founded by Rev. Thomas Young Darling in 1857. In 1910, there were 300 students in the high school and 400 pupils in the branch school.[146] After India's Independence, the school was handed over to the Municipal administration of Vijayawada and was named as "Gandhi Municipal High school."

Bishop Azariah played a major role in the development of education in the Anglican dioceses of Kistna and Dornakal. He was the motivating force behind the appointment of nearly 100 to 150 teachers in rural schools. Under his leadership, groups of villages were placed under a lay teacher to look after education in the schools.[147] In 1927, in Khammamet, 16 new schools were opened where 922 pupils were instructed, besides 543 Christian adults were attending the night schools.[148]

The American Evangelical Lutheran Mission (AELM) believed that India's evangelization must be carried out by a body of trained native workers filled with Christian spirit, qualified with adequate education and matured with experience. The General Council of the Pennsylvania Ministerium and the General Synod organized an educational network that was noteworthy and remarkable for the upliftment of the depressed castes from the last part of the 19th century. The foundation for such a network was laid along with evangelistic work in 1842 by Rev. Christian Frederick Heyer of the Pennsylvania Ministerium. Upon his arrival in Guntur in 1841, Rev. Heyer took charge of the school in the Collector's compound. Indeed this was the beginning of the future mighty educational network of the AELM. It may be noted that the colonial government's cooperation, particularly through the Collector, Henry Stokes Esq., who was solicitous about the education of the people, especially Christian converts, of coastal Andhra, continued to sustain the AELM enterprise.[149] The first schools started with 20 Christian boys each at Gurajala, Polepalli and Dachepalli by Rev. Heyer.[150] In 1844 Rev. L. P. Valett and Rev. Walter Gunn of the General Synod worked with Rev. Heyer to start seven schools in the Guntur area.[151] Though the education received by the pupils in the early years was modest, but honest and fair efforts were made to impart better education in the subsequent years.

Rev. Heyer employed caste Hindu teachers in the beginning. However, he wished to employ educated, intelligent converts and so he began to train young men under his pastoral care to be future Gospel workers and to that effect, he started a boys' boarding school in 1849 in Gurjala. A few names at the boys' boarding school were Jacob, Matthew, Nelaprolu Paulus, Barnabas and Rettivardu.[152] He employed trained native Mala convert teachers in the mission schools: for example, Samuel was assigned to the Veldurti school, Malapati John in the Polepalli school, Devasikamani to the Gurjal school and Mr. Jacob to the Tumurucotta school and Appiah was employed as a colporteur.[153]

Our records show that better educational mobility led to greater occupational mobility raising the economic standard of the converts. Almost all the educated, trained former students of the mission schools got employed either in mission's institutions or in government ones. In 1858, there were fifty five boys who were under instruction by seven native Christian teachers in the AELM schools in Guntur and nearby villages.[154] The government's grants-in-aid scheme also supported the missionaries in their efforts to educate the poor and the downtrodden people who otherwise could not even afford decent livelihood.[155] At the same time, missionaries were cautious that the government's grants-in aid did not interfere with the Christian orientation of their schools. In other words, mission schools were careful not to compromise with their ideals for the sake of getting the financial aid from the government.[156]

Dr. Lemon L. Uhl who served for fifty years from 1873 at Guntur, had distinguished himself in both evangelistic and educational work as supervisor of the English and Vernacular schools.[157] He took utmost interest in the education department and tried to improve the standard of the schools, besides reopening the Anglo-Vernacular school in 1873. He also had given utmost attention for the education and training of future pastors and preachers.[158] Later, under Rev. L. B. Wolf's principal-ship, the main Anglo-Vernacular school at Guntur was upgraded to a junior grade college and was named as the 'Andhra Christian College' with affiliation to Madras University, in 1885.[159] Though the school was started to admit students from all caste backgrounds, opposition to admitting depressed castes came from the Hindu pupils. In the hostels, they refused to sit with the depressed castes on the same benches, nor would occupy the same room with them.[160] But the missionaries gradually succeeded in convincing the parents of the Hindu students to allow their children to forego caste prejudices.

The desire for education was so intense among all castes that by the end of the first month itself, Hindu students began to join the college.[161] At the end of the year 1873, there were eighty-five students, of whom seventeen were Christians. The number of students rose to one hundred twenty seven, of whom ninety-four came from various Hindu castes and thirty three were Christian pupils.[162] In the year 1920, the college was upgraded to a higher grade college. Under the visionary leadership of the principals namely, Dr. J. Roy Strock, Rev. V. C. H. John, Rev. C. H. Swavely and Rao Saheb Dr. T. S. Paulus, the reputation of the college spread far and wide. Due attention was also given to the development of Christian character among the Christian students to provide leadership for the growing church.[163]

In the Rajahmundry, when Rev. Heyer took charge of the Anglo-Vernacular school in 1855, it had an enrolment of 68 pupils. There Rev. William E. Snyder acted as the manager of the Telugu schools which numbered seven in 1856, and had native Christian teachers.[164] All the schools had many native Christian teachers. In Rajahmundry also, the practice of training prospective preachers in boarding schools was introduced after the example of Rev.

Heyer in Guntur.[165] In early 1860, the number of converts in Rajahmundry was relatively fewer than that of the Guntur congregation, yet the number of pupils in schools continued to grow. Even the Anglo-vernacular school had an enrollment of eighty students. There were one hundred and sixty pupils in the boy's schools and forty-five pupils in the girl's school with thirteen Christian teachers.[166] In the surrounding areas of Rajahmundry, schools were conducted at Dowlaishwaram and Muramunda that were attended by about thirty pupils each. The sons and daughters of baptized Christians were admitted in these schools, but it appears that the missionaries also admitted un-baptized children as free boarding pupils.[167]

In the year 1870, there were seven native Christian teachers with 138 pupils in twelve of the mission schools at Rajahmundry, Muramanda, Jegurupadu, Metta, Peddapuram, Gowripatnam, Velpur, Narsapur, Palakol, Jagannathapuram, Peravaram and Lolla.[168] In 1879, the mission school at Rajahmundry had twenty-three pupils, both boys and girls. This school had special course on religion besides the normal subjects. These were Bible History, New Testament, Luther's Small Catechism, Telugu Language, Telugu History, Grammar, Geography, Arithmetic and Writing.[169] In 1883, the Dowlaishvaram School, which was begun by Rev. Heyer, was restored thanks to the enthusiasm of a retired engineer, Mr. Theodore Van S Tavern.[170] By the middle of the 20th century, the schools maintained by the AELM at Rajahmundry were the Luthergiri Theological College, Women's Bible Training School, two normal training schools, three high schools for boys, two high schools for girls, three nurses' training schools, four trade schools (agriculture, carpentry, weaving and lace making), seventeen higher elementary schools and eight hundred and ninety two elementary schools with an enrolment of 46,809 pupils, which demonstrated the spread and depth of the educational enterprise of the missionaries.[171] Certainly, the strenuous efforts of the missionaries seem to have mediated much socio-economic advancement among the converts and others. The missionaries took pride in their 'Christian boys' as these turned out to be the future leaders of the Christian communities. They were also greatly gratified that their dreams were being realized through education.[172]

The geographical territory of the American Baptist Missionary (ABM) touched the towns of Nellore and Ongole and the surrounding vast number of villages. In 1840, Rev. Samuel S. Day founded the American Baptist Telugu Mission in Nellore. With his acquired proficiency in Telugu language, he was able to interact with the local people.[173] Rev. Day opened several day schools in which English and Telugu were taught, besides instruction on Christian principles. The number of students was two hundred and seventy.[174] The educational enterprise in Nellore began with Rev. John Anderson, (Principal of the St. Andrew's School in Madras) who founded the 'Free Church Mission School for Boys' in Nellore in 1841 to pursue two principles: (a) inculcation of the Gospel teachings on pupils and (b) equal freedom of admission to all castes.[175] Similar to that of other missionary societies, the primary object of this school was to admit not only the Christian youth but also non-Christian caste Hindus.[176] In 1849, the mission schools had an enrolment of two hundred and fifty children and two hundred, in the Sabbath school.[177]

The boarding and day schools made good progress. There was a practice of paying the parents a small sum of money to encourage them to send their children to schools. This was done given the situation of extreme poverty of the parents who could not otherwise afford to send their children to school. The children were retained by their parents to assist them in earning daily wages through coolie work. Besides, the value of education was not understood by these illiterate parents. At the same time the missionaries desired to impart on the children Christian principles to facilitate the spread of the Gospel.[178] The ABM's educational services were largely conducted for the convert Madigas as the vast body of inquirers came from this caste.[179]

The pioneer of the ABM's evangelistic work in Ongole, Rev. J. E. Clough started an Anglo-Vernacular school in 1867 with a grant-in-aid of Rs. 288. This school developed into two separate institutions, one for boys and another, for girls. Two Anglo-Indian women, Ms. Sarah Kelly and Ms. Amelia Dessa had worked as headmistresses.[180] Devoting his energies more to evangelistic work, Rev. Clough closed down this school and began to train a body of native workers to quicken the spread of the Gospel among the inhabitants of Ongole. This enhanced conversions among the depressed caste Madigas in 1870s.

Subsequently, native demand for schools came from the Madiga converts. In order to sustain the results of conversion, the missionaries felt the need to undertake training of the converts in Christianity with Bible instruction, along with primary civil education.[181] A large number of schools were established in Ongole. In 1877 there were 42 schools which increased to 83, in 1878 and further, to 176, in 1880 with a total number of 2100 pupils.[182]

When a Christian boy was admitted into the school, caste pupils protested by walking out of the school, along with their fellow non-Christian boys. But this made no difference to the missionaries who remained firm in their conviction of equality of all castes. Besides, they had the confidence in the capacity of the converts to receive education.[183]

The Boy's school at Ongole was revived in 1875 by Rev. Clough in the changed circumstances of the rising demand for schools.[184] This school had seen many obstacles during the terrible famine of 1877. It was permanently opened as a high school for the whole mission, in May 1880 under the headship of Rev. W. I. Price, followed successively by Rev. Edward A. Kelley and Rev. W. R. Manley.[185] The school had one hundred students in 1880 out of whom twenty seven students were convert Christians.[186] In 1883, the school was raised to a second grade college with affiliation to the University of Madras with the provision to teach the First Arts course.[187] On his furlough in 1891, Dr. Clough presented a petition to the Baptist Executive Committee requesting that the high school be raised to the grade of a college and a grant of fifty thousand dollars, be given.[188] The missionaries believed that an up-gradation of the High school would be useful both for the Christian students who would get priority in admission and non-Christian students to take benefits of Higher education.[189] Subsequently, the high school was raised to a regular college in 1893, with Lower Secondary and Senior Secondary departments, with an enrolment of 357 students under Prof. Lewis E. Martin as the Principal.[190]

Rev. J. E. Clough also did remarkable service in gathering hundreds of famine orphans into the mission schools and orphanages.[191] The school functioned fruitfully and produced good results in annual examinations under Madras University.[192] It had sufficiently met the higher education needs of the Christian converts. Apart from Telugu, the main course of study also included study of English grammar and literature as the missionaries believed that if pupils learnt a language other than their own, they would be better educated. Bible recitation was a regular part of the course in all classes.[193] In 1916, there were sixty-five students in the sixth form out of whom fifty-seven pupils were allowed to take the public exam.[194] In 1922, Mr. Rowland reported that the total enrolment of the High school was 253 boys, of whom 126 pupils were Christians. The good results of the Secondary School Leaving Certificate public examination held in March, 1922 gave greater satisfaction to the missionaries.[195] The high school at Ongole was the only institution of the kind between Nellore and Guntur and the only one for the whole of the Telugu Baptist mission. The staff of the school comprised of Eurasian and native teachers.[196] The school did not make distinctions based on one's caste or religion.[197] The system of grant-in-aid by the government was much appreciated by the missionaries as they felt that it had brightened the chances of education of the Malas and Madigas. The mission took advantage of this aid by the government.[198] Luckily for the missionaries, much of the aid from the government came at a time when diminished aid was available from the 'Home missions'. This timely aid not only sustained their educational work, but also helped to further it.

The Free Church Mission school of Nellore named, the Coles Ackerman Memorial High School, came under the management ABM missionaries in 1887.[199] It had 350 students and 25 teachers then.[200] It was held in four large buildings, built largely from the generous donations of Dr. Coles of the New York City.[201] Agricultural education was undertaken in this school where the pupils learnt plowing, irrigating, planting seeds and other necessary operations related to agriculture, thereby enabling them to earn enough remuneration to pay for their fees and boarding. In 1912, there were 320 pupils whose number increased to 800 in 1916, and therefore arranging accommodation for all was difficult.[202]

In 1883, a school-house was built by Rev. Maplesden at Narasaraopet.[203] Later, thanks to the efforts of Mrs. Powell and Miss Linker, the school was developed into a 'Central Boarding School' for both Narasaraopet and Vinukonda.[204] In the subsequent years, there were one hundred and thirteen pupils in the school from where ten pupils were sent to the Ramapatnam Seminary for theological training.[205] Rev. W. Powell also established a boarding school for boys in Narasaraopet in 1883 with fifty pupils. There were thirty village schools in the vicinity of Narasaraopet and most of the inquirers in this mission field were from the Madiga caste.[206]

In 1920, Miss Lena Alberta Keens took charge of the school and in 1930, the school was named as 'the Hird Memorial school' to honor the Hird family which had donated huge funds for the development of the school. This was an elementary school for boys and girls until the year 1942, but was upgraded as a middle school in 1943.[207] There was also an 'alphabet class' (sort of kindergarten) conducted for the benefit of Christian boys in Ongole, in order to prepare them to get admission to class one. Two other primary schools were held in Ongole and Kothapatnam that served as feeder schools for the Ongole high school.[208] In Vinukonda, Rev. George N. Thomssen built a building in 1882 that served two purposes: of serving as chapel and as the school-house.[209] The establishment of five elementary boarding schools at Allur, Kavali, Udayagiri, Kanigiri and Cumbum by the Lone Star Mission in 1922 with an enrolment of 2,634 pupils further helped spread education among the converts.[210] Thus, through an extensive network of boys' elementary schools, higher elementary schools and boarding schools, the missionaries endeavored to provide education to the Mala and Madiga converts' children.

Overall, education of the Christian males enabled them to achieve social mobility through occupational mobility. The prospect of getting job as preachers and teachers with a pass in the eighth grade made the parents enthusiastic to make some sacrifices for the education of their children. Often the students earned not only their own boarding and clothing but also supported other mission schools through their newly acquired industrial skills in agriculture, poultry farming, gardening, etc.[211] Suffice it to say that the advancement of education among the Malas and Madigas owed much to the free education provided by the missions.[212]

5.7.2 Education of the Females

Female education was not given any importance in traditional Indian society. Hence, the approach of the missionaries in giving equal importance to education of girls surprised many, including the largest beneficiaries, the Mala and Madiga communities. Education of girls, as per the understanding of the missionaries, was like 'building a permanent church', and hence necessary.[213] The London Missionary Society's native female boarding school at Vizagapatam had twenty five boarders, mainly from the depressed castes from villages, besides a few day scholars. In 1853, under pressure from caste Hindus, a caste girls' school was started by Mrs. Hay.[214] In 1865, in Chicacole, there was a native female day school with 23 girls under instruction.[215] In the year 1868, there was a school each at Vizagapatam (217 boys and 51 girls), Vizianagaram (35 boys and 23 girls) and Chicacole (85 boys and 23 girls) respectively.[216] The Anglo-Vernacular school at Vizagapatam along with another high school was maintained by the Canadian Baptist Mission to serve the educational needs of the Christian converts.[217] One remarkable feature of the LMS schools was the continued reinforcement for a strong foundation of female education in coastal Andhra. By the end of 1899, the missionary education figures at Vizagapatam was 9 schools, 13 Christian teachers of whom 5 were female teachers and 1,113 scholars both male and female.[218] The curriculum was comprised of scripture lessons, English and Telugu grammar and composition, Geography, History and solving of simple equations.[219]

In 1910, the number of schools in Vizagapatam was six, with 1,295 boys and 156 girls, when its mission was handed over to the CBM. The remarkable service in the education of women in these schools was testified by the Education Inspector. He had noted both quality of character formation (self-respecting, Christian life) and quantity in terms of percentage increase in pass rates in the Presidency.

The Bobbili Boarding School for Girls' catered to the educational needs of the converts' children in the northern fields of the mission, under the supervision of Rev. R. E. Gullison.[220] In 1912, through the efforts of Dr. Sanford, the school acquired three acres of land and got constructed two good buildings under the supervision of Ms. Elliott, who also built a permanent school building with dormitories.[221]

The Canadian Baptist Mission had a large mission territory between Vizagapatam in the North to Vuyyuru in the South. However there were limited numbers of schools for girls. Therefore, Rev. John Craig opened a boarding school for girls at Cocanada, where 154 students were enlisted for instruction.[222] Another boarding school for girls at Tuni, a town north of the Godavari, was started under Mrs. Garside's care.[223] In 1886, the

Timpany Memorial School was enlarged to receive the growing number of pupils with government's grants-in-aid, and was placed under the care of Miss Ellen A. Folsom.[224] In 1896, a girls' primary school was started in Cocanada in a modified house.[225] The school was upgraded to higher elementary school in 1905 and was recognized by the government. The Vuyyuru girls' boarding school catered to the educational needs of the Christian girls from the Vuyyuru and Avanigadda towns and the surrounding villages. In 1924, a new building was constructed and was renamed as the Canadian Baptist Jubilee School, where 360 students were on the roll call.[226] In 1942, an additional 157 boarders joined this school after completing their fourth standard from village schools.[227]

The Church Missionary Society's Sharkey Girls' School at Masulipatnam was established in the year 1847 by the missionary couple, Rev. Edmund Sharkey and Mrs. Ann Amelia Sharkey in Masulipatnam. Caste distinctions were not allowed to be kept. Girls from all caste backgrounds had attended this school.[228] Mrs. Sharkey devoted her energies for the cause of this school until her death in 1878. During her time education of girls gained much importance in practice. In 1879, the school was revived and was named as Sharkey Memorial School.[229] This school was regarded as the 'Mother school of the CMS Mission.'[230] It was recognized by the government which granted a sum of Rs.242/- for the support of education of girls, especially from the depressed castes.

During the cyclone of 1864, Ms. Gregory braved her own life to save many young girls.[231] In 1902, due to a surge in the number of converts, the school was upgraded to the secondary level up to the third form and the students appeared for Matriculation exams in 1909. A training course was conducted to train female teachers to work in village schools.[232] In 1929, a CMS boarding school was established in Bezwada (Vijayawada) by Miss Young from New Zealand. This school catered to the educational needs of the Christians from the surrounding villages.[233] The school was renamed as 'Bishop Azariah High School' in 1931, as a mark of respect for the first Indian Anglican Bishop, Rev. Vedanayagam Samuel Azariah of Dornakal Diocese, for the valuable services rendered by him. This boarding school had Christian students from near and far towns and villages such as Machilipatnam, Eluru, Gollapalli, Gudivada, Pamarru, Kanchikacharla, Mylavaram, Nuzvid, Gannavaram, Mylavaram, Nadigama, Chintalapudi, Gudivada, Vuyyuru and Kondapalli.

With regard to the American Evangelical Lutheran Mission's contribution towards girls' education, a girls' school was founded by Rev. Heyer in 1842 with fifteen girls who were first taught by a young Hindu teacher.[234] Rev. Erias Unangst and Mrs. Unangst took charge of the Guntur girls' school, with about 40 girls, who were taught by three native teachers namely Walter, Ruth and Rebecca.[235] Mrs. Unangst took deep interest in the education of Christian girls and women and did achieve excellent results and efficiency.[236] The Silvanus Stalls Girls School was established in 1907 in Guntur with generous donations from Dr. Silvanus Stall.[237] By the year 1935, there were 33 mission schools in Tenali, 23 in Narasaraopet, 17 in Chirala and 15 schools in Repalle that were engaged in the teaching of students up to VIII standard. After completing their formal education in secondary schools, some of them proceeded to the Training institutions.[238]

By the year 1924, there were 632 girl students in the AELM elementary and boarding schools at Guntur, Bapatla, Markapur, Cumbum, Narasaraopet, Vinukonda, Palnadu, Repalle, Sattenpalli and Tenali.[239] One third of the number of students received mission support.[240] For day scholars who came from a distance of a mile or more, noon day meals were provided.[241] Quality of education in the mission schools was carefully maintained through a system of grading according to the academic achievements of students tested through annual examinations.[242]

In the AELM's Rajahmundry station, there were thirty-two scholars with two teachers at the girls' school in 1856. The pupils were taught vernacular reading and writing, multiplication tables and plain sewing.[243] In 1881, a separate girls' boarding house was opened in the missionary bungalow of Rev. Artman with thirteen girl inmates. They were taught not only regular school curriculum but also vocational crafts such as sewing and knitting under Mrs. Artman's supervision.[244] The Dowlaishvaram girls' school functioned with 40 girls. The Rajahmundry girls' school worked with full capacity, with some 120 pupils. In 1902 school built good buildings having better facilities.[245] In January 1904, Miss. Emily L. Weiskotten started a school for girls of the *Panchama* caste (outcaste) with 13 non-Christian girls who were taught by Christian teachers at Lakshmivarampetta, Rajahmundry.[246] The Hunter Commission of 1881 made an important recommendation that female education be treated as a subject of legitimate charge on the local, municipal and provincial funds. The Commission also recommended that the conditions of aid to the girls' schools to be more flexible to apply higher rates in case of the schools established for low-caste girls.[247] These schools were visited monthly by government schools inspector as these were run under the grants-in-aid scheme.

In 1894, Ms. Agnes Schade organized a separate boarding school for girls who were withdrawn from their former school which was made exclusive for boys. With 134 students it was under the supervision of Rev. Rev. Calvin F. Kuder.[248] Some other upgraded elementary schools included the Lutheran High School at Dowlaishvaram and Bethany Girls high School at Bhimavaram, under the leadership of Dr. Mrs. A. Neodorffer.[249] The number of girls' boarding schools maintained by the AELM at its

Rajahmundry mission station and surrounding areas was four hundred and thirty elementary schools and seven high schools.[250]

In 1925, the number of boarding girls at the Rajahmundry AELM Mission were: the Central Girls' School: 191, Luthergiri Mission School: 49, Samalkota Girls' School: 97, Narsapur Girls' School: 24, Bhimavaram Girls' School: 117, Tallapudi Girls' School: 160, Parvathipur Girls' School: 192 and Yeleshwaram Girls' School: 6.[251] In 1932, the Commission for Women's Education, under Ms. Alice van Doren examined the Christian secondary schools with a view to introducing domestic science as a subject of learning which was perceived to be relevant for girls.[252] In 1939, the Central school was upgraded into a high school and was named as Schade Girls High School.[253] By 1942, there were 42 schools in Godavari District and some of the schools got upgraded either as higher elementary or high schools. The latter were the Whittern Girl's High School at Samalkot, Lutheran High School at Agarthipalem, Lutheran High School at Peddapuram and Schade Girl's High School at Rajahmundry.[254]

In 1848, Rev and Mrs. Day and Rev. L. Jewitt started a girls' boarding school in Nellore. The first woman to get education was Julia, who helped the missionaries in Gospel preaching.[255] The American Baptist Mission opened a girls' school in Ongole, under Mrs. Clough's supervision with ten pupils in 1866, which became a boarding school for girls.[256] The Woman's Baptist Foreign Missionary Society of the West supplied funds for the construction of school buildings and was supervised Rev. Edwin Bullard and Mrs. Bullard during the years 1886 to 1887. Education of the Madiga girls and women was an important feature in the upliftment and empowerment of that caste.[257]

The Girls' boarding school in Nellore was started by Mrs. Day in 1848 and functioned with the help of non-Christian native teachers. In 1874, a devastating flood damaged the school as also other mission properties. The rebuilding of the school was undertaken through a generous help from the Woman's Board of Boston to the tune of $2,300.[258] The school had functioned as a secondary school for girls for the entire ABM mission stations with full capacity with thirty boarding girls.[259] The school was managed under the efficient guidance of Ms. Ella J. Draper, Ms. Olive E. Jones and Ms. F. E. Carman.[260] Compulsory manual training made the students self-supporting; the students acquired skills in industrial crafts such as lace work, sewing, house work, embroidery, etc.[261] In 1920, the girls' school was under the charge of Ms. Dessa.[262] During the year 1920, the school was up till the 6th form grade and had boarding occupancy of sixty-five scholars.[263] The teachers in the school were Christians except for a Telugu pundit who was a Hindu.[264] Due to increasing number of students, the problem of insufficient accommodation arose, but was solved with the generous financial help of the Woman's Board of Boston.[265]

Situated between Ongole and Nellore, the town of Ramapatnam presented an ideal field to serve Christians from both the regions. In 1870, Rev. A. V. Timpany started a system of developing lands for building schools and houses for the benefit of the villagers. The responsibility for building school-houses was entrusted to native preachers, deacons and head men of the village.[266] When Ms. Peabody was sent as a missionary in 1872 to Ramapatnam, she started a girls' boarding school with six girl inmates that increased to forty-five in 1875.[267] The expansion of schools among for girls not only raised the standard of education but provided them with remunerative occupations.

According to the statistical tables of the year 1900 for the Protestant Missions in India, Burma, and Ceylon, there were 106,266 women and girls under instruction in mission schools throughout India, which shows that at least one-fifth of the total number of female scholars and students were under instruction.[268] The events that occurred in the second half of the 19th century had witnessed a change in the traditional perception about women and a change in the role of women in family and society.[269]

Ms. Agnes Schade's Boarding School for Girls was built in 1897 in Rajahmundry with fifty Christian boarders, who were trained to teach in the Zenana and to do other useful crafts.[270] The girls' boarding schools served as medium for the preparation of Christian girls to assist in the Zenana classes. It was with the help of the educated native Christian women, the lady missionaries organized Zenana missions in the Rajahmundry region for the purpose of education of caste girls, as well as girls from depressed castes, thereby enabling many beneficiaries to achieve social progress. Miss Agnes Christenson rendered her services to the school for two terms from 1921-22 and 1938-45 and Ms. Salma Anderson was the manager of the school from 1922-27.[271] Thus the significant progress of the Mala and Madiga girls in education owed to the free education provided in the elementary and high schools.[272]

In the field of Zenana training, Christian women were trained to be Zenana teachers and care-givers to Hindu castes and Mohammadan women's households. The caste Hindus particularly the *Brāhmins* and *Vaishyas* and a few other castes, kept their women in seclusion who were difficult to reach. The Lady missionaries and the Bible women could gain easy access to the Zenana homes. In 1870, a caste girls' school was founded by Rev. J. H. Harrison at Bezwada with financial assistance from the Zamindar of Nuzvid.[273] The Church of England Zenana Missionary Society (CEZMS) was founded in 1880 and was separated from the interdenominational Indian Female Normal School Society.[274]

The responsibility of conducting Zenana schools for caste women was taken up by the ladies of the CEZMS with the help of convert Christian women and opened schools at Jaggiahpet, Bezwada, Amalapur and Rajamundry.[275] Working in close co-operation with the CMS, the Mission's vision was to reach women by means of Zenana visiting, providing medical services, establishing female Hindu and Muslim schools. In order to do these tasks the lady missionaries employed native Christian women who were trained to become Bible women. In order to spread the Zenana work, a female missionary or a Bible woman had to be professional and secular in thought who could link their cause to the progress of science and medicine.[276] The AELM gave Zenana training for Christian women within the missionary schools that added valuable strength to missionary work.[277]

The credit for educating the womenfolk in India could certainly be attributed to the efforts of Christian missionaries.[278] Education of the girls was considered to be the most effective weapon for breaking down social evils of caste, child-marriage and enforced widowhood. Christian missionaries gave encouragement not only for the education of girls from the depressed castes but also for the caste Hindu and Mohammadan women. Owing to the efforts of the Christian missionaries the first generation girls from the Mala and Madiga castes gained education up to the fourth or fifth forms and entered into the government service as teachers, preaching assistants and Bible women.[279] In the opinion of a regional historian, Prof. Vaikuntham, the disciplinary life style and social habits of the missionary ladies who had worked as teachers, doctors, nurses, wardens and Bible women, influenced the people of Andhra. By taking initiatives to start groups such as Women's Help Societies and Mother's Union', they had strived to enlighten the womenfolk in coastal Andhra.

5.7.3 Technical Education

The importance of imparting technical education to the converts was felt as an urgent need as the converts had often suffered from economic helplessness due to wide spread poverty and recurring famines and also due to the ostracism by their employers following their conversion.[280] The attempt to incorporate Industrial education was recommended in the Report of the Famine Commission of 1877-78.[281] The Government too had recognized the imperative need of Industrial education and appointed an Industrial Education Commission in 1901. The Commission had recommended an Industrial Education Policy to be adopted with a common curriculum in which promotion of manual training was recognized as part of the school curriculum.[282]

Both the English and American Missionary societies took special interest in the development of Industrial education. Skill building was introduced from fifth standard onwards in areas of agriculture and related activities such as vegetable gardening, fruit growing and cattle rearing.[283] Christian missionaries showed much interest in the welfare of the depressed caste converts for their material improvement and taught them the practical aspects of self-help and sustained livelihood through industrial training.[284] Missionary institutions had imparted manual and vocational training in practical subjects like agriculture, carpentry, gardening, telegraphing, lace making, weaving, and leather work.[285] The missionaries also found that the depressed castes were far more teachable in industrial pursuits and hence the growth of industrial education among them.[286] Industrial education also became an important medium to provide work for both Christian converts as well as others. This opened up new channels of employment for the converts, who had lost their jobs as a consequence of their conversion.[287]

Education with practical training was emphasized by all the missionary societies in coastal Andhra for two specific reasons. One reason was to make the Christian community independent from their caste masters and the other was to accomplish the task of self-sufficiency without any expense to the mission's treasury. The Manual Instruction Department at Samalkota Seminary and the Industrial Training School at Cocanada were maintained by the CBM. Rev. H. Dixon Smith gave special training in the field of industrial work at Cocanada where he had made arrangement for a carpentry and blacksmith training school with a regular curriculum in 1889.[288] In 1899, Mr. Davis transferred the Industrial Department from Samalkota to Cocanada where training in industrial pursuits was already in place at the Cocanada Industrial School.[289] Training was given in areas such as printing, bookbinding, leather-work, wood-carving, weaving, tailoring, shoemaking, blacksmithing, carpentry, cabinet-making, lace-making, embroidery, typewriting, and stenography.[290] It was understood by the missionaries that through practical education converts could secure employment in various vocations.

Thus, the educational work of the CBM not only achieved good results but also facilitated new lease of life and personal joy to the converts. The CBM missionaries had mainly worked among the Mala and Madiga caste converts by conducting village elementary schools, boarding schools, Bible training schools, normal and nurse training institutions and made every effort to turn the Christian converts into an effective and efficient workforce in the Godavari and Krishna delta regions.[291] The educational work of the CBM was a typical example of the socially transformative work among the Malas and the Madigas which influenced the life and conduct of the converts leading to progress and upliftment. With simplest elements of knowledge combined with spiritual instruction, the missionaries had aimed to bring change among the students. And the students in return applied the lessons from the Bible as well as from vocational professions in their practical life with earnest devotion.

In the field of Industrial education, vocational schools were started at Dummagudem and Chintalapudi in 1904 by the CMS missionaries to give manual training for the converts in vocational subjects. The wives of the missionaries were also active in the field of education and training of the Christian women in vocational pursuits which contributed for the latter's economic self-sufficiency.[292] The lace-making industry at Dummagudem benefited many village households. The mission school at Dornakal had a weaving unit from where the students took a loom, and with the yarn supplied by the mission they were able to market their finished articles.[293] The CMS had worked in close association with the Church of England Zenana Missionary Society (CEZMS) in providing vocational education for women at the Industrial School at Masulipatam.[294] In the girls' orphanage at Masulipatnam, the CEZMS lady missionaries conducted industrial training.[295] The Dornakal training school gave practical training for girls in needlework and lace-making at Dummagudem and Khammamet.[296]

According to the Report on Public Instruction in Madras Presidency for the year 1911-12, the government emphasized on the scheme of Industrial education by constructing new buildings and increasing the number of staff.[297] Some non-government secondary schools were allotted grants for vocational and pre-vocational training.[298] Certain Municipalities in Coastal Andhra had maintained technical and industrial classes attached to them. The growth of cotton mills, tanneries and railway workshops contributed largely to the growth of industrial education and training.

The AELM's General Synod had maintained an Industrial school for women and conducted trade classes for boys at the Lam Industrial Centre where training was given in fields such as carpentry, weaving, hatchery, animal husbandry, leather work and mat making.[299] Agricultural training was given to students to learn the methods of plowing, planting seeds and irrigation. The newly acquired skills enabled the students to receive remuneration which helped them not only to pay their school fees but also increased their self-confidence and even improved their physique.[300] In the Industrial School for Women at Narasaraopet, instruction was given in the fields of lace-making and embroidery.[301] At the Sattenapalli Higher Elementary School there was a weaving instruction class where 22 boys learned the techniques of weaving for six hours a week. The sale proceeds were used for purchase of new machines.[302] A qualified weaving instructor was engaged by the American Lutheran Mission to tour in the villages to advocate better methods of weaving. Courses were taught for spinning quality cloth to enable weavers to practice the profession of weaving on a manufacturing scale.[303] The Industrial training contributed to the improvement of traditional occupations such as weaving and leather work among the Malas and Madigas because of which they were able to work independently and to improve their earnings.[304]

The Industrial training work in the AELM's Rajahmundry mission was started in 1852 by Rev. and Mrs. Cutter, who were not only the founders of an education network but also the driving force behind the teaching of lace manufacture to the Christian girls and promoted export of their products to the missionaries' home country.[305] In Mrs. Schmidt's sewing class, boys and girls learnt the art sewing, for which the missionaries provided the learners with needles and thread. In the early part of 1878 the first lace was sent from Rajahmundry to Philadelphia under Mrs. Schmidt's supervision.[306] The teaching of lace making as a cottage industry evolved into a most practiced craft in the Godavari district which enabled the women to become self-sufficient wage earners. Mrs. Catharine Taylor McCready taught Christian women and girls in the crafts of crochet work, knitting and lace making in Tallapudi and in the neighboring villages.[307] In 1907, three women from Bhimavaram were sent to Madras to learn more advanced techniques of lace making from the Lace school conducted by the Church of Scotland Mission.[308] Dr. H.C. Schmidt was also credited for the building of an industrial school with carpentry and blacksmith-shops, a saw-pit and a lumber-yard in the Rajahmundry mission compound in 1876, with the help of his Schleswig friends and the Executive Committee in America.[309] He undertook training courses for the Christian boys at the Mission Boarding School in order to build a house-boat for preaching tours.[310]

In 1895, a vocational school was established at Samalkota where students were trained in carpentry that helped them gain employment in building churches and designing church furniture (altars, pulpits and baptismal fonts), school buildings, hospitals, ship building, furniture making, etc.[311] Rev. Frederick James McCready was interested in the teaching of tile-making which enabled the students to construct roofs of churches and schools. He understood that the Madiga converts were very poor, and they desired better living conditions which they were deprived of as a consequence of their conversion. Therefore he proposed to start a workshop in Tallapudi and made it a regular branch of the mission work.[312]

The Rajahmundry Mission Conference, held in 1918, passed a Resolution to make industrial education a part of the mission work with a regular budget and made Ms. Charlotte B. Hollerback in-charge.[313] This initiative was mainly meant for the poor Christian women of the AELM churches.[314] In 1923, Mr. Hauller Bauch founded the Dorcas Home for the women from unfortunate circumstances and strived to teach various craft works such as tailoring, embroidery, stitching of gowns and shawls, lace work, crochet work, darning, towels, floor mops, school bags, pillow covers, hand kerchiefs, gowns, shawls, etc.[315] In 1923, Ms. Alice J Nickel started a vocational school and taught weaving, tailoring, lace-making and gardening for destitute women. Manual training was made compulsory in boarding schools where vocational courses such as training for Railway works and commercial works such as typing, book-keeping, accountancy, commercial correspondence and domestic science for girls, were undertaken.[316] Mr. Gollapalli Devadasu was sent to the school of Engineering at Calcutta with a stipend of Rs. 180, for higher training.[317]

Regarding improvement in agricultural work, students were required to read books on topics associated with rural life, understand the village map and to acquire knowledge about village accounts in order to understand the demands by the employer. This strategy helped students to understand business transactions with the landlords to whom they had to pay rent and also with the grain dealers with whom they had to dispose of their crops.[318] Vocational courses on improved methods of weaving, agriculture and poultry were also undertaken.

The ABM's Rev. F. P. Manley, Rev. L. C. Smith and Mr. Fred G. Christenson took a lead in the development of industrial work in Nellore. The students became physically strong with improved physique and self-supporting, having received remuneration for their work and in turn, were able to pay for their own boarding and clothes.[319] They had also taken part in supporting other schools of the ABM.[320]

Dealing with leather was the traditional occupation of the Madigas. Upon the Madigas' conversion, missionaries of the American Baptist Mission held varied views on retaining or not retaining this supposedly 'polluting' occupation. At a conference held in Guntur, a section of the missionaries argued that the occupation was intimately connected with the depressed condition of the Madigas and therefore it should be discouraged altogether. Another section of the missionaries opined that the Madigas should certainly be encouraged to continue this profession quite usefully and turn it into a worthy occupation by learning better methods of tanning leather. Such an encouragement would free their '*tied*' position and would become one of the most valuable means of livelihood for the Madigas.[321] Since the work was in a crude fashion, better methods of tanning were taught by creating separate work-rooms away from their dwelling places. The Leather Trades Institute at Madras had enrolled a large number of students where improved methods of working with leather were taught with good results.[322] The updated methods of production helped the Madigas to get better wages from their masters. The Coles Ackermann Boys' High School at Nellore had an Industrial Department where agriculture and poultry farming led the students to undertake useful works.[323] Students took care of the undeveloped plots under the possession of the missionaries and developed them into vegetable gardens and farms.[324]

Mention may also be made of the American Baptist Missionary Union's manual training facilities in wood-work at Kanigiri, Darsi and Bapatla where all kinds of household furniture were manufactured. In the Faith Orphanage at Ongole, which was an independent industrial mission in charge of the Rev. H. Huizinga, industrial instruction was undertaken to teach manufacture of aluminum ware for the inmates.[325] The ABM had not only provided general education for the converts but also strived to make them self-sufficient by providing industrial training and inculcated the habit of self-help. The recommendations of the Fraser Commission on Village Education (1919), the Report of the Commission on Christian Higher Education in India or the Lindsay Commission on Colleges (1931), the Rural Uplift Survey by Butterfield and the Agricultural Institute at Bapatla gave a lead in imparting practical education and ensuring adequate livelihood for the Malas and Madigas.[326] Therefore, through the good network of technical institutions, avenues for differentiated employment were made possible with high level of efficiency among the Mala and Madiga Christian converts.

The Financial help from the American Board of Missions helped to sustain the educational institutions of the AELM. Mention may be made of the subsidies given in 1935 to the ULT College (Rs. 1600), Andhra Christian College (Rs. 26000), high schools (Rs. 16647), teacher training and middle schools (Rs. 4886), higher elementary schools (Rs. 12700), boarding schools (Rs. 25000), industrial schools (Rs.300) and to the Lam Agricultural Farm (Rs. 1975, besides stipends worth Rs. 4000.[327]

In the field of Medical education, the resolutions of the AELM recommended that encouragement be given to Christian girls to enter Nurses' training and to pursue three months' special training at the Welfare Centre in Madras. Women students were allowed to pursue a medicine degree only after two years of college work.[328] Rev. F. W. Armstrong had started the Allyn Hospital and Nurse Training School in 1878 in Pithapuram although medical evangelism was only taking root in the soil.[329] Dr. Anna Degenring, worked as a medical missionary for the American Hospital in Nellore and Ms. Annie Magilton and Ms. Dorrie worked as in-charges of the training school for pupil-nurses at Nellore between the years 1915-1922.[330]

5.7.4 Theological Education

Theological education was one of the most important means for the development of a native church. Theological education was needed since Christian instruction in government schools was excluded. In order to establish a body of Christian workers instilled with the ideals of Christian faith, theological colleges were established to teach the art of preaching the Gospel in the native language. In the preparation of native preachers, a course of study was designed which comprised certain portions of the Bible with written and oral examination. Once the candidates graduated in this course, they were employed either as preachers or as village teachers.[331]

For an efficient system of training of preachers Rev. Lyman Jewett of the American Baptist Mission started a theology training school in Nellore in 1865.[332] By the end of 1870, there were fifty pupils in that training school.[333] At the Missionary Conference in 1870 in Ramapatnam a Resolution was adopted towards opening a theological seminary as an immediate necessity for the Telugu Mission. Under the leadership of Rev. A. V. Timpany, a seminary was begun with fifteen students in 1872 and was named the Brownson Theological Seminary.[334] In 1878, there were seventy-three male and fifty-four female trainees in this Theological seminary.[335] In order to ensure qualification and efficiency as ministers of the Gospel, a course study of six years was designed by Rev. Timpany, of which the first three years were to be spent as preparatory training and the last three years, for studying proper theological subjects.[336] But the course design was never strictly followed for two reasons: a) trainee-pupils could not fully comprehend higher theological concepts of the religion and so they cared only for a few years of Biblical study, and b) despite their limited education, missionaries hastened to send the pupil-trainees as preachers and teachers to villages due to pressing evangelical needs.[337]

Rev. McLaurin of the CBM opened a Theological Seminary at Samalkota in 1882 for training native converts to become catechists and Gospel workers.[338] By 1912, the Seminary had trained men for the ministry with growing enrolment each year. It was shifted to Cocanada under the leadership of Rev. H. E. Stillwell in 1912.[339] The initiative to set up a 'Union Theological Seminary' was realized in 1920, under auspices of the CBM and ABM at Bezwada due to its strategic and geographical importance.[340] The Eva Rose York Bible Training School for women was established in 1922 at Palakonda and was later shifted to Tuni in 1925 where girls took to Bible training, financially supported with a small stipend.[341] The Bible Training School of the AELM was initially established at Mangalamandiram in Guntur.[342] However it was discontinued in 1927 when the Charlotte Swenson Memorial Bible Training School was established at Rajahmundry by the missionaries of the Augustana Lutheran mission.[343]

The Lutheran Seminary at Rajahmundry worked under the supervision of Rev. E. Pohl in an excellent manner as was attested by the Inspector of Government Schools in 1892.[344] In 1892, there were 10 teachers and 150 pupils at the Seminary with boarding facility. Preference was given to young boys who had passed the second class in village schools. The Seminary had lower primary, upper primary and lower secondary with seventh class or third form (being the highest). The boys acquired a high standard of education that enabled them to teach their fellowmen.[345] The subjects taught were World Geography, English, Algebra, Elementary Geometry, Simple Physics,

Catechism, Old Testament history, Bible History, New Testament Readings, Luther's small Catechism, and English grammar, along with practice in reading and writing.[346] In 1883, Ms. Emma Rauschenbusch was stationed in Ongole where she undertook supervision of the Bible-women's work.[347] In July 1921, a Bible Training School was opened in Nellore in a new building.[348] Miss Margarita Moran and Ms. Genevra Brunner worked in the Bible Training School for Women and rendered valuable evangelistic service among the women in the Nellore mission station.[349]

5.7.5 Teacher Training Education

In order to prepare a body of teachers, Normal Teacher Training was needed so that students could be enabled to gain a fair amount of general education. Teacher Training was conducted for Christian men and women. Some schools were equipped with Normal Training Departments to train pupils to become village school teachers. These departments were recognized by the Education Department in Madras Presidency.[350] The Christian Normal School at Cocanada was held under the supervision of Rev. R. C. Bensen. This served as a good educational asset for the mission which needed many teacher-evangelists.[351] Samalkota became an important town for the CBM's activities, where Ms. Ellen A. Folsom had conducted a Teacher Training Institute.[352] The Bettie Elementary Training School at Cocanada was also conducted by the CBM.[353]

The AELM had maintained the Men's Normal Training School and the Elementary Women's Normal Training School in Guntur.[354] The other Missions (ABM and CMS) availed of these training facilities by sending their students for teacher training.[355] The AELM also maintained a school for the blind both male and female at Rentachintala.[356] The AELM had a boys' orphanage within the premises of the Boys' Boarding School at Guntur. During the year 1883, Rev. Artman added a Normal Training Centre to the boys' school at Rajahmundry. In 1904, a Women's Normal Training School was opened by Miss Schade and attached it to the Central Boarding Girls' School of Rajahmundry, where teaching was conducted up to lower secondary grade.[357] The Training School for Masters was established in 1908 with twenty-one pupils and the number of normal pupils comprised of both Christian youths and employee-teachers of the Mission kept growing.[358]

The CMS mission established the Preparandi Teacher Training Institute for Men and the Sharkey Training Institute for Women at Masulipatnam.[359] In 1918, on the occasion of the diamond jubilee of the Noble School, another teacher training centre was started by Rev. Penn in its premises and the institute continued till 1971 and was credited for training hundreds of teachers.

The Charlotte Swenson Bible Training School and the Industrial Home for Women were built in 1926 in memory of Miss Charlotte Swenson's missionary services in Rajahmundry.[360] The School did well under the successful principalships of Ms. Christian Eriksson (1926-1928), Ms. Hildegarde Swanson (1928-1930), Ms. Hilda Kaercher (1930-1931) and Ms. Jesse Cronk (1937-1939).

In the beginning, the ABM employed many non-Christian teachers as there was a lack of trained Christian teachers.[361] To serve the growing demand for Christian teachers in village schools, Mrs. Clough's Normal Training school was founded with four teachers in Ongole in 1875, with 97 students both men and women.[362] In 1908, this training school had 140 students (90 men and 50 women) who were trained as preachers and teachers.[363]

The Normal Training School in Bapatla was started under the aegis of the American Baptist Foreign Missionary Society (ABFMS) under the supervision of Rev. Bullard and Mrs. Edwin Bullard in 1888 for training of teachers for village schools, as there was an intense requirement for village school teachers.[364] The school provided two-year teacher training programme for both higher and lower grade teacher–pupils. In 1916, there were 64 students from the ABM mission stations. There were attempts to make quality improvements in terms of efficiency and functioning.[365]

The ABFMS Women's Training School at Guntur was established to provide large numbers of staff for their schools.[366] In 1884, an Urdu school was founded for the training of women to do evangelistic work among Muslim households. Another training school for women in Ongole was started in 1892 to supply qualified teachers to village schools. Men and women converts belonging to the Madiga caste undertook training to preach and teach in the mission's villages.[367] In 1926, three native Bible women were entrusted with work among Mohammedan women.[368] The Higher Elementary Training School for mistresses at Nellore had three-fold functions: as a Bible school, as a Normal school and as an Industrial school.[369] An amount of $3,500 was donated by Mr. William Bucknell of Philadelphia for establishing the ABFMS Girls' Training School in Nellore in 1886. A prominent task of this school was to give the pupils instruction in Zenana teaching and Bible work. In 1884, Ms. Jennie E. Wayte was designated to conduct the Zenana educational work in Nellore which was supported by the Woman's Board of Boston.[370] Teaching was conducted primarily in English. Many students who were graduated from this school were trained as teachers and Bible women.[371] In 1920, the lady missionaries of the ABFMS, Ms. Tencate and Ms. Ethel M. Ross together maintained the Training School as well as the Model School attached to it. A Kindergarten Normal Training School was opened in 1920 which was developed into a Model Kindergarten in which the first four Telugu girls undertook Kindergarten Normal training.[372] A Normal school at Kanigiri was started by Mr. Brock for training teachers to meet the demand for teachers in Christian hamlets.

5.7.6 Indianisation of Education Management

Till about 1910 the missions societies somewhat kept the status quo of all their educational institutions. The period between 1910 and 1950 witnessed great change in terms of transfer of management (to Indians), nature (on national lines) and need (growing need for village education). Also, government agencies and even non-Christian agencies began to pay more attention towards the education of the Depressed Castes. Hence, missionary educational sphere came to an inevitable stage of 'devolution' since 1910. During the World Missionary Conference at Edinburgh (1910), the aims and objectives of Christian education throughout the world, particularly in India, were discussed.[373] It was said that 'Indianisation' of Christianity and its institutional system can occur only if native Christians were allowed to manage administration.[374] Parallel to the great tide of the Indian freedom struggle, the Indian Christian community strived to Indianize Christianity. Indian Christians demanded that church affairs and church institutions be 'controlled by Indians', 'shaped by Indians' and 'carried by Indians.'[375] At the same time, the foreign missionary societies started to consolidate their work among native communities and began to prepare themselves for an eventual transfer of administration and authority to the hands of Indian Christian leadership. The National Christian Council (1924) (formerly the National Missionary Council, 1914), under the leadership of K. T. Paul, V. S. Azariah and V. Santiago had planned to indigenize the Church affairs.

Most missionary educational institutions gradually came under Indian Christian leadership, but continued to get foreign missionary support in close association with Provincial Church Councils under the head of 'Christian Education'. The missionaries had proposed to amalgamate their activities with social work and rural reconstruction programs for upholding and strengthening the Indian Church. The rural reconstruction programs were planned programmes in favour of rural communities providing education, health care, and socio-economic upliftment.[376]

During the 10th meeting of the National Christian Council, it was recommended to envisage a complete 'literate Church', by organizing literacy campaigns with the local Churches providing personnel and funds. The Council had urged the Churches and missions to raise the standard of elementary schools in rural areas. It was recommended that each Church earmark a scholarship fund to enable talented boys and girls, whose families were poor to secure the best education.[377] Industrial education was much valued and encouraged so that people could set up suitable cottage industries. Improved methods of agriculture on co-operative basis were encouraged. It was also resolved to continue Christian instruction to both Christian and non-Christian students.[378]

While handing over the responsibility of education to the Indian Christians, the foreign missionaries had adopted a policy of 'responsible handover' of the educational institutions. As requested of them, they continued to give their guidance through debates and discussions. As the Church of South India was being set up (1947), the foreign missionaries were in a dilemma: whether to join the newly formed Church (CSI) or to remain where they were. Some missionaries, with years of experience in the field of education decided to resign as they thought that their continued presence would hinder the proposed transfer of power.[379] The missionaries understood the political undercurrents among the Indian Christians and felt they should leave the management, particularly of educational institutions, to the Indian Christians.[380]

The contribution of Christian missionaries for the educational development of the Malas and the Madigas during the period 1850-1950 was enormous and invaluable. It was a medium for effecting social transformation.[381] Edgar Thruston noted in 19019 that, "the condition of the Malas has, in recent times, been ameliorated by their reception into mission schools".[382] According to Dr. S. F. Smith, an observer of the Baptist Telugu mission, with Christianity and elementary education, the Christian converts formed the bone and strength of the Telugu country.[383] The missionaries believed that by imparting education to the converts, the Malas and the Madigas would wipe out the perceived low caste nature of the newly emerging Church.[384] The educational efforts of the Christian missionaries complimented their conversion work the outcomes of which were adopting of good habits and good manners, horning of skills and putting in hard work, maintaining better cleanliness, etc., by the Mala and Madiga converts. Their changed life style seems to have brought much credit for the converts.

The Bishop of Dornakal Rev. Azariah, who had observed the Christian community evolve into a large constituent body of school masters and school mistresses in South India, said that there is probably no other community that has such a large proportion of its educated men and women engaged in the work of imparting primary education. Men and women in teaching profession could be seen in government, municipal and district board schools providing education to the young of India.[385] Educational growth and development should lead to a new identity and meaningful employment for the betterment of the individual as well as the society. The largest number of scholars enrolled in institutions such as training schools and technical schools were from the Christian converts.[386]

In conclusion, education work, more than any other works, pushed up the poor people on the socio-economic scale. It was the most signal contribution of the missionaries to the Malas and the Madigas. In a statement prepared for the Parliament in 1923, the Government had observed:

> In this benevolent and essential work, designed for the uplift of one-fifth of the total population of India, a voluntary agency has been particularly successful. The work of the various Christian missionary societies is beyond all praise. Not only had they established a large number of schools for the education of the depressed classes, they had resolutely insisted that pupils from this social stratum should be admitted side by side with members of the higher castes into colleges under mission control.[387]

5.8 Education of Non-Christian Malas and Madigas

In the matter of education of the Malas and Madigas by missionaries, no distinction was made between converts and non-converts, and both groups were allowed to join in their educational institutions, until the beginning of the 20th century. Non-converts were encouraged to convert at their own will. For example in 1889, in the AELM educational institutions nearly half of the pupils were non-Christian Malas and Madigas and the missionaries welcomed such a composition of student body for rapid evangelization.[388] Missionary attempts at social reform by creating awareness about the evils of caste system, particularly untouchability, were aimed at all Depressed Castes. So it did not matter whether the latter were converts or non-converts. During the first part of the 20th century, apart from missionaries there were Hindu social reformers who attempted to remove these social evils. Gandhi for one, named them 'Harijans' (meaning children of Hari=God) in an attempt to elevate them nominally.

Missionary education stimulated the Depressed Caste students to realize that through education and social participation they could also be emancipated from caste restrictions and traditional bondages. The government's commitment through the system of grants-in-aid and liberal free education to these castes was a way of supporting missionary efforts.[389] Besides, the social reformers both from within and outside the Depressed Castes had been either students of Christian missionary schools or had been associated with missionaries and because of which they recognized the importance of reforming the condition of the Depressed Castes. They realized that conversions took place also because of caste oppression within the Hindu fold. And so removal of the caste disabilities would prevent these castes from leaving the Hindu fold. The foremost among the social reformers in Andhra were Sri Raghupathi Venkata Ratnam Naidu, Sri Kasinadhuni Nageswara Rao Panthulu, Sri Vellanki Krishna Murthy, Sri Nallapati Hanumantha Rao and Sri Vemuri Ramji Rao. A movement of self-help generated among the Depressed Castes due to the efforts of Harijan reformers like Bhagya Reddy Varma, Arige Ramaswamy, Vemula Kurmayya, B. S. Venkata Rao and Narralasetty Devendrudu. In the struggle for equal opportunity, justice and removal of caste-based evils, it was Dr. B. R. Ambedkar who provided the most significant leadership for the Depressed Castes all over India. Thanks to him, these castes were guaranteed equal rights and equal citizenship under the Constitutional of India.

Government initiatives in the field of education such as establishment and maintenance of schools, grant of scholarships, stipends, free books, slates and clothing, waiving of examination fees and maintenance of free hostels at important towns contributed much for the growth education among the Malas and Madigas. Grants were provided to some private bodies that were engaged in social and economic uplift of these communities.[390] The management of these schools was classified as municipal, district board, aided missionary and aided private schools and unaided schools.[391] Under the Appendix VIII of the White Paper for Madras Presidency the following sections of the Depressed Castes, *Adi-Andhra*, Madigas, *Malasdasu*, Malas and *Panchamas*, became eligible for the ameliorative measures undertaken by the Labour Department.[392]

In almost every town of coastal Andhra districts, there were Harijan schools with boarding facilities which were supported by well-to-do *Harijans*. There was also a policy pursued by the Education Department to open schools for the Depressed Castes in those localities where no schools existed or where the existing schools were inaccessible to the Depressed Caste students. Scholarships and fee remissions were awarded for the deserving students of the Harijan communities. The government enforced this policy with some disciplining measures such as:

a) Recognition shall not be granted to any school situated in a locality which was inaccessible to the members of the depressed castes.
b) Recognition may be withdrawn for any school, whether under public or private management, which refuse admission to any pupil merely on the ground of the caste or community.[393]

The Department of Labour in cooperation with the Harijan Welfare Department made provisions for maintenance of numerous Harijan hostels by sanctioning boarding grants for eligible communities.[394] A hostel for boys was established at Masulipatnam which was maintained by the Government with 50 students.[395]

In 1942, the Government instructed the Director of Public Instruction to amend the Madras Education Rules so that a pupil belonging to the 'Scheduled Castes' (Non-Christian Harijans) may be retained and fee concessions be given for a second year in case he or she fails in the previous year.[396] The Report of Public Instruction of 1949-50 gave an account that the number of Harijan students studying in all secondary schools was 27,076 boys and 4,522 girls. The number of scholars studying in Arts and Science colleges were 684 men and 57 women, 148 men and 24 women in Professional colleges and 939 men and 399 women underwent teacher training.[397] The number of public institutions intended for the Harijans rose from 10,429 to 10,874 and the strength of students rose from 302,804 to 312,515 for the whole of the Madras state, for the reporting year.[398]

The Harijan Welfare Department also undertook the following measures to ameliorate the condition of the Depressed Castes: provision of house sites, maintenance of schools, grant of scholarships, stipends, boarding grants, grants for purchase of books, tanks for supply of drinking water, sanitary amenities and street lighting.[399] Under Section 92 of the Madras Educational Rules, half fee concession was granted to poor pupils belonging to the Scheduled Castes in all secondary schools and colleges and no fee was collected in elementary schools. For obtaining grant of half-fee concession, students were required to produce 'poverty certificates' that had to be signed either by an honorary magistrate, a president of local board or a District educational council member, Chairman of a Municipal Council, or an officer of the Revenue Department not lower rank than a Deputy Tahsildar.[400] There was no change in the policy of the Education Department with regard to establishing and maintenance of schools except in the direction towards making the schools more efficient and utilizing the budget allotment for the purpose of greater advantage to the Harijan communities.[401] A number of scholarships were granted to eligible Harijan students and converted Harijan students under the Harijan Welfare Department for pursuing industrial, professional and commercial courses.[402] As per the Census of 1951, there was an ever increasing demand for more schools and colleges in places where the existing institutions were unable to cope with the requirement.[403] A total of 179 boarding schools in all the principal towns of the Coastal Andhra were running with government grants in 1951.[404]

Studies have shown that due to encouragement and growth of education among the Depressed Castes in colonial India they were able to move forward socially and economically.[405] Education played a leading role to claim their place in the Indian society as equal citizens for equal opportunities. It was due to the liberal policies of the British government and Christian missionary undertaking that education became a tool to uplift themselves from their depressed position. Regarding the social mobility among the Malas, Hibbert Ware, a missionary scholar noted:

> From the very beginning, they were leaders, uneducated indeed, but men of character and talents, were not wanting. Under the influence of education this community had produced several

hundreds of school masters, besides a small band of catechists, and even clergy.[406]

Thus, education initiated and brought a substantial change in the lives of the converts as Mrs. Ellen M. Kelly observed that education brought change in the life of the Malas and the Madigas where social barriers had crumbled and "people of the highest caste do not now look upon these Mala and Madiga converts with the same horror and repugnance that they felt some years back."[407] Education created an affirmative stimulus among the Malas and the Madigas for social progress which was evident in their awakened resolve to achieve a new social identity.[408]

II

5.9 Missionary Humanitarian Service in Health Care

'Health' has been described as not only the mere absence of disease or infirmity but also a state of complete physical, mental and social well-being of the individual.[409] The ancient medical systems of *Ayurveda* and *Siddha* were truly Indian science of healing which dealt mainly with the health of an individual through the three humors of the body.[410] With little evidence of in-patient treatment of the sick in ancient and medieval India, health care was essentially an individual discretion and preference wherein people were treated with some herbs and natural remedies and for hundreds of miles, there were no hospitals in the countryside.[411]

During the period of this study, the general health condition of the common people in the country was filled with ignorance and neglect in the treatment of severe diseases such as cholera and smallpox. The conception that diseases are caused by gods and goddesses made the people to perform rituals, sometimes elaborate and expensive, to appease the gods and goddesses. The village physicians followed inhuman practices on helpless human beings by burning the wounded flesh, rubbing pepper into sore eyes and the use of mercury which made the patients suffer intense agony.[412] The early Colonial administration too did not make any provisions for public health but restricted itself to the treatment of only the servants of the Company.[413] Once the Colonial Government took up the responsibility of civil governance in India, it set up modern hospitals and public health care centres in cities and villages. But the need of the people far exceeded fulfillment. Further, for the poorest of the marginalized sections of society, access to modern medicines was a near impossibility. It is here one must appreciate the health care services of the Christian missionaries which were preferentially available to the marginalized depressed class communities. In this section we shall review the enormous humanitarian medical service rendered by the respective missionary bodies under our study.

5.9.1 Medical Evangelism

Medical Evangelism and the work of healing may be viewed as the fruitful effects of Christianity, where advances in the medical field were applied by the missionaries for the betterment of the lives of the people who sought their help.[414] The term 'Medical Missionary' refers to the system of dispensing medicines for the sick and availing the opportunity of organizing evangelistic effort among the patients.[415] At the Centenary Protestant Missionary Conference at London, in 1888, it was declared that the medical missions be recognized as not merely as benevolent agencies and auxiliary part of the missionary work, but as an embodiment of the essential teachings of the Gospel.[416] The duties of a medical missionary were to conduct itinerating trips, visiting villages and conducting both medical and evangelical duties.[417]

In coastal Andhra, as also elsewhere in India, the Christian medical missionary enterprise was not an agency to supplement or support the main missionary enterprise, nor was it only a means of attracting men to listen to the Christian message: it was a part of and an expression of that message itself.[418] It was an approach of the missionaries to reach out both the converts and the non-converts to communicate the truth as well as to remove superstitious beliefs. In this duty of the missionaries, the Mala and Madiga converts assisted the missionaries in various capacities in hospitals and Zenana Homes for not only medical work but also to share the gospel.[419]

5.9.2 Growth of Medical Evangelism in Coastal Andhra

The contribution of the Protestant medical missionaries to the well-being of the Mala and the Madiga converts seems to have been quite significant which fact can be gleaned from the available records on health condition in coastal Andhra for the period of our study. The provision for medicines in case of ailments such as cholera, flu and smallpox improved the standards of health among the people. Though vaccination was introduced early in the 19th century (the first vaccine for smallpox was developed in 1796), it was not until the year 1880 that an organized effort was made to establish public health as an active agency of the Government.[420] However, missionary medical interest existed since the middle of the 19th century. Since 1845, Rev. Heyer, M.D. of the AELM used his physician skills to treat hundreds of people in the Palnadu area.[421] Medical evangelistic work became a source of spreading the Gospel for the AELM, ABM, CBM and CMS missionaries.

5.9.3 The Growth of the Missionary Hospitals

Though the government initiative in public health created a feeling of wellness and confidence especially where hospitals and dispensaries were established in large towns,[422] there was insufficient number of government hospitals and dispensaries to treat women and children. The growth of a network of Mission hospitals served to remove the insufficiency.[423] Missionaries of all denominations used simple fever remedies and cholera mixtures to relieve the distress of the people. Small tracts of medical works were published in Telugu to be used by the native workers while offering assistance to the poor people.[424] During times of famines, it became the duty of the missionary to give food for the starving and medicine to the sick.[425] The patients who were treated at these mission hospitals often returned to their homes with a Christian message of divine healing that paved the way for effective spreading of the Gospel in the villages.[426] The missionaries' wives who often were also trained nurses, rendered efficient assistance in treating females.[427] The hospitals and dispensaries gave medical help for the people in times of plagues, famines and epidemics like cholera, flu, and smallpox. It was noted that the missionaries responded to the needs and distresses of the people by offering their medical services day and night.[428]

i) Missionary General Hospitals

The mission hospitals in coastal Andhra were intended to serve two purposes: to serve the growing number of converts and to witness the Gospel among non-Christians.[429] Mission hospitals played an important role in the social, moral and spiritual progress of the village Christians.[430] The Canadian Baptist missionaries established hospitals at Akidu, Narsapatnam, Pithapuram, Yellamanchili, Samalkot and Kotipalli. The CBM's medical practitioners namely Dr. Hulet, Dr. Cameron, Miss Harrison, Miss Mason, Dr. Allyn, Dr. Smith, Dr. Wolverton, Dr. Jessie Findlay and Dr. Zella Clark not only served the Christians but also the caste Hindus.[431] The Good Samaritan Hospital was opened in Chicacole in 1899 to fulfill the long cherished medical needs of the mission.[432] The medical services of the Canadian Mission got strengthened in 1900 when Dr. Woodburne and Miss Gertrude Hulet joined the mission. Miss Hulet rendered her medical work at Vuyyuru from 1904 where she built a small hospital in 1906.[433]

As mentioned earlier, the first American Lutheran missionary to Guntur, Rev. C. F. Heyer, M.D., provided medical aid to the people in Guntur and Palnad areas.[434] The medical work of the Lutheran mission saw speedy growth after 1885 with the opening of a dispensary in Guntur and its vicinity area of Mangalagiri where the number of patients who were treated exceeded more than a thousand people.[435] Since 1888, new dispensaries in the mission stations were opened with the aim to reach a wider population especially females.[436] Dr. Edman of Samalkota urged the mission authorities for the establishment of a Mission hospital due to the caste-based difficulties faced by the Malas and the Madigas at the hands of the indifferent caste Hindu dressers in the government hospitals.[437] According to Miss Julia Harpster, treatment was conducted under the skillful hands of the physicians and the untiring care of the nurses who were also in-charges of the daily Bible instruction. She further wrote that the patients often returned to their homes not only healed in body, but with a changed heart.[438] The method of preaching the Gospel at the dispensaries was that: a Bible woman would read the Bible for the waiting patients and the lady doctor talked to the women patients with a scripture message.[439]

Rev. Dr. Erias Unangst of the AELM mission made great use of his medical skills to reach different classes of patients who suffered from various types of common diseases. He had the habit of carrying a supply of medicines, and had the company of a native compounder to dispense medicines under his direction.[440] His service as missionary doctor earned him great popularity in the district.

In 1910, the Lutheran dispensaries treated more than twenty thousand patients in Rajahmundry where Gospel messages were heard not only by the patients but also by their accompanying relatives. Dr. Betty A. Nilsson opened a dispensary in Dowlaishvaram in 1911 to fulfill the growing medical needs of the region.[441]

In 1947, the United Lutheran Christian Mission was managing the Augustana Hospital in Bhimavaram, the Bear Hospital in Chirala, the Kugler Hospital and the Evangeline Booth Hospital in Guntur.[442] In 1950, the Andhra Evangelical Lutheran Church at Guntur maintained one hospital each at Guntur, Chirala, Rentachintala, Rajahmundry, Bhimavaram and Tarlupadu besides a Tuberculosis Sanatorium at Visrantipuram, Rajahmundry.[443]

The CMS' medical work ran in close collaboration with the government. In 1903, Lady Curzon initiated the 'Victoria Memorial Fund' for the training of nurses and in 1906, a Nursing Association was started by Lady Minto.[444] In 1947, a hospital with a first-class diagnostic clinic, was opened in Bezwada (Vijayawada) through the generous gifts of Rev. Canon Dhanwada Anantam.[445]

The American Baptist missionaries also realized the considerable medical needs of a large number of Christians in the areas of their preaching. Rev. Clough dealt with the epidemic of cholera with much efficiency at the Coolie camp in 1877 by giving doses of cholera medicines.[446] In 1893, the Baptist Mission hospital was started under the aegis of Rev. Clough and Rev. David Downie. Dr. Robert Williams worked with thiamin (the beri-beri vitamin), which he used to treat vitamin deficiency diseases in Andhra.[447] In 1916, upon the recommendation of the South India Mission Conference and the Reference Committee for the Telugu Field, a hospital was built in memory of Rev. Clough that served the growing medical demand of thousands of Christian adherents and boarding schools inmates.[448] This hospital treated a number of patients, both Christian and non-Christian ones, who suffered from epidemics like cholera, bubonic plague, relapsing fever, influenza, smallpox, typhus and malaria.[449] Patients were said to have expressed their gratitude over the medical services of the missionaries. Thus, the role of these hospitals in improving the health of the native converts was remarkable and dynamic.

ii) Missionary Women's Hospitals

The main intention of establishing Women's hospitals was to provide assistance to women at the time of childbirth and to care infants. For the benefit of the female patients, Dr. Pearl Smith Chute of the CBM's Akidu station made earnest efforts to provide medical help for the female patients who could not go far off to get help from the hospitals.[450] Dr. Chute's services were remarkable for her treatment of about 1,642 patients with the help of a European matron.[451] Dr. Zella Clark served in the Sompetta mission and treated over 52,000 patients.[452]

At the Guntur Women's Hospital, all classes of people were treated, including European, Eurasian, native Christian, *Brāhmin*, *Súdra* and Mohammedan. The Women's Missionary Societies of the Pennsylvania Ministerium and the Augustana Synod had worked in collaboration with each other. Since 1884, they were managing were six hospitals with local dispensaries, nine out-station dispensaries and one sanatorium.[453]

Dr. Anna Sarah Kugler, M.D., of the AELM was a renowned medical missionary, who was filled with intelligent spirit and interest in medical work. In 1883, she established a mission dispensary which was later developed into a hospital for women in 1897.[454] In 1893, a donation of Rs.45000/- was secured to build a permanent hospital. Dr. Kugler worked as the supervising doctor for 40 years and her noble work was appreciated by one and all.[455] The hospital was later named as 'Kugler Hospital' in 1930 in her respectful memory.[456]

The Swedish Augustana Synod recommended in 1895 that Miss Charlotte Swenson be sent to India as a medical missionary.[457] The Nurses Training School at Guntur was established by Miss Katherine Fahs. A similar school was established in 1897 and kept under an Indian Christian doctor in Rentachnitala. In the year 1902, the "Medical Home" (along with a residence for the medical missionary) was built on the road from Rajahmundry to Dowlaishwaram with a generous contribution from the Women's Missionary Society of the Pennsylvania Ministerium and the Women's Missionary Society of the Swedish Augustana Synod.[458] Dr. Lydia Woerner established the Lutheran Mission Dispensary for Women and Children at Rajahmundry in 1902. During her tenure there she had made 432 visits to patients' houses and performed 84 surgical operations.[459] She also conducted Sunday schools for patients and children in the Medical Home.[460]

Dr. Julia Van Der Veer shared the medical work of Dr. Lydia Woerner in 1905.[461] Dr. Mary Baer was another notable doctor who founded a hospital for women and children at Chirala in 1906. In addition to the hospital, houses were built for native assistants and Bible women to facilitate Bible teaching for the patients.[462] In 1908, Dr. Sigrid A. Esberhn and Betty A. Nilsson were sent by the Women's Missionary Society of the Augustana Synod to serve in Rajahmundry and Dowlaishvaram areas.[463] Miss Agatha Marie Dorothea Tatge who was specialized in Hospital Economics undertook the management of the mission's department of Nursing in Rajahmundry Women and Children's hospital in 1911.[464] The supplies for hospitals and dispensaries were solicited through Miss Mary Miller, the chairman of the India Box Committee of the Women's Missionary Society of the General Council.[465] Dr. Mary Baer also opened mission-hospitals for women and children at Rentachintala and Tarlupadu in 1920 and 1923 respectively.[466] There was an effort for the establishment of a Christian Medical School also.[467] The medical services of Dr. Ida Scudder in Guntur were remarkable as she used her automobile "Samaritan Car" which was equipped with a dispensary and material to aid in Gospel preaching.[468] In 1930, Ms. Borthwick was authorized to acquire a plot of five acres of land for the Bhimavaram dispensary and an appeal was made to the Women's Missionary Society of the Augustana Synod for a grant of Rs.3000.[469] The Augustana Hospital at Bhimavaram was built in 1934 and Dr. Mary Moses was placed as in-charge of the hospital which, under her capable leadership, catered to the medical needs of men, women and children.[470]

The CMS at Dummagudem also engaged in training of nurses since 1885, under the direction of Miss Graham, a trained nurse, to help missionaries Rev. and Mrs. Cain. Modest hospitals were managed at Kammamett, Dummagudem, and Bezwada under the devoted labours of the CEZMS nurses.[471] The notable CZEMS lady missionaries were Miss Penny, Miss Turnbull and Miss Digby at Khammamett and Miss Alexander and Miss Symonds at Kammamett.[472] They gave comforting moments for the poor Mala and Madiga women of the surrounding villages.[473] With their benevolent undertaking, the medical missionaries raised the value of human life and the sacredness of womanhood.[474]

The American Baptist Mission conducted medical work for women at Bapatla and Ramapatnam since 1886. Miss E. J. Cummings toured the villages for both evangelistic and medical work.[475] The medical work of Dr. Lena A. Benjamin, a senior missionary of the American Baptist mission, was much in demand as she had worked in the hospital for women and children and also as Superintendent of the Training School for Nurses.[476] She had achieved considerable progress in her work of treating obstetrical cases and conducting operations.[477] Ms. Lilian Wagner rendered her useful work at the Ramapatnam dispensary by not only treating the Seminary students and their wives but also toured the surrounding villages.[478] The Bible-women at the hospital took the opportunity to bring the Gospel to a large number of patients. The medical help provided for women brought immense relief from physical sufferings and provided comfort not only to the Christian Mala and Madiga women but anybody who sought the help of the medical missionaries.

The home medical services provided by the lady missionaries were mainly meant for women and children who were confined in homes. Trained Christian women from the Mala and the Madiga communities were employed as assistants and nurses by the lady missionaries in Zenana medical work.[479] It is a recognizable feature that the services of the Bible-women in Zenana homes were widely accepted and respected for their experience in teaching and thoroughness of work.[480] It was further stated that without the help of these trained women workers, Zenana work and hospital work would not have been possible as male missionaries were not allowed into the Zenanas.

There was a great increase in the number of vaccinations including the vaccination of infants.[481] However, the frequent occurrence of malaria, cholera, small pox, dysentery and diarrhea was blamed on frequent festival gatherings where flooded rivers caused the spread of infection in Kistna and Guntur districts. The government initiated to station Deputy Inspectors of Vaccinations in these districts.[482] Health weeks were conducted at the Dornakal diocese where musical health dramas were played and booklets on sanitation and precautionary methods were sold and bought.[483]

5.9.4 Missionary Mercy Institutions

The sad condition of the lepers drew the attention of the missionaries whose efforts were directed towards opening of asylums for them.[484] Called as 'Mercy Colonies', these settlements of lepers were a demonstration of the missionaries' ideals of humanity and social Christianity. Despite many practical difficulties, these institutions of mercy worked as auxiliary units that were conducted by the AELM and the ABM. In these homes were accommodated widows, deserted wives and crippled women, along with their children and young girls. One such institution was the Dorcas Home at Samalkota which was in later years shifted to Rajahmundry to be a part of the Industrial Home.[485] The CMS Orphanage was conducted at Masulipatnam where twenty-five hundred orphans and other destitute children took relief.[486] At the AELM's orphanages at Guntur, residents took vocational training in cottage industries.[487] At the ABM's Christian Herald Orphanage and Faith Orphanage, skills in leather and aluminum work were taught.[488]

Leprosy was a common disease and occurred frequently among the Depressed Castes owing to their occupations such as field labour and leather work.[489] Missionary medical help came as a relief for them. As field personnel on the ground, the missionaries felt obliged to take the responsibility of healing the famine orphans not only from the Mala and the Madiga castes, but from all castes. The missionary could teach what he was able to teach, that is, the good news of the Bible without giving much thought for results, in terms of conversion, but imbibed by philanthropic motive.[490]

The missionaries received a large contribution from the Maharajah of Pithapuram towards the Bethesda Leper Home in 1898.[491] The Bapatla Leper Asylum had 28 women and 48 men among whom there were also converted Christians.[492] Under the committed leadership of Rev. J. E. Davis and Miss S. I. Hatch, the Ramachandrapuram Leper Home was started in 1899, where 25 lepers were admitted. Miss Flora Clarke founded the Vizianagaram Leper Home on a site of one hundred acres that was obtained from the Rajah of Vizianagaram on the main road leading towards Bimlipatnam.[493]

5.9.5 Medical Education for Christian Converts

An important aspect of missionary medical service was imparting medical training to native converts. The missionaries realized that the vast medical needs of the women in Andhra could not be met by foreign medical missionaries alone. Therefore they began to train native men and women medical personnel who largely belonged to the convert communities. On the other side, medical training opened more employment opportunities for Mala and Madiga converts as doctors, nurses, compounders and physician assistants. Trained convert women worked as superintendents of nurses, Bible women and ayahs.[494] The Christian compounders relieved the medical missionary who was often under great pressure, by administering medicines to patients under direction of physicians.[495]

Though the Christian missionary enterprise was meant for all castes, it was more available to the Mala and the Madiga converts due to the latter's proximity and network with the missionaries. Opportunities were created to bring the bright native Christian students into a sphere of medical training with full curriculum and rigorous requirements for the benefit of their communities.[496] The Telugu Christian doctor, Dr. Joshee who worked at the Ramachandrapuram Mission Hospital, was given medical education under the care of and financial assistance from Miss Hatch.[497]

Medical mission statistics show that at the end of 1933, there were over 11,000 Indian and 500 foreign mission workers in the Telugu area. Medical work was conducted in 89 hospitals and dispensaries, where 500,000 patients were treated annually.[498]

The mission hospitals and dispensaries were not only places of comfort for the sick but also served as centres of modern medical practices.[499] The missionary medical methods helped in giving impetus to scientific practices.[500]

5.10 Conclusion

In conclusion, the medical work of the missionaries uplifted health care among men and women, who also learned the values of cleanliness and sanitation as preventive measures.[501] Health care practices got changed, scientific understanding of diseases increased, obsolete and obnoxious customs and rituals related to healing of diseases were abandoned. Change of living styles and better hygienic living space seem to have helped the depressed caste converts to achieve greater immunity against common diseases.[502] Thus, medical missions became important agencies that improved the health condition of both converts and non-converts by alleviating their physical sufferings and pain.

Endnotes and References

1 James M. Thoburn, *The Christian Conquest of India* (New York: Young People's Missionary Movement, 1906), 183.

2 M. L. Orchard, *Canadian Baptists at Work in India* (Toronto: The Missionary Education Department of the Foreign Mission Board, 1922), 132.

3 Syed Mahmood, *History of English Education in India: 1781 to 1893* (Aligarh: Mao College, 1805), 11.

4 R. C. Majumdar, ed. *The History and Culture of the Indian People* (Bombay: Bharatiya Vidya Bhavan, 1965), 31.

5 *The American Baptist Quarterly* V(2 and 3), (June- September 1986): 135.

6 Edward W. Uthe, "Educational Foundations," in *Foundations for Educational Ministry*, Vol. III, ed. Evenson C. Richard (Minneapolis: Fortress Press, 1971), 130.

7 M. S. Gore, *Education and Modernization in India* (Jaipur: Rawat Publications, 1982), 2.

8 Charles Elmer Gehlke, *Emile Durkheim's Contributions to Sociological Theory* (New York: Columbia University, 1915), 53.

9 See Rudolph H. Fischer, "Conversion and Social Mobility in Nineteenth Century South Canara and Malabar," in *Religion in South Asia: Religious Conversion and Revival Movements in South Asia in Medieval and Modern Times*, (2nd edn.), ed. G. A. Oddie (New Delhi: Manohar Publication, 1991); P. C. Jain, *Christianity, Ideology and Social Change among Tribals: A Case Study of Bhils in Rajasthan* (Jaipur: Rawat Publications, 1995); Jose Kalapura, "Change of Socio-economic Structure: A Paradigm of Dalit Mobility (A Case Study of the Ravidasis of Bihar)," in *Dalits and Peasants: the Emerging Caste-Class Dynamics,* ed. Ashish Ghosh (New Delhi: Gyan Sagar Publications, 1999); Shyam Lal, *Tribals and Christian Missionaries* (New Delhi: Manak Publications, Pvt. Ltd., 1994); Sushil Madhav Pathak, *American Missionaries and Hinduism, (1813-1910)* (New Delhi: Munshiram Manoharlal, 1967); Jaiprakash Raghaviah, *Basel Mission Industries in Malabar and South Canara (1834-1914): A Study of its Social and Economic Impact* (New Delhi: Gian Publishing House, 1990); K. N. Sahay, *Christianity and Culture Change in India* (New Delhi: Inter India, 1986); Dasarathi Swarno, *The Christian Missionaries in Orissa: Their Impact on Nineteenth Century Society* (Calcutta: Punthi Pustak, 1990) Augustine Kanjamala, *Religion and Modernization of India: A Caste Study of Northern Orissa* (Indore: Satprakashan Sanchar Kendra, 1981).

10 Edward W. Uthe, op. cit., 132.

11 Richard Lovett, *The History of the London Missionary Society (1795-1895)*, Vol. II (Oxford: Oxford University Press, 1899), 109.

12 Ingham Kenneth, *Reformers in India, 1793-1833*: *An Account of the Work of Christian Missionaries on behalf of Social Reform* (Cambridge: Cambridge University Press, 1956), 61.

13 L. B. Wolf, *After Fifty Years or An Historical Sketch of the Guntur Mission of the Evangelical Lutheran Church of the General Synod in the United States of America* (hereafter, *After Fifty Years*) (Philadelphia: The Lutheran Publication Society, 1896), 186.

14 John Clark Marshman, *History of India from the earliest period to the close of the East India Company's Government* (Calcutta: The School Book Society, 1873), 309.

15 S. Nurallah and J. P. Naik, *A Student History of Education in India 1800-1973* (New Delhi: McMillan, 1974), 38.

16 Norman Goodall, *A History of London Missionary Society* (Oxford: Oxford University Press, 1954), 459.

17 Richard Lovett, op. cit., 34.

18 I. W. Francis, *Madras District Gazetteers: Vizagapatam* (Madras: The Government Press, 1907), 63.

19 S. N. Mukerji, *History of Education in India: Modern Period* (Baroda: Acharya Book Depot, 1955), 35.

20 H. Sharp and J. A. Richey, ed. *Selections from the Educational Records of the Government of India*, Vol. 1 (Calcutta: The Government Press, 1920), 65.

21 *Manual of the Administration of the Madras Presidency*, Vol. I (Madras: The Government Press, 1885), 566-68.

22 S. Sathianathan, *History of Education in the Madras Presidency* (Bombay: Srinivasa Varadachari and Co, 1894), 6.

23 Ibid., 8.

24 Ibid., 20.

25 The Act of Parliament for the better Government of India, received Royal assent on 28th August 1833. Syed Mahmood, op. cit., 49.

26 John Clark Marshman, op. cit., 14.

27 S. N. Mukerji, op. cit., 99.

28 The Wood's Despatch was the first authoritative declaration by the British Parliament about the educational policy to be followed in India. S. N. Mukerji, op. cit., 133.

29 J. Talboys Wheeler, *India under British rule from the Foundation of the East India Company* (London: Macmillian, 1886), 278.

30 S. Satthianathan, op. cit., 33.

31 S. N. Mukerji, op. cit., 155.

32 Ibid., 278.

33 S. Satthianathan, op. cit., 190.

34 Ibid., 190.

35 M. Sargur Doss, *Educational Policy in Madras Presidency 1800-1900* (Madras: Unpublished Ph. D thesis, Madras University, 1961), 271.

36 *Government of India Records: Education*, Home, Nos 9-12 (February 5, 1858), 9.

37 H. Sharp and J. A. Richey, ed. op. cit., 25.

38 Ibid., 25, 141.

39 A. Biswas and S. P. Agarwal, *Development of Education in India: A Historical Survey of Educational Documents before and after Independence* (New Delhi, Concept Publishing, 1986), 30.

40 R. C. Majumdar, et al, *An Advanced History of India* (Delhi: McMillan, 1978), 867.

41 *Indian Educational Policy 1913: Being a Resolution Issued by the Governor General in Council on 21st February 1913* (Calcutta: The Government Press, 1915), 17.

42 A. Biswas and S. P. Agarwal, op. cit., 36.

43 Panchanandas Mukherji, *Indian Constitutional Documents, Containing the Government of India Acts, 1915 and 1916,* Vol. II (Calcutta: Thacker Spink, 1915), Introduction.

44 *Indian Educational Policy 1913: Being a Resolution Issued by the Governor General in Council on 21st February 1913* (Calcutta: The Government Press, 1915), 3-4 & 10.

45 V. S. Azariah, "The Bishop's Letter," *The Dornakal Diocesan Magazine* (December 1934): 1.

46 *Report on Indian Constitutional Reforms* (London: HM Stationery Office, 1918), 15.

47 A. Biswas and S. P. Agarwal, op. cit., 835.

48 Yagati Chinna Rao, "Education and Identity Formation among Dalits in Colonial Andhra," in *Education and the Disprivileged: Nineteenth and Twentieth Century India*, ed. Sabyasachi Bhattacharya (New Delhi: Orient Longman, 2002), 65.

49 C. V. Dikshitulu, "Madarasu Prabhutvamu: Vidyasakha Vyayamu," (Education Expenditure of the Madras Government), *Bharathi* (2), (July, 1938): 88.

50 Y. Vaikuntam, *Education and Social Change in South India and Andhra* (Madras: New Era Publications, 1982), 181.

51 B. D. Bhatt and J. C. Aggarwal, *Educational Documents in India: 1813-1968: Survey of Indian Education* (New Delhi: Arya Book Depot, 1969), 37.

52 G. Syamala,"Uttama Upadhyayani Tadi Nagmma," in *Nalla Poddu* (Hyderabad: Book Trust, 2003), 42.

53 Yagati Chinna Rao, op. cit., 98.

54 B. D. Bhatt and J. C. Aggarwal, op. cit., 37.

55 Ibid., 64.

56 Ibid., 59.

57 *Government of India Resolution on Indian Educational Policy*, 1904, Para 31 in K. S. Vakil and S. Natarajan, *Education in India* (New Delhi: Allied Publishers, 1966), 160.

58 *Administration Report of the Harijan Welfare Department for 1948-49* (Madras: The Government Press, 1949), 2.

59 Krishna Kumar and Joachim Oesterheld, eds., *Education and Social Change in South Asia,* (Hyderabad: Orient Longman, 2007), 49.

60 Ibid., 63.

61 Kapil Fathima Kutty, *Education and Social Change in India* (New Delhi: Radiant Publishers, 1990), 4.

62 I. W. Francis, op. cit., 16.

63 Charles Lawson, *Memories of Madras* (London: Sonnenschien and Co Publishers, 1905), 216.

64 *The Godavari District Records,* Andhra Pradesh Archives (Hyderabad: Government of Andhra Pradesh, 1935), 221.

65 Charles E. Grover, *Results of Educational Census, Madras-1871* (Madras: The Government Press, 1872), 60.

66 L. B. Wolf, *After Fifty Years,* op. cit., 228.

67 M. L. Orchard and K. S. McLaurin, *The Enterprise: The Jubilee Story of the Canadian Baptist Mission in India: 1874-1924* (hereafter, *The Enterprise*) (Toronto: The Canadian Baptist Foreign Mission Board, 1925), 230.

68 J. A. Sharrock, *South Indian Missions* (Westminster: SPG Publications, 1910), 221.

69 James M. Thoburn, op. cit., 173.

70 Frederik Gledstone, *Andhra Christian Church Founders: Robert Turlington Noble* (Madras: Diocesan Press, 1941), 10.

71 David Downie, The Lone Star: The History of the Telugu Mission of the American Baptist Missionaries Union (1838-1927) (Philadelphia: The American Baptist Publication, 1892), 24.

72 Stephen Neill, A History of Christianity in India: 1707-1858 (Cambridge: Cambridge University Press, 1984), 320.

73 M. Sargur Doss, op. cit., 362.

74 G. A. Oddie, "Christian Conversion in the Telugu Country, 1860-1900: A Case Study of one Protestant Movement in the Godavari Krishna Delta," *The Indian Economic and Social History Review* XII (63), (1975): 70.

75 *Government of India Records: Education*, Home, Nos 9-12, (February 5, 1858), 9.

76 Henry Morris, *A Descriptive and Historical Account of the Godavari District in the Presidency of Madras* (London: Trubner & Co Publishers, 1878), 100.

77 *A Descriptive and Historical Account of the Godavari District in the Presidency of Madras* (London: Trubner & Co Publishers, 1878), 230.

78 *The Church Missionary Atlas, Containing an Account of the various countries in which the Church Missionary Society Labours and of its Missionary Operations* (London: Seeley Jackson and Halliday Publishers, 1879), 102.

79 Frederik Gledstone, op. cit., 6.

80 George Drach and Calvin F. Kuder, *Telugu Mission of the General Council of the Evangelical Lutheran Church in North America Containing a Biography of the Rev. Christian Frederick Heyer* (hereafter, *Telugu Mission General Council*) (Philadelphia: General Council Publication House, 1914), 49.

81 Ibid., 77.

82 Henry Morris, op. cit., 39.

83 Ibid., 103.

84 Harlan P. Beach, *India and Christian Opportunity* (New York: Student Volunteer Movement for Foreign Missions, 1908), 195.

85 David Downie, op. cit., 125.

86 S. Sathianathan, op. cit., 16.

87 Ibid., 32.

88 Rev. Alexander Duff displayed his deep conviction for vernacular education. The enthusiasm he displayed for English higher education created an idea that Rev. Duff cared little for the establishment of the vernacular primary schools: see William Paton, *Alexander Duff: Pioneer of Missionary Education*, (New York: George H Doran Company, 1922), 101.

89 Henry Morris, op. cit., 92.

90 Ibid., 96.

91 Jabob Chamberlin, In the Tiger Jungle and Other Stories of Missionary Work among the Telugus of India (New York: Fleming H. Revell, 1896), 95.

92 Hibbert G Ware, *Christian Missions in the Telugu Country* (Westminster: The SPG Publications, 1912), 103.

93 Susan Billington Harper, "The Dornakal Church on the Cultural Frontier," in *Christians, Cultural Interactions and India's Religious Traditions,* eds. Brown, Judith M. and Robert Eric Freykenberg (Grand Rapids, Michigan: W.B. Eerdmans Publishing Company, 2002), 113.

94 L. B. Wolf, *After Fifty Years,* op. cit., 225-226.

95 Julia M. Harpster, *Among the Telugoos: Illustrating Mission Work in India* (Philadelphia: Lutheran Publication Society, 1902), 36.

96 Hibbert G. Ware, op. cit., 103.

97 A. Satyanarayana, *Dalits and Upper Castes: Essays in Social History* (New Delhi: Kanishka Publishers, 2005), 61.

98 Y. Vaikuntam, op. cit., 32.

99 *Government Order No 68, Educational, Proceedings of Education Department*, February 1, (Madras: 1893), 1-8.

100 Y. Vaikuntam, op. cit., 181.

101 "Government Order No 504 Educational," in *The Proceedings of the Education Department,* August 22 (Madras: 1884), 64A-64C.

102 *Report of the Public Instruction in the Madras Presidency for the Year 1905-06*, Vol. I (Madras: 1906), 18.

103 Chartres J. Molony, *Census of India, 1911, Part I, Report* (Madras: The Government Press, 1913), 296.

104 A. G. Fraser, et al, *Village Education in India: The Report of a Commission of Inquiry* (London: Oxford University Press, 1920), 15.

105 S. N. Mukerji, op. cit., 156.

106 S. Nurallah and J. P. Naik, op. cit., 61.

107 Yagati Chinna Rao, op. cit., 102.

108 Y. Vaikuntam, op. cit., 182.

109 D. F. Carmichael, *A Manual of the District of Vizagapatam in the Presidency of Madras* (Madras: Lawrence Asylum Press, 1869), 355.

110 Khandavalli Balendu Sekharam, *Andhras through the Ages* (Madras: Sri Sarawathi Press, 1973), 355.

111 Ibid., 355.

112 Gujjarlamudi Krupachary, *Telugu Sahityaniki Kristavula Seva* (Guntur: Navodaya Publishers, 1988), 29.

113 I. W. Francis, op. cit., 63.

114 Richard Lovett, op. cit., 138.

115 Harriet Groves, *Memoir of Anthony Norris Groves: Compiled Chiefly from His Journals and Letters*, Third Edition (Bristol: James Nisbet and Co, 1869), 644.

116 J. Mangamma, *The Rate Schools of Godavari* (Hyderabad: A.P State Archives, 1973), 34.

117 John Craig, *Forty Years among the Telugus: A History of the Mission of the Baptists of Ontario and Quebec, Canada to the Telugus, South India 1867-1907* (Toronto: The Canadian Baptist Foreign Mission Board, 1908), 17, 153.

118 Henry Morris, op. cit., 40.

119 Harriet Groves, op. cit., 650.

120 *Memoir of Anthony Norris Groves: Compiled Chiefly from His Journals and Letters*, Third Edition (Bristol: James Nisbet and Co, 1869), 314.

121 John Craig, op. cit., 173.

122 Ibid., 49.

123 Kapil Fathima Kutty, op. cit., 23-24.

124 Ibid.

125 M. A. Sherring, *The History of Protestant Missions in India from their Commencement in 1706 to 1881* (London: The Religious Tract Society, 1884), 418.

126 John Craig, op. cit., 58.

127 Ibid., 75.

128 M. L. Orchardand K. S. McLaurin, *The Enterprise*, op. cit., 308.

129 *Among the Telugus and Bolivians: A Report of the Canadian Baptist Foreign Mission Board on the Indian and Bolivian Fields with Directory and Statistics of 1942* (Toronto: Canadian Baptist Overseas Mission Board, 1941), 84.

130 Ibid., 84.

131 Eugene Stock, *History of the Church Missionary Society: Its Environment, Its Men and Its Work* (hereafter, *History of CMS*) Vol. I (London: The CMS Publications, 1899), 177.

132 Ibid., 318.

133 Ibid., 328.

134 Y. V. Krishna Rao, "Delta Shipli Sir Arthur Cotton" in *Andhra Pradesh Darshini* (Hyderabad: Vishalandra Publishing House, 1976,) 303.

135 Eugene Stock, *History of CMS,* Vol. II, op. cit., (London: The CMS Publications, 1899), 530-531.

136 D. Raghava Rao, *Machlipatnam Charitra*, (Vetapalem: Sri Sarawatha Nikethanam, 2001), 266.

137 Eyre Chatterton, *A History of the Church of England in India since the Early Days of the East India Company* (London: SPCK Publishers, 1924), NP.

138 Eugene Stock, *History of CMS,* Vol. II, op. cit., 548.

139 Eyre Chatterton, op. cit.

140 Helen H. Holcomb, *Men of Might in India Missions: The Leaders and their Epochs 1706-1899* (New York: Young People's Missionary Movement, 1901), 281.

141 Henry Morris, op. cit., 37.

142 Ibid., 38-39.

143 Ibid.

144 M. A. Sherring, op. cit., 416.

145 Ibid.

146 *The Church of South India, Krishna Godavari Diocese*: 100th Harvest Festival Issue, 1911-2010 (Vijayawada: 2010), 19.

147 Ibid.

148 "Khammamet District 1927", *The Dornakal Diocesan Magazine*, May (Dornakal: Diocesan Press, 1927), 6.

149 George Drach and Calvin F. Kuder, *Telugu Mission General Council*, op. cit., 49.

150 Ibid., 79.

151 W. G. Polack, *In to All the World: The Story of Lutheran Foreign Missions* (St. Louis, Missouri: Concordia Seminary, 1930), 112.

152 George Drach and Calvin F. Kuder, *Telugu Mission of the General Council,* op. cit., 80.

153 Ibid., 80.

154 Ibid., 120.

155 L. B. Wolf, *After Fifty Years,* op. cit., 220.

156 George Drach and Calvin F. Kuder, *Telugu Mission of the General Council* op. cit., 108.

157 W. G. Polack, op. cit., 114.

158 L. B. Wolf, *After Fifty Years,* op. cit., 129.

159 W. G. Polack, op. cit., 144.

160 Ibid., 240.

161 Ibid.

162 Ibid.

163 *Minutes of the Council of the India Mission of the United Lutheran Church in America,* January 11 (1935), 7.

164 Ibid., 108-109.

165 Ibid., 103.

166 Ibid., 120.

167 Ibid., 124.

168 Ibid., 178.

169 Ibid., 189-190.

170 Ibid., 214.

171 Augusta Highland, *India* (Rock Island, IL: Board of Foreign Missions, Lutheran Augustana Synod Centennial Committee, 1945), 19.

172 *Minutes of the Council of the India Mission of the United Lutheran Church in America,* January 11 (1935), 221.

173 M. L. Orchard and K.S. McLaurin, *The Enterprise*, op. cit., 128.

174 David Downie, op. cit., 41.

175 M. A. Sherring, op. cit., 410.

176 Ibid., 42.

177 S. F. Smith, *Missionary Sketches: A Concise History of the Work of the American Baptist Missionary Union* (Boston: W. G. Corthell Publishers, 1883), 196.

178 David Downie, op. cit., 55.

179 Ibid., 195.

180 James Millard Baker, *Contending the Grade in India* (Ashville: The Biltmore Press, 1947), 290.

181 John E. Clough, *Social Christianity in the Orient: The Story of a Man, A Mission and a Movement* (New York: The Macmillan Company Publishers, 1914), 349.

182 David Downie, op. cit., 4.

183 John E. Clough, op. cit., 331.

184 David Downie, op. cit., 85.

185 Edmund F. Merriam, *A History of American Baptist Missions* (Philadelphia: The American Baptist Publication Society, 1900), 150.

186 John E. Clough, op. cit., 330- 331.

187 Edmund F. Merriam, op. cit., 151.

188 David Downie, op. cit., 126.

189 Ibid., 126.

190 Ibid., 132. Also John E. Clough, op. cit., 375.

191 James S. Dennis, *Christian Missions and Social Progress: A Sociological Study of Foreign Missions, Vol. II* (New York: Fleming H. Revell, 1899), 395.

192 David Downie, op. cit., 59.

193 Ibid., 125.

194 *The American Baptist Foreign Mission Society Report* (The South India Mission, 1917), 97.

195 A. T. Fishman, *Culture Change and the Underprivileged: A Study of the Madigas in South India under Christian Guidance* (Madras: The Christian Literature Society for India, 1941), 72-73.

196 David Downie, op. cit., 125.

197 Ibid., 126.

198 James Millard Baker, op. cit., 226.

199 *Report of the Deputies to India in 1888-1889: Opinion of the Missionaries in 1890* (Edinburgh: The Edinburgh Press, 1891), 80.

200 *The Nellore Station and Field of the American Baptist Telugu Mission, South India* (Nellore: The American Baptist Telugu Mission, 1922), 51.

201 Ibid., 51.

202 *The American Baptist Foreign Mission Society Report* (The South India Mission, 1917), 97.

203 David Downie, op. cit., 192.

204 *The Hird School Souvenir and Magazine*, 25th Anniversary of Hird School (Narasaraopet: 1973-74), 1.

205 David Downie, op. cit., 90.

206 Ibid., 193.

207 *The Hird School Souvenir and Magazine*, op. cit., 1.

208 David Downie, op. cit., 125.

209 Ibid., 194.

210 *History of the Lone Star* (Madras: American Baptist Telugu Mission, 1922), 77-78.

211 Ibid., 74.

212 *Minutes of the AELC Executive Committee*, April (1925), 7.

213 M. L. Orchard and K. S. McLaurin, *The Enterprise*, op. cit., 74.

214 D. F. Carmichael, op. cit., 356.

215 *The Report of the Directors to the Seventy first General Meeting of the London Missionary Society*, (London: W. Steven Printers, 1865), 73.

216 Ibid., 102.

217 M. L. Orchard, op. cit., 188.

218 *The One Hundred Fifth Report of the London Missionary Society* (London: Yates and Alexander Printers, 1900), 167.

219 D. F. Carmichael, op. cit., 356.

220 M. L. Orchard, op. cit., 92.

221 M. L. Orchard and K. S. McLaurin, *The Enterprise*, op. cit., 309.

222 Pathuri Joseph, *Bharatiya Baptist Prarambha Charitra Parishodhana* (Ohio: Transworld Ministries, 2005), 57.

223 M. L. Orchard and K. S. McLaurin, *The Enterprise*, op. cit., 232.

224 M. L. Orchard, op. cit., 102-103.

225 Kapil Fathima Kutty, op. cit., 23.

226 M. L. Orchardand K. S. McLaurin, *The Enterprise*, op. cit., 285.

227 Ibid., 285.

228 B. E. Devaraj, *Bharata Desa Kraisthava Sangha Charitra*, Andhra Christian Theological Literature Council (Tenali: A.S.R. Power Press, 1969), 141.

229 Gerald H. Anderson, *Biographical Dictionary of Christian Missions* (Grand Rapids, Michigan: W. B. Eerdmans Publishing Company, 1999), 614.

230 *The Church Missionary Gleaner* (London: Seeley Jackson and Halliday Publishers, 1881), 106.

231 D. Raghava Rao, op. cit., 273.

232 Eyre Chatterton, op. cit.

233 Susan Billington Harper, *In the Shadow of the Mahatma: Bishop V.S Azariah and the Travails of Christianity in British India* (Richmond, Surrey: Curzon Press, 2000), 215.

234 George Drach and Calvin F. Kuder, *Telugu Mission of the General Council*, op. cit., 64.

235 Ibid., 120: Walter was the headmaster, Ruth, the wife of missionaries' butler Henry and Rebecca, was wife of Stephen, the first Mala convert.

236 L. B. Wolf, *After Fifty Years*, op. cit., 238.

237 J. Mangamma, *The Rate Schools of Godavari, op. cit., 49.*

238 *Minutes of the Council of the India Mission of the United Lutheran Church in America*, January 11 (Guntur: 1935), 5.

239 *Minutes of the Council of the India Mission of the United Lutheran Church in America,* October (Guntur: 1924), 2.

240 Ibid., 35.

241 Ibid., 4.

242 *Minutes of the Council of the India Mission of the United Lutheran Church in America*, January 11 (Guntur: 1935).

243 *Minutes of the Council of the India Mission of the United Lutheran Church in America,* October (Guntur: 1924), 109.

244 Ibid., 205.

245 Julia M. Harpster, op. cit., 86.

246 Ibid., 344.

247 S. Satthianathan, op. cit., 193.

248 George Drach and Calvin F. Kuder, *Telugu Mission of the General Council*, op. cit., 311.

249 K. L. Madhusudhan Rao, *Andhra Evangelical Lutheran Church Souvenir* (1987-1989), 3.

250 *Minutes of the AELC Executive Committee* (October 1927), 13.

251 *Minutes of the Council of the Indian Mission of the United Lutheran Church in America* (Guntur: 1925), 13.

252 Ms. Alice B Van Doren was the Educational Secretary of the National Christian Council of India, in The Social Setting of Christian Conversion in South India: The Impact of the Wesleyan Methodist missionaries on the Trichy-Tanjore Diocese with special Reference

to the Harijan communities of the Mass Movement Area 1820-1947, Sundarraj Manickam (Wiesbaden: Franz Steiner Verlag, 1977), 146.

253 C. H. Swavely (ed), *One Hundred Years in the Andhra Country* (Madras: Diocesan Press, 1942), 315.

254 K. L. Madhusudhan Rao, op. cit., 2.

255 John Craig, op. cit., 15.

256 David Downie, op. cit., 79.

257 John E. Clough, op. cit., 191.

258 David Downie, op. cit., 69.

259 Ibid., 69.

260 *The Nellore Station and Field of the American Baptist Telugu mission, South India* (Nellore: The American Baptist Telugu Mission, 1922), 11.

261 David Downie, op. cit., 74.

262 *History of the Lone Star*, (Madras: American Baptist Telugu Mission, 1922), 77-78.

263 *The Nellore Station and Field of the American Baptist Telugu mission, South India* (Nellore: The American Baptist Telugu Mission, 1922), 45.

264 *The American Baptist Foreign Mission Society Report* (Nellore: The South India Mission, 1917), 98.

265 Ibid.

266 John Craig, op. cit., 22.

267 David Downie, op. cit., 137.

268 Harlan P. Beach, op. cit., 262.

269 U. V. Shakeela, *Perceptions of Women's Emancipation in Nineteenth Century India* (Pondicherry: Unpublished Ph.D Thesis), 1.

270 George Drach and Calvin F. Kuder, *Telugu Mission of the General Council*, op. cit., 322. Also Pierce R Beaver, *Pioneers in Mission: The Early Missionary Ordination Sermons, Chargers And Instructions* (Grand Rapids, Michigan: W.B. Eerdmans, 1966), 205-206.

271 Augusta Highland, op. cit., 20.

272 *Minutes of the AELC Executive Committee*, April (1925), 7.

273 *The Missionary Services of CMS Missionary Harrison*, Mission Festival Celebrations (Vijayawada: CSI Krishna-Godavari Diocese, 2010), 26.

274 *The Church Missionary Atlas, Containing an Account of the various countries in which the Church Missionary Society Labours and of its Missionary Operations* (London: Church Missionary Society Publications, 1896), 125.

275 Irene H. Barnes, *Behind the Purdah: The Story of C.E.Z.M.S Work in India* (New York: Thomas Y Crowell Company, 1897), 244.

276 Antoinette Burton, "Contesting the Zenana: The Mission to Make Lady Doctors for India: 1874-1885," The *Journal of British Studies* 35, July (1996): 395.

277 Richard Lovett, op. cit., 63.

278 Opinion of Prof. Rekha Pande, Department of History (Hyderabad: University of Hyderabad, 01/08/2013).

279 G. Syamala, *Nalla Poddu* (Hyderabad: Book Trust, 2003), 33.

280 James S. Dennis, op. cit., Vol. III (New York: Fleming H. Revell, 1906), 95.

281 S. Nurallah and J. P. Naik, op. cit., 385.

282 Ibid., 104.

283 J. Mangamma, op. cit., *The Rate Schools of Godavari, 52.*

284 George Jay Lapp, *The Christian Church and Rural India* (Calcutta: YMCA Publishing House, 1938), 23.

285 *Report of the Public Instruction in the Madras Presidency for the year 1908-09*, Vol. I (Madras: The Government Press, 1909), 26.

286 Julius Jefferys, The *British Army in India: Its Preservation* (London: Longman and Roberts Publishers, 1858), 385.

287 *Report of the Commission 1 carrying the Gospel to all the Non-Christian World*, World Missionary Conference of 1910 (Edinburgh: Oliphant Anderson and Ferrier Publishers, 1910), 160.

288 Ibid., 321.

289 Ibid., 308.

290 James S. Dennis, op. cit., Vol. III, 108.

291 M. L. Orchard, op. cit., 102.

292 Jocelyn Murray, "The Role of Women in the Church Missionary Society: 1799-1917," in *The Church Missionary Society and World Christianity 1799-1999,* eds. Kevin Ward and Brain Stanley (London: Curzon Press, 2000), 87.

293 D. Tickell, "Poverty among Village Christians," *The National Christian Council Review* XIII, (January to December, 1935) (Mysore: Wesley Press, 1935), 623.

294 James S. Dennis, op. cit., Vol. III, 108.

295 *The Directory of Christian Missions in India, Burma and Ceylon*, 14th edn (Ajmer: The Scottish Mission Press, 1924), 299.

296 Eyre Chatterton, op. cit.

297 *Report on Public Instruction in the Madras Presidency For the year 1911-12 and for the Quinquenium 1906-07 to 1911-12*, Vol. I, Parts I and II (Madras: The Government Press, 1938), 45.

298 *Law Department (Education) Despatch Abstract, 1924, G.O No 10, 6-1-1925.*

299 L. B. Wolf, *After Fifty Years,* op. cit., 228.

300 *The Nellore Station and Field of the American Baptist Telugu Mission, South India* (Nellore: The American Baptist Telugu Mission, 1922), 59.

301 *Minutes of the AELC Executive Committee,* April 1925, 1.

302 *Minutes of the Council of the India Mission of the United Lutheran Church in America* (Guntur: October, 1925), 15.

303 D. Tickell, op. cit., 624.

304 Ibid., 625.

305 J. Mangamma, *The Rate Schools of Godavari,* op. cit., 50.

306 George Drach and Calvin F. Kuder, *Telugu Mission of the General Council*, op. cit., 184-184.

307 Ibid., 284.

308 Ibid., 360.

309 Ibid., 176.

310 Ibid., 175.

311 Ibid.

312 Ibid., 284.

313 J. Mangamma, *The Rate Schools of Godavari,* op. cit., 50.

314 C. H. Swavely (ed), op. cit., 269.

315 Gujjarlamudi Krupachary, op. cit., 41.

316 Austin A. D'Souza, *Anglo Indian Education, A Study of its Origins and Growth in Bengal Up to 1960* (Bombay: Oxford University Press, 1976), 159.

317 *AELM Routine Minutes,* General Work Budget, Appendix A, 31-3-1931 (1930-31), 3.

318 "Government of India Resolution on Indian Educational Policy of 1904," Para No 8 in *Education in India,* K.S. Vakil and S. Natarajan (New Delhi: Allied Publishers, 1966), 156.

319 James Millard Baker, op. cit., 133.

320 David Downie, op. cit., 74.

321 Ibid., 625.

322 *Report on the Administration of the Madras Presidency During the Year 1921-22 (*Madras: The Government Press, 1923), 187.

323 *The Nellore Station and Field of the American Baptist Telugu Mission*, South India (Nellore: The American Baptist Telugu Mission, 1922), 11.

324 James Millard Baker, op. cit., 133.

325 Ibid., 110.

326 V. S. Azariah, "The Christian Contribution to India," *The National Christian Council Review*, XVII (Jan-Dec, 1939): 120.

327 *Minutes of the AELC Executive Committee, Joint Finance Committee Bulletin,* No 30, 20 January (Rajahmundry: 1936), 5.

328 *Minutes of the AELC Executive Committee,* October (1928), 40.

329 John Craig, op. cit., 136.

330 *The Nellore Station and Field of the American Baptist Telugu Mission, South India* (Nellore: The American Baptist Telugu Mission, 1922), 11.

331 James Millard Baker, op. cit., "Contending the Grade in India," 81.

332 S. F. Smith, op. cit., 202.

333 David Downie, op. cit., 66.

334 John Craig, op. cit., 21-22.

335 S. F. Smith, op. cit., 213.

336 David Downie, op. cit., 143.

337 Ibid., 143.

338 Ibid., 56.

339 M. L. Orchard, op. cit., 97.

340 M. L. Orchard and K. S. McLaurin, *The Enterprise*, op. cit., 313.

341 *Among the Telugus and Bolivians: A Report of the Canadian Baptist Foreign Mission Board on the Indian and Bolivian Fields with Directory and Statistics of 1942* (Toronto: Canadian Baptist Overseas Mission Board, 1941), 66.

342 *Minutes of the AELC Executive Committee,* April (1925), 1.

343 Augusta Highland, op. cit., 15.

344 George Drach and Calvin F. Kuder, *Telugu Mission of the General Council*, op. cit., 285.

345 Ibid., 287.

346 Ibid.

347 Herbert Waldo Hines, *Clough: The Kingdom Builder in South India* (Philadelphia: The Freedom Press, 1929), 156.

348 *The Nellore Station and Field of the American Baptist Telugu Mission, South India* (Nellore: The American Baptist Telugu Mission, 1922), 11.

349 Ibid.

350 *The Directory of Christian Missions in India, Burma and Ceylon,* 14th edn (Ajmer: The Scottish Mission Press, 1924)), 292.

351 M. L. Orchard, op. cit., 95.

352 B. V. Subbamma, *Christ Confronts India: Indigenous Expression of Christianity in India* (Madras: Diocesan Press, 1973), 10.

353 *The Directory of Christian Missions in India, Burma and Ceylon*, 14th edn (Ajmer: The Scottish Mission Press, 1924), 266.

354 Ibid.

355 Julia M. Harpster, op. cit., 36.

356 *The Directory of Christian Missions in India, Burma and Ceylon*, 14th edn (Ajmer: The Scottish Mission Press, 1924), 292.

357 George Drach and Calvin F. Kuder, *Telugu Mission of the General Council*, op. cit., 343.

358 Ibid., 367.

Also see *The Directory of Christian Missions in India, Burma and Ceylon*, 14th edn (Ajmer: The Scottish Mission Press, 1924), 266.

359 *The Directory of Christian Missions in India, Burma and Ceylon*, 14th edn (Ajmer: The Scottish Mission Press, 1924), 266.

360 C. H. Swavely (ed), op. cit., 155.

361 Ibid., 70.

362 S. F. Smith, op. cit., 213; Also John E. Clough, op. cit., 121.

363 *Report of the American Baptist Telugu Mission* (Madras: 1908), 27.

364 *The Directory of Christian Missions in India, Burma and Ceylon*, 14th edn (Ajmer: The Scottish Mission Press, 1924), 266.

365 *The American Baptist Foreign Mission Society Report* (1917), 98.

366 *The Directory of Christian Missions in India, Burma and Ceylon*, 14th edn (Ajmer: The Scottish Mission Press, 1924), 266.

367 R. P. Jones, *The Year Book of Missions in India, Burma and Ceylon* (Madras: The Christian Literary Society, 1912), 283.

368 K. L. Richardson, "The Church and Native Culture: A Telugu Lutheran Perspective," *Indian Journal of Theology* (Kolkata: The Serampore College, 1993): 82.

369 David Downie, op. cit., 74.

370 Ibid.

371 *The Nellore Station and Field of the American Baptist Telugu Mission, South India* (Nellore: The American Baptist Telugu Mission, 1922), 25.

372 Ibid., 41.

373 H. T. Gairdner, *Edinburgh 1910: An Account and Interpretation of the World Missionary Conference* (Edinburgh: Oliphant Anderson and Ferrier, 1910), 19.

374 *The National Christian Council Review* (Mysore: Wesley Press, 1933), 74.

375 Bengt Sundkler, *Church of South India: The Movement Towards Union, 1900-1947* (London: The Lutterworth Press, 1954), 48.

376 *Proceedings of the Seventh Meeting of the National Christian Council* (Madras: Diocesan Press, 1937), 61.

377 *Proceedings of the Tenth Meeting of the National Christian Council of India, Burma and Ceylon* (Mysore: Wesley Press, 1946), 52.

378 Ibid.

379 Bernard Thorogood, *Gales of Change: The Story of London Missionary Society 1945-1977* (Geneva: World Council of Churches Publications, 1994), 106.

380 A. Mathew, *Christian Missions, Education and Nationalism: From Dominance to Compromise, 1870-1930* (New Delhi: Anamika Prakasan, 1989), 189.

381 A. T. Fishman, op. cit., 24.

382 Edgar Thurston, *Castes and Tribes of Southern India*, Vol. IV, K-M (Madras: The Government Press, 1909), 331.

383 *Culture Change and the Underprivileged: A Study of the Madigas in South India under Christian Guidance*, (Madras: The Christian Literature Society for India, 1941), 213.

384 John E. Clough, op. cit.,118.

385 V. S. Azariah, "The Christian Contribution to India," op. cit., XVII, (Jan-Dec 1939): 120.

386 *Report on Public Instruction in The Madras Presidency for 1901-11*, Vol. I (Madras: The Government Press, 1911), 15.

387 Rushbrook L. F. Williams, *India in 1922-23: A Statement Prepared for Presentation to Parliament in accordance with the Requirements of the 26th Section of the Government of India Act* (Calcutta: The Government Press, 1923), 224.

388 L. B. Wolf, *After Fifty Years,* op. cit., 224.

389 N. Jayapalan, *History of Education in India* (New Delhi: Atlantic Publishers, 2000), 96.

390 Ibid.

391 *Report on Public Instruction in the Madras Presidency for the Year 1936-37 and for the Quinquenium 1931-32 to 1936-37,* Vol. II, Parts I and II (Madras: The Government Press, 1938), 41.

392 *The Harijan Uplift of the Government of Madras* (Madras: The Government Press, 1938), 1.

393 "G. O. No. 1446, Law and Education on 16th July 1935" in *The Harijan Uplift of the Government of Madras* (Madras: The Government Press, 1938), 3.

394 For a list of Harijan hostels see *Administration Report of the Harijan Welfare Department, 1948-49* (Madras: The Government Press, 1949), 24-32.

395 Krishna Kumar and Joachim Oesterheld eds. op. cit., 28.

396 "Educational Developments for the Year 1942," *The National Christian Council Review* (Mysore: Wesley Press, 1943): 292.

397 *Report on Public Instruction for the Year 1949-50* (Madras: The Government Press, 1951), 39.

398 *The Administrative Report of the Harijan Welfare Department for 1950-51* (Madras: The Government Press, 1951), 4.

399 Ibid., 23.

400 "G. O. No. 1101, Education on 14th May 1938" in *The Harijan Uplift by the Government of Madras* (Madras: The Government Press, 1938), 9.

401 *The Administration Report of the Harijan Welfare Department 1948-49* (Madras: The Government Press, 1949), 4.

402 Ibid., 10.

403 R. A. Gopalaswami, *The Census of India*, 1951, Vol. I, Part I-A, Report (New Delhi: The Government of India Press, 1955), 152.

404 *Administration Report of the Harijan Welfare Department for the Year 1950-51*, Appendix B (Madras: The Government Press, 1952), 25.

405 Regunta Yesuratnam, *Bharatavanilo Kraisthava Sangham* (Hyderabad: Telugu Kraistava Vedanta Sahiti Samiti, 1998), 59.

406 Hibbert G. Ware, op. cit., 83.

407 James S. Dennis, op. cit., Vol. II, 231.

408 George Jay Lapp, op. cit., 5.

409 Rajah B. Manickam, *Christianity and the Asian Revolution* (Madras: The CLS Publication Society, 1954), 60.

410 A. L. Basham, *A Cultural History of India* (New Delhi: Oxford University Press, 1975), 148.

411 Sushil Madhav Pathak, op. cit., 18, 12.

412 W. G. Polack, op. cit., 116.

413 Edward Blunt, Social Service in India: An Introduction to Social and Economic problems of the Indian Peoples (London: His Majesty's Stationary Office, 1939), 184.

414 Hibbert G. Ware, op. cit., 163.

415 L. B. Wolf, *After Fifty Years*, op. cit., 187.

416 James Johnson, ed. *Report of the Centenary Conference on Protestant Missions of the World Held in Exeter Hall*, Vol. II (London: James Nisbet, 1888), 104.

417 Rutter J. Williamson, *The Healing of the Nations: A Treatise on Medical Missions* (New York: The Student Volunteer Movement for Foreign Missions, 1899), 82.

418 Sundara Raj Manickam, op. cit., 168.

419 L. B. Wolf, *After Fifty Years,* op. cit., 202.

420 Edward Blunt, op. cit., 185.

421 George Drach and Calvin F. Kuder, *Telugu Mission of the General Council*, op. cit., 80.

422 W. G. Polack, op. cit.,116.

423 George Drach and Calvin F. Kuder, *Telugu Mission of the General Council*, op. cit., 305.

424 Ibid., 189.

425 Ada C. Chaplin, *Our Gold Mine: The Story of American Baptist Missions in India* (Boston: W. G. Corthell, 1889), 407.

426 Augusta Highland, op. cit., 15.

427 John Craig, op. cit., 106.

428 M. L. Orchard, op. cit., 130.

429 Dr. L. L. Uhl, Life Views from the India Field (Philadelphia:The Lutheran Publication Society, nd).

430 V. S. Azariah and Henry Whitehead, *Christ in the Indian Villages* (London: Student Christian Movement Press, 1930), 114.

431 M. L. Orchard, op. cit., 138.

432 M. L. Orchard and K. S. McLaurin, *The Enterprise*, op. cit., 76.

433 John Craig, op. cit., 138.

434 L. B. Wolf, *After Fifty Years,* op. cit., 188.

435 Ibid., 193.

436 Ibid.

437 George Drach and Calvin F. Kuder, *Telugu Mission of the General Council*, op. cit., 291.

438 Julia M. Harpster, op. cit., 44.

439 L. B. Wolf, *After Fifty Years,* op. cit., 194.

440 Ibid., 189.

441 George Drach and Calvin F Kuder, *Telugu Mission of the General Council*, op. cit., 377.

442 J. Mangamma, *Andhra Desamulo Kraisthava Missioanrila Seva* (hereafter, *Andhra Desamulo*) (Hyderabad: Telugu Academy Publishers, 1992), 57.

443 C. H. Swavely, *Mission to Church in Andhra Pradesh: The Andhra Evangelical Lutheran Church* (New York: The Board of Foreign Missions, 1962), 21.

444 J. Mangamma, *Andhra Desamulo*, op. cit., 55.

445 *Annual Report of the Committee of the Church Missionary Society for Africa and the East, 1947-48* (London: The CMS Publications, 1948), 86.

446 Herbert Waldo Hines, op. cit., 127.

447 James Millard Baker, *Contending the Grade in India*, op. cit., 52.

448 Ibid., 151.

449 Ibid., 171.

450 M. L. Orchard and K. S. McLaurin, *The Enterprise*, op. cit., 250.

451 John Craig, op. cit., 107.

452 M. L. Orchard, op. cit., 144.

453 Augusta Highland, op. cit., 24.

454 George Drach, ed. *Our Church Abroad: The Foreign Missions of the Lutheran Church in America* (Philadelphia: United Lutheran Publication House, 1926), 67.

455 J. Mangamma, *Andhra Desamulo*, op. cit., 56.

456 M. Moses, *Andhra Pradesh Kraisthava Sangha Charitra* (Tenali: Kraisthava Satya Grandhasala, 2004), 54.

457 George Drach and Calvin F. Kuder, *Telugu Mission of the General Council*, op. cit., 313.

458 Ibid., 338.

459 Ibid., 337.

460 Ibid., 347.

461 Ibid., 350.

462 George Drach and Calvin F. Kuder, *The Guntur Mission: A Review of a Year's Work* (The Board of Foreign Missions of the General Synod of the Evangelical Lutheran Church in America, 1915), 17.

463 George Drach and Calvin F. Kuder, *Telugu Mission of the General Council*, op. cit., 365.

464 Ibid., 380.

465 Ibid., 361.

466 W. G. Polack, op. cit., 115.

467 *Minutes of the AELC Executive Committee* (1914), 3.

468 Clarence Valentine Sheatsley, *Our Mission Field in India: 1873-1943* (Columbus, Ohio: Lutheran Book Concern, 1921), 131.

469 *Minutes of the Executive Committee of the Council of the India Mission of the United Lutheran Church in America* (1930), 2.

470 Augusta Highland, op. cit. 27.

471 Irene H. Barnes, op. cit., 209. Also see *The Annual Report of the Committee of the Church Missionary Society for Africa and the East*, 1947-48 (London: The CMS Publications, 1948), 86.

472 Irene H. Barnes, op. cit., 252.

473 Ibid., 180.

474 Rutter J. Williamson, op. cit., 56.

475 David Downie, op. cit., 149.

476 *The Nellore Station and Field of the American Baptist Telugu mission, South India* (Nellore: The American Baptist Telugu Mission, 1922), 11.

477 *The Report the American Baptist Foreign Missionary Society* (Boston: Foreign Mission Rooms, 1917), 108.

478 Ibid.

479 George Drach and Calvin F. Kuder, *Telugu Mission of the General Council*, op. cit., 268.

480 Julia M. Harpster, op. cit., 58.

481 *Report on Vaccination in the Madras Presidency for the year 1901-02* (Madras: The Government Press, 1902), 221.

482 *Report on the Administration of the Madras Presidency during the Year 1921-22* (Madras: The Government Press, 1923), 221 and 226.

483 V. S. Azariah and Henry Whitehead, op. cit., 46.

484 John Craig, op. cit., 109.

485 Martin L. Dolbeer, *A History of Lutheranism in Andhra Desa: The Telugu Territory of India*, Board of Foreign Missions (New York: United Lutheran Church in America, 1959), 334.

486 James S. Dennis, op. cit., Vol. II, 395.

487 Martin L. Dolbeer, op. cit., 334.

488 James Millard Baker, *Contending the Grade in India*, op. cit., 81.

489 H. A. Stuart, *Census of India*, 1891, Vol. XIII (Madras: The Government Press, 1893), 167.

490 Julia M. Harpster, op. cit., 82.

491 J. Mangamma, *Andhra Desamulo Kraisthava,* op. cit., 57.

492 "Report of Ms. Brummer" in *The Minutes of the AELC Executive Committee* (April 1927), 8.

493 M. L. Orchard, op. cit., 149.

494 Julia M. Harpster, op. cit., 48.

495 John Craig, op. cit., 188.

496 Rutter J. Williamson, op. cit., 57.

497 Ibid., 137.

498 *Proceedings of the Fifth Meeting of the National Christian Council* (Mysore: Wesley Press, 1933), 89.

499 M. L. Orchard, op. cit., 136.

500 Rutter J. Williamson, op. cit., 55.

501 Ibid., 58.

502 Ibid., 71.

Chapter 6

Mediating Socio-economic and Socio-religious Structural Changes: Christian Mission, Malas and Madigas

6.1 Introduction

As the title indicates, this chapter deals with two aspects of social changes: socio-economic and socio-religious, dealt in two sections. The changes seem to have been structural because they were long-lasting, not transient or short lived. These changes were like the structure of a building: strong, permanent and added a new dimension to their social identity. In short, even if the economic level of these two communities were to deteriorate or their religious identity changes, the social mobility and status change will not digress to the older order. In other words, mere advancement in economic standard would not have automatically added social change. Or, in the realm of religion mere change in religion, would not have made their social status higher. What gives foundational credibility for higher social status is good behaviour, good habits, cultural refinement, etc, which only education and religion can provide. Hence, I have described the changes as socio-economic and socio-religious.

It has been noted earlier that the economic problems of the Depressed Castes were basically related to the entrenched social structures entwined within the caste system wherein economic resources were kept far from their reach. In the village economic situation, the Malas were traditional agricultural labourers with total dependence on land-owning castes for their livelihood. And the Madigas were leather working occupational labourers. Both groups had very limited economic resources. Under the patron-client *jajmani* system to which they were tied to, in the caste-based village economic system, there were few channels for adopting alternative occupations or enhancement of existing occupational income through modernization or expansion of production.

As already noted, with the mediation of the Christian missions, arrangements for improvement of existing occupations were made on one hand, and on the other, channels for adopting alternative occupations, in place of hereditary occupations were available. Because, of a package of developmental and educational interventions of the missionaries, a substantial number of Malas and Madigas found greater opportunities for attaining socio-economic mobility.

In the first section, I shall discuss the process and results of this mediatory intervention in the lives of the Malas and Madigas. I do not claim that the entire economic mobility achieved by these communities was exclusively due to the mediation of the Missions. There were opportunities offered by the Colonial Government, as for instance, employment in its service sectors such as the railway, bureaucracy, military, public works, relief works, etc, which also offered channels of alternative employment to these and other communities. Besides, as part of the general population, these communities must also have benefitted from the modern infrastructure such as railway, telegraph, transportation facilities, etc., which were created by the Colonial administration. Introduction of new methods of production and expansion of economic activities would have benefitted them, as well as others, within the general economic advancement in India. Among many of the regenerative aspects of British rule in India were the effacement of the village self-government and commercialization of economic activities, which aspects also provided occupational mobility and choice of new occupations for the Malas and Madigas. Improved state of communications, for example laying out of extensive network of roads and construction of railroads and navigable canals increased the chances of better employment which generated greater income and economic mobility among the population of the country in general. But, the fact is that it was the Mission which enabled a majority of the members of these communities to acquire better educational qualification which, in turn, made them competent to get employed in the government or private sectors.

The question is did the economic development take place because of their conversion? One cannot make a total claim that such a development took place because of conversion. But the data show that the proportion of those who achieved educational mobility which facilitated occupational mobility and hence economic mobility were converts, whereas non-converts did not achieve mobility at an equal level. It was noted earlier that although the Mission's educational facilities were available to all (converts and non-converts of all castes) these were preferentially available to the converts who were mainly from the Malas and Madigas. Some observers have opined that the Depressed

Castes' Christian conversion resulted in their material improvement and enhanced social status due to the progress achieved in education.[1] The converts who had received the fruits of missionary education found employment as teachers, catechists and evangelists, medical staff and railway employees, public servants in government departments and as tradesmen.[2] Missionary societies also worked as patrons for the economic betterment of the Malas and Madigas by encouraging them to take up non-caste ascribed alternative occupations or by creating improved facilities for bettering production of industrial goods through industrial training and vocational training.[3]

The dynamics of this process may be observed: in the first place, thanks to mission's mediation, some of the traditional agricultural production methods were improved through use of better irrigation facilities, better implements, better marketing, etc; so also, improved methods of production of village industrial goods were facilitated, as for instance, leather goods; in other cases, facility for adopting alternative occupations was made available by the missions, such as lace-making, brick-making, tile-making, knitting, tailoring, carpentry, etc, which were not caste-bound hereditary occupations of either Malas or Madigas. Still in other cases, channels for acquiring new, alternative, blue or while collar jobs were made available to the educated Malas and Madigas, such as teaching in private or government schools, preaching in mission's own intuitions, being catechists in mission's institutions, nursing in private or government hospitals, dispensaries; employed service in the military, police, railway, telegraph, etc. of the government. That is to say, a whole lot of Malas and Madigas, a majority of whom were converts, were employed by the mission at various levels in mission' own institutions or were enabled to acquire educated employment in the government departments, through the most powerful empowering tool of education.

I must also emphasis that none of the changes would have taken place, had they not been made conscientious of their worth as persons with dignity and worth as equal any other. This awareness creation was the key aim of Christian preaching: that God is creator of all, and all humans are his children, and hence all are equal. This was available to all those who came into contact with the missionaries. The changes were effected by the people themselves: the missionaries were only agents who mediated such change using Christian religious superstructure such as ideas, religious teachings, tenets of faith, preaching, personal example, commitment, sacrifice, etc., besides offering the physical and institutional infrastructure, such as schools, colleges, dispensaries, hospitals, industry, etc.

In the second section, I deal with the apparent socio-religious changes. In this area one is more certain about the powerful intervention of mission on one hand, and the conscientious decision of the converts to abandon their certain established rites, rituals, customs and traditions which they had been observing for centuries, in lieu of adopting new rites, rituals, customs and traditions which were part of the process of conversion. It may be noted that conversion was not a one-time change from one religion to another. Change from Hindu religion to Christian religion was a one-time event of baptism. But the process of becoming a Christian is life-long. Hence, certain religious rituals, customs and practices were continued by the converts even after conversion. Unless equal and alternative rites, rituals and traditions are offered to the converts, the tendency of continuity remains. What I have noted in the religious life of the converts are certain rites, rituals and practices which were overtly opposed to the Christian tradition were abandoned, although some converts might have covertly continued them in the domestic realm. At the same time, certain received rites, rituals and practices were adopted as sign of being a Christian.

With regard to practices in cultural life, some of the acceptable ones were retained, while some unchristian ones were rejected. Externally, therefore, the culture of converts did not undergo rapturous changes as happened in Goa after the conversion. In socio-religious rituals and rites of passage such as in marriage, mingling of indigenous practices and customs were retained, while the rite changed to a prescribed form of Christian marriage rite. Overall, they remained, totally local, indigenous, Indian Malas and Madigas, except for the fact that their religious practices were changed. With regard to external aspects of social change the living styles, manner of organization of life, ordering of life, etc., underwent changes thanks to Christianization. For instance, certain habits such as theft of cattle, certain dances, etc., which were morally unacceptable to Christian culture were abandoned. At the same time, cleanliness which is hailed as a 'Christian' virtue was practiced. So also, certain social manners which behoove a Christian were accepted due to group pressure or individual conviction. In short, after a hundred-year-long Christianization of the Malas and Madigas, one could observe recognizable socio-cultural-religious changes in the everyday life of these two communities, besides the new nominal identity as Christians.

I

6.2 Mediating Economic Mobility

An examination of the economic condition in coastal Andhra in the first half of the 19th century gives us an understanding that, in the stratified village peasant system, the Malas and the Madigas were part of the large rural proletariat, who were held in conditions of semi-bondage under the dominant upper caste peasants.[4] In a wide canvas, after the colonial takeover of village administration, the government tried to maximize its revenue from agriculture and exacted the revenue in cash instead of kind. This put pressure on the upper peasantry to enhance production and the burden naturally fell on the agricultural labourers.[5]

The Malas were the primary agricultural labour class who carried out most of the village agricultural activities being employed by their *Súdra* employers.[6] But the Madigas were a caste-based occupational caste whose traditional duties were curing and tanning hides and manufacturing leather articles. Both groups were remunerated in kind the amount of which was just enough to sustain daily life.[7] The remuneration was so low that they often had to borrow money from money-lenders at high interest rates to spend for social functions and obligations such as marriages and funerals. The illiterate borrowers were often cheated by the money lenders who pushed up the amount borrowed. This forced them to borrow more money and they fell into a vicious circle and remained in never ending debt bondage. When the missionaries came to the scene, what was so obvious was entrenched impoverishment and poverty of both Malas and Madigas.

The missionaries who came in close touch with the poverty in the villages devised methods for Malas and Madigas to advance in both traditional occupations and alternative occupations such as in cottage industry. Steps were devised to improve the traditional occupations sectors such as cultivation, weaving and leather work.[8] Pursuance of vocational and industrial work needed skill training. For this the missionaries first set up agricultural and industrial training centres for them. Both men and women were given practical training in economically productive occupations such as lace-work, carpentry and other cottage industries.[9]

It was expected that the people would be able to break the fetters of poverty once alternative avenues of employment were generated.[10] The missionaries themselves set up cottage industries to give employment to the working class. Besides, with adequate training the people were absorbed into clerical and bureaucratic jobs in mission's own institutions such as schools, hostels, dispensaries, etc.[11] Quite a lot of trained personnel found employment in the government. Consequently, the economic condition of the Malas and the Madigas in villages underwent many positive changes.

One can estimate the apparent economic progress of the Malas and the Madigas from the government reports and accounts. Missionary accounts and minutes also provide information regarding the economic development of the Malas and Madigas. According to Henry Morris, "education was used as an effective mechanism to know about the rights and to advance their own understanding of village economic operations both in terms of remuneration and debt management."[12] The influence of primary education benefited the converts and raised their capacity for earning and the standard of living. In a survey conducted by the Mass Movement Commission in 1933, it was found that graduates who were in responsible and remunerative positions were the sons and grandsons of poor and illiterate converts.[13]

6.3 Initiatives in the Traditional Sector

6.3.1 Promotion of Agriculture

In the agricultural sector, better farming methods were applied and the quantity of land under cultivation was increased.[14] Those who had remained either as tenants-at-will or tenancy occupants continued the tasks of ploughing, sowing, weeding and harvesting. Both men and women took part in agricultural activities.[15] There was an increase of cultivated tracts, almost 978 % or in actual terms from 28,000 acres to 302,000 acres in the Godavari delta. Similarly, there was 1195% or from 19,000 acres to 246,000 acres increase in the Kistna delta area.[16] According to Morris Henry, the improvement in agricultural methods benefited not only the agricultural castes but also the agricultural labour castes.[17]

The endeavour of the missionaries in agricultural work of the converts was to make them independent of their caste-masters and making them self-supporting. In this pursuit they worked in collaboration with the Colonial government which had charted out various programmes in education for enhancing agriculture. The Colonial government had proposed a two-way approach in the courses of study in rural schools: 1) to train children in agricultural operations and 2) to enable them to protect themselves in the financial transactions with the landlords and village dealers, who often cheated them.[18] The primary education that was provided in missionary schools was also aimed to providing improved knowledge about agricultural practices. An agricultural department was instituted in boarding schools where vegetables and spices were grown that made each institution self-sufficient.[19] A garden was also attached to teach lessons in plant rearing, which became a part of the curriculum.[20] A system of 'halftime' was introduced when children of the ryots attended the morning classes and worked in the fields of the school garden, during the rest of the day.

The opening of industrial training in carpentry and iron work facilitated the pupils to learn the making of agricultural implements, carts, wheels and water lifts. They were also taught how to manage all kinds of agricultural machinery.[21] Improved implements and tools helped the farmer converts achieve a larger degree of independence.

The Village Education Commission of 1918 had emphasized on education which was relevant to rural needs. The Commission also urged to strengthen primary education in rural areas. The importance of incorporating vocational courses especially in agriculture, spinning and housekeeping, in the middle school curriculum was emphasized.[22] The Farm Labourers' School at Anakapalle had attempted to impart agricultural education to the agricultural labourers employed in the government agricultural stations.[23] Elementary school teachers were sent on deputation to the agricultural stations at Anakapalle and Samalkota by the taluk boards for training in courses such as agricultural and allied activities.[24]

In their efforts to improve the economic situation of the convert Malas and Madigas, the missionaries negotiated with the government to distribute unoccupied lands either on lease or by deed. In the Vuyyuru station, 2000 acres of land was received through the Co-operative Society. In the Akidu staton, Dr. Wolverton helped the Christians obtain over 300 acres of land and Mr. Cross helped Christians in Avanigadda with 175 acres of land between the years 1920 and 1922.[25] The missionaries' aim of securing lands for the Christians was to help them redeem themselves from debts which they owed to the farmers.[26] Agricultural Cooperative Societies were organized by the missionaries with the support of the government not only for providing agricultural credit but also to give practical demonstration in improved methods of agriculture and for the distribution of seeds and manure (see Table 6.1, below).[27]

In the vocational school of CMS' Dornakal diocese, training was given in areas of agriculture and weaving and other allied industries.[28] The American Evangelical Lutheran Mission (AELM) at Guntur established an agricultural settlement at the Lam Reserve School where boys were given instruction in the best agricultural practices and allied occupations.[29] The School was conducted not only with own annual budget but also managed to gain a government subsidy.[30] Practical agricultural pursuits such as keeping of poultry yards and stock yards were taught in the school.[31] At the Rajahmundry Industrial Home, besides agriculture, efficient ways of stock raising paved the way to high growth in dairy making industry.[32] The oil pressing mills (twelve in the Godavari district, two in the Kistna district and two in the Guntur district) provided employment in the agricultural sector for the Christians.[33]

At the Ongole Mission School, activities in agricultural works included a substantial part of the school curriculum. The girls particularly took part in three hours' daily work in the school garden. This initiative gave excellent results not only in making agricultural products, but also created better health and finer morale among the pupils.[34] Rev. James Baker developed an eleven-acre garden in Ongole which was placed under the care of the girls and boys at the Mission's schools.[35] By teaching them to keep their rooms and grounds clean and self-cooking, the girl boarders were made fit for household duties. By teaching habits of cleanliness, order and punctuality, the inner character was modified for producing better results.[36]

6.3.2 Increase Irrigation: Increase Production

The Colonial administration recognized the fact that to curb the evil effects of famine, the economics of irrigation was the answer.[37] New irrigation works were undertaken in the Godavari and Kistna delta, which were river-diversion works of a gigantic nature. The agricultural sector experienced expansion in cultivation since the construction of these great river anicut systems began. This particular system of irrigation presented a marvelous contrast to the immense tracks of arid waste lands in peninsular India.[38] The initiative to start canals by means of locks for every few miles added value to the lands under cultivation[39] and the embankments, water channels, canals, tanks and wells provided an effectual remedy for drought conditions and adverse seasons.[40] The gradual increase of areas under cultivation proved a great advantage for the land holding castes as well as the tenants.[41]

Between the years 1845-1865, the quantitative and quanlitative improvements in the agriculture sector resulted in a state of abundance in coastal Andhra.[42] Due to the irrigation channels, paddy transplantation and sugar plantation immensely increased and contributed for the economic power of the region, which also benefitted the Malas and the Madigas, by way of gaining more employment.[43] Colonel Arthur Cotton employed sub-officers and about nine thousand native labourers, both men and women, for particular tasks such as of contractors, bricklayers and stone-masons.

The beneficiary towns of Rajahmundry, Samalkota, Cocanada, Coringa and Mandapeta were also the principal towns of three missionary societies: the Godavari Delta Mission, the Canadian Baptist Mission and the American Evangelical Lutheran Mission.[44]

Since 1865, canal construction works were undertaken such as of the Nellore tank, the side channels from Duggirla to Nizampatnam, the Akidu canal, the Samalkota canal, the canal drainage of the Ellore, the widening of the main canal from Bezwada via Kankipadu to Masulipatam, etc. These works offered employment to thousands of Malas and Madigas.[45] During the acute famine of 1877-78 in the Nellore region, people had suffered due to severe staving conditions. The depressed sections suffered more as they could not procure or store grain from their caste employers.[46] The canal digging work that was undertaken by Rev. Clough for the Government created employment opportunities for the Madiga Christians as well as non-Christians. As a result they escaped starvation.[47] A large number of labourers were employed in camps to work in relief projects of the government such as the digging of the Buckingham Canal as an extension of the Madras canal up to Bezwada via Nellore.[48] In Rev. Clough's words, "wages were good, men saved up a few rupees, went home and sent other members of their families."[49] According to Robert O. Fuller, a member of the American Baptist Mission's Executive Committee, the missionary's execution of public works saved many people from starvation.[50]

6.3.3 Agricultural Settlements and Training

The establishment of agricultural settlements was a measure recommended by the Madras Christian Conference as means of cultivating industrial value.

Christian families were placed under the direct care of a pastor and were expected to attend regular worship and instruction.[51] One such settlement was the Lam Agriculture Reserve Settlement of the AELM near Guntur where improvement in agricultural practices was encouraged among the converts.[52] The American Baptist Missionary Society maintained the Bapatla Agricultural Settlement at Bethapudi.[53] The Coles Ackerman Agricultural School in Nellore had trained students to gain experience in farm and crop management.[54] Rev. James Baker also acquired a 167 acre tract of land located at the north side of Ongole, which was named as Bakerpuram, where the tract was divided into five-acre plots and were given to capable coolies who, until then, had worked for petty farmers.[55]

In all boarding schools, gardening work such as proper manuring, weeding, deep ploughing and rotation of crops were compulsorily taught. The students succeed in raising better crops enough not only for their own consumption but also for sale locally as well as for sending to other boarding schools in far off places by railroads. Industries allied to agriculture were started to supplement the income. Village industries such as rope making, mat making, fruit growing and market gardening were started to provide allied occupations for the residents of the settlements.[56] The missionaries encouraged the converts to acquire small strips of land for cultivation and used to distribute lands availed from the government, to the depressed people.

6.3.4 Weaving

There was a popular criticism that the colonial government forced the farmers to cultivate cotton and jute for commercial purpose of export by providing irrigation facilities. This was supposedly to supply raw materials for the British looms.[57] Though the imports from England affected the fine linen industry in India, the production of coarse cloth in which the Malas specialized as a hereditary occupation did not decline and efforts were made for more sophisticated production of the same with power-loom application.[58] Since the last quarter of the 19th century, several British merchants realized the cost effective ways of manufacturing cloth within the Indian territories instead of carrying raw cotton to England and bringing finished goods to India and therefore, the development of much larger cotton textile industry in India.[59]

Traditionally, the Malas were weavers for the *Súdra* traders, who supplied the raw material for them.[60] According to Romesh Dutt, the wives of the caste Mala cultivators were great spinners.[61] They were guaranteed regular work and a certain amount of remuneration. With the growth of mechanization of the weaving industry, cotton spinning mills (two in Godavari and five in Guntur) and a cotton handloom factory at Vizagapatam were established.[62] Jute presses as an allied agricultural activity were established, one in Ganjam, two in Godavari and two in Guntur.[63] Carpet and weaving factories were established at Tadepalligudem and Ellore by the American Evangelical Lutheran Mission.[64] Weaving factories were also conducted at Cocanada and Nellore by the Canadian Baptist Mission and the American Baptist Foreign Mission Society.[65] In 1909, inquiries were made as to improve handlooms through which the workers might get higher profits.[66] Training courses were conducted in collaboration with industrial schools where improved implements and weaving methods were taught.[67]

In the Dornakal diocese's training school, teaching of modern weaving practices steadily grew from where products were supplied on local demand.[68] The Lutheran Augustana Mission conducted a Trade school of weaving at Rajahmundry.[69] A one-year course for artisans and a two-year course for supervisors were conducted at the Textile Institute in Madras where eligible candidates were sent by the missionaries.[70] Further, the introduction of Khadi, weaving and spinning provided people with more work. Improved charkas (spindles) made their way to a number of Christian homes to supplement their family needs.[71] Efforts were directed to provide free outlet for the weavers so that they could work independently of their *Súdra* landlords for better wages.[72] The Government Textile Institute at Madras provided instruction for supervisors in power spinning, weaving, dyeing and finishing.[73]

The following table (6.1) with comparative data indicates the occupational status of the Malas and Madigas during the year 1910-11:[74]

Table 6.1: Occupations of Malas and Madigas

Occupation	Malas		Madigas	
	Number per 1000 workers engaged in each Occupation	Number of Female workers for 1000 Male workers	Number per 1000 workers engaged in each Occupation	Number of Female workers for 1000 Male workers
Agricultural labourers	609	1079	473	1009
Cultivators and Tenants	206	548	–	–
Miscellaneous labourers	84	1287	80	1067
Land Owners and Tenants	22	508	19	981
Cotton Weavers	21	729	–	–
Raising of Farm Stock	13	247	–	–
Leather Workers and Sellers of Sandals	–	–	191	229
Cultivators: Owners and Tenants	–	–	165	418
Sellers of Bark etc.	–	–	7	55,255
Others	45	508	53	188

Source: tabulated from Mission sources

6.3.5 Leather-Work

The leather-work in coastal Andhra was rendered by the Madigas for the *Súdras*. The Madigas tanned the hides, sewed sandals, manufactured leather buckets and trappings used for the bullocks (Table 6.1).[75] Leather industry in coastal Andhra was much encouraged by the American Baptist Missionaries as a majority of the converts of the Baptist Mission belonged to the Madiga caste. The missionaries observed that much of the leather work was done in the same old fashion and hence there was felt the need for introducing modern methods to increase production for consumption beyond the village.[76] The Leather Trade Institute gave special instruction and assistance to the tanners, and even conducted experiments on the use of indigenous tanning methods. A number of tanneries were established in coastal Andhra: two in Ganjam, one in Godavari, besides one leather factory.[77]

The fiber factory at Bapatla was under the supervision of Rev. G. N. Thomssen who provided employment for some 200 to 300 people. The Christian Industrial School conducted by Rev. H. Huizinga in Ongole provided training to young men in large numbers in professional trades such as fiber making, blacksmithing, carpentry and gardening.[78] Rev. J. M. Baker started an Industrial Organization to finance the program of self-support. Rev. Fishman had observed that between the years 1881 and 1905, the movement for self-support was emphasized in education, along with economic betterment, of the Christians.[79] Regarding the economic condition of the Madiga Christians in Markapur, Rev. Marsh had observed in 1916 that thanks to the apparent adoption of new ideals of self-support and self-respect, there was much improvement in the material and economic condition of the Christians.[80]

The new CMS Industrial Settlement near Bezwada was situated at Vidya Nagar and a Central Training School was established there.[81] The school was specialized in the manufacture of leather goods which ensured enormous economic upliftment of the poor Christians. The industrial schools manufactured beautiful and useful articles such as purses, wallets, notecases, ladies' handbags and suitcases.[82]

6.4 Adopting Alternative Professions

As mentioned earlier, since the middle of the 19th century, the traditional economic occupations of the Malas and the Madigas were disrupted due to the disintegration of the village economic system and so they had to find alternative employment in other sectors such as in private or public service sectors. The growth of commercialization of agriculture and the disruption of the village economy gave rise to occupational mobility into new occupations among the Malas and the Madigas. The employment gained by educated Malas and Madigas was mainly as teachers, medical staff and clerical staff in various government offices including the police, military, railway, telegraph departments. In addition, the Tahsildars and District Labour offices looked after their welfare by providing them with vacant land for cultivation or for houses.[83]

6.4.1 Teaching in Educational Establishments

One of the notable contributions of the missionary societies to the converts was training both men and women to increase their capacity for the teaching professions or for evangelistic work.[84] In a report to the American Baptist Mission in 1907, Rev. J. Heinrichs had observed that;

> In many parts of the Mission there seem to be a desire among the *Súdras* for schools taught by the Christian teachers. With traits such as that of sincere and faithful services, the services of the Christians were appreciated by the caste people.[85]

In the initial years of the missionary enterprise, native teachers from non-depressed caste communities were employed by the missionaries due to lack of educated people from the depressed caste converts. But as education gained momentum among the converts, the missionaries directed their efforts to secure efficient teachers from the converts and looked for more promising pupils for instruction in the normal schools.[86] The first Malas to be employed as teachers were Mr. Stephen and Mr. Nicodemus who were in-charge of the newly established school on the outskirts of Guntur in 1847.[87] To mention a few other examples, Mr. Samuel was appointed at the Veldurti school, Mr. John, at the Polepalli school, Mr. Devasikamani, at the Gurjal school and Mr. Jacob, at the Tumurucotta school.[88]

The schools in these towns (Gurjal, Polepalli, Veldurti and Macherla), had many Christian students who were taught by Christian teachers. In 1854, the General Synod in Guntur conducted special training for men and devised a course of study to make them competent for the work in the Mission.[89] In 1857, twenty men and two women were employed on salaries, varying from Rs 2-6, to work in the Mission schools at Guntur, Palnad, Gurjala and Rajahmundry.[90] In 1858, the President of the Synod had recommended immediate attention to the necessity of training more native workers to answer to the need in native ministry.[91] In 1881, the American Evangelical Lutheran Mission employed 95 Christian preachers and teachers in its 59 schools where nearly 1,965 students were under instruction.[92] The village school teachers who were employed by the missionaries were all Christian converts.[93] The schoolmasters in the village schools were educated in the boarding schools of the Mission at Guntur, Masulipatnam, Ongole, Nellore, Cocanada, and Samalkota.[94]

The CMS' Vernacular Teacher Training at Masulipatam had supplied skilled teachers to various districts.[95] During the year 1912, the Dornakal diocese had employed 100 lay teachers to work in 75 villages.[96] In 1924, at the Hindu Girls' School in Guntur there were 38 Christian teachers.[97] In the higher elementary and middle schools, 66 teachers were of Christian backgrounds.[98]

There were nearly one hundred and fifty village school teachers employed by the American Baptist Mission in Ongole.[99] There were also nearly 1,986 Christian teachers in non-Christian primary schools.[100] The growing body of educated lay men and women graduated at the secondary level with Secondary School Leaving Certificates (SSLC) with additional Elementary Teacher Training were appointed as teachers.[101] For the teaching posts in the subjects of Mathematics, Economics and History, the qualification needed was SSLC, Inter-trained, Bachelor of Arts (BA) studied, BA Passed or BA Passed in one part, and so on.[102] Salaries for school teachers were given according to their educational qualifications. For example, a teacher with SSLC Trained was paid Rs. 42, a Primary Teacher Trained with Rs.17, a BA Passed, with Rs. 90 and Rs. 51 for a Head Mistress.[103]

Regarding female teachers, if a student qualified in her primary level of instruction, she was sent for training as a school mistress in the teacher training institutes in the towns of Nellore, Ongole, Bapatla, Guntur, Masulipatnam, Cocanada and Rajahmundry.[104] Often they were married to preachers, who were graduated from Boys' schools and were employed as preachers and teachers in their own or adjacent villages.[105] Rev. Schmidt had advocated employment of teachers in villages from which they hailed or in which there were at least ten Christian families.[106]

The remuneration of village teachers was nominal as some were voluntary teachers, others were paid in kind. The payment depended on the collective interest and decisions of the local congregation regarding the education of their children and also on their affordability.[107] However, many teachers were paid from the foreign funds and from the Mission treasury.[108] Overall, our data show that a substantial number of native converts were educated by the Mission, and were made competent to undertake alternative occupations such as teaching either in Mission's own institutions or in government one, which clearly indicates the upward occupational mobility due to educational advancement.

6.4.2 Employment in Health Sector

Medical work required qualified doctors and nurses. All the medical undertakings of the Mission in Coastal Andhra were encouraged and obliged to facilitate training of native personnel so that the missionaries could free themselves to engage in spiritual ministry. The development of medical and nursing professions gave a lot of employment opportunities to the qualified converts as medical helpers and assistants. The missionary medical enterprise helped not only in improving the health condition of the converts, but also provided employment for them. In 1898, at the Star of Hope Hospital, Dr. Pearl Smith and a trained Indian assistant doctor worked at the in-patient department and also engaged in Gospel preaching.[109] Trained nurses and mid-wives were also employed in public health institutions and private nursing homes of the Zenanas. The introduction of medical work among the Malas and the Madigas made deep impact in improving the health of the Malas and Madigas. Consequently, their work efficiency and work quality increased.[110]

Regarding missionary contribution to training of health personnel, the candidates had to have passed their III Form to be able to undergo nurses' training. Those who had passed their VI form were sent for training in the Raney Hospital in Madras.[111] Trained women helpers took the tasks as dispensers and chloroformists. There was one nurse training school at Guntur and three, in Rajahmundry.[112] In 1942, the American Lutheran Mission and its allied bodies employed 40 graduate nurses and 121 pupil nurses in its three hospitals.[113] The AELM had employed three missionary doctors, seventeen Indian doctors and seven missionary nurses. Miss. Hilma Levine and Miss Verna Lofgren from the Augustana Synod contributed much to the training of nurses.[114] The influence and conduct of the Christian medical staff not only helped curing the patients, who were often influenced by the Christian value of service. Apparently some of them even sought conversion to Christianity.

6.4.3 Employment in Preaching Ministry

Due to the magnitude of the evangelistic work and acute shortage of foreign missionary personnel, utilizing the service of native converts became a necessity for all the missionary societies in Colonial Andhra.[115] Therefore, trained native converts were employed as Gospel workers to expand the evangelical activities of the missionary societies.[116] The quantitative growth of native church members naturally increased the number of ordained and un-ordained preachers. With zeal and passion for Gospel work, many were oriented to undergo training to become pastors, catechists, colporteurs and bible-women. The aim of native evangelistic work was to help the missionaries through preaching and teaching on the Christian religion.[117]

The AELM in Guntur trained and employed a large number of native workers to help the foreign missionaries. The Bible Colporteur was a grass root Christian worker. The village Christian school teacher was expected to impart both elementary secular knowledge and Biblical knowledge.[118] Catechists and evangelists carried on the work of preaching and conversing with the people under the direction of the missionary in an area of ten or more contiguous villages or in un-touched villages with non-Christian population.[119] The preachers conducted Gospel preaching activities not only in their own villages but also in adjacent villages where there were as many as five hundred converts under their spiritual care.

In March 1847, the first native catechist Nicodemus was employed.[120] The CMS mission had set up a sub-committee to employ a large body of native lay agents for Gospel work in 1880 due to the rising number of native Christians and congregations. After about two decades there were 450 native preachers who worked as full time evangelists.[121] Preachers engaged in street preaching, stopping at various locations on the village street, singing, preaching and teaching. They were also required to visit Christian homes in the evenings when people returned from farm work.[122] The mission also employed two hundred Bible women who used to visit the homes of caste Hindus and preached the Gospel. Only women preachers could get access to the Zenanas, women's wards in dispensaries and hospitals or caste Hindu girls' schools.[123]

As for the ABM's missionary fields, there were thirty three ordained preachers and thirty un-ordained Gospel workers besides several hundred deacons.[124] Rev. Clough mentions about the 'Ongole method' of self-support system for employing large numbers of native Gospel workers. In this system, a quarterly subsidy was given to support the preachers thereby reducing the financial difficulties of the Mission.[125] The salary of the different grades of native pastors was determined by the Mission at Rs 12 to 18. The catechists and sub-catechists received a salary between Rs 3 to Rs 10.[126] The sources of funding were many: foreign funds, mission's treasury funds, and native congregational donations.[127] Full time Bible-women were paid from the Mission's budget amount and half-time Bible-women's salary was borne by the Mission's Women Budget fund.[128]

6.4.4 Military and Police Services

In traditional Indian caste-based society, the Depressed Castes did not have a space in the military as they, as well as several others castes, were not considered as fighting classes. But, Indian History under the Muslim rule shows that irrespective of caste, able bodied men with right orientation were employed in the military. And these proved right that talent does not count on caste. In many battles, Muslim military personnel belonging to different ethnic groups, occupational groups or clans or castes, won battles led by the so-called Hindu fighter castes (*Kshatriyas-Rajputs*). The British, hailing as they were from a European Christian background, did not consider caste as a qualification for enlistment in the military. They enlisted thousands of the so-called 'low' caste persons in their Madras Regiment whose men were deputed to suppress the so-called 'Sepoy Mutiny (First War of Independence) led by Hindu upper caste military personnel as well as powerful local Muslim rulers. So also, the British enlisted a large of 'low' caste Mahars from Maharasthtra and set up the Mahar Regiment which achieved great victory over the Brahmin-led Peshwa Raj's army of Poona in 1818. These historic military events in Indian history has proved beyond doubt that talent for fighting does not depend on caste, but good physique, and more than that endurance and right motivation, besides empowering and brave leadership. During the British Colonial rule lakhs of members of the Depressed Castes were enabled to demonstrate their talent in fighting enemies under military service.

With their endurance and physical strength, the Malas and Maldigas in Colonial Andhra provided good manpower to the colonial Indian Army.[129] They found employment in the Indian Army's service sectors. They were deputed to Mesopotamia to participate in the First World War on behalf of the British.[130] The earliest British army employees were recruited from those people who had an aptitude for mingling freely with foreigners.[131] The Inspector of Police at Vizagapatam headquarters was brought up in the London Mission Orphanage who was an exemplary Christian and occupied a respectable position in that town.[132] According to the Memorandum on the Progress of the Madras Presidency, a number of people from the Depressed Castes were enlisted to be the sepoys and in the domestic establishments of the European residents as cooks, nurses and horse keepers.[133] The sepoys in the Indian army belonging to Depressed Castes had the reputation of being the best of the recruits from the population of South India.[134] However, the prospect of higher level of military employment leading to political power was low, as the basic qualification of these castes was inadequate to hold higher posts.[135] Nevertheless the military and the police sector provided ample channels of better and more dignified employment which definitely enabled them to achieve higher economic and social mobility.

6.4.5 Employment in Public Works

During the second half of the 19th century, the frontiers of world commerce expanded and pulled the Indian villages into a wider economic system. The growth of commerce necessitated the development of transportation systems and the need for transporting merchandise increased. The disintegration of village communities due to the colonial administrative integration of the country furthered the requirement of road works.[136] Colonial Public works were also meant to provide relief by providing immediate employment to a multitude of people. In the last part of the 19th century, millions of people were suffering under famine conditions. Due to the initiative of Rev. Clough, hundreds of Madigas (converts) found employment in the public works during the great famine of 1877.[137] A variety of public works were undertaken by the government in various towns of colonial Andhra such as Vizianagaram, Cocanada, Bezwada and Nellore. The diverse works were building district munsif's courts, post offices, jails, sub-magistrate's cutcheries, college buildings, school-houses, police stations, police hospitals, roads, bridges, and so on. Building water supply facilities, drainages, ports and marine works were also undertaken.[138]

6.4.6 Employment in Railway Construction

The introduction of Railways in India occupies a very prominent place in the history of Colonial Administration's efforts to create a surface network over the whole country through modern transportation systems.[139] The Railways were the biggest employer of workers in India then. It also became the chief source of employment for the natives. In colonial Andhra, Railway workshops were established at Ganjam, Vizagapatam, Godavari and Nellore.[140]

The construction of railway lines was undertaken in various towns of colonial Andhra such as Bezwada, Masulipatnam, Samlakota, Vizagapatam, Cumbum, Bitragunta and Gudur, by the Madras Railway and the Madras and Southern Maharatta Railway Company Ltd.[141] These Railway companies provided employment opportunities for a large number of Christian Malas and Madigas as well.[142] Railway contracts were undertaken by the missionaries themselves to secure work for the Christians.[143] According to Rev. Pickett, in the Guntur area, the Malas joined as Railway workers and were engaged in a variety of works.[144] Rev. Clough had insisted for a line to pass through Ongole for the proposed railroad between Madras and Calcutta. When the Railway engineers came to survey for a new railroad they found Rev. Clough's observations were good about the proposed location.[145] The Malas and the Madigas were employed as railway lines men, guards, points men, signal men, shunters and dockyard staff.[146] The railway labour force was of three main categories: a) Skilled artisans who were usually recruited by work subordinates; b) Gang men on the permanent way, recruited from neighboring villages by the permanent-way inspectors; c) Unskilled staff in stations and goods-sheds, recruited by station-masters and traffic inspectors.[147] The majority of these workers came from the agricultural labour classes.[148] During the early years of Railway line construction, labourers were supplied with food and clothing by the railway companies, which was a great relief for poor Malas and Madigas.[149]

6.5 Entering into Industrial Enterprise

6.5.1 Mission's Industrial Enterprise

One may naturally ask what had these men of religion to do with industry. Christian evangelism was a package of offers to people inviting them to listen to the Gospel, understand its message of God's mercy to both sinners and saints and accept salvation of the believer. The package aimed not only the religious, spiritual wellbeing of the people, but also their material wellbeing. It is these twin aims that rationalized the missionary's assistance in industrial, vocational, material aspects of the lives of people, along with spiritual aspects. Industrial Evangelism in colonial Andhra developed many initiatives, such as setting up industrial units for brick-making, tile-making, lace-making, poultry rearing, cottage manufacturing, etc.[150] Training schools to generate instructors and workers in industrial works also were set up. Opportunities were available to the Christian converts to learn vocational skills in boarding schools so that they could raise their economic status.[151] The training schools were gradually made financially independent and even helped support other mission schools.[152] Every branch of Industrial work was promoted to enhance self-reliance, strengthen self-respect and to gain consciousness that they need no more be dependent upon others but could support themselves.[153]

The training in missionary industrial and vocational schools facilitated the Malas and the Madigas to undertake new occupations to achieve occupational mobility and employment variation. The undertaking of various Industrial pursuits was a valuable effort for the Christian converts for two reasons. They provided work not only for the converts but also opened up new branches of employment for those who had lost their traditional occupation, having turned away by their employers, as a consequence of their baptism.[154] Industrial training proved to be a successful initiative as the trained converts gained employment in railway workshops and other organized industrial undertakings.[155]

6.5.2 The Industrial Mission Aid Society

The Industrial Mission Aid Society, a non-profit society, was formed in 1895 for the purpose of developing native industries for which facilities were arranged for industrial training and technical education. Much attention was directed towards growth of printing industry, book-binding, brick and tile manufacture.[156] In civil society, a variety of factories such as rice mills, railway workshops, brick and tile making, printing presses, sugar factories, leather and tanning industries were started.[157] The missionary societies took advantage of these facilities and encouraged and sponsored training of converts in industrial pursuits such as textile making, carpentry, mechanical engineering, welding, etc.[158]

As per the Indian Factories Act of 1881, the Government, under the Department of Labour, created opportunities for employment in many of its undertakings. This helped the trained Malas and Madigas to avail the employment opportunities.[159] Consequently, as the data show, there was a decrease in the number of field labourers, whereas there was an increase in the numbers in learned professions. This indicates a degree of occupational mobility.[160]

Agro-industries in colonial Andhra also provided opportunities to the Malas and Madigas for employment. For instance, quite a few rice mills (3 in Ganjam, 1 in Vizagapatam, 11 in Godavari, 26 in Kistna, 19 in Guntur and 13 in Nellore 3), sugar factories (one each in Ganjam and Godavari), cotton mills and tobacco industries (4 in Godavari), provided ample employment for men and women.[161]

Similarly cottage industries, such as brick making, tile making, furniture making, printing press, book-binding, lace-making, etc., managed by the missions or the government absorbed a substantial number of skilled Malas and Madigas. The developmental works such as construction of roads, railways, canals, etc., by the government also created employment opportunities for them. That the industry-oriented development progammes of the mission seem to have enhanced upward occupational mobility and economic mobility is noted in many documents. This was one of the success stories of the Christian missions in colonial Andhra. We shall examine this aspect in some detail.

6.5.3 Development through Cottage Industries

The missionary bodies in Andhra also set up cottage industrial units mainly to create employment opportunities for the Christians and to make them self-sufficient.[162] The wide gap between industry and education was reduced when the missionaries introduced practical training with the application of improved machinery.[163] Various industries such as printing, leather manufacture, brick-making, aluminum work, tailoring, lace-making and so on were started with investment made by the mission. Besides, carpentry, weaving units, and burning of lime and brick as a cottage industry were introduced.[164]

Industries of practical nature were started for girls also in missionary boarding schools where if a girl failed to complete the full course of study, she was given training in sewing, lace-making and gardening to help her in future life.[165]

The initiative to start cottage industries was taken mainly to engage famine orphans in useful, revenue yielding employment. Due to frequent occurrence of famines and natural calamities, many adult lives were lost which necessitated the opening of orphanages to take care of the orphan children.[166] Eventually, these were to be occupied. The industrial work in Guntur grew out of an orphanage where efforts were made to teach the orphan boys in occupations such as carpentry, tailoring, weaving and motor driving.[167] The children at the Christian Herald Orphanage (1901) and the Faith Orphanage of Rev. Henry Huizinga learnt skills in leather and aluminum work.[168]

Among the diverse industries, leather industry became competitive with modern means of production, which seem to have helped a large number of Madigas.[169] Rev. Frederick James McCready of the American Lutheran Mission took much interest in the employment of converted but poor Madigas in the brick and tile-making manufacturing industries at Tallapudi and Samalkota.[170] Due to the growing demand for construction of buildings for schools, chapels, missionary houses, it became a necessity to manufacture bricks and tiles to be used for buildings.[171] Large sheds were set up for making tiles for which a number men and women were employed. Tiled school-houses and chapels were built in place of leaf-thatched roofs. Though these constructions were modest, they generated a lot of employment for the Mala and Madiga Christian converts.[172]

Mission records show that three among all the industries—carpentry, printing and lace-making—aided much to improve the economic life of the Malas and Madigas. I shall describe these with some details.

6.5.4 Carpentry

The growth of woodworking industry as a cottage industry in colonial Andhra had its origins in the developing needs of the communities. There was increasing demand in the mission for making buildings for houses, hospitals, residences, chapels, etc. The missionaries employed a lot of converts who were trained in these skills. Building masons and carpenters were in high demand. The untrained ones were often given guidance by the experienced missionary, who was occasionally a carpenter and an architect.[173] The boys in boarding schools were intimated into these skills.[174] Some of the elder graduates later became building contractors.[175]

In the Godavari delta region, the tows such as Cocanada, Narsapur, Koringa, Amalapur, Ellore and Dummagudem, were linked through reverine means of transport.[176] Boats and small ships were used for transportation of goods and passengers. Construction of boats and ships needed a lot of skilled carpenters, most of whom were Christians. The American Evangelical Lutheran Mission employed the school boarder boys and native Christian youth as carpenters and blacksmiths.[177] In April 1876, Rev. Schmidt undertook the building of a house-boat called "Dove of Peace", 40 feet long and 12 feet wide, was built entirely with the help of the boarding school boys and native Christians. This house-boat was used in traversing the canals for Gospel preaching in the island villages. The American Lutheran Mission in Rajahmundry maintained carpenter and blacksmith-shops, a saw-pit and a lumber-yard.[178]

The Cocanada Carpentry School for boys was established under the guidance of Rev. Craig and Rev. Dixon Smith of the Canadian Baptist Mission. The school had a large workshop with twenty carpentry desks fitted with tool kits. The school had a regular curriculum for a five-year course, in which three years were for instruction and two years for employed practical internship in factories.[179] A wood-working factory was built nearby the school to give practice for the students.[180] Almost all the missionary societies in Colonial Andhra had sent many of their students to the Canadian Baptist Mission's Carpentry School at Cocanada.[181]

As for the CMS, its Dornakal diocese reportedly employed over 1200 men and women who had received training in agriculture or weaving or carpentry at the Dornakal Vocational School.[182] There were two wood factories at Nellore and an iron working factory at Vizagapatam where tables, chairs, almirahs, cots and other furniture were manufactured and sold in the local markets.[183]

6.5.5 Printing Industry

There were no printing presses in coastal Andhra before the last part of the 19th century. Missionaries needed printing presses to print Christian literature in local languages for dissemination of Bible teachings. Christian literature in Telugu was printed by the Madras Auxiliary Bible Society at Madras. To overcome this handicap, missionaries in coastal Andhra appealed to their Home Committees for founding printing presses. During Rev. J. H. Harpster's missionary tenure, a printing press at Rajahmundry was donated by Mr. William P. M. Braun of Philadelphia through which a number of Christian literary works were printed and distributed.[184] In 1874, the Canadian Baptist Mission established a printing press and a Book binding facility to cater to the printing needs of the mission.[185] The American Lutheran Mission at Guntur set up its own printing and publishing house.

Once printing presses were set up, employment opportunities were created for the converts in book printing and book-binding occupations. The CMS Dove Press at Masulipatnam and the ABM Press at Ramapatnam printed Christian Gospel tracts using the skills of the Christians workers.[186] Besides, the missionaries endeavored to promote the arts of Book Keeping, type writing and shorthand where job placement was created in the central and provincial administration.[187] According to Rev. Malcolm Orchard, Christians were entwined with the economic life in the Godavari district where eight thousand of them had earned a comfortable living.[188]

6.5.6 Lace-making Industry

Lace work as a cottage industry created new avenues of vocational employment for the Malas and Madigas[189] It became one of the methods through which Christian women (boarding girls, Christian widows and orphans) acquired skills in lace-making. This occupation seems to have lifted them out of the depressed economic conditions and enabled them to become self-reliant and independent.[190] The art of needlework was introduced as early as 1845 by Mrs. Walter Gunn of the AELM to a small group of Hindu girls.[191] After the death of her husband Rev. Walter Gunn at Guntur in 1854, she had continued to manage the girls' school where she imparted both elementary education and proficiency in the art of sewing.[192] But the foundation of the lace-making industry was laid by AELM's Mrs. Schmidt at the Rajahmundry Girls' Boarding School, in 1878.[193] This was the largest one of its kind. Mrs. Schmidt supplied materials such as needles and thread to make lace which were exported to America.

The sale proceeds were made over to the women lace workers.[194] In times of famines, earnings from lace work had provided relief to the converts. Widowed women, poor girls and physically challenged women were employed in this industry.[195] The wives of other missionaries also taught the Christian girls the art of sewing.[196] Lace work industry was a very self-supporting venture.

The towns of Rajahmundry, Narsapur and Bhimavaram emerged as big centers of lace industry with regular exports to the western countries. In 1887, Mrs. Schmidt sent lace to America having secured many orders on her furlough.[197] The lace produced there was of high standard of excellence.[198] From 1892, at Tallapudi, Mrs. McCready engaged herself in teaching crochet, knitting and lace-making.[199] Under the efficient management of Mrs. Harpster, boxes of lace were sent to America which were received with great enthusiasm and more orders were placed. It was reported that the lace making industry created employment opportunities for as many as two hundred and forty women,[200] by 1908. An Industrial Home for women was also located at Rajahmundry near the Charlotte Swenson Memorial School where lace-making work was supervised by Mrs. A. F. A. Neodoerffer and Miss. Holerbach. Lace industry was also conducted at the Dorcas Home for Widows in Rajahmundry.[201]

Miss Elliott of the Bobbili Boarding School reported about the excellent skills of the girls in making beautiful lace. They did lace making outside the school hours as well, in order to earn more income for themselves.[202] The wives of the preachers and teachers were also among the lace makers to supplement their salaries for the needs of the family.[203] The lace industry in the Ramachandrapuram station was introduced in the year 1910 by Mrs. D. A. Gunn. By 1920 there were more than one hundred women employed in the lace-making industry there.[204] The salaries of the lace makers ranged from Rs. 6 to 12 per month.[205] At the Canadian Baptist Mission's Girls' Boarding School at Akidu, Vuyyuru, Cocanada and Bobbili, girls learnt sewing, mat-weaving, gardening and lace-making.[206]

The industrial activities of the CMS can be traced to Rev. Noble, who had convinced the CMS Home Committee on the importance of reviving the industrial school as an important aid to the missionary enterprise.[207] In Rev. Nicholson's Industrial School, carpentry, blacksmithy and brick-laying were taught to the Christian children.[208] The CMS' Zenana Missionary Society had engaged in industrial education of women, chiefly widows.[209] The Industrial School at Masulipatam made arrangements for training women converts in crochet making.[210] The Dornakal Vocational Training School was started in 1907 as a mission boarding school of the Indian Missionary Society of Tinnevelly (IMST).[211] At Dummagudem and Khammamett, classes were held for teaching needlework and lace-making to women.[212]

Sometimes, village Christians found it difficult to find market for their finished goods. Therefore, the missionaries initiated efforts to ensure better sale of their products through proper distribution channels. The co-operative societies started by the missionaries also helped a great deal in this regard.[213] The sale of lace was managed by either the lady missionaries or the wives of male missionaries, who exported the finished products to their home countries. The Augustana Women's Missionary Society had consistently helped in the export sale of lace work to America and had even arranged an exhibition of the lace from India at the Chicago World's Fair in 1895.[214] The money realized from the sales was invested back home for further development of women's work.[215]

Embroidery as a cottage industry was also undertaken by the Christian women in the Godavari delta areas.[216] The efforts of Ms. Flora Clarke were noteworthy, for she had purchased not only a knitting machine but also obtained an auto-knitter from Canada in 1917. She had also arranged for further training of women with a special course in Madras. Eventually, she handed over the management of the Knitting factory to the Christian women.[217] At the Narasaraopet Industrial School, a wide variety of products were manufactured: darned net, bed tape, machine and hand sewing linen work, etc.[218] In sum, the missionaries had created more avenues for economic development and upliftment of the converts through practical training.

6.5.7 Financing through Co-Operative Societies

For the economic independence of the Christians, the Madras Missionary Conference urged the establishment of co-operative banks, making use of Government's Cooperative Credit Association Scheme. Dr. J. R. Stillwell, Mr. Gordon, Dr. Wolverton and Mr. Cross were the principal organizers of these societies in Krishna and Godavari Mission stations.[219] The Mission banks helped train the converts in financial practices of thrift and saving.[220]

The Indian Cooperative Societies Act, passed in 1904, aimed to guide, recognize and monitor the co-operative credit societies.[221] The local governments had appointed Registrars for monitoring such societies. Due to the trust the government had on the missionaries, some societies were entrusted to the management of local missionaries.[222] The latter exercised caution while granting loans as the borrowers tended to utilize the borrowed money for non-productive purposes which would have further added to their financial distress.[223] The credit societies also granted the members loans at reasonable rates of interest to enable them to pay back the debts taken from elsewhere, so that they could become free of their debt-bondage.[224] The co-operative societies assisted the producers in marketing and selling of their products. They also maintained depots where tools and implements were procured for distribution at nominal rates to the members.[225] In 1928, Miss A. B. Van Doren introduced an agenda of rural reconstruction in the National Christian Council. This initiative was to recognize the problems of rural Christians and provide avenues for reconstruction wherever possible for the welfare of the community.[226] Further, the appointment of the Royal Commission on Agriculture in 1928 made provision for grants for agriculture, which helped many cultivators.[227]

The Rural Reconstruction Committees of the missionary societies looked after the affairs of the Mission Co-Operative Societies.[228] The rural reconstruction programs were concrete expressions of the Christian principle of love of neighbour through practice of philanthropy. Functionally it meant assisting people to acquire education, helping them in health care, uplifting their economy through co-operative credit societies, and so on.[229] The Vuyyuru Co-operative Society was formed in 1920 with the objective of securing land for the Christian converts and to relieve them from their debts to the *Súdra* farmers.[230] The Cooperative Society of the American Baptist Mission in Donakonda under Rev. J. A. Curtis did remarkable work by helping village Christians get out of their poverty. Loan capital for productive employment was made available for agriculture, industry and commerce.[231] Cooperative societies of other missionary societies such as at Bezwada (CMS), Guntur (AELM), Eluru (CMS), Kakinada and Tuni (C.B.M), also did commendable work for rural communities.[232] According to Rev. Azariah, rural poverty could be won over by people by correcting themselves in moral practices such as alcoholism, excessive marriage expenses and imprudent habits of eating, dressing, giving and spending above one's income.[233] Our data show that economic upliftment was achieved thorough reduction in wasteful expenditure during weddings, funerals and other functions. By following temperate practices, money was saved and better health was achieved. A number of Christians had testified that much less was spent at their weddings than in their pre-conversion days.[234]

The economic upliftment of the Malas and the Madigas was achieved in the traditional sectors of agriculture and its allied activities as well as in non-agricultural industrial pursuits. The converted Malas and the Madigas were able to achieve economic mobility in agricultural and industrial sectors in all the districts of Coastal Andhra. As a result they were able to have comfortable livelihood, besides freedom from the bondages of traditional economic ties.[235] The economic condition of the Christians in Markapur town (Guntur district) was noted by the District Collector in 1916. He was impressed by economic improvement of the Madiga Christians and credited it largely as a result of new ideals.[236]

The Missionary endeavours to ameliorate the economic condition of the Malas and the Madigas took place on a scale that had never occurred before. This was noted by many Hindu reformers and social scientists. According to Srinivasa Raghava Aiyangar, the Inspector-General of Registration of the Madras Presidency, "the best thing that can happen to them is conversion either to Christianity or to Muhammadan religion, for there is no hope for them within the pale of Hinduism."[237] But with no given record of the Malas' and the Madigas' conversion to Islam, the work of improving the condition of the convert Malas and the Madigas was entirely left in the hands of the Christian missionaries alone. On the other hand, efforts of the social reformers in Andhra namely Sri Raghupathi Venkata Ratnam Naidu, Sri Chilakamarthi Lakshmi Narasimham and Sri Unnava Lakshmi Narayana largely played an important role in the removal of untouchability and upliftment of the non-convert Malas and the Madigas.[238]

In conclusion, the economic upliftment and occupational mobility achieved by the Malas and the Madigas seem to have been due a new awakening and understanding among them consequent to their acceptance of a different moral order, set of values and ideals available to them through conversion. It has been noted above and has been substantiated by contemporary documents and reports that the Malas and Madigas were provided with diverse opportunities and channels of empowerment by the missions both for better performance in their traditional occupations and entering into new professions. According to Rev. J. E. Chute, who had worked in the Akidu Mission field, "whatever the economic prosperity the Christian community possessed had been acquired mostly subsequent to their conversion. Every church and every convert to Christianity is a sure sign of a better day coming."[239]

II

In this section, I deal with the apparent social, religious and cultural changes among the Christian Malas and the Madigas.

6.6 Culture Change Explained

Culture is "a set of values, artifacts and modes of human interaction in an integrated pattern of human life in which the creative freedom of a people is expressed and implemented."[240] It is a subjective set of orientation towards particular beliefs and values where traditions are a pattern of a cumulative process of transmission, adjusting and applying the values and beliefs through time with a system of symbols and signs.[241] Culture change is a rapid process of modification in a person's beliefs and systems of knowledge and material tools that have evolved independently or through contact with people from a different culture of their own.[242] Culture change involves freezing of the existing patterns by overcoming resistances and opening up for the adoption of new forms of life.[243]

In the process of Christianization, the Malas and Madigas had been infused with an urge for social change either by abandoning old customs and habits, adopting new ones, besides accepting new norms of life, belief system and religious practices. Though their ethnic and social identity remained, they acquired a new religious identity as Christians. The life of the convert Christians can be seen as an expression of their Christian faith within the given social milieu and Indian culture.

Religio-cultural change among the Malas and the Madigas occurred when they eliminated certain pre-conversion practices such as idol worship, animal sacrifices, etc., and adopted new norms of Christian living and forms of worship the stimulus for this was given by the Christian missionaries, through diverse ways of Christianization such as preaching, suggesting new practices and customs and monitoring of their moral lives.[244] The Gospel preaching of the missionaries gradually transformed the character and lives of the Mala and Madiga converts.[245] A new world view was accepted as they began to lead a Christian life besides acquiring the new Christian identity.[246] The changes were seen not only in the religious realm but also in social, cultural and material life.[247]

The institutional contexts of constructing a new Christian community centred around the church and its ambient institutions which were new and different from the existing institutions of the pre-conversion Hindu religion. The mission functionaries acted as gurus, patrons and even as custodians of their moral and religious life. Although they were men of religion, they were also totally involved in the social, cultural and material life of the converts.

I do not claim that all these changes were mediated exclusively by the mission functionaries. Socio-religious change takes place through the conscientious decision of the individual although collective conviction, group stimulus besides external impetus may be present. When so many individuals changed, one can say that the total society changed. Socio-cultural transformation occurs through conscious actions of the subjects who become convinced that the old order of structures and norms are no longer relevant and adopt a new order of society.[248] What is noticed in the socio-religious life of the Malas and the Madigas after conversion was a two-way action: a) abandoning of certain un-Christian practices and b) adopting certain Christian forms of worship, practices along with moral and religious principles and tenets of faith. This process did not involve the abandonment of their Indian culture, while adopting a new religious culture. In some cases, the utilitarian forms of pre-convert religion and social customs were retained and adapted to suit the new status as converts especially in matters of wedding ceremonies and many social customs.[249] The dynamics of the socio-religious change that seems to have occurred among the Mala and Madiga convert communities are examined in this section.

6.7 Christianization of Rites, Rituals and Practices

6.7.1 *Rejection of Pre-conversion Religious Practices and Beliefs*

The process of conversion among the Malas and the Madigas involved the disintegration of the existing traditional culture complexes, and the adoption of a new form of culture based on new perception and self-realization of the individuals.[250] Among the many changes, I have studied only a few which were more conspicuous in the converts.

6.7.2 Abandoning Idol Worship

Christian missionaries advocated that idol worship was anathema in the Christian way of worship. On the other hand, consecrated statues of Lord Jesus, Mother Mary, and saints are only revered, not worshipped in the Catholic Religion. These sacred objects help the believer to transport his/her spirit to true God. Thus they have only a mediatory role.[251] The practice of animistic idol worship, serpent worship, festive processions, rituals of immoral practices, etc., were to be totally left behind by the new converts.[252] Traditional caste-bound religious duties of these two castes, for instance, carrying idols, playing music in front and rear side of religious processions, dancing to the beats of the drums, playing the drums, swearing for the appeasement of deities, and so on had to be abandoned by the converts.[253] As mentioned in Chapter 2, these were religious functions, but socially bound duties assigned to particular castes. The participation of the Malas and the Madigas was a necessary social function. The Madiga performed the *Sivam* dance under the influence of drugs and uttered strange words to give a sign that the spirit of the idol was in him. Once he became a Christian he refused to perform it, or was asked by the Christian priest to abandon it. Mission chronicles had recorded the following attitude of village elders, "We cannot beat those drums. We cannot have anything to do with idol-worship. We are Christians."[254] In the town of Markapur (Guntur District) the Christian Madigas refused to repair the broken leather drum to be played on the occasion of idol-worship. They stood firm, saying that "we are now Christians and cannot have anything to do with idol-worship."[255] In the CMS' Khammamet and Dornakal villages (North Kistna), prospective converts admitted to Bishop Azariah that, "we are tired of worshipping these idols."[256] Besides, Christians had to face the anger of the caste masters when the former refused to perform traditional duties during village festivals and so were denied their customary dues as a form of punishment.[257]

The ritual of bowing down to the idol requesting for help for an undetected robbery was abandoned.[258] The renunciation of idol worship was meant refusal to accept the sacrificial meat.[259]

The traditional Madiga *Chindu* dance was discouraged by the missionaries as it involved provokingly suggestive movements to cause affront to the

Malas. Since continuance of such dance made a breach of peace in the villages, Christian teachers and preachers had to intervene to prevent feuds among the Malas and the Madigas.[260] The missionaries also discouraged playing the musical instrument of *Tappeta*, a hand held drum that was used for all village festivals, besides the Madiga performing the *Chindu* dance. However, at certain festive occasions the converts were allowed to play the instrument.[261]

Belief in the new religion put new obligations on the converts to follow Christian forms of worship, reject customs and beliefs that were incompatible with it and to demonstrate new conviction and put on outward conformity of the inward conviction. A catechist was appointed to reside in the villages near the new converts' homes to teach and reinforce Gospel essences in daily life.[262] The consent of the Christians to cut off the *Juttu* (the lock of hair on the top of the head) and erase vermilion marks from the foreheads of women testified as outward signs of acceptance of the new faith.[263] In a few cases when an individual converted into Christianity, his family members attempted to discourage any physical changes that reflected the new faith citing strong family ties.[264] Beliefs in religious merit that can be acquired through pilgrimages to sacred spots, almsgiving and animal sacrifices had to be given up,[265] although pilgrimage and almsgiving were practiced in Christianity as works of piety and charity.

The Christians (with few exceptions) remained firm in their faith during the occurrence of Cholera in 1906 in the Masulipatnam region, when their Hindu relatives and neighbours offered large numbers of goats and fowls, as propitiatory sacrifices.[266] It was believed that such sacrifices would heal the cholera affected. At the same time, the Christian religious functionaries had to give alternative arrangements of healing from cholera. It was reported that this compelled them to bring in medical missionaries to deal with it. The matter was discussed at the Missionary Conference in 1910 to deal with the frequent occurrence of diseases among the people.[267] In the Akidu station, the faith of the Christians was tested when a *Brāhmin* priest asked for a donation of one rupee for the erection of a temple for a local deity, which request was spurned by the Christians.[268]

6.7.3 Adopting Christian Forms of Worship

Indigenous church worship was embedded with deep faith and used the forms of thought and modes of action familiar to its own environment.[269] Whether in a mud and thatched humble structure or in tile-roofed, stone-walled building, worship services were conducted with utmost devotion and commitment. The Christian converts in coastal Andhra adapted to the new form of worship on Sundays and other important sacred days. The worship service was led by the convert village headman accompanied with playing of musical instruments. People gathered on the floor and worshipped either by kneeling or prostrating.[270] Voluntary offertories were received in the native style wherein a large earthen pot was provided to receive the donations of grain or money.[271] Rice, vegetables, first fruits of garden crops, cattle and poultry were brought to the altar for offering.[272] The generosity of the people in giving to the church was much appreciated by the missionaries. They were aware that many converts were poor daily wage earners and yet contributed generously for the support of the church.[273]

6.7.4 Observance of Sunday as Rest Day

In order to attend the church worship services, converts needed to comply with the Christian doctrine of observing Sunday as a rest day.[274] This new practice caused much opposition from the *Súdra* employers.[275] Assurances were taken from the new converts to observe Sunday as a day of rest and adherence to the same.[276] Accusations of 'insubordination' were raised by the Hindu *Súdras* who had never before seen the Mala and Madiga subordinates taking the Sunday off, and attempted to punish the converts by denying their right of share of the grain. Nevertheless, despite bearing the economic loss, Christians showed much courage in staying away from work on Sundays.[277]

6.7.5 New Religious Nominal Identity

Before the converts were baptized, they had non-Christian names which were often the names of their Hindu deities.[278] Upon baptism new names were adopted that signified their conversion to Christianity. In some cases converts had added their Christian names to their old names or took entirely new Christian names.[279] For example, Taleru Marayya took the name of Thomas Gabriel,[280] Karre Potarazu was named Peter.[281] Karre Andrew and Karre Samuel and such other names like Bezwada Paul, Ongole Abraham, Virdulala Jonah, Kuchipudi Yacob, Todeti Abraham, Mālapati John, Nelaprolu Paulus, Thota Joseph, Baddepudi Abraham, Thaluri Daniel, Bezzam Yohan and Sreeram Solomon and so on became customary for the converts which gave a new nominal identity to the Christians. The earlier system of giving dual names on the twenty first day of the child's birth during the purudu ceremony was gradually eliminated.[282]

6.7.6 Creating a Christian Space

The local church was both a sacred place and a centre for community gathering. It became a source of inspiration for the converts under the foster care of the missionaries and native preachers. People gathered there in crowds for worship services and sang tunes from an anthology of Telugu lyrics. It was a symbol of Christian presence in an otherwise totally Hindu religious space. It became a novel feature in each village with a sizeable number of Christians who gathered in community worship on Sundays.[283] Christian festivals were celebrated with musical dramas and dances based on the stories of Biblical heroes which attracted a huge number of crowds. The Christians held Gospel processions accompanied by music and reading of scripture verses.[284] Be it Christmas, Easter, Good Friday, or any Sunday, Christians had exhibited a devotional spiritual tide.[285]

Simultaneously there was distancing from the pre-conversion religious sites and places: the converts were told not to attend Hindu or Muslim festivals. In churches, converts were to discard anything that was associated with their old forms of worship. Church architecture was distinctively Christian.[286] In the beginning, village churches were built in oblong and barn-like shape and appearance, and were made with mud, with thatched roofs supported by jungle-wood.[287] Gradually as their economic situation improved, church buildings, schools, hospitals, etc., were made of bricks and mortar with tiled roofs.[288] Substantial structures of stone and teak-wood were undertaken in the building of churches, schools, hospitals and seminaries.[289] These physical structures were symbolic of the structural changes in the socio-religious realm.

6.7.7 Christianized Marriages and Caste Regulations

Much before the passing of the Child Marriage Restraint Act or the Sarda Act in 1929, the government had enacted the Indian Christian Marriage Act in 1872 (Act 15 of 1872), wherein laws related to solemnization of a marriage between persons professing Christian religion were enacted. The solemnization of a Christian marriage could only be done by an ordained minister or a person holding a license.[290] It was mentioned in Part VI of the Act that the age of man intending to be married shall not be under twenty-one years and the age of the woman intending to be married shall not be under eighteen.[291] The licensed pastors who were to solemnize the marriage of the Christians had to ascertain the age of the bride and the bridegroom by referring to their record of baptisms. In the absence of such records, Village Register of Births and Deaths was referred.[292]

With respect to inter-religious marriages that is, marriage between Christians with non-Christians, there was no prohibition imposed on a person professing Christianity from marrying a non-Christian in a non-Christian ceremony.[293] However, without affecting the essential tenets of Christianity, converted Christians willingly married non-Christians of their own *kulam* (clan) for two reasons: to make the spouse and her family follow the Christian faith and also to keep their traditional caste loyalties intact.[294] But it was always a standard practice that while marrying a non-Christian by a Christian, the non-Christian partner must be admitted into baptism first in order for the marriage to be solemnized.[295] Since the Mala and the Madiga converts made up only a small portion of the entire caste in the beginning, quite a lot of inter-religious marriages took place, unless the Christians made deliberate efforts to find a Christian partner from anywhere. However, when the number of Christians increased such marriages became fewer. Also, traditional child marriages and uncle-niece marriages which were common in south India were opposed by the missionaries.[296] Early marriages and infant marriages were not common among the converts and a widow could remarry without any social restriction.[297]

It was observed in Coastal Andhra that Christians exhibited flexibility in caste relations across religions. Converts belonging to the same caste community continued to have social and family interaction especially during rites of passages. This enabled them to maintain family ties and caste traditions.[298] In other words conversion to a non-Hindu religion did not entail social disruption. This was not possible when conversions occur in small numbers. In mass conversion places, a majority of the converts were able to maintain the same social relations, and community interactions, contracted same caste marriages and participated in rites of passages of members belonging to the same clan though they professed different religions. Continuity of caste bonds helped maintain strong social affiliations. This in a way helped spread Christianity through kin and family affiliations.[299] Some historians have opined that the continuity factor was so strong as though conversion had never occurred.[300]

6.7.8 Constructing an Indian Christianity

For its long-term continuation on the Indian soil, Christianity needed to be naturalized as Indian. Though initiated by foreign church functionaries, the local Christianity emerged in a contextual setting by assimilating indigenous customs and cultural patterns of the people which normally did not contradict Christian values. Contextualization of Christianity called for dynamic changes by incorporating the customs of the land. This approach in a way gave a sort of continuity with the pre-conversion Indian culture. This inspired their non-convert relatives and members of extended families to join the ranks of the church.[301] Indianisation of Christianity was a good method to enable the converts to continue to claim their Indian culture after a change of religion. Indigenous customs which did not go against the tenets of faith were retained and the social order was generally maintained.[302] Cultural expressions such as dance, music, art, architecture, etc were Christianized but not abandoned. Gospel messages were presented in an *inculturated* way to the non-Christian caste-mates and people of other castes. Elements of native traditions and ceremonies were retained in worship practices and social relations.[303]

Social and cultural symbols were retained in the CMS Dornakal Diocese, whose Bishop V. S. Azariah had formulated an Indigenized marriage ritual accommodating certain traditional customs, keeping the local community sensibilities. The wedding ceremony was to be held in a church or chapel.

The marriage rite consisted in tying the traditional *tāli* or marriage badge to the bride's neck by the bridegroom.[304] This was similar to the pre-conversion Hindu custom and was strongly desired by the people. But it was Christianized ingeniously by inscribing the cross symbol on the golden disc which was heart-shaped.[305] He had also suggested incorporation of inculturated Telugu hymns for the occasion as for example, *Mangalame Yesunaku* (Auspicious Jesus) and *Devara Nee Deevenalu* (Bless these newlyweds).[306] The Fifth Lambeth Conference decreed that as long as the marriage was free from all idolatrous practices, there would be no objection in adopting native forms of marriage and christianize them with a due registration of the marriage.[307] The Mala and the Madiga converts subscribed to a new religion and were attached to the new faith but preferred to and were encouraged to maintain continuity of their *Indianness* socially and culturally asserting themselves as 'Indian Christians'.

6.8 Adopting New Social Norms and Styles of Life

6.8.1 Rejecting Traditional Habits: Carrion Consumption

The consumption of *tsachina mamsamu* (carrion) was strongly disapproved by the missionaries. The Madigas had to deal with the dead cattle in a village for which he would get the hide from which, after processing, he would make leather goods, sandals, trappings and leather buckets. He had the right to the carcass of the dead cattle as part of the bargain. He would consume it and so was considered ritually low in Hindu society which believes everything dead as impure. The origin of this practice by the Madigas varied from legendary curses of the Hindu sages to the distressed famine conditions which compelled them to consume carcass for survival. It was a source atmospheric filth and pollution in the physical surroundings as well as injurious to the health of the Madigas. The missionaries discouraged this habit on every ground that the meat of dead animals was dangerously unhygienic and its renunciation was one of the preconditions to be admitted into the Church.[308] Candidates who were ready for baptism were examined if they had agreed to abstain from this practice. According to Rev. Clough, the American Baptist Missionary, discarding of the consumption of carrion was enforced in a stringent way.[309] The loathsomeness of the food was much resented by the converts within their immediate non-Christian family circles where Christian families refused to share the earthen plates with their non-Christian relatives on the grounds that, "we turn sick when you touch our food. You are unclean."[310] In some parts of the Nellore district, the Christians formed over half of the Madiga population. "This changes their habits of life and also their social position. Eating of carrion is now forbidden, as well as beating of drums at Hindu festivals."[311]

The rejection of this practice laid the foundation for cleaner living hamlets, cleaner surroundings and cleaner physical life and spiritual life.[312]

The issue of abandoning of the practice of consuming carrion was discussed at the World Missionary Conference at Edinburgh in 1910 which advised the missionaries that a restraint on beef-consumption by the Depressed Castes would remove an obstacle in the acceptance of Christian faith by the Hindus.[313]

6.8.2 Discarding of Morally Degraded Habits

In the words of Rev. Clough, "Christianity brought the sword of change that had cut through the social evils that the Malas and the Madigas had to suffer with."[314] The wave of conversions of the Malas and the Madigas resulted in the abandoning of some of the morally degraded habits such as stealing of cattle and grain, vegetables and tobacco.[315] Instead, the converts demanded for better wages from their *Súdra* masters who were told that so far they had been supplementing their inadequate wages by the stolen supplies from the employer's farm and as converted men, they would not go on in their old ways.[316]

For a clean physical life, the four 'demons' of dirt, disease, debt and drink were to be discarded. Besides, for economic betterment, habits such as drinking, smoking, quarrelling, cheating, gambling were discouraged and alternatively clean and healthy habits were to be promoted through temperance practices and thrift practices. The reports say that these steps had brought change in the converts' material life style also.[317]

The demand for animal skins and meat frequently forced the Madigas to indulge in cattle-theft and cattle poisoning. An unethical practice, *Tuppu Kuli* or 'payment for clues' was prevalent. Cattles were stolen and were driven for long distances to a hiding place for a day or two in the hills or forests. The owner, who was completely ignorant about the whereabouts of his cattles, would approach the nearest go-between individual by offering a reward or *Tuppu Kuli* if the cattle were found.[318] In the districts of Kistna, Guntur and Nellore, this practice was much prevalent. Cattle stealing became very profitable: and so tackling this practice was difficult. Hence, a compromise was reached that the thief would himself fetch the cattle for a price.[319]

The converts had given up such unethical practices. According to the government sources, there was a reduction in cattle theft and cattle poisoning in Nellore and Guntur districts.[320] In 1945, the decrease in cattle theft was reported to be at 7.2%,[321] and in 1949, a further reduction to 3.2% was reported.[322]

6.8.3 Abstaining from Socially Harmful Habits

Christian missionaries played an active role in the promotion of temperance practices among the Mala and the Madiga converts and the prospective converts, by opposing the consumption of liquor and alcohol.[323] Special Committees on Temperance, Mental and Social Hygiene promoted the cause of abstention from such consumption habits.[324] Awareness of physiology and personal hygiene was highlighted not only in connection with alcohol consumption but also with regard to tobacco and opium consumption. In some villages, converts had given up the practice of consuming alcohol and appealed the *Súdras* to get the liquor shops removed from their villages.[325] In some cases, the converts gave up the practice of beef eating also.[326] In the Canadian Baptist Mission's Akidu station, the missionaries expected the converts to become total abstainers. The missionaries had initiated a prohibition movement and cooperation of the *Súdras* was solicited through a petition to close the liquor shops in various villages of the mission field.[327]

Mrs. Ellen M. Kelly of the American Baptist Missionary Union (ABMU) reported that total abstinence was insisted upon the Baptist Church members in Ongole, where in the Christian Temperance League both men and women were admitted as members.[328] Teaching on the subject of temperance in schools was encouraged and the Inspecting officers addressed the teachers on the importance of instilling the habits of temperance on pupils. A curriculum on moral values was drawn up to be followed in the missionary schools. In order to take the message to the pupils, various methods were employed to illustrate the benefits of temperance through pictures and vernacular pamphlets.[329]

6.8.4 Cleanliness of Physical Surroundings

Training in cleanliness and wellness seems to have changed the appearance of the Mala and Madiga hamlets.[330] The hamlets used to be filled with filth and were known for foul odour. Cleanliness as a value was taught by the missionaries to the converts. And the preachers and teachers insisted the converts on its practice in practical life. Continuous Christianization seems to have shown its results, for it was noted by a Tahsildar that the home and its ambience was generally kept clean in the Christian hamlets, unlike in the past. He had attributed this to the efforts of the Christian teachers and the Bible women.[331] This newly cultivated habit was observed in the way things were ordered in everyday life like, using cleaner dress, cleaning of houses and so on. This was also perceived by the ambient society: a high caste Hindu opined thus: "we dare no longer to use foul language. The Christians would not work for us if we did."[332] So also, it was reported that cases of poisoning of cattles, use of abusive language and drunken brawls became uncommon.[333] Exposure of a good number of converts to outside world also effected a change of mindset. The spread of ideas regarding the value of education, hygiene and sanitation practices were also attributed to the native soldiers who had returned from their service in World War I either from Europe or from Mesopotamia.[334] The perceptible change in society was noted by Carol Graham: cleanliness in place of squalor, temperance instead of drunkenness, a concerted effort towards clean-living, honest dealing and truthfulness, above all the discovery of the most precious of human possessions, sell-respect were the outward results of inward spiritual transfiguration.[335]

6.8.5 Change in Social Behaviour

The converts seem to have acquired cultured manners and adopted acceptable behaviour. That this change was noticed by the non-Christian neighbours is clear from the testimony of a rich Hindu landowner at Chattannavaram, who at the time of his death asked his grandchildren never to do anything without consulting Matangi Abraham, a poor Christian whom he had trusted in all his money matters because "he was a Christian.'[336] Christians were considered to be more reliable in the dealing with the cooperative credit societies.[337] Mr. E. A. H. Blunt was quoted in the Census Report of 1911, that the Indian Christians had exercised greater cleanliness in dress and habits. In a generation or two, the converts became better in physical appearance than their predecessors.[338] The exemplary upward social mobility achieved by the convert brethren did influence the non-converts who also desired to better their pathetic condition.[339]

A missionary of the American Baptist Mission opined that the changed life style of the converts apparently facilitated respectful inter-caste interaction and mitigated caste conflicts.[340] The impact of conversion was such that upper castes were also drawn to become Christians, though they initially thought that Christianity was a religion only of the 'low' castes. This was testified by Rev. Pickett, who did a scholarly study on the impact of mass conversions in India during the early part of the 20th century: 'none of these people would have become Christians if they had not first seen what happened to the Malas.[341] About ninety per cent of all higher caste converts attributed their conversion wholly, or in part, to the influence upon them of changes they had observed in the converts from the Depressed Castes.[342]

Further, the presence of a good number of well-educated, trained women commanded respect not only in the Mala and Madiga communities, but also in the ambient caste communities. Such women were considered as a big asset in the hamlets, and were even invited by the caste women to teach them.[343]

Overall, the Mala and the Madiga villages in Coastal Andhra had experienced much social transformation since their conversion. While exceptions exist, social change in a society becomes perceptible when it is reflected in a majority of the members of that society. Contemporary observations were noted in mission records as well as in government records which attribute palpable changes such as frugal spending, simple weddings, practice of temperance, maintenance of cleanliness, rejection of carrion consumption, rejection of cattle thieving, etc., in the convert communities.[344] The Mala and the Madiga converts were motivated by the simple and modest lives of the missionaries, who offered them with the knowledge of Christianity and inspired them to lead a better living style and a higher morality in society.[345]

6.9 Conclusion

Just as there was much socio-economic changes thanks to the upward educational mobility and occupational mobility, there were perceptible changes in the socio-religious and cultural realms, which were not just cosmetic but structural, as if an edifice.

The socio-cultural and religious practices and customs had become permanent markers of a new social space established by the Christian community. The socio-religious changes were also visible, as noted above, in the realm of moral progression and living out of higher moral values, practice of virtues, etc. In conclusion, the apparent culture change among the Mala and the Madiga converts was seen in various aspects of life: in social relations, in cultural expressions and in religious expressions, rituals, festivals and worship. In the opinion of Anthony Copley, converts of depressed caste origin certainly had moved upward on the social scale which furthered a quality social base for the modern Indian society.[346]

Endnotes and References

1 Duncan B. Forrester, *Caste and Christianity: Attitudes and Policies on Caste of Anglo-Saxon Protestant Missions in India* (Richmond, Surrey: Curzon Press, 1980), 75.

2 "Mass Movements and Economic Reconstruction," *The Dornakal Diocesan Magazine* 11 (3), (March 1934), (Dornakal: Diocesan Press, 1934): 17.

3 Eyre Chatterton, *A History of the Church of England in India since the Early Days of the East India Company* (London: SPCK Publishers, 1924).

4 Irfan Habib, "Colonization of the Indian economy 1757-1900," *The Social Scientist* 3 (8), March (1975): 25.

5 Ibid., 35.

6 Athelstane Baines, *Ethnography*: *Castes and Tribes* (Strassburg: Karl J Trubner Publishers, 1912), 9.

7 Hibbert G Ware, *Christian Missions in the Telugu Country* (Westminster: The SPG Publications, 1912), 81.

8 W.G. Polack, *Into All the World: The Story of Lutheran Foreign Missions* (St. Louis, Missouri: Concordia Seminary, 1930), 89.

9 James S. Dennis, *Christian Missions and Social Progress: A Sociological Study of Foreign Missions*, Vol. II (New York: Fleming H. Revell, 1899), 13.

10 James S. Dennis, ibid., Vol. III (New York: Fleming H. Revell, 1906), 97.

11 Eugene Stock, *The Romance of Missions: Beginnings in India* (London: The Society for Promoting Christian Knowledge, 1917), 84.

12 Henry Morris, *A Descriptive and Historical Account of the Godavari District in the Presidency of Madras* (London: Trubner & Co Publishers, 1878), 101.

13 "Mass Movements and Economic Reconstruction," *The Dornakal Diocesan Magazine* XI (3), (March (1934): 16.

14 Srinivasa S. Raghavaiyangar, *Memorandum of the Progress of the Madras Presidency during the Last Forty Years of British Administration* (Madras: The Government Press, 1893), 94.

15 "Description of the Madras Riot by Mr. Bourdillon in 1853," in Raghavaiyangar, Ibid., xxiii.

16 Raghavaiyangar, ibid., 45.

17 Henry Morris, op. cit., 101.

18 A. Andrew, *Indian Problems Concerned with Education, Agriculture and Land Reven*ue (Madras: G. A. Natesan and Co, 1905), 25.

19 M. L. Orchard, *Canadian Baptists at Work in India* (Toronto: The Missionary Education Department of the Foreign Mission Board, 1922), 88.

20 Ibid., 26.

21 Ibid., 38.

22 A. Mathew, *Christian Missions, Education and Nationalism: From Dominance to Compromise, 1870-1930* (New Delhi: Anamika Prakasan, 1989), 197.

23 D. Ananada Rao, *Results of Demonstrations of Agricultural Improvements in the Madras Circle carried out in 1924-1927* (Madras: The Government Press, 1929), 2.

24 *Operations of the Department of Agriculture in the Madras Presidency for the year 1918-1919* (Madras: The Government Press, 1919), 3.

25 M. L. Orchard, op. cit., 117.

26 Ibid., 121.

27 *Report on the Administration of the Madras Presidency during the Year 1930-31* (Madras: The Government Press, 1932), 64. Also M. L. Orchard and K. S. McLaurin, *The Enterprise: The Jubilee Story of the Canadian Baptist Mission in India: 1874-1924* (Toronto: The Canadian Baptist Foreign Mission Board, 1925), 318.

28 Eyre Chatterton, op. cit.

29 *Minutes of the Council of the India Mission of the United Lutheran Church in America*, St. Mathews Church (Guntur: April 21-29 1927), 19.

30 *Executive Committee Meetings of the American Evangelical Lutheran Church: Joint Finance Committee Bulleti*n, No 30 (Rajahmundry: January 20, 1936), 5.

31 A. Andrew, op. cit., 38.

32 "Minutes of the Third Convention," in *The Andhra Evangelical Lutheran Church* (Guntur: September 19-26 1929), 14.

33 W. Francis, *The Census of India, 1901, Vol. XV, Part I, Report and Part II, Imperial Tables (*Madras: The Government Press, 1902), 206. Also in *Part II, Imperial Tables.*

34 James Millard Baker, *Contending the Grade in Indi*a (Ashville: The Biltmore Press, 1947), 134.

35 Ibid., 133.

36 M. L. Orchard and K.S. McLaurin, op. cit., 2.

37 William Digby, *Prosperous British India: A Revelation from Official Records* (London: T. Fisher Unwin Publishers, 1901), 144.

38 Sir Arthur Cotton, *The Madras Famine with Appendix Containing a Letter from Ms. Florence Nightingale and Other Papers* (London: Marshall Simpkin & Co Stationers, Undated), 10.

39 Julius Jefferys, *The British Army in India: Its Preservation* (London: Longman & Roberts Publishers, 1858), 269.

40 Henry Morris, op. cit., 293.

41 Baden B. H Powell, *The Land Systems of British India: Being a Manual of the Land Tenures and of the systems of Land Revenue Administration prevalent in the several Provinces*, Vol. I (Oxford: Clarendon Press, 1892), 384.

42 *Manual of the Administration of the Madras Presidency, an Illustration of the Records of Government and the Yearly Administration Reports* (Madras: The Government Press, 1885), 80.

43 Sir Arthur Cotton, op. cit., 87.

44 George Drach and Calvin F. Kuder, *Telugu Mission of the General Council of the Evangelical Lutheran Church in North America Containing a Biography of the Rev. Christian Frederick Heyer* (hereafter, *Telugu Mission General Council*) (Philadelphia: General Council Publication House, 1914), 96.

45 *Report on the Administration of the Madras Presidency during the Year 1867-68* (Madras: Fort St. George Gazette Press, 1868), 190-194.

46 Ada C. Chaplin, *Our Gold Mine: The Story of American Baptist Missions in India* (Boston: W. G. Corthell, 1889), 408.

47 John E. Clough, *Social Christianity in the Orient: the Story of a Man, a Mission and a Movement* (New York: The Macmillan Company Publishers, 1914), 23.

48 Emma Rauschenbusch Clough, *While Sewing Sandals Or Tales of a Telugu Pariah Tribe* (London: The Selwood Printing Works, 1899), 274.

49 John E Clough, op. cit., 247.

50 Ibid., 302.

51 "Report of the Madras Conference: 1902," in Harlan P. Beach, *India and Christian Opportunity* (New York: Student Volunteer Movement for Foreign Missions, 1908), 146.

52 *Minutes of the Executive Committee: Council of the India Mission of the United Lutheran Church in America*, October 24-31 (Guntur: 1923), 8.

53 *Directory of Christian Missions in India, Burma and Ceylon,* November, 1924, 14th Edition (Ajmer: The Scottish Mission Press, 1924), 260.

54 *The Nellore Station and Field of the American Baptist Telugu Mission, South India* (Nellore: The American Baptist Telugu Mission, 1922), 57.

55 James Millard Baker, *Contending the Grade in India* (Ashville: The Biltmore Press, 1947), 135.

56 "Report of the Madras Conference: 1902," in Harlan P. Beach, *India and Christian Opportunity* (New York: Student Volunteer Movement for Foreign Missions, 1908), 147.

57 M. P. Gandhi, *The Indian Cotton Textile Industry, Its Past, Present and Future* (Calcutta: G.N. Mitra Publishers, 1928), 43.

58 Raghavaiyangar, op. cit., 129.

59 M. P Gandhi, op. cit., 52.

60 Hibbert G. Ware, *Christian Missions in the Telugu Country* (Westminster: The SPG Publications, 1912), 33.

61 Romesh Dutt, *The Economic History of India Under Early British Rule*, Sixth Edition, Kegan Paul (London: Trench and Trubner Publishers, 1901), 217.

62 W. Francis, *Census of India, 1901, Vol. XV-A, Part II, Imperial Tables* (Madras: The Government Press, 1901), 251.

63 Ibid., 252.

64 *Directory of Christian Missions in India, Burma and Ceylon*, November, 1924, 14th Edition (Ajmer: The Scottish Mission Press, 1924), 259-260.

65 Ibid.

66 Hibbert G. Ware, op. cit., 82.

67 F. M. Noble, "The Economic Situation and Self-Support," in *The National Christian Council of India Proceedings* (Mysore: Wesley Press, 1930), 257.

68 "Co-Education at Dornakal," *The Dornakal Diocesan Magazine* 5 (10), (October (1928), (Dornakal: Diocesan Press, 1928): 14.

69 Augusta Highland, *India* (Rock Island, IL: Board of Foreign Missions, Lutheran Augustana Synod Centennial Committee, 1945), 19.

70 "Minutes of the Executive Committee," in *The Council of the India Mission of the United Lutheran Church in America* (Guntur: 1930), 15.

71 Ibid., 256.

72 Ms. D. Tickell "Poverty among Village Christians," in *The National Christian Council Review*, Vol. XIII (Mysore: Wesley Press, 1935), 624.

73 *Report on the Administration of the Madras Presidency during the Year 1939-40* (Madras: The Government Press, 1940), 147.

74 Chartres J. Molony, *Census of India, 1911, Part II, Imperial and Provincial Tables* (Madras: The Government Press, 1913), 219.

75 Emma Rauschenbusch Clough, op. cit., 40.

76 John E. Clough, op. cit., 388.

77 W. Francis, *Census of India, 1901, Vol. XV-A, Part II, Imperial Tables* (Madras: The Government Press, 1902), 252.

78 A. T. Fishman, *For This Purpose: A Case Study of the Telugu Baptist Church in Its Relation with South India Mission of the American Baptist Foreign Mission Societies in India* (hereafter, *For This Purpose*) (Madras: Diocesan Press, 1958), 50.

79 Ibid., 51.

80 Ibid., 64.

81 "The Bishop's Letter," in *The Dornakal Diocesan Magazine* (11), (Nov 1928), (Dornakal: Diocesan Press, November 1928): 3.

82 "Vidya Nagar, 1935," in *The Dornakal Diocese Magazin*e XIII (7), (July 1936), (Dornakal: Diocesan Press, 1936): 12.

83 W. S. Hunt, *India's Outcastes A New Era* (London: The CMS Publications, 1924), 67.

84 "Mass Movements and Economic Reconstruction," in *The Dornakal Diocesan Magazin*e 11 (3) (March 1934), (Dornakal: Diocesan Press, 1934): 17.

85 A.T. Fishman, *For This Purpose*, op. cit., 64.

86 Initially, Rev. Heyer had employed four native teachers, all heathen, but apparently, they used their employment in Mission schools as stepping-stone for some civil service in the government: George Drach and Calvin F. Kuder, *Telugu Mission General Council*, op. cit., 54.

87 Ibid., 77.

88 Ibid., 80.

89 L. B. Wolf, *After Fifty Years or An Historical Sketch of the Guntur Mission of the Evangelical Lutheran Church of the General Synod in the United States of America* (hereafter, *After Fifty Years*) (Philadelphia: The Lutheran Publication Society, 1896), 169.

90 Ibid., 169.

91 Ibid., 170.

92 M. A. Sherring, *The History of Protestant Missions in India from their Commencement in 1706 to 1881* (London: The Religious Tract Society, 1884), 415.

93 Julia M Harpster, *Among the Telugoos: Illustrating Mission Work in India* (Philadelphia: Lutheran Publication Society, 1902), 99.

94 Hibbert G Ware, op. cit., 114.

95 Eugene Stock, *The History of the Church Missionary Society: Its Environment, Its Men and Its Work* (hereafter, *History of CMS*) Vol. III (London: The CMS Publications, 1899), 175.

96 Eugene Stock, ibid., Vol. IV (London: The CMS Publications, 1916), 244.

97 *Minutes of the AELC Executive Committee*, Item No. 11, April (Guntur: 1925), 2.

98 Ibid., 7.

99 John E Clough, op. cit., 335.

100 A. T. Fishman, *For This Purpose,* op. cit., 61.

101 *Minutes of the AELC Executive Committee*, October (Guntur: 1928), 4.

102 *Minutes of the Council of the Indian Mission, The United Lutheran Church in America,* October (Guntur: The United Lutheran Church, 1935), 11.

103 *Minutes of the Council of the Indian Mission, The United Lutheran Church in Americ*a, January (Guntur: The United Lutheran Church, 1925), 13.

104 J. Mangamma, *Andhra Desamulo Kraisthava Missioanrila Seva* (Hyderabad: Telugu Academy Publishers, 1992), 76.

105 Julia M Harpster, op. cit., 36.

106 George Drach and Calvin F Kuder, *Telugu Mission General Council,* op. cit., 211.

107 James Millard Baker, *Contending the Grade in India* (Ashville: The Biltmore Press, 1947), 73.

108 L. B. Wolf, *After Fifty Years,* op. cit., 259.

109 Ibid., 250.

110 Augusta Highland, op. cit., 31.

111 *The American Lutheran Mission's Report of the Hill Conferences on the Knubel-Miller Conference*, February 27- 28 (Guntur: 1928), 8.

112 Augusta Highland, op. cit., 19.

113 Ibid., 24.

114 George Drach and Calvin F. Kuder, *Telugu Mission General Council,* op. cit., 24.

115 John E. Clough, op. cit., 388.

116 David Downie, *The Lone Star: The History of the Telugu Mission of the American Baptist Missionaries Union (1838-1927)* (Philadelphia: The American Baptist Publication, 1892), 208.

117 *The Church Missionary Intelligencer of Missionary Information: A Monthly Journal of Missionary Information*, Vol. VIII (London: The CMS Publications, 1872), 201.

118 George Drach and Calvin F Kuder, *Telugu Mission General Council*, op. cit., 266.

119 Ibid.

120 Ibid., 77.

121 Julia M. Harpster, op. cit., 22.

122 Augusta Highland, op. cit., 24.

123 Julia M Harpster, op. cit., 60.

124 John E Clough, op. cit., 335.

125 Ibid., 356.

126 L. B. Wolf, *After Fifty Years,* 304.

127 Ibid., 259.

128 *Minutes of the American Lutheran Evangelical Church in Indi*a, October (Guntur: 1923), 8.

129 Julius Jefferys, *The British Army in India: Its Preservation* (London: Longman & Roberts Publishers, 1858), 384.

130 The military services of an Māla, V. Francis of Kondapalli, Kistna district as told to his family.

131 Barbara R Joshi, *Democracy in Search of Equality: Untouchable Politics and Indian Social Change* (Delhi: Hindustan Publishing Corporation, 1982) 35.

132 James S. Dennis, Vol. III, op. cit., 345.

133 Raghavaiyangar, op. cit., 85.

134 Ibid., 156.

135 Stephen P Cohen, "The Untouchable Soldier: Caste, Politics, and the Indian Army" in *The Journal of Asian Studies* 28(3), (May 1969): 467.

136 F. G. Bailey, *Caste and the Economic Frontier: A Village in Highland Orissa* (Manchester: Manchester University Press, 1957), 6.

137 John E Clough, op. cit., 144.

138 *Report on the Administration of the Madras Presidency During the Year 1890-91* (Madras: The Government Press, 1891), 109.

139 Romesh Dutt, op. cit., 311.

140 W. Francis, *Census of India*, 1901, Vol. XV-A, Part II (Madras: The Government Press, 1902), 257.

141 Arnold Wright (ed.), *Southern India: Its History, People, Commerce, and Industrial Res*ources (New Delhi: Asian Educational Services, 1914), 536.

142 David Downie, op. cit., 174.

143 Ibid.

144 J. W. Pickett, *Christian Mass Movements in India* (Lucknow: The Lucknow Publishing House, 1933), 129.

145 Herbert Waldo Hines, *Clough: The Kingdom Builder in South India* (Philadelphia: The Freedom Press, 1929), 164.

146 Ibid., 283.

147 Ibid., 289.

148 Ibid., 284.

149 Ibid., 283.

150 M. L. Orchard, op. cit., 127.

151 *The American Lutheran Mission's Report of the Hill Conferences on the Knubel-Miller Conference*, February 27- 28 (Guntur: 1928), 4.

152 David Downie, op. cit., 74.

153 M. L. Orchard, op. cit., 170.

154 *World Missionary Conference, Report of Commission 1: Carrying the Gospel to all the Non-Christian World* (Edinburgh: Oliphant Anderson and Ferrier, 1910), 160.

155 *Report of the Indian Industrial Commission Mission 1916-18* (Calcutta: The Government Press, 1918), 97.

156 James S. Dennis, Vol. III, op. cit., 98.

157 *Report on the Administration of the Madras Presidency during the Year 1930-31* (Madras: The Government Press, 1932), 109.

158 *Standing Committee Meetings of the Andhra Evangelical Lutheran Church*, No 20, October (1931), 21.

159 *Report on the Administration of the Madras Presidency during the Year 1921-22* (Madras: The Government Press, 1923), 188.

160 Ibid., 216.

161 W. Francis, *Census of India, 1901, Vol. XV-A, Part II, Imperial Tables* (Madras: The Government Press, 1902), 255.

162 "AELM Routine Minutes", in *The General Work Budget of 1930-31*, Appendix A (Guntur: 1931), 4.

163 "Lord Crowe, Secretary of State for India, Revenue Dispatch, No. 24, 12 March 1912" in *The Report of the Indian Industrial Commission Mission 1916-18* (Calcutta: The Government Press, 1918), 71.

164 *The Report the American Baptist Foreign Missionary Society* (Boston: Foreign Mission Rooms, 1917), 109.

165 *The American Lutheran Mission's Report of the Hill Conferences on the Knubel-Miller Conference* (Guntur: February 27- 28, 1928), 6.

166 James S. Dennis, Vol. III, op. cit., 393.

167 Martin L Dolbeer, *A History of Lutheranism in Andhra Desa: The Telugu Territory of India, Board of Foreign Missions* (New York: United Lutheran Church in America, 1959), 334.

168 James Millard Baker, *Contending the Grade in India* (Ashville: The Biltmore Press, 1947), 81.

169 Chartres J Molony, *Census of India, Madras, 1911, Vol. I, Part I, Report* (Madras: The Government Press, 1913), 211.

170 Drach and Kuder, *Telugu Mission General Council*, op. cit., 311.

171 John Craig, *Forty Years among the Telugus: A History of the Mission of the Baptists of Ontario and Quebec, Canada to the Telugus, South India 1867-1907* (Toronto: The Canadian Baptist Foreign Mission Board, 1908), 262.

172 M. L. Orchard, op. cit., 125.

173 M. L. Orchard and K. S. McLaurin, op. cit., 61.

174 "Co-Education at Dornakal" in *The Dornakal Diocesan Magazine* 5(10), (Dornakal: Diocesan Press, October 1928), 15.

175 M. L. Orchard and K. S. McLaurin, op. cit., 320.

176 George Drach and Calvin F. Kuder, *Telugu Mission General Council*, op. cit., 196.

177 Ibid., 175.

178 Ibid., 176.

179 M. L. Orchard and K. S. McLaurin, op. cit., 321.

180 Ibid.

181 *Minutes of the Council of the Council of the India Mission of the United Lutheran Church in America* (Guntur: October 6-20 1927), 14.

182 Eyre Chatterton, op. cit.

183 W. Francis, *Census of India, 1901, Vol. XV-A, Part II, Imperial Tables* (Madras: The Government Press, 1901), 253.

184 George Drach and Calvin F Kuder, *Telugu Mission General Council*, op. cit., 357.

185 S. F. Smith, *Missionary Sketches: A Concise History of the Work of the American Baptist Missionary Union* (Boston: W. G. Corthell Publishers, 1883), 210.

186 *Directory of Christian Missions in India, Burma and Ceylon*, November 1924, 14th Edition (Ajmer: The Scottish Mission Press, 1924), 233.

187 James S. Dennis, Vol. III, op. cit., 466.

188 M. L. Orchard, op. cit., 125.

189 Alice B Van Doren, "Christian Mass Movements in India: A Review" in *The National Christian Council Review* (Mysore: Wesley Press, 1933), 139.

190 M. L. Orchard, op. cit., 121-122.

191 George Drach and Calvin F Kuder, *Telugu Mission General Council*, op. cit., 63.

192 Ibid., 100.

193 Ibid., 268.

194 C. H. Swavely (ed.), *One Hundred Years in the Andhra Country: A history of the India Mission of the United Lutheran Church in America, 1842-1942* (Madras: Diocesan Press, 1942), 269.

195 *Minutes of the AELC Executive Committee*, Item 19 (Guntur: October 1925), 41.

196 Ibid., 268.

197 George Drach and Calvin F Kuder, *Telugu Mission General Council*, op. cit., 43.

198 *Report on Public Instruction in the Madras Presidency for the year 1911-12 and for the Quinquenium 1906-07 to 1911-12*, Vol. I, Parts I and II (Madras The Government Press, 1938), 46.

199 George Drach and Calvin F Kuder, *Telugu Mission General Council*, op. cit., 284.

200 Ibid., 360.

201 "General Work Committee Meetings", in *The General Work Meetings of the AELC* (Guntur: 1935), 8.

202 Ibid., 92.

203 M. L. Orchard, op. cit., 121-122.

204 Ibid., 124.

205 "Minutes of the Third Convention of the Andhra Evangelical Lutheran Church" (Guntur: September 19-26, 1929), 14.

206 M. L. Orchard, and K. S. McLaurin, op. cit., 286.

207 John Noble, *A Memoir of the Rev. Robert Turlington Noble: Missionaries to the Telugu People in South India* (London: Seeley Jackson and Halliday Publishers, 1867), 258.

208 Ibid., 268.

209 James S. Dennis, Vol. III, op. cit., 108.

210 Irene H. Barnes, *Behind the Purdah: The Story of C.E.Z.M.S Work in India* (New York: Thomas Y Crowell Company, 1897), 174.

211 "Co-Education at Dornakal" in *The Dornakal Diocesan Magazine* 5 (10), (Dornakal: Diocesan Press, October 1928), 13.

212 Eyre Chatterton, op. cit.

213 F. M. Noble, op. cit., 257.

214 "Minutes of the Executive Committee" in *The Council of the India Mission of the United Lutheran Church in America* (Guntur: 1930), 15.

215 J. W. Pickett, op. cit., 133.

216 F. M. Noble, op. cit., 262-265.

217 M. L. Orchard and K. S. McLaurin, op. cit., 323.

218 "Minutes of the Third Convention" in *The Andhra Evangelical Lutheran Church*, September 19-26 (Guntur: 1929), 14.

219 Harlan P Beach, *India and Christian Opportunity* (New York: Student Volunteer Movement for Foreign Missions, 1908).

220 Ibid., 229.

221 Dattatreya Diskalkar, *Contribution of Agricultural Education to Economic Development of India, Department of Economics and Sociology* (Kansas: Kansas State University, 1963), 26.

222 Frederick A Nicholson, "Report regarding the possibility of introducing Land and Agricultural Banks in the Madras Presidency: 1895," in *The Economic Transition of India*, ed. Theodore Morison (London: John Murray Publishers, 1911), 84.

223 A. T. Fishman, *For This Purpose,* op. cit., 65.

224 Sometimes in association with the Y.M.C.A: see M. L. Orchard, op. cit., 120.

225 F. M. Noble, op. cit., 257.

226 George Jay Lapp, *The Christian Church and Rural India*, (Calcutta: The YMCA Publishing House, 1938), 11.

227 Dattatreya Diskalkar, op. cit, 26.

228 "Minutes of the Executive Committee" in *The Council of the India Mission of the United Lutheran Church in America* (Guntur: January 1935), 20.

229 *Proceedings of the Ninth Meeting of the National Christian Council* (Mysore: Diocesan Press, 1944), 65.

230 M. L. Orchard, op. cit., 120.

231 A. T. Fishman, *For This Purpose,* op. cit., 65.

232 *Directory of Christian Missions in India, Burma and Ceylon*, November, 1924, 14th Edition (Ajmer: The Scottish Mission Press, 1924), 236.

233 A. T. Fishman, *For This Purpose,* op. cit., 64.

234 "Mass Movements and Economic Reconstruction" in *The Dornakal Diocesan Magazine* 11(3), (March 1934), (Dornakal: Diocesan Press, 1934), 19.

235 M. L. Orchard, op. cit., 125.

236 A. T. Fishman, *For This Purpose,* op. cit., 64.

237 Raghavaiyangar, op. cit., 85.

238 V. Ramakrishna, *Social Reform in Andhra, 1848-99*, (Delhi: Vikas Publishing House, 1983), 213.

239 "Mass Movements and Economic Reconstruction" in *The Dornakal Diocesan Magazine*, 11(3), (March 1934), (Dornakal: Diocesan Press, 1934), 117.

240 George F McLean, "Culture and Religion" in *Culture Evangelization and Dialogue,* ed. George F. McLean, et al, (Washington: The Council for Research in Values and Philosophy, 2003), 21-22.

241 Thomas H Groome, *Christian Religious Education* (San Francisco: Harper & Row Publishers, 1980), 110.

242 Bronislav Malinowski, *The Dynamics of Culture Change: An Inquiry into Race Relations in Africa* (New Haven: The Yale University Press, 1945), 1.

243 Duncan G. Zaltman and J. Holbeck, "Innovations and Organizations" in *Social Change and Social Research: An Indian Perspective,* ed. R. S. Mann (New Delhi: Concept Publishing Company, 1988), Op cit, 61.

244 Clyde Woods, "Culture Change" in *Social Change and Social Research: An Indian Perspective*, ed. R. S. Mann (New Delhi: Concept Publishing Company, 1988), 60.

245 Norman S Buchanan and Ellis S Howard, *Approaches to Economic Development* (New York: The Twentieth Century Fund, 1955), 87.

246 Thomas H Groome, op. cit., 115.

247 William Fielding Ogburn, *Social Change with Respect to Culture and Original Nature* (New York: B. W. Huebsch Publishers, 1923), 269.

248 George F McLean, "Culture and Religion" in ed. George F. McLean et al, *Culture Evangelization and Dialogue* (Washington: The Council for Research in Values and Philosophy, 2003), Op cit, 18.

249 *The Dornakal Diocese Magazine* (Dornakal: Diocesan Press, October 1928), 3-4.

250 Archibald G. Baker, *Christian Missions and a New World Culture* (Chicago: Willett Clark and Co Publishers, 1934), 192.

251 Hibbert G Ware, *Christian Missions in the Telugu Country* (Westminster: The SPG Publications, 1912) (Westminster: The SPG Publications, 1912), 188.

252 A. T. Fishman, *For This Purpose,* op. cit., 83.

253 Julia M Harpster, op. cit., *Among the Telugoos: Illustrating Mission Work in India* (Philadelphia: Lutheran Publication Society, 1902), 76.

254 John E Clough, op. cit., 169.

255 Herbert Waldo Hines, *Clough: The Kingdom Builder in South India* (Philadelphia: The Freedom Press, 1929), 90-91.

256 V. S. Azariah and Henry Whitehead, *Christ in the Indian Villages* (London: Student Christian Movement Press, 1930), 32.

257 *The Dornakal Diocesan Magazine* 7 (9), (September 1930), (Dornakal: Diocesan Press, 1930), 9.

258 Emma Rauschenbusch Clough, op. cit., 308.

259 David Downie, op. cit., 136.

260 Hibbert G Ware, op cit, 93.

261 A. T. Fishman, *For This Purpose* , op. cit., 185.

262 Jacob Chamberlain, *In the Tiger Jungle and other Stories of Missionary Work among the Telugus of India* (New York: Fleming H. Revell, 1896), 129.

263 John E Clough, op. cit., 147.

264 Ibid, 183.

265 Richard Lovett, *The History of the London Missionary Society, 1795-1895*, Vol. II (Oxford: Oxford University Press, 1899), 7.

266 John Craig, op cit, 143.

267 M. L. Orchard, and K. S. McLaurin, op. cit., 299.

268 John Craig, op cit, 142.

269 B. V. Subbamma, *Christ Confronts India: Indigenous Expression of Christianity in India* (Madras: Diocesan Press, 1973), 276.

270 *The Dornakal Diocesan Magazine*, October 1928, op cit, 3.

271 Eugene Stock, Vol. II, op. cit., 420.

272 *The Dornakal Diocesan Magazine*, October 1928, op cit, 3.

273 Ibid, 6.

274 Hibbert G Ware, op cit, 208.

275 Herbert Waldo Hines, *Clough: Kingdom Builder in South India,* op. cit., 92.

276 Emma Rauschenbusch Clough, op. cit., 147.

277 Ibid, 177.

278 P. Y. Luke and John B Carman, *Village Christians and Hindu Culture: Study of Rural Church in Andhra Pradesh, South India* (New Delhi: ISPCK Publishers, 1969), 190.

279 David G. Mandelbaum, *Society in India: Change and Continuity*, Vol. 2 (Berkeley: University of California Press, 1970), 445.

280 John Craig, et al, *Telugu Trophies*, op. cit., 8.

281 John Craig, op. cit., 270.

282 P. Y. Luke and John B Carman, op. cit., 191.

283 Hibbert G Ware, op. cit., 210.

284 L. B. Wolf, *After Fifty Years,* op. cit., 312.

285 Carol Graham, *Azariah of Dornakal* (London: S.C.M. Press Ltd, 1946), 59.

286 A. T. Fishman, *For This Purpose,* op. cit., 80.

287 Eugene Stock, Vol. III, op. cit., 471.

288 M. L. Orchard and K. S. McLaurin, op. cit., 279.

289 John Craig, op. cit., 114.

290 *The Indian Christian Marriage Act, 1872.* http: //ncw.nic.in/acts/ The Indian Christian Marriage Act 1872-15 of 1872. pdf, 25: accessed on 05 March 2011

291 Ibid, 25.

292 L. B. Wolf, op. cit., 313.

293 http: //ncw.nic.in/acts/ The Indian Christian Marriage Act 1872-15 of 1872. pdf.: accessed, on 05 March 2011.

294 A. T. Fishman, *For This Purpose,* op. cit., 83.

295 P. Y. Luke and John B Carman, op. cit., 193.

296 A.T. Fishman, *Culture Change and the Underprivileged: A Study of the Madigas in South India under Christian Guidance* (Madras: The Christian Literature Society for India, 1941) 176.

297 H. A. Stuart, *Census of India*, 1891, Vol. XIII (Madras: The Government Press, 1893), 310.

298 Lionel Caplan, *Class and Culture in Urban India* (Oxford: Clarendon Press, 1987), 156.

299 Andrew Wingate, *The Church and Conversion* (Delhi: ISPCK, 1997), 84.

300 Ibid, 251.

301 B. V. Subbamma, op. cit., 28.

302 David Mosse, *Caste, Christianity and Hinduism: A Study of Social Organization and Religion in Rural Ramand*, D. Phil Thesis (Oxford: University of Oxford, 1986), 89 and 100.

303 Heike Liebau, "Indianisation and Education: Reaction from Protestant Christians of the Madras Presidency to the Lindsay Commission Report," in *Education and Social Change in South Asia,* eds.. Krishna Kumar and Joachim Oesterheld (Hyderabad: Orient Longman, 2007), 46.

304 The *tali,* which is usually about the size of a dime sixpence, is worn round the woman's neck.

305 Susan Billington Harper, *In the Shadow of the Mahatma: Bishop V. S. Azariah and the Travails of Christianity in British India* (Richmond, Surrey: Curzon Press, 2000), 196.

306 Susan Billington Harper, "The Dornakal Church on the Cultural Frontier," in *Christians, Cultural Interactions and India's Religious Traditions,* eds., Brown, Judith M. and Robert Eric Freykenberg (Grand Rapids, Michigan: W.B. Eerdmans Publishing Company, 2002), 196.

307 *The Dornakal Diocese Magazine* V (10), (Dornakal: Diocesan Press, October 1928), 3.

308 A. T. Fishman, *For This Purpose,* op. cit., 80.

309 John E Clough, op cit, 165.

310 Emma Rauschenbusch Clough, op. cit., 151.

311 Edgar Thurston, *Castes and Tribes of Southern India*, Vol. IV, K-M (Madras: The Government Press, 1909), 308-309.

312 John E Clough, op. cit., 166.

313 A. T. Fishman, *For This Purpose,* op. cit., 80.

314 John E Clough, op. cit., 166.

315 V. S. Azariah and Henry Whitehead, op. cit., 38.

316 Ibid, 42.

317 Samuel Jaya Kumar, *Dalit Consciousness and Christian Conversion: The Work of SPG Missionaries, Historical Resources for a Contemporary Debate, Mission Theology in an Asian Context* (Delhi: The ISPCK Publishers, 1999), 256.

318 Edgar Thurston, op. cit., 67.

319 *Report on the Administration of the Police of the Madras Province 1905* (Madras: The Government Press, 1906), 9.

320 *Report on the Administration of the Police of the Madras Province 1910* (Madras: The Government Press, 1911), 20.

321 *Report on the Administration of the Police of the Madras Province 1945* (Madras: The Government Press, 1947).

322 *Report on the Administration of the Police of the Madras Presidency 1949* (Madras: The Government Press, 1949), 11.

323 James S. Dennis, Vol. II, op. cit., 458.

324 *Proceedings of the Eighth Meeting of the National Christian Council* (Nagpur: Central India Printing Works, 1940), 79.

325 "Extracts from the Minutes of Fourth Session of the Dornakal Diocesan Council held in Bezwada on December 1927," *The Dornakal Diocesan Magazine* 3, March 1928, (Dornakal: Diocesan Press, 1928), 4.

326 *The Dornakal Diocesan Magazine* IX (9), (Dornakal: Diocesan Press, September 1930), 9.

327 Ibid, 119.

328 James S. Dennis, Vol. II, op cit, 120.

329 *Administration Report of the Abkari Revenue for the year 1915-16* (Madras: The Government Press, 1917), 4.

330 "Mass Movements and Economic Reconstruction," in *The Dornakal Diocesan Magazine* XI (3), March (Dornakal: Diocesan Press, 1934), 19.

331 John Craig, op. cit., 115.

332 *The Dornakal Diocesan Magazine* 4(5), (Dornakal: Diocesan Press, 1928), 4.

333 Ibid, 6.

334 A. T. Fishman, *Culture Change and the Underprivileged,* op. cit., 173.

335 Carol Graham, op. cit., 56.

336 *The Dornakal Diocesan Magazine* (Dornakal: Diocesan Press, May 1928), op. cit., 8.

337 *The Dornakal Diocesan Magazine* (Dornakal: Diocesan Press, March 1934), op. cit., 18.

338 *The Dornakal Diocesan Magazine* 5(10), (October 1928), (Dornakal: Diocesan Press, 1928), 4.

339 Sherwood Eddy, *India Awakening* (New York: Missionary Education Movement, 1911), 100.

340 *The Dornakal Diocesan Magazine* (Dornakal: Diocesan Press, October 1928), op. cit., 6.

341 J. W. Pickett, op. cit., 52-53.

342 Ibid, 60.

343 *The Church Missionary Society Gazette* (London: The CMS Publications, 1919), 6.

344 Emma Rauschenbusch Clough, op. cit., 292.

345 M. L. Orchard and K. S McLaurin, op. cit., 101.

346 Anthony Copley, *Religion in Conflict: Ideology, Cultural Contact and Conversion in Late Colonial India* (New York: The Oxford University Press, 1997), 56.

Chapter 7

Conclusion and Epilogue

We have reviewed the conversion and social change among the Depressed Castes of Andhra Pradesh, especially the Malas and Madigas, during the period 1850-1950. Though there were many socio-religious reform movements which envisaged bringing about equality in society during the ancient and medieval periods, it was during the modern period, especially during the colonial period, reform became actualized in the life of the Depressed Castes. This was mainly because they were able to have access to and participate in the socio-economic and educational resources which were made available to them thanks to the mediation of the missionaries who played a key role.

The missionaries came to evangelise and conversion was the response of the people. Both Protestant and Catholic missionaries had well-networked systems of evangelization which essentially included humanitarian, liberative and empowerment programmes. Though the services of the missionaries were available to all, it was the most marginalized sections of society which largely responded to their evangelization through conversion, accepting their religion. A large segment of the Malas and Madigas seem to have made conscious decisions to break away from the fetters of the contemporary religiously-sanctioned caste system under Hinduism, and converted to Christianity.

Based on large amounts of statistical and historical data including Census data, we examined the mechanisms and dynamics of conversion and the post-conversion religious, social, economic, educational and occupational changes among the Malas and Madigas. It was noted that besides education, employment channels, training in skills and health care, besides philanthropic activities resulted in the overall socio-economic upliftment of the Malas and the Madigas.

We also attempted to understand the ethnographic, social, religious, cultural, economic and educational status of the Malas and Madigas in pre-conversion period. The roles of the missionaries, their organizations, strategies and services pastoral engagement, etc., were examined using a large amount of mission sources.

This concluding chapter has two parts: Section I will give an overview of the findings of this research on conversion and the apparent social change of the Depressed Classes; Section II is an epilogue on the predicament of the converts in the post-Independence period, that is, from 1950s.

I

7.1 Christian Mission, Conversion and Change

7.1.1 Mission Agencies

There were Catholic and Protestant missionary organizations which worked among the Depressed Classes. However, the present research focused only on six Protestant missionary societies namely, 1) the London Missionary Society (Vizagapatam), 2) the Canadian Baptist Mission (Cocanada), 3) the Godavari Delta Mission (Dowlaishvaram and Narsapur), 4) the Church Missionary Society (Masulipatnam and North Kistna), 5) the American Evangelical Lutheran Mission (Guntur and South Kistna) and 6) the American Baptist Mission (Nellore and Ongole). Each mission society had different territory as its operating area, within the Colonial Coastal Andhra, the geographical territory of this study.

The missionary work in Andhra was informed by evangelistic vision of a new society based on Christian values, which was shared by all the above-mentioned missionary societies, though there might have been variations in their approach, perception of the ground realities and methods. Overall, all of them engaged in preaching, teaching of the Bible, and making Christian communities. The package of mission work consisted of not only building churches and chapels for worship, but also opening educational institutions, hostels, training institutes, and medical centres.

The Christian missionaries also tried to fulfill their social obligations with humanitarian works. They understood that it was their duty to feed the hungry, give drink to the thirsty, visit the sick and so on, as the Bible teaches. There was no other way to serve humanity.[1] The missionaries used humanitarian works as part of evangelical works.[2] Within the primary aim of preaching the Gospel, the missionaries translated into action practical Christianity through their services. Thus, in the perception of the people, they came to be identified with the type of service they engaged in: evangelistic missionaries, educational missionaries, medical missionaries, itinerant missionaries, industrial missionaries, zenana missionaries, and so on.[3]

Mission records are replete with narratives on the remarkable personal qualities of some of the missionaries. Their character was marked by self-denial, selfless devotion to duty, unquestioning fidelity for the establishment of the mission, and deep love for their flock (people).[4]

The missionary occupied an important place in the lives of the people. Both Christians and Hindu caste people alike felt that they had someone with them far above the ordinary.[5] During times of natural calamities the missionaries became a ray of hope not only for the Depressed Castes but also for the caste people who trusted the missionaries with their valuables.[6] During their missionary work they had had to suffer often personal losses, diseases and face unsuitable weather conditions.[7]

Along with the foreign missionaries there was a large body of native preachers and leaders whose combined work augmented group conversions in Colonial Andhra. The pioneers of group conversions had maintained strong faith and led the movement in a steadfast way.

7.1.2 Missionaries and Caste

In the beginning, the missionaries had earnestly attempted to convert caste Hindus for two reasons: to bring the prosperous caste people into the Christian faith and to elicit their support in mission work. At the same time, they were convinced that they would work among the poor, who were generally of 'low' castes. Indeed, they experienced that few among the caste Hindus converted, whereas a large majority of the poor castes, particularly the Malas and the Madigas welcomed the message of redemption and liberation.[8] They also realized that caste, more than religious faith and traditions, hindered the higher castes to convert, because caste is a perennial socio-religious structure with its tenacious hold over the everyday life of the people and continues to define the social and ritual status of a person even today. History has shown that caste distinction and discrimination continues to remain even when people changed religion. Though the missionaries did not accept caste-based status ascriptions, the converts, hailing from different castes as they were, continued to maintain caste distinctions in the church. They realized that conversion was also guided by caste considerations.

7.2 Dynamics and Factors of Conversion

We have explored the course of the conversions of the Malas and the Madigas, both individual and group ones, in the preceding chapters. Individual conversions of a few over a period of time cannot be considered as a mass movement. But as we have seen in the preceding chapters, individual conversions led to regular occurrence of group conversions due to kin/family, clan/caste affinities, which became a pulling factor. Just as group social reform movements were taking place in the Hindu society during late nineteenth and early twentieth centuries, group conversion movements to Christianity also were taking place in several parts of India from mid 19th century to roughly about 1930s.[9] These movements were triggered by the coming of the Christian missionaries.

It is a surprising factor that Christianity became an answer to various social, economic, religious and spiritual problems in the second part of the 19th century. Whether it was from the prosperous river deltas or from the drought stricken arid region, the Malas and the Madigas had one intention: to embrace Christianity. But it is often commented that the conversions among the Deprived Classes were not out of conviction, but of convenience meaning, to secure socio-economic mobility which was made possible due to the work of the Christian missionaries who not only preached a new religion, but offered channels for human development.

Scholars have identified diverse factors ranging from spiritual zeal to material gain, quest for social liberation to desire for attaining economic upward mobility, yearning for freedom from caste-based occupational bondage to seeking freedom to acquire alternative occupations for socio-economic development, quest for human dignity amidst degrading 'out-casted' existence in Hindu society, and so on. From our data, it is evident that a majority of the Malas and the Madigas chose alternative occupations seeking liberation from caste bondages as other means of social change was closed for them.[10] Often multiple factors were present in a single conversion.

7.2.1 Caste and Conversion

An examination of the course of the group conversion movements can provide us with insights into the relation between conversion, social relations and inter-caste dynamics. In the late nineteenth century, the numbers involved in group conversion movements were unusually large as converts came in caste groups rather than as family groups or groups of individuals.[11] It was evident that the Malas and the Madigas had chosen an alternative route of social change under the leadership of prominent persons or community leaders.[12] There might also have been a desire not to be left out, when many members of the community were moving ahead. There might have been an eagerness to be identified with the new religion, which was accepted by a substantial numbers among them.[13] We have discussed the work and strategies of the missionary societies in Chapter 3. It may be understood that the beneficiaries of the missionary aid might have felt more empowered having received better education, training, health care, etc.

Individual conversion was liable to immediate excommunication often from one's own family or clan and definitively from one's own caste, and from the larger village community. This implied subsequent lose of the means of livelihood, and ostracisation. Therefore group conversion was preferred because it gave a sort of security and group strength to the converts. One can see a sort of tribal spirit in group conversions.[14] All these factors together seem to have played in augmenting group conversions, which eventually became a movement when many group conversion instances occurred.

In group conversion, the sluggish nature of individuality was won over by corporate action while changing allegiance towards a new religion.[15] The ties of kinship were also preserved through endogamous marriage relationships.[16] In Andrew Wingate's opinion, "a vital relationship exists between the family, friends, ethnic group, religious community and neighbourhood, which create a sense of identity."[17]

In the case of the Malas and Madigas, kin/family and clan/caste affinities were evident as our data on conversions show. This is substantiated in the processes of group conversions. If one caste converted to a particular Church, another caste which considered itself either below or above that caste, would invariably convert to another Church, not the same Church. Here the Church's identity and teaching were subsumed because caste affinity was stronger. Thus, caste linkages were a major factor of conversion.[18] People tended to move within their caste boundaries *en masse* towards conversion.[19] The motive was primarily to protect themselves from the persecution of the upper caste employers and to continue their congregational life based on caste allegiances.

7.2.2 Aspiration for an Egalitarian Society

The ideal of equality of all human beings inclusive of the 'outcastes' might have been experienced by them in the lived life of the missionaries. The Christian missionaries had established a relation between scriptural writings and hope of an egalitarian society in the here and now which seem to have made an appeal to their listeners.[20] Thus, this message of salvation seems to have touched the Malas and Madigas who otherwise were considered 'outcastes' in the contemporary Hindu society. For centuries, they had lived a subaltern life, having internalized their society-imposed lowliness and rejection or fate.

Thus, beyond the material advancement achieved through the mediation of the missionaries, was the enlightening of their minds, gaining of abilities, gaining more confidence in themselves and above all, the touching experience of the heart—the acceptance of the Malas and Madigas as persons with dignity by the endearing, welcoming and accepting attitude of the missionaries—all these together seem to have created a new consciousness among those who came across with the missionaries. This seems to be the reason why groups of families and villagers decided to forego their centuries-old socio-cultural structures and the religions of their ancestors—Hinduism—and accept an alien religion, Christianity. A proper perception of the teachings or doctrinal

Christianity might not have been there, but the experience of Christianity as the lived religion of the missionaries seems to have been deep. This was the birthing of a new consciousness among the Malas and the Madigas.

7.2.3 Conversion, New Consciousness and New Identity

This new social consciousness seems to have goaded the Malas and the Madigas to make conscious efforts, individually and collectively, to liberate themselves from the given depressed condition, to a better level of life.[21] Social consciousness is a byproduct of 'self-consciousness with reference to the one self.[22] New consciousness occurs from the mobility of a few individuals' exposure to new ideas and impacting those ideas upon their own people.[23]

Group conversion movements of the Malas and the Madigas into Christianity were apparently attempts to achieve a new collective identity as Christians, rejecting the existing identity as 'outcastes' and distancing themselves from their past faiths. At the same it was also their attempt towards upward mobility for a qualitative change in life.

The growth of social consciousness and the aspiration for social change among the Christian converts of the Malas and the Madigas during the second half of the 19th century was a by-product of their interaction with the Christian missionaries. Social change is a process where an idea or ideas is/are perceived as an illuminating influence for social mobilization.[24]

The late nineteenth century group conversion movement was characterized by elements of spiritual restlessness, quest for new faiths and striving for betterment of life.[25] Given their experience of inclusion-exclusion within Hinduism, it was not hard for them to convert, though it entailed several challenges and even sufferings.[26] The resolve to join the ranks of the new faith rose from a conviction about the essential truths of the Gospel.[27] Certain other material motives for attaining social, educational upward mobility also played a role in their decisions.[28] Overall, the deprived condition of the people and their quest for a better life on one hand, and the purposive, goal-oriented, external action of the missionaries on the other, seem to have brought about the change in the Malas and Madigas. The 'push and pull factors' may be referred here: the push factors constituted the existential oppressive social, economic and religious structures of the Malas and the Madigas; the pull factors comprised of the new consciousness, new understanding of another religion and aspirations for a better life and future.[29]

Historically the birth of the new social consciousness among the Mala and the Madiga Christian converts can be explained in terms of a combination of some historically contingent factors. In the case of Colonial Andhra the new consciousness did not erupt into incipient or sporadic revolts, nor was it articulated as protest conversions. Quite differently, the conversions in Andhra were mobility-oriented and voluntary.

Some scholars tended to have given undue weightage to the quest for social and economic upward mobility of the Depressed Castes, undermining their quest for spirituality. In the several case studies we have on record, the primary factor of spiritual thirst among the Malas and the Madigas was not given due importance.[30] The search for higher principles of life to satisfy their spiritual needs was indeed a remarkable feature in some of the individual conversions among the Depressed Castes.[31]

Thus, group conversion movements in Andhra seem to have occurred as a result of many contingent factors of both spiritual and non-spiritual nature. The lead for the group mobility movements came from the leading men of the clan.[32] The dire poverty, wretched homes, unremitting toil and physical sufferings were also behind the Malas' and Madigas' conversion into Christianity.[33] The fact that many converts remained steadfast under severe pressure was a sign that they were not actuated by want of immediate gains and temporal benefits.[34] The most important outcome of the group conversion movements was the accomplishment of spiritual gain, thanks to the evangelistic activities. The series of movements created avenues for the Malas and the Madigas to move out of their traditional spaces into alternative and new spaces in society.[35]

In other words, the group conversion movement among the Malas and the Madigas was an attempt to create a new identity for themselves and was the beginning of a great change in all aspects of life that was characterized by educational mobility, occupational mobility and social mobility.

Thousands of Malas and Madigas who had passed through the missionary schools had experienced change in their lives through education and improved economic conditions. It was a collective decision of a number of individuals that enabled them to become Christians, while maintaining full ties with their non-Christian relatives, thereby enabling the latter to follow the faith after suitable instruction.[36] The aim has always been transformation of the collective towards upward status or position with the help of an external agency. In the case of the Malas and Madigas of Coastal Andhra, the most significant external agency which mediated their upward socio-religious and socio-cultural mobility, was the missionary society.[37]

7.2.4 Cost of Conversion

Christianity's arrival seems to have disrupted the existing caste-based occupational structure and notions of purity and pollution. This was the main cause of harassment, intimidation and persecution of the converts by the caste Hindus. Often Christians had to face indiscriminate vengeance by the upper castes whose aim was to disturb the lives of the converts. The social hardships that were endured by the Depressed Castes were mitigated due to availability of alternative choice of occupations after their Christian conversion.[38] The active identification, sympathy and intervention on the part of the Christian missionaries worked as a shock absorber for the persecuted converts.

7.3 Christianization and Making of the Christian Communities

Just as there was much socio-economic changes thanks to the upward educational mobility and occupational mobility, there were perceptible changes in the socio-religious and cultural realms, which were not just cosmetic but were structural. The apparent culture change among the Mala and the Madiga converts was seen in various aspects of life: in social relations, in cultural expressions and in religious expressions, rituals, festivals and worship. In the opinion of Anthony Copley, converts of depressed caste origin certainly had moved upward on the social scale which furthered a quality social base for the modern Indian society.[39]

Church functionaries strived to construct a cohesive, united community of Christians out of disparate caste converts, through Christianization of the converts. After witnessing change among the Malas and the Madigas, it was noticed by the missionaries that these castes had desired for development and above all attempted to escape from their degraded status in society.[40] The missionaries became the forbearers of change in terms of introducing a new faith and in creating an aspiration for better life. They exhibited a sincerity of purpose with ingenious methods and enthusiasm.[41] By combining the proselytizing and philanthropic services the missionaries had laid a foundation for an assimilative incorporation of the Depressed Castes into a church community.[42]

Visible evidence of social change was observed in the life and character of the converts who gave up some of their harmful habits on one hand, and attained higher economic status, on the other.[43] Every individual was considered as an integral part of the local church and therefore the person's consent and co-operation was enlisted.[44]

The changes were effected by the people themselves: the missionaries were only agents who mediated such change using Christian religious superstructure such as ideas, religious teachings, tenets of faith, preaching, personal example, commitment, sacrifice, etc., besides offering the physical and institutional infrastructure, such as schools, colleges, dispensaries, hospitals, industry, etc.

The importance of the Christian press and literature as missionary instruments was perceived by all missionary societies which worked in Colonial Andhra. These instruments were used to strengthen the faith of the Christians and to evangelize the non-Christians.

In the field of socio-religious changes, one is more certain about the powerful intervention of mission on one hand, and the conscientious decision of the converts to abandon their certain established rites, rituals, customs and traditions which they had been observing for centuries, in lieu of adopting new rites, rituals, customs and traditions which were part of the process of conversion.

Externally, the culture of converts did not undergo rapturous changes. In socio-religious rituals and rites of passage such as in marriage, mingling of indigenous practices and customs were retained, while the rite changed to a prescribed form of Christian marriage rite. Overall, they remained, totally local, indigenous, as Indian Malas and Madigas, except for the fact that their religious practices were changed.

In short, after a hundred-year-long Christianization of the Malas and Madigas, one could observe recognizable socio-cultural-religious changes in the everyday life of these two communities, besides the new nominal identity as Christians.

7.4 Education, Empowerment and Social Mobility

The Christian missionary enterprise in coastal Andhra from mid 19th century had several enabling tools for social empowerment in their package of evangelization of the people. Conversion aimed at not just change of religion, but change in life many aspects—social, economic, educational, cultural and so on. In fact, a major engagement of the mission was providing education to the people. Though the education service of the missionary was available to all, it was preferentially available to the convert Malas and Madigas in the mission area. So also, health care of the sick was considered a humanitarian service by the missionary.

In my study of the impact of conversion and social change among the Malas and Madigas of coastal Andhra, I found that a major part of the mission resources were spent on education and health care. Educational ministry always appealed the missionaries as it enabled the converts to read the Bible and to become preachers and teachers. The Christian converts also always looked for a school for their children and the missionaries promptly made efforts to help the new Christian communities.[45] It can be explicitly stated that missionary educational institutions particularly served the convert and non-convert Malas and Madigas with an evangelistic motive. Credit also must go to the determination of the Malas and Madigas to get educated in order to move upward on the social scale. Among the most significant outcomes of the mass conversions in Colonial Andhra was the desire of the people to get education for their children rather than tending the cattle of the landlord.[46]

Education work, more than any other works, pushed up the poor people on the socio-economic scale. It was the most signal contribution of the missionaries to the Malas and the Madigas. The main reason for the missionaries' success in gaining the hearts of the converts was their emphasis on the values of individualism and equality of all human beings that were often accompanied by attempts at socially uplifting them through programs related to education, health care and economic development. In order to educate and instruct the new converts, the missionaries gave priority to training of teachers and pastors to work in village congregations.

In education, no distinction was made between converts and non-converts, and both groups were allowed to join in their educational institutions, until the beginning of the 20th century. Non-converts were encouraged to convert at their own will. Due to encouragement and growth of education among the Depressed Castes in colonial India they were able to move forward socially and economically. Education played a leading role to claim their place in the Indian society as equal citizens for erase equal and replace by growing opportunities.[47] It was due to the liberal policies of the British government and Christian missionary undertaking that education became a tool to uplift themselves from their depressed position.

An important aspect of the missionary medical service was to impart medical training to the native converts. Medical training opened more employment opportunities for Mala and Madiga converts as doctors, nurses, compounders and physician assistants. Trained convert women worked as superintendents of nurses, Bible women and ayahs.[48] Medical work of the missionaries uplifted health care among men and women, who also learned the values of cleanliness and sanitation as preventive measures.[49] Health care practices got changed, scientific understanding of diseases increased, obsolete and obnoxious practices (for instance, witchcraft) and rituals related to healing of diseases were abandoned. Change of living styles and better hygienic living space seem to have helped the Depressed Caste converts to achieve greater immunity against common diseases.[50] Thus, medical missions became important agencies that improved the health condition of both converts and non-converts by alleviating their physical sufferings and pain.

As already noted, with the mediation of the Christian missions, arrangements for improvement of existing occupations were made on one hand, and on the other, channels for adopting alternative occupations, in place of hereditary occupations were available. Because, of a package of developmental and educational interventions of the missionaries, a substantial number of Malas and Madigas found greater opportunities for attaining socio-economic mobility.

Our data show that the proportion of those who achieved educational mobility which facilitated occupational mobility and hence economic mobility were converts, whereas non-converts did not achieve mobility at an equal level. Some observers have opined that the Depressed Castes' Christian conversion resulted in their material improvement and enhanced social status due to the progress achieved in education.[51] The converts who had received the fruits of missionary education found employment as teachers, catechists and evangelists, medical staff and railway employees, public servants in government departments and as tradesmen.[52] Missionary societies also worked as patrons for the economic betterment of the Malas and Madigas by encouraging them to take up non-caste ascribed alternative occupations or by creating improved facilities for bettering production of industrial goods through industrial training and vocational training.[53]

The marginalized communities were able to achieve much progress in life through education and remunerative employment. To sum up, the Christian missionary undertakings in Coastal Andhra was not just for evangelization of the people, meaning preaching of the Gospel, but to show practical Christianity by empowering the poor and the rejected in society through material means.[54]

II

7.5 Malas and Madigas in Post-Independence Period: Uplifted by the Missionaries, Overlooked by the Constitution Makers

In the preceding pages of this book, we have seen the story of the convert Malas and Madigas in Andhra Pradesh during nearly one hundred years in the pre-Independence period. Their history is one of liberation from social, economic and religious bondage and substantial upward socio-economic and occupational mobility. In this section we shall examine their predicament in the post-Independence period.

Several scholars have studied the plight of the Christian converts from the Depressed Classes (or 'Scheduled Castes' (SCs) or Dalits).[55] Rajpramukh is of the opinion that conversion to Christianity has not redeemed 19 million Dalit Christians from social discrimination and untouchability. It has only added to their misery.[56] As Christians, they continue to suffer and live all human misery both in the society and also in the Church. This is because conversion disqualifies a Dalit Christian the constitutionally guaranteed protection and privileges given to the Hindu, Buddhist and Sikh Dalits.

The Constitution of India has laid down that "the State shall promote with special care the educational and economic interests of the weaker sections of the people and in particular of the Scheduled Castes and Scheduled Tribes and shall protect them from social injustice and all forms of exploitation".[57] Article 341 of the Constitution of India envisaged that the President may with respect to any State or Union territory, and where it is a State after consultation with the Governor thereof, by public notification, specify the castes, races or tribes or parts of or groups within castes, races or tribes which shall for the purposes of this Constitution be deemed to be Scheduled Castes in relation to that State or Union Territory, as the case may be.[58]

Further, the Constitution (Scheduled Castes) Order, 1950, paragraph 2 states that subject to the provisions of this order, the castes, races or tribes or parts of, or groups within, castes or tribes specified in the Schedule to this order shall in relation to the States to which those parts respectively related, be deemed to be Scheduled Castes so far as regards members thereof resident in the localities specified in relation to them in those parts of that schedule.

Paragraph 3 of the Order also states that "notwithstanding anything contained in paragraph 2, no person who professes a religion different from the Hindu, the Sikh or the Buddhist religion shall be deemed to be a member of a scheduled caste."[59] Regarding the educational facilities granted by the government for the students belonging to the Scheduled Castes, government scholarships were to be awarded in public schools of state managed and state aided educational and technical institutions.[60]

Thus, provisions were made in the Constitution of India whereby non-convert Depressed Castes were placed in the category of the 'Scheduled Castes' and received the benefits of reservation and other protective measures to improving their social and economic position.[61] The exclusion of Christian SCs from reservation in education and employment for the Scheduled Castes has negatively affected them. The constitutional guarantees of the Right to Freedom of Religion, Article 25 (1), states that "subject to public order, morality and health and to the other provisions of this part, all persons are equally entitled to freedom of conscience and the right freely to profess, practice and propagate religion."[62] Freedom of conscience to follow their choice of faith was denied to people from Scheduled Castes, who desired to convert to Christianity.

The main setback on the interests of the Indian Christians was put forward with the 'Constitution (Scheduled Castes) Order, 1950' which excluded Dalit Christians from the 'Scheduled Castes' category. The order stated that, "no person who professes a religion different from 'Hinduism' shall be deemed to be a member of the Scheduled Castes" (Ministry of Law Notification No. S.R.O. 385: The Gazette of India Extraordinary, Part II, Section 3, 1950:163). The order was amended in 1956 by the Parliament to include "the Hindu or the Sikh" and it was further amended in May 1990 to include "the Hindu or the Sikh or the Buddhist". However, there is no exclusion on grounds of following the Christian religion for the Scheduled Tribes who reside mainly in the seven states of Northeast India and Central and Eastern India.

Despite the fact that Christian missionaries contributed to the social, educational and economic upliftment of the Christian converts since the middle of the nineteenth century, it was a small portion when compared to the large proportion of the Depressed Castes' population. Moreover, continuity of that progress was very much needed in independent India. The deprivation of representation in democratic institutions and denial of reservations in educational institutions and no quota in public employment have hampered and continue to hamper the material development of Dalit Christians. At the same time, Dalit Christians also had failed to develop strong political leadership; they focused only on the possession of control of the church affairs from the foreign missionaries rather than on safeguarding the interests of the Dalit Christians.[63]

Later, the issue of Dalit Christians was brought up in a petition before the Government for its consideration. Under clause (1) of article 340, the President appointed a "Backward Classes Commission" under the Chairmanship of Kakasaheb Kalelkar to determine a criterion to be adopted in considering whether any sections of the people should be treated as socially and educationally Backward Classes, to prepare a list of such classes, and to determine whether Christians from the Depressed Castes were to be regarded as Backward Castes/Classes.[64] But unfortunately, again, the Government of India did not implement the report of the Backward Classes Commission, giving the reason that 'it was too vague'. Instead it adopted a criterion prescribed by the Commission for determining which classes other than the Scheduled Castes and Scheduled Tribes might be regarded as 'Backward Classes' for the fulfillment of the spirit of the Constitutional articles 15(4) and 16(4). Further, the Government of India went on to advise the state governments to render every possible assistance to those classes whom the state governments might consider "socially and economically backward."[65] Even the "Carry Forward Rule" to regulate the appointment of persons of Backward Castes in the public employment in the absence of persons from Scheduled Castes and Scheduled Tribes was rejected by the Honourable Supreme Court on the grounds that "reservation for Backward Classes each year should not be excessive so as to create a monopoly or to interfere unduly with the legitimate claims of the other communities."[66]

Therefore, non-Christian Dalits (Scheduled Castes) belonging to Hindu, Sikh or Buddhist religions, had legal provisions guaranteed by the Constitution ensuring proportional legislative representation and remedial benefits in education and government employment.

Dalit Christians, however, are "twice deprived," suffering from their given Dalit status (in its post-conversion phase), and from discrimination by state mechanisms. Therefore, a socio-economic gap has grown between Dalit Non-Christians and Dalit Christians in matters of educational opportunities and employment avenues. However, such challenges are reduced to some extent in the private sector where a number of Dalit Christians have better job opportunities and therefore economic stability for their families. Dalit unity and collective resistance are challenged where the support of the Dalits is divided among the political parties for electoral gains. Another challenge emanates from the Hindu fundamentalists who see India as predominantly

"Hinduistic" by ignoring the fact that Christianity has been part of India for many centuries.

Therefore, the concept of social justice, with the objective of removing all inequalities and affording equal opportunities to all citizens in social affairs and economic development, was left undefined by the Constitution makers. It should be re-evaluated to broaden the base of reservations to incorporate Dalit Christians into the realm of reservations. The idea of social impartiality may be followed and implemented by disconnecting any constitutional connection between the state and a religion. Dalit Christians should receive the same concessions and benefits as Dalits in other religions. In the light of India's secular-nationalist agenda, discrimination based on religion should be put to an end by giving representation for Dalit Christians in the democratic institutions, creating reservations in educational institutions and making a quota in public employment. Since the very nature of reservations is to reduce socio-economic disparities between people, an all-inclusive social policy may reduce class divisions, both economic and social, between the non-Christian Dalits (Scheduled Castes) and Christian Dalits.[67]

7.5.1 The Ground Reality for the Dalit Christians

The Indian Government has refused to include Christian Dalits in its list of Scheduled Castes, thus denying the Christians the basic rights. The fact that the Government has designated Hindu, Sikh and Buddhist Dalits as the Scheduled Castes, and refused to do the same for Christian Dalits, shows that Christian Dalits are being penalised for being Christians. The Constitution of India maintains clearly that India is a secular state and every person has a right to practice any religious faith. However, Dalit Christians obviously suffer discrimination because of their faith.[68] Although, the general socio-economic conditions of a Dalit Christian is in no way different from that of a Hindu, Sikh or Buddhist Dalit, the Indian Government and some Hindu fundamentalists refuse to recognize the miserable condition of Dalit Christians. For centuries Dalit Christians have been carrying the burden of oppression in common with the other Dalits; but now the Indian Government has brought in a distinction between one kind of Dalit and the other, offering one kind of treatment to Hindu Dalits, Sikh or Buddhist and a different treatment to Christian Dalits.[69]

7.5.2 Struggle for Equality under the Constitution

The Christian Churches in India have been fighting against this unfair discrimination since the independence of our country. Many commissions appointed by the Government of India have studied the actual situation of Dalit Christians in Indian society and have concluded that Dalit Christians suffer the same economic and social disabilities as other Dalits. The Commissions have highlighted the fact that Dalit Christians are 'twice discriminated', both by the State and by the Church. The Commissions recommended that the Government include Dalit Christians in the Scheduled Caste list, but so far the Government of India has not taken these recommendations seriously. For the last fifteen years, Christian communities have been appealing to the Government to consider the issue of Dalit Christians and to include them in the Scheduled Caste list in order to be eligible for certain advantages under 'protective discrimination' guaranteed by the Constitution. On more than one occasion many delegations of different Churches approached the successive Presidents of India, Prime Ministers and other politicians to plead on behalf of Dalit Christians. The ground for denial of such a status is the fallacious explanation offered by the politicians that Christianity does not recognize any caste differentiation in its rank and file; hence no suffering on the basis of caste stigma and discrimination.[70]

However, the reality is otherwise. Dalit Christians suffer the same socio-economic disabilities like the Dalits of Hindu faith. The change of religion did not change much their social, economic and educational status. Most of the Dalits, Hindus and the Christians, often live together side by side in their localities. Whenever there is any unrest or violence, the Caste people do not discriminate between Hindu Dalits and Christian Dalits. Even Caste Christians do not consider Dalit Christians as their equals. Though Dalit Christians undergo the same unjust caste discrimination as Hindu Dalits, Christian Dalits are deprived of the privileges of protection of Civil Rights Act and Prevention of Atrocities Act 1989. In other words, they suffer under the hierarchised caste system even after conversion to Christianity.[71]

7.5.3 Caste Discrimination within the Church

Caste discrimination is present not only in the Hindu religion but also in an egalitarian religion like Christianity. The existence of caste elements in multifarious forms within the Christian Churches is confirmed by Anthony Raj in his study of the Dalit Christians of Cuddapah District of Andhra Pradesh. He says that the Dalits accepted the new faith in Jesus Christ with a hope that it would give them a new identity and they would be considered as God's children. But in reality, it has remained only a dream even within the Church.[72] Conversion has not altered much the fate and plight of Dalit Christians. "They continue to be *Harijans*; but Christian *Harijans*.[73] There is no inter-dining between these groups.[74]

According to Alexander, "even after conversion, the lower caste converts were continued to be treated as Harijans, by all the sections of the society, including the Syrian Christians, even though with conversion the former ceased to be legally Harijans and untouchables."[75] Kananaikil also criticizes the caste discriminations existing among the Christians themselves. He says, "Perhaps the most crucial area where the Church reveals its weakness, is that of caste in the Church. Converts to Christianity brought with them their caste prejudices."[76] He also criticizes the attitude of the government in not extending the privileges of SC Hindus to SC Christians.

There are deep-rooted prejudices among certain Christian groups against members of the Dalit Christians.[77] An open letter written in 1982 by the Catholics of Scheduled Caste Origin, in Ramnad district, in Tamil Nadu, addressed to all the Catholic bishops and lay Christian leaders, brings out the acuteness of the problem of caste discrimination being practiced among Christians even today.[78] Instances of Dalit Christians converting to Islam or Buddhism show that they are disappointed with the treatment they get within the Church.

In conclusion, we can say that, even when exposed to class mobility and occupational mobility, Dalit Christians in Andhra Pradesh and elsewhere are continuing to suffer caste discrimination and prejudiced treatment in the Church and even in the wider society.

Endnotes and References

1 Graham Taylor, *Religion in Social Action* (New York: Mead and Co Publishers, 1913), 88.

2 David W. Bebbington, *Evangelism in Modern Britain: A History from the 1730s to the 1980s* (London: Unwin Hyman Publishers, 1989), 2-3.

3 Edward A. Lawrence, *Modern Missions in the East: Their Methods, Successes and Limitations* (New York: Harper Brothers Publishers, 1895), 43.

4 George Drach and Calvin F. Kuder, *Telugu Mission of the General Council of the Evangelical Lutheran Church in North America Containing a Biography of the Rev. Christian Frederick Heyer* (Philadelphia: General Council Publication House, 1914), 50.

5 M. L. Orchard and K. S. McLaurin, *The Enterprise: The Jubilee Story of the Canadian Baptist Mission in India: 1874-1924* (Toronto: The Canadian Baptist Foreign Mission Board, 1925), 309.

6 John E. Clough, *Social Christianity in the Orient: The Story of A Man, A Mission and A Movement* (New York: The MacMillan Company, 1914), 255.

7 Frederik Gledstone, *Andhra Christian Church Founders*: *Henry Watson Fox* (Madras: Diocesan Press, 1941), 9.

8 George Drach and Calvin F. Kuder, op. cit., 159.

9 Anon, *The Depressed Classes: A Chronological Documentation,* Part I-XI, 1931-1937, (Kurseong: St Mary's College (presently Vidyajyoti College of Theology, Delhi), 1937): 1-587+ xx.

10 Duncan B. Forrester, "The Depressed Classes and Conversion to Christianity, 1860-1960" in *Religion in South Asia,* ed. G. A. Oddie (Delhi: Manohar Publishers, 1977), 45; Also in M. N. Srinivas, "Caste in Modern India," *The Journal of Asian Studies* 16 (4), (1957): 531.

11 Duncan B. Forrester, op. cit., 35.

12 J. J. Ellis, "Christward Movements in South India," in *The Social Setting of Christian Conversion in South India: the Impact of the Wesleyan Methodist Missionaries on the Trichy-Tanjore Diocese with special reference to the Harijan Communities of the Mass*

Movement Area 1820-1947, ed. Sundara Raj Manickam (Wiesbaden: Franz Steiner Verlag, 1977), 100.

13 Andrew Wingate, *The Church and Conversion* (Delhi: ISPCK Publishers, 1997), 82.

14 John E. Clough, op. cit., 280.

15 W. S. Hunt, *India's Outcastes: A New Era* (London: The CMS Publications, 1924), 5.

16 Sundara Raj Manickam, op. cit., 100.

17 Andrew Wingate, op. cit., 259.

18 L. Stanislaus, *The Liberative Mission of the Dalit Christians* (Delhi: ISPCK Publishers, 1999), 143.

19 M. A. Sherring, *The History of Protestant Missions in India from their Commencement in 1706 to 1881* (London: The Religious Tract Society, 1884), 409.

20 W. S. Hunt, op. cit., 86.

21 Warner Fite, "The Social Implications of Consciousness," *The Journal of Philosophy, Psychology and Scientific Methods* 10 (14), (1913): 367.

22 Charles H. Cooley, "Social Consciousness," *The American Journal of Sociology* 12 (5), (1907): 676.

23 Barbara R. Joshi, *Democracy in Search of Equality: Untouchable Politics and Indian Social Change* (Delhi: Hindustan Publishing Corporation, 1982), 34.

24 R. S. Mann, *Social Change and Social Research: An Indian Perspective* (New Delhi: Concept Publishing Company, 1988), 18.

25 Lewis R. Rambo, *Understanding Religious Conversion* (New Haven: Yale University Press, 1993), 168.

26 *The Church Missionary Intelligencer of Missionary Information: A Monthly Journal of Missionary Information* VIII (London: The CMS Publications, 1872): 45.

27 C. B. Webster, *Dalit Christians: A History* (Delhi: ISPCK, 1994) 33.

28 Chad M. Bauman, *Christian Identity and Dalit Religion in Hindu India* (Grand Rapids, Michigan: W. B. Eerdmans Publishing Company, 2008), 74.

29 Anthony Copley, *Religion in Conflict: Ideology, Cultural Contact and Conversion in Late Colonial India* (New York: The Oxford University Press, 1997), 54.

30 L. Stanislaus, op. cit., 143.

31 Samuel Jaya Kumar, *Dalit Consciousness and Christian Conversion: The Work of SPG Missionaries, Historical Resources for a Contemporary Debate, Mission Theology in an Asian Context* (Delhi: ISPCK Publishers, 1999), 238.

32 Gustav Warneck, *Outline of a History of Missions from the Reformation to the Present Time: Contribution to Modern Church History* (New York: Fleming H. Revell, 1901), 404.

33 Robert Hall Glover, *The Progress of World-Wide Missions* (New York: Harper and Brothers Publishers, 1924), 23.

34 J. P. Jones, *The Yearbook of Missions in India, Burma and Ceylon* (Madras: Christian Literature Society of India, 1912), 255.

35 Alice B. Van Doren, "Christian Mass Movements in India: A Review in Laymen's Foreign Missionary Inquiry Reports," in *The National Christian Council Review* (Mysore: Wesley Press, 1933), 139.

36 This was an observation made specifically for the Malas and Madigas. See Donald McGavran, *Understanding Church Growth* (Grand Rapids, Michigan: W. B. Eerdmans Publishing Co, 1970), 298.

37 *The New Encyclopedia Britannica*, Vol. X, 15th Edition (Chicago: Encyclopedia Britannica Incorporation, 1997), 921.

38 John E. Clough, op. cit., 126.

39 Anthony Copley, op. cit., 56.

40 G. A. Oddie, "India: Missionaries, Conversion, and Change," in *The Church Missionary Society and World Christianity 1799-1999,* ed. Kevin Ward and Brian Stanley (London: Curzon Press, 2000), 251.

41 Gustav Warneck, op. cit., 37.

42 Ibid., 404.

43 D. F. Pocock, *Essays on the Caste System by Celestin Bougle* (Cambridge: The Cambridge University Press, 1971), 82.

44 F. Whittaker, "Evangelism: Opportunities and Difficulties in Relation to Mass Movements," in *The National Christian Council Review* XVII (Mysore: Wesley Press, 1939), 125.

45 *A Descriptive and Historical Account of the Godavari District in the Presidency of Madras* (London: Trubner & Co Publishers, 1878), 230.

46 G. A. Oddie, "Christian Conversion in the Telugu Country, 1860-1900: A Case Study of One Protestant Movement in the Godavery Kistna Delta," *The Indian Economic and Social History Review* XII, (1975): 73.

47 Regunta Yesuratnam, *Bharatavanilo Kraisthava Sangham* (Hyderabad: Telugu Kraisthava Vedanta Sahiti Samiti, 1998). 59.

48 Julia M. Harpster, *Among the Telugoos: Illustrating Mission Work in India* (Philadelphia: Lutheran Publication Society, 1902), 48.

49 Rutter J. Williamson, *The Healing of the Nations: A Treatise on Medical Missions* (New York: The Student Volunteer Movement for Foreign Missions, 1899), 58.

50 Ibid., 71.

51 Duncan B. Forrester, *Caste and Christianity: Attitudes and Policies on Caste of Anglo-Saxon Protestant Missions in India* (Richmond, Surrey: Curzon Press, 1980), 75.

52 "Mass Movements and Economic Reconstruction," *The Dornakal Diocesan Magazine* 11 (3), (March 1934), (Dornakal: Diocesan Press, 1934): 17.

53 Eyre Chatterton, *A History of the Church of England in India since the Early Days of the East India Company* (London: SPCK Publishers, 1924).

54 K. K. Kuruvilla, "The Christian Approach to the Unprivileged," *The National Christian Council Review* XV (Mysore: Wesley Press, 1937): 547.

55 The Constitution of India accorded in 1950 a new nominal identity 'Scheduled Castes', to the Depressed Classes. However, since 1970s certain leaders among them have preferred to use the term *Dalits*, in place of Scheduled Castes. Since this term has gained much currency in the present time, we use this term in our discussion hereafter. These belong to different religious persuasions. Hence, Scheduled Caste converts to Christianity are called Dalit Christians. On studies on Dalit Christians, see S. Lourduswamy, *Equal Rights to All Dalits (with special reference to Dalit Christians)* (New Delhi: Centre for Dalit Studies, 2001); Bosco SJ, Aariz Mohammed, Selva Rathinam, SJ, L. A. Samy, Joe Xavier, SJ, & Franklin Caesar Thomas, *Constitutional Rights of Dalit Christians and Muslims* (Chennai: LTD Media, 2010).

56 K. E. Rajpramukh, *Dalit Christians of Andhra: Under the Impact of Missionaries* (New Delhi: Serials Publications, 2008), 80; also John C. B. Webster, *The Dalit Christians: A History*, second edition (Delhi: ISPCK, 1994).

57 L. M. Shrikant, *Report of the Commissioner for Schedule Castes and Scheduled Tribes for the Year 1951* (New Delhi: Government of India, 1956), 116.

58 Santha K. Varikoti-Jetty, "Indian Christians from the Depressed Castes Background and Challenges to Their Christian Identity," *Mission Studies* 34 (2017): 337.

59 Ibid., 338.

60 Shrikant, op. cit., 116.

61 Venkateswaran S., *Census of India, 1951, Madras and Coorg, Vol. III, Part II-B, Tables* (Madras: The Government Press, 1953), 147.

62 Varikoti-Jetty, op. cit., 338.

63 Ibid., 338-339.

64 D. D. Basu, *Commentary on the Constitution of India* (Calcutta: S. C. Sarkar & Sons, 1964), 156.

65 Ibid., 156–157.

66 J. N. Pandey, *Constitutional Law of India* (Allahabad: Central Law Agency, 1993), 145-46.

67 Varikoti-Jetty, op. cit., 340.

68 Rajpramukh, op. cit., 81.

69 Ibid., 81-82.

70 Ibid., 82.

71 Ibid., 81.

72 Y. Antony Raj, *Social Impact of Conversion: A Comparative Sociological Study on the Christians of Scheduled Caste Origin and Scheduled Caste Hindus* (Delhi: ISPCK, 2001), 18.

73 Harijan (meaning children of God): a term used for Depressed Classes by M. K. Gandhi, but objected to by them due to its pejorative connotation.

74 Antony Raj, op. cit., 19.

75 K. C. Alexander, "The Problem of Caste in the Christian Churches of Kerala," in *Caste Among Non-Hindus in India*, ed. Harjinder Singh (New Delhi: National Publishing House, 1977), 54.

76 Jose Kananaikil, *Christians of Scheduled Caste Origin: In Search of Justice* (New Delhi: Indian Social Institute, 1986), 20; See also, Walter Fernandes, *Caste and Conversion Movements in India* (New Delhi: Indian Social Institute, 1981); M. E Prabhakar, "In Search of Roots: Dalit Aspirations and the Christian Dalit Question (Perceptions of the Andhra Poet Laureate, Joshua)," *Religion and Society*, XLI (March 1994): 2-20.

77 Sebasti L. Raj, and G. F. Xavier, *Caste Culture in Indian Church* (New Delhi: Indian Social Institute, 1993).

78 Dr. Nandi Joseph, *Dalit Reality of the Indian Catholic Church* (Chennai: Foundation for Dalit Literature, 2001); M. E. Prabhakar, "Caste in Andhra Churches–A Case Study of Guntur District, *Religion and Society*, XXXIX (September 1987): 31- 51.

Appendix A

Maps of the Missionary Mission fields in Colonial Coastal Andhra

1. ***The London Missionary Society's Mission Field in Coastal Andhra (marked):***[1]

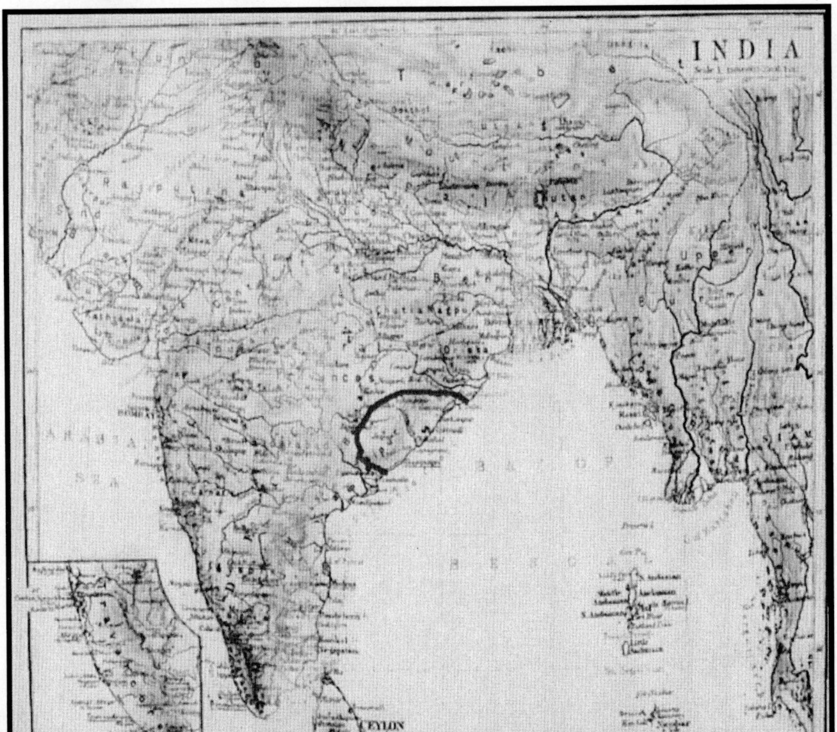

2. *The Canadian Baptist Mission's Mission Field:*[2]

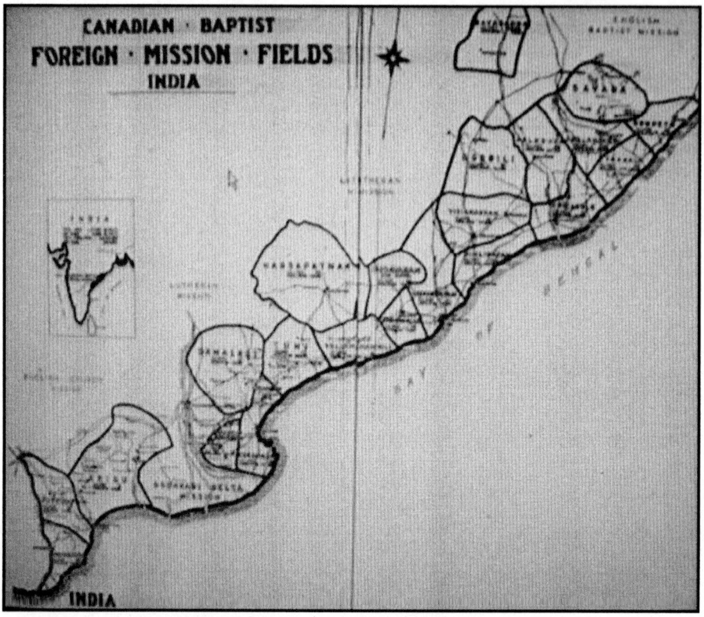

3. *The Godavari Delta Mission's Mission Field:*[3]

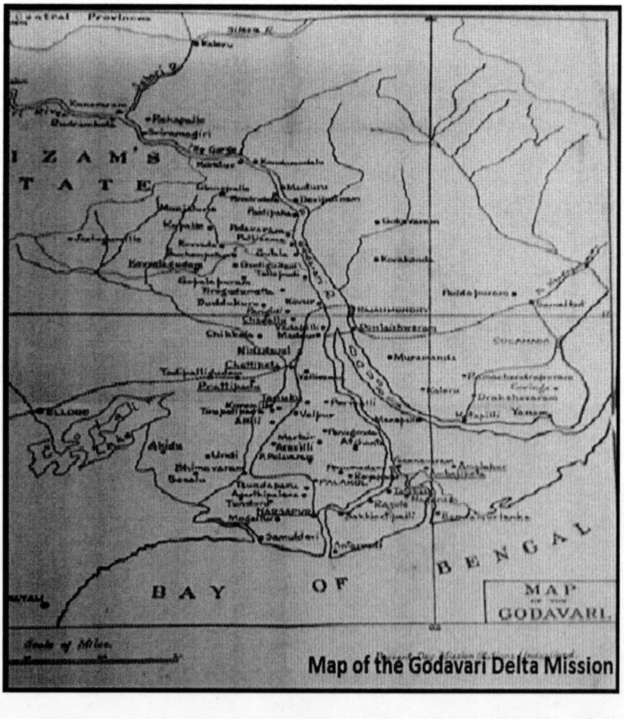

4. *The Church Missionary Society's Telugu Mission Field (marked):*[4]

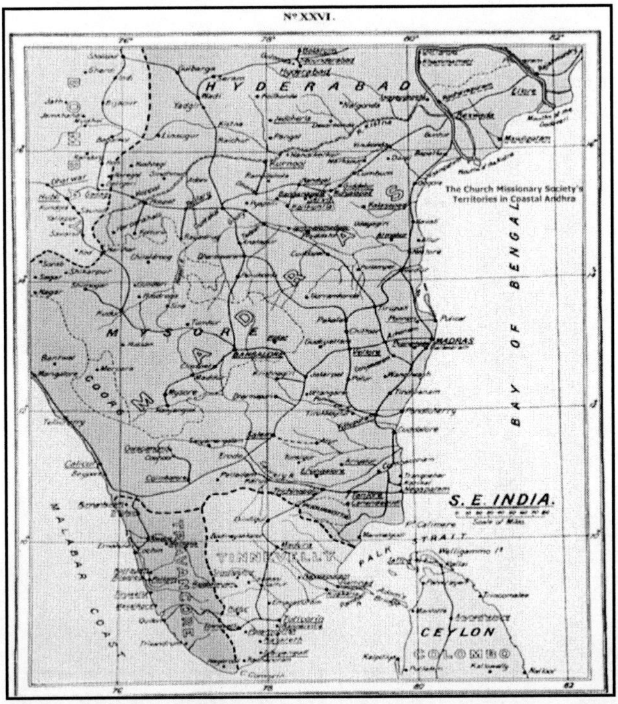

5. *The American Evangelical Lutheran Mission's Guntur Mission Field:*[5]

MAP OF THE GENERAL COUNCIL'S TELUGU MISSION FIELD

6. *The American Evangelical Lutheran Mission's Rajahmundry Mission Field:*[6]

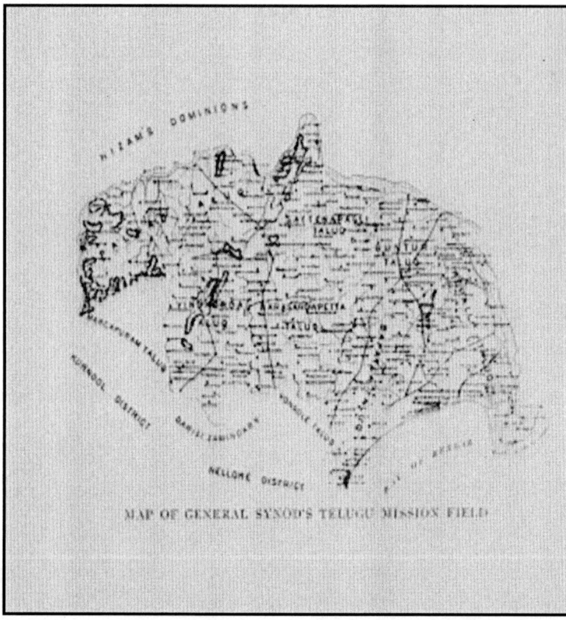

7. *The American Baptist Mission's Telugu Mission Field (marked):*[7]

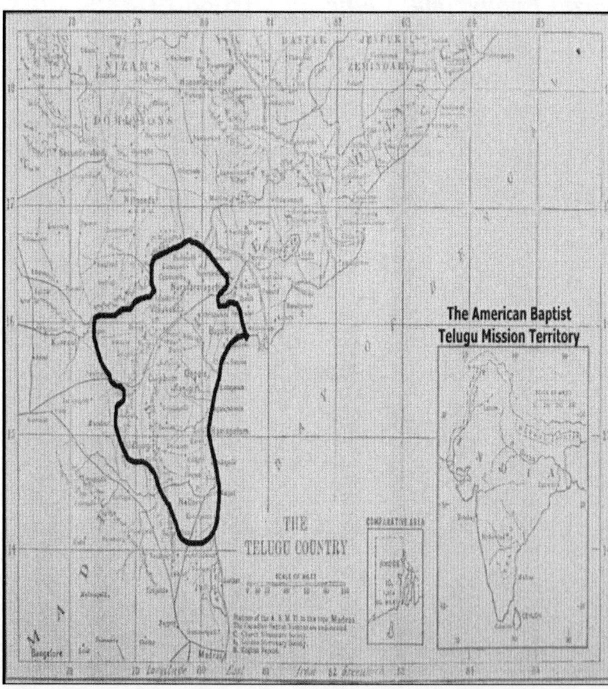

Map References

1 Richard Lovett, *The History of the London Missionary Society (1795-1895)*, Vol. II (Oxford: Oxford University Press, 1899), to face, 33.

2 M. L. Orchard and K.S McLaurin, *The Enterprise: The Jubilee Story of the Canadian Baptist Mission in India*, 1874-1924 (Toronto: The Canadian Baptist Foreign Mission Board, 1925), Cover.

3 E. B. Bromley, *They were Men Sent from God* (Bangalore: The Scripture Literature Press, 1937).

4 *The Churchman's Missionary Atlas* (Westminster: The Society for the Propagation of the Gospel in Foreign parts, 1912), 60.

5 George Drach and Calvin F Kuder, *Telugu Mission of the General Council of the Evangelical Lutheran Church in North America Containing a Biography of the Rev. Christian Frederick Heyer (*Philadelphia: General Council Publication House, 1914), 130.

6 Ibid.

7 David Downie, *The Lone Star: The History of the Telugu Mission of the American Baptist Missionaries Union (1838-1927)* (Philadelphia: The American Baptist Publication, 1892), frontispiece.

Appendix B

Photographs of Missionaries

1. ***Missionaries of the London Missionary Society:***[1]

A. Des Granges (Vizagapatam)

Rev. John Hay

Mrs E. Porter

2. ***Missionaries of the Canadian Baptist Mission:***[2]

Rev. John McLaurin

Mary Bates McLaurin

3. *Missionaries of the Godavari Delta Mission:*[3]

Sir Arthur Cotton

Rev. Anthony Norris Groves

William Bowden

MR. AND MRS. WILLIAM BOWDEN
taken in 1871

4. *Missionaries of the Church Missionary Society:*[4]

Rev. H. W. Fox

Rev.Canon F.N Alexander

H.J. Tanner (1885-1895)

Rev. E.S.Tanner
Arch Deecan
Bezwada

Bishiop V.S. Azariah

Miss Dugdale

Missionaries of the CMS

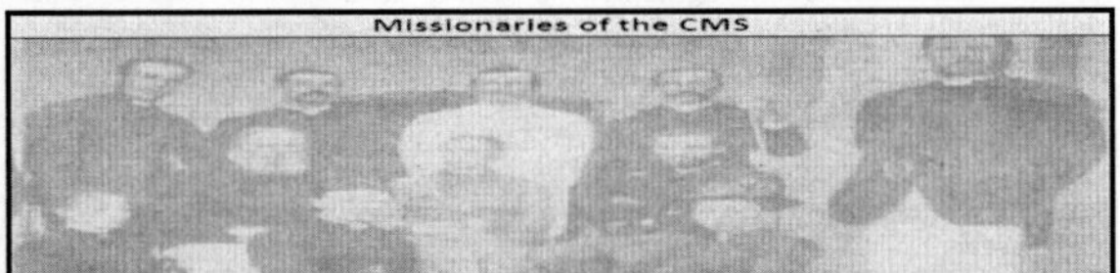

5. *Missionaries of the American Evangelical Lutheran Mission:*[5]

Rev. Dr. Christian Frederick Heyer

Rev. Horace B. Artman

Rev. Iver K. Poulsen

Rev. H.C. Schmidt

Rev. Augustus. B. Carlson

Rev. William Groening

Rev. Dr. J.H. Harpster

Rev. E.Pohl

AELM General Council Missionaries at Rajahmundry

A Missionary's Home in Rajahmundry

6. *Missionaries of the American Baptist Mission and other Areas of Mission Work:*[6]

Rev. Lyman Jewett

Rev. John E. Clough

Mrs. Harriet Clough

Yerraguntla Periah

On Prayer Meeting Hill, Ongole, 1854

Preaching at Ongole

Baptisms at Gundlakamma River, Ongole

THE CHAPEL AT ONGOLE

The church home of 15,000 members.

AT HOME

ON TOUR

7. *Missionary Schools:*[7]

GIRLS' BOARDING SCHOOL, GUNTUR.

Teachers and Pupils of the Boys' Boarding School

The Vizagapatam High School.

Boarding School Girls.

The Nellore Girls' High School

Pupils and Teachers of the Girls' High School

CHARLOTTE SWENSON MEMORIAL BIBLE SCHOOL

Central Boarding School

8. *Missionary Hospitals:*[8]

Dr. Anna Sarah Kugler, M.D

Dr. Agnes Schade with a Lady Missionary

BUILDING IN RAJAHMUNDRY RENTED FOR USE AS A MISSION DISPENSARY

The Guntur Women's Hospital

Zenana Bible-women with Dr. Kugler and Ms. Fannie Dryden

STAFF OF BETHESDA HOSPITAL, PITHAPURAM, IN 1922

Dr. R. G. Smith is centre of third row from bottom with missionary nurses Mrs. Smith, Miss Sanford, Evelyn Smith Armstrong and Indian assistant nurses in second row from bottom

9. *Industrial and Training Schools:*[9]

Mrs. H.C. Schmidt and her Sewing Class

A River Boat

A GROUP OF LACEMAKERS

In the Bible Training School Garden

THE INDUSTRIAL SCHOOL, COCANADA

10. *Some Aspects of Indian Christianity:*[10]

A NATIVE CHRISTIAN FEAST, CHRISTMAS DAY.

Jewett Memorial Baptist Church, Ongole

SOME OF THE ONE THOUSAND TELUGU WORKERS.

INDIAN MISSION WORKERS OF EARLY DAYS

The bareheaded man is Karré Peter, while on his right is Rev. Jonathan Burder

Endnotes

1 Richard Lovett, *The History of the London Missionary Society, 1795-1895*, Vol. II (Oxford: Oxford University Press, 1899), Frontispiece.

2 M. L. Orchard and K. S McLaurin, *The Enterprise: The Jubilee Story of the Canadian Baptist Mission in India: 1874-1924* (Toronto: The Canadian Baptist Foreign Mission Board, 1925), 138 & 148.

3 E. B. Bromley, *They Were Men Sent from God* (Bangalore: The Scripture Literature Press, 1937), 179.

4 *The Church of South India, Krishna Godavari Diocese*, 100th Harvest Festival Issue 1911-2010 (Vijayawada: 2010).

(i) Eugene Stock, *History of the Church Missionary Society: Its Environment, Its Men and Its Work,* Vol. I (London: The CMS Publications, 1899), 92.

(ii) Eugene Stock, *History of the Church Missionary Society: Its Environment, Its Men and Its Work*, Vol. II (London: The CMS Publications, 1899), 176.

(iii) Sherwood Eddy, *India Awakening* (New York: Missionary Education Movement, 1911), 204.

5 L. B. Wolf, *After Fifty Years or An Historical Sketch of the Guntur Mission of the Evangelical Lutheran Church of the General Synod in the United States of America* (Philadelphia: The Lutheran Publication Society, 1896), various pages.

6 David Downie, The Lone Star: *The History of the Telugu Mission of the American Baptist Missionaries Union (1838-1927)* (Philadelphia: The American Baptist Publication, 1892), 39 & 86.

7 L. B. Wolf, Op cit., 212.

Julia M Harpster, *Among the Telugoos: Illustrating Mission Work in India* (Philadelphia: Lutheran Publication Society, 1902), 34 & 42.

Augusta Highland, *India* (Rock Island, IL: Board of Foreign Missions, Lutheran Augustana Synod Centennial Committee, 1945), 21.

8 L. B. Wolf, Op cit.,158.

*The Nellore Station and Field of the American Baptist Telugu mission, South India (*Nellore: The American Baptist Telugu Mission, 1922), 36.

9 George Drach and Calvin F Kuder, *Telugu Mission of the General Council of the Evangelical Lutheran Church in North America Containing a Biography of the Rev. Christian Frederick Heyer* (Philadelphia: General Council Publication House, 1914), 175 & 361.

10 Sherwood Eddy, op. cit., 99.

Bibliography

I. Government/Official Sources

1. "Ministry of Law Notification No. S.R.O. 385," in *The Gazette of India*, Extraordinary, Part II, Section 3 (Calcutta: August 10, 1950).
2. "The Government Order No 504 Educational," in *The Proceedings of The Education Department*, August 22 (Madras: The Government of Madras, 1884).
3. "The Government Order No 68, Educational," in *The Proceedings of Education Department*, February 1 (Madras: The Government of Madras, 1893).
4. *Administration Report of the Abkari Revenue (1915-16)* (Madras: The Government Press, 1917).
5. *Administration Report of the Harijan Welfare Department (1948-49)* (Madras: The Government Press, 1949).
6. Boag, G. T., *Census of India, Vol. XIII, Imperial and Provincial Tables*, Madras (Madras: The Government Press, 1922).
7. Carmichael, D. F., *A Manual of the District of Vizagapatam in the Presidency of Madras* (Madras: Lawrence Asylum Press, 1869).
8. Cornish, W. R., *Census of the Madras Presidency*, 1871, *Census Results, Supplementary Tables*, Vol. II (Madras: The Government Gazette Press, 1874).
9. Cotton, Elizabeth Reid, Lady Hope, *General Sir Arthur Cotton, R.E., K.C.S.I, His Life and Work* (London: Hodder Stoughton, 1900).
10. Cotton, Sir A., *The Madras Famine with Appendix Containing A Letter from Ms. Florence Nightingale and Other Papers* (London: Marshall Simpkin and Co Stationers, Undated).
11. Digby, William, *Prosperous British India: A Revelation from Official Records* (London: T. Fisher Unwin Publishers, 1901).

12. *Dr. H. C. Mukherjee's Address in the Constituent Assembly of India, Constitution Assembly Debates*, Vol. IV (New Delhi: 1947).
13. *Ecclesiastical Proceedings, Government of India, Home, No. 13-1* (Calcutta: Government Press, April 1, 1871).
14. Elwin, D. H., *Census of India, 1941, Vol. II, Part I, Tables* (Simla: The Government Press, 1942).
15. Francis, I. W., *Madras District Gazetteers: Vizagapatam* (Madras: The Government Press 1907).
16. Francis, W., *Gazetteer of South India*, Vol. 1 (New Delhi: Mittal Publications, 1988).
17. Gait, E. A., *Notes on Census Returns of Hindus* (Simla: The Government Press, 1910).
18. Gait, Edward Albert, *Census of India 1901, Education, Table VIII*, Part II (Madras: The Government Press, 1901).
19. *Godavari District Records, Andhra Pradesh Archives* (Hyderabad: Government of Andhra Pradesh, 1935).
20. Gopalaswami, R. A., *Census of India, 1951, Vol. I, Part I-A, Report* (New Delhi: The Government Press, 1955).
21. *Harijan Uplift by the Government of Madras, G.O. No. 1101, Education* (Madras: Government Press, May 14, 1938).
22. *Harijan Uplift by the Government of Madras: GO. No. 1446, Law and Education* (Madras: The Government Press, July 16, 1935).
23. *Home-Education Proceedings, Government of India, Education, No. 9-2* (Calcutta: Government Press, February 5, 1858).
24. Hutton, J. H., *Census of India, 1931, Provincial Tables* (Madras: The Government Press, 1931).
25. India Constitutional Reforms, *Report of the Reforms Enquiry Committee*, 1924 (London: H. M. Stationary Office, 1925).
26. *Indian Educational Policy 1913: Being a Resolution Issued by the Governor General in Council* (Calcutta: The Government Press, February 21, 1915).
27. *Law Department (Education) Despatch Abstract, 1924*, G.O No. 10 (1925).
28. Mackenzie, Gordon, *A Manual of the Kistna District in the Presidency of Madras* (Madras: Lawrence Asylum Press, 1883).
29. *Manual of the Administration of the Madras Presidency, an Illustration of the Records of Government and the Yearly Administration Reports* (Madras: The Government Press, 1885).
30. *Manual of the Administration of the Madras Presidency*, Vol. I (Madras: The Government Press, 1885).

31. McIver, Lewis, *Census of India*, 1881, Madras Presidency, Operations and Results, Vol. II (Madras: The Government Press, 1882).
32. *Memorandum on Some of the Results of Indian Administration during the Past Thirty Years of British Rule in India* (Madras: Government Press, 1889).
33. Mitra, H. N. ed., *The Government Act of 1919: Rules there under and Government Reports* (Calcutta: Annual Register Office, 1921).
34. Molony, J. Chartres, *Census of India*, 1911, Part I, *Report* (Madras: The Government Press, 1913).
35. Molony, J. Chartres, *Census of India, 1911, Part II, Imperial and Provincial Tables*, Vol. XII (Madras: The Government Press, 1913).
36. Morris, Henry, *A Descriptive and Historical Account of the Godavari District in the Presidency of Madras* (London: Trubner and Co Publishers, 1878).
37. *Operations of the Department of Agriculture in the Madras Presidency for the year 1918-19* (Madras: The Government Press, 1919).
38. Rao, Ananada D., *Results of Demonstrations of Agricultural Improvements in the Madras Circle carried out in 1924-1927* (Madras: The Government Press, 1929).
39. *Report of the Public Instruction in the Madras Presidency for the Year 1905-06*, Vol. I (Madras: The Government Press, 1906).
40. *Report of the Public Instruction in the Madras Presidency for the year 1908-09*, Vol. I (Madras: The Government Press, 1909).
41. *Report on Indian Constitutional Reforms* (London: H. M. Stationery Office, 1918).
42. *Report on Native News Papers Examined by the Translators to the Government of Madras,* No 89 (Madras: Government Press, 1899).
43. *Report on Public Instruction for the Year 1949-50* (Madras: The Government Press, 1951).
44. *Report on Public Instruction in the Madras Presidency for the year 1911-12 and for the Quinquenium 1906-07 to 1911-12, Vol. I, Parts I and II* (Madras: The Government Press, 1938).
45. *Report on Public Instruction in the Madras Presidency for the Year 1936-37 and for the Quinquenium 1931-32 to 1936-37, Vol. II, Parts I and II* (Madras: The Government Press, 1938).
46. *Report on Public Instruction in the Madras State for the year 1950-51* (Madras: The Government Press, 1953).
47. *Report on the Administration of the Madras Presidency during the Year 1867-68* (Madras: Fort St. George Gazette Press, 1868).

48. *Report on the Administration of the Madras Presidency during the Year 1890-91* (Madras: The Government Press, 1891).
49. *Report on the Administration of the Madras Presidency During the Year 1910-11* (Madras: The Government Press, 1911).
50. *Report on the Administration of the Madras Presidency During the Year 1921-22* (Madras: The Government Press, 1923).
51. *Report on the Administration of the Madras Presidency during the Year 1930-31* (Madras: The Government Press, 1932).
52. *Report on the Administration of the Madras Presidency during the Year 1939-40* (Madras: The Government Press, 1941).
53. *Report on the Administration of the Police of the Madras Presidency during the Year 1949* (Madras: The Government Press, 1949).
54. *Report on the Administration of the Police of the Madras Province 1905* (Madras: The Government Press, 1906).
55. *Report on the Administration of the Police of the Madras Province 1910* (Madras: The Government Press, 1911).
56. *Report on the Administration of the Police of the Madras Province 1945* (Madras: The Government Press, 1945).
57. *Report on the Vernacular Papers Examined by the Translators to the Government of Madra*s, No 27, July (Madras: Government Press, 1909).
58. *Report on Vaccination in the Madras Presidency for the year 1901-02* (Madras: The Government Press, 1903).
59. Risley, H. H., *Census of India*, 1901, Vol. I, Part I, Report (Calcutta: The Government Press, 1903).
60. S., Venkateswaran, *Census of India, 1951, Madras and Coorg,* Vol. III, Part II-B, Tables (Madras: The Government Press, 1953).
61. Sharp, H. and J. A. Richey, eds., *Selections from the Educational Records of the Government of India*, Vol. 1 (Calcutta: The Government Press, 1920).
62. Shrikant, L. M., *Report of the Commissioner for Schedule Castes and Scheduled Tribes for the Year 1951* (New Delhi: Government of India, 1951).
63. Shrikant, L. M., *Report of the Commissioner for Schedule Castes and Scheduled Tribes for the Year 1951* (New Delhi: Government of India, 1956), 116.
64. Srinivasa, Raghavaiyangar S., *Memorandum of the Progress of the Madras Presidency during the Last Forty Years of British Administration* (Madras: The Government Press, 1893).
65. Stuart, H. A., *Census of India*, 1891, Vol. XIII (Madras: The Government Press, 1893).

66. *The Administrative Report of the Harijan Welfare Department 1950-51, Statement IV, Part II* (Madras: The Government Press, 1951).
67. *The Government of India Act of 1935* (Calcutta: H. M. Stationery Office, 1936).
68. The *Government of India Records: Education, Home*, No 9-12 (February 5 1858).
69. *The Government of India Resolution on Indian Educational Policy of 1904.*
70. *The Harijan Uplift of the Government of Madras* (Madras: The Government Press, 1938).
71. *The Imperial Gazetteer of India*, Vol. 12 (Oxford: Clarendon Press, 1909).
72. *The Imperial Gazetteer of India, Vol. 15, Karachi to Kotayam* (Oxford: Clarendon Press, 1908).
73. *The Imperial Gazetteer of India*, Vol. 16 (Oxford: Clarendon Press, 1909).
74. *The Imperial Gazetteer of India*, Vol. 2 (Oxford: Clarendon Press, 1909).
75. *The Imperial Gazetteer of India*, Vol. 24 (Oxford: Clarendon Press, 1909).
76. *The Imperial Gazetteer of India, Vol. 5, Karachi to Kotayam* (Oxford: Clarendon Press, 1909).
77. *The Imperial Gazetteer of India: The Indian Empire, Descriptive, Vol. I* (Oxford: Clarendon Press, 1909).
78. *The Madras State Administration Report of 1951-52, Part II* (Madras: The Government of India Press, Madras, 1954).
79. *The Report of the Indian Industrial Commission Mission 1916-18* (Calcutta: The Government Press, 1918).
80. The *Statistical Abstract Relating to British India from 1876/7 to 1885/6* (London: H. M. Stationary Office, 1887).
81. Thurston, Edgar, *Castes and Tribes of Southern India*, Vol. IV, K-M (Madras: The Government Press, 1909).
82. Thurston, Edgar, *Castes and Tribes of Southern India*, Vol. VI, P-S, (Madras: The Government Press, 1909).
83. Venkateswaran, S., *Census of India*, 1951, *Madras and Coorg, Vol. III, Part II-B*, Tables (Madras: The Government Press, 1953).
84. Williams, L. F. Rushbrook, *India in 1922-23: A Statement Prepared for Presentation to Parliament in accordance with the Requirements of the 26th Section of the Government of India Act* (Calcutta: The Government Press, 1923).

85. Yeats, N. W. M., *Census of India, 1931, Vol. XIV, Madras, Part II, Imperial and Provincial Tables* (Madras: The Government Press, 1932).
86. Yeats, N. W. M., *Census of India, 1941, Vol. 1, Part 1* (Madras: The Government Press, 1942).

II. Church/Mission Sources: Books

1. *Among the Telugus and Bolivians: A Report of the Canadian Baptist Foreign Mission Board on the Indian and Bolivian Fields with Directory and Statistics of 1942* (Toronto: Canadian Baptist Overseas Mission Board, 1941).
2. *Annual Report of the Committee of the Church Missionary Society for Africa and the East: One Hundred and Forty Fifth Year, 1943-44* (London: The CMS Publications, 1944).
3. Barnes, H. Irene, *Behind the Purdah: The Story of C.E.Z.M.S Work in India* (New York: Thomas Y Crowell Company, 1897).
4. Beach, Harlan P., *A Geography and Atlas of Protestant Missions: Their Environment, Forces, Distribution Methods, Problems, Results and Prospects at the Opening of the Twentieth Century*, Vol. I (New York: Student Volunteer Movement For Foreign Missions, 1901).
5. ________, *India and Christian Opportunity* (New York: Student Volunteer Movement for Foreign Missions, 1908).
6. ________, *The Findings of the Continuation Committee Conferences held in Asia, 1912-1913* (New York: Student Volunteer Movement for Foreign Missions, 1913).
7. Beaver, R. Pierce, *Pioneers in Mission: The Early Missionary Ordination Sermons, Chargers And Instructions* (Grand Rapids, Michigan: W. B. Eerdmans Publishing Company, 1966).
8. Bebbington, David W., *Evangelism in Modern Britain: A History from the 1730s to the 1980s* (London: Unwin Hyman Publishers, 1989).
9. Bromley, E. B., *They Were Men Sent from God* (Bangalore: The Scripture Literature Press, 1937).
10. Cecil, John Grimes, *Towards an Indian Church: The Growth of the Church of India in Constitution and Life* (London: Society for Promoting Christian Knowledge, 1946).
11. Chamberlain, Jacob, *In the Tiger Jungle and other Stories of Missionary Work among the Telugus of India* (New York: Fleming H. Revell, 1896).
12. ________, *The Kingdom in India: Its Progress and Its Promise* (London: Fleming H. Revell, 1908).
13. Chaplin, C. Ada, *Our Gold Mine: The Story of American Baptist Missions in India* (Boston: W. G. Corthell, 1889).

14. Chatterton, Eyre, *A History of the Church of England in India since the Early Days of the East India Company* (London: SPCK Publishers, 1924).
15. Clayton, A. C., *Christian Literature in India and Ceylon: An Account of the Christian Literature Published in the Vernacular Languages and in English by Protestant Missions* (Madras: The Christian Literature Society, 1920).
16. Clough, Emma Rauschenbusch, *While Sewing Sandals or Tales of a Telugu Pariah Tribe* (London: The Selwood Printing Works, 1899).
17. Clough, John E., *Social Christianity in the Orient: the Story of a Man, A Mission and a Movement* (New York: The Macmillan Company Publishers, 1914).
18. Craig, John, *Forty Years among the Telugus: A History of the Mission of the Baptists of Ontario and Quebec, Canada to the Telugus, South India 1867-1907* (Toronto: The Canadian Baptist Foreign Mission Board, 1908).
19. Craig, John, J. R. Stillwell, I. C. Archibald and A. E. Baskerville, *Telugu Trophies: The Jubilee Story of Some of the Principal Telugu Converts in the Canadian Baptist Foreign Mission in India from 1874 to 1924* (Toronto: The Canadian Baptist Publication Society, 1925).
20. Culross, James, William Carey (London: A. C. Armstrong and Sons Publishers, 1882).
21. Dawson, W. J., *The Evangelistic Note* (London: Fleming H. Revell, 1905).
22. Dennis, James S., *Christian Missions and Social Progress, A Sociological Study of Foreign Missions*, Vol. I (New York: Fleming H. Revell, 1897).
23. ________, *Christian Missions and Social Progress: A Sociological Study of Foreign Missions*, Vol. II (New York: Fleming H. Revell, 1899).
24. ________, *Christian Missions and Social Progress: A Sociological Study of Foreign Missions*, Vol. III (New York: Fleming H. Revell, 1906).
25. *Directory of Christian Missions in India, Burma and Ceylon*, November, 1924, 14 Edition (Ajmer: The Scottish Mission Press, 1924).
26. Dolbeer, M. L., *One Hundred Years in the Andhra Country* (Madras: Diocesan Press, 1942).
27. ________, *A History of Lutheranism in Andhra Desa: The Telugu Territory of India, Board* of Foreign Missions (New York: United Lutheran Church in America, 1959).
28. Downie, David, *The Lone Star: The History of the Telugu Mission of the American Baptist Missionaries Union (1838-1927)* (Philadelphia: The American Baptist Publication, 1892).

29. Drach, George and Calvin F. Kuder, *Telugu Mission of the General Council of the Evangelical Lutheran Church in North America Containing a Biography of the Rev. Christian Frederick Heyer* (Philadelphia: General Council Publication House, 1914).
30. *Educational Papers: Supplement to the South India Missionary Conference Report*, 1 May 1879, No. 1737 (Madras: Addison and Co, 1880).
31. Edward Lawrence, *Modern Missions in the East: Their Methods, Successes and Limitations* (New York: Harper Brothers Publishers, 1895).
32. Elmore, Wilber Theodore, *Dravidian Gods in Modern Hinduism: A Study of the Local and Village Deities of Southern India* (New York: Published by the Author, 1915).
33. Fishman, A. T., *For This Purpose: A Case Study of the Telugu Baptist Church in Its Relation with South India Mission of the American Baptist Foreign Mission Societies in India* (Madras: Diocesan Press, 1958).
34. ________, *Culture Change and the Underprivileged: A Study of the Madigas in South India under Christian Guidance* (Madras: The Christian Literature Society for India, 1941).
35. Frank, Penny, *The Church in Madras: The History of the Ecclesiastical and Missionary Action of the East India Company in the Presidency of Madras from 1805 to 1835* (London: John Murray Publishers, 1912).
36. Gairdner, H. T., *Edinburgh 1910: An Account and Interpretation of the World Missionary Conference* (Edinburgh: Oliphant Anderson and Ferrier Publishers, 1910).
37. Gledstone, Frederick, *Andhra Christian Church Founders: Robert Turlington Noble* (Madras: Diocesan Press, 1941).
38. ________, Frederick, *Andhra Christian Church Founders: Henry Watson Fox* (Madras: The Diocesan Printing Press, 1941).
39. ________, *Andhra Christian Church Founders: John Goldingham: the Collector of Kistna* (Madras: Diocesan Press, 1940).
40. ________, *Andhra Christian Church Founders: Sharkey Jeevitha Charitra* (Madras: Diocesan Press, 1941).
41. ________, *Andhra Christian Church Founders: The Life Story of Thomas Young Darling* (Madras: Diocesan Press, 1941).
42. Glover, Robert Hall, *The Progress of World-Wide Missions* (New York: Harper and Brothers Publishers, 1924).
43. Goodall, Norman, *A History of London Missionary Society* (Oxford: Oxford University Press, 1954).

44. Groves, Anthony N., *Journal of a Residence at Bagdad During the Years 1830 and 1831* (London: James Nisbet Publications, 1832).
45. Groves, Harriet, *Memoir of Anthony Norris Groves: Compiled Chiefly from His Journals and Letters*, Third Edition (Bristol: James Nisbet Publishers, 1869).
46. Harpster, Julia M., *Among the Telugoos: Illustrating Mission Work in India* (Philadelphia: Lutheran Publication Society, 1902).
47. Harris, J. C., *Couriers of Christ: Pioneers of the London Missionary Society* (Westminster: Livingstone Press, 1931).
48. Highland, Augusta, *India* (Rock Island, IL: Board of Foreign Missions, Lutheran Augustana Synod Centennial Committee, 1945).
49. Hines, Herbert Waldo, *Clough: The Kingdom Builder in South India* (Philadelphia: The Freedom Press, 1929).
50. Hough, James, *The History of Christianity in India: From the Commencement of the Christian Era*, Vol. V (London: James Nisbet Publishers, 1845).
51. ________, *The History of Christianity in India: From the Commencement of the Christian Era*, Vol. II (London: Nisbet Publishers, 1845).
52. Houghton, Ross C., *Women of the Orient: An Account of the Religious, Intellectual, and Social Condition of Women* (New York: Cranston and Stowe Publishers, 1877).
53. Johnson, James ed., *Report of the Centenary Conference on Protestant Missions of the World Held in Exeter Hall,* Vol. II (London: James Nisbet, 1888).
54. Jones, J.P., *The Yearbook of Missions in India, Burma and Ceylon* (Madras: Christian Literature Society of India, 1912).
55. ________, *The Year Book of Missions in India, Burma and Ceylon* (Madras: The Christian Literary Society, 1912).
56. Kaye, John William, *Christianity in India: An Historical Narrative* (London: Smith Elder and Co, 1859).
57. Latourette, Kenneth Scott, *History of the Expansion of Christianity*, Vol. VI (New York: Harper and Brothers Publishers, 1938).
58. Lawrence, Edward, *Modern Missions in the East: Their Methods, Successes and Limitations* (New York: Haprer Brothers Publishers, 1895).
59. Lawson, Charles, *Memories of Madras* (London: Swan Sonnenschien and Co, 1905).
60. Lillingston, Frank, The *Brahmo Samaj and Arya Samaj in their bearing upon Christianity* (London: The Macmillan Company Publishers, 1901).

61. Lovett, Richard, *The History of the London Missionary Society* (*1795-1895)*, Vol. I (Oxford: Oxford University Press, 1899).

62. ________, *The History of the London Missionary Society, 1795-1895*, Vol. II (Oxford: Oxford University Press, 1899).

63. Marshman, John Clark, *History of India from the earliest period to the East India Company's Government* (Edinburgh: William Blackwood and Sons Publishers, 1873).

64. ________, *History of India from the Earliest period to the Close of the East India Company's Government* (Calcutta: School Book Society, 1873).

65. *Mass Movement Work in India: Findings of a Conference of the CMS Mass Movement Commission*, Bezwada, Nov 21-28, 1928 (Kottayam: The CMS Press, 1929).

66. Mateer, Samuel, *The Gospel in South India: On the Religious Life, Experience, and Character of the Hindu Christians* (London: The Religious Tract Society, 1880).

67. ________, *The Land of Charity: A Descriptive Account of Travancore and its People with Special Reference to Missionary Labour* (London: John Snow and Company, 1887).

68. Edmund F. Merriam, *A History of American Baptist Missions* (Philadelphia: The American Baptist Publication Society, 1900).

69. Murdoch, John, *Catalogue of the Christian Vernacular Literature in India: With Hints on the Management of Indian Tract Societies* (Madras: Caleb Foster Publishers, 1870).

70. Noble, John, *A Memoir of the Rev. Robert Turlington Noble: Missionaries to the Telugu People in South India* (London: Seeley Jackson and Halliday Publishers, 1867).

71. Orchard, M. L., *Canadian Baptists at Work in India* (Toronto: The Missionary Education Department of the Foreign Mission Board, 1922).

72. Orchard, M. L. and K. S. McLaurin, *The Enterprise: The Jubilee Story of the Canadian Baptist Mission in India: 1874-1924* (Toronto: The Canadian Baptist Foreign Mission Board, 1925).

73. Paton, William, *Alexander Duff: Pioneer of Missionary Education* (New York: George H. Doran Co Publishers, 1922).

74. Polack, W. G., *In to All the World: The Story of Lutheran Foreign Missions* (St. Louis, Missouri: Concordia Seminary, 1930).

75. *Progress of Education in India: 1927-32,* Tenth Quinquennial Review, Volume I, in *Report of the Canadian Baptist Telugu Missions* (Madras: M.E. Publishing House, 1900).

76. Rao, Madhusudhan K. L., *The Andhra Evangelical Lutheran Church Souvenir* (1987-1989).
77. *Report of Commission 1 Carrying the Gospel to all the Non-Christian World*, World Missionary Conference of 1910 (Edinburgh: Oliphant Anderson and Ferrier Publishers, 1910).
78. *Report of the Canadian Baptist Telugu Missions* (Madras: M.E. Publishing House, 1900).
79. *Report of the Deputies to India in 1888-1889, Opinion of the Missionaries in 1890* (Edinburgh: The India Mission of the Free Church of Scotland Press, 1891).
80. Rogers, Olive, *The Origins of the Godavari Delta Mission and Its Distinctive Tenets* (Secunderabad: The Andhra Christian Theological College, 1980).
81. Rutherford, John, *Missionary Pioneers in India* (Edinburgh: Andrew Elliot Press, 1896).
82. Sharrock, J. A., *South Indian Missions* (Westminster: The SPG Publications, 1910).
83. Sheatsley, C. V., *Our Mission Field in India: 1873-1943* (Columbus, Ohio: Lutheran Book Concern, 1921).
84. Sherring, M. A., *The History of Protestant Missions in India from their Commencement in 1706 to 1881* (London: The Religious Tract Society, 1884).
85. Smith, George, *Life of Alexander Duff*, Vol. I (New York: A.C. Armstrong and Sons Publications, 1879).
86. Smith, S. F., *Missionary Sketches: A Concise History of the Work of the American Baptist Missionary Union* (Boston: W. G. Corthell Publishers, 1883).
87. *Statistical Tables of Protestant Missions in India, Burma and Ceylon* (Calcutta: The Baptist Mission Press, 1902).
88. Stevenson, Fleming, *The Dawn of the Modern Mission* (Edinburgh: A. C. Armstrong and Sons Publishers, 1888).
89. Stewart, Edith Anne, *The Life of St. Francis Xavier: Evangelist, Explorer, Mystic* (London: Headley Brothers Publishers, 1917).
90. Stock, Eugene, *A Short Handbook of Missions* (London: Longmans Green and Company, 1904).
91. ________, *History of the Church Missionary Society: Its Environment, Its Men and Its Work,* Vol. I (London: The CMS Publications, 1899).
92. ________, *History of the Church Missionary Society: Its Environment, Its Men and Its Work,* Vol. II (London: The CMS Publications, 1899).

93. _______, *History of the Church Missionary Society: Its Environment, Its Men and Its Work,* Vol. III (London: The CMS Publications, 1899).
94. _______, The *History of the Church Missionary Society: Its Environment, Its Men and Its Work,* Vol. IV (London: The CMS Publications, 1916).
95. _______, *The Romance of Missions: Beginnings in India* (London: The Society for Promoting Christian Knowledge, 1917).
96. Sutton, Amos, *Orissa and its Evangelization: Interspersed with Suggestions Respecting the More Efficient Conducting of Indian Missions* (Boston: William Heath Publishers, 1850).
97. Swavely, C. H. ed., *One Hundred Years in the Andhra Country*: A history of the India Mission of the United Lutheran Church in America, 1842-1942 (Madras: Diocesan Press, 1942).
98. _______, ed., *The Lutheran Enterprise in India* (Madars: Federation of Evangelical Lutheran Churches in India, 1952).
99. _______, *Mission to Church in Andhra Pradesh*: *The Andhra Evangelical Lutheran Church* (New York: The Board of Foreign Missions, 1962).
100. *The American Baptist Missionary Union, Fifty Seventh Annual Report: With the Proceedings of the Annual Meeting held in Chicago,* May 23 (Boston: Missionary Rooms, 1871).
101. *The Church Missionary Atlas*, No XXVI (Westminster: The Society for the Propagation of the Gospel in Foreign Parts, 1912).
102. *The Church Missionary Atlas: Containing an Account of the various countries in which the Church Missionary Society Labours and of its Missionary Operations* (London: The CMS Publications, 1896).
103. *The Church Missionary Atlas: Containing an Account of the various Countries in which the Church Missionary Society Labours and of its Missionary Operations* (London: Seeley Jackson and Halliday Publishers, 1879).
104. *The Church Missionary Society Gazette* (London: The CMS Publications, 1919).
105. *The Church Missionary Gleaner* (London: Seeley Jackson and Halliday Publishers, 1881).
106. *The Church Missionary Gleaner,* Volume XIX (London: The CMS Publications, 1869).
107. *The Church Missionary Intelligencer of Missionary Information*: *A Monthly Journal of Missionary Information,* Volume VIII (London: The CMS Publications, 1872).
108. *The Church Missionary Intelligencer, A Monthly Journal of Missionary Information* (London: James Nisbet and Co. Publishers, 1860).

109. *The Church Missionary Intelligencer,* Vol. XVII (London: Seeley Jackson Halliday Publishers, 1892).
110. *The India Mission of the Free Church of Scotland* (Edinburgh: The Foreign Missions Committee, Edinburgh Press, 1891).
111. *The Missionary Jubilee: An Account of the Fiftieth Anniversary of the American Baptist Missionary Union with Commemorative papers and Discourses* (New York: Sheldon and Company Publishers, 1871).
112. *The Missionary Register of the Church Missionary Society* (London: W. Watts Publishers, 1852).
113. *The Nellore Station and Field of the American Baptist Telugu mission, South India* (Nellore: The American Baptist Telugu Mission, 1922).
114. Thoburn, James M., *The Christian Conquest of India* (New York: Young People's Missionary Movement, 1906).
115. Thomson, A., *Great Missionaries: A Series of Biographies* (London: T. Nelson and Sons Publishers, 1870).
116. Thorogood, Bernard, *Gales of Change: The Story of London Missionary Society 1945-1977* (Geneva: World Council of Churches Publications, 1994).
117. Ware, G. Hibbert, *Christian Missions in the Telugu Country* (Westminster: The SPG Publications, 1912).
118. Warneck, Gustav, *Outline of a History of Missions from the Reformation to the Present Time: Contribution to Modern Church History* (New York: Fleming H. Revell, 1901).
119. Williamson, J. Rutter, *The Healing of the Nations: A Treatise on Medical Missions* (New York: The Student Volunteer Movement for Foreign Missions, 1899).
120. Wolf, L. B. (ed.), *Missionary Heroes of the Lutheran Church* (Philadelphia: The Lutheran Publication Society, 1911).
121. Wolf, L. B., *After Fifty Years or An Historical Sketch of the Guntur Mission of the Evangelical Lutheran Church of the General Synod in the United States of America* (Philadelphia: The Lutheran Publication Society, 1896).
122. Wolf, L. B., "Lutheran Missions and Missionaries before Carey: From 1555 to 1800," in *Missionary Heroes of the Lutheran Church*, ed. L. B. Wolf (Philadelphia: The Lutheran Publication Society, 1911).
123. World Missionary Conference, *Report of Commission 1: Carrying the Gospel to all the Non-Christian World* (Edinburgh: Oliphant Anderson and Ferrier Publishers, 1910).

124. Yeats, Thomas, *Indian Church History; Or An Account of the First Planting of the Gospel in Syria, Mesopotamia and India* (London: Maxwell Bell Yard Publishers, 1818).

III. Missionary Reports, Documents and Articles

1. "AELC Executive Committee Meetings," *The Joint Finance Committee Bulletin* (1928).
2. "AELC Executive Committee Meetings," *The Joint Finance Committee Bulletin,* No. 30 (Rajahmundry: January 20, 1936).
3. "AELC General Work Committee Meetings, General Work," *The Council of the India Mission of the United Lutheran Church in America* (Guntur: 1935).
4. "AELM Routine Minutes," *The General Work Budget of 1930-31*, Appendix A (Guntur: 1931).
5. "Co-Education at Dornakal," *The Dornakal Diocesan Magazine*, No. 10, Vol. 5, October (*Dornakal: Diocesan Press, 1928*).
6. "Educational Developments for the Year 1942," *The National Christian Council Review* (Mysore: Wesley Press, 1943).
7. "Educational Work: Elementary Education," *The Minutes of the Executive Committee,* AELC (Guntur: 1925).
8. "Extracts from the Minutes of Fourth Session of the Dornakal Diocesan Council held in Bezwada on December 1927," (1928).
9. "From the Bishop's Letter Bag: For their Children's Education," Vol. IX, No. 9, September (1930).
10. "Khammamet District-1927," *The Dornakal Diocesan Magazine*, Vol. 4, No. 5, May (*Dornakal: Diocesan Press*, 1928).
11. "Mass Movements and Economic Reconstruction," *The Dornakal Diocesan Magazine,* Vol. XI, No. 3, March (1934).
12. *Minutes of the Council of the India Mission of the United Lutheran Church in America*, held at St. Mathews Church, 21-29 (Guntur: April 1927).
13. "Minutes of the Council of the Indian Mission," *The United Lutheran Church in America* (Guntur: October 1924).
14. "Minutes of the Executive Committee," *The Council of the India Mission of the United Lutheran Church in America* (Guntur: October 1923).
15. "Minutes of the Executive Committee," *The Council of the India Mission of the United Lutheran Church in America* (Guntur: 1930).
16. "Minutes of the Executive Committee," *The Council of the India Mission of the United Lutheran Church in America* (Guntur: January 1935).

17. "Minutes of the Third Convention of the AELM," Guntur (September 19-26, 1929).
18. "Report of Ms. Brummer," *The Minutes of the AELC Executive Committee* (Guntur: April 1927).
19. "The Bishop's Letter," *The Dornakal Diocesan Magazine,* No. 11-12, December (*Dornakal: Diocesan Press*, 1934).
20. "The Bishop's Letter," *The Dornakal Diocesan Magazine,* No. 11, November (*Dornakal: Diocesan Press*, 1928).
21. "The Church in Rural India," *The Dornakal Diocesan Magazine*, Vol. 5, No. 10, October (*Dornakal: Diocesan Press*, 1928).
22. "Vidya Nagar, 1935," *The Dornakal Diocesan Magazine*, No. 7, Vol. XIII, July (*Dornakal: Diocesan Press*, 1936).
23. *American Baptist Quarterly*, Vol. V, No. 2 and 3, June-September (1986).
24. Azariah, V. S., "Christian Education," *The National Christian Council Review* (Mysore: Wesley Press, 1943).
25. Azariah, V. S., "The Christian Contribution to India," *The National Christian Council Review*, Vol. XVII, Jan-Dec (Nagpur: Central India Printing Works, 1939).
26. Azariah, V. S., "The Christian Approach to the Unprivileged," *The National Christian Council Review*, Vol. XV (Mysore: Wesley Press, 1937).
27. Chellaswamy, F. S., "Occupational Training," *The National Christian Council Review* (Mysore: Wesley Press, 1946).
28. *C.M.S. Annual Reports* (1891-1892).
29. Dolbeer, M. L., "The Caste Mass Movement in the Telugu Area," *The National Christian Council Review* (Mysore: Wesley Press, 1933).
30. Doren, Van, B. Alice, "Christian Mass Movements in India: A Review, in Laymen's Foreign Missionary Inquiry Reports," *The National Christian Council Review*, Vol. I, (Mysore: Wesley Press, 1933).
31. "Anon," *History of the Lone Star, The American Baptist Telugu Mission* (Madras: Baptist Mission Press, 1922).
32. Kuruvilla, K. K., "The Christian Approach to the Unprivileged," *The National Christian Council Review*, Vol. XV (Mysore: Wesley Press, 1937).
33. Mathew, C. P., "Mahatma Gandhi and Christian Missionary Work," *The National Christian Council Review*, January to December 1937, Vol. XV (Mysore: Wesley Press, 1937).
34. *Minutes of the Council of the Council of the India Mission of the United Lutheran Church in America* (Guntur: October 6-20, 1927).

35. *Minutes of the Council of the Indian Mission of the United Lutheran Church in America* (Guntur: 1925).
36. *Minutes of the Council of the Indian Mission*, The United Lutheran Church in America (Guntur: January 1935).
37. *Minutes of the Executive Committee*, Item No. 11 (Guntur: April 1925).
38. Noble, F. M., "The Economic Situation and Self-Support," *The National Christian Council of India Proceedings* (Mysore: Wesley Press, 1930).
39. *Proceedings of the Eighth Meeting of the National Christian Council* (Nagpur: Central India Printing Works, 1940).
40. *Proceedings of the Fifth Meeting of the National Christian Council* (Mysore: Wesley Press, 1933).
41. *Proceedings of the Fifth Meeting of the National Christian Council* (Mysore: Wesley Press, 1933).
42. *Proceedings of the National Christian Council Review*, Vol. XVIII (Mysore: Wesley Press, 1940).
43. *Proceedings of the National Christian Council,* Vol. XVIII, 1939-40 (Mysore: Wesley Press, 1940).
44. *Proceedings of the Seventh Meeting of the National Christian Council* (Madras: Diocesan Press, 1937).
45. *Proceedings of the Sixth Meeting of the National Christian Council* (Nagpur: Central India Printing Works, 1934).
46. *Proceedings of the Tenth Meeting of the National Christian Council of India, Burma and Ceylon* (Mysore: Wesley Press, 1946).
47. *Proceedings of the Tenth Meeting of the National Christian Council of India, Burma and Ceylon* (Mysore: Wesley Press, 1946).
48. *Report of the American Baptist Telugu Mission* (Madras: Baptist Mission Press, 1908).
49. *Report of the Hill Conferences on the Knubel-Miller Conference,* AELM (Guntur: AELM Press, February 27- 28, 1928).
50. Smiley, C. H., "God at Work in the Telugu Area," *The National Christian Council Review*, Vol. XIII, January to December (Mysore: Wesley Press, 1935).
51. Smiley, C. H., "God at Work in the Telugu Area," *The National Christian Council Review*, Vol. XIII, Jan-Dec (Mysore: Wesley Press, 1935).
52. *Standing Committee meetings of the Andhra Evangelical Lutheran Church*, No. 20, and (October 1931).
53. *The Guntur Mission: A Review of a Year's Work* (Guntur: The Board of Foreign Missions of the General Synod of the Evangelical Lutheran Church in America, 1915).

54. Tickell, D., "Poverty among Village Christians," *The National Christian Council Review,* Vol. XIII (Mysore: Wesley Press, 1935).

IV. Secondary Sources: Books and Papers

1. A Father, *History of the Telugu Christians* (Trichinopoly: St. Joseph's Industrial School Press, 1910).
2. Alexander, K. C., "The Problem of Caste in the Christian Churches of Kerala," in *Caste Among Non-Hindus in India*, ed. Harjinder Singh (New Delhi: National Publishing House, 1977).
3. Alexander, Susan, *The Attitudes of British Protestant Missionaries Towards Nationalism in India: With Special Reference to Madras Presidency, 1919-1927* (New Delhi: Konark Publishers, 1994).
4. Ambedkar, Babasaheb, *Why go For Conversion*? (Bangalore: Dalit Sahitya Academy, 1984).
5. Anderson, Gerald H., *Biographical Dictionary of Christian Missions* (Grand Rapids, Michigan: W. B. Eerdmans Publishing Company, 1999).
6. Anderson, J. D., *The Peoples of India* (Cambridge: The Cambridge University Press, 1913).
7. Andrew, A., *Indian Problems concerned With Education, Agriculture and Land Revenue* (Madras: G. A. Natesan and Co, 1905).
8. Anon, *The Depressed Classes: A Chronological Documentation,* Part I-XI, 1931-1937 (Kurseong, Delhi: St Mary's College, Presently Vidyajyoti College of Theology, 1937), 1-587+ xx.
9. Azariah, V. S. and Rev. Henry Whitehead, *Christ in the Indian Villages* (London: Student Christian Movement Press, 1930).
10. Baago, Kaj, *A History of the National Christian Council of India: 1914-1964* (Mysore: Wesley Press, 1965).
11. Bailey, F. G., *Caste and the Economic Frontier: A Village in Highland Orissa* (Manchester: The Manchester University Press, 1957).
12. Baines, Athelstane, *Ethnography: Castes and Tribes* (Strassburg: Karl J Trubner Publishers, 1912).
13. Baker, Archibald G., *Christian Missions and a New World Culture* (Chicago: Willett Clark and Co Publishers, 1934).
14. Baker, James Millard, *Contending the Grade in India* (Ashville: The Biltmore Press, 1947).
15. Balendu Sekharam, Khandavalli, *Andhras through the Ages* (Madras: Sri Sarawathi Press, 1973).
16. Barber, Bernard, "Social Mobility in Hindu India," in *Social Mobility in the Caste System in India: An Interdisciplinary Symposium, Comparative*

Studies in Society and History, Supplement III, ed. Silverberg, James (The Hague: Mouton Publishers, 1969).

17. Barnett, L. D., *A Catalogue of the Telugu Books in the Library of the British Museum* (London: Longmans and Co Publishers, 1912).
18. Basham, A. L., *A Cultural History of India* (New Delhi: The Oxford University Press, 1975).
19. Basu, D. D., *Commentary on the Constitution of India* (Calcutta: S. C. Sarkar and Sons, 1964).
20. Basu, D. D., *Commentary on the Constitution of India*, Vol. V (Calcutta: S.C. Sarkar Sons Publishers, 1964).
21. Bauman, Chad M., *Christian Identity and Dalit Religion in Hindu India* (Grand Rapids, Michigan: W. B. Eerdmans Publishing Company, 2008).
22. Beck, Brenda E. F., "The Right-Left Division of South Indian Society," in *Right and Left: Essays on Dual Symbolic Classification,* ed. Rodney Needham (Chicago: The University of Chicago Press, 1973), 779-798. Accessed on 02 June 2012, http://www.jstor.org/stable/2943087.
23. Bendix, Reinhard, *Max Weber: An Intellectual Portrait* (Berkeley: University of California Press, 1977).
24. Beteille, Andre, *Castes: Old and New:* Essays *in Social Structure and Social Stratification* (New Delhi: Asia Publishing House, 1969).
25. Bhargava, K. D., *Selections from Educational Records of the Government of India, Vol. IV, Technical Education in India, 1886-1907* (New Delhi: The National Archives of India, 1968).
26. Bhatt, B. D. and J. C. Aggarwal, *Educational Documents in India: 1813-1968*: *Survey of Indian Education* (New Delhi: Arya Book Depot, 1969).
27. Biswas, A. and S. P. Agarwal, *Development of Education in India* (New Delhi: Concept Publishing House, 1986).
28. Blunt, Edward, *Social Service in India: An Introduction to Social and Economic Problems of the Indian Peoples* (London: H.M. Stationary Office, 1939).
29. Bosco SJ., Aariz Mohammed, Selva Rathinam SJ., L. A. Samy, Joe Xavier SJ. and Franklin Caesar Thomas, *Constitutional Rights of Dalit Christians and Muslims* (Chennai: LTD Media, 2010).
30. Bose, Anima, *Higher Education in India in the 19th Century: The American Involvement, 1883-1893* (Calcutta: Punthi Pustak, 1978).
31. Boskoff, Alvin, "Social Change: Major Problems in the Emergence of theoretical and Research Foci," in *The Modern Sociological Theory in Continuity and Change, eds.* Howard Becker and Alvin Boskoff (New York: Holt, Rinehart and Winston, 1957).

32. Brewer, John D., *Ethnography* (Philadelphia: The Open University Press, 2000).
33. Brian, Stanley ed., *Missions, Nationalism and the End of the Empire* (Grand Rapids, Michigan: William B. Erdman Publishers, 2003).
34. Briggs, Henry George, *The Nizam: His History and Relations with the British Government*, Vol. I (Delhi: Manas Publications, 1985).
35. Brown, Charles Philip, *A Telugu-English Dictionary*, Second Edition (Madras: Society for Promoting Christian Knowledge, 1903).
36. Buchanan, Norman S. and Ellis S. Howard, *Approaches to Economic Development* (New York: The Twentieth Century Fund, 1955).
37. Buenes, Alexander, *Travels into Bokhara: Being the Account of a Journey From India to Cabool, Tartary and Persia*, Vol. III (London: John Murray Publishers, 1834).
38. Burrow, Trigant, *The Social Basis of Consciousness* (London: Kegan Paul, Trench and Trubner Co. Publishers, 1927).
39. Caldwell, Bruce J., *Jajmani System: An Investigation* (New Delhi: Hindustan Publishing Corporation, 1991).
40. Caplan, Lionel, *Class and Culture in Urban India* (Oxford: Clarendon Press, 1987).
41. Chaudhari, Nirad, "The Continent of Circe: An Essay on the Peoples of India," in *Dalits and Social Mobilization,* Siva Prakasam, M. N. (Delhi: Rajput Publications, 2002).
42. Chenchayya, P. and Raja M. Bhujanga Rao Bahadur, *A History of Telugu Literature* (Calcutta: The Association Press, 1928).
43. Cohn, S. Bernard and Marriott McKim, Alan R. Beals eds., *The Changing Status of a Depressed Caste Village India; Studies in the Little Community Comparative Studies of Cultures and Civilizations* (Chicago: The University of Chicago Press, 1955).
44. Copley, Anthony, *Religion in Conflict: Ideology, Cultural Contact and Conversion in Late Colonial India* (New York: The Oxford University Press, 1997).
45. D'Souza, A. Austin, *Anglo Indian Education, A Study of its Origins and Growth in Bengal Up to 1960* (Bombay: The Oxford University Press, 1976).
46. Deliege, Robert, *The Untouchables of India*, Translated by Nora Scott (Oxford: The Berg Publishers, 1999).
47. Dena, Lal, *A Study of Missionary Movement in Northeast India With Particular Reference to Manipur and Lushai Hills 1894-1947* (Shillong: The Vendrame Institute, 1988).

48. Dhanagare, D. N., *Peasant Movements in India 1920-1950* (Delhi: The Oxford University Press, 1983).
49. Dikshit, Kashinath Narayan, *Pre-Historic Civilization of the Indus Valley* (Madras: University of Madras, 1967).
50. Dirks, Nicholas B., *Colonialism and the Making of Modern India* (New Jersey: The Princeton University Press, 2001).
51. Dubois, Abbe J. A., *Description of the Character, Manners and Customs of the People of India, and of their Institutions, Religious and Civil* (London: Longman and Hurst Publishers, 1817).
52. Dubois, Abbe J. A., *Hindu Manners, Customs and Ceremonies*, Third Edition (Oxford: Clarendon Press, 1906).
53. Dubois, Abbe J. A., *Letters on the State of Christianity in India: In which the Conversion of the Hindoos is Considered as Impracticable: To Which is Added a Vindication of the Hindoos, Male and Female* (London: Longman Company Publishers, 1823).
54. Dumont, Louis, *Homo Hierarchicus: The Caste System and Its Implications* (Chicago: The University of Chicago Press, 1970).
55. Durkheim, Emile, *Education and Sociology* (New York: The Free Press, 1956).
56. Dutt, Nripendra Kumar, *Origin and Growth of Caste in India*, Vol. I (Calcutta: Firma K.L Mukhopadhyay, 1968).
57. Dutt, Romesh, *The Economic History Of India Under Early British Rule*, Sixth Edition, Kegan Paul (London: Trench and Trubner Publishers, 1901).
58. Eddy, Sherwood, *India Awakening* (New York: Missionary Education Movement, 1911).
59. Ellis, J. J., "Christward Movements in South India," in *The Social Setting of Christian Conversion in South India: The Impact of the Wesleyan Methodist Missionaries on the Trichy-Tanjore Diocese with special reference to the Harijan Communities of the Mass Movement Area 1820-1947*, Manickam, Sundara Raj (Wiesbaden: Franz Steiner Verlag, 1977).
60. Fernandes, Walter, *Caste and Conversion Movements in India* (New Delhi: Indian Social Institute, 1981).
61. Fischer, Rudolph H., "Conversion and Social Mobility in Nineteenth Century South Canara and Malabar," in *Religion in South Asia: Religious Conversion and Revival Movements in South Asia in Medieval and Modern Times*, (2nd ed.), ed. G. A. Oddie (New Delhi: Manohar Publication, 1991).
62. Forbes, J., *Oriental Memoirs :* A *Narrative of Seventeen Years Residence in India* (London: R. Bentley Publishers, 1834).

63. Forrester, Duncan B., "The Depressed Classes and Conversion to Christianity, 1860-1960," in *Religion in South Asia,* ed. G. A. Oddie (Delhi: Manohar Publishers, 1977).
64. Forrester, Duncan B., *Caste and Christianity: Attitudes and Policies on Caste of Anglo-Saxon Protestant Missions in India* (Richmond, Surrey: Curzon Press, 1980).
65. Frederick A. Nicholson, "Report regarding the possibility of introducing Land and Agricultural Banks in the Madras Presidency: 1895," in *The Economic Transition of India,* Morison, Theodore (London: John Murray Publishers, 1911).
66. Gehlke, Charles Elmer, *Emile Durkheim's Contributions to Sociological Theory* (New York: The Columbia University Press, 1915).
67. Gibbs, M. E., *The Anglican Church in India* (Delhi: The ISPCK Publishers, 1972).
68. Giddens, Anthony and Jonathan Turner ed., in *Social Theory Today* (Cambridge: The Polity Press, 1987).
69. Gladstone, J. W., *Protestant Christianity and People's Movements in Kerala: A Study of Christian Mass Movements in Relation to Neo-Hindu Socio-Religious Movements in Kerala, 1850-1936* (Trivandrum: The Seminary Publications, 1984).
70. Gore, M. S., *Education and Modernization in India* (Jaipur: Rawat Publications, 1982).
71. *Gould, Harold* A., *The Hindu Caste System* (Delhi: The Chanakya Publications, *1987*).
72. Graham, Carol, *Azariah of Dornakal* (London: S.C.M. Press Ltd, 1946).
73. Greville, Charles Francis, *British India Analyzed: The Provincial and Revenue Establishments*, Vol. 3 (London: R. Faulder Publishers, 1795).
74. Grimes, Cecil John, *Towards an Indian Church: The Growth of the Church of India in Constitution and Life* (London: SPCK Publishers, 1946).
75. Groome, Thomas H., *Christian Religious Education* (San Francisco: Harper and Row Publishers, 1980).
76. Grover, Charles E., *Results of Educational Census, Madras-87* (Madras: The Government Press, 1872).
77. Gupta, A. R., *Caste Hierarchy and Social Change: A Study of Myth and Reality* (New Delhi: Jyotsna Prakasan, 1984).
78. Habermas, Jurgen, *Religion and Rationality, Essays on Reason, God, and Modernity* (London: The Polity Press, 2002).
79. Habib, Irfan, *The Agrarian System of Mughal India* (New Delhi: Asia Publishing House, 1963).

80. Haferkamp, Hans and Neil J. Smelser ed., *Social Change and Modernity* (Berkeley: University of California Press, 1992).

81. Hammond, Philip E., *Religion and Personal Autonomy* (Columbia: University of South Carolina Press, 1992).

82. Hardgrave, R. L., *Essays in the Political Sociology of South India* (New Delhi: The Usha Publications, 1979).

83. Harper, Marvin Henry, *The Methodist Episcopal Church in India: A study of Ecclesiastical Organization and Administration* (Lucknow: The Lucknow Publishing House, 1936).

84. Harper, Susan Billington, *In the Shadow of the Mahatma: Bishop V.S. Azariah and the Travails of Christianity in British India* (Richmond, Surrey: Curzon Press, 2000).

85. Harper, Susan Billington, "The Dornakal Church on the Cultural Frontier," in *Christians, Cultural Interactions and India's Religious Traditions,* eds. M. Judith Brown, and Robert Eric Freykenberg (Grand Rapids, Michigan: W.B. Eerdmans Publishing Company, 2002).

86. Hastings, Adrian, "The Clash of Nationalism and Universalism with in Twentieth Century Missionary Christianity," in *Missions, Nationalism and the End of Empire,* ed. Brian Stanley (Grand Rapids, Michigan: W.B. Eerdmans Publishing Company, 2003).

87. Heimsath, Charles H., Indian *Nationalism and Hindu Social Reform* (Princeton: The Princeton University Press, 1964).

88. Holland, T. and Jadunath Sarkar, *Economics of British India* (Calcutta: M.C. Sarkar and Sons Publishers, 1917).

89. Homans, George Caspar, *Social Behavior: Its elementary Forms* (New York: Harcourt and Brace Publishers, 1974).

90. Horner, Norman A., *Protestant Cross Currents in Mission: The Ecumenical-Conservative Encounter* (New York: Abingdon Press, 1968).

91. Hrangkhuma, E., *Christianity in India: Search for Liberation and Identity* (New Delhi: ISPCK Publishers, 1998).

92. Hunt, W. S., *India's Outcastes: A New Era* (London: The CMS Publications, 1924).

93. Hunter, William Wilson, *A Brief History of the Indian Peoples* (Oxford: Clarendon Press, 1893).

94. Hunter, William Wilson, *The Indian Empire: Its People, History and Products* (London: Trubner and Ludgate Hill Publishers, 1886).

95. Hutton, John Henry, *Caste in India: Its Nature, Function and Origins* (Cambridge: The Cambridge University Press, 1946).

96. Ingham, Kenneth, *Reformers in India 1793-1833* (Cambridge: The Cambridge University Press, 1956).

97. Jain, P. C., *Christianity, Ideology and Social Change among Tribals: A Case Study of Bhils in Rajasthan* (Jaipur: Rawat Publications, 1995).
98. Jayapalan, N., *History of Education in India* (New Delhi: Atlantic Publishers, 2000).
99. Jefferys, Julius, The *British Army in India: Its Preservation* (London: Longman and Roberts Publishers, 1858).
100. Jones, William, *Institutes of Hindu Law or the Ordinances of Menu: According to the Gloss of Culluca: Comprising the Indian System of Duties, Religious and Civil* (London: Printed by Order of the Government, 1796).
101. Joseph, Dr. Nandi, *Dalit Reality of the Indian Catholic Church* (Chennai: Foundation for Dalit Literature, 2001).
102. Joshi, Barbara R., *Democracy in Search of Equality: Untouchable Politics and Indian Social Change* (Delhi: Hindustan Publishing Corporation, 1982).
103. Juergensmeyer, Mark, *Religion as Social Vision: The Movement Against Untouchability in 20th Century Punjab* (Berkeley: The University of California Press, 1982).
104. Jurgen, Habermas, *Religion and Rationality: Essays on Reason, God, and Modernity* (London: The Polity Press, 2002).
105. Kalapura, Jose, "Change of Socio-economic Structure: A Paradigm of Dalit Mobility (A Case Study of the Ravidasis of Bihar)," in *Dalits and Peasants: the Emerging Caste-Class Dynamics,* ed. Ashish Ghosh (New Delhi: Gyan Sagar Publications, 1999).
106. Kamble, J. R., *Rise and Awakening of Depressed Classes in India* (Delhi: National Printing Press, 1979).
107. Kananaikil, Jose, *Christians of Scheduled Caste Origin: In Search of Justice* (New Delhi: Indian Social Institute, 1986).
108. Kananaikil, Jose, *Scheduled Castes in the Constituent Assembly: Rebirth in a New Nation* (New Delhi: The Indian Social Institute, 1983).
109. Kanjamala, Augustine, *Religion and Modernization of India: A Caste Study of Northern Orissa* (Indore: Satprakashan Sanchar Kendra, 1981).
110. Kaye, John William, *Administration of the East India Company: A of Indian Progress* (London: Richard Bentley Publishers, 1853).
111. Ketkar, Shridhar V., *The History of Caste in India: Evidence of the Laws of Manu on the Social Conditions in India During the Third Century A. D, Interpreted and Examined*, Vol. I (New York: Taylor and Carpenter Publishers, 1909).
112. Khadavalli, Lakshmi Ranjanam, *The Andhras through the Ages* (Hyderabad: Sri Saraswati Book Depot, 1973).

113. Kahn, Zafar, "Social Justice and the Indian Constitution: Ambedkar's Perspective," in *Ambedkar on Law, Constitution and Social Justice,* ed. Mohammad Shabbir (New Delhi: Rawat Publishers, 2008.
114. Klass, Morton, *Caste: The Emergence of South Asian Social System* (Delhi: Manohar Publishers, 1980).
115. Kumar, Dharma, *Land and Caste in South India: Agricultural Labour in the Madras Presidency* (London: The Cambridge University Press, 1965).
116. Kumar, Krishna and Joachim Oesterheld ed., *Education and Social Change in South Asia* (Hyderabad: Orient Longman, 2007).
117. Kuppuswamy, B., *Social Change in India* (New Delhi: Vikas Publishing House, 1972).
118. Kutty, Kapil Fathima, *Education and Social Change in India* (New Delhi: Radiant Publishers, 1990).
119. Laird, M. A., Missionaries *and Education in Bengal 1793-1837* (Oxford: Clarendon Press, 1972).
120. Lal, A. K. ed., *Social Exclusion* (New Delhi: The Concept Publishers, 2003).
121. Lal, Shyam, *Tribals and Christian Missionaries* (New Delhi: Manak Publications, Pvt. Ltd., 1994).
122. Lapp, George Jay, *The Christian Church and Rural India* (Calcutta: The YMCA Publishing House, 1938).
123. Liebau, Heike, "Indianisation and Education: Reaction from Protestant Christians of the Madras Presidency to the Lindsay Commission Report," in *Education and Social Change in South Asia,* eds. Krishna Kumar and Joachim Oesterheld (Hyderabad: Orient Longman, 2007).
124. Lillingston, Frank, The *Brahmo Samaj and Arya Samaj in their bearing upon Christianity* (London: The Macmillan Company Publishers, 1901).
125. Lourduswamy, S., *Equal Rights to All Dalits (with special reference to Dalit Christians*) (New Delhi: Centre for Dalit Studies, 2001).
126. Luke, P. Y. and John B. Carman, *Village Christians and Hindu Culture: Study of Rural Church in Andhra Pradesh, South India* (New Delhi: ISPCK Publishers, 1969).
127. Lynch, Owen M., *The Politics of Untouchability: Social Mobility and Social Change in a City of India* (Delhi: The National Publishing House, 1974).
128. Mahmood, Syed, *History of English Education in India: 1781 to 1893* (Aligarh: Mao College, 1805).
129. Majumdar, Bimal Kanthi, *The Military System in Ancient India* (Calcutta: The World Press Limited, 1955).

130. Majumdar, P. K., *Commentary on the Constitution of India* (New Delhi: Orient Publishers, 1977).
131. Majumdar, R C., et al, *An Advanced History of India* (Delhi: The McMillan Publishing Company, 1978).
132. Majumdar, R. C. ed., *History and Culture of the Indian People: The Vedic Age* (Mumbai: Bharatiya Vidya Bhavan, 1996).
133. Majumdar, R. C. ed., *The History and Culture of the Indian People* (Bombay: Bharatiya Vidya Bhavan, 1965).
134. Malinowski, Bronislaw, *The Dynamics of Culture Change: An Inquiry into Race Relations in Africa* (New Haven: The Yale University Press, 1945).
135. Mandal, Jagadish Chandra, *Poona Pact and the Depressed Classes* (Calcutta: Sujan Publications, 1999).
136. Mandelbaum, David G., *Society in India: Change and Continuity*, Vol. 2 (Berkeley: University of California Press, 1970).
137. Mangamma J., *The Rate Schools of Godavari* (Hyderabad: A.P. State Archives Monograph, 1973).
138. Manickam, Rajah B., *Christianity and the Asian Revolution* (Madras: The CLS Publication Society, 1954).
139. Manickam, Sundar Raj, *Studies in Missionary History: Reflections on a Culture-Contact* (Madras: Christian Literature Society, 1988).
140. Manickam, Sundar Raj, *The Social Setting of Christian Conversion in South India: The Impact of the Wesleyan Methodist missionaries on the Trichy-Tanjore Diocese with special Reference to the Harijan communities of the Mass Movement Area 1820-1947* (Wiesbaden: Franz Steiner Verlag, 1977).
141. Mann, R. S., *Social Change and Social Research: An Indian Perspective* (New Delhi: Concept Publishing Company, 1988).
142. Mathew A., *Christian Missions, Education and Nationalism: From Dominance to Compromise, 1870-1930* (New Delhi: Anamika Prakasan, 1989).
143. Mathews, Basil, *The Church takes Root in India* (New York: Friendship Press, New York, 1938).
144. Mazumder, Nogendra Nath, *A History of Education in Ancient India* (Calcutta: The Macmillan Company Publishers, 1916).
145. McGavran, Donald Anderson, ed., *Church Growth and Christian Mission* (New York: Harper and Row Publishers, 1965).
146. McGavran, Donald, *Understanding Church Growth* (Grand Rapids, Michigan: W.B. Eerdmans Publishing Co, 1970).

147. McLean, George F. and John K. White, *Imagination in Religion and Social Life*, Vol. III (Washington: The Council for Research in Values and Philosophy, 2003).
148. McLean, George F., "Culture and Religion," in *Culture Evangelization and Dialogue,* ed. George F. McLean et al. (Washington: The Council for Research in Values and Philosophy, 2003).
149. Mendelsohn, Oliver and Marika Vicziany, *The Untouchables: Subordination, Poverty and the State in Modern India* (Cambridge: The Cambridge University Press, 1998).
150. Mishra, N., *Scheduled Castes Education* (Delhi: Kalpaz Publications, 2001).
151. Moffatt, Michael, *An Untouchable Community in South India: Structure and Consensus* (New Jersey: The Princeton University Press, 1979).
152. Morison, Theodore, *The Economic Transition of India* (London: John Murray Publishers, 1911).
153. Morris, Henry, *Charles Grant: Director of the East India Company and Member of Parliament* (Madras: M.E. Publishing House, NY).
154. Mott, John R., *The Decisive Hour of Christian Missions* (New York: Student Volunteer Movement for Foreign Missions, New York, 1910).
155. Mukerji, S. N., *History of Education in India: Modern Period* (Baroda: Acharya Book Depot, 1955).
156. Mukherji, Panchanandas, *Indian Constitutional Documents, Vol. II Containing the Government of India Acts, 1915 and 1916* (Calcutta: Thacker Spink and Co Publishers, 1915).
157. Murray, Jocelyn, "The Role of Women in the Church Missionary Society: 1799-1917," in *The Church Missionary Society and World Christianity 1799-1999*, eds. Kevin Ward and Brain Stanley (London: Curzon Press, 2000).
158. Naito, Masao, *Marga: Ways of Liberation, Empowerment, and Social Change in Maharashtra* (New Delhi: Manohar Publishers, 2008).
159. Neill, Stephen, *A History of Christianity in India: 1707-1858* (Cambridge: The Cambridge University Press, 1984).
160. Nock A. D., *Conversion: The Old and the New in Religion from Alexander the Great to Augustine of Hippo* (Oxford: Clarendon Press, 1933).
161. Nurallah, S. and Naik J. P., *A Student History of Education in India 1800-1973* (New Delhi: McMillan Publishing Co, 1974).
162. Oddie, G. A., "Christian Conversion among Non-Brahmins in Andhra Pradesh, with Special Reference to Anglican Missions and the Dornakal Diocese, c. 1900-1936," in *Religious Conversion and Revival Movements*

in South Asia in Mediaeval and Modern Times, ed. G. A. Oddie (New Delhi: Manohar Publishers, 1977).

163. Oddie, G. A., *Social Protest in India: British Protestant Missionaries and Social Reforms 1850-1900* (New Delhi: Manohar Publishers, 1979).
164. Oddie, G. A., "India: Missionaries, Conversion and Change," in *The Church Mission Society and World Christianity 1799-1999,* eds. Kevin Ward and Brian Stanley (Grand Rapids, Michigan: W. B. Eerdmans Publishing Company, 2000).
165. Ogburn, William Fielding, *Social Change with Respect to Culture and Original Nature* (New York: B. W. Huebsch Publishers, 1923).
166. Oomen T. K., *State and Society in India: Studies in Nation Building* (New Delhi: Sage Publications, 1990).
167. Oomen, T. K., *Protest and Change, Studies in Social Movements* (London: Sage Publications, 1990).
168. Oppert, Gustav, *On the Original Inhabitants of Bharatavarşa or India* (London: Archibald Constable and Co, 1898).
169. Packer, J. I., *The Church of South India and Reunion in England, Conference of Evangelical Churchmen* (London: Church Book Room Press, 1968).
170. Pandey, J. N., *Constitutional Law of India* (Allahabad: Central Law Agency, 1993).
171. Pasupuleti, Manasseh, *A Historical Overview of Christianity in the Telugu States and its Impact on Telugu Language, Literature and Culture* (Hyderabad: Andhra Christian Theological College, 2015).
172. Pathak, Sushil Madhav, *American Missionaries and Hinduism* (Delhi: Munshiram Manoharlal Publishers, 1967).
173. Pathak, Sushil Madhav, *American Missionaries and Hinduism (1813-1910)* (New Delhi: Munshiram Manoharlal, 1967).
174. Paul, Rev. R. C., *History of the Telugu Christians* (Madras: Good Pastor Press, 1929).
175. Philips, G. E., *The Gospel in the World* (London: The Duckworth Publishers, 1939).
176. Pickett, J. W., *Christ's Way to India's Heart* (Lucknow: The Lucknow Publishing House, 1938).
177. Pickett, J. W., *Christian Mass Movements in India* (Lucknow: The Lucknow Publishing House, 1933).
178. Pickett, J. W., et al, *Church Growth and Group Conversion* (California: The William Cary Library, 1936).
179. Plutarch, *Alexander* (New York: Philips and Hunt Publishers, 1883).

180. Pocock, D. F., *Essays on the Caste System by Celestin Bougle* (Cambridge: The Cambridge University Press, 1971).
181. Powell, Baden, B. H., *The Land Systems of British India: Being a Manual of the Land Tenures and of the systems of Land Revenue Administration prevalent in the several Provinces*, Vol. I (Oxford: Clarendon Press, 1892).
182. Raghaviah, Jaiprakash, *Basel Mission Industries in Malabar and South Canara (1834-1914): A Study of its Social and Economic Impact* (New Delhi: Gian Publishing House, 1990).
183. Raghuvanshi, V. P. S., *Indian Society in the Eighteenth Century* (Delhi: Associated Publishing House, 1969).
184. Rai, Lajpat, *The Arya Samaj: An Account of its Origin, Doctrines and Activities* (Delhi: Longman Greens and Co, 1915).
185. Raj, Dharma, Jacob S., *Colonialism and Christian Missions: Post-Colonial Reflections* (Delhi: The ISPCK Publishers, 1993).
186. Raj, Y. Antony, *Social Impact of Conversion: A Comparative Sociological Study on the Christians of Scheduled Caste Origin and Scheduled Caste Hindus* (Delhi: ISPCK, 2001).
187. Raj, Sebasti L. and G. F. Xavier, *Caste Culture in Indian Church* (New Delhi: Indian Social Institute, 1993).
188. Rajprakukh, K. E., *Dalit Christians of Andhra: Under the Impact of Missionaries* (New Delhi: Serials Publications, 2008).
189. Ram, Nandu, *Encyclopedia of Scheduled Castes in India* (New Delhi: Gyan Publishing House, 2007).
190. Ramakrishna, V., *Social Reform in Andhra, 1848-99* (Delhi: Vikas Publishing House, 1983).
191. Rambo, Lewis R., *Understanding Religious Conversion* (New Haven: The Yale University Press, 1993).
192. Rao, P. Raghunadha, *History of Modern Andhra Pradesh* (New Delhi: Sterling Publishers, 1988).
193. Rao, Y. Sudershan, *Andhra between the Empires* (Hanmakonda: Sulekha Publishers, 1991).
194. Rao, Y. V. Krishna, "Delta Shipli Sir Arthur Cotton," in *Andhra Pradesh Darshini* (Hyderabad: Vishalandra Publishing House, 1976).
195. Rao, Y. V. Krishna, *Andhra Pradesh Darshini* (Hyderabad: Vishalandra Publishing House, 1976).
196. Ricards, R., *India or Facts Submitted to Illustrate the Character and Condition of the Native Inhabitants*, Vol (London: Smith Elder and Company Publishers, 1829).

197. Rosalind, O'Hanlon, *Caste, Conflict and Ideology* (Cambridge: The Cambridge University Press, 1985).
198. Roth, Guenther and Claus Wittich, *Max Weber: Economy and Society: An Outline of Interpretive Sociology* (Los Angeles: The University of California Press, 1978).
199. S., Venkateswaran, *Census of India, 1951*, *Madras and Coorg,* Vol. III, Part II-B, Tables (Madras: The Government Press, 1953).
200. Sahay, K. N., *Christianity and Culture Change in India* (New Delhi: Inter India, 1986).
201. Samuel, Jayakumar, *Dalit Consciousness and Christian Conversion: The Work of SPG Missionaries, Historical Resources for a Contemporary Debate, Mission Theology in an Asian Context* (Delhi: The ISPCK Publishers, 1999).
202. Saradamony, K., *Emergence of a Slave Caste: Pulayas of Kerala* (New Delhi: People's Publishing House, 1980).
203. Satthianathan, S., *History of Education in the Madras Presidency* (Madras: Srinivasa Varadachari and Co Publishers, 1894).
204. Satyanarayana, A., *Dalits and Upper Castes: Essays in Social History* (New Delhi: Kanishka Publishers, 2005).
205. Satyanarayana, A., "The Contribution of Benjamin Schultze to Telugu Language and Learning," in *Halle and the Beginning of Protestant Christianity in India,* ed. Gross Andreas, et al. (Halle: Verlag der Franckschen Stiftungenzu, 2006).
206. Sebastian, Fr. S. Joe, S.J., *The Jesuit Carnatic Mission: A Foundation of Andhra Church* (Secunderabad: Andhra Jesuit Province Society, 2004).
207. Sebastian, Kim C. H., *In Search of Identity: Debates on the Religious Conversion in India* (New Delhi: The Oxford University Press, 2003).
208. Shabbir, Mohammad, *Ambedkar on Law, Constitution and Social Justice* (New Delhi: Rawat Publishers, 2008).
209. Shafer, Robert, *Ethnography of Ancient India* (Wiesbaden: Harrassowitz Publishers, 1954).
210. Shah, K. T., *Foundations of Economics in India* (Bombay: Vora and Co Publishers, 1954).
211. Shantz, Douglas H., *An Introduction to German Pietism: Protestant Renewal at the Dawn of Modern Europe* (Baltimore: The John Hopkins University Press, 2013).
212. Sharma, B. A. V. and K. Madhusudhan Reddy, eds., *Reservation Policy in India* (New Delhi: Light and Life Publishers, 1982).
213. Sharma, Raj Bahadur, *History of Christian Missions: North India Perspective* (New Delhi: Mittal Publications, 2005).

214. Sharma, Sanjay Prakash, *Dalit Society and Upliftment* (New Delhi: Mohit Publications, 2004).
215. Sheatsley, Clarence Valentine, *Our Mission Field in India: The Report* (Ohio: Lutheran Book Concern, 1921).
216. Shrikant, L. M., *Report of the Commissioner for Schedule Castes and Scheduled Tribes for the Year 1951* (New Delhi: Government of India, 1956).
217. Singh, N. K., *Global Encyclopedia of the South Indian Dalit's Ethnography* (New Delhi: Global Vision Publishing House, 2006).
218. Smith, George, *The Conversion of India from Pantaenus* to *the Present Time, A.D. 193- 1893* (New York: Young Peoples' Missionary Movement, 1903).
219. Smith, Vincent A., *The Early History of India: From 600 BC to the Muhammadan Conquest* (Oxford: Clarendon Press, 1957).
220. Solomon, Thanugundla, *Structures of the Church in Andhra Pradesh: An Historico-Juridical Study* (Secunderabad: Karuna Sri Printers, 1997).
221. Sorokin, Pitirim A., *Social and Cultural Dynamics: A Study of Change in Major Systems of Art, Truth, Ethics, Law and Social Relationships* (New Jersey: The Transaction Publishers, 1962).
222. Srinivas M. N., *Caste: In its Twentieth Century Avatar* (New Delhi: The Penguin Books India Ltd, 1990).
223. Srinivas, M. N., *Caste in Modern India:* And Other Essays (New Delhi: Asia Publishing House, 1962).
224. Srinivas, M. N., *Religion and Society among the Coorgs of South India* (New Delhi: Asia Publishing House, 1952).
225. Srinivas, M. N., "Studying one's own Culture: Some Thoughts," in *The on Living in a Revolution and Other Essays* (New Delhi: Oxford University Press, 1992).
226. Stanislaus, L., *The Liberative Mission of the Dalit Christians* (Delhi: The ISPCK Publishers, Delhi, 1999).
227. Stanley, Brian, *The World Missionary Conference, Edinburgh 1910* (Grand Rapids, Michigan: William B. Eerdmans Publishing Company, 2009).
228. Subbamma, B. V., *Christ Confronts India: Indigenous Expression of Christianity in India* (Madras: Diocesan Press, 1973).
229. Sundkler, Bengt, *Church of South India: The Movement Towards Union, 1900-1947* (London: The Lutterworth Press, 1954).
230. Swarno, Dasarathi, *The Christian Missionaries in Orissa: Their Impact on Nineteenth Century Society* (Calcutta: Punthi Pustak, 1990).

231. Taylor, Graham, *Religion in Social Action* (New York: Mead and Co. Publishers, 1913).
232. *The New Encyclopedia Britannica*, Vol. 10, 15th Edition (Chicago: The *Encyclopedia Britannica* Incorporation, 1997).
233. Thurston, Edgar, *Castes and Tribes of Southern India*, Vol. IV, K-M (Madras: The Government Press, 1909).
234. Thurston, Edgar, *Castes and Tribes of Southern India*, Vol. VI, P-S, (Madras: The Government Press, 1909).
235. Tylor, Edward Burnett, *Primitive Culture: Researches into the development of Mythology, Philosophy, Religion, Art, and Custom*, Vol. 1 (London: J Murray Publishers, 1871).
236. Uthe, Edward W., "Educational Foundations," in *Foundations for Educational Ministry*, Vol. III, ed. Evenson C Richrad (Minneapolis: Fortress Press, 1971).
237. Vaikuntam, Y., *Education and Social Change in South India and Andhra, 1880-1920* (Madras: New Era Publications, 1982).
238. Vakil, K. S. and S. Natarajan, *Education in India* (New Delhi: Allied Publishers, 1966).
239. Walter, Fernandes, *Caste and Conversion Movements in India* (New Delhi: Indian Social Institute, 1981).
240. Webster, John C. B., *Dalit Christians: A History* (Delhi: ISPCK, 1994).
241. Weinstein, Jay, *A Social and Cultural Change: Social Science for a Dynamic World* (Lanham, Maryland: Rowman Littlefield Publishers, 2005).
242. Wheeler, J. Talboys, *India under British Rule from the Foundation of the East India Company* (London: The Macmillan Co. Publishers, 1886).
243. Whitehead, Henry, *The Religious Life of India: The Village Gods of South India* (Calcutta: The Association Press, 1921).
244. Wiebe, Paul D., *Christians in Andhra Pradesh: The Mennonites of Mahbubnagar* (Bangalore: The Christian Literature Society, 1988).
245. Williams, Monier, *A Sanskrit-English Dictionary* (Oxford: Clarendon Press, 1872).
246. Williams, Monier, *Brahmanism and Hinduism or Religious Thought and Life in India: As Based on The Veda and Other Sacred Books of The Hindus* (London: John Murray publishers, 1892).
247. Wingate, Andrew, *The Church and Conversion* (Delhi: ISPCK, 1997).
248. Wiser, William, *The Hindu Jajmani System: A Socio-Economic System Interrelating Members of a Hindu Village Community in Services* (Lucknow: The Lucknow Publishing House, 1958).

249. Wright, Arnold ed., *Southern India: Its History, People, Commerce, and Industrial Resources* (New Delhi: Asian Educational Services, 1914).

250. Yagati, Chinna Rao, "Education and Identity Formation among Dalits in Colonial Andhra," in *Education and the Disprivileged: Nineteenth and Twentieth Century India,* ed. Sabyasachi Bhattacharya (New Delhi: Orient Longman Publishers, 2002).

251. Zimmerman, Carle C., *Sociology of Underdevelopment* (Jaipur: Rawat Publications, 1976).

V. Journal Articles

1. Ames, Edward Scribner, "Religion in Terms of Social Consciousness," *The Journal of Religion,* I (3), (May 1921): 264-270. Accessed on 28 October 2013, http://www.jstor.org/stable/670262.

2. Azariah, V. S., "Evangelization and its Challenge," *The Andhra Christian Council Meeting, The National Christian Council Review* (Mysore: Wesley Press, 1933).

3. Bawden, H. Heath "The Social Character of Consciousness and Its Bearing on Education," *The Elementary School Teacher,* IV (6), (February 1904): 366-376. Accessed on 08 March 2012, http://www.jstor.org/stable/993018.

4. Beaglehole, J. H. "The Indian Christians: A Study of a Minority," *The Modern Asian Studies,* 1 (1), (1967): 59-80. Accessed on 10 December 2012, http://www.jstor.org/stable/311585.

5. Beaglehole, J. H., "Sir Thomas Munro," *The Indo British Review,* II (1968): 9-30.

6. Brubaker, Richard L., "Barbers, Washer men, and Other Priests: Servants of the South Indian Village and Its Goddess," *History of Religions*, 19 (2), (November 1979): 128-152. Accessed on 13 October 2013, http://www.jstor.org/stable/1062270.

7. Burton, Antoinette, "Contesting the Zenana: The Mission to Make Lady Doctors for India (1874-1885)," *The Journal of British Studies*, (35), (July 1996): 368-97. Accessed on 04 April 2014, http://www.jstor.org/stable/175919.

8. Carroll, Lucy, "Sanskritization, Westernization and Social Mobility: A Reappraisal of the Relevance of Anthropological Concepts to the Social Historian of Modern India," *The Journal of Anthropological Research*, XXXIII (4), (1977): 355-371. Accessed on 04 April 2014, http://www.jstor.org/stable/3629747.

9. Cohen, Stephen P., "The Untouchable Soldier: Caste, Politics, and the Indian Army," *The Journal of Asian Studies*, XXVIII (3) (May 1969):

453-468. Accessed on 12 September 2013, http://www.jstor.org/stable/2943173.

10. Cooley, Charles H., "Social Consciousness," *The American Journal of Sociology*, XII (5) (March 1907): 675-694. Accessed on 07 November 2012, http://www.jstor.org/stable/2762377.
11. Dann, Robert Bernard, "The Legacy of Anthony Norris Groves," *The International Bulletin of Missionary Research*, XXIX (4), (October 2005): 198-202. Accessed on 05 February 2014, http://www.internationalbulletin.org/issues/2005-04/2005-04-198-dann.pdf.
12. Desai, Mahadevan ed., *Harijan*, (5), (Poona: 13-3-1937).
13. Dikshitulu, C. V., "Madarasu Prabhutvamu: Vidyasaklha Vyayamu," *Bharathi*, (2), (July 1938).
14. Dirks, Nicholas B., "Castes of Mind," *Representations*, (37), (1992): 56-78. Accessed on 05 Febraury 2014, http://www.jstor.org/stable/2928654.
15. Fite, Warner, "The Social Implications of Consciousness," *The Journal of Philosophy, Psychology and Scientific Methods*, X (14), (July 3, 1913): 365-374. Accessed on 02 March 2014, http://www.jstor.org/stable/2012909.
16. Forrester, Duncan B., "Indian Christian Attitudes to Caste in the Twentieth Century," *The Indian Council of Historical Review,* IX (1), (June 1975).
17. Frykenberg R. E., "On the Study of Conversion Movements: A Review Article and a Theoretical Note," *The Indian Economic and Social History Review,* XVII (1980): 122-138.
18. Gipson, Tracy G., "Anthony Norris Groves and the Godavari Delta Mission," *The Indian Church History Review* (June 1984): 58-73.
19. Habib, Irfan, "Colonization of the Indian Economy 1757-1900," *The Social Scientist*, III (8), (March 1975): 23-53.
20. Halbwachs, Maurice, "Individual Consciousness and Collective Mind," *The American Journal of Sociology*, XLIV (6), (May 1939): 812-822. Accessed on 25 May 2012, http://www.jstor.org/stable/2769413.
21. Hurst, Charles E., "Race, Class, and Consciousness," The *American Sociological Review*, 37 (6), (December 1972): 658-670. Accessed on 25 May 2012, http://www.jstor.org/stable/2093577.
22. Kumar, Dharma, "Caste and Landlessness in South India," *The Comparative Studies in Society and History*, IV (3), (April 1962): 337-363.
23. Miller, William and J. C. R. Ewing, "Christian Education in India," *The American Journal of Theology*, XIV (3), (July 1910). Accessed on 06 June 2012, http://www.jstor.org/stable/3154995.

24. Nicholson, Sydney, "Social Organization of the Malas: An Outcaste Indian People," *The Journal of the Royal Anthropological Institute of Great Britain and Ireland*, (56), (1926): 91-103. Accessed on 03 January 2011, http://www.jstor.org/stable/2843602.
25. Noel, Gist P., "Caste Differentials in South India," *The American Sociological Review*, 9 (2), (April 1954): 26-37. Accessed on 03 January 2011, http://www.jstor.org/stable/2088393.
26. Oddie, G. A., "Christian Conversion in the Telugu Country, 1860-1900: A Case Study of one Protestant Movement in the Godavari Krishna Delta," *Indian Economic and Social History Review*, XII (63), (1975).
27. Oommen, George, "Dalit Conversion and Social Protest in Travancore, 854-890," *The Bangalore Theological Forum*, XXVII (3 & 4), (September – December 1996).
28. Oommen, T. K., "Sources of Deprivation and Styles of Protest: The Case of the Dalits in India," *The Contributions to Indian Sociology*, XVIII (1984).
29. Powell, Baden, B. H., "The Origin of Zamindari Estates in Bengal," *The Quarterly Journal of Economics*, (1), (October 1896): 36-69.
30. Prabhakar M. E., "In Search of Roots: Dalit Aspirations and the Christian Dalit Question (Perceptions of the Andhra Poet Laureate, Joshua)," *Religion and Society*, XLI (March 1994), 2-20.
31. Prabhakar, M. E., "Caste in Andhra Churches-A Case Study of Guntur District," *Religion and Society*, XXXIX (September 1987), 31- 51.
32. Prabhakar, M. E., "Caste-class and Status in Andhra Churches and Implications for Mission Today: Some Reflections," *Religion and Society*, Vol. XXVIII (3), 17.
33. Raju, Bezzam David, and N. Suresh Babu, "Lutheran Medical Missionary Enterprise In Guntur District," *The A. P. History Congress Proceedings*, Guntur, 15 (1996).
34. Richardson, K. L.,"The Church and Native Culture: A Telugu Lutheran Perspective," in *The Indian Journal of Theology* (Kolkata: The Serampore College, 1993).
35. Specker, Konrad, "Madras Handlooms in the Nineteenth Century," *The Indian Economic and Social History Review,* XXVI (2), (April-June 1989). Accessed on 10 July 2013, http://ier.sagepub.com/content/26/2/131.
36. Srinivas, M. N., "A Note on Sanskritization and Westernization," *The Far Eastern Quarterly,* (1956): 481-96. Accessed on 10 February 2012, http://www.jstor.org/stable/2941919.
37. Srinivas, M. N., "Caste in Modern India," *The Journal of Asian Studies*, XVI (4), (1957): 529-548. Accessed on 13 June 2011, http://www.jstor.org/stable/2941637.

38. Subramaniam, V., “Consequences of Christian Missionary Education,” *The Third World Quarterly*, 1 (3), (July 1979). Accessed on 20 January 2013, http://www.jstor.org/stable/3990283.
39. Thapar, Romila, “The Theory of Aryan Race and India: History and Politics,” *The Social Scientist*, 24 (1/3), (1996): 3-29. Accessed on October 2013, http://links.jstor.org/sici?sici=0970-0293.
40. Jetty, Santha K. Varikoti, Indian Christians from the Depressed Castes Background and Challenges to Their Christian Identity, Mission Studies, 34(3), (2017), 327-344. doi: https://doi.org/10.1163/15733831-12341522.
41. Whittaker, F., “Evangelism: Opportunities and Difficulties in Relation to Mass Movements,” *The National Christian Council Review*, Vol. XVII (Mysore: Wesley Press, 1939).
42. Woodburne, Angus Stewart, “The Indianization of Christianity,” *The Journal of Religion*, 1 (1), (January 1921). Accessed on 28 May 2013, 66-75. http://www.jstor.org/stable/1195391.

VI. Secondary Sources in Telugu: Books

1. Devaraj, B. E., *Bharata Desa Kraisthava Sangha Charitra*, Andhra Christian Theological Literature Council (Tenali: A.S.R. Power Press, 1969).
2. Jagannadham, Pervaram (ed.), *Dr. Babasaheb Ambedkar Rachanalu-Prasangalu: Congress anjd Gandhi Antarani variki Emi Chesaru*? (*What Congress and Gandhi have done to the Untouchables?*), 9 (Hyderabad: The Government of Andhra Pradesh Publications, n.d).
3. Krupachary, Gujjarlamudi, *Telugu Sahityaniki Kristavula Seva* (Guntur: Navodaya Publishers, 1988).
4. Mangamma, J., *Andhra Desamulo Kraisthava Missioanrila Seva* (Hyderabad: Telugu Academy Publishers, 1992).
5. Moses, M., *Andhra Pradesh Kraisthava Sangha Charitra* (Tenali: Kraisthava Satya Grandhasala, 2004).
6. Pathuri, Joseph, *Bharatiya Baptist Prarambha Charitra Parishodhana* (Ohio: Transworld Ministries, 2005).
7. Ranjanam, Lakshmi, Khadavalli, *Andhrula Charitra Samskriti* (Madras: Bala Sarawathi Book Depot, 1966).
8. Rao, Raghava D., *Machlipatnam Charitra* (Vetapalem: Sri Sarawatha Nikethanam, 2001).
9. Syamala, G., *Nalla Poddu* (Hyderabad: Hyderabad Book Trust, 2003).
10. Tathapudi, David, *Telugu Baptist Mission History* (n.d).

11. Yendluri, Dr. Kalaprapoorna, *Telugunata Dalita Udyamamu* (Hyderabad: Samantara Publications, 2009).
12. Yesuratnam, Regunta, *Bharatavanilo Kraisthava Sangham* (Hyderabad: Telugu Kraisthava Vedanta Sahiti Samiti, 1998).

VII. Telugu Articles

1. "Jewett Vision," *The Journal of the Jewett Memorial Baptist Church, Ongole* (May 2012).
2. *Bezwada Baptist Sangha Golden Jubilee Souvenir* (1906-1956).
3. Daivasirvadam, G., "Dhayajeevi Canaon Dhanwada Anantam," *The Church of South India* (Krishna Godavari Diocese Magazine, 2010).
4. Rao, Kasinadhuni Nageswara, Unnava Lakashmi Narayana, *Mālapalli* (1922).
5. Rao, Y. V. Krishna, "Delta Shipli Sir Arthur Cotton," in *The Andhra Pradesh Darshini* (Hyderabad: Vishalandra Publishing House, 1976).
6. *Schade Satavarshikotsavapu Vela, Centenary Celebrations Souvenir*, Schade Girls High School, Rajahmundry (1894-1994).
7. Syamala, G., "Uttama Upadhyayani Tadi Nagmma," in *Nalla Poddu* (Hyderabad: Hyderabad Book Trust, 2003).
8. *The Church of South India, Krishna Godavari Diocese, 100th Harvest Festival Issue 1911-2010* (Vijayawada: 2010).
9. *The Hird School Souvenir and Magazine, 25th Anniversary of Hird School* (Narasaraopet: 1973-74).
10. Yagati, Chinna Rao, "Dalit Vidya Agencila Patra," in *Dalita Udyama Charitra* (Hyderabad: Hyderabad Book Trust, 2007).

VIII. Unpublished Ph. D. Dissertations

1. David, Mosse, "Caste, Christianity and Hinduism: A Study of Social Organization and Religion in Rural Ramand", (D. Phil Dissertation, The University of Oxford, 1986).
2. Doss, M. Sargur, "Educational Policy in Madras Presidency 1800-1900" (Ph. D Dissertation, The Madras University, 1961).
3. Padmakar, Dattatreya Diskalkar, "Contribution of Agricultural Education to Economic Development of India" (Ph. D Dissertation, The Kansas State University, 1963).
4. Shakeela, U. V., "Perceptions of Women's Emancipation in Nineteenth Century India" (Ph. D Dissertation, The Pondicherry University, 2003).

IX. Web Sources

1. The Constitution (Scheduled Castes Order), Accessed on 10 February 2011, http://lawmin .nic.in/ld/subord /rule4a.htm.
2. The Indian Christian Marriage Act, (1872), Accessed on 05 March 2011, http://bdlaws.minlaw.gov.bd/pdf.
3. Shah, Dr. Vinod, *Christian Contribution to India in the Area of Health*, Accessed on 15 June 2011, www.eha-health.org/resources.
4. Demand to Amend the Constitution, Accessed on 07 November 2011, http://www.sabrang.com/cc/archive /2010/apr10/chapter9.pdf.
5. Article 67: Clause 5, Accessed on 05 February 2013, http://indiankanoon.org/docfragment/1629071.
6. Article 149: Clause 3, Accessed on 10 January 2012 http://indiankanoon.org/doc/1173345.
7. Caligiuri, Amanda, *Hidden in Plain Sight: Plaque in Christ Chapel*, Gettysburg College, Philadelphia, 2006, http://www.gettysburg.edu/library/gettdigital/hidden/Caligiuri_paper.pdf. (Accessed on 08 July 2013).

X. Oral Interviews

1. Interview held on 14/07/2012 with Rev. Dr. Sunil Bhanu, President of The Andhra Evangelical Lutheran Church, Guntur, Andhra Pradesh regarding AELC support from ELCA.
2. Interview held on 09/07/2012 with Prof. Bezzam David Raju, Head of the Department, Department of History, Acharya Nagarjuna University, Guntur, Andhra Pradesh regarding the Medical work in the Guntur town by the AELM Missionaries.
3. Interview held on 01/08/2013 with Prof. Rekha Pandey, Head of the Department, Department of History, University Hyderabad (formerly in the State of Andhra Pradesh) regarding the contribution of the Christian missionaries towards the education of women.
4. Interview held on 25/11/2013 with Rev. Dr. Chilkuri. Vasantha Rao, Theologian and Principal (former) of the Andhra Christian Theological College, Hyderabad, Telangana, regarding the subject of culture change among the Christian converts.
5. Interview held on 05/02/2014 with Rev. Dr. U. David Uday Kumar, Principal of the Gurukul Theological Seminary and College, Chennai, Tamilnadu, regarding the liberating influence of the work of the Christian Missionaries in Coastal Andhra.
6. Interview held on 29/08/2015 with Rev. Dr. Tathapudi Mathews Emmanuel, Principal of the Andhra Christian Theological College, Hyderabad, Telangana, regarding the extent of missionary influence on the *Malas* and *Madigas* Christian converts.

Index

D

E

J

K

L

M

S

T

U

V

W